Frank Norris

The American Critical Tradition 7
M. Thomas Inge, *General Editor*

Frank Norris

The Critical Reception

Edited by Joseph R. McElrath, Jr.,
and Katherine Knight

Burt Franklin & Co., Inc.

Published by Burt Franklin & Co., Inc.
235 East Forty-fourth Street
New York, New York 10017

© 1981 Burt Franklin & Co., Inc.

All rights reserved.
No part of this book may be reproduced
in whole or in part by any means,
including any photographic, mechanical,
or electrical reproduction, recording, or information
storage and retrieval systems,
without the prior written consent of the publisher,
except for brief quotations for
the purposes of review.

Library of Congress Cataloging in Publication Data

Main entry under title:

Frank Norris, the critical reception.

(The American critical tradition ISSN 0-163-1470)
Bibliography: p.
Includes index.
 1. Norris, Frank, 1870–1902—Criticism and
interpretation. 2. American literature—20th
century—Book reviews. I. McElrath, Joseph R.
 II. Knight, Katherine, 1944–   III. Series:
The American critical tradition (New York, 1978–
     PS2473.F68   813'.4   78-26966
         ISBN 0-89102-150-7

Manufactured in the United States of America

General Editor's Preface

When we speak of a writer's reputation in critical terms, we should recognize that he actually has two: the response of book reviewers and critics during his own lifetime to each of his works as it was published, and the retrospective evaluation of his achievement by literary historians and academic critics in the decades after his career is concluded. The primary concern of modern scholarship has been the latter, on the assumption that the passage of time is essential before a writer's achievement can be objectively viewed and assessed. The purpose of the volumes in the American Critical Tradition series, however, is to provide overviews of the critical reputations earned by major American authors in their own times. Such overviews are necessary before the full impact of a writer's influence can be properly evaluated and an understanding of how he related to his contemporary cultural milieu achieved.

The few efforts hitherto made in summarizing a writer's contemporary critical standing have usually been based on a reading of sample reviews or vague impressions retained by veterans of the era. Seldom have literary historians gone back to locate and read all or most of the comment elicited by a career in progress. In the present volumes, the editors have sought to unearth every known review of each book in the contemporary newspapers, journals, and periodicals, and to demonstrate the critical response chronologically through reprint, excerpt, or summary. Exhaustive checklists of reviews not included in the text are appended to each chapter, and the editor has provided an introduction summarizing the major trends observable in the criticism. The results not only elucidate the writer's career, but they reveal as well intellectual patterns in book reviewing and the reception of serious writing by the American reading public. Each volume is, therefore, a combined literary chronicle and reference work of a type previously unavailable.

M. Thomas Inge
General Editor

Contents

General Editor's Preface v

Introduction ix

Acknowledgments xxv

Yvernelle (1891) 1

Moran of the Lady Letty (1898) 11

McTeague (1899) 29

Blix (1899) 57

A Man's Woman (1900) 81

The Octopus (1901) 111

The Pit (1903) 183

A Deal in Wheat (1903) 299

The Responsibilities of the Novelist (1903) 309

The Third Circle (1909) 323

Vandover and the Brute (1914) 335

Posthumous Items of Importance: A Checklist 365

Index 367

Introduction

I

When Frank Norris died in San Francisco on October 25, 1902, at the age of thirty-two, he was considered one of America's most promising novelists. He had come to Mount Zion Hospital with the symptoms of appendicitis: Peritonitis developed; the infection had advanced too far for remedy. Thus ended the most productive phase of his brief life. Within less than three years—1898 to 1901—he had seen five of his novels published. *The Pit* would be posthumously issued in January 1903, after its serialization in the *Saturday Evening Post* was completed. Norris had not taken the literary world by storm; but once he finally got going in 1898, his assault on the establishment had been relentless. His apparent goal had been to establish himself through journalistic and belletristic activities, similar to those of Richard Harding Davis and Stephen Crane, as another of the boy wonders of the 1890s. But it was not until the time of his death that his work would begin to have the impact on the marketplace that the Van Bibber stories and *The Red Badge of Courage* had had early in Davis's and Crane's careers.

Like Davis and Crane, Norris displayed extraordinary energy in his chosen profession of writing; it was no coincidence that Norris's heroes—Ward Bennett, Annixter, Curtis Jadwin, and Condy Rivers—were remarkably "driven" characters. In his work Norris seemed to be repeatedly lashing himself into something like a "fine frenzy." When he died he was planning a third volume of his Epic of the Wheat—*The Wolf*, which would succeed the very sizable prior volumes, *The Octopus* and *The Pit*. Writing was his full-time occupation, and while producing the novels of 1898–1901, he had continued production of the essays and stories that were his bread and butter in the days before he gained entry to the East Coast publishing world. After his death a selection of his literary essays would appear in *The Responsibilities of the Novelist* (1903) and some of his many tales would be gathered in *A Deal in Wheat* (1903) and *The Third Circle* (1909). In 1902 he was also in possession of the lengthy novel, *Vandover and the Brute*, which would not be published until his brother, Charles G. Norris, placed it at Doubleday, Page and Company in 1914.

Norris had written much, and he was beginning to "make it" in 1902 after years of dogged determination. The road to the status of major writer had been a long one for him. When J. B. Lippincott published his narrative poem *Yvernelle: A Legend of Feudal France* in late 1891, he may have expected something like Davis's overnight success. In many of the reviews, however, more attention was paid to the illustrations, the quality of paper, and the binding than to the literary achievement. The *New York Herald* was typical of reviewers' responses when it devoted fully half of its attention to the "dainty" appearance of the book: "It is full of fine pictures by good artists, a pleasing innovation being several full page plates in colors, the subjects being female heads; the print, paper and binding are of the best, and the result is a holiday book of the better kind." In light of such reviews it is no wonder the consensus today is that the lavishly manufactured volume was more a vanity publication than anything else. Gertrude Norris had underwritten some portion of its production costs apparently, and *Yvernelle* is usually seen as merely an act of encouragement from a fond mother with artistic inclinations. Gertrude was enamored of Sir Walter Scott; young Frank, recently returned from art study in France to literary study at Berkeley, had produced a work more typical of his mother's tastes in romance than of the sensibility that would fashion the later realistic and naturalistic novels. Norris's beginning, then, is not taken as much of a true beginning.

But there is reason to believe that Frank himself took the event quite seriously and had cause to suppose that he had actually initiated a career. One needs to be careful when belittling his real achievement of 1891 in light of the financing of the publication. For, to a measurable degree, the publisher acted as though *Yvernelle* were more than an act of maternal indulgence. Lippincott treated the work, priced at $3.50 (twice the price of most trade books), as a potential profit-maker in the Christmas gift-book market. In the *Chicago Inter Ocean* of December 19, 1891, for instance, one finds that the publisher had purchased thirty-two lines of advertising space headed by two lines in upper case: "A HANDSOME BOOK" and "YVERNELLE" sought to attract the attention of a real audience to a real book for sale. Lippincott distributed review copies and also printed a promotional brochure for the post-Christmas market. Moreover, Norris probably was encouraged by the parts of reviews not focusing on the physical makeup of *Yvernelle*. The *New York Herald* declared that his work was one "of the best narrative poems that has appeared in a long time." *The Critic* observed that the "lines have plenty of swing and music, and the narrative advances steadily without any break in the movement of the verse"; the *San Francisco Chronicle* admired the "stirring verse" and Norris's skill in creating dramatic effects; and the *Overland Monthly* also noted instances in which the tale embodied "a good deal of dramatic force." For a first effort by a literary unknown, Norris's book might have fared worse.

Introduction

With one real book on his shelf, Norris devoted himself to the magazines and newspapers through 1896. His work was appearing while he was still a student at Berkeley; and after a year at Harvard, 1894–95, he embarked on the then fashionable and attention-winning adventure of reporting from South Africa at the time of the Jameson raid. It was a bit of journalistic derring-do of the Davis and Crane variety; and we can suppose that it helped earn him a place on the San Francisco weekly, *The Wave*, for which he wrote regularly between 1896 and early 1898. During those two years he did fine first-person reportage (still very much neglected by Norris scholars today) and produced fictional sketches and tales, but the big break did not materialize. Themes written at Harvard indicate that he had begun to work on the material that became *McTeague, Vandover,* and *Blix,* but by late 1897 it seemed as though he had stalled and his prospects included the possibility of remaining in the position of what is vaguely described as a "subeditor" for a minor West Coast weekly publication for the rest of his career.

McTeague had not proved suitable for a publisher as of 1897, and Norris turned from that remarkable composition to play what proved a winning card. "Gaudy," "meretricious," "fantastic," "puerile"—these are terms that often come to mind when discussing *Moran of the Lady Letty*. But this adventuresome, outlandish, eye-catching potboiler saved the day. Norris began writing and immediately serializing the chapters in January 1898; and before *The Wave* serialization concluded, and the act of composing it was completed, Norris was on his way to New York City to work for the S. S. McClure syndicate, to be a salaried reader for Doubleday and McClure, and to begin his career as a popular novelist in earnest—whereupon he seemed to stall again. His assignment by McClure to report on the Spanish-American War helped his career very little. *Moran* appeared in September 1898, shortly after Norris's untriumphant return from Cuba. It received both positive and negative notices. None was especially long, and no reviewer acted as though Norris had created "high" art. But as in the case of *Yvernelle*, reviewers were impressed by the dramatic sense displayed in this piece of adventure-romance writing. The characterizations of Ross Wilbur and Moran Sternersen were generally considered "striking." George Hamlin Fitch of the *San Francisco Chronicle*—who took Norris to task in reviews of his later works—expressed an almost unreserved admiration for Norris's story-telling ability: "No better story of adventure has been printed in many a day." The *Washington Times* reviewer, who was highly supportive of Norris's work as volume after volume appeared, greeted his first novel with the declaration that "there has been nothing in American fiction just like this tale of adventure." He then proceeded to celebrate the novelty of the conception of *Moran*. Quite a few reviews struck this note; but there were also many that offered the opposite opinion, citing the derivative nature of Norris's tale. *Yvernelle* had brought Scott and Byron to mind; *Moran*, as *The Independent* observed, seemed "dyed with the accepted colors well known to Bret Harte, Stevenson and Joaquin Miller, not to mention Charles Warren Stoddard." *Moran* also recalled Kipling's *Captains Courageous* for several reviewers. Some sophisticated reviewers responded with tongue in cheek; some allowed their tongues to protrude, as when *The Literary World* expressed relief over Moran's departure from the tale via the knife of Hoang. *Moran*—or *Shanghaied*, as the British edition was entitled—received mixed reviews.

McTeague followed in 1899, receiving some noteworthy praise and some markedly heated statements of outrage. The praise came mainly from those with progressive literary concerns who appreciated the advent of realism in fiction. John D. Barry of *The Literary World*, for example, ranked *McTeague* "among the few great novels" produced in America, and he celebrated Norris's "profound insight into character," "brilliant massing of significant detail," and sense of "dramatic force." Then he sanctioned Norris's treatment of the unpleasant in life—whereupon Barry's editors rejoined, in a second *Literary World* review, that "grossness for the sake of grossness is unpardonable." Such a negative response by 1890s reviewers with "genteel" and "ideal" standards of judgment is well known today to have been typical. *McTeague* is frequently employed as a touchstone in discussions of the "war" between the realists and the so-called romantics at the end of the nineteenth century. The fact that Norris had to eliminate a pants-wetting scene from *McTeague* for its second printing is a memorable token of the effect of reviewer outrage over what the *Boston Evening Transcript* termed a novel of "unrelieved pain and grossness." What has not been so widely recognized is the degree of positive reaction that *McTeague* created, as recorded in this present volume. In anticipation of a pattern that was to develop fully in 1901 and 1903, when *The Octopus* and *The Pit* were published, reviewers began to link Norris's name with Zola, Balzac, and Dickens—though, admittedly, not always to Norris's advantage.

In spite of such serious treatment by even the nay-sayers, *McTeague* was not a great success. Neither *Moran* nor *McTeague* proved a true *cause célèbre*, though William Dean Howells publicly approved of both. He had read *Moran* with what he termed breathlessness, and he was gratified to find such an *American* book. He questioned the necessity of an almost exclusive focus on the ugly in *McTeague*; yet his main emphasis had to do with the way in which Norris had rendered "little miracles of observation." Still, even with Howells's approval, Norris created only a minor sensation.

By the end of 1899, however, Norris had produced a more significant effect upon the literary establishment with the publication of *Blix*. September 1898, February 1899, September 1899—this was the rapid sequence of publication. Published as the novels were in staccato fashion,

Norris's name became familiar through a remarkable process of accretion. Appearing within a span of one year, the novels did not allow reviewers to forget the author. Moreover, together, the novels made a specific impression that would have been less likely if the accustomed interludes between publications had occurred.

The reviewers were not allowed to forget Norris, but most importantly they were not allowed to forget the substance of *Moran* and the quite different substance of *McTeague* before Doubleday surprised them with a novel very different from the first two. Typical of many reviews is the point made in the *New York Commercial Advertiser*: "It is a genuine pleasure to read a new story by Mr. Frank Norris, for they always abound in the unexpected. In each of the three volumes which already stand to his credit, he has succeeded in striking a new and successful vein." The *St. Paul Pioneer Press* began its review in the same manner: " 'Blix,' the third story published by Frank Norris, is likewise a demonstration of a third capacity in its author." In the *San Francisco Chronicle* George Hamlin Fitch went so far as to avow that *Blix* was the "height of literary art." The first stage in Norris's rise was thus achieved by the end of 1899. The reviewers, on the whole, were somewhat stunned by this writer who refused to be pinned down as a Stevensonian yarn-spinner, a Zolaesque naturalist, or a smiling Howellsian realist. *Blix* was unanticipated, and the refrain that rose from the review columns had to do with the extraordinary *versatility* of this young writer who might try heaven knows what in his next novel. Because he was the first to sound this major chord in a prepublication notice of *Blix*, Isaac F. Marcosson of the *Louisville Times* merits quotation here: "With the presentation of 'Blix' this writer will have displayed a versatility at once striking and remarkable.... Truly it is a varied work that he is building."

It was a minor "arrival." As of 1899 William Dean Howells was still in the minority in regard to his estimation of the author of *Moran* and *McTeague*. Even as late as 1901, with the publication of *The Octopus*, Howells's early high regard for Norris was not the consensus opinion. But as the *Moran, McTeague*, and *Blix* sections of this volume will indicate, Norris *had* arrived as a budding boy wonder on the score of versatility. It was then something of a calamity that Norris squandered his gains and earned a good deal of ill will by allowing the publication of *A Man's Woman* in January 1900. In his correspondence he himself admitted that *A Man's Woman* was slovenly put together. But published it was, and what was most remarkable about reviewer response was that it did not have more of a debilitating effect upon Norris's career. True, some reviewers found points to admire in the work, but the outrage that greeted *McTeague* in polite circles was restated in treble volume in reviews of this novel.

Norris had fumbled his way through the tale. It was, and is, judged an aesthetic failure. But at the turn of the century Norris's cardinal sin was in going too far, in following his unequaled flair for extravagance and what would then have been termed bad taste. The hero and heroine *look* grotesque; they behave grotesquely; and the story of how their love progresses is plain-and-simple strange. *A Man's Woman* includes a vivid and tactile description of surgery on a diseased hip bone that is still capable of producing a visceral response in some readers.

The novel also goes too far in its description of the extreme physical suffering of the members of an Arctic expedition. In *McTeague* Norris had with exquisite (and perhaps malevolent) understatement dealt with Trina's loss of fingers because of blood poisoning. At the close of Chapter 18 the need for amputation was established, and the next chapter began in the most matter-of-fact tone: "One can hold a scrubbing-brush with two good fingers and the stumps of two others even if both joints of the thumb are gone, but it takes considerable practice to get used to it." Such a flourish is vintage Norris for those who have noted his talent for constructing bizarre situations during his days on *The Wave*. In *A Man's Woman* Norris again selected amputation as a subject, giving Richard Ferriss's loss of both hands graphic treatment. Norris's boldness had increased, though, and he decided to give a darkly humorous twist to the real calamity: He created a shudder-inducing bit of comedy by having the principal characters forget about Ferriss's lack of hands. We wince as we observe Ward Bennett, caught up in the enthusiasm of one moment, extending a hand to Ferris, inviting him to shake. And Lloyd Searight later becomes angry with Ferris for not extending a hand to help her down from a carriage. These moments constitute perhaps the bravest comedic descents into the deliberately "tasteless" in all of nineteenth-century American literature.

Norris had, as the reviewer for the *New York Times* phrased it, constructed a "chamber of horrors." James L. Ford concluded his *Providence Journal* review with the reflection that Norris might better employ his peculiar talents "in some honest, well-paid labor, such as the preparation of catalogues of undertaker's supplies." Oddly enough, it was his best-selling book through 1900—an indication, perhaps, of just how well his first three novels and the Doubleday press releases had fashioned his public image. For, on its own, the book could only be excused as the crude beginnings of an amateur, of contemporaneous interest mainly because of the popular appetite for works dealing with the quest to reach the North Pole.

Luckily, Norris had established himself securely enough to weather the storm. By then he was sufficiently secure to be able to compensate for the artistic debacle with his next two works. As Norris performed his field research for *The Octopus*, he must have known that he would have to make up for his mistake. That he once again focused upon the complexities of

Introduction

male-female relationships—a topic that he had handled badly in *A Man's Woman*—seems one indication that he was going to do more than penance for his sins. In the Annixter-Hilma relationship developed in *The Octopus*, he artfully transcended the mistakes of *A Man's Woman*; and in his later fashioning of the central relationship of *The Pit*, he proved even more mature an artist than in *The Octopus*. With these two works Norris recovered lost ground and demonstrated a newly developed strength in his writing that earned him the status of a major writer.

Between 1901 and 1903 Norris's reputation began to loom large, and its growth occurred in three major stages. Already known as a versatile and sensational writer, the author of *The Octopus* was viewed as a writer of epic imagination and energy. With *McTeague* he had been termed Zolaesque, the reviewers having in mind the traits of Zola's *L'Assomoir*. When *The Octopus* appeared, Norris was again termed Zolaesque, but this time the reviewers were alluding to the Zola of works such as *Germinal*. *The Outlook* recalled *Fécondité* and *Paris*; and like the *Overland Monthly* and the *Bookman* (America), it immediately linked Norris's plans for a trilogy with the literary practice of Zola. The *Bookman* also alluded to *Le Ventre de Paris*, *L'Argent*, and *La Bête Humaine* to give its readers an idea of the sort of writing to which Norris had turned.

Norris's new canvas was a large one, of Homeric breadth, and the first volume of his Epic of the Wheat caused reviewers to begin alluding to the notion of the "Great American Novel" so long expected in literary columns. There were negative responses, of course. A. Schade Van Westrum, in *The Book Buyer*, found *The Octopus* too reminiscent of Zola's method. "The trick of repetition of certain adjectives, phrases and descriptions, so wearisome in 'Fécondité,' is here, but kept within bounds." This positive qualification was not offered by all reviewers. William Morton Payne, for instance, informed readers of *The Dial* that Zola's and Norris's style is "essentially inartistic": "With [Norris], as with M. Zola, realism means the piling up of great masses of trivial fact, reporting in place of true characterization, and enforcement of his argument by the bludgeon rather than by the rapier." In spite of such chiding, however, Norris had—as with *Blix*—caught the reviewers by surprise. *Munsey's Magazine* opined that with *The Octopus*, "Frank Norris has put himself a long stride ahead of the author of 'McTeague.'" *The Athenaeum* declared, "'McTeague' and 'Blix' are novels which have given Mr. Norris some standing in England; but, creditable as these were, they by no means prepared one for so important a piece of work as 'The Octopus.'" Norris, the sensationalist who had cannily designed his first four novels to keep readers and reviewers guessing as to what new extravagance he would turn to next, had succeeded in offering yet another "new venture in fiction."

It would be a mistake to make too much of the effect *The Octopus* had on

Norris's reputation in 1901, for it did not establish him as a great writer, as one might now suppose it did. What is clear is that the reviewers began to assume a different tone toward Norris. He was obviously aiming at something great in that large and energetic novel, and it simply could not be dismissed offhand. The result was that even those reviewers who were not especially impressed by the actual achievement of the work expressed their discontent in a manner that might be employed in critical discussions of Zola, George Moore, Flaubert, Ibsen, or Howells. Norris was no longer the mere author of *Moran* or of a breezy little love idyll called *Blix*. What is also clear, though, is that the response to *The Octopus* might have been greater. Sales of *The Octopus* topped those of *A Man's Woman*, but still it was not until the publication of *The Pit* in 1903 that the grand arrival took place. Again Norris's reputation grew by a process of accretion. *The Octopus* was not *The Red Badge of Courage*.

Viewed from the vantage point of 1903 and the massive response to *The Pit, The Octopus* must have been something of a disappointment. Doubleday had advertised heavily. Press releases, beginning in 1899, had paved the way. The result, for example, was that the *Washington Times* announced in its literary paragraphs, as early as July 16, 1899, that Norris had left San Francisco to do research in the San Joaquin Valley; and on March 24, 1901, it was announced that *The Octopus* would deal with the Mussel Slough affair and the effects of railroad trusts in California. Doubleday was feeding the literary columnists. A large party was being prepared for Norris and the Doubleday accountants over a period of almost two years, but the "event" did not truly materialize. It was not that nobody came to the party; it was just that fewer than must have been expected attended, and several did not dress for the occasion.

The next stage of the growth of Norris's reputation came at his death. As the early posthumous writings about Norris indicate, his stature increased as writers took up a dirge that began: "If only he had lived, . . ."* *The Octopus* was foremost in the writers' minds, but most recalled the majority of the prior works and lamented the loss of a writer who was clearly past the apprentice stage and who seemed so promising.

"If only he had lived" was sounded again and in greater volume as *The Pit* appeared in bookstores in January 1903. Most students of Norris's work do not view *The Pit* as *the* masterpiece today, but in 1903 it was seen as a happy culmination of Norris's artistic development. Individuals such as Albert Bigelow Paine were so impressed that they chose to deny the fact that the wheat trilogy would never be finished. In the *Bookman* (America),

---

*Because of the format of the "American Critical Tradition" series of which this book is a part, the memoirs and eulogies that appeared upon Norris's death are not reprinted. They should be consulted, however, if one wishes the fullest possible picture of Norris's impact upon his generation. A checklist of such relevant items appears on pp. 365-66.

he concluded that Norris's "great work seems completed as it stands;—the Epic of the Wheat is finished." This time almost everyone came to the party, properly dressed. For *The Pit* it was tails and ties and, lamentably, black armbands. Once again the "Great American Novel" was alluded to frequently. The *New York Herald* was typical:

> The book of the week . . . is Frank Norris's "The Pit." Indeed, it promises to be the book of the year, mayhap of the decade. Enthusiastic critics may even declare that it comes . . . close to being the great American novel to which we have all been looking forward for—how many years?

Norris had clearly entered the list of serious contenders. *The Pit* was handled as though it was high art. And if it was not the "Great American Novel," it was at least—as the *Chicago Inter Ocean* suggested—*the* novel of a great young American city, Chicago. Norris's oft cited faults of verbosity, rhetorical inflation, redundancy, and lack of reserve were belabored in reviews of *The Pit* by the *Brooklyn Daily-Eagle*, the *New York Sun*, and the *New York Times*. Norris never ascended to a level of Jamesian "fineness" in his writing. But the fact remains that in *The Pit* Norris had won the day.

Norris's sensibility frequently proved to be an ironic one: Trina "wins" a lottery prize in *McTeague* only to have the stroke of good fortune trigger latent personality traits that are destructive to her and her husband; Annixter transcends his boorish personality in *The Octopus* only to be gunned down by representatives of the railroad trust; and Jadwin and Laura lose all only to win a chance at a new, better life. Life's ironies, large and small, were a main ingredient of Norris's short fiction and novels. Thus it is chillingly ironic to note that after all the disappointments and years of labor, Norris finally arrived in a grand manner six months after his demise. The situation might have been fictionally developed by Norris himself. Those reading this volume will note that the section comprising responses to *The Pit* is not much smaller than the total length of all the sections devoted to his earlier works. And there is not only a quantitative difference to be observed here; qualitatively the estimates of *The Pit* are quite different from those of earlier works, including those of *The Octopus*. Not all of the reviews are reverential, but a tone of reverence is to be found throughout the section comprising reviews of *The Pit*.

When his work was finally beginning to draw the attention afforded to Davis and Crane, Norris's career was over.

II

What followed during the years in which Norris should have lived to build upon the firm foundation of six novels, many literary essays, and many more short stories was a large group of memoir-eulogy essays. By his contemporaries he was not forgotten. His reputation did not begin to decline until the middle years of the twentieth century, when his own generation began to pass away. As the reviews indicate, *A Deal in Wheat* (1903), *The Responsibilities of the Novelist* (1903), and *The Third Circle* (1909) did not add significantly to Norris's reputation. In fact, one who reads the reviews of these collections may easily conclude that the degree of positive response they received was mainly a result of what had transpired with the publication of *The Pit*. Reviews of *A Deal in Wheat* regularly refer to the author as the creator of *The Octopus* and *The Pit*, and many describe the volume as a collection of apprentice pieces. Frederic Taber Cooper voiced a dominant opinion in the *Bookman* (America):

> They impress one as fragments, rather splendid fragments too, trials of the author's strength, before he launched forth upon a really serious work. Take, for instance, ["A Deal in Wheat"]. It was palpably written for practice, a sort of five-finger exercise in preparation for Mr. Norris's last volume, *The Pit*—and from this point of view it is brimful of interest. But taken as a story, it is at once too long and too short.

With the help of Will Irwin, who introduced *The Third Circle* by focusing upon its tales as products of Norris's apprentice days, that volume received like treatment. Reviewers found the work of interest because it illuminated the initial steps in the "making of a novelist." *The Responsibilities of the Novelist* was also viewed as a gloss upon the career of a novelist who translated the literary theories expressed in that collection of essays into practice in *The Pit*. Moreover, one sees a reversion to the earlier situation of Norris around 1899. The reviews of the collections are few, and the expansive character of *Pit* reviews is replaced by the brevity typical of *Moran* reviews. When *Vandover and the Brute* was published in 1914, a similar situation developed. As with *The Octopus*, Doubleday once again sought to pave the way for a large procession of admirers of *Vandover*. Charles G. Norris wrote a promotional pamphlet designed to trigger a sensation over the story of how the long-lost manuscript was miraculously recovered from the fires of the 1906 San Francisco earthquake and accidentally identified in 1913. But as the *Vandover* reviews are read, it becomes clear that Norris had ceased to be a felt force in the literary world. Norris's mid-1890s boldness in *Vandover* seemed rather "normal" to readers of realistic fiction in 1914.

Where Norris remained vital was in the memories of his turn-of-the-century contemporaries, whose enthusiasm found its final expression in the prefaces to the ten-volume Argonaut edition of Norris's works published by Doubleday in 1928. And it was not until the 1950s that scholars with belletristic and literary-historical concerns began in significant numbers to revive Norris's popularity—if only on university campuses. Norris was, after all, clearly a pivotal figure in the transition from nineteenth-century American literature to modern literature. It is partially to this still-growing group of students of Norris that this volume is addressed.

One thing that the volume is intended to achieve is the provision of a better-informed point of view on the actual situation of Norris in the turn-of-the-century literary world, in which the forces of romanticism, realism, and naturalism were coalescing to shape the character of modern fictional prose-writing. What was Norris's relationship with the literary establishment, and most important, what effect did that relationship have on the development of Norris's craft? As a would-be popular writer, to what grandstand was Norris playing? What did the grandstand want, and demand? To what degree did Norris fashion his work to accommodate audience demands? Conversely, to what degree and at what moments did Norris sensationally violate, and vandalize, his audience's most cherished assumptions about the nature of literature? What shaping influence did Norris's work have on American literature? These are questions to which the here recorded contemporary reception of Frank Norris's works seems to offer some answers.

For example, did Norris fashion *Blix* the way he did in order to appease the genteel critics who had found *McTeague* an affront to good taste and public morality? At least one reviewer boldly suggests that he did thus play to the grandstand. Did Norris attempt to establish himself as an innovative writer honestly calling into question genteel standards of art? Reviews of *McTeague* and *A Man's Woman* seem to indicate that he did. As such questions arise, the reader will, one hopes, perceive not a static situation in 1899 and 1900 but, as Norris would have phrased it, the living, pulsating, vivid drama of Norris's dual struggle for success both on the establishment's terms and on his own antiestablishment terms.

III

We have here the materials for a fuller portrait of Norris in his own time, but this collection of writings should not be presumed a total or "definitive" one. Readers should not be surprised to find, several years from now, notices or reprints of newly discovered reviews of Norris's works in journals such as *American Literary Realism*. The present compilation represents more than five years of searching in contemporary books, magazines, and newspapers; but one should not assume that all of the critical response to Norris has been recovered. For instance, many reviews gathered by a clipping service are now in the Frank Norris Collection at the Bancroft

Library, Berkeley, California. Inadequate identification of the reviews and the inaccessibility of many newspapers of Norris's time have made it impossible to include those items here. Moreover, all newspapers have not been surveyed. That would take decades.

There are two other reasons for the reader to exercise a degree of caution when using this volume. The first has to do with the fact that reviews of *The Pit* are relatively easy to find. They are, literally, all over the place, and one can safely presume that a very true picture of the critical response to *The Pit* is afforded here. Reviews of *Yvernelle* and the other prior works do not seem so omnipresent. A researcher may spend many fruitless hours attempting to locate even one-line mentions of *Moran*, and he would certainly expect to find more reviews of *McTeague* than are included here. Moreover, one would think that the wave of popularity at the top of which *The Pit* rode would carry *The Responsibilities of the Novelist* and *A Deal in Wheat* into more popular regard. Apparently it did not. But I remain skeptical, and readers may have a right to suspect that the picture of Norris's grand leap to popularity with *The Pit* is somewhat exaggerated. Admittedly, the picture is partially a result of the *absence* of similar responses to *Blix, A Man's Woman*, and *The Octopus*, as well as of the inferior quality of the pre-*Pit* reviews. It seems only fair, then, to suggest to the reader that further searching in magazines and newspapers may alter the present picture to some degree.

Second, skepticism should inform one when considering what is meant by the "critical reception of Frank Norris." It is the kind of skepticism that ultimately grips any historian. The only hard data that we can recover are the paragraphs and essays left behind by the literary establishment. We know that Norris's sales climbed steadily from 1898 to 1903; we know that *The Pit* was truly a best-seller. But as to contemporary regard, all that we have is the opinion that gradually evolved in review after review and in posthumous estimates. As to posthumous estimates, we can presume that we are receiving in the main some sincere, reliable accounts of the impression Norris made as of 1902–3. But when we turn to the reviews, problems arise. They all have to do with the puffery, the strutting, and, in general, the media manipulations common to the publishing world then and now.

Those familiar with the small amount of Norris correspondence that has survived already know that it suggests the author's willingness to distort the facts of his life and work so as to enhance his image. He was not reluctant to write to reviewers such as Howells and Isaac F. Marcosson of the *Louisville Times* and feed them fact mixed with half fictions. Quite a few reviews in the present collection seem to be thus shaped by Norris's hand. However, when we read of Norris having graduated from Berkeley and from Harvard (neither statement is true), and of his adventures as a war correspondent, we also begin to suspect that Doubleday press releases

Introduction   xxi

were even more actively bending facts here and there to suit purposes of image-fashioning. Those familiar with the known facts of Norris's life will find "stretchers" offered to review-readers throughout this volume. The reviewers repeatedly used the hype that Norris and Doubleday were sending them; and one therefore begins to wonder how accurate a reflection of actual responses to Norris's *works*, especially the early ones, the reviews afford. Consider the fact that Doubleday printed in *McTeague* a biographical sketch of the author, which reviewers mined. It reads thus:

A NEW AMERICAN AUTHOR

It may as well be stated at the outset that this is a harsh, almost brutal story. It deals with a class of people who are beyond a question "common," and the author is far too conscientious an artist not to depict them as they really are.

MCTEAGUE; A STORY OF SAN FRANCISCO. BY FRANK NORRIS
But it is difficult to believe that anyone could read "McTeague" without realizing its overwhelming presentation of the modern curse of Money. It is by no means a tract or a sermon: it is a study in human development; and the very minuteness of its accuracy at once makes a convincing picture of contemporary life in the lower middle-class of a great city, and enforces the tremendous truth it contains. This truth comes from the story, not the story from any "lesson" which the author has set out to inculcate.

Mr. Norris has produced a novel of contemporary American life more real, vital, sustained, and dramatic than anything which has appeared for a long time. It deals with a phase of the West hitherto almost untouched: the Coast city with its strange conglomerate of inhabitants and lying upon the verge of a land where "civilization" sloughs off from the natural man without a struggle. It is a strenuous and tragic tale, yet there are passages, notably those dealing with the German-American Sieppes, which show a keen, irresistible humorous faculty. Moreover, the pathos and romance in the love-story of the two shy old people in the big flat, "Old Grannis" and little Miss Baker, have a delicacy of touch and feeling that stand out the more strikingly for the grim surroundings.

MR. NORRIS'S FIRST BOOK.
Mr. Howells speaks of "Moran of the Lady Letty" as an "extremely clever book," and says that "whoever desires a thrill may find it in this fresh and courageous invention, which has some divination of human nature, as different in man-nature and woman-nature, and some curious glimpses of conditions."

A RECENT CRITICISM OF THE AUTHOR'S WORK.
In a second notice of the book the *Louisville Times* has an interesting discussion of Western literature and of Mr. Norris as follows:

"In a recent paper on the development of purely local literary life in the United States Mr. William Dean Howells said that 'it was left for California to evolve the notion of something American which was neither vaunting nor shamed,' Mr. Howells believing that the distinctive original colonial material was developed in a sort of apologetic spirit. We are all willing to admit that Bret Harte was the pioneer of that evolution that has recorded itself in a varied and characteristic fiction. But Harte is away from the scenes that he first depicted, and the negatives of the Western land are growing dimmer and dimmer to that distant London view. Whether Frank Norris is his successor or not remains to be seen, but this most promising young writer has begun a work that bears every evidence of an artistic and highly successful fruition.

"The few who first saw in 'Moran of the Lady Letty' a quickness of style and a refreshing originality were convinced that its author was not a mere literary amateur. Something in the crisp narrative suggested vigor, the ability to do better things and to say the right thing at the right time. The original limited audience is becoming larger every day, and the verdict that 'Moran' was one of the best sea tales in many a day is having an emphatic endorsement.

"Norris believes sincerely in the possibilities of the Golden West, and his 'McTeague' is a more serious story than the first book that bore the name of the young Californian. Norris says that 'Moran' was a trial. It has encouraged him to something better. Very modestly he writes: 'I have faith in the possibilities of San Francisco and the Pacific coast as offering a field for fiction, not the fiction of Bret Harte, however, for the country has long since outgrown the "red shirt" period. The novel of California must be now a novel of city life, and it is that novel that I hope some day to write successfully.' And it may be typical of Frisco without the 'Purple Cow' to lead it to fame.

"The author of 'Moran of the Lady Letty' is eminently a type of the young men with whom the future of American fiction rests. He is a Harvard man, class of '95. Immediately after his graduation he became staff correspondent of the San Francisco *Chronicle* and was assigned to Africa to do the Uitlander insurrection. With three other journalists he was ejected from the country by the Boer Government after the failure of the Jameson raid. He settled in San Francisco as associate editor of *The Wave*, an illustrated weekly, for which he wrote 'Moran' as a serial. It attracted the attention of S. S. McClure, who put the Western man on his magazine staff and he went to Cuba with the Shafter expedition. He is now in New York.

" 'Moran of the Lady Letty' has strongly impressed itself as a brilliant sea tale. It is masterly, that fine picture of the Brunhilde of the salt water, a heroic figure, strong, reliant, brave, and in the end so inexpressibly tender. Only Louis Becke, with his glowing color of the South Seas, could vie with Norris in that portraiture."*

---

*A careful search of the *Louisville Times* did not reveal the actual publication of this statement, obviously written by one of Norris's strongest and earliest supporters, Isaac F. Marcosson.

Introduction

   This lengthy quotation merits full presentation because, as those already familiar with reviews of *McTeague* will recognize, the blurb expresses all of the positive points developed by reviewers. Doubleday had thus provided lively copy for those who had to meet press deadlines; for the lazier reviewers and those truly pressed for time Doubleday, in effect, wrote much of the text that would fill newspaper columns. At the least it provided a first draft. For *The Octopus* and *The Pit* Doubleday again worked hard to manipulate the character of reviewer response. As the *Vandover* reviews illustrate, Charles G. Norris's story of the recovery of the lost manuscript enlivened what might have otherwise been dull review columns. There will be occasionally noted, then, a quality of sameness in clusters of reviews, which should cause the reader to pause now and then when considering the character of Norris's critical reception.

   This is especially true in the case of *Blix*, which has been identified as the work that marked the first step in Norris's "arrival." I opined that the reviewers were somewhat stunned by the versatility of the young author who turned from *Moran* to *McTeague* to *Blix*—writing remarkably different books. The reviews clearly lead to one conclusion: that in late 1899 Norris had stepped over the threshold. *But* the pattern of national reviewer response causes some suspicion. What was in the press release that accompanied review copies of *Blix*? We should not be surprised to discover one day that Doubleday had viewed Norris as a versatile writer who seemed to be willing to try anything in his art and that the Doubleday press release functioned as a parent text for reviews.

   Although the nature of critical reception to Norris is to be found in these pages, judgment should be tempered by the apparent facts that reviewers were reading each other, were reading press releases from Doubleday, and were riding their personal hobbyhorses, as well as reading (in whole or in part) Norris's works. "Avalanche" effects also require attention, as in the case of *The Pit* when it became *de rigeur* to appreciate Norris's large intentions and achievements and to pose the question of what would have happened if this promising author had not died.

   Gore Vidal's key question in *1876*, regarding the ability of anyone actually to reconstruct the past, comes to mind. Perhaps, it is suggested in that novel, Julius Caesar's history of the Gallic Wars was merely a campaign biography, designed to create a firm base for political advancement. Perhaps. Perhaps not. All historians can do is make estimates by offering imaginative reconstructions founded on surviving data that are sometimes of a dubious character. Here we have a good deal of surviving data on the reception of Frank Norris, and all that can be derived is a probably valid approximation of what it was like as Norris became a force in the literary world.

IV

The reviews were lightly, and silently, edited when simple spelling and obvious typographical errors were encountered. When lines or word groups were obviously omitted by accident from the texts, we have indicated that fact with "[sic]." Reviews are complete, except for a few instances where ellipses indicate omission of absolutely irrelevant material. And given the character of the section devoted to *The Pit*, the decision not to abridge requires some explanation and, perhaps, defense. Some readers may wonder why it was necessary to reproduce in full the passages from *The Pit* quoted by reviewers. These quotations, in themselves, reveal some essential facts about Norris's image in 1903. Repeatedly the reviewers turn to the same lengthy, melodramatic, and ultrarealistic passages, thus clearly indicating to us what was viewed as the essence of Norris's art. In one review, passage A is celebrated; in the next, passage A is damned; but the fact that passage A, embodying what was viewed as uniquely Norrisean, is the constant tells us what impressed his audience, positively or negatively. For that reason the temptation to excise lengthy quotations from the reviews was resisted.

JOSEPH R. MCELRATH, JR.

Tallahassee, Florida

Acknowledgments

James D. Hart must be first in any list of contributors to the serious study of Frank Norris. The Frank Norris Collection at the Bancroft Library of the University of California was developed by him; and much of the work performed on this volume in 1971–72 was made possible by his generous sharing of information with those of us involved in the Frank Norris edition project at the University of South Carolina. Joseph Katz heads that project, and he made available to us his Norris files for photocopying—thus saving us a good deal of energy that we might have had to expend in obtaining materials through the interlibrary loan system. When we did have to turn to interlibrary borrowing, the staff of the Strozier Library of Florida State University made the situation as pleasant as it could be. We especially thank Anne Page Mosby, Carol Woolverton, Tricia Simonds, Betty De Carlo, and Cathy Cooper.

The Strozier Library, the University of South Carolina Library, and the Alderman Library of the University of Virginia kindly allowed us to photograph title pages in their copies of the works of Frank Norris.

YVERNELLE

A LEGEND OF FEUDAL FRANCE
BY FRANK NORRIS

"Cui me moribundam deseris, hospes?"
—ÆNEID

ILLUSTRATED

PHILADELPHIA
J. B. LIPPINCOTT Company
1892

Yvernelle

"Yvernelle."
The Publishers' Weekly, 40 (November 21-28, 1891), 36.

In the poem called "Yvernelle, a legend of feudal France," Mr. Norris has studied to good purpose the times and scene of his characters and events, which are purely fictitious, and has made of his dream of the days of tournaments a stirring poem of adventure and romantic love with a tragic climax. His hero is a fiery French youth, Sir Caverlaye of Voysvenel, who is reproached by Guhaldrada, a dark countess of old Spain, who thinks he has tired of her. In her bitter pride she sends him away with a curse.

The author says this idea came to him in reading Goethe's "Dichtung und Wahrheit." The banished knight knew he had been faithless and untrue to his first love, Yvernelle, whom he had left in his native France while he lingered at the side of the bewitching countess. The curse makes him afraid to return to Yvernelle. His wanderings and feats of valor make a very pretty song, full of life and color.

Messrs. Lippincott Co. have made one of their chief holiday books of this mediaeval picture of the feelings and sufferings and joys that are the same yesterday, today and for ever. A handsome illuminated title-page in many colors imitates some rich old missal. The text is clear and printed on heavy coated paper and looks very rich. Among the artists who have illustrated the many scenes of battle and chivalry and romance are J. J. Bissegger, who has done the half-title and caption for list of artists, notes and cantos; John J. Boyle, who has made the modellings for frontispiece, half-titles to cantos, etc.; F. S. Church, C. W. Dewey, F. Diehlman, E. H. Garrett, Will H. Low, E. Maene and Walter Shirlaw, all of whom have furnished characteristic illuminations of the old-fashioned text. The book is bound in several styles and makes a very important gift-book from an artistic standpoint. This narrative poem, a free and flowing fancy of the days of knight errantry, is skilfully worded, the author having well mastered all the technical difficulties of his art, and clothing his thoughts easily and fittingly in smooth verse. Some very telling points the author makes comparing the feudal baron of yore with the money-kings of today:

> Time there was when squire, page and knight,
> Portcullis, keep and barbican were real;
> When tournaments were things of daily sight,
> And chivalry arrayed in flashing steel;

And time there was when the brave
    errant-knight
  Was not a fancy of a minstrel's tale,
But fought in very earnest for the right,
    Or wandered wide to find the Holy
    Grail;
Or when on bridge or road, backed by
    his page,
  He held his post with ever-ready
    lance,
And pledged himself all comers to
    engage
  To win the favor of his lady's glance.

"New Publications." *Lippincott's Magazine*, 48 (December 1891), 647–48.

It has been and it will be the good fortune of few authors to have their writings published with an elegance in any degree comparable to that which distinguishes Mr. Norris's "Yvernelle." This narrative poem—a free and flowing fancy of the days of knight-errantry—has been made all splendidly beautiful by the magic touch of the artist's hand. The three illustrations in color are marvels of reproduction, worthy of fine framing; and the plentiful decorative designs, printed in monotint, show an excellence of drawing and an illustrative value highly meritorious. The volume, indeed, in every detail—in the superior quality of the paper, the faultless printing, the lavish margin, and the rich and tasteful binding—calls for unstinted praise. Its romantic text relates to the ever-glorious days of chivalry,—tells a moving tale in fluent and melodious verse of the loves and battles of a valiant knight who loses his heart in two lands. We are at first not so sure that the gallant Sir Caverlaye deserves our compassion, much less our admiration: he comes to know himself, however, and resolves to forsake the "dark countess of old Spain" and return to the "blue-eyed Yvernelle," and all our sympathy goes out to him, and we watch with bated breath the course of his adventurous journey into France, his great fight in the forest with the brother of Guhaldrada, and his furious gallop through the wild night to the door of the church wherein the fair Yvernelle stands ready to take the veil.

" 'Yvernelle.' " *The Critic*, 19 (December 5, 1891), 316.

"Yvernelle" is a legend of feudal France, told in octosyllabic couplet verse by Mr. Frank Norris, and handsomely illustrated by Messrs. Church, Dewey, Dielman, Garrett, Low, Shirlaw and other artists. The author knows how to tell a story and also how to write in the manner of Sir Walter. His lines have plenty of swing and music, and the narrative advances steadily without any break in the movement of the verse. The mediaeval character of the legend is well sustained, and there is plot and incident enough to make the story interesting. The illustrations, particularly the two heads—one by Low, the other by Dielman,—which are reproduced in color, contribute much to the beauty of the book and make it among the most attractive of the holiday volumes. It will please those who are fond of pictures quite as much as those who are fond of rhymed legends; and people who like both will be doubly pleased.

"Literature."
San Francisco Chronicle, December 6, 1891, p. 9.

In "Yvernelle" Frank Norris of San Francisco has written in verse a legend of feudal France. The tale is that of the fortunes of Sir Caverlaye of Voysvenel, a noble French knight, who falls under the influence of a Spanish damsel. When his passion is spent he breaks with her and returns to his former love, the lady Yvernelle, but he comes back with the Spanish woman's curse, which has power to blight his love. Of the way he removed this ban and won his bride just as she was on the point of entering a nunnery the poet tells in stirring verse. The measure is the rhymed heroic verse that Scott and Byron used so effectively. Mr. Norris handles it with great skill. He has the dramatic instinct, and in the great scenes—such as the curse of the Spanish woman, the return of the knight to France, the combat in the lists and the ride to save Yvernelle from the nunnery—the verse bends to his will and reflects the fire and passion of the actors in this dramatic story. The poem is suffused with the genuine spirit of chivalry, so that it needs not the details of heraldry to convince the reader that the author has made a loving study of mediaeval life and knightly customs.

The book has evidently been illustrated under the author's supervision, for everything is in keeping with the story. The modelings in bas-relief by John J. Boyle will interest anyone who loves ancient armor, while the designs by Church, Dewey, Garrett, Low and Shirlaw are unusually strong and appropriate. Dielman has given a portrait of Guhaldrada the Spanish damsel, and Low a portrait of Yvernelle, both in color. The book is superbly printed and bound.

"Weekly Record of New Publications."
The Publishers' Weekly, 40 (December 12, 1891), 987.

The romantic verse relates to the ever-glorious days of chivalry, and tells a moving tale of the loves and battles of a valiant knight who loses his heart to two ladies, one of whom is Yvernelle. The three illustrations in color are excellent reproductions, and the plentiful decorative designs show illustrative value and correctness of drawing. All the details of paper, print and binding are of artistic merit.

"Book News of the Week."
New York Herald, December 13, 1891, p. 26.

One of the best narrative poems that has appeared in a long time is "Yvernelle," by Frank Norris. It is a story of the Middle Ages, the scenes being laid in France, but there is nothing ancient about the rhyme or rhythm, both of which are delightfully smooth and flowing. Artistically the book is as dainty as the verse; it is full of fine pictures by good artists, a pleasing innovation being several full page plates in colors, the subjects being female heads; the print, paper and binding are of the best, and the result is a holiday book of the better kind.

"The Reviewer."
Columbus Dispatch,
December 16, 1891,
p. 8.

"Yvernelle"—a poem of the age when knights contended for honor and deathless fame, when ladies fair bestowed their smiles upon the victor and disregarded the vanquished, when chivalry reigned supreme and all feudal France was keenly sympathetic to chivalrous deeds—has been written by Frank Norris and as it appears from the house of J. B. Lippincott Company it is one of the handsomest books of the year. The poem is of remarkable beauty in thought and expression and in itself has all the elements to command attention. But illustrated as it is, and redundant with all the charms of the most advanced artistic skill, it has hardly a parallel in the magnificent array of Christmas books.

"Current Literature."
Chicago Inter Ocean,
December 19, 1891,
p. 11.

One of the most artistically illustrated holiday books of the year is "Yvernelle" before mentioned [in an advertisement] in our columns. It is a legend of feudal France. It is a poem of great strength and beauty. It is a royal love story, where true love as usual does not run smoothly, yet satisfies, when "all is well that ends well." Several eminent artists in their specialties contribute to the beautiful pages, among them Boyle, Church, Dewey, Dielman, Garrett, Low, Shirlaw, and others. The artists and poet and publishers have conspired to make the book both beautiful and entertaining.

"Songs of the Poets."
Cincinnati Commercial Gazette,
December 19, 1891,
p. 13.

... Another handsomely executed book, from the decorative point of view, is a narrative poem by Frank Norris. The tale told in Mr. Norris' graceful verse is a legend of feudal France. A very pretty love story is worked out, and there is much spirit and action in its relation. The poem is intensely dramatic, and Mr. Norris has given a very good picture of the life and customs of feudal France, in which medieval knights and lovely women stand out in high relief. Mr. Norris' poem is superbly illustrated. So thoroughly in touch with the text are the illustrations that it is evident the latter were done under Mr. Norris' supervision. The names of such artists as Church, Boyle, Garrett, Will Low and Shirlaw are signed to the illustrations. That is all that need be said as to their artistic worth. J. B. Lippincott & Co., Philadelphia, are the publishers.

K. B. Oracle.
"A Letter About Books."
The Wave, 7
(December 26, 1891),
9.

Here is a holiday book that surprises

me. It is by Frank Norris, a student over at Berkeley, one of whose stories—"The Jongleur of Taillebois"—appeared in the Christmas issue of this journal. It is a romantic story of chivalrous love and devotion, related in verse, called by the name of the heroine, "Yvernelle." Without considering the youth of the author, this is an exceedingly clever piece of work, exhibiting very considerable verbal dexterity and a decided power of composition besides imaginative power of no common order. In narrative poetry one generally finds a prolixity of words and a paucity of action, but "Yvernelle" is full of life, color, incident. There are some passages of descriptive writing that show touches of real poetic fire and fancy—the hunting scene, the meeting of Sir Caverlaye and Yvernelle in Canto I, the burial of the hermit and the downfall of Guhaldrada in Canto II, the ride of Sir Caverlaye to Kaerenrais and the description of the cloisters wherein Yvernelle is about to assume the veil in Canto III, are admirably done. The book is published in artistic style and its illustrations are quite the finest of the holiday publications I have seen this season. There are three illuminated heads, one by Dielman, of Guhaldrada, another of Yvernelle by Will H. Low, really exquisite work. Besides, there are photogravure illustrations, captions, decorations, that make this volume one well worth the having. I certainly congratulate Mr. Norris.

"Recent Verse."
Overland Monthly, 19 (January 1892), 106.

"Yvernelle," by Frank Norris, is a legend of chivalry founded on a passage from Goethe, in which a curse is laid by a deserted woman on the woman whose lips shall next touch those of her reluctant lover. Yvernelle falls under the curse and the story is devoted to the purging of the lover's sin through mortal combat and mastery of self and his final happy union with Yvernelle. The book is a marvel of the printer's art. The binding is in white and gold, and the illustrations are exquisite both in design and in reproduction. The illuminated figures by Dielman, Shirlaw, and Will H. Low, are especially fine. The text is interesting, sparkles here and there with an apt and pretty figure, and in the fight in the second canto, and in Sir Caverlaye's ride, rises to a good deal of dramatic force.

"The Books of 1891: Art Books."
The Publishers' Weekly, 41 (January 30, 1892), 204.

We devote so much space to this class of books in our Christmas Number that we shall not endeavor to do more in the present review than to name the leading illustrated works.... Frank Norris' "Yvernelle"....

"Recent Poetry."
The Nation, 54 (March 31, 1892), 254.

Then there is the highly wrought romance of chivalry, of which the most obvious recent type is "Yvernelle, a

Legend of Feudal France," by Frank Norris (Philadelphia: Lippincott), a book whose wealth of costly illustrations only makes the verse seem tamer.

Ella S. C. Michels. "California Writers and Literature." *The Story of the Files* (San Francisco: Co-operative Printing Co., 1893), pp. 359–60.

Mr. Frank Norris, a student at the University of California, has written "Yvernelle, a Legend of Feudal France," in rhymed couplets. Mr. Norris is only 21 years old, but he has already a more than local reputation. A long residence abroad seems to have saturated him with the spirit of France of the Middle Ages; and "Yvernelle" reflects very truthfully the "valor, love, romance and poetry" of those fascinating times.

When squire, page and knight,
Portcullis, keep and barbican were real.

"Yvernelle" is a strong performance for a man of 21; there are several episodes marked in dramatic force, and some descriptive passages which, perhaps, show the writer at his best, and hint of some pleasant surprises for the future. Of such is:

Within a forest's tangled heart,
Far from the fief of Brittomarte,
Some three leagues as the swart crow flies,
A little stone-built bridge there lies—
A relic of the Roman day
When Caesar's legions held their sway
Of Gaul—when Roman skill and art
Subdued the might of Gallic heart.
Scarce wider than the dun deer's leap,
Than his slim fetlock not as deep,
With dimpling cheek and laughing eye
The little stream goes dancing by.
Beneath its rippling wavelets fleet
The hemlocks bathe their gnarled feet;
O'er it the oaks their strong arms cast
To shield it 'gainst the boist'rous blast.

Of Frank Norris the *Boston Home Journal* says:

Frank Norris shows a familiarity with the old knightly chronicles in this romantic poem, and recounts with all the flavor and fascinating interest of the old chronicles, in fluent and melodious verse, the loves, battles and adventures of a valiant knight. His great fight in the forest, the furious gallop on the invincible horse, Bayard, through the wild night to the door of the church wherein the fair and despairing Yvernelle stands ready to take the veil, are recounted in a style of surpassing power.

The *Overland Monthly* says:

"Yvernelle," by Frank Norris, is a legend of chivalry founded on a passage from Goethe, in which a curse is laid by a deserted woman on the woman whose lips shall next touch those of her reluctant lover. Yvernelle falls under the curse, and the story is devoted to the purging of the lover's sin through mortal combat and mastery of self and his final happy union with Yvernelle. The book is a marvel of the printer's art—the binding is in white and gold and the illustrations are exquisite, both in design and reproduction. The illuminated figures by Dielman, Shirlaw, and Will Low are especially fine. The text is most interesting—sparkles with apt and pretty figures, and in the second canto and in Sir Caverlaye's ride, rises to a good deal of dramatic force.

CREPUSCULUM

I hear them say our little life's "a day"—
That, born with light, at dusk it dies away.
I hear them say that Death is that Life's night—
That we but wax and wane with changing light.
O Blind! The Day's not yet, this Life of ours
Is still the night's slow retinue of hours;
Its sorrows, nightmares, phantasms of shade;
Its pleasures, dreams that only form to fade.
Our Life's a night through which we blindly grope
With outstretched palms, hoping 'gainst failing hope.
Death ushers in the dawn of Life's true day;
Though gray the eve, so is the morning gray.
Be thou uplift, O Heart! Death's visage wan
Is lighted not with twilight but with dawn.—*Frank Norris.*

Eleanor M. Davenport. "Some Younger California Writers." *The University of California Magazine*, 3 (November 1897), 80–82.

Frank Norris is one of the younger school of writers, the school which writes up-to-date stories, and which, in San Francisco, appears first in the Overland Monthly, and later signs its name to articles appearing in the Argonaut.

At the age of seventeen Mr. Norris went to Paris to study art, for he was convinced that his talents lay entirely in that direction. For two years he lived the life of the picturesque Latin Quarter, drawing and painting and extending his knowledge of France and its people. He just escaped being a good artist. Why, it would be difficult to say, for his illustrations have a certain expression and spirit which is attractive, even though they are apt to be out of drawing, and his decorative work is good. It has always been hard for Mr. Norris to shut himself up with pen and paper and say, no, to all the calls of a delightfully alive world, for he has what a physiognomist calls the *sense* of human nature, that is, a love of people and the study of the vagaries of character. Perhaps it is this very love of human nature which prevented his making any mark as an artist; perhaps if he had been more faithful to his easel and less interested in experiencing the life of a French student, he would have remained an artist and never have attempted story writing. At any rate when he returned to

San Francisco, he was quite ready temporarily to sacrifice art to a college education.

Accordingly he entered the University of California with the class of '94, joined Delta Xi of Phi Gamma Delta and became a prominent member of the Skull and Keys. It was during his college course that he first seriously turned his attention to literature, and published his first book, "Yvernelle," a romantic tale in verse, which many consider superior to anything he has done since. He also wrote a junior farce for his class, made many illustrations for the University magazines and annuals, and did some very clever acting in various plays.

In the fall of '95, just before the Jamieson raid, Mr. Norris went to South Africa as a special correspondent for Harper's Weekly and the San Francisco Chronicle. He did some remarkably good work for those papers and was rapidly establishing his reputation as a journalist, when suddenly his communications ceased. For five weeks nothing was heard of him, and then he emerged from the revolution, having been mixed up in it just enough to cause the government to request him to leave. He came back to San Francisco with but one visible mark of his adventures—a rattlesnake tattooed on his right wrist.

Since his return from South Africa Mr. Norris has identified himself with The Wave, and the connection has been of mutual benefit, The Wave having raised its standard to an attractive, illustrated magazine, and Mr. Norris having made himself a place in the literary world through its pages.

How much of a place, we have yet to see. It is undeniable that his stories are read all over the United States, and that they are invariably crisp and entertaining. Mr. Norris has always been original in matter, but it is only lately that he has formed a style distinctly his own. When in college, his work savored strongly of Davis, and later his intense admiration for Kipling was apparent, but thanks to the discipline of regular contributions, Frank Norris' work can now be easily recognized even under the disguise of five different *noms de plume*. Vivid, graphic description is his strong point; he can make the most impossible tales plausible, and one cannot read his horrors, be thrilled for the moment and then forget them. Such a story as "The Third Circle" will haunt one waking and sleeping for days, and make him quake every time he thinks of Chinatown. Indeed Mr. Norris has made such a specialty of horrors, that one wonders whether he is capable of anything else, whether he is going to confine himself to scare heads, or cultivate a broader field with some space in it for the pleasant side of life.

At present Mr. Norris' readers are looking forward to the appearance of "Ways That Are Dark," a collection of short stories, illustrated by the author, which is now in press, and which will enable them to form a more just idea of his possibilities.

Notes

Moran of
The Lady Letty

A STORY OF ADVENTURE OFF
THE CALIFORNIA COAST :: ::

BY
FRANK NORRIS

NEW YORK
DOUBLEDAY & McCLURE CO.
1898

Moran of the Lady Letty

"Weekly Record of New Publications."
The Publishers' Weekly, 54 (October 1, 1898), 520.

Ross Wilbur, a young society man of San Francisco, was, in rogue's parlance, "shanghaied" and carried on board *The Bertha Millner*, a twenty-eight-ton keel schooner, commanded by Captain Kitchell, a brutal white man, whose crew consisted entirely of coolies. An account of Wilbur's exciting voyage on *The Bertha Millner* is given, with a graphic description of the capture of the derelict *Lady Letty*, and the tragic history of Moran, who is, aside from Wilbur, the most interesting personage in the singular novel.

George Hamlin Fitch.
San Francisco Chronicle, October 2, 1898, p. 4.

No better story of adventure has been printed in many a day than "Moran of the Lady Letty," by Frank Norris, the young San Francisco writer, who is well-known on this Coast by his short stories and sketches. The book is brought out by Doubleday & McClure Company of New York in good style, but it is a pity that the publishers did not illustrate it, as the tale is full of material for striking pictures. They have given it a handsome dress, however, and the book ought to be a success, unless the public has wearied of stirring stories of adventure.

Nearly all the action of the story takes place along the coast of Lower California and in Magdalena bay. The plot is simple, but strong, and is marred by only a few improbabilities, which the author could easily remove. The hero, Ross Wilbur, is a wealthy young San Franciscan, fresh from college, who is shanghaied on the water front and taken to sea in a dirty schooner, whose crew is made up of Chinese coolies. They are under a master who is worthy of a place in any of Clark Russell's sea novels. Captain Kitchell is a clean-cut type of the unscrupulous adventurer, and one is sorry when the exigencies of the plot end his brutal but masterful career. The cruise is for sharks' livers, which are tried out for oil, and almost at its beginning a derelict is sighted. Boarded by the captain and Wilbur, she is found to be the Lady Letty. The only persons found are the dead Norwegian captain and a young sailor lad, whom Wilbur discovers to be a girl in man's disguise. A squall comes on, sinks the derelict and the villainous Captain Kitchell, and leaves Wilbur on board the schooner with Moran, the daughter of the Norwegian master of the Lady

Letty. This girl, bred to the sea and her father's constant companion in his voyages, is a new type in fiction. A thorough sailor, she is strong as a man and has a supreme contempt for the politeness of the young hero. She stamps upon his pretty sentiment and, as the only navigator, takes command of the vessel. Wilbur, of course, falls in love with her, but of this, of their adventures with pirates, of the awakening of Moran's dormant womanly nature and of their return and the girl's tragic fate, only a mere mention should be given here, as the reader ought to enjoy the surprises of the story and its keen dramatic interest.

Defects there are in the tale, but these are not grave. The hero, almost at the outset of the story, orders a Manhattan cocktail in a water-front saloon, and is so careless of his surroundings as to permit his rough companion to drug his liquor. No self-respecting young American, with any knowledge of city life, would dream of taking a cocktail on any city water front. If he had to drink there he would take his whisky straight, as less dangerous to the system. Again, in the scene on the schooner the Chinese pirates are represented as without firearms, yet Wilbur and Moran permit these coolies to board the vessel, when one good man with a sharp cutting spade such as the shark-fishers used could have kept off a dozen. Then in the fight on the beach Wilbur is represented as throwing away in the excitement of battle a loaded pistol, after firing one shot, and jumping in among a lot of Chinese hatchet-men. In real life he would have potted as many heathen as he could with bullets, and then used the heavy revolver as a weapon, for every one knows it is far more effective in a hand-to-hand fight than a knife.

But these and other minor blemishes do not seriously hurt the interest of the story. In its unforced realism and its sustained dramatic strength the story is worthy to take rank with Stevenson's "The Wrecker" or "The Ebb Tide." From the outset it gets a firm grip on you, and there is no escape from its uncanny power. Its sea characters, its Chinese and its society people are all true to life. They impress you as real. Even Moran, the heroine, who at first seems an impossible figure, becomes genuine flesh and blood. The style is strong, clear, terse and yet full of color and picturesqueness. No one has painted so well the Lower California coast as Norris in the few short descriptive passages which he introduces. Take it all in all, this is a great story, and not the least of its merits is that it gives promise of better work to come.

"Novels and Tales."
The Outlook, 60 (October 8, 1898), 394–95.

A dramatic story of the sea is Mr. Frank Norris's *Moran of the Lady Letty*. Moran, a Norse maiden, is discovered on board a deserted bark by a schooner belonging to the Six Companies of San Francisco, whose mate is a society man who was "shanghaied" by the aid of knock-out drops. A love story follows.

"Briefer Notices."
Public Opinion, 25 (October 13, 1898), 473.

"Moran of the Lady Letty," is a somewhat enigmatical title, so it may be well to explain that the *Lady Letty* was the name of a ship and that Moran was the name of a girl who was the sole living being found aboard the ship when she was encountered by Ross Wilbur, a darling of San Francisco society. Wilbur was Shanghaied and awoke to find himself at sea aboard a schooner that was out for fishing or piracy on a small scale if a favorable opportunity occurred. The captain of the schooner being happily drowned, Wilbur found himself second in command of the schooner, for Moran was of the masterful mold and assumed control under all circumstances. This is as much of Mr. Frank Norris's tale as we shall tell. We will add only that Wilbur obtained Moran's affection by the old-time method of worsting her in a hand to hand fight and so securing her respect. That he lost her after she was won was probably a piece of good fortune for both. The tale is readable, but not above the average.

"Literature."
The Independent, 50 (October 20, 1898), 1129.

This book has the stamp of the Pacific upon it, so that the sub-title, *A Story of Adventure Off the California Coast*, is superfluous. It is a romance dyed with the accepted colors well known to Bret Harte, Stevenson and Joaquin Miller, not to mention Charles Warren Stoddard. There are beach-combers, very picturesque indeed, Chinamen of the conventional sort, and Moran the strange heroine. The story is amateurish in tone, but not ill told, and it will be read with pleasure by those who are not sticklers for the finished art of the masters in fiction. If the author is young we may yet have good work from him.

"Recent Fiction."
Washington Times, October 30, 1898, p. 20.

"Moran of the Lady Letty" is a story by Frank Norris, of San Francisco, and was originally published in the *New York Sun*. It is not a long story, but possesses the rare merit of novelty. It is safe to say that there has been nothing in American fiction just like this tale of adventure. The novelty is not in the style but in the subject. The heroine, Moran, is a Norwegian girl of twenty-two, who has followed the sea with her father all her life; who fights, swears and sails a ship like a man, and a very rough man at that, and who is, in short, simply a reincarnation of an ancient Viking woman. By a strange chance she is thrown into the company of a Yale graduate, an athlete and society man, shanghaied and carried into the South Pacific on a shark-fishing vessel. With the aid of a crew of Chinese the two manipulate the vessel, the captain having been eliminated by one of those devices known to romance. Falling in with a set of beach-combers of the most degraded Chinese type, they make a bargain—or rather Moran does—for a part of the carcass of a sperm whale. Finding in this carcass a lump of ambergris worth a good-sized fortune, they determine to secure it, and, to save their lives as well as their fortune, are forced to fight a pitched battle with their half-human, savage allies. It is a return to the primitive life of humanity. It is the story of a type of high civilization of the nineteenth century —a man morally, mentally, and physically thoroughbred—thrown head first into the conditions of the Middle Ages, or even of the life before the Middle Ages—the days when Thorfin Karlsefne sailed among icebergs in a sea-serpent galley. So wild and daring a conception would occur to few writers, and only one in a hundred to whom it occur would be able to work it out. Mr. Norris seems to be equal to his task. The story is vivid, strong, forceful, as the hero himself might have told it. The man who can write such a tale as this should be able to do other good work of an unusual sort. It is one of the best sea tales of the year.

" 'Moran of the Lady Letty.' "
Buffalo Morning Express, November 20, 1898, p. 18.

This is a story of the Pacific Coast, which, in its main lines, recalls Kipling's "Captains Courageous." It is about a San Francisco society youth who is shanghaied and carried off in a sailing vessel engaged in the shark fishery off Lower California. During the cruise he helps to rescue a Scandinavian girl, Moran, from a derelict. The captain of the fishing schooner is lost, leaving only the youth and the girl and the Chinese crew. The girl has Viking blood in her veins, and takes command of the schooner, and leads an attack on a party of Chinese pirates, and otherwise distinguishes herself on an exciting voyage. The story is steep in places, but it has the taste of the sea in it, and it enthralls the reader.

Geraldine Bonner. "A Californian's Novel."
The Argonaut, 43 (November 21, 1898), 7.

One evening last winter, in New York, I was looking over the *Evening Sun*, when I came upon a chapter of "Moran of the Lady Letty." It was chapter six toward the second half of the story, and I had read nothing that came before it, yet it held my attention with its brusque and almost defiant sharpness of phrase and the lurid picturesqueness of its setting.

"Good for California!" I thought; "I must see the rest of this."

But fate willed otherwise. For several subsequent evenings I was reft from the *Evening Sun* by engagements, and when these were over the *Evening Sun* was reft from me by other members of the family who got it first. When I finally did get hold of it, "Moran of the Lady Letty" had run its course, and the mystery of what caused the *Bertha Millner* to rise up and tremble as she lay moored to the kelp in Magdalena Bay remained a genuine mystery to me.

At intervals since then I have speculated about it, and once, hearing two girls at a lunch discussing the book, I eagerly asked for a solution of the unusual performances of the *Bertha Millner*, and strange as it may seem, though they both had read it through, they neither of them could remember this particular point. The other day I got the book myself and read it from cover to cover, and then I knew why two up-to-date and intelligent young women had overlooked what seemed to me, in my ignorance, to have been the main point of the story.

It is a curious thing that one of the chief faults of the Californian writers should be a lack of sincerity. This is curious, because the Californians themselves, "in their habits as they live," are remarkably sincere. In fact, I think I should put this attribute as at once their best and their strongest. A sincerity sometimes defiant, sometimes indifferent, sometimes carelessly self-reliant, marks the race. Californians are, as a rule, true to themselves, whether they are serenely apathetic, or cheerfully nonchalant, or violently and aggressively unconventional. They do things because they like to do them, and that sums up their entire creed.

That the works of their writers should be marked by a peculiar, meretricious extravagance I think rises from the fact that most Californians, and certainly all Californian writers, have it on their consciences that they have got to live up to the reputation of the State as a place where astonishing, lurid, and tremendous things have always happened. Outside California the Californians of the gentlest and quietest species have been forced by public expectation into the most surprising and embarrassing pranks. It is like the Americans in Paris. No one will believe in them until they begin to indulge in the strange, wild antics that the French novelists ascribe to them.

So the Californian writers feel that nothing ordinary or humdrum must come from the land of suns and snows. Mrs. Atherton, viewing her distant home through English spectacles, writes of heroines who must not disappoint her English readers—girls who never get out of the superlative degree; whose lovers, if they were ranged in line, would stretch from Lotta's Fountain to the ferry; whose riches are past the dreams of avarice; and who in behavior mingle the childish barbarity of M'liss with the sophisticated fascinations of Mrs. Skaggs.

Mr. Norris's muse has had little to do with the devious ways of society. He is a romanticist of the savage type. Belles and ball-rooms have had no attractions for him. He likes the darkling by-ways of the Barbary Coast. The lean-bodied, slinking grisette of the local Latin Quarter, furtively stealing along by the walls, with shawled head and side-glancing black eyes, has more attractions for his pen than the scented, corseted, silk-lined siren of his own world. He writes fierce, dark tales of the lawless beings who dwell in tenements that hang by the eyelids on the ledges of Telegraph Hill. The haunted, inner chambers of Chinatown, thick with opium smoke and dim with mystery, appeal to his sense of the horrible. The water-front, with the great ships sticking their noses over the wharves; the swarthy sailor-men, with their brown faces and their strange, clear eyes; the alluring scents and the thousand voices of the sea—exert over him their exultant and uplifting charm.

But his work has always shown the effort of attempting to give reality to the unusual. It has lacked the power of convincing, and, like Mrs. Atherton's—with brilliancy and cleverness—has missed the sincerity which impresses the reader. I have not read all, but have read a good many of Mr. Norris's stories, and in almost all of them have felt the absence of the imaginative force which compels us to accept and receive these wild tales of strange people.

But in "Moran of the Lady Letty" Mr. Norris at last got real control of his story, and for the first half was the master of it. I suppose every writer has felt that buoyant sensation of mastery which comes with the knowledge that he has control of his work; that the tale is following his lead; that it is docile to his command, and under his guidance is sweeping forward, steadily and confidently, toward its climax. And I also suppose that no honest writer living—from the impatient amateur who has never yet been published to the great master who has his disciples and his imitators—has not known the misery of feeling his story quietly slip through his fingers without a moment of warning, break away from him, shake off his guiding and controlling hand, and dash forward on its once wavering course, shattering itself as it plunges onward.

This is what "Moran of the Lady Letty" did. For the first half the author had his idea completely under his control, and it moved forward with strength, firmness, and an exultant force and sincerity. Then, suddenly, just about in the middle of the story, he lost command of it and never regained it to the end. I think that it was the introduction of the Eternal Feminine, as represented by Moran—the massive and monumental heroine—that broke up the harmonious relations between the author and his work. Mr. Norris knew whereof he dealt when he wrote of the little schooner nosing her way through the crisp, green seas; of the humming of the wind in the strained cordage; of the miracle of gold-leaf sunrises and flaming sunsets; of the silent, oily calms, and star-strewn midnights on the breast of the still and tremendous Pacific.

Up to the finding of the derelict the book is alive, full of vitality, and vigor, and truth. The chill, wild breath of the trades sweeps through it, the rustling rush of seas crushed under the *Bertha Millner*'s bows sounds from page to page. We feel the still heats of noonday, the enormous quietude of evening. The few figures that move against this canvas, blazing with the colors of the vast ocean floor and the vast sky dome, are natural and simple with the elemental simplicity of those who go down to the sea in ships. We follow the narrative, caught and carried away by its swinging, onward rush, with quick, curious sympathy. The fascination of the Pacific is there, the sense of mystery that blows across it from the strange and wonderful East—the mysterious East whence so many things that are weird, and evil, and beautiful, and terrifying, come.

If Mr. Norris could write a whole book, and keep it on the key as he has kept "Moran of the Lady Letty" up to, say, the fifth chapter, he would be one of those writers who are to reveal the genius of the West to the incredulity of the East. We are proud of him as it is, and I, for one, offer him my congratulations and prophesy for him a success that will be all round, not go half way and then stop, as it has done in the case of "Moran."

For "Moran" grows into a disappointment. After the introduction of the heroine the story ceases to move forward. It becomes a series of adventures, more or less episodical and unnatural. Mr. Norris's descriptive talent, which is simple, strong, and vivid, stands him in good stead in these hurried chapters, where improbable incident crowds on incident, and where the tale suddenly appears to have quitted this part of the globe entirely, and to be taking place in some wild and distant land at some remote period of the world's development. There is no progression in the characters at all. They step on and they step off the stage; they do astounding things; battle, murder, and sudden death rage about them, and they remain as wooden as figure-heads on ships. The charm, the air of an elastic and buoyant life that marked the earlier chapters entirely disappears. Toward the end the feeling that the author was conscious of the falseness of his work, and grew tired of it, and hurried it up, struck me at least very strongly. Mr. Norris is too clever not to have felt what a mess he had got his people into when he tried to introduce a Valkyrie from German mythology to a little San Francisco *débutante* in white canvas shoes and a pink shirt-waist.

The sincerity of the story was lost when Moran took the stage. Moran, as an idea, is very fine. A sea-story, wild and free as the foam-crested billows, with a heroine, untamed, unconquered, fierce in her splendid independence as the winds that tore her hair, honest as the sun that tanned her cheek, was an original and harmonious conception. But Mr. Norris would not let well alone, and in order to draw her in the few, firm lines that befit the primitive type, made her appear as a sort of gigantic, mythological figure—a Titanic demi-goddess built on the scale of a huge statue. In order to bring her off her pedestal and make her fit into the background of an evil-smelling, dirty, begrimed trading schooner, he makes her drink whisky, wear men's clothes, and when talking stand with her thumbs in her belt.

But the most unconvincing thing about Moran is her hair. I am an expert on hair, and I declare, over my signature, that Moran's hair is the most improbable of the many improbable things in the book. It is "rye-colored," and she has two braids of it as thick as a man's arm. Now, there are men's arms and men's arms. There is Sandow's arm and the arm of the living skeleton at the circus. If Moran had two braids that fell to her knees, each as thick as an arm of Sandow, she would have had some difficulty in carrying them around. As she is the strongest and most energetic of women, we will have to suppose the arm referred to was that of the living skeleton at the circus.

Moran, in her sou'wester and blue jeans, wears her hair in two braids, sometimes hanging forward over her shoulders. In the high moments of storm and tempest the braids lash out on the elements, at others they fall peacefully over her shoulders to her boot-tops. Once Mr. Norris gives us a glimpse of her while performing her morning toilet, and after braiding her rye-colored tresses, she knotted them. I have seen braids of hair tied up with little blue ribbons, like Christmas presents, and I have seen them turned up and fiercely bound around with what is technically known as "combings"; but to knot them I Never. It can't be done.

I.F.M. [Isaac F. Marcosson].
"A Splendid Story of the Sea."
Louisville Times, November 26, 1898, p. 7.

If you want to read a bracing sea story, a story that for cleverness, color and all those things that make a book really fascinating to the reader of fiction, then read "Moran of the Lady Letty." The author, Frank Norris, has done nothing before to startle the literary world. The name of the book at hand is not calculated to arouse any particular interest. It is a splendid sea story, told in brilliant style, and it is one of that lamentably small number of recent offerings in fiction that with the end is a sincere regret that there is no more.

In the first place, Mr. Norris has a delightful style. It is not pretentious; it does not soar; but it is undeniably clever, and it makes an impression. And then Mr. Norris has quite a capital story, refreshing in its originality, sustained to the very end and there is almost a quarrel with him because he has killed a superb creature. Moran is a Brunhilda [sic] of the high seas, a glorious creature and a daughter of the Vikings. She lives like a man, walks the decks like a man and in the hour of danger faces it like a man. The sea is her highway; the winds her lover until she meets a San Francisco swell who has been kidnapped aboard a schooner and compelled to work. Moran's ship is lost, her father drowned and then begins the friendship between this magnificently isolated creature and the clubman. It is an unusual story and Mr. Norris has told it in captivating style. Love makes all things vulnerable and it kindled the spark in the breast of this queen of the seas, and the woman is asserted in the end. It is a strong analysis, this laying bare of Moran's heart, but it is intensely human. She died as she lived, alone on the deck with the salt air playing about her cheeks and the sea murmuring at her feet. "Moran of the Lady Letty" is one of the best sea tales of the year.

bibulous purpose he accompanies the stranger to a low sailor's boarding house, where he is promptly drugged, "shanghaied," and taken on board a fishing schooner with a Chinese crew. Their adventures lie chiefly with sharks and pirates, but Ross is instrumental in saving from a derelict the young woman who gives her name to the story. She is daughter to the dead captain, an expert navigator, strong as a man, profane and masculine, and given to lying. The only feminine things about her are two long braids of yellow hair which, we would think, must have been much in the way of her daily avocations. She and Ross share many dangers together, and strange to say, fall in love with each other, but the incongruity and impossibility of the sentiment is so marked that it is a relief when one of the Chinese sailors knifes Moran and sends her body off to sea in the smack to find an ocean grave after the pattern of her Viking forefathers. To imagine her civilizing into a female gilded youth, with a knowledge of dress, deportment, salted almonds, and tea-table chatter, is too great a stretch of human fancy.

"Moran of the Lady Letty."
The Literary World, 39 (November 26, 1898), 404.

Frank Norris is the author of this "story of adventure off the California coast." A very queer story it is. Its hero, Ross Wilbur, a gilded youth who leads germans, goes down to the wharves at night to meet a friend's yacht, and casually accepts an offer to drink made him by a dirty and suspicious character on whom he has never set eyes before. For this

William Dean Howells. "American Letter: Some Recent Novels."
Literature, 3 (December 17, 1898), 577–78.

In a way, all portraiture of life on the terms that fiction proposes is impossible. Life cannot give any one its confidence literally and really as the novelist says it has done in a certain case; it is essentially incapable of being so interviewed. But unless you grant the preposterous premise that it can be shown in its deepest intimacies by fiction, you simply cannot have fiction; the thing ends before it has begun.

The question, after the premise is granted, is how much impossibility shall colour situations, characters, and incidents. For myself, after I have supposed the case, after I have once made the immense concession asked of me by the art, I like to have the artist keep to the closest verisimilitude in everything. I feel that in supposing he can represent life at all, I have done enough, and that he is then bound not to falsify its motives and circumstances at all. It is for some such reason as this that between two extremely clever stories by two rather new writers I choose one for greater praise and the other for less; and I cannot allow that they are of kindred quality because the less praiseworthy approaches the more praiseworthy in its methods. That approach is rather too much like the homage which vice pays to virtue for my austere morality.

I

I am obliged to own that I read the two books I mean with almost the same breathlessness; if anything I gasped rather more in the crucial moments of "Moran of the Lady Letty" than in those of [Will Payne's] "The Money Captain"; but I do not consider even my own gasps criticisms; for the gasps of other people I have no more regard than for their goose-flesh. Still, "Moran" is a clever little story, and if the reader does not mind granting, after the working hypothesis, that a young society man in San Francisco can be drugged, cast aboard a fishing-schooner, and articled with a belaying-pin for a voyage to the waters of Southern California, there to take sharks for their livers in the employ of the Chinese Six Companies, I cannot deny that he will find a good deal of reality in the society man himself, as well as in the pirate-souled skipper, and the several Chinese cooks who manage the crew. As for the incidents, they follow one another with a profusion and a rapidity which leave one little leisure for question of their probability, from the time the skipper and the hero board a derelict vessel which promptly blows up with the skipper and leaves the hero in charge of the gigantic sea-girl Moran. She is the daughter of the Norse captain of the derelict, she was born and brought up on the ocean, and she has always lived the life of a man. She promptly takes command of the schooner, and the hero becomes her mate and remains no more than her comrade till she turns upon him in the madness of a hand-to-hand fight with Chinese pirates, and finds him more than her match in a sort of Siegfried scuffle. She then duly owns her love, but the vigilance of the author prevents her marriage with the hero when they return to civilization, and he again becomes a society man. The captain of the Chinese pirates is her prisoner on board the schooner, and while the hero is gone to tea on a neighbouring yacht he seizes the chance to make fight for the lump of ambergris which first caused her trouble with him and his crew. Moran has no longer the strength of former days; her love has sapped her courage; she has instinctively become dependent on a man for her defence, and she falls under the Chinaman's knife.

In simply stating the scheme of any romanticistic story one has an unkind air of mocking it; but I should sincerely deprecate this in the case of "Moran of the Lady Letty," to which I am grateful for some rapid passages of time, to say no less. The story gains a certain effectiveness from being so boldly circumstanced in the light of common day, and in a time and place of our own. Whoever desires a thrill may find it in this fresh and courageous invention, which has some divinations of human nature, as differenced in man nature and woman nature, and some curious glimpses of conditions. You are aware, in these, of a San Francisco world, as in "The Money Captain" you are aware of a Chicago world, interestingly unlike other worlds on either shore of the Atlantic.

II.

The Chicago novel, however, keeps one illusion to the last, and does not, like the San Francisco romance, break an outer to get at an inner illusion. The working hypothesis suffices the author, and after that he makes as little demand upon the reader's imagination as any novelist I know....

"Literary Chat." *Munsey's Magazine*, 20 (January 1899), 653.

A story betrays many things about its author, little facts about his personality that he is quite unconscious of registering. One may catch glimpses of him over the hero's shoulder, and make very good guesses at his manner of bearing himself from his manner of shaping his phrases.

No man with a light, careful footstep could have written "Moran of the Lady Letty." It goes at a sure, strong pace, straight at the object wanted, and one hears the sound stump of heels in every page. It is the pace of one whose feet push the ground away from them with their surplus vigor.

It is to the sense of fresh vitality that this book of high adventure owes half its charm. It is a thing built of flesh and blood, bone and muscle. It has a mind of its own, and a temper. It goes to sea for adventures, and finds them, too, strange, picturesque events new to the world of fiction, part of them taken, no doubt, from the experiences of some weather-beaten old sea captain, since man's imagination does not furnish such odd yet plausible properties without the help of living facts.

Moran herself, "sired of the surges," moves like some splendid valkyrie through the story

> shunning men and shunned of women, a strange, lonely creature, solitary as the ocean whereon she lived, beautiful after her fashion; as yet without sex; proud, untamed, splendid in her savage primal independence—a thing untouched and unsullied by civilization. Her purity was the purity of primeval glaciers. ... Wilbur found himself... wondering to just what note the untouched cords would vibrate; just how she should be awakened one morning to find that she—*Moran*, sea rover, virgin unconquered, without law, without land, without sex—was, after all, a woman.

It is a sincere story as well as a quick, stirring one, written with a convincing belief in its people and events, and not without a certain scorn of the probabilities. One reads it with a sense of salt on the lips—and, once, in the eyes. The author, Frank Norris, is a young Californian with a strong taste for adventure that has already taken him from South Africa to Cuba, and a strong fist for the wielding of a pen. He has made a good beginning in fiction.

"Among New Books." *Chicago Daily Tribune*, February 2, 1899, p. 8.

"Moran of the Lady Letty" opens with the declaration that it is to be a story of a battle, at least one murder, and several sudden deaths, and the program is certainly carried out to a finish. It is a story of adventure off the California coast, written by Frank Norris, a San Franciscan himself, and is published by the Doubleday & McClure company.

There is no time lost in admiring scenery or any other side play from the time young Wilbur, dainty society swell and Yale athlete, is kidnapped and kicked into the forecastle of a filthy little longshore schooner, until his eventful return at the end of the book. And the adventures are not common; far from it. A fearless, powerful young Norwegian girl is rescued from a derelict, and by reason of strange chance and forceful seamanship she becomes Captain of the little schooner and its crew of six Chinamen and one city swell. Then there are adventures with Chinese "beach-combers," culminating in a pitched battle on the shore of Lower California, in which this curious woman, frenzied by the war spirit, attacks the young athlete, gets all the masculinity knocked out of her in a catch-as-catch-can fight with him, and learns to love him in that moment—probably the most remarkable method of lovemaking on record. The style of the story is always lively.

"Novels of the Week." *The Spectator*, 82 (March 18, 1899), 386.

...*Shanghaied** is a strange tale of a young Californian dandy, fresh from Yale, who is drugged in a San Francisco crimping-house and carried off to sea in a pirate schooner. His strange alliance with a Norwegian Amazon, rescued from a derelict, supplies an element of barbaric romance in a narrative which reminds one in its main motive of Mr. Kipling's *Captains Courageous*.

"Shanghaied." *The Academy*, 56 (March 18, 1899), 328.

To be Shanghaied is to be drugged, and decoyed as a sailor on board an American ship. Once on board, the mate's fists or revolver instill seamanship. In this story a gilded youth of San Francisco suddenly finds himself on a vessel commanded by a drunken, bullying captain. His adventures form the book, which is of American origin, and incisively written.

"Fiction." *The Dundee Advertiser*, March 30, 1899, p. 2.

Amongst what may be called extreme

**Moran* was published in England by Grant Richards with the title *Shanghaied*.

adventure stories recently issued Frank Norris's "Shanghaied" will take a very high, if not premier, position. In the first place, it is refreshingly original and clever. Next, the action is both brisk and surprising. Thirdly, it is extremely picturesque and riotously redolent of the sea, and of strange waters, too. Lastly, it introduces a character whose like has not before appeared in fiction. This is a young Norwegian woman who affects male attire, and displays extraordinary courage and endurance in many surprising and terrible adventures through which she passes with the hero. The latter is a society man of San Francisco, who is shanghaied or carried to sea in a schooner bound on a curious little trading trip to the coast of lower California. On the way a disabled steamer is encountered. The captain's corpse lies in the cabin, and the only living person aboard is a young seaman. The latter is discovered by our hero to be a woman. This is only the beginning of surprises. The story ends tragically with the death of the fair Norwegian, and the close is as dramatic as the beginning. So strong and remarkable a book should quickly become popular.

"A Good Story."
The New Age, 19 (March 30, 1899), 155.

"Shanghaied," by Frank Norris (Grant Richards; 3s. 6d). Frank Norris's story of adventure off the Californian coast is a remarkably well written piece of work. Ross Wilbur, a young man of the highest San Francisco society, is "shanghaied," i.e., drugged, and taken on board the "Bertha Millner," a "two topmast twenty-eight-ton keel schooner," with the result that he learns things. The captain of the schooner, Kitchell by name, teaches Wilbur the first lesson by throwing him down a hatchway and allowing him two minutes to change his clothes in. "He went down the forward hatch at the toe of Kitchell's boot—silk-hatted, melton-overcoated, patent-booted, and gloved in suedes. Two minutes later there emerged upon the desk a figure in oilskins and a sou'wester. There was blood upon the face of him and grime of an unclean ship upon his bare hands. It was Wilbur, and yet not Wilbur. In two minutes he had been, in a way, born again. The only traces of his former self were the patent-leather boots still persistent in their gloss and shine that showed with grim incongruity below the vast compass of the oilskin breeches." Captain Kitchell comes to grief in the course of the adventure, and is eaten by sharks; we are sorry for this, as the Captain was uncommonly good company, especially when sober, whilst the rest of the crew were silent Chinamen. Wilbur is not left solitary, however, for when Kitchell disappears, Moran, of the "Lady Letty," is rescued from a derelict. Moran Sternersen is a descendant of Scandinavian Vikings, and she and Wilbur have great times, and naturally enough fell in love with each other. In due course they take the schooner back to San Francisco, and then when we are looking forward to a fresh chapter, our story is all too soon finished, for Moran is dead. Excellently told is the reappearance of Ross Wilbur in polite society, but indeed, the whole story is excellent and of unflagging interest, and it is to us a welcome oasis in the desert of dull fiction. We do not remember having seen any of Mr. Frank Norris's books before; we shall certainly look forward with pleasure to his next volume—there is a vigorous, descriptive power, a brightness, and withal a humour displayed in "Shanghaied" that likes us well.

"Shanghaied." *Bookman* (England), 16 (April 1899), 22.

"Shanghaied" is a stirring tale well told. The interest is sustained throughout from the first chapter to the last, and the tragedy at the end is as dramatically effective as it is unexpected. The heroine, a modern Amazon, without sex and without fear, is a highly original conception. Mr. Norris has not made her quite real to us, but has gone far towards it. We are sorry that Captain Kitchell has to be killed so early in the story. There is a gruesome fascination about this truculent ruffian, who robs a dead man of his false teeth, and then, having qualms of conscience, cannot bury the body till he has replaced them upside down. The book is full of exciting incidents, the fight with the Chinese "beach combers" being particularly good. "Shanghaied" is certainly a story to be read. We shall await Mr. Norris' next work with much interest.

"Shanghaied." *Edinburgh and Glasgow Scotsman*, April 6, 1899, p. 2.

Mr. Frank Norris's new story of adventure is briskly and brightly told, and as the scene is somewhat novel, and thrilling incidents are crowded thick on a small canvas, it provides a capital entertainment for any one who can appreciate good story telling. To be "shanghaied" is to be seized by sailor men, carried aboard ship, and made to slave like a coolie on the pain of brutal ill-treatment at the hands of a tyrannous captain. This was the fortune of Ross Wilbur, a wealthy Chicago club man. Having gone down to the docks to meet a long-absent friend, and having made acquaintance with a suspicious character to kill the time, he finds himself aboard the "Bertha Millner," with only one white man, the captain, and a crew of Chinese coolies. Like a true American he accepts the situation, along with the oilskins, dirt, and other concomitants of life on a boat that is bound for the lonely coast of California, there to secure sharks' livers which in time will be made in Chicago into the finest cod liver oil. It is a beastly existence; yet it is not altogether dull. For they fall across a derelict with a strange, yellow-haired Scandinavian sailor lad as the only occupant. A storm destroys the derelict and the captain; Moran, the sailor boy, turns out to be a strapping young woman; there is no end of fighting and adventures with sharks, Chinese pirates, and submarine disturbances; and generally the story hums along. Wilbur falls in love with the Scandinavian girl; but she, in spite of her heroic virtues, is of another world than his, and one feels that her tragic and sudden death at the end is the best thing for both of them. The story, being told by Wilbur in the first person, takes the form of a slice of wild and unheard-of adventure sandwiched into the ordinary life of a fashionable man about town. The sudden change in environment is the cause of an equally sudden change of temperament in the man, and one is constantly reminded that under the broadcloth of the city fashionable lurk the passions and virtues of the primeval savage. Moran is a strong and original character, powerfully depicted. Like Wilbur, the reader grows to enjoy the spectacle of the lonely Californian coast line, with its myriads of loathsome sharks; and even the Chinese coolie, with his strange pidgin English, becomes not altogether unlovely. This effect is due to the vigorous and terse style of the descriptive writing, and the air of reality in which the writer has, by his art, succeeded in investing an inherently improbable tale.

"New Novels: Shanghaied."
London Daily Telegraph, April 7, 1899, p. 3.

Ross Wilbur is "shanghaied"—that is to say, he leaves an afternoon tea-party in San Francisco, and is promptly drugged and conveyed on board the Bertha Millner, where, under the threats of Captain Kitchell, he exchanges his silk hat and frockcoat for oilskins and a sou'-wester. Then follows a voyage of much incident and originality. Captain Kitchell goes down in the Pacific on a derelict which he had found and appropriated, and Ross Wilbur is forced by the Chinese crew to set sail for Magdalena Bay and shark-fishing. He acts as the mate of the Bertha Millner, but the captain's place is taken by Moran Sternerson—Moran the Norse maiden, the daughter of a Hundred Vikings, sea-rover and sailor, sexless, strong, and ferocious. A more oddly assorted pair than the City-bred club man and this strange girl have seldom been sent on a voyage together. They reach Magdalena Bay, and commence the business of shark fishing. There follows an encounter with a Chinese junk manned by beachcombers, the discovery of ambergris of great value, the sinking of the Bertha Millner, and the desertion of the Chinese crew. And lastly a battle on the shores of the Bay, which ends in a single combat between Ross Wilbur and Moran Sternerson. Moran is beside herself with excitement:

> Her eyes were blazing under her thick frown like fire under a bush; her arms were bared to the elbow; her heavy ropes of hair flying and coiling from her in all directions; while with a voice hoarse from shouting she sang, or rather chanted, in her long-forgotten Norse tongue, fragments of old sagas, words and sentences meaningless even to herself. . . . Once more she had lapsed back to the old Vikings and sea rovers of the tenth century—she was Brunhilde again, a shield-maiden, a Valkyrie, a Berserker and the daughter of Berserkers; and, like them, she fought in a veritable frenzy, seeing nothing, hearing nothing, every sense exalted, every force doubled, insensible to pain, deaf to all reason.

The conflict ends in a hard-won victory for Ross Wilbur, and Moran loves him for conquering her. Oddly enough, the man loves her too, in spite of—or, perhaps, because of—her red face and hands, her massive frame, her hair yellow to whiteness, and eyes "blue, with a glint of ice in them." She is different to anything he had ever known. They go back to San Francisco, and there Moran is murdered. The author gives a beautiful description of the dead girl lying on the deck of the little schooner which is racing out to the Pacific. "She went out with the tide, out with the storm; out, out, out to the great grey Pacific that knew her and loved her, and that shouted and called for her, and thundered in the joy of her."

Mr. Frank Norris has written a delightful book in "Shanghaied." It is fresh, breezy, original, and full of interest. The author is thoroughly at home with his subject, and, in scenes like that of the fight between Wilbur and Moran, or in the picture he draws of the lonely, deserted, heat-ridden Magdalena Bay, he shows some vivid descriptive power.

"Shanghaied."
Glasgow North British Daily Mail,
April 10, 1899,
p. 2.

It is not often that even the professed novel of adventure thrills the reader and holds his attention as this one does. To the attractions of a somewhat novel set of incidents and characters Mr. Norris has added that of a highly picturesque and vigorous style, and between the two any attempt on the part of the reader to lay the book aside for purposes of natural rest or refreshment is irresistibly overborne. Ross Wilbur, a young and wealthy San Franciscan gentleman, is "Shanghaied"—that is, has a drink he takes with a casual sailor drugged, and when he next wakes up he finds himself on board a small and dirty vessel, with a crew of Chinamen, commanded by a brutal and unscrupulous captain; their destination, he learns, is the Californian coast, where a harvest of sharks' livers and the resultant oil are indicated as the objective source of profit. On the road they fall in with a derelict, the only living occupant of which is a girl of Norse descent, huge in frame and of manlike strength and courage. The wicked captain being opportunely drowned, Wilbur and this strange female, Moran Sternersen, are compelled by the Chinese crew to continue the voyage, for Moran is an accomplished navigator, and none of them are capable of filling the dead captain's place. From this point right on to the end the tale is of thrilling interest, one event following another with breathless rapidity. The character of Moran dominates the reader—it is so original and so boldly drawn; her actions are so unexpected and her abilities so unique that they hold one's attention by a species of fascination, and while we deplore her fate we at the same time admit that no other course was left open to the author. A female Berserker in modern life would have been an anachronism.

J.D.
" 'Shanghaied.' "
London Star,
April 22, 1899,
p. 1.

"Shanghaied" (Grant Richards), by Mr. Frank Norris, is a splendid sea story. It describes the strange adventures of Ross Wilbur off the California coast after he was "shanghaied," that is to say, drugged and forced to serve Captain Kitchell as a common seaman on the Bertha Millner. Kitchell is a delightful ruffian. It is a pity that he dies so soon after Moran comes on the scene. She is a wonderful Amazon, fierce, fearless, and ferocious as one of her berserker ancestors, and in her Mr. Norris has drawn one of the most original heroines in recent fiction. Nothing less than love tamed or tempered her savagery, and indeed Wilbur had to hit her between the eyes with his fist, and so prove his physical superiority, before she yielded to her womanhood. Her end is very dramatic. Of the many sensations in the story, the fight with the beach-combers is the most thrilling; but the most horrible incident is the torturing of Hoang. Moran was determined to make him talk, and this is how she did it. A file was thrust endways into his mouth, and his jaws were bound tightly together. "Some few inches of the file protruded from his lips. Moran took this end and drew it out between the beach-comber's teeth, then pushed it back slowly." I will not harrow you by going into more detail, but you may imagine that by the time Hoang's teeth were filed down to the gums he was willing to talk. Later on, when he murders Moran, can you blame him? But sheer brutality is not unnatural, for it is a polite error to think that gentleness, tenderness, and refinement are the attributes of women. Indeed, some think that the average man is "softer" than the average woman. In novels, at any rate, the dice are loaded too heavily in favor of what a great, if unknown humorist, has called "the fair sex."

" 'Shanghaied.' " *Saturday Review* (England), 87 (June 3, 1899), 696.

"Shanghaied" is a skilfully told tale of shark-fishing and primitive passion in unfrequented seas. A Norse girl, Moran, of the derelict "Lady Letty," and a "shanghaied" (kidnapped) 'Frisco exquisite are the chief characters, but the breezy sketch of the roaring skipper, Kitchell, stands by itself as one of the best things in a book which despite its undoubted cleverness is too reminiscent—in the way that many a popular orchestral selection is reminiscent—to quite meet the craving for novelty its author apparently set out to satisfy.

"Shanghaied." *The Athenaeum*, April 14, 1900, p. 461.

Ever since the unfortunate Dantes in "Monte Cristo" was snatched from the wedding-feast at Marseilles the incident has been found useful. In "Shanghaied" a smart young man of San Francisco society is drugged, and pressed on board of a ship engaged in a more or less nefarious trade. His adventures are of the exciting and blood-curdling kind usual in tales of the sea, but they have some decidedly novel features. When the poor fellow gets back to civilization he no longer cares for it. The rough sea life has changed his nature. It is hard to believe that such a thing is possible, but Mr. Norris tells his story well and may convince some readers. At all events, his book is short and vigorous.

Notes

McTeague

A Story of San Francisco

By FRANK NORRIS

AUTHOR OF "MORAN OF THE LADY LETTY"

NEW YORK
DOUBLEDAY & McCLURE CO.
1899

McTeague

"A New and Promising American Novelist." *New York Tribune*, March 5, 1899, p. 14b, "Illustrated Supplement."*

"McTeague" is in large measure a "slum" novel, and, like every other book in that category, it is more repellent than one thinks fiction ought to be. On the other hand, the author has a sincerity which makes his work sympathetic, and even when the tale is most sordid and distasteful it commands the reader's interest. Though Mr. Norris is obviously forming himself as a novelist, feeling his way toward the production of first-rate work, he already has merits of an uncommon sort. Thus McTeague, the giant dentist who is the central figure in the book, is anything but attractive when he is first introduced; but Mr. Norris contrives to make him so real that we soon follow his development with eager curiosity. It is a grim evolution through which the dentist passes from quiet vegetation and simple honesty to drunken passion and cowardly murder. The curse of gold is at the bottom of the man's fall, which is facilitated by the pure animalism of his nature. Left to work out his destiny as a cheap dentist, McTeague might have died in his bed, but when, on the eve of his marriage, his betrothed wins $5,000 from the lottery, the seeds of moral collapse are implanted in the breasts of both. The woman is a miser. Adversity lures McTeague on to get at the money his wife is hoarding. The gradual growth of unhappiness in the household is admirably indicated by the author; and, in fact, it is in his treatment of this matter and in his portraiture of McTeague and Trina that he persuades us to expect strong work from him in the future.

We feel the more confident of his taking a conspicuous position because the glaring faults of this narrative are such as may easily be corrected by experience. Some of these faults may even, if properly treated, prove foundations for better things. For example, the detail is now excessive, sometimes absurdly so, but at least it shows that Mr. Norris sees clearly and can put what he sees vividly on paper; and he only needs to learn selection to make his descriptions entirely satisfactory. Also, while he is learning what to leave out, he might include philosophical platitudes in his index expurgatorius. On page 92 there is an observation fairly comic in its jejune character. Then there are inexplicable repetitions of words and phrases, brought in to go with certain personages, and that way lies artificiality—a fault to which the au-

*Reprinted in *The Literary News*, 20 (April 1899), 109.

thor further shows that he is liable by painting some of his figures more with an eye to a certain effect than to absolute truth. Old Grannis and Miss Baker, whose love affair is supposed to supply an idyllic contrast to the coarse existence of the McTeagues, would do very well as foils to that pair if they had not been made almost imbecile in their timidities. In short, the author's untutored talent is inclined to overshoot the mark from beginning to end; but it is better to have too much power than too little, and Mr. Norris has a fresh vigor which is captivating enough in these days of mediocrity. We only hope that he will not jump to the conclusion that because his book is in some ways good it is necessarily a masterpiece. He cries aloud in this story for disinterested advice, for some one who will make him work hard at the elimination of his crudities. His greatest peril lies in the direction of the self-satisfaction so easily aroused by the flattery which in these days awaits just such a promising novice as he happens to be.

"A Story of San Francisco." *New York Times,* March 11, 1899, p. 150, "Saturday Review of Books and Art."

To be definite, to produce an absolutely clear impression of the subject at hand, seems to be the foremost aim of the school of realists to which Mr. Norris belongs. When George Moore wrote "Esther Waters" he sacrificed every other charm of style, even the sharp wit of his critical essays, to this one quality of precision. Chiefly by statement naked of adornment, and partly by the cheaper method of iteration, the person and the scene were pressed firmly into the reader's mind. The result was that no one who read the book can remember it vaguely. The mention of it instantly recalls the whole distinct dreary picture, with its uncompromising outlines and details. We speak of "Esther Waters," because this book "McTeague" is the only American novel to our knowledge that resembles it in subject and style. Each has a motive that in the last analysis conveys a moral lesson. In Mr. Moore's book the gambling passion, in Mr. Norris's the passion of the miser is followed from the ugly start to the uglier conclusion. Both writers have chosen to portray the life of the common and unintelligent people who have been neglected in literature largely because their aspect is exceedingly uninteresting and promises small reward for the labor of exhaustive study. In "McTeague," as in "Esther Waters," the process of development turns out to be the process of degeneration; in the one case the woman is responsible for the miserable outcome, in the other the man. The English writer goes back of the individual to the structure of society in which he moves to account for his downfall. The American is content to show the individual and his environment without investigation of causes.

Mr. Norris puts himself out of the way of temptation to anything like "pretty" writing by his choice of situations. McTeague is a dentist, and Trina Sieppe falls from a swing and knocks out a front tooth. That is the beginning. The first love scene is laid in the operating room, to the orchestral accompaniment of scraping instruments and "purring" burrs; and the details are most unlovely. Mr. Norris succeeds, however, in bringing McTeague through the first phase with his rude flag of honest intention—flying. He is never again more than a brutelike creature of great bones and sinews and evil inherited traits. But it cannot be forgotten—and this is the value of Mr. Norris's plain method—that once the good in him struggled with the bad and gained the mastery.

The story progresses from the period of the courtship, in itself an abomination to the fastidious, through the successive stages of an infelicitous married life, with increasing sordidness, brutality, and misery. By the time the dark termination is reached the beginning seems almost gay in its absence of lugubrious incident. Mr. Norris is certainly not deficient in a sense of humor. The account of the wedding supper is a masterpiece of pure comedy; not refined, for nothing would be more incongruous than refinement in connection with that broadly farcical scene; but restrained to the point of stiffness, and irresistibly diverting. It is a supper that deserves a place at the lower end of the social line headed by Mr. Meredith's brilliant festivities.

The same spirit of humor prompts the description of the theatre "treat"; but a false note is struck in the introduction of details that are purely vulgar, without necessary connection with the intrinsic vulgarity of the whole episode. To reverse Swinburne's phrase, Mr. Norris gives us an ounce of good fresh humor to a pound of more questionable ingredients. It is obviously a part of his plan to keep the tone of his writing in harmony with the tone of his subject, the style being for him not the man, but the subduing of the man to what he works in.

It is also part of his plan to represent the importance of concrete portraiture. We see again and again Trina's narrow milk-blue eyes, her little out-thrust chin, her heavy huge tiara of black hair. Again and again we are reminded of McTeague's enormous red hands, "hard as wooden mallets, the hands of the old-time car-boy," and of his big red ears, his thick red neck, his great square-cut head. Again and again, too, we hear the story of the gold service from Maria Miranda Macapa, and the favorite phrases of the class to which McTeague belongs are fifty times reiterated. Mr. Norris seems positively to court weariness on the part of his readers by this droning repetition of details. When the book is closed, however, we realize that the impression has been pounded in; that the life of these people, removed, as far as the east is from the west, from all the refinements of higher civilization, has become a part of our intellectual equipment, familiar in its most intimate aspects. It is not wise to condemn a method strong enough to produce this result; but it seems to us to be a method that must be regarded as a preparation for art, and not as art itself. There is no doubt of its value as a groundwork, and from the writer who employs it we invariably look for fusion and synthesis in his later style. Although "McTeague" is pretty hard reading and not a book to enjoy, it contains testimony to a talent that may turn out to be genius. It is a monument of industry and fidelity to fact, and those whose curiosity concerning their fellow-man extends to the lower middle-class life of San Francisco will be rewarded for weathering its difficulties. In one respect Mr. Norris lets himself go with joyous abandonment. He revels as freely as Mr. Kipling in the jargon of special trades and finds place for a quantity of words that are not in the dictionary. His conscientiousness is so pervasive that we are entirely willing to take his word for their accuracy. It would be impossible to suspect him of "miscallin' technicalities."

"Among the New Fiction: A New 'Great American Novel.' "
Buffalo Morning Express, March 12, 1899, p. 18.

"McTeague," the new novel by Frank Norris, who wrote "Moran of the Lady Letty," is a good story. Whether it is a great story is open to debate, although there are critics who would decide at once in the affirmative. But though it has its weaknesses, it also has its strength; and it is certain that Mr. Norris's next book will be worth watching for.

"McTeague" is a story of San Francisco. It is a study in the lower half of life. McTeague is a half-trained dentist, who is finally compelled by the city to suspend practice, because he has no diploma. Most of the other characters of the story are dwellers in a lodging-house in a quarter of small tradespeople. The book is a study of the relations of McTeague and his wife. He has a big body and only half the ordinary amount of wits. She is a clever, anaemic girl of German parentage, who wins $5,000 in a lottery and develops into a miser. He loses his profession, and at the end of a struggle between his shiftlessness and her miserliness, he kills her. He runs away from San Francisco, becomes a miner, and finally dies in Death Valley in trying to escape the officers of the law.

The strength of the story is in its episodes, rather than in it as a whole. Many of these episodes have great dramatic qualities. They remind the reader of Stephen Crane's studies of life. They are minute, photographic, outspoken, full of humor. The picnic with Mrs. McTeague's family, the visit of Mrs. Sieppe to the variety show, McTeague's wedding feast and other chapters live in the memory as entertaining facts. The love affair of the old spinster and the old bachelor, in the lodging-house, is of mingled pathos and humor. But the plot does not develop in an easy and natural way. The curse of gold is the leading motive and finally wrecks several of the chief characters of the story; but its workings are not delineated in such a way as to be convincing. The fate that befalls Mrs. McTeague and the others is plausible, but not inevitable. This gives the story the aspect of melodrama. Some portions of the book are pure melodrama, like the episode of Maria Macapa and the junk-dealer Zerkow—an episode which is, none the less, one of the most striking portions of the book.

Mr. Norris is not a Dickens, but his novel has refreshing vitality and originality. Next time he should do still better. He is a Harvard man, '95, who reported the Uitlander trouble in the Transvaal. Then he did newspaper work in San Francisco and finally went to Cuba with Shafter, as a member of the staff of McClure's Magazine. He is now in New York.

I.F.M. [Isaac F. Marcosson]. "The Story of McTeague." *Louisville Times*, March 13, 1899, p. 6.

A golden light lured men on to our Western land, where in the full radiance of the setting sun they found wealth and just as often failure. The story of that region has found its record in fiction through the medium of a few scattered short stories, which have dealt in the purely picturesque rather than the real aspect of life. It is a rich field, that California land, where great mountains frown on the east and the peaceful sea laps on the west, a land of sunshine and flowers, with a poetic Latin past, when fat friars ambled and vesper bells tinkled from adobe missions. The evolution has been rapid; civilization has relegated the red-shirted miner to the background, and he belongs now to a type that has exhausted itself in our native fiction. As the great metropolis of California reared its proud structures and gathered from many lands its varied people, there rose in its midst the new Westerner, not the rough-handed delver after gold; not the busy promoter; but a coarse, prosaic creature, who was the product of those early, semi-savage days. It is this man that Frank Norris exploits in his new book, "McTeague." It is a story of San Francisco, and is the artistic evidence of the determination of its author to build out of the Western city life the fiction of California.

That this book is strong, virile, throbbing with life, and brutally lifelike is no surprise. There were those who saw in "Moran of the Lady Letty" the hallmark of a coming man; the emphatic indication that finer and greater things were to be expected. Moran, a magnificent creature of will and tenderness, drenched by the ocean brine, is hardly a companion figure for McTeague. Where Moran yielded in her isolation and was warmed by the quick rush of love, McTeague is always the savage. Norris proclaims himself a member of the realist band; the coterie that finds for life's canvas no dab of impressionism but the quick flow of color that only follows the bold stroke. "McTeague" puts its author in the rank of our best younger authors. If it is a harsh, uncompromising study of humanity, it is undeniably the work of the sincere artist who knows whereof he writes.

* * *

Fiction has been best described as an abstract of life. Therefore characters in fiction must be reproductions of humanity. If the life reflected is ordinary and the instinct commonplace, there can be no quarrel with the man who faithfully reproduces. McTeague's story is the semi-translation of a savage. The man is a great, coarse-grained hulk, the elements of his life as driver boy at a mine ever dominant in his make-up and his actions. He is a dentist in a poor district. One of his accomplishments is a gentle way of extracting teeth with his fingers. The brute force is always cropping out. His chief delight before a woman came into his life was to gorge himself with food, drink his fill of steam beer and then lie torpid and stupid, and inert in a cloud of cheap tobacco smoke. Truly this is not a very inspiring figure about which to weave the threads of a story. It can only be harsh, discordant, almost repulsive. But then, again, it is life, and if the mirror is to be held up, the image must not be dodged.

McTeague pursues his ponderous way. He is the creature of his environment. There is scarcely any variety in the monotony of his life. The cable cars trundle by his door by day, and at night the ducks and geese cackle in the market near his office. He drinks more beer, pulls more teeth and becomes more stupid. Then the woman crosses his path. She has the kindness to fall out of a swing and break off a tooth. She sits in his professional chair. He feels her hot breath, and her hair brushes against his face. He is too coarse to be thrilled, but something moves his sluggish nature. It is beauty and the beast. She lies before him asleep from gas; she is helpless, and the conflict is waged between animal and spirit. The woman wins. Her touch becomes magnetic, her breath scented, and her hair gives off a sweet fragrance McTeague loves. The woman demurs. Then he simply gathers her up in his great brute arms, crushing her into submission. She scarcely feels love. Rather is it concession to strength. Thus McTeague loves and proposes. The woman tries to bring the man up to her level. She partially succeeds. Then they marry. The translation of the savage has begun.

* * *

Money becomes the curse of McTeague's life. He is professionally debarred and the retrograde movement begins. It is a vivid, realistic picture that Norris draws with the return of the savage again. The beer becomes whisky, the brain becomes thick; the arms that once crushed in the delirium of love now strike in the frenzy of drink. These people are "lost in the tide that always ebbs."

McTeague's translation is stopped. Then comes the conflict between man and woman—the woman sunk below her level, the man at his normal stage. There can only be one ending. McTeague is the fugitive murderer, now drunk with blood. And if this book possessed no other merit than the final picture, it will have served the purpose. It is the awful silence of Death Valley, and in the gleaming sun the white alkali meets the horizon on every side. Here, hunted, mad with thirst, McTeague meets his pursuer, the man who ruined his life. It is a fierce battle that is waged out on that death field of baking acrid powder under the pitiless sun. And McTeague is handcuffed to the dead man alone in that burning desert. It is a truly awful picture, and Norris has done it with a powerful pen.

* * *

This harsh story is not without its touch of sentiment. Nothing could be more tender than the romance of the two old people, who live in adjoining rooms, who know the silence of love for years and yet fear to break that silence. Each knows the habits of the other. When one binds his papers at night the other makes her tea and, with only a thin wall between them, they sit out the evening. And this goes on for years. But the day comes when even the second childhood cannot prevail against timidity, and these two old people, the one with the flush mounting to the faded cheeks and the other with wrinkled hands trembling with joy, walk together through the twilight of their lives. This is the leaven of the book.

It is a powerful, dramatic story that Frank Norris offers in "McTeague." His people are flesh and blood and they enact the tragedy of their rude lives vividly before you. They are exasperatingly alive. They do not demand sympathy, but they arouse intense interest. Through comedy, pathos, success, failure, they are the same human creatures. Norris writes with terse strength and appealing force; with vigor and disdaining all pretensions to style. His marvelous technical knowledge at once suggests Kipling. His comprehension of dialect is admirable, and his humor is delightful and refreshing. "McTeague" is a distinct advance in his art.

"Briefer Notices." *Public Opinion*, 26 (March 16, 1899), 347.

There is no denying the fact that the McClures have a fine faculty for the discovery of new writers of fresh ideas and style. Frank Norris was one of the writers discovered in 1898 by this firm; his "Moran of the Lady Letty," as we advised our readers at the time it was published, is an exceedingly clever story, thoroughly original, and for a romance of its kind, very well constructed. This author has now published another story, "McTeague, A Story of San Francisco," which displays much the same talent that was observable in his first book. But we must express regret that he should have followed the fashion set by so many of our younger writers in searching out the degraded side of humanity. Truth may be clean and pleasant as well as soiled and brutal. It is a good story, as we have said, but we trust that Mr. Norris's next plot will fall in more pleasant places.

John D. Barry. "New York Letter." *Literary World*, 30 (March 18, 1899), 88–89.

The Doubleday & McClure Company has lately brought out in *McTeague, a Story of San Francisco*, a volume which seems to me worthy to rank among the few great novels produced in this country. Before reading the story I had heard it well spoken of; but I was astounded by its profound insight into character; its shrewd humor; its brilliant massing of significant detail, and by its dramatic force. Many readers would consider the subject too unpleasant to be treated in fiction; but for those who do not go to fiction merely to be amused and diverted, and who believe that fiction may profitably be made an expression of life, *McTeague* will be a revelation. An authoritative reviewer recently spoke of it as a study of people who were on the verge of the criminal class. This statement, apparently made as a reproach, was hardly fair. But even if it were absolutely true, why should the author be blamed? People on the verge of the criminal classes, as well as the criminal classes themselves, offer excellent material for serious study in fiction. "I can't understand," said a novelist the other day, "why reviewers are always blaming writers for making their disagreeable characters true, instead of praising them for making the characters express their evil meaning as they do in life." Mr. Frank Norris has been blamed and will unquestionably be blamed again and again for choosing the theme of *McTeague*; but it is only just to him to say that he has handled his material fearlessly, that he has steadfastly followed out his premises to the end. His characters are all common, and they make a picture of the common life in the San Francisco of today that, for clearness and vigor, leaves very little for criticism. Every figure is perfectly realized; every episode has its significance. The main theme, the relations between McTeague and the little German-American girl who becomes his wife, are indicated with extraordinary fidelity, the man's natural brutality, brought out through misfortune, being thrown into play with the woman's instinctive economy, stimulated into wild avarice by the chance that has won for her a five-thousand-dollar prize in a lottery. The description of the wedding feast of these two people is one of the strongest pieces of writing that I have ever read. It is the kind of writing that, in its vivid presentation of the comic and the pathetic, makes the reader feel like laughing and crying at the same time. The subordinate interests are very skillfully woven into the work of the narrative. Perhaps the strange love affair between little Miss Baker, the retired dressmaker, and old Grannis, conducted in silence on either side of the partition that separates their rooms, has a little of the unreality of romance; and the marriage between the drudge, Maria Macapa, and Zerkow, the miser, founded on the story told by Maria of a wonderful gold service of one hundred pieces, contains a curious suggestion of the more extravagant fancies of Dickens. But both these motives are made absorbingly interesting, and many readers will find in the love of the two old people an exquisite poetry and pathos. The book deserves a great success, and it ought to place Mr. Norris in the first rank among our writers, beside Mary Wilkins, and Howells, and Stephen Crane. Indeed, *McTeague* is in treatment not unlike Stephen Crane's work, though without the least suggestion of imitation and without, too, the least suggestion of that striving for effect that Crane's writing shows. The style is wholly free from trickiness, and is simple and virile, evidently the natural expression of the author's thought. It is by no means, however, a mature and finished style, and in this regard Mr. Norris is sure to develop. Now and then the reader sees the author pulling the strings, so to speak, standing off and explaining the characters in a way that suggests superiority. This is a fault to which I have already referred in these columns, in connection with the work of nearly all our writers of fiction. Mr. Norris would have gained in power if he had not only projected his characters and allowed them to explain themselves as much as possible, but also used, whenever he spoke in his capacity as author, language wholly in harmony with theirs.

After reading *McTeague* I remembered that the name of Frank Norris had been connected with a volume published several months before, so I soon looked it up. It astonished me too, because it was so unlike the other book and yet so good. *Moran of the Lady Betty* [sic] is an adventure story that Stevenson might not have been ashamed to sign. It is capitally written, it moves swiftly, it has several nice sketches of character, and it tells a fine and thoroughly original tale of the sea. A man who could write both those books certainly has a rare versatility. In the last number of *McClure's*, too, Mr. Norris has a short story, "This Animal of a Buldy Jones," in still another vein, telling of an adventure in the art-student life of Paris.

Since reading these stories I have

learned something about Mr. Norris himself. He was born in Chicago ("but of course he couldn't help that," he writes of "Buldy Jones," who was born in the same place), and, as a young boy, he went with his family to live in San Francisco. Ten years ago, when about eighteen, he went to Paris and studied for a year at Julian's. This explains the "Buldy Jones" story. He gave up the idea of becoming a painter, however, and he studied for a time at the University of California, and for one year at Harvard, entering with the class of '95. It was at Harvard that he began *McTeague*, writing it, oddly enough, as a short theme in the composition course conducted by Professor Gates, to whom the book is dedicated. Two years ago, after his return to San Francisco, and after a period of service on the *Chronicle* there, he decided to make a book of the sketch, and he joined a friend who was working a mine in the mountains, where he could write in solitude. After three months the novel was completed. *Moran of the Lady Betty*, though published first, was written after *McTeague*. For a time Mr. Norris served as one of the editors of the San Francisco *Wave*, coming to New York about a year ago at the invitation of the Doubleday & McClure Company to take a position on their staff. He has, I hear, two new books ready for publication.*

*A response to this estimate appears on pp. 45–46.

"Books of the Week: Novels and Tales." *The Outlook*, 61 (March 18, 1899), 646–47.

Mr. Frank Norris, the author of "Moran of the Lady Letty," has published through the Doubleday & McClure Company (New York), a study of San Francisco life under the title *McTeague*. The work shows distinct power. It is an effort to deal with real life at first hand, and so far as this goes it indicates a sound instinct on the part of the writer. It is a misfortune that he should have devoted so much skill and virility to the description of a life so essentially without spiritual significance, and so repulsive in its habit and quality. There is, it is true, a touch of idealism in the relations of the two elderly lovers who appear in the story; otherwise the reader is immersed in a world of bald and brutal realism from beginning to end, and is brought into association with men whose vulgarity and brutality are unrelieved by any higher qualities. This is a serious artistic defect. Mr. Kipling has often given us studies of coarse and even vulgar men, but he has always exhibited them at some point as possessing deep human feeling, a sense of duty, courage, fellowship, or humor. In Mr. Norris's story there is not a trace of these higher qualities. With the single exception of the two lovers, it is a monotony of brutality from beginning to end. If it is faithful to life, it is entitled to the credit due to sincerity; but its power is misdirected. In two instances at least, the story descends to descriptions of incidents which have no place in print; to comment upon or even suggest them is vulgar to the last degree. It is to be hoped that Mr. Norris will find subjects better worthy of his power.

"Weekly Record of Publications." *The Publishers' Weekly*, 55 (March 18, 1899), 509.

The curse of the modern greed of money is represented in this story of the lower middle-class life of a great city, which is told with the brutal realism of a Zola. The scene is San Francisco, with its strange conglomerate of inhabitants. A few gleams of humor are introduced in describing a German family, but the serious and tragic predominates. The author is a Harvard man of the class of '95, who has seen much of rough life in Africa as well as in the west. His former work, "Moran of the *Lady Letty*," was highly praised by W. D. Howells.

"A Rough Novel." *Boston Evening Transcript*, March 22, 1899, p. 10.

The equipment for a modern realistic novel writer is the knowledge of some particularly seamy places in life, a power of detailed description of sordid or nasty things, an intense desire to make them real to the reader—and a few words of praise from Mr. Howells. The theory seems to be that culture is acquired in order to revert perversely to a morbid contemplation of those things from which culture ought to have enfranchised us. This is a use which is obviously made of culture by some persons, but it is a discouraging fact that it is so. Mr. Morrison in his "Slum Stories" touches the genuine chords of terror and pity. His books are helpful social studies and might inspire beneficent action. But Frank Norris occupies himself, not with the poor, but with the vulgar. They are not themselves readers and are not likely to enjoy his photography. Can it be possible that many persons can be found to enjoy gloating over bourgeois doings, and to absorb the details of the disgusting episodes which Mr. Norris presents? The sights and sounds and even smells of low living are described harshly and brutally—the pages reek of beer, old clothes, stuffy bedding and nameless horrors. The hero is a half-educated monster who figures as a dentist. Having attracted to him a girl whose anaemic type is graphically described, he marries her and after a process of disenchantment, alienation and separation, murders her to obtain a sum of money she has in her possession. He flies and is finally captured on the Alkali plains by a former rival. Mr. Norris exhibits a familiarity with the terminology of dentistry, the dens and dives and cheap streets of San Francisco and the geography and atmospheric conditions of the burning desert.

The tragic moments are described with undeniable vigor, and there is no criminal incident that does not freshen up and relieve the mean things which fill the narrative, and thus become positively welcome. The story contains one bit of realism which transcends anything yet perpetrated by this school. Probably Mr. Norris aims to be the American Balzac, but there must be relief to the picture of squalor which the great author of the Comedie Humaine makes the background of a charming ideality. "McTeague" is unrelieved pain and grossness, yet there are probably readers whose interest is only excited by a series of shocks such as this book administers to taste, sensibility and the moral sense.

William Dean Howells. "A Case in Point." *Literature*, N.S. No. 11 (March 24, 1899), 241–42.

The question of expansion in American fiction lately agitated by a lady novelist of Chicago with more vehemence than power, and more courage than coherence, seems to me again palpitant in the case of a new book by a young writer, which I feel obliged at once to recognise as altogether a remarkable book. Whether we shall abandon the old-fashioned American ideal of a novel as something which may be read by all ages and sexes, for the European notion of it as something fit only for age and experience, and for men rather than women; whether we shall keep to the bounds of the provincial proprieties, or shall include within the imperial territory of our fiction the passions and the motives of the savage world which underlies as well as environs civilisation, are points which this book sums up and puts concretely; and it is for the reader, not for the author, to make answer. There is no denying the force with which he makes the demand, and there is no denying the hypocrisies which the old-fashioned ideal of the novel involved. But society, as we have it, is a tissue of hypocrisies, beginning with the clothes in which we hide our nakedness, and we have to ask ourselves how far we shall part with them at his demand. The hypocrisies are the proprieties, the decencies, the morals; they are by no means altogether bad; they are, perhaps, the beginning of civilisation; but whether they should be the end of it is another affair. That is what we are to consider in entering upon a career of imperial expansion in a region where the Monroe Doctrine was never valid. From the very first Europe invaded and controlled in our literary world. The time may have come at last when we are to invade and control Europe in literature. I do not say that it has come, but if it has we may have to employ European means and methods.

It ought not to be strange that the impulse in this direction should have come from California, where, as I am always affirming rather than proving, a continental American fiction began. I felt, or fancied I felt, the impulse in Mr. Frank Norris' "Moran of the Lady Letty," and now in his "McTeague" I am so sure of it that I am tempted to claim the prophetic instinct of it. In the earlier book there were, at least, indications that forecast to any weather-wise eye a change from the romantic to the realistic temperature, and in the later we have it suddenly, and with the overwhelming effect of a blizzard. It is saying both too much and too little to say that Mr. Norris has built his book on Zolaesque lines, yet Zola is the master of whom he reminds you in a certain epical conception of life. He reminds you of Zola also in the lingering love of the romantic, which indulges itself at the end in an anticlimax worthy of Dickens. He ignores as simply and sublimely as Zola any sort of nature or character beyond or above those of Polk Street in

San Francisco, but within the ascertained limits he convinces you, two-thirds of the time, of his absolute truth to them. He does not, of course, go to Zola's lengths, breadths, and depths; but he goes far enough to difference his work from the old-fashioned American novel.

Polite readers of the sort who do not like to meet in fiction people of the sort they never meet in society will not have a good time in "McTeague," for there is really not a society person in the book. They might, indeed, console themselves a little with an elderly pair of lovers on whom Mr. Norris wreaks all the sentimentality he denies himself in the rest of the story; and as readers of that sort do not mind murders as much as vulgarity, they may like to find three of them, not much varying in atrocity. Another sort of readers will not mind the hero's being a massive blond animal, not necessarily bad, though brutal, who has just wit enough to pick up a practical knowledge of dentistry and to follow it as a trade; or the heroine's being a little, pretty, delicate daughter of German-Swiss emigrants, perfectly common in her experiences and ideals, but devotedly industrious, patient, and loyal. In the chemistry of their marriage McTeague becomes a prepotent ruffian, with always a base of bestial innocence; and Trina becomes a pitiless miser without altogether losing her housewifely virtues or ceasing to feel a woman's rapture in giving up everything but her money to the man who maltreats her more and more, and, finally, murders her.

This is rendering in coarse outline the shape of a story realised with a fulness which the outline imparts no sense of. It abounds in touches of character at once fine and free, in little miracles of observation, in vivid insight, in simple and subtle expression. Its strong movement carries with it a multiplicity of detail which never clogs it; the subordinate persons are never shabbed or faked; in the equality of their treatment their dramatic inferiority is lost; their number is great enough to give the feeling of a world revolving around the central figures without distracting the interest from these. Among the minor persons, Maria Macapa, the Mexican chorewoman, whose fable of a treasure of gold turns the head of the Polish Jew Zerkow, is done with rare imaginative force. But all these lesser people are well done; and there are passages throughout the book that live strongly in the memory, as only masterly work can live. The one folly is the insistence on the love-making of those silly elders, which is apparently introduced as an offset to the misery of the other love-making; the anti-climax is McTeague's abandonment in the alkali desert, handcuffed to the dead body of his enemy.

Mr. Norris has, in fact, learned his lesson well, but he has not learned it all. His true picture of life is not true, because it leaves beauty out. Life is squalid and cruel and vile and hateful, but it is noble and tender and pure and lovely, too. By and by he will put these traits in, and then his powerful scene will be a reflection of reality; by and by he will achieve something of the impartial fidelity of the photograph. In the meantime he has done a picture of life which has form, which has texture, which has color, which has what great original power and ardent study of Zola can give, but which lacks the spiritual light and air, the consecration which the larger art of Tolstoy gives. It is a little inhuman, and it is distinctly not for the walls of living-rooms, where the ladies of the family sit and the children go in and out. This may not be a penalty, but it is the inevitable consequence of expansion in fiction.

[Willa Cather.] "Books and Magazines." *Pittsburgh Leader*, March 31, 1899, p. 8.

The great printing presses of the country go on day and night, year after year, grinding out the mediocre. When in all this output of ink and paper, these thousands of volumes that are rushed upon the booksellers' shelves, one appears which contains both power and promise, the reader may be pardoned some enthusiasm. Excellence always surprises; we are never quite prepared for it. In the case of "McTeague; A Story of San Francisco," it is even more surprising than usual. In the first place, the title is not alluring, and not until you have read the book can you know that there is an admirable consistency in the stiff, uncompromising commonplaceness of that title. In the second place the name of the author is as yet comparatively unfamiliar, and finally the book is dedicated to a member of the Harvard faculty, suggesting that whether it be a story of San Francisco or Dawson City, it must necessarily be vaporous, introspective and chiefly concerned with "literary" impressions. Mr. Norris is, indeed, a "Harvard man," but that he is a good many other kinds of a man is self-evident. His book is, in the language of Mr. Norman Hapgood, the work of "a large human being, with a firm stomach, who knows and loves the people."

In a novel of such merit as this, the subject matter is the least important consideration. Subject matter abounds. Every newspaper contains the essential material for another "Comedie Humaine." In this case "McTeague," the central figure, happens to be a dentist practicing in a little side street of San Francisco. The novel opens with this description of him:

"It was Sunday, and, according to his custom, on that day, 'McTeague' took his dinner at 2 in the afternoon at the car conductors' coffee joint, on Polk street. He had a thick, gray soup, heavy, underdone meat, very hot, on a cold plate; two kinds of vegetables, and a sort of suet pudding, full of strong butter and sugar. Once in his office, or, as he called it on his sign-board, 'Dental Parlors,' he took off his coat and shoes, unbuttoned his vest, and having crammed his little stove with coke, he lay back in his operating chair at the bay window, reading the paper, drinking steam beer, and smoking his huge porcelain pipe, while his food digested; crop-full, stupid and warm." "McTeague" had grown up in a mining camp in the mountains. "He remembered the years he had spent there trundeling heavy cars of ore in and out of the tunnel under the direction of his father. For thirteen days out of each fortnight his father was a steady, hard-working shift boss of the mine. Every other Sunday he became an irresponsible animal, a beast, a brute, crazy with alcohol." His mother cooked for the miners. Her one ambition was that her son should enter a profession. He was apprenticed to a traveling quack dentist, and, after a fashion, learned the business.

"Then one day at San Francisco had come the news of his mother's death; she had left him some money—not much, but enough to set him up in business; so he had cut loose from the charlatan and had opened his 'Dental Parlors' on Polk street, an 'accommodation street' of small shops in the residence quarter of the town. Here he had slowly collected a clientele of butcher boys, shop girls, drug clerks, and car conductors. He made but few acquaintances. Polk street called him the 'Doctor,' and spoke of his enormous strength. For 'McTeague' was a young giant, carrying his huge shock of blonde hair six feet three inches from the ground; moving his immense limbs, heavy with ropes of muscle, slowly, ponderously. His hands were enormous, red and covered with a fell of stiff yellow hair; they were hard as wooden mallets, strong as vices, the hands of the old-time car-boy. Often he dispensed with forceps and extracted a refractory tooth with his thumb and finger. His head was square-cut, angular; the jaw salient, like that of the carnivora.

"But for one thing, 'McTeague' would have been perfectly contented. Just outside his window was his signboard—a modest affair—that read: 'Doctor McTeague. Dental Parlors. Gas Given.' but that was all. It was his ambition, his dream, to have projecting from that corner window, a huge gilded tooth, a molar with enormous prongs, something gorgeous and attractive. He would have it some day, but as yet it was far beyond his means."

Then Mr. Norris launches into a description of the street in which "McTeague" lives. He presents that street as it is on Sunday, as it is on working days, as it is in the early dawn when the workmen are going out with pick-axes on their shoulders, as it is at 10 o'clock when the women are out, marketing among the small shopkeepers, as it is at night when the shop girls are out with the soda fountain tenders and the motor cars dash by full of theater-goers, and the Salvationists sing before the saloon on the corner. In four pages he reproduces in detail the life in a by-street of a great city, the little tragedy of the small shopkeeper. There are many ways of handling environment—most of them bad. When a young author has very little to say and no story worth telling, he resorts to environment. It is frequently used to disguise a weakness of structure, as ladies who paint landscapes put their cows knee-deep in water to conceal the defective drawing of the legs. But such description as one meets throughout Mr. Norris' book is in itself convincing proof of power, imagination and literary skill. It is a positive and active force, stimulating the reader's imagination, giving him an actual command, a realizing sense of this world into which he is suddenly transported. It gives to the book perspective, atmosphere, effects of time and distance, creates the illusion of life. This power of mature and comprehensive description is very unusual among the younger American writers. Most of them observe the world through a temperament, and are more occupied with their medium than the objects they watch. And temperament is a glass which distorts most astonishingly. But this young man sees with a clear eye, and reproduces with a touch firm and decisive, strong almost to brutalness. Yet this hand that can depict so powerfully the brute strength and brute passions of a "McTeague," can deal finely and adroitly with the feminine elements of the story. This is his portrait of the Swiss girl, "Trina," whom "McTeague" marries: " 'Trina' was very small and prettily made. Her face was round and rather pale; her eyes long and narrow and blue, like the half-opened eyes of a baby; her lips and the lobes of her tiny ears were pale, a little suggestive of anaemia. But it was to her hair that one's attention was most attracted. Heaps and heaps of blue-black coils and braids, a royal crown of swarthy bands, a veritable sable tiara, heavy, abundant and odorous. All the vitality that should have given color to her face seemed to have been absorbed by that marvellous hair. It was the coiffure of a queen that shadowed the temples of this little bourgeoise."

The tragedy of the story dates from a chance, a seeming stroke of good fortune, one of those terrible gifts of the Danae. A few weeks before her marriage, "Trina" drew $5,000 on a lottery ticket. From that moment her passion for hoarding money becomes the dominant theme of the story, takes command of the book and its characters. After their marriage the dentist is disbarred from practice. They move into a garret where "Trina" starves her husband and herself to save that precious hoard. She sells even his office furniture, everything but his concertina and his canary bird, with which he stubbornly refused to part, and which are destined to become very important accessories in the property room of the theater where this drama is played. This removal from their first home is to this story what "Gervaise's" removal from her shop is to "L'Assommoir"; it is the fatal episode of the 3d act, the sacrifice of self-respect, the beginning of the end. From that time the money stands between "Trina" and her husband. Discouraged and humiliated, hating her for her meanness, demoralized by his idleness and despair, he begins to abuse her. The story becomes a careful and painful study of the disintegration of these two souls, the woman's corroded by greed, the man's poisoned by disappointment and hate. And all the while this same painful theme is played in a still lower key. "Maria," the housemaid, who took care of "McTeague's" dental parlors in his better days, was a half-crazy girl from somewhere in Central America, she herself did not remember just where. But she had a wonderful story about her people once owning a dinner service of pure gold with a punch bowl you could scarcely lift, which rang like a church bell when you struck it. On the strength of this story "Zerkow," the Polish junk man, marries her, and believing that she knows where this treasure is hidden, bullies and tortures her to force her to disclose her secret. At last "Maria" is found with her throat cut, and "Zerkow" is picked up by the wharf with a sack full of rusty tin cans, which in his dementia he must have thought the fabled dinner service of gold.

From this it is a short step to "McTeague's" crime. He kills his wife to get possession of her money and escapes to the mountains. While he is on his way south, pushing toward Mexico, he is overtaken by his murdered wife's cousin and former suitor. Both men are half mad with thirst, and there in the desert waste of Death Valley, they spring to their last combat. The cousin falls, but before he dies he slips a hand-cuff over "McTeague's" arm, and so the author leaves his hero, in the wastes of Death Valley, a hundred miles from water, with a dead man chained to his arm. As he stands there, the canary bird, the survivor of his happier days, to which he had clung with stubborn affection, begins "chittering feebly in its little gilt prison." This reminds one a little of Stevenson's use of poor "Goddedaal's" canary in "The Wrecker." It is just such touches that bring out the high lights in a story and separate excellence from the commonplace. They are at once dramatic and revelatory, and lacking them, a novel which may otherwise be a very good one, lacks its chief reason for being. The fault with many worthy attempts at fiction lies not in what they are, but in what they are not. Mr. Norris' model, if he will admit that he has followed one, is clearly no less a person than M. Zola himself. Yet there is no discoverable trace of imitation in his book. He has simply taken a method which has been most successfully applied in the study of French life, and applied it in his study of American life, as one uses the same algebraic formulae to solve different problems. It is perhaps the only truthful literary method of dealing with that part of society which environment and heredity hedge about like the walls of a prison. It is true that Mr. Norris now and then allows his "method" to become too prominent, that his restraint occasionally savors of constraint. Yet he has written a true story of people, courageous, dramatic, full of matter, and warm with life. He has addressed himself seriously to art, and he seems to have no ambition to be clever. His horizon is wide, his invention vigorous and bold, his touch heavy and warm and human. This man is not limited by literary prejudices; he sees the people as they are, he is close to them and not afraid of their unloveliness. He has looked at truth in the depths, among men begrimed and besotted, and still found her fair. "McTeague" is an immense achievement for a young man. It may not win at once the success which it deserves, but Mr. Norris is one of those who can afford to wait.

E. D. Beach. "New and Entertaining Fiction." *The Book Buyer*, 18 (April 1899), 244.

An interesting figure, surely, McTeague, dentist, of San Francisco, who dined at two o'clock daily with the car conductors, gorging himself with a thick soup, hot meat on a cold plate, and a suet pudding, emphasized by bad butter and plenty of sugar. One sees in the first paragraph that here is realism. Perhaps McTeague is a literal, strong transcript of some actual dentist in San Francisco. This one, when he has finished his dinner, carries home to his "dental parlors" a pitcher of beer, encourages the stove, unbuttons his waistcoat, and goes to sleep over a pipe of tobacco. Surely a new figure about which to write a book and perhaps worth while, though he snores. There can be no doubt that this story is vigorously told. We find on page 183 that somebody "loved McTeague with a blind, unreasoning love that admitted of no doubt or hesitancy." What a person, with what a capacity for sentimentality under difficulties! We are inclined to separate ourselves from the snoring, and to allow it to become distant and vague. Who is there that will not vanish, if possible, under the provocation of a snore? Who is so strong as not to be willing to flee from the dentist? *McTeague* is the title of the book. Mr. Frank Norris wrote it. It is published by the Messrs. Doubleday & McClure.

Edward and Madeline Vaughn Abbot.
"McTeague."
The Literary World, 30 (April 1, 1899), 99.*

It is seldom that we have any opportunity to differ from our New York correspondent, but with his enthusiastic estimate of *McTeague* in the last number of the Literary World we must confess ourselves somewhat out of sympathy. At the time Mr. Barry's letter was received we had seen only the outside of Mr. Norris's book, and as soon as time permitted we turned to it with all our expectations roused in its favor by Mr. Barry's high recommendation. With much that Mr. Barry says we must agree; Mr. Norris is undeniably a powerful writer. He has drawn his characters with rare skill; he has told their stories in most graphic fashion; he has presented the actuality of their life in San Francisco or the wildernesses of California mountains with all its sordidness, its wretchedness, and crime. That huge, stupid animal, McTeague the dentist, his anaemic little wife Trina, the quaint old maid seamstress and the equally quaint old bachelor dog doctor, the repulsive Jew junk dealer, all stand out from the pages with the individuality of life, and the inevitable consequences of misused life follow in their tracks. With relentless truth we are made to follow the decay of McTeague's prosperity, and accompanying it the decay of his own manhood. Stupid he was always, but the one victory he won over his animal nature was the prelude to uninterrupted defeats and a final descent into the very depths of animal brutality. Even more terrible was Trina's wretched life, for she had something to start with in mind and spirit, and the slatternly figure, maimed already through her husband's cruelty—which the story leaves face downward in a pool of blood, battered to death by her husband's fists—was once as neat and trim a little woman as you could find, and the idol of her big husband's heart. One has not the consolation of saying that in real life it could not have happened so. Trina's sordid miserliness, which worked the mischief, was the natural outcome of unnecessary petty economy in a character like hers, and in McTeague's elemental nature hate was quickly stirred and brutally followed. No stronger picture could be given of the evil that lies rooted in the love of money.

That Mr. Norris has written an exceptionally strong and powerful novel we do not wish to deny. Neither do we hold that an author may not choose harsh and brutal subjects. But we do believe that highest art is not merely a question of execution, and that the spirit with which the brutal or the beautiful is treated is the quality that redeems or damns. To our thinking, with all our genuine admiration for its exceptional qualities, *McTeague* cannot be classed among great novels, for the spirit that animates is false to the highest standards. We can pardon, accept even with intellectual pleasure, loathsome details that are necessary to the artistic progress of the story, but grossness for the sake of grossness is unpardonable.

Mr. Norris has written pages for which there is absolutely no excuse, and his needless sins against good taste and del-

---

*A response to Barry, pp. 35–37.

icacy are fatal spots upon his work. *McTeague* undoubtedly will be widely read—it is too remarkable to pass speedily into oblivion; but we pray that a kind fate may bring it only to those of vigorous mind and, shall we say it, strong stomach. Norris has reason to be proud of his work, but the world will not be proud of it in the distant tomorrow which irrevocably sets true value on books of today.

"Literature."
The Independent, 51 (April 6, 1899), 968.

There is a certain fascination in a book like this—the fascination of murder and other hideous crimes. Most of the characters presented are worthless where not positively bad; it is a novel of spasms, jerks, and hitches, and everybody talks brokenly, as if at a loss for words. Sensational from beginning to end, the story reeks in blood and does not lack dramatic power of a rude sort, while at the end a hopeless situation stands out unrelieved by any softening effect of perspective. Such a story will find its audience, perhaps a large one, but no person will be the better for reading it. It has no moral, esthetical or artistic reason for being.

"A Western Realist."
Washington Times, April 23, 1899, p. 20.

When Frank Norris, a young Western man, made his appearance in literature a year ago with "Moran of the Lady Letty," there were people who prophesied for him an uncommonly brilliant career, for that tale had an originality, a vividness, and a power about it which made an impression on the reader.

Mr. Norris has now brought out a novel of an entirely different character, which he calls "McTeague; A Story of San Francisco," and nothing stronger in the way of realistic fiction is to be found in American literature.

The story is not a pleasant one in any possible sense of the word. There is nothing pretty in it except the heroine, and she is only moderately pretty for the space of two or three chapters. The hero—if he can be called by that name—is only about half human. The minor characters are the more or less warped and distorted specimens of humanity to be found in the side streets of a big city. But every character and situation in the story is absolutely true to life. Mr. Norris would probably resent being called the American Zola, as a man of his vigor and independence usually does resent being compared to some foreign celebrity or other; but it is a fact that his work comes near being to San Francisco what that of Zola is to Paris. It is fearless, strong and full of artistic spirit. There are not many men who care to spend a year in painting a muck-heap, but when one does, it is reasonably certain that the painting will be good. And McTeague and his companions are a sort of human garbage collection.

McTeague is a huge, overgrown, sluggish, dull-witted animal, who, through the restless ambition of his mother, has been led to become a dentist instead of fulfilling his natural destiny of manual labor. He is not vicious; he is simply a big brute with some human feelings, endowed with self-consciousness. He meets a little Swiss girl, Trina Sieppe, cousin of a quick-witted, socialistic, shifty friend of his, Marcus Schouler. This is probably the first instance in literature of a courtship beginning in a dentist's parlor. McTeague and Trina are finally betrothed, and soon after the engagement Trina wins a $5,000 prize in a lottery. This fortune eventually develops miserly instincts in Trina, and when, three or four years after the marriage, McTeague is forbidden to practice because he has no diploma from a dental college, she becomes more and more miserly and insists on the most rigid economy for them both. As the author points out, she had during the first years of their married life cultivated refined tastes in him, which she now refuses him the means to gratify, and the result is a blind, unreasoning irritation and fury against her on the part of the man. He ill-treats and finally deserts her, taking with him all of her savings which he can find—the $5,000 is invested in a safe place. After his departure she begins once more to save, and her passion for money finally results in her obtaining possession of her little fortune, all in gold, that she may have the delight of handling the pieces. Finally, McTeague returns once more, and this time kills her, escaping with the money in a canvas sack. He also with fatuous, feeble instinct, carries with him a canary in a gilt cage, a possession from which he has never parted. His irrational impulse of flight takes him into one of the desert tracts of the southwest, and he is tracked by Marcus Schouler, who has long borne a grudge against him for marrying Trina. The two have a fight in the wilderness, and with a dying impulse Marcus handcuffs their wrists together, so that the huge, misshapen, half-reasoning barbarian is left to die from thirst and heat in the place called Death Valley, chained to the dead body of his worst enemy. It is a grewsome tale.

The descriptive power of the author is something marvelous, and his grasp of character equally sure. From McTeague, the giant, to the timid little dog-doctor, Old Grannis; from Trina, with her half-developed civilization and strong ancestral and racial instincts, to the crazed Mexican woman, Maria Macapa, there is not a false touch in the portraits. These people are not the poor folk of the story books, or the ideal Americans; they are real people, of types which are fast becoming common in American cities; common, sordid, vulgar, full of half-understood racial tendencies inherited from Old World ancestors, veneered with a superficial intelligence and culture due to American institutions; sometimes capable of great acts in a great crisis, but hopelessly incapable of real refinement till at least three generations of them have lived, learned, and suffered in a free land. McTeague was not fit to be a dentist, but under certain circumstances his son might have been. Trina, with her quick, alert, intense, and narrow nature, might have been a different woman had she been given larger interests. Her married life was spent in a city flat, where her only ambition was toward cheap gentility. Had she lived in a small village, where her husband might have used his muscles instead of his poor, bewildered, sluggish brain; where she had social life of her own instead of the sham society of the lodging-house; had she possessed three or four children to break up her tendency toward miserliness and give McTeague something to occupy his emotions, if not his brain, that couple might have been happy to the end of their days, and the rude strength that was in both of them might, in their descendants, have been refined into something worth cultivation. In other such marriages this has happened; but the McTeagues were among the failures.

Some of the reviewers who have commented upon this book have tried to represent it as a tract teaching the sin of stinginess, but it is safe to say that Mr. Norris meant it for nothing of the kind. The McTeagues are simply an example of the disastrous working of hereditary tendencies in the wrong place. Trina's ancestor, who bequeathed to her a saving spirit and tireless industry, was a Tyrolese peasant, busy, blithe, and useful to the community. McTeague's ancestor was an animal, capable of being moved either to vice or virtue by the superior mind. He could easily have been led to heroic actions by anyone who knew how to awaken his better impulses and coax his human self into being, he could as easily be roused to fury by that surest weapon of the cruel—ridicule. His often repeated expression, "I'll teach 'em they can't make small of me," is one of the sure touches which indicate the sort of man he was. Had he possessed less brute strength he might have been a thinker. Accustomed to rely on his fists for argument, he had never accustomed himself to think. Hence he beat and finally killed Trina; hence he fought with Marcus; hence he never troubled himself to reason, not being used to the process. He went through life very much as he practiced his profession; he pulled teeth with his fingers because it was less trouble than using the proper instrument, and also made him a reputation for strength. He is not a pleasant figure, nor could he have been an admirable one; but he is very real, and a distinct addition to literature.

Jeanette Gilder. "The Lounger." *The Critic*, 34 (May 1899), 398.

Mr. McClure's latest discovery is the author of "McTeague," Mr. Frank Norris. Mr. Norris was one of the editors of *The Wave*, an interesting periodical published in San Francisco. To meet the requirements of his paper he wrote a serial called "Moran, of the Lady Letty." Mr. McClure saw it and he sent for its author, who came as quickly as most young authors do when the call is to New York. Mr. Howells, who also has the true sportsman's sense where American literature is concerned, had his genial eye on the young man. He found a "new thrill" in Mr. Norris's work and he said so in print. Now "McTeague," which I believe was actually written before the other book, has appeared, and everybody is talking about this strange and impressive story. It is not a pleasant story, but when I began reading it I went on to the end without laying it down, though the clock warned me that the small hours had set in. It is a realistic story, horribly realistic, but it is never coarse; it is also a strong story, and yet it has none of those peculiarities that some young authors, and some old ones too, I regret to say, seem to think the ear-marks of strength. Mr. Norris, who I believe is only eight and twenty, has a future before him. As we are so fond of names of comparison in this country, I should say that he might be called the American Balzac. A re-reading of the chapter describing the wedding of McTeague and Trina has confirmed me in this opinion.

"Novels That Are Being Talked About."
The Publishers' Weekly, 55 (May 27, 1899), 840.

C. E. Raimond, the name that appears on the title-page [of *The Open Question*], is the pseudonym of Elizabeth Robins, an American woman living in England, who has personated on the stage several of the characters of Ibsen's dramas. Her book deals with heredity, and is a special plea against the marriage of near relations and persons suffering from incurable disease. The argument is cleverly and strongly presented, but the question remains an open question at the end. Sad as is the subject, and hopelessly as it is treated, the book nevertheless abounds in most enjoyable reading-matter, and is a notably intellectual effort. The character drawing is incisive and picturesque, while the wit and wisdom in which the conversations are so rich make the rereading of many of the pages an unalloyed pleasure.

Mrs. Gertrude Atherton's "A Daughter of the Vine" is another "heredity" story, with a background of California life in the forties. "The Californians," a more cheerful story from her clever pen, deals altogether with the love affairs and social triumphs of two pretty girls. Frank Norris became known to novel-readers within the year by his "Moran of the *Lady Letty*." His latest and much talked about story is "McTeague." Sordid life in San Francisco, with characters taken from the lowest stratum of society, whose ignorance and vulgarity are emphasized by their love of money and pursuit of it, are what he there writes about. Mr. Frank Norris belongs to the realistic school, his Zola-like touches leaving nothing unknown of the repulsiveness of his subject. As an antidote to these pessimistic estimates of life we offer Maurice Hewlett's charming story of "The Forest Lovers," as innocent and delightful as a fairy tale, and Miss Mary Johnston's "Prisoners of Hope," both marked successes of the year, the latter being a fresh and vigorous story of Virginia in 1663, when Sir William Berkeley was Governor.

Nancy Huston Banks. "Two Recent Revivals in Realism."
Bookman (America), 9 (June 1899), 356–57.

The passing of morbid realism has never been quite so complete as the healthy-minded hoped it would be, when it was swept out of sight five or six years ago by the sudden on-rush of works of ideality and romance, which arose like a fresh, sweet wind to clear the literary atmosphere. In this resistless new movement toward light and hope and peace, these black books were cast aside and forgotten, and there was fair hope for a time that the celebration of the painful and the unclean had passed from fiction forever.

But now, just as hope approached security, two novels appear, surpassing almost all examples of realism in modern story-writing, and rivalling the utmost efforts of the ancients in this peculiar respect. It is said that Aristophanes makes reserved mention of certain matters which one of these tales discusses with freedom; but the current novel reader's acquaintance with Aristophanes is too remote for that precedent to do much toward lessening this recent shock. It is also urged in extenuation of the other of these two extraordinary works, that Flaubert and Balzac made studies for publication along the same lines, but—to a good many normal minds—their having done so does not alter the fact that there is an appreciable difference between the artistic description of a subject in the dissecting room and the actual presentation of it face to face.

And this is what both these new realistic novels do in their somewhat different ways. Both are despairing utterances of the pain of the world, the tragedy of living. Both stories deal exclusively with hopeless conditions of mental, moral and physical disease; both are written with convincing brilliancy and power; both have enough bitter wit to deepen the unlifting gloom; both fail to offer a remedy for the horrors they drag the screen from.

Much alike on these points, the books are markedly unlike on others. For example, Mr. Norris has woven his story with a double thread, whereas Mrs. Dudeney's has but one [in *Lady Rose's Daughter*]. Mr. Norris now and then leaves the lead of his motive, going wholly outside and beyond it to touch the untouchable, without any apparent purpose or result—other than the repulsion of the reader. Mrs. Dudeney's work, on the contrary, is never coarse, notwithstanding the fearless direction with which she follows her theme. Mr. Norris's manner is hard and cold, making scarcely any appeal other than keen intellectual appreciation. Mrs. Dudeney, on the other hand, writes with sympathy so complete, so tender, so exquisite as to justify—if any writing could—the telling of such untellable truths. There is sympathy, too, in her choice of subject, for the woman whose sufferings and sins are the motive of her work is a victim rather than a criminal, and worthy of respect throughout; while the female miser of Mr. Norris's story who suffers and makes others suffer merely in order that she may save money, is a most ignoble figure from first to last.

And yet after pointing out all these differences and resemblances it would be hard to say which of the two books is more absorbingly interesting. *McTeague* seizes and holds in a vise-like grasp that is almost painful from the beginning to the end of the story of this monster of a dentist and his pretty, shallow, vulgar little wife, whose avarice wrecks their lives—for the love of money is the root of all evil in Mr. Norris's book. . . .

But, having so conceded the fine quality of the works, the strength and vitality of the stories, it becomes permissible to regret the misuse of such eminent power, to protest against the intrusion of the clinic into fiction, and to question the success of the books as fiction. To discuss these regrets and protests and questions in detail would be to thresh old straw, and yet recurrence to the old contention seems to be demanded by the unexpected revival of realism in its most unendurable form, which these two notable recent novels appear to foreshadow.

"McTeague."
The Literary Era, 6 (June 1899), 178.

Mr. Norris's former book, "Moran of the Lady Letty," won warm praise from some of the best critics, among them Mr. W. D. Howells. This new novel is a powerful and forceful one, being a sustained study in the development of several human lives, which certainly evinces something nearly akin to genius. The story is harsh, even brutal at times, owing to its environment; but never perhaps has the curse of money been more overwhelmingly presented by an American writer.

"Summer Reading."
Review of Reviews (America), 19 (June 1899), 749.

Several months ago there appeared a very bright, original and wideawake story of sea adventurers off the California coast, from the pen of a new writer, Mr. Frank Norris, entitled *Moran of the Lady Letty*. It won prompt attention from the discriminating who like to welcome really strong, fresh, and vital work in American fiction. That first story has been followed by another entitled *McTeague: A Story of San Francisco*. This story moves in a wholly different sphere, but, even more strongly than its predecessor, it shows power and directness of method. It is about the most unpleasant American story that anybody has ever ventured to write. It is a study of life and character among a class of people that story-tellers generally avoid, or at least seldom select for their chief characters. McTeague is an ill-born lad of the mining country, who learns something of dentistry as a trade from a traveling dentist who makes the rounds of the camps. The young fellow finally opens an office as a dentist on a side street in San Francisco, where he lives in his office and takes his meals at a third-class restaurant near by. He falls in love with a girl of German-American family who happens to find her way into his dentist's chair, and their marriage leads to ever-increasing wretchedness through the development of the brutal side of McTeague's nature, and of a miserly quality in that of his wife. It is unnecessary to follow this story to its hideous end. Mr. Norris has shown us in this powerful study of life an ability that it is to be hoped he may henceforth use in the writing of books that will be not less true but a good deal more agreeable.

Charles F. Lummis. "Another California Novel."
Land of Sunshine, 11 (July 1899), 117.

Perhaps one reason why so many reviewers of the day are so optimistic is that they do not read through (if they really read at all) the books they "review." It is hard to conceive of any mind so resilient that it could return instantly to benevolence from such a test. On the other hand, these critics who can so easily acquit them of a duty probably know nothing of the keen comfort their more slavish fellow finds in a sound book amid the weary wilderness. It is a very cheap critic who is afraid to find fault; it is a very miserable one who likes to.

Wha—wha—what? Is things what they seem, or is visions about? Here for years we have gone hungry for a California novel big enough to make a mouthful; and of a sudden the whole table falls on us, a comestible avalanche. In thirteen years there have not been as many California novels of serious consideration as already punctuate this year of grace and odd numbers—*The Procession of Life, A Soul in Bronze*—and now *McTeague, a Story of San Francisco*. Evidently civilization is not a total failure, nor the Caucasian irremediably played out. For here are three books that California can and will add to its slim fiction shelf with pride. And the best of it is, perhaps, that all three are growth in the unforeseen. It would not be half so promising if Bret Harte got back a flash of his old fire.

Precisely like Mr. Vachell and Miss DuBois, Mr. Frank Norris has emerged into open type before, and with credit. But precisely like them, again, he bursts upon us now with every quality of a surprise. All three have just turned out their masterpieces—to date. There could be no sounder fulcrum for the hope that all three will astonish us again—and we shall not again be so easy.

McTeague is a hideous story. It deals wholly with humans so uninformed of humanity at their best, so sodden at their worst with the thing we flatter ourselves to call brutality (meaning something so base that no brute but man ever dreamed of it), as to be haunting. In the whole 450 pages there is not a rift in the sullen horizon. It is a depressing story to the humanist; and as to California it is about as characteristic as any Peter Funk shop on Kearney street.

But it is a story. "McTeague," the giant quack dentist, "Trina" his sordid doll of a wife, "Marcus Schouler" the man whose brains as well as his heart are in his mouth—they are genuine characters. "Schouler" doubtless is more a caricature than a character; yet at times he is the one thing needful. The ancient lovers are also a Dickensesque exaggeration, but a tolerable one. And the story as a story is literally strong. Above all, it is character drawing of a high order. A simple but consistent plot, a firm hand in its development, and generally admirable restraint in the tragedy—these are part of Mr. Norris's endowment. Far less than either of the stories ranked with it, is *McTeague* of California. But quite as much as they, it is a human document, a fine and a powerful piece of work, an honor to its smith and a matter of pride to those of us who love literature, love California and respect honest craft.

"Novels of the Week." *The Spectator*, 83 (November 4, 1899), 662.

We cannot congratulate Mr. Frank Norris on *McTeague*, a robust, but extraordinarily repulsive, story of low life in San Francisco. The central figure is a quack dentist, who after his marriage "reels back into the brute," batters his wife to death, kills her avenger, and perishes miserably of thirst in the burning wastes of the alkali desert. The brutality of some of the scenes is quite indescribable. Mr. Norris showed along with a certain undisciplined violence, such promise in his earlier novel that we regret to find him in his present venture appealing mainly to the instincts to which the bull-ring owes its continued existence. In *McTeague* he is simply an animal painter, who, while he entirely fails to touch the heart, is often completely successful in turning the stomach.

"Literary Notes." *Washington Times*, November 12, 1899, p. 8, part 2.

The November "Bookman" contains a long and interesting article on Frank Norris by Frederic Taber Cooper.* Inevitably Norris is compared to Kipling—it is getting to a point where every new novelist will have to be compared with Kipling, which, on serious thought, seems rather absurd. But considering Mr. Cooper's general ability as a writer, it does seem a little queer that he should say that Norris "has a fantastic ideal of womanhood undreamed of by him who wrote 'The Vampire.'" Why should it be assumed by a lot of semi-intelligent critics that "The Vampire," with its savage satire, embodied the author's "ideal of womanhood"? Anyone who reads it with even ordinary attention ought to see that it is a particular woman—the vampire woman—who is under discussion, and that the Mrs. Patsy Campbell type is no more Kipling's ideal than the McTeague type is Mr. Norris'. There are a good many vampire women in the world, or the poem would not have been so widely read—a great many men recognized their own bitter experience in the description—but when looking for ideal women it would be more sensible to take "William the Conqueror" or Dinah Shadd or Miriam of the dream-world for an example. And these women are as good and true and loving as any in literature.

*See pp. 81–86.

"American Fiction." *The Athenaeum*, December 2, 1899, p. 757.

McTeague, by Frank Norris (Grant Richards), is a story of life in San Francisco, in which the California forms of English speech are many, and sometimes puzzling. For instance, a coffeehouse is a "coffee-joint"; "Steam beer" is a drink for which we do not know the English equivalent, but it is declared to be far inferior to bottled beer; a person dies owing to being "corroded with alcohol" after being "crazy with alcohol" every other Sunday; a lady says "Um hum" in answer to the question "Cleaning house to day?" McTeague, the chief personage, when protesting against unfair treatment, remarks, "They can't make small of me," and the lady whom McTeague marries calls upon him to "love me, big, big." Trina Sieppe is the young lady's name; her parents are German Swiss; her father addresses his wife as "mommer," and she says to her daughter, "Kiss your mommer." McTeague himself is a Californian Caliban, who practises as a dentist without a diploma, and is able to pull out a tooth with his finger and thumb. Trina, whom he marries, pays a dollar for a lottery ticket and draws a prize of five thousand dollars. She devotes her whole soul to adding to her fortune, a tragedy being the consequence. No personage in this melodramatic tale is pleasing, yet the story is vigorously told and readable.

" 'McTeague.' "
Saturday Review (England), 88 (December 9, 1899), 14, Supplement D9.

As a social study Mr. Frank Norris has chosen a San Franciscan type of life which is repulsive in the sordidness of its vulgarity; he gives his readers a picture of human nature in its brute aspect. There are some minor offences against art, and we can scarcely conceive it possible to find much more unpleasant characters to delineate. The drab monotone of the story is unrelieved.

"McTeague."
The Academy, 57 (December 23, 1899), 746.

Mr. Norris, aware of his strength, uses it brutally. *McTeague* is a narrative of lower middle-class life in San Francisco. The hero is a quack dentist, a great, coarse, simple-minded animal of a fellow, who marries an attractive girl of stingy and avaricious temperament. Trina possesses a fortune of five thousand dollars, won in a lottery, and though McTeague loses his livelihood by Government edict against unlicensed dentistry, she will not let him touch her capital. Together they descend, he growing more brutish, she more miserly. In the result he kills her for her five thousand dollars, and decamps. At the end of the book he commits another murder, and we have him handcuffed to a corpse in the middle of a desert valley, where death certainly awaits him. The existence of nether San Francisco is described with grim and fearless vigour. No sordid detail is omitted, no revolting episode glossed over. We do not ask, if the subject is to be handled at all, that it should be trifled with, but we do ask that Mr. Norris's vision should comprise something beyond the gross animalism of humanity; we do ask for something of the spirit.

Let us add that Mr. Norris has a genuine imaginative talent. That was shown in his *Shanghaied*, a fine book that preceded *McTeague*.

Frederic Taber Cooper. "Literature, American and English."
The International Year Book: 1899 (New York: Dodd, Mead & Co., 1900), p. 489.

... *The Greater Inclination*, by Mrs. Edith Wharton, a collection of short stories exhibiting in the highest degree that rare creative power called literary genius, met with much appreciation from the critical portion of the public, and was declared by one eminent critic to be "the one work of fiction belonging to the present year which is equal to the very best in its own class." *McTeague*, by Frank Norris, was the only important representation of the realistic novel that the year produced. The story is a strange and impressive one, and depicts with power and vigor the sordidness and brutality of life. *The Market Place*, Harold Frederic's posthumous novel, though not of sustained excellence throughout, is a vivid study of the modern financial world, and took high rank among the fiction of the year....

"McTeague."
Bookman (England), 17 (January 1900), 121.

From the every-day routine of his life in the "Dental Parlours" on Polk Street, through the comedy of his courtship and marriage, through the finely commonplace tragedy of his ruin and subsequent moral deterioration, to his horrible death, handcuffed to the enemy he has killed, on the leper-white alkali desert—we have followed the career of McTeague with an interest that increased to the end. McTeague himself, the tame giant in whom the primitive barbarian, long dormant close under the surface, was to be roused at last to such dreadful issues, is drawn with a bold and masterly hand; every one of Mr. Norris's characters lives, indeed, and is really human. The passing of Trina from girlhood to womanhood, and the development after her marriage with McTeague of a prevailing miserliness in her disposition, are traced with an admirable cunning; the ludicrous Sieppe family, the contemptible Marcus Schouler, the gentle old Miss Baker, the shy old Mr. Grannis, and all the dwellers in and about the tenement house on Polk Street, grow upon our comprehension in clearest detail—we know them and the very atmosphere they breathe. The realistic novelist is too apt to think he heightens the effect of his realism by suppressing the sentimental or romantic aspects of life that are, after all, as real as its more sordid features; on the other hand, the romancist is apt to miss the truth as widely by ignoring the common and unlovely realities of existence that are inseparable even from romance. Happily, Mr. Norris has a conscience, and is too much of an artist to lapse into such timorous compromises. The unemphasised realism and romance of his story are not the realism and romance of a biassed imagination but simply of life itself, and what is sordid and even repellent, and what is sweet and tender, and something that is earthy and something that is heavenly, are blended in his men and women and woven into the fabric of his story as they are blended and woven in actual human experience. It is a cleverly written story and one that we are glad not to have missed reading.

BLIX

by FRANK NORRIS
Author of McTeague
Moran of the
Lady Letty
etc.

New York
Doubleday & McClure Co.
1899

Blix

I.F.M. [Isaac F. Marcosson]. "The Gossip of Book Land." *Louisville Times*, March 25, 1899, p. 8.

Each succeeding work of that clever young Westerner, Frank Norris, gives an added and gratifying assurance of the fulfillment of the promise that his first work in fiction held out. There has been occasion to say pleasant things of his "Moran of the Lady Letty," and more recently of his strong study in realism, "McTeague," and now it is just as agreeable to write a word about his coming book. It will be called "Blix," and, as Norris very characteristically and consistently writes, "it belongs to no school; it is not naturalism and it's not romanticism—it's just a story." No forecast could be more emphatic. From what I understand from Mr. Norris, that forthcoming work will be clean, wholesome and natural and a pure love story without any silly sentimentality.

With the presentation of "Blix" this writer will have displayed a versatility at once striking and remarkable. "Moran" is a fresh, bracing story of the sea that fairly splashes with salt water; "McTeague" is grimy with life's wretchedness and yet is not morbid. Now will come this immaculate romance of honest loving hearts. Truly it is a varied work that he is building.

"Novels of the Week." *New York Commercial Advertiser*, September 23, 1899, p. 11.

It is a genuine pleasure to read a new story by Mr. Frank Norris, for they always abound in the unexpected. In each of the three volumes which already stand to his credit, he has succeeded in striking a new and successful vein: *Moran of the Lady Letty*, which first drew attention to him, was a frankly slap-dash sort of romance story of adventure, in which shipwrecks and Chinese pirates figured prominently; *McTeague*, which followed close upon it, is a book of such an utterly different calibre that it is difficult to realize that it is from the same hand—a cruel, relentless tale of sordid life, told with the uncompromising brutality of a Maupassant. *Blix* marks another epoch in Mr. Norris's development. While staged with all the realism of minute detail which characterizes his previous work, the story itself is a refreshing little idyl of contemporary life, redolent with healthy, happy human nature. It deals with the love affairs of two young people, belonging to the "younger set" of San Francisco society, who after a flirtation of eighteen months, frankly confess that they do not love each other, conclude to have "no more nonsense," and then settle down to the dangerous experiment of remaining comrades. The story of how this comradeship ripens, through all sorts of strange adventures—idyllic outings into the country, and delightful tête-à-tête dinners at out-of-the-way Mexican restaurants,—into something warmer than they themselves suspect, is told with a delicacy unlooked for in the author of *McTeague*. The book takes its title from the heroine or rather from the name which the hero elects to bestow upon Travis Bessemer, because "it sounds bully and snappy and crisp and bright and sort of sudden"; and most readers will agree that it is eminently suited to a girl who "radiates health," and is "as trig and trim and crisp as a crack yacht." We shall probably have a good deal more to say about this book at a later date; meanwhile we can heartily indorse it as one of the brightest and most enjoyable novels of the month.

"Weekly Record of Publications."
The Publishers' Weekly, 56 (September 23, 1899), 388.

The author of "McTeague" has imagined a heroine of nineteen, with strength of body and strength of mind and most lovable womanly qualities, to whom the hero gives the name of "Blix" because there is so much "snap" and "go" about her. After several months of companionship the girl and the editor of the Sunday supplement of a San Francisco paper agree that they are not lovers, but they become chums and friends. They go about a great deal, and the Chinese district, the shipping districts, and the resorts where gambling is carried on, are described. "Blix" is an influence for good, and makes a man of her chum.

Annie W. Sanborn.
"Books."
The St. Paul Pioneer Press, October 1, 1899, p. 18.

"Blix," the third story published by Mr. Frank Norris, is likewise a demonstration of a third capacity in its author. In "Moran of the Lady Letty" we had an audacious but eminently successful novel of adventure. In "McTeague" the same pen produced a realistic study of life in one of its least attractive and repaying phases. In "Blix" we have yet more realism, but this time it is of an invigorating sort. Its points and peaks are tipped with the rose color of youthful idealism.

It is, in its elements, a very simple tale, dealing with the companionship of a young man and woman of San Francisco. The girl, Travis Bessemer, is nineteen, pretty, chic and sensible. She keeps house for her father and a younger brother and sister. The youth, Condy Rivers, is a newspaper man, a special writer on the Times, bitten with the craze for authorship and hampered in his progress by two things—a passion for gambling and a lack of the mainspring that keeps him well up to a sustained purpose. The two have been amusing themselves by one of those moderate, half-platonic flirtations in which neither party is deeply involved and from which a lapse into ordinary friendship is not attended with any anguish whatever.

The story opens by describing a Sunday in the Bessemer household in which the members of the family are presented to the reader for the first and last time. Rivers drops in, according to habit, to the Sunday night supper. After it is over Travis, sitting with him in the parlor, informs him that she has made up her mind to drop society because at a club dance the night before she was practically forced into a dance with a man partially intoxicated, a member of the "set" to which she belonged. She has also made up her mind to do away with all "nonsense" which being interpreted means that her relations with Condy are to assume a perfectly matter-of-fact basis, no candy, no flowers, no hand-kissing, no pretence at sentiment. In the course of the conversation she forces the astonished young man into a confession that he doesn't really love her and never did.

From this point the author's energies are delightfully employed in showing how altogether enchanting and satisfactory the "matter-of-fact" relation can become when the right people are in it. Their intercourse becomes that of comradery. They lay aside conventions, go fishing together in their old clothes, play absurd pranks on the people who write newspaper "personals" and altogether become thorough boy and girl again. A great deal of wholesome fun is the result. Out of door life, sensible hours, frank, friendly talk, bring them closer to each other than ever before. Travis, whose nickname "Blix" is bestowed on her in the middle of one of their pranks, becomes the young man's guide and mentor as well as chum. She cures him of gambling by a method all her own and inspires him to do his best and most successful writing. All this sounds commonplace enough and it is a happy thing to feel that it is, in one sense, commonplace. But not even a quoted page or two could reproduce the freshness, the vividness, the whole effect of young audacious, confident, righteous life that emanates from this book. It is not without some incongruities, even some cheapnesses. But we prefer not to enumerate them but rather to pay complete tribute to the real triumph of the book, which is a triumph of everlasting good in that it has made inexperienced virtue more thoroughly gay and joyous than any sophisticated vice that ever lent its spurious charm to romance.

"Blix."
Baltimore Sun,
October 2, 1899,
p. 10.

Mr. Frank Norris has written in "Blix" just what such a woman's name would imply—a story of a frank, fearless, girl comrade to all men who are true and honest. How she saves the man she fishes and picnics with in a spirit of outdoor platonic friendship makes a happy and pleasant story, and a perfect contrast to the author's "McTeague."

"The Book Table."
Detroit Free Press, October 2, 1899, p. 7.

To read a book and wish there was more of it is a high tribute to the author's ability to entertain. And that is the compliment the reader will pay to Frank Norris' new story, "Blix." Nothing could well be further removed from "McTeague" and "Moran of the Lady Letty" than this charming little love idyll. Yet it abounds in what W. D. Howells, speaking of "McTeague," called "touches of character, both fine and free, little miracles of observation, vivid insight, simple and subtle expression." "Blix" is a much more agreeable book than the tragedy of the San Francisco dentist; its realism is of quite another character, and will be found "delicious" instead of repellent. It is a leaf from the drama of commonplace life.

The purpose—if such were in its author's mind—of the story is to show how much stronger and more enduring is the bond that brings two young people to the gate of marriage when it is based on comradeship and goodfellowship rather than on sentiment. Incidentally he indicates how much influence a bright girl may exert over a young man of good impulses but rather inconstant character, simply through comradeship and tact, allied with an understanding of his weaknesses. Condé Rivers and Travis Bessemer were lovers, and were beginning to find the bond irksome. Mutual confession made it possible for them to change the relation to friendship and be "done with foolishness." Through the new relationship the real love comes. This is a charming story, crisp and spicy, with touches of humor, and full of subtle comprehension of human nature. It is another index of Mr. Norris' versatility.

George Hamlin Fitch. "Among the New Books."
San Francisco Chronicle, October 8, 1899, p. 4.

The Doubleday & McClure Company of New York brings out a story by Frank Norris, entitled "Blix," which furnishes a most remarkable contrast to the hard realism of "McTeague" and the wild adventure of "Moran of the Lady Letty." Blix is the pet name of Travis Bessemer, a young San Francisco girl, given her by Condé Rivers, a man ten years older than she, who starts out swearing to be her comrade and naturally ends by becoming her lover. The two decide to abandon society and seek amusement in unusual places, and they find it in jaunts to all kinds of out-of-the-way places in San Francisco. Rivers is a newspaper man with an ambition to be a novelist, and the girl helps him in his work by her suggestions. She also cures him of the gambling habit by learning poker and playing with him whenever he feels the passion for gambling coming upon him.

This is a bald outline of a very delightful love idyll which contains more of the local color of San Francisco than any other novel that is in print. There is no set descriptive work, but with the lightest and deftest touch Mr. Norris has put in sketches here and there of the many peculiar features of San Francisco life, while that view of the bay and the

Golden Gate from the heights of Pacific avenue has never been made so real before. The author has been equally happy with his characters, who strike one as natural and as acting and talking as they might act and speak in real life. The only jarring note is found in a certain Zolaesque description of the heroine—an insistence upon the feminine odor which she exhaled that reminds one disagreeably of an episode in Cherbuliez's "Samuel Brohl & Co." in which the adventurer appraises some of the heroine's belongings rather above their value because of the "odor femina" which clings to them.* This dwelling upon purely fleshly charms of the heroine would fit well into a French novel of the period, but it is alien to this story and it will be apt to rasp the nerves of any sensitive reader.

Very sharp and clear-cut are all the portraits in this story. The Bessemer household is particularly well-done, but the clearest and best picture is that of the nineteen-year-old daughter of the house—a girl that one feels it would be good to know because of her wholesome strength and her freedom from nerves. Here are a few lines of this picture:

> She was young, but tall as most men, and solidly, almost heavily built. Her shoulders were broad, her chest was deep, her neck round and firm. She radiated health; there were exuberance and vitality in the very touch of her foot upon the carpet, and there was that cleanliness about her, that freshness, that suggested a recent plunge in the surf and a "constitutional" along the beach.... Her lips were full and red, her chin very round and a little salient. Curiously enough, her eyes were small—small, but of the deepest, deepest brown, and always twinkling and alight, as though she were just ready to smile or had just done smiling, one could not say which.... She was as trig and trim and crisp as a crack yacht; not a pin was loose, not a seam that did not fall in its precise right line.

Equally good is the reason given by Rivers for calling his companion Blix, because, " 'it sounds bully, and snappy, and crisp, and bright, and sort of sudden; sounds—don't you know, this way?' and he snapped his fingers." The descriptions of fishing in Lake Pilarcitos, of the trip to the Presidio and the whole episode of the marriage romance that began in the Mexican restaurant—all of these are so wonderfully well done that the reader's interest is secured as completely as though he were absorbed by the most stirring adventure. This is the height of literary art, and the man who is a master of it is capable of great things. When Mr. Norris takes up a large theme that touches the life of the people, we may expect to see his literary skill, his power of minute observation and his knowledge of human nature combine to bring forth a great novel.

*Lest Norris seem more "modern" a writer than he actually was, it should be noted that the allusion is to the odoriferous cashmere hood of the heroine in this romance.

"Blix."
The Outlook, 63 (October 14, 1899), 419.

"McTeague" was a powerful and disagreeable book; the author's "Blix" is a refreshing contrast. It is a slight story and has some improbabilities and crudities, but it is light-hearted, jolly, and its man and maiden, if a little Bohemian in their jollifications, are clean-minded, healthful-bodied people whose frolics are harmless and amusing.

"A California Novelist." *Washington Times*, October 15, 1899, p. 8, part 2.

Within the past year the reading world has been made aware that there is a new American novelist in sight, and that he "comes out of the West." Since Bret Harte and the Forty-niner no one has written of California life with the vigor and accuracy of Mr. Frank Norris; and the best of it is that he is not in the least like Bret Harte, or very much like anyone but himself. His "McTeague," following close on his tentative adventure story "Moran of the Lady Letty" settled his right to a place in American literature; and he has now presented a third novel, "Blix," which is in some respects the finest and likely to be the most popular of the three.

The noticeable thing about these three books—the thing which strikes the reader at sight—is their wide difference from each other. It is an unprecedented thing in literature. Here is an author, practically unknown, who makes something of a reputation by a story of adventure dealing with types absolutely new in fiction; the heroine a woman Viking, the hero a nineteenth-century college man, the incident one wild turmoil of moving events by sea and land, and the atmosphere realistic to the last degree. His next work is a powerful character study of San Francisco types which are yet the types of almost any large American city; a grewsome, half-disgusting, but perfectly accurate analysis of a semi-barbarous modern man, done with the realism of Zola and the idealism of Balzac all steeped in an atmosphere which can be nothing but American. Now we find this author turning from adventure and slum study to picture an exquisite, tender, yet humorous love-idyl of the City of the Golden Gate. The only thing which these novels have in common is their fidelity to nature. No one can prophesy what Mr. Norris' next venture will be; but it is safe to say that it will be good. There is one quality which is his in full measure, which is seldom possessed by either the saga man or the analyst; and that is the power to comprehend a woman. Wherever he touches feminine character he does it with as sure and confident a hand as in dealing with men; and his intuition rarely is at fault.

"Blix" is the nickname given by her lover to Travis Bessemer, a California maiden, serene, happy, beautiful and full of strength—the American girl at her best. She is a blossom of San Francisco gardens, but she might have grown in Chicago, Boston, New Orleans or New York and varied but slightly from the type. There is nothing phenomenal or abnormal about her. Her traits are possessed in some degree by thousands of charming girls all over this land; and yet she is an individual; one could never mistake her for anyone else. The same is true of Condy Rivers, the other character in the book—for to all intents and purposes there are but two. He is the writer-man; in certain peculiarities of dress, manner and temperament he is the Western type, but in him half the newspaper men and novelists of the country will recognize salient qualities of their own.

It would be spoiling the feast in store for the reader if one were to sketch the plot of this charming little love story, for it is in the unexpected turns and doublings of this plot, as well as in the character-drawing, that the interest of the book lies. It is thoroughly original and as thoroughly natural, from the first page to the last; and not for two minutes at a time can the reader say what is going to happen next, or what the two people most concerned will take it into their heads to remark. The comedy is odd and bright and rippling; the pathos—what there is of it—is delicately reserved; and the whole movement of the story is free, joyous, and confident. If Mr. Norris can write as careful and powerful novels of Eastern as of Western life, he may yet turn out to be that long-looked-for man, the man whom, perhaps, we lost too early in Harold Frederic—the man who will write the great American novel.

"Blix" gives the impression of having been written swiftly and rather easily, with great enjoyment. There is a hint of the author's own experience in novel writing here and there, and one gets an inkling of the methods by which "Moran" was accomplished. It may be for this reason that one or two unaccountable slips from accuracy occur in this book, for nothing of the sort is to be found in "McTeague." Curiously enough they occur in the author's dealing with Kipling, for whom he has evidently a great admiration, almost a passion. He describes an afternoon in a Chinese restaurant where Condy read to Blix some marvelous tales, and she "fell under the charm of the little spectacled colonial, to whose song we all must listen and to whose pipe we all must dance," and he causes these tales to be read from "a paper-covered volume" entitled "Life's Handicap." In this collection he finds "The Strange Ride of Morrowbie Jukes," and "The Return of Imri." Now, it may be that a special California edition of this work was published; but there was no other edition of it which appeared in paper, and the one generally circulated does not contain the "Morrowbie Jukes" story. Moreover, "The Return of Imray"—which Mr. Norris misspells—is hardly the sort of story which even Condy Rivers would select to read to a girl at luncheon-time in a restaurant. It is a perfectly proper tale, but the snakes and ghosts and corpses are rather too numerous to make it agreeable as an appetizer. Perhaps there was a reason for Mr. Norris' doing these things, but it is not apparent. It is a small matter, but the rest of the book is so finished in its realism that this tiny false touch jars on one.

"Blix" will be a revelation to those who have not read between the lines of the author's earlier works. It is fresh and simple and wholesome, full of ideality and high thought, without being sentimental or metaphysical, and the vein of drollery which runs through it gives life, vivacity and a certain careless strength and abandon to the whole. Perhaps Mr. Norris' next undertaking will be to give us something purely humorous. He could do it, and it would be worth doing; and it is one of the things which he has not yet done. Or he may turn his attention to the political novel; and there his opportunities would be simply unparalleled. Whatever he does next, he has already done so much that the curiosity of the public is piqued, and it desires to see more of him.

"An Idyl of San Francisco."
The Argonaut, 45 (October 16, 1899), 9.

Frank Norris will not fail to write a great novel for lack of trying many fields. He led off with a sea story, followed that with his Zolaesque tragedy of Polk Street, and now he has written in "Blix" what his publishers term a "charming little California love idyl." But he does not seem to have hit it off yet. There is observation, and character study, and the story-teller's knack in his tales, but they are all marred by signs of immaturity.

This immaturity crops up in "Blix" in the attempt to ascribe a social status to the two young people about whom the story is written which they could not have occupied. Condé Rivers is described as a newspaper man, twenty-eight years of age, and a member of the Bohemian Club, but he is as coltish as a college boy in his freshman year. His besetting vice is poker, and he is youthful enough to be willing to borrow the necessary money to take a hand in a game. His newspaper work apparently fills in five or six hours a day, and the rest of his time is devoted to what he and Blix call "functions"—dances, dinners, teas, and theatre-parties. For a year and a half he has been taking Blix to the theatre on Monday nights and calling on her Wednesday and Sunday evenings, when her widowed father and younger brother and sister are promptly huddled away to remote corners of the flat, and Blix and her "company" are left alone in the "parlor," with its "drapes" and gilded catstails. They have been carrying on this species of flirtation, spiced with a mutual pretense of love, for eighteen months.

And Blix is only nineteen. She must have begun young. There are girls of sixteen in San Francisco, as elsewhere, who go to the theatre unchaperoned and receive young men alone in their homes regularly twice a week. But they do not go in the class of society in which Mr. Norris places Condé and Blix. She is not "out" yet, but she is a member of the "Saturday Fortnightly" club and has invitations for at least three other "functions" a week. One wonders how such a young woman would be "brought out" and what change it would make in her mode of life.

Thus much one must say in defense of the class of San Francisco society in which Mr. Norris assumes to place his hero and heroine. For the rest, "Blix" is a very "charming little California idyl." The young couple have been flirting with one another for a year and a half in the manner approved in "ball-party" circles. But the girl has unusual good sense, and when she demands that they drop the silly pretense, they fall into a delightful comradeship. He takes her down to the wharves on one of his newspaper "details"—to write up a whaleback ship—and on their return they take tea in a gorgeous Oriental restaurant in Chinatown. A few days later they go on a fishing-trip—these two alone—and, on their return to town, dine together in a little restaurant in the Mexican quarter. They make regular expeditions to a life-saving station near the ocean-beach, and from the old salt in charge Rivers derives material for a novel of adventure, which Blix hears read chapter by chapter as it is written, and criticises to its considerable benefit. Altogether, they enjoy an ideal companionship in their intellectual tastes as well as in their material life, and in the three months which the tale includes the old flirtatious pretense is replaced by a genuine love that strengthens and improves them both.

"Literature."
The Independent, 51 (October 19, 1899), 2830.

The story of a young newspaper man and how he gained him a wife through the usual process of courtship, yet did not realize that it was really courtship until at the very last, when platonic symptoms suddenly developed into an irresistible case of matrimonial fever. The hero has the inevitable literary bee in his bonnet meantime, and finally prints a story in his paper which makes his fortune. There are many delightful touches and points of freshness and lifelikeness which mark the work as unusual and full of promise.

"Briefer Notices."
Public Opinion, 27 (October 26, 1899), 538.

The very simplicity and unassuming frankness of "Blix," the latest production of Mr. Frank Norris, is the book's greatest attraction. It is the story of a very level-headed young San Francisco girl and a young journalist who promises to turn out well if he will continue to follow the girl's advice. When we leave them they are starting for the east, the girl to study medicine and the man to fill a position that has been offered him in New York. By this time, it is fairly safe to say, they are happily married, having met with the success they promised themselves to achieve before that event should take place.

"Blix."
Overland Monthly, 34 (November 1899), 474-75.

Frank Norris has written a new novel and called it *Blix*. The book is a surprise, inasmuch as many of us have been looking for something big from Frank Norris, and this attempt of his is no fulfillment of such an expectation. Is it because he has not taken enough pains? Or has he already measured his capacity for careful and sustained effort?

Blix is vastly interesting (Mr. Norris could not write anything that was otherwise)—clean, sweet, and wholesome, full of light and color. Who can stroll and peer around Chinatown and the Mexican and Latin quarters in San Francisco—having once read one of Mr. Norris's sketches of these neighborhoods—without being continually reminded of this young man's remarkable descriptive powers? He has immortalized the squalid picturesqueness of the dingy alleys with their splashes of Oriental reds, blues, and yellows; the brilliant balconies; the narrow passageways opening upon unexpected dens of weird people and things; and has cast over the undeniable grime and unpleasantness a glow of romance which for those who can appreciate it changes the aspect of this part of the city.

In *Blix* there are many incidents which will not be forgotten by the San Franciscan who has enjoyed investigating the places described. Among these stands out conspicuously the dinner at the Mexican restaurant: not an item of the quaint old apartment has escaped the author; and besides, the errand which took "Blix" Bessemer and Condy Rivers there, though far from being original, is irresistibly funny. This can also be said of the consequences of their scheme, which have the added advantage of being both unique and dramatic.

Blix Bessemer is a first-rate heroine—strong, true, boyish in her camaraderie with her friend, but womanly and loving-hearted, and beautiful withal. She has the sort of mentality that counts in a woman's influence with men; the reasoning ability and discrimination that taught her she was wasting time in fashionable society, and which suggested her learning to play poker that she might night after night keep Condy Rivers, whose great weakness was gambling, away from objectionable associates. She wins his money with ease, skill, and apparent unscrupulousness, and saves it for his rainy day, which comes when he resigns his newspaper position in order to find time to write a book. In short, Miss Bessemer is a splendid woman, and not at all an impossible one.

Mr. Norris has given a rather peculiar impression with regard to San Francisco society, by representing this young girl of nineteen as having moved in a "swell" set for some two years (her mother is dead and she has no chaperone), and continually repeats the statement that she is not yet "out." It sets us wondering what will be especially needed to accomplish her début. At the same time, several other points are brought out concerning the behavior of certain young men at society functions that are unfortunately only too true.

Mr. Norris may have known a girl like Blix, but it would be hard to believe that a man like Condy Rivers has ever come under his personal observation. Rivers is not made of good enough stuff to stand up well beside the royal-natured woman who works untiringly and with beautiful tact to make something of him. To begin with, he is twenty-eight years old, is a graduate of the State University, and has been through a finishing year at Yale; he holds a responsible position on a big daily, and is supposed to be a genius as a short-story writer. Despite these advantages he has the manners and apparent mental development of a schoolboy of sixteen, irrelevant, uncertain, and shallow,—positively silly at times.

Condy Rivers and Blix grow weary of a flirtation of a year's standing, and are forced to admit to each other that they are bored. Upon deciding to separate, they suddenly find that they are very good friends in place of disillusioned lovers. They decide to drop out of their social environments, and in lieu of cotillions and afternoon functions, substitute tramping and fishing excursions, rambles along the water-front and aboard ships, dinners and luncheons in out-of-the-way places, where she pays for the entertainment with money won from her companion at poker. And, by the way, the fishing expedition is one of the most inspiring descriptive bits in the story.

The upshot of this frank and Bohemian intercourse, and Blix's steady resolve and undertaking to make a man out of Condy in spite of discouragements, is that within three months they fall earnestly in love with each other, and no one will be unpleasantly jarred by the fact that it is Blix who first speaks.

For one who knows so much about the

journalistic world as Frank Norris must, his conception of the responsibilities of a newspaper man is rather startling. Condy Rivers is depicted as drawing $100 a month salary, but it is a puzzle to discover what he does to earn it, as he spends nearly all his daytime with Miss Bessemer and most of his nights playing poker, and still contrives to keep on good terms with his managing editor!

From a logical standpoint the author of *Blix* cannot be particularly complimented on its construction, and he has been careless enough to put some unnecessarily bad English into the conversation of his characters; some of the passages that are intended to be witty, sound cheap and hackneyed; even the incident of the origin of the name "Blix" falls flat. On the whole, however, this little volume is bound to please, for there is in it the true ring of a good story. Nevertheless we are sure Frank Norris can do better work than this, for in proportion to his reputation as a story-writer and what is hoped for his future, this latest book is not an eminent success. And so we trust that it is but the herald of something larger, higher and more worth his while.

Charles F. Lummis. "Another Success by Norris." *Land of Sunshine*, 11 (November 1899), 353.

Evidently Frank Norris has come to stay, and bringing his welcome with him. It is but a few months since we reviewed his remarkable novel *McTeague* (now gone into its fourth edition); and already comes a new San Francisco story from his pen, with the mystifying title *Blix*. It is almost the swing of the pendulum from *McTeague*; not so powerful, certainly, as that ghastly study in sodden brutality, but far more comfortable reading. Indeed the grisly note is avoided altogether; and *Blix* is a direct, simple, yet ingenious and loveable love-story, with little more than the two central characters. Mr. Norris's descriptions are usually good, and not too much dwelt upon; his character drawing is literally excellent. We have a right to hope large things of a young man who already shows up so handsomely.

A. Schade Van Westrum. "A Bundle of Good Stories." *The Book Buyer*, 19 (November 1899), 298.

Mr. Norris has made a new venture—that of the love idyl, and he has done so deliberately, for the traces of spontaneity in the story are few, though it contains many telling touches of romance, and is, indeed, as a *tour de force*, rather clever. We are not acquainted with the San Francisco dialect, but find here a rising young journalist and *littérateur* talking in the same disjointed, asyntactic fashion as did McTeague, and like him, prefacing many of his remarks with "huh!" And Blix herself shares this peculiarity with him to a large extent. Another puzzle in the book are San Francisco's social "sets," which, we fear, are judged from the society column of the young journalist's daily paper, which evidently still clings to the superannuated rule that all persons whose names stray into its pages must be "society leaders" and belong to the "best set," the "junior set," or the "golf crowd." The social side of the book (we say it subject to correction) seems to be crude and badly jumbled. As to the disjointed dialogue in the story, that may be the result of a too conscientious aiming at realism. But if this be so, the experiment may be said to be a failure. A striking analogy could be drawn between Mr. Norris's beginnings in literature and those of Mr. Stephen Crane—an analogy that will be found to grow more marked as one follows it up in detail.

Willa Cather. "Books and Magazines." *Pittsburgh Leader*, November 4, 1899, p. 5.

Last winter that brilliant young Californian, Mr. Norris, published a remarkable and gloomy novel, "McTeague," a book deep in insight, rich in promise and splendid in execution, but entirely without charm and as disagreeable as only a great piece of work can be. And now this gentleman, who is not yet 30, turns around and gives us an idyll that sings through one's brain like a summer wind and makes one feel young enough to commit all manner of indiscretions. It may be that Mr. Norris is desirous of showing his versatility and that he can follow any suit, or it may have been a process of reaction. I believe it was after M. Zola had completed one of his greatest and darkest novels of Parisian life that he went down to the seaside and wrote "La Reve," a book that every girl should read when she is 18, and then again when she is 80. Powerful and solidly built as "McTeague" is, one felt in that the realistic method was carried almost too far, that Mr. Norris was too consciously influenced by his French masters. But "Blix" belongs to no school whatever, and there is not one shadow of pedantry or pride of craft in it from cover to cover. "Blix" herself is the method, the motive and the aim of the book. The story is an exhalation of youth and spring; it is the work of a man who breaks loose and forgets himself. Mr. Norris was married only last summer, and the march from "Lohengrin" is simply sticking all over "Blix." It is the story of a San Francisco newspaper man and a girl. The newspaper man "came out" in fiction, so to speak, in the drawing room of Mr. Richard Harding Davis, and has languished under that gentleman's chaperonage until he has come to be regarded as a fellow careful of nothing but his toilet and his dinner. Mr. Davis' reporters all bathed regularly and all ate nice things, but beyond that their tastes were rather colorless. I am glad to see one red-blooded newspaper man, in the person of "Condy Rivers," of San Francisco, break into fiction; a real live reporter, with no sentimental loyalty for his "paper," and no Byronic poses about his vices, and no astonishing taste about his clothes, and no money whatsoever, which is the natural and normal condition of all reporters. "Blix" herself was just a society girl, and "Condy" took her to theaters and parties and tried to make himself believe that he was in love with her. But it wouldn't work, for "Condy" couldn't love a society girl, not though she were as beautiful as the morning and terrible as an army with banners, and had "round full arms," and "the skin of her face was white and clean, except where it flushed into a most charming pink upon her smooth, cool cheeks." For while "Condy Rivers" was at college he had been seized with the penchant for writing short stories, and had worshiped at the shrines of Maupassant and Kipling, and when a man is craft-mad enough to worship Maupassant truly and know him well, when he has that tingling for technique in his fingers, not Aphrodite herself, new risen from the waves, could tempt him into any world where craft was not lord and king. So it happened that their real love affair never began until one morning when "Condy" had to go down to the wharf to write up a whaleback, and "Blix" went along, and an old sailor told them a story and "Blix" recognized the literary possibilities of it, and they had lunch in a Chinese restaurant, and "Condy," because he was a newspaper man and it was the end of the week, didn't have any change about his clothes, and "Blix" had to pay the bill. And it was in that queer old tea house that "Condy" read "Blix" one of his favorite yarns by Kipling, and she, in a calm, offhanded way, recognized one of the fine technical points in it, and "Condy" almost went to pieces for joy at her doing it. That scene in the Chinese restaurant is one of the prettiest bits of color you'll find to rest your eyes upon, and mighty good writing it is. I wonder, though, if when Mr. Norris adroitly mentioned the "clack and snarl" of the banjo "Condy" played, he remembered the "silver snarling trumpets" of Keats? After that, things went on as such things will, and "Blix" quit the society racket and went to queer places with "Condy," and got interested in his work, and she broke him of wearing red neckties and playing poker, and she made him work, she did, for she grew to realize how much that meant to him, and she jacked him up when he didn't work, and she suggested an ending for one of his stories that was better than his own; just this big, splendid girl who had never gone to college to learn how to write novels. And so how, in the name of goodness, could he help loving her? So one morning, down by the Pacific, with "Blix" and "The Seven Seas," it all came over "Condy," that "living was better than reading, and life was better than literature." And so it is; once, and only once, for each of us; and that is the tune that sings and sings through one's head when one puts the book away.

Willa Cather. "Books and Magazines." *Pittsburgh Leader*, November 11, 1899, p. 9.

After reading such a delightful newspaper story as Mr. Frank Norris' "Blix," it is with assorted sensations of pain and discomfort that one closes the covers of another newspaper novel, "Active Service," by Stephen Crane. . . .

"Recent Publications." *New Orleans Daily Picayune*, November 12, 1899, p. 3, part 2.

Mr. Norris has found congenial subjects in turning to California for the characters who figure in this charming little idyll of love and adventure in the west, in which the chief figure is a reporter-novelist. Mr. Norris' work has a distinction which has already led Mr. Howells—a discerning critic, if a kind one—to praise it highly. There is no doubt that it is rapidly becoming a really important element in the development of American fiction.

I.F.M. [Isaac F. Marcosson]. "Blix and Her Story." *Louisville Times*, November 13, 1899, p. 6.

When Frank Norris published his first book, "Moran of the Lady Letty," a year ago, there was impressed on American literature a new and virile force. It proclaimed a profound disdain of conventional things. It was full of throbbing life such as life really is. And when "McTeague" followed shortly there was evident at once the artistic fulfillment of the promise that the initial work held out. No two books could have been more different. "Moran" was pungent with the salt of the sea and a fine story of adventure. "McTeague" was grimy with life's uncompromising realism. As different as was "McTeague" from "Moran" so is the new book "Blix" different from both of its predecessors.

Norris started out as the historian of his native Western land, the sunset country beyond the Rockies, but in a single work he has outstripped that first ambition. He belongs not to the literature of California, but to the whole national literature if the bundle of widely varied elemental forces that contribute to our letters may be given the dignity of a truly national literature. This literature needs men like Norris whose art is keyed to every emotion and whose brilliant force adjusts itself to every phase of fast-developing character.

* * *

All this foreword is scarcely necessary to introduce "Blix"—the book would surely assert itself and command more than the ordinary interest paid to the passing book. It is a glorious story, glorious because it is so keen, so vivid. And yet it is a simple love story that baffles analysis. One would just as soon try to explain the fragrance of a flower. It is not the sort of a love story that steals over the senses like the murmurous music of a lute, but it vibrates with the majestic din of a great cathedral organ. It fairly thrills with the pure melody of the affection that knows the heart and the mind and one page of it is worth all the silly sentimentality with which so many books are deluged.

To begin with Blix is a splendid creature. She is just "a good, sweet, natural, healthy minded, healthy bodied girl, honest, strong, self-reliant and good-natured." Now of all the rank and file of heroines where could you find one who could be more productive of healthy love? There is no nonsense, and yet she is not "strong minded" as most of these misguided "strong-minded women" are. She is Norris' tenderest woman, wholly unlike the tawny-maned Moran or the pathetic Trina McTeague. This is the woman in the story.

Then you have the man. He is a newspaper man, bright, clever, resourceful. He swears by Kipling, which is the first point in his favor; he is a stickler for detail, which shows that he is a good newspaper man, and he is fond of Blix, which indicates a proper appreciation of glorious womanhood. About these two people there is evolved the story of "Blix."

In this book Norris has done admirably what many have vainly tried to do. People have always struggled with love as they have battled with life, and with many love and life have meant the same. Only in the depths of people's hearts have been recorded those tragedies. It is a serious proposition to hold the leash on love. It is one thing to be "jolly good fellows" with a congenial girl, to have no nonsense, and another to resist that indefinable something that speaks out from her and envelops the man with its delicious fascination that tugs at his heart, brings the ache to his throat and fills him with the infinite yearning for that one great affection. It discredits friendship. It is in the end triumphant Love always.

This very thing, the attitude so to speak, is the basis of "Blix," and brilliantly has Norris developed it. To the men who have tried it, to the men who lived it, and to the men and women who long for the comradeship that means only friendship, this book will have a meaning eloquent and inspiring.

* * *

It wouldn't be fair to tell the story of "Blix" here, however strong the temptation to write about it. One closes the book with a full joy in the heart and the fine exhilaration that fresh, healthy people have been living fresh, healthy lives. On one side is sturdy, intellectual, ambitious, loving manhood; on the other, this splendid girl, a thoroughbred, if one ever gave grace and womanliness to a book. It is the man who thinks he alone is passing through the furnace of abnegation, but the woman's heart is just as tender. Each feels that "life is better than literature and love is the greatest thing in life." And when it did come, it seemed to have always been there. It was love's dawn with a new year when new life was riotous in all things.

* * *

Norris' characters are never photographs; they are actual people. His sentences seem to be forged of gleaming steel. He always says just the right thing, and no man, perhaps save Kipling, who writes to-day has so gorgeous a use of words. Norris does not go in for the spun gold and fine linen of the stylist, but unconsciously he weaves a marvelous fabric that reflects every color of the rainbow and about which there blows the real atmosphere of life. He can make you feel the glaring, desolate awfulness of Death Valley with the same ease that he pictures the salt spray as it flecks the deck, and he can take you by the hand and lead you step by step through the highways and hedges from the "Latin Quarter" to "Chinatown." Earth, air, sky and people are on his palette. But practically all this has been said of him in this column long ago, before many other people were as willing to take him as the "American realist" as now. The fact remains that "Blix" is a remarkable performance.

John Kendrick Bangs. "The Compleat Novelist." *Literature*, 5 (November 17, 1899), 449–50.

Every man who has enough of the child in him to keep his nature sweet tries to "see the wheels go wound" in whatever interests him. The layman, however, cannot know how a novel is written except he be told, and it is therefore kind of the practitioners of this "gentle art" to reveal the hidden works of contemporary fiction. But for fear the unsophisticated layman might miss some of the finer points, and be misled by the glitter of the jewelled bearings, the bilious critic who feels it his duty to say "Ha, Ha!" and set right people who imagine vain things, may also be permitted to peep and then have his say.

Mr. Frank Norris has taken the public into his confidence regarding the writing of realistic fiction in his latest novel, "Blix" (The Doubleday and McClure Company). The hero of his story, Condy Rivers, is a newspaperman who has a turn for writing excellent but unsalable fiction. It is but natural that the reader should suspect that Condy Rivers's literary methods are those of the author of "Blix," especially as Rivers finally succeeds. But that is not the way "the wheels go wound" at all. Mr. Norris's methods are diametrically opposite to those of his hero. His hero, in his noblest moods, never dreams of "scalping" a newspaper clipping when in need of facts. He goes direct to nature for both essentials and details. By so doing he proves himself to be a true realist. Yet what does Mr. Norris do? He permits his hero to get acquainted with a certain Captain Jack, who appears to be an incarnate Sunday Supplement. This worthy straightway proceeds to "fill him with tin whistles." He gives him an incident for his great novel that is guaranteed to be "something new and queer, something that ain't ever been written up before." Alas for the unsuspecting realistic novelist! Captain Jack tells him the story of the vessel loaded with whiskey that sank in the mud of the Mississippi about fifty years ago.

Since then the river has changed its course, and untold gallons of whiskey, ripened in the wood, are buried in the sand about five miles inland. This liquor, at a conservative estimate, must now be worth at least twenty dollars a quart, and the adventurers of the great novel are to dig it up and make their fortunes. Condy Rivers swallows this story joyously, even though realistic writers are generally believed to be so alert that they write their suspicions rather than their observations. And yet this whiskey trove story appeared with a wealth of details in a New York Sunday paper a couple of years ago, and there are connoisseurs in the city whose mouths still water at the thought of that fine old ripe whiskey that never materialised out of the limbo of space-writing.

Then there is the story of Captain Jack's wife. Her conversations are arranged in alphabetical order. On each new visit the hero and heroine find that she has advanced a letter, and are much puzzled until they discover that she bought an encyclopedia on the instalment plan, and that as each book is delivered she reads it. This accounts for the fact that on their first visit she discusses the Alps; on the second, bacteriology; on the third, crystals; on the fourth, Denmark, etc. Just when this excellent jest originated it would not be safe to venture an opinion; but if the creation had been done in alphabetical order, a professor of "the higher criticism" might be able to establish the fact that the joke was at least contemporary with the jackal, jellyfish, jabberwock, and all the other creatures with names beginning in "J."

But that is not the worst. When Blix, the unconventional heroine, and Condy Rivers first interest themselves in the fortunes of Captain Jack and his wife, or rather the lady who afterward became his wife, they get rid of a superfluous man by sending him a telegram which reads:

"All is discovered. Fly at once."

Of course the man flies, and never is seen again.

When last the writer saw this anecdote it was credited to Dr. Conan Doyle, and was rather better than in its present form, for the author of "Sherlock Holmes" had addressed the telegram to the most stainless bishop of his acquaintance, who promptly "passed off the map."

But the intention is not to prove that Mr. Norris plagiarised. To use such material as has been referred to is quite defensible, but why did he not let his hero do the same? There are many excellent writers who have large scrap-books and use them freely, and the opinion is growing that when the "Great American Novel" is finally written it will be written in collaboration with Mr. Romeike. Mr. Norris evidently believes so, although he does not allow Rivers to believe anything of the kind.

Joseph Edgar Chamberlin. "With a Paper-Cutter." *Boston Evening Transcript*, November 22, 1899, p. 12.

Mr. Frank Norris's "Blix" bears somewhat the same relation to his "McTeague" that Mr. Stephen Crane's subsequent work has borne to "The Red Badge of Courage;" and yet it is not so bad as that, for "Blix" at least has a good deal of honest fun in it. "McTeague" was a story of blood and brutality, but it had genuine power. "Blix" reads as if the author had tired of having people reproach him for writing such a gloomy and terrible story, and had said: "Go to; I will write a real jolly novel." Here and there we find in it touches of the strength that was in "McTeague," but they are few and far between, and the story sometimes comes very near being trashy. Blix is an astonishingly clever girl of nineteen, who does the most wonderful things; for instance, she learns in two days how to play poker so well that she regularly beats her lover, who is a confirmed poker-player, and wins his money away from him until she sickens him of the game, and then gives him back the money just when he most needs it—to enable him to take a vacation from his newspaper work and write a great story. For Condy Rivers is a newspaper man and is, like most of the newspaper men that have ever appeared in modern fiction, a very disagreeable person. The book has a wofully made-up flavor all the way through.

Not so "McTeague." "McTeague" is more or less shocking, but it is convincing all the way through—even where the men fight in the desert. "Blix" has a forced and artificial style. People "foregather" in places, and never attend parties, but always and forever "functions," and you now and then come upon a real reporter's phrase. More's the pity, after "McTeague," which was written in a pithy, direct, well-weighted style—evidently according to the recipe of "L. E. Gates of Harvard University," to whom the book is ironically dedicated. "Blix" is put forth as an idyl, but it is not so good an idyl as one that is imbedded in "McTeague"—simply thrown in for good measure—the beautiful story of the love of old Grannis and Miss Baker.

"Blix" I fear is distinctly a letting down from "McTeague." Mr. Norris is writing something more of course. I shall be curious to see if "McTeague" gave us his measure, or "Blix."

D.
"Blix."
Pacific Monthly, 8 (December 1899), 82.

A famous physician of New York is said to have introduced a lecture on nervous diseases with the remark, "Gentlemen, this world is full of four things: Sin and sorrow and books and neurasthenia." A reading of Frank Norris' latest novel will easily convince one that it is a book that does not belong to the calamity class.

In marked contrast to his earlier work, "McTeague," its tone is hopeful and the ethical purpose is predominant—to show the latent possibilities in the average man, when developed by the love of a good woman. Mr. Norris is a realist and paints his characters as he sees them, actual flesh and blood people. The hero, Condy, is a young journalist with no special purpose in life until "Blix" Bessemer comes into it. "Blix" is a sensible girl, sisterly and resourceful, who discovers when circumstances would part them, that Condy is necessary to her happiness. Her efforts to cure him from gambling are both novel and interesting, and might serve as a model for reformers who realize the almost hopeless task of fighting this evil. The other characters are well drawn. Mr. Bessemer, with his twin fads, homeopathy and mechanism of clocks, and Captain Jack Hoskins, with the true sailor's penchant for spinning "yarns." The captain's wife is as unique, in her way, as Stockton's "Pomona." She is a queer mixture of sentimentality and common sense, with a wonderful fund of knowledge, only limited by the slow issues of the "Encyclopedia" in installments, to which she subscribed. The work is a fine bit of character sketching. The author is a genuine lover of nature, and his descriptions of points of interest in and about San Francisco, where the scene of the story is laid, will appeal to all readers familiar with that cosmopolitan town. This romance lacks the exciting events of "McTeague," and may be considered weak in comparison, but coarseness and brutality do not necessarily constitute strength.

M.
"Blix."
Pacific Monthly, 8 (December 1899), 82.

No matter how well told and clever a story may be, we never forgive the author who, having the power to do so, fails to make his heroine beautiful. Therefore, we, the readers of that entertaining little book entitled "Blix," naturally bear malice toward Mr. Frank Norris. Compared to the horrible realism of "McTeague," this story is almost ideal. It would be admirable but for one glaring and wholly unnecessary fault that continually stares us in the face, or, to be more literal, blinks at us from every other page. If Mr. Norris had, in delineating the physical charms of his leading character, casually mentioned that her eyes were not of the usual size and then forever after held his peace regarding them, he might have been pardoned. However, he neglects no opportunity to remind us that her eyes are small. He even goes out of his way to call attention to the fact that they are little and twinkling. He makes a noble, sensible, lovable, physically perfect creature, and then deliberately ruins his creation with a pair of tiny orbs that twinkle. If she had to have a defect, why not have given her a moral one? Or, if the exigencies of the case called for a physical blemish, she might have walked on crutches, worn a wig, or blondined her hair. She might have been totally blind—no eyes at all are preferable to eyes that suggest rodents. The character of the heroine does not harmonize with her eyes. I refuse, therefore, to consider her seriously. She is incongruous. Let her creator confess that he has no sense of the fitness of things and then stop writing books.

"Talk About Books." *The Chautauquan*, 30 (December 1899), 329.

The crisp little story "Blix," by Frank Norris, is as guiltless of problem as a story well can be, and has just enough plot to hold it together. Its minor characters are little more than rifts in the background against which we see the two principals. The account of these two, however, the writer of short stories, who, the author tells us, "had begun by an inoculation of the Kipling virus, had suffered an almost fatal attack of Harding Davis, and had even been affected by Maupassant," and the lighthearted, wholesome western girl, nicknamed "Blix," furnish an hour's excellent entertainment.

"The Christmas Bookstalls." *Boston Evening Transcript*, December 6, 1899, p. 14.

A San Francisco journalist and a young woman whom he desires to marry wander about the city and its environs, until she discovers that her wishes accord with his. The most entertaining incident in the book is borrowed from "The Autocrat of the Breakfast Table," but no footnote states the terms of the loan.

"Blix." *The Academy*, 58 (June 23, 1900), 534.

"A Love Idyll," by the able author of *Shanghaied* and *McTeague*. Blix is the nickname of the heroine, given to her by Condé Rivers when they decide on a Platonic friendship. Blix is San Francisco girlhood at its whitest, ripest, best. Condé writes stories, and is just "convalescing from Maupassant" when we meet him. Blix's family, the Bessemers, supply some delightful youngsters. Novels are written, and sunsets dye the floor of the Pacific. The story makes for fun and happiness.

"Literature."
Illustrated London News, 117 (July 7, 1900), viii.

"Blix" is a singularly fresh and pleasant book, and it is quite free from any taint of decadence; it is delightful to meet with a heroine so wholly free from all false sentiment; she is never, even for a moment, introspective (happy creature!), nor does she seem to imagine that she is doing anything out of the common; and yet she makes a man of her clever, impetuous, but unstable lover. Clear-eyed love saw his weakness, and set herself to cure it. Do not run away with the notion that Blix sermonised—Condy would never have stood that; instead, she threw herself into his pleasures and pursuits, taking advantage to the full of that wholesome freedom which is the birthright of the young American girl. Blix was not particularly clever—or particularly anything: just a natural, healthy girl, eminently sane, and with a mind of her own; a woman who dispensed, on occasion, with the minor conventions, very much as the dragonfly sheds his skin that he may wing his unfettered way in the sunlight. There is a charm and quality in Mr. Norris's style that lures the reader on from page to page: his word pictures are crisp and vivid, and San Francisco becomes known to us as we wander in China Town, or walk down Clay Street with Blix and Condy. We laugh with them when they are gay—which happily is not seldom—and when the culminating moment does arrive and love declares itself, we are happy and relieved. Mr. Norris is to be congratulated on having given us a pleasant book.

"Novels of the Week."
The Spectator, 85 (July 7, 1900), 19.

Inverting the Virgilian order, Mr. Norris passes from the clash of arms and the life of action to the idyllic vein,—from *McTeague* and *Shanghaied* to the uneventful love romance of two young Americans of what we should call middle-class rank. If, however, the story is devoid of violent sensation, it leaves nothing to be desired to the English reader on the score of unconventionality. To begin with, the scene is laid in San Francisco, where the "decalogue of mode" differs as widely from that of Mayfair as the surroundings of the Golden Gate from those of the Marble Arch; to go on with, Condy Rivers—there is something strangely ludicrous in the collocation to English ears—is a San Franciscan journalist and short-story writer, "who had begun by an inoculation of the Kipling virus, had suffered an almost fatal attack of Harding Davis, and had even been affected by Maupassant." As for the heroine, Travis Bessemer, *alias* "Blix," she is best described as a "thorough good sort." After eighteen months' flirtation with the hero, she decides that it is no use pretending that they are in love with each other; henceforth they are to be chums, good friends but nothing more. Rivers readily agrees, and the plan answers so splendidly that in a very short time he has irrevocably lost his heart to his genial and sensible playmate. The record of their excursions and picnics is exceedingly bright and pleasant, and the lapses from good taste are so surprisingly few and far between, when one remembers his last book, that we confidently look forward to the time when Mr. Norris will be wholly reconciled to the value of reticence. Meantime he has given us a capital and enjoyable story, excellent in feeling and sincere in sentiment, containing one or two very fine pieces of description, a singularly weird episode in the life of a diver, and a most generous and gracious tribute to the genius of Mr. Kipling.

"Fiction: Some American Heroines."
The Academy, 59 (August 11, 1900), 111–12.

When a man seeks to define the charm of woman he finds that his task is synthesis rather than analysis. Clothes become her in a literal as well as a colloquial sense, the grace of nature is inwoven with the grace of artifice so cunningly that he cannot separate them. She is concealed by that which expresses her and expressed by that which conceals her. Her many moods (though some be doubtless products of calculation and design) by their very variety hint at a spontaneity in which her beauty persuades him to believe. In the end it is easier to abandon the attempt to define her and to take out of Celia's mouth the exclamations which offended Rosalind in "As You Like It": "O wonderful, wonderful, and most wonderful wonderful! and yet again wonderful, and after that, out of all hoping!"

But in this indefatigable age even glamours are classified, and women, though never to be wholly explored, can be mentally segregated.

She of America may be profitably studied in the three novels before us, for it is safe to say that, in each case, by dint of the author's knowledge of her environment, she could not be mistaken for a native of any other land than her own. In Blix and Selma, the heroine of *Unleavened Bread*, two extremes confront one another, but both are products of the democratic spirit. Blix is woman strengthened by liberty to love better, more helpfully; Selma is woman hardened and falsified by ambition till she becomes, if the phrase be admissible, a sort of leech or parasite of the democratic spirit. In depicting Selma Mr. [Robert] Grant has produced a work of art so symmetrical and sincere that it deserves also to be called a work of science. She has a secret perception that republicanism consists in the existence of a place for Selma at the top of American society whence she can look down on the aspiring friends whose presumption she despises. Thrice was she married; but each time the husband was a stepping-stone. The offence of her first husband against her, though solitary and contritely regretted, found her inexorable. She had neglected him for a Congress of Women's Clubs, and he pleaded his loneliness. "Here," she said, slipping off her wedding-ring, "this belongs to you." It was, of course, her "soul" that revolted, but she promptly married, after her divorce, an architect of delicate talent, whom she would have made play Andrea Del Sarto to her Lucrezia. Upon his death she married a third time, the bridegroom being a lawyer—a man of straw, but imposingly stuffed. Him we see mounting the political ladder of the United States as Congressman, Governor, and Senator. It was Selma who made him Senator. It was done at the sacrifice of his honour as a gentleman. "The eternal verities are concerned," she said. That was Selma's way. She canted her way through everything to gain position and notoriety. A social evening was nothing to her unless she could recite "O why should the spirit of mortal be proud?" She was incapable of the maternal feeling. Her second husband more than once detected her "looking at the babies with a wistful glance. She was really admiring their clothes, yet the thought of how prettily she would have been able to dress a baby of her own was at times so pathetic as to bring tears to her eyes, and cause her to deplore her own lack of children as misfortune." Selma was lovely, but the awful vulgarity of her soul would creep out to defile it despite her cleverness. The varnish of a new American town is smelt in her; it is the spoor-scent by which we track her. She is convinced of her own worthiness and the virtue of the quack-loving energy which is hers. Wherefore the author, while doubtless disliking her extremely, can but leave her seraphically "penetrating the future even into Paradise." For ourselves we may truly say that not "Bel-Ami" himself, whom in feminine, respectable fashion she more than a little resembles, leaves in the wake of his crowning triumph quite so implacable an odour as this same Selma, uncynical and chaste though she is.

Gladly we turn to Blix, who is loved by her author with a Pygmalion-passion, which vivifies without a prayer to the gods. He is never tired of showing the strength of his visualisation of this daughter of San Francisco. She wore instead of a belt "the huge dog-collar of a St. Bernard." In its way that's as good a touch of domestic life as the painting of Amy's boots in *Little Women*. Our eyes rise from the dog-collar to the "hightight band of white satin" which she wore round her throat, and then they see the "honest yellow hair," and the "sloe-brown glittering little eyes." She induced a tenderness "for all the good things of the world," and she set to work to manufacture a man out of her conceited, fiction-spinning lover. She cured him of gambling and of promise-breaking. To her indirectly he owed his best inspiration, a story too good to be retailed as a sketch. Shop—literary shop—is a dangerous element to introduce into fiction. This, too, was made in a shop, the reader is apt to think. But Blix triumphs. Because she is so tender, so gay, so truthful; because she preferred comradeship to the philanderings of lukewarm love, we forgive the fanfare which announces her final awakening. "The moment that had been in preparation for the last few months, the last few years, the last few centuries, behold! it had arrived." It was a moment that came after innumerable holidayings with her lover. Listen to her as she sits on a log within sight of "the old fort at the entrance of the Golden Gate," "clasping her hand upon her knees, and rocking to and fro":

> "Oh, Condy, and you thought of a *lunch*—you said it was shoes— and you remembered I loved stuffed olives too; and a book to read. What is it?—*The Seven Seas*. No, I never *was* so happy. But the mouth-organ—what's that for?"
>
> "To play on. What did you think—think it was a can-opener?"

Neither Blix nor Selma could have fully understood Nannie Ditmer of

[James Newton Baskett's] *As the Light Led*. She was sectarian and stated her grievance against her lover thus: "What'd he want to go and make a Methodist of himself right in my face for?" She attracts the reader's attention at an early stage by pinching a notch out of the wing of a fly to make it match the other. "I can't stand a one-sided thing," she remarked. She was a very sensitive girl, and when her lover visited her at school, "kind of country-like—pants in his boot-tops and all that," as one of her companions observed, she flouted him dreadfully, not knowing that his mother was dying. But she was clever and recognised the weakness of a showy man. "He heightened the burnish of many things, but he was not part of them. . . . He could not stretch himself and make a dead scene quiver into life."

Of these three heroines she is the most surrounded by the properties of romance, though *Blix* ends with a most candid creak of optimistic machinery. Nannie is nearly frozen to death, she has brain-fever; there is a prairie fire, a cattle pest. The author is a poet in his way, yet "where were heroism without catastrophes?" he seems to ask. It would be hard to say if, in the language of a character in *Blix*, Mr. Smith's story is "a snorkin' good" one, but it is certainly interesting and gracious. It contains, by the way, some extraordinary dialect.

Here we must leave our women. None of them is the woman of Charles Dana Gibson's pencil and Mrs. Burton Harrison's pen. We imagine them to be less hotel-seasoned than theirs. They are Americans, and they are heroines. Cosmopolis knows none such.

A Man's Woman
By FRANK NORRIS

New York
Doubleday & McClure Co.
1900

A Man's Woman

Frederic Taber Cooper. "Frank Norris, Realist." *Bookman* (America), 10 (November, 1899), 234–38.

Even if *Captains Courageous* were really so much below Mr. Kipling's usual level as some zealous critics have contended, it would still have placed lovers of fiction in his debt, if only for having brought the romance of sailor life again into favour. It opened up a golden opportunity to a host of new writers, and more than one of the younger reputations of today are due to this renaissance of stories of the sea. Morgan Robertson's *Spun Yarn* and Joseph Conrad's *Nigger of the Narcissus* are instances which come at once to mind, while a more recent, and in some ways a more significant, example, is Frank Norris's *Moran of the Lady Letty*—a book which no less an authority than Mr. Howells has heralded as the forerunner of a new era in American fiction. Impartially considered, *Moran* is scarcely a masterpiece—just a strong, fresh idyl of the sea, conceived with a reckless disregard for plausibility, but full of the dash of waves and the pungency of salt breezes, and amply redeemed by the brave, frank, loyal character of that "daughter of a hundred Vikings," Moran herself.

But the real significance of Mr. Norris's first book lies far less in the plot than in the resourceful vigour of his language and the admirable accuracy of minor details; and more interesting than the undoubted promise that it contains is the promptness with which that promise is being redeemed. Mr. Norris is a young man to have attained his present measure of success, being still in the vicinity of thirty; and the very versatility which his work exhibits is an indication that he is yet engaged in testing his strength and seeking his true path. Three other novels have followed *Moran* in rapid succession, each offering a fresh surprise and dealing with an utterly different theme, but showing at the same time a steady gain in power along the lines which stamped the first book as a work of sterling merit *McTeague*, which immediately followed it, is frankly, brutally realistic; a study of heredity and environment, symbolising the greed of gold, and dominated throughout by the gigantic figure of the dull and brutish dentist, ox-like, ponderous and slow. *Blix*, which has just been issued in book form, offers a sharp contrast. It is a sparkling little love story, clean and wholesome, the chronicle of an unconscious courtship between a young couple who begin by agreeing that they do not love each other, and then make the dangerous experiment of trying to be simply and frankly good comrades. *A Man's Woman*, now running serially in the San Francisco *Chronicle* and the New York *Evening Sun*, is the most ambitious effort that

Mr. Norris has yet made. The central figures are an Arctic explorer, whose heart is divided between two passions, his love for a woman and his ambition to reach the northern pole; and a woman, "a grand, noble, man's woman," strong enough to subordinate her own love for him to the furtherance of that ambition. The story abounds in dramatic situations, of an intensity often bordering on the repellent; while the convincing pictures of gruesome suffering amid the desolate ice-plains of the far north cannot fail to be recognised as a remarkable *tour de force*. Here is a single passage which admirably conveys the flavour of the whole book:

> There were six of them left, huddled together in that miserable tent.... Their hair and beards were long, and seemed one with the fur covering of their bodies. Their faces were absolutely black with dirt, and their limbs were monstrously distended and fat—fat as things bloated and swollen are fat. It was the abnormal fatness of starvation, the irony of misery, the huge joke that Arctic famine plays upon those whom it afterward destroys. The men moved about at times on their hands and knees; their tongues were distended, round and slate-coloured, like the tongues of parrots, and when they spoke they bit them helplessly.

Yet varied and uneven as these four volumes are, they nevertheless afford a fair criterion of Mr. Norris's powers and limitations. They prove him, first of all, to be a man who appreciates the dynamic force of words, and who can bend them to his own use—a man who can see life as it is, the earnest, pulsating life of today, and is courageous enough to regard the function of the novel as something higher than a mere pastime for the Young Person. It would be an interesting study, if space allowed, to trace the genesis of Mr. Norris's style, for many different influences have helped to form it. Somewhere in his writings he says of one of his characters, a young journalist: "He had begun by an inoculation of the Kipling virus, had suffered an almost fatal attack of Harding Davis, and had even been affected by Maupassant," but was "now convalescing and had begun to be somewhat himself"; and if we do not force the parallel too far, this will apply fairly well to the author of *Moran* himself; for Kipling, Davis and Maupassant have each left their imprint upon him. To be sure, he "began to be somewhat himself" at a rather early stage; even *That Animal of a Buldy Jones*, that slight *esquisse* of the Paris Latin Quarter, which appeared in *McClure's Magazine*, bears the unmistakable hall-mark of individuality. Much of his independence, no doubt, is due to his journalistic training and the experiences incidental to it; one can hardly have had a share in such thrilling scenes as Jameson's raid and the siege of Santiago without gaining a broader view of the relativity of things. But of the writers who have helped to form him, Kipling is one of the most obvious. Like Kipling, Mr. Norris is marked by an exuberant virility; his books are essentially men's books, his heroines, with the exception of McTeague's Trina, are essentially men's women. Yet it is just here that he and Kipling part company, for Mr. Norris has a fantastic ideal of womanhood undreamt of in the philosophy of him who wrote *The Vampire*.

As for his indebtedness to Maupassant, no one can read far in *McTeague* without discovering that its author's literary creed is realism. And yet, paradoxical as it may seem, he has an obstinate and often exasperating vein of romanticism running through all his work. It is his pet failing, his besetting sin, so to speak. A disciple of Zola and of Maupassant, a high-priest, as it were, of Things as They Are, he adheres doggedly to the blunt truth and at times is brutally outspoken, never softening or palliating a thought where he conceives it essential to the fidelity of his picture; occasionally his very imagery verges upon coarseness, as when he describes the ships along the city's waterfront, "their flanks opened, their cargoes, as it were, their entrails, spewed out in a wild disarray of crate and bale and box." And yet every now and again this same acute, clear-visioned writer will perversely sacrifice not only truth, but even verisimilitude for the sake of a melodramatic stage effect, even at the risk of "an anti-climax worthy of Dickens," as Mr. Howells has characterised the closing scene in *McTeague*.

Nevertheless, it is beyond question that Frank Norris is a realist by instinct and by creed. As between the two French masters, however, his realism is less that of the author of *Le Horla* than it is that of Zola, the Zola of *Germinal* and *Pot-Bouille*—a realism with a half-unconscious symbolism underlying it. It has often been pointed out how each of Zola's novels is dominated by a central symbol, some vast personification, which is constantly kept before the reader. Similarly, to take but one of Mr. Norris's novels, the symbol in *McTeague* is the spirit of greed represented by gold: we find it in the lottery prize which Trina wins; in the huge gilded tooth of the dentist's sign; in the Polish Jew, Zerkow, "The Man with the Rake, groping hourly in the muck heap of the city for gold, for gold, for gold"; in the visionary gold dishes of Maria Macapa's diseased fancy, "a yellow blaze like fire, like a sunset"; and finally in the coins on which Trina delighted to stretch her naked limbs at night, in her strange passion for money, and which finally lured both McTeague and his enemy to their death in the alkali desert. Another resemblance to Zola is the swing and march of phrase and sentence; the exuberant wealth of noun and adjective; the insistent iteration with which Mr. Norris develops an idea, expanding and elaborating, and dwelling upon it, forcing it upon the reader with accumulated synonym and metaphor, driving it home with the dogged persistence of a trip-hammer. Here is a passage which, brief as it is, will illustrate this quality:

> Outside, the unleashed wind yelled incessantly like a sabbath of witches, and spun about their pitiful shelter and went rioting past, leaping and somersaulting from rock to rock, tossing handfuls of dry, dustlike snow into the air; folly-stricken, insensate, an enormous, mad monster gambolling there in some hideous dance of death, capricious, headstrong, pitiless as a famished wolf.

So far, Mr. Norris has shown small interest in psychological problems—in self-questioning, introspective men, in neurotic, high-strung women, the product of our complex modern civilisation. It is only in *A Man's Woman* that he has verged upon analytic methods; and even here his characters are too simple and primitive to give him sufficient scope. To save the woman he loves from fancied danger, Bennett sacrifices the life of his best friend as ruthlessly as that of the fractious horse which he fells with his geologist's hammer. Had they been every-day, commonplace people, the shadow of that friend's death would have lain between them, barring the way to happiness. Bennett and Lloyd brush it aside with an ease that savours of the stone age. His characters are none of them troubled with an over-refinement of sentiment; they are for the most part normal beings, with a healthy animality about them, rugged, rough-hewn men, and dauntless, self-sufficient women. He deals by preference with primitive characters, dominated by single passions. He paints upon a broad canvas and with bold strokes, and his figures often have something of the Titan about them. From Buldy Jones to Bennett, his favourite heroes are cast in this giant mould, big of bone and strong of sinew, with square-cut head and a salient "prognathous" jaw. Such an one had Captain Kitchell, in *Moran of the Lady Letty*; so, too, had McTeague:

> A young giant, carrying his hugh shock of blond hair six feet three inches from the ground; moving his immense limbs, heavy with ropes of muscle, slowly, ponderously. His hands were enormous, red and covered with a fell of stiff, yellow hair. His head was square-cut, angular; the jaw salient, like that of the carnivora.

Bennett, too, the savage, indomitable Bennett, is of the same brotherhood: "His lower jaw was huge, almost to deformity, like that of a bull-dog, the chin salient, the mouth close-gripped, the great lips indomitable, brutal. The forehead was contracted and small, the forehead of men of single ideas, and the eyes, too, were small and twinkling, one of them marred by a sharply defined cast."

In dealing with women, it is Norris's wont to paint pleasanter pictures, but here, too, he dwells mainly on physical attributes. He never wearies of describing their features, the colour of their hair and eyes, the odour of their neck and arms, their "whole sweet personality." It is curious to see what a fascination woman's hair seems to have for Mr. Norris; it fairly haunts him like an obsession. He dwells upon it constantly, lingeringly; it is the one great charm of each and all of his heroines, and he never lets us lose sight of it for an instant—they are forever smoothing it, braiding it, putting it up or down; it enters into and lends a colour to their every mood. Moran Sternerson has "an enormous mane of rye-coloured hair," which "whipped across her face and streamed out in the wind like streamers of the northern lights." Travis Bessemer, in *Blix,* "trim and trig and crisp as a crack yacht," also has yellow hair, "not golden nor flaxen, but plain, honest yellow"; "sweet, yellow hair, rolling from her forehead." Lloyd Searight, in *A Man's Woman*, has auburn hair, "a veritable glory; a dull red flame, that bore back from her face in one grand, solid roll, dull red like copper or old bronze, thick, heavy, almost gorgeous in its sombre radiance." Even small, delicate, anaemic Trina McTeague has "heaps and heaps of blue-black coils and braids, a royal crown of swarthy bands, a veritable sable tiara, heavy, abundant, odorous. All the vitality that should have given colour to her face seemed to have been absorbed by this marvellous hair."

But it is not alone the scent of feminine hair and neck and arms on which Mr. Norris likes to dwell; his pages are redolent with smells of all sorts and conditions—a veritable carnival of odours. McTeague's dental parlours exhaled "a mingled odour of bedding, creosote and ether"; in *Blix*, the Chinese quarter suggests "sandalwood, punk, incense, oil and the smell of mysterious cookery." Here again is the fragrance of the country in midsummer, as set forth in *A Man's Woman*:

> During the day the air was full of odours, distilled as it were by high noon. The sweet smell of ripening apples, the fragrance of warm sap and leaves and growing grass, the smell of cows from the near-by pastures, the pungent ammoniacal suggestion of the stable back of the house, and the odour of scorching paint blistering on the southern walls.

And as a companion-piece to the foregoing, here is an unsavoury bit from the same volume, a glimpse into Bennett's tent in the Arctic regions, redeemed by the dramatic suggestion of the closing words:

> The tent was full of foul smells: the smell of drugs and of mouldy gunpowder, the smell of dirty rags, of unwashed bodies, the smell of stale smoke, of scorching sealskin, of soaked and rotting canvas that exhaled from the tent cover—every smell but that of food.

It is his gift of depicting the physical side of life, the smells and sounds and tastes of the external world around us, which makes Mr. Norris so convincing, even when he gives free rein to his imagination. He recognises with great frankness the potent part that the senses still play in our modern social cosmogony; and he seems to enjoy pointing out that in spite of our boasted civilisation, *La Bête Humaine* is still very near the surface in these end-of-the-century days. He prefers, when possible, to isolate his men and women, to get them away from the veneer of modern refinement and set them face to face with nature and their own passions. He delights in "the great reach of the ocean floor, the unbroken plane of the blue sky, and the bare green slope of land—three immensities, gigantic, vast, primordial," scenes where "the mind harks back unconsciously to the broad, simpler, basic emotions, the fundamental instincts of the race." He is nearly always at his best when describing the elemental, unchanging aspects of nature; the "golden eye of a tropic heaven," "the unremitting gallop of unnumbered multitudes of grey-green seas"; the "remorseless scourge of the noon sun" in the alkali waste of Death Valley, where "the very shadows shrank away, hiding under sage-bushes," and "all the world was one gigantic, blinding glare, silent, motionless." Best of all, perhaps, is such a picture as this of the limitless desolation of the Arctic ice fields:

> In front of the tent, and over a ridge of barren rock, was an arm of the sea, dotted with blocks of ice, moving silently and swiftly onward; while back from the coast, and back from the tent, and to the south and to the west and to the east, stretched the illimitable waste of land, rugged, grey, harsh, snow and ice and rock, rock and ice and snow, stretching away there under the sombre sky, forever and forever, gloomy, untamed, terrible, an empty region—the scarred battlefield of

chaotic forces, the savage desolation of a prehistoric world.

The rugged amplitude of passages like these has led more than one critic to advise Mr. Norris in all seriousness to leave the life of the city and confine himself to the mountains, the ocean and the plains, wherein they insist that his true strength lies. This verdict, however, is open to serious question: it is true that Mr. Norris's strength lies in depicting life on a gigantic scale, and he has turned instinctively to these wild regions because here at least he is untrammelled, with limitless space for his spacious canvas and broad, sweeping strokes; and, nevertheless, it is an equally stupendous task, and one requiring much the same talents, to portray humanity on a large scale, the thronging crowds in the streets, pushing and eddying, the whirl and bustle of the department stores, the ceaseless traffic along the busy arteries of trade, all the motley, complex life of a great city. It is just here that Zola stands unrivalled; it is here that so many others have tried and failed. Herrick, in *The Gospel of Freedom*, and Payne, in *The Money Captain*, have tried to do it in part for Chicago. Norris, in *McTeague*, has given good earnest of what he is capable of doing for San Francisco. He is admirable at grasping and depicting the physiognomy of a street or of a room, so as to give you the illusion that you must have known them well yourself in some unremembered period of the past. McTeague's dental rooms, with the stone pug-dog and steel engraving of the Court of Lorenzo di Medici, "bought because there were a great many figures for the money;" the Bessemers' stiff little parlour, in *Blix*, "peopled by a family of chairs and sofas robed in white druggets," with the inevitable bunch of gilded cat-tails in the inverted section of a painted sewer-pipe; the Chinese tea-rooms and Luna's restaurant, where Blix and Condy loved to end the day, with "the solemn rites of a supper Mexican"—these and many like them are pictures drawn in indelible colours, which we could not forget, though we tried never so hard.

American life is growing more tense, more strenuous, year by year. There are titanic forces at work here among us as well as in the far north—the clamorous spread of population, the pitiless laws of competition, the growing powers of the trusts, grinding and fashioning our social fabric with a power as steady and relentless as the vast floes which Bennett saw crushing and grinding the ponderous blocks of northern ice. Here is Mr. Norris's true field; he has already shown how he can grapple with huge problems; let him confine himself to depicting the hourly struggle of man against man in the social and industrial world. He has many of the qualifications needful; it rests largely with himself to determine whether he will become an enduring figure in the development of a representative American fiction.

"Mr. Norris's Ultra Realism."
New York Times, February 10, 1900, p. 82, "Saturday Review of Books and Art."

Conan Doyle once said: "We talk so much about art, that we tend to forget what this art was ever invented for. It was to amuse mankind—to help the sick and the dull and the weary." The majority of our novelists must emphatically dissent from this, for one and all—with a few shining exceptions—seem to have taken for their motto the blood-curdling announcement of the Fat Boy in "Pickwick," "I wants to make your flesh creep."

Mr. Norris's hero is an arctic explorer, his heroine a trained nurse, and he avails himself to the utmost of these opportunities to make our "flesh creep." The experiences in the arctic are a skillful mosaic of the worst sufferings of various expeditions. We have portrayed the extremes of cold and hunger, limbs amputated, dying and imploring companions deserted on the ice—terrible pictures of suffering and brutality. We turn for relief to the trained nurse, and we are made almost literally to assist at a fearful operation, every preparation, every detail, every movement of the surgeon and the nurse being given with a minuteness that is simply sickening. That removal of the child's hip joint is as

> Photographically lined
> On the tablets of our mind

as if we had been the nurse herself. After all this, it is, perhaps, a mere trifle to see a horse brained with a hammer, and to go through two cases of typhoid fever with almost as much attention to minutiae as was given to the operation.

We respectfully submit, Is this art?

But, steadying our nerves with restoratives, or handing the instruments to somebody else while we take a quiet little faint, let us accept Mr. Norris's canons of art and turn from the horrors to the romance.

Strong and original the book undoubtedly is, holding the reader's interest to the end. Nevertheless, it fairly bristles with faults. The hero is not only ugly—but let Mr. Norris describe him: "His lower jaw was huge almost to deformity, like that of the bull-dog; the chin salient, the mouth close gripped, with great lips, indomitable, brutal. The forehead was contracted and small—the forehead of men of single ideas—and the eyes, too, were small and twinkling, one of them marred by a sharply defined cast." Beyond force and endurance, Capt. Ward Bennett possesses no qualities to atone for this villainous physiognomy. The scene in which he consigns his best friend to certain death in order to snatch the nurse from a contagion already fully risked is brutal beyond belief. That nurse, the "man's woman," is the opposite of the type commonly supposed to be a man's woman. Her characteristics, many of them fine, are distinctively masculine. The author seems to be resolved that we shall not admire what appear to be self-sacrifice and generosity in his heroine, for he takes pains to tell us that she was not inspired by philanthropy nor a great love of humanity, but she wanted "to count in the general economy of things." Ferris, whom his creator rather carelessly casts aside, is the one really noble character of the story. It is singular that at first much is made of his unselfish falsehood, and that it is afterward wholly ignored and dropped, as if Mr. Norris had changed his mind as regards the working out of his plot.

There are some fine scenes in the book, notably, the one in which Lloyd drives into the pole of the arctic chart the worn banner of the former expedition. But why persistently call the

Stars and Stripes "the stars and bars," the name which was borne by the flag of the short-lived Confederacy?

As we close the story, we cannot help wondering whether it was not written to see how much ultra-realism in what is painful and repulsive a long-suffering public intends to endure. It is a pity that a strong and capable pen should do these things. A novel is neither a chamber of horrors nor a surgical journal.

"Books of the Week." *Providence Journal*, February 11, 1900, p. 15.

Realism without reality is the phrase which best sums up the character of much modern fiction. There is an abundance of detail, but no coherent drawing; exactness in the unessentials and exaggeration in the general effect. It is this kind of realism which Mr. Frank Norris affects. Mr. Norris is still a young man, but, as Mr. Howells kindly points out, he has "arrived." Such being the case, a mere reviewer is bound to approach his work with baited breath and whispering humbleness. But with the liveliest desire in the world to praise, it is impossible not to be struck with the fact that Mr. Norris's "arrival" puts a number of most respectable writers hopelessly behind the procession. The art of fiction as practiced by the author of "A Man's Woman" is a very different thing from the art of Jane Austen or Thackeray or Mr. Hardy. It may be superior, that is no doubt a matter of taste.*

Mr. Norris's novel opens with a vivid sketch of the sufferings of the members of an Arctic expedition making their way southward over trackless fields of ice. Everything is set down with great precision of detail—what they ate and drank, how many miles they travelled, all the physical sufferings they had to endure. Their leader is the protagonist of the drama that is to follow. Ward Bennett, we are told, "was an ugly man. His lower jaw was huge almost to deformity, like that of a bull-dog; the chin salient, the mouth close-gripped, with great lips, indomitable, brutal. The forehead was contracted and small, the forehead of men of single ideas, and the eyes, too, were small and twinkling, one of them marred by a sharply defined cast." Nothing could daunt this man. When he stood face to face with "the titanic primal strength of a chaotic world" and saw the ice hummocks in every direction, he moved his arm forward like a huge piston. Through his clenched teeth his words came slow and measured. "But I'll break you, by God! believe me, I will." It is as if one of our friends of transpontine melodrama were speaking. Mr. Norris's realism is quite as convincing as that of Messrs. Sims and Pettitt. Fortunately for the comfort of the reader he gets away speedily from the tale of Arctic miseries. Bennett and his friend Ferriss are both rescued by a whaling vessel, though poor Ferriss has lost both his hands and got the fatal germ

*The first paragraph of this review was reprinted in "Literary Notes," *St. Paul Pioneer Press*, March 5, 1900, p. 4.

of typhoid fever in his system, and so return to San Francisco and to Lloyd Searight, whom they both love. Lloyd Searight is the "man's woman"—why, we do not know, for men do not as a rule care for what is unfeminine. Where, by the way, did she get such a name? That she is destined to mate with Bennett is clear. The merest old-fashioned romancer could not set the machinery of the tale working more naively than Mr. Norris does. Miss Searight has a fortune of her own; she has built a great house for nurses, and she herself is one of the occupants. The description of her personal appearance is remarkable:

> She was tall and of a very vigorous build, full-throated, deep-chested, with large, strong hands and solid, round wrists. Her face was rather serious; one did not expect her to smile easily; the eyes dull blue, with no trace of sparkle, and set deep under heavy, level eyebrows. Her mouth was the mouth of the obstinate, of the strong-willed, and her chin was not small. But her hair was a veritable glory, a dull-red flame, that bore back from her face in one great solid roll, dull red, like copper or old bronze, thick, heavy, almost gorgeous in its sombre radiance. Dull-red hair, dull-blue eyes and a faint, dull glow forever on her cheeks, Lloyd was a beautiful woman with much about her that was regal, for she was very straight as well as very tall, and could look down upon most women and upon not a few men.

This is certainly a remarkable description, though some carping person might object that an ability to write good English should be among the conditions of "arrival" at the goal of the novelist. The dull red girl is, as has been said, a nurse, and a very competent one. Indeed, the novel is in a way a complete manual of nursing. In "McTeague," the book in which Mr. Norris first won fame, there is a beautiful description of filling teeth. But the account of the operation for hip disease in this story is far superior as a piece of exquisite realistic art:

> Street located the head of the thigh-bone with his fingers and abruptly thrust in the knife, describing Sayre's cut, going down to the bone itself. Farnham turned back the flap made by the semi-circular incision, and with a large, broad-bladed, blunt-edged knife, slightly curved upon the flat, pulled the soft tissues to one side. Street, without looking away from the incision, held the knife from him, and Lloyd took it and laid it on the table with her left hand, at the same time passing the bistoury to him with her right. With the bistoury the surgeon, in half a dozen strokes, separated the surrounding integuments from the diseased head of the bone. But by this time the wound was full of blood. Street drew back, and Lloyd washed it clear with one of the gauze sponges, throwing the sponge in the pail under the table immediately afterward. When the operation was resumed the surgeon went into

the incision again, but this time with the instrument called the periosteal elevator peeling off the periosteum, and all the muscles with it, from the bone itself. Meanwhile Lloyd had gone to the foot of the table and had laid hold of the patient's leg just above the knee, gripping it with both her hands. Dr. Street nodded to her, signifying that he was ready, and Lloyd, exerting her strength, pulled down upon the leg, at the same time turning it outward. The hip-joint dislocated easily, the head of the bone protruding. While Lloyd held the leg in place, Farnham put a towel under this protruding head, and the surgeon, with a chain-saw, cut it away in a few strokes. And that was all—the joint was exsected.

The nurse and surgeons eased their positions immediately, drawing long breaths. They began to talk, commenting upon the operation, and Lloyd, profoundly interested, asked Street why he had, contrary to her expectations, removed the bone above the lesser trochanter. He smiled, delighted at her intelligence.

"It's better than cutting through the neck, Miss Searight," he told her. "If I had gone through the neck, don't you see, the trochanter major would come over the hole and prevent the discharges."

"Yes, yes, I see, of course," assented Lloyd.

And equally we all see. The popularization of medical science has gone on at a great rate, thanks to the zeal of the novelists.

But the climax of the story is reached when it is about half finished. Ward Bennett finds that Lloyd has gone to nurse poor Ferriss, whose case of typhoid is particularly virulent. He fancies that her own life is in danger and posts after her to compel her to come back. Incidentally, we get more medical information. "Quinine for the regular morning and evening doses, sulphonal and trional for insomnia, ether for injections in case of anaemia after hemorrhage, morphine for delirium, citrite of caffein for weakness of the heart, tincture of valerian for the tympanites, bismuth to relieve nausea and vomiting, and the crushed ice wrapped in flannel cloths for the cold pack in the event of hyperpyrexia." But this is by the way. All Lloyd's precautions go for nothing. Bennett appears, and insists that she shall leave the house at once. The fact that Ferriss is his dearest friend does not move him. He clings with dogged obstinacy to the one point, giving an exhibition of manners that is truly delightful. Indeed the man is such an unconscionable brute that the reader longs ardently for some one to kick him. But no one rises to that opportunity. On the contrary Bennett falls ill and is nursed in turn by Lloyd, and recovers and marries her, and goes north on another expedition, leaving her behind. This is the gist of the tale. How it is told our readers can judge from the extracts we have given. Whether it was worth telling they can settle for themselves.

"'A Man's Woman.'"
San Francisco Chronicle, February 16, 1900, p. 24.

Readers of the "Sunday Chronicle" are familiar with Frank Norris's "A Man's Woman," for the story appeared in its columns in serial form. It is not a story, however, which should be cut up, as its power comes out fully only when read at a sitting. The crucial incident we do not think is credible, but aside from this there are no improbabilities, and the story moves forward with the sureness of fate. It differs absolutely from anything that Norris has written, but the hero has some qualities akin to McTeague. Two specialities Norris has mastered for this work. One is Arctic exploration, and the other the life of the female trained nurse. Into both he has put so much of dramatic power that he forces the reader to see as clearly his explorers battling with the elements in the frozen north as the expert nurse fighting with all the aid of science for the life of a patient.

The story turns on the masterfulness of Ward Bennett, an Arctic explorer as big as Nansen, and as full of enthusiasm in his work, and on his passion for Lloyd Searight, a trained nurse, who is his physical and mental counterpart. The Arctic episodes, which form the opening chapters, are written with great power. Imagination never conceived anything more grim and terrible than the retreat of Bennett's party over the hummocky ice. Nothing in Nansen's book or in Greely's narrative approaches it in ghastly details. Ferriss, the bosom friend of Bennett, has both hands amputated, and in this maimed condition, believing that the whole party is doomed, he tells Bennett that Lloyd Searight is in love with him. The next day the party is rescued, but what isn't explained is why Ferriss permits his lie to stand, when the simpler and manlier way would have been to explain that he had misrepresented the facts to cheer and comfort his friend.

On their return to civilization Bennett proceeds at once to find Miss Searight. He is described as a man with so much of the primordial cave man in his composition that he cannot conceive of anything preventing him from realizing his desires. We will not follow the plot, but let it suffice to say that his dominating influence is not unnatural until it reaches the point where he bars Miss Searight from attending his friend Ferriss, who has typhoid fever. Although she has been in the sickroom and therefore has come within danger of contagion, he forbids her to return to the room, and when a servant calls for her and she tells Bennett his friend will die unless she can attend him, he refuses to let her pass and forces her to go back to town. This we find incredible in a civilized man. If Bennett had been a Congo savage it would have been perfectly natural; but in his case, powerful as was the bestial side of him, it would not have warped him and made him abandon his chum to death, nor can we believe that a woman of Miss Searight's fine, generous nature could have been won over to forgive him this atrocious, unnatural act because of his remorse when himself delirious with fever.

If we allow these impossible acts the story is a great one, with few but clearly drawn characters, and with a dramatic power in all its main scenes that carries the reader along to the end. Again and again in this book we find evidences of Norris' genius for putting things in a way which sears them into the memory. His repetition of certain physical traits of his main characters, a bit of realism in which Zola excels, is only one of his literary devices to make his figures stand out with the reality of life. The novel is well worth reading, and it shows an advance in literary workmanship over anything Norris has yet done.

"The New American Novelist."
Washington Times, February 18, 1900, p. 8, part 2.

If there is any one man among the younger writers of today for whom it is safe to predict a brilliant future, that man is Frank Norris. Mr. Norris' published work has been so wide in range, so finished in style, and so original in every way, that it is almost certain that he will be known in future years as one of the few great novelists of America. Those who read "Moran of the Lady Letty," "McTeague," and "Blix" have been awaiting with interest the advent of "A Man's Woman." This young writer—he is not far beyond thirty—gives one the impression of having much good material in reserve, and powerful as some of his work has been, the reader instinctively feels that he may be expected to write, at some time in the future, a book which will fully establish his claim to greatness.

Whether "A Man's Woman" does this must be a matter of opinion. It certainly comes so near doing it that the careful critic may doubt whether or not to call the book a great novel. Compared with "McTeague" it suffers in certain respects; but that story of the San Francisco common people, with all its sombre, grewsome power and unflinching realism, was less ambitious than this later work, and does not compare with it in depth and subtlety of motive. "Blix" was an exquisite, idyllic love story, as unstudied as a rhodora blossom, and involved no extraordinary psychological problems. "Moran" was an adventure tale pure and simple. But in "A Man's Woman" Mr. Norris has attacked most daringly a subject involving tremendous difficulties, and the judgment of the public upon his success will depend very largely on individual temperaments, personal experience, and acuteness of perception. There is likely to be a wide difference between the opinions of men and those of women in regard to the book. This is due to the fact that the plot involves incidents which a man will naturally regard in one way and a woman in another. The book ought to create some discussion in literary clubs.

The plot is simple, almost elemental in its bareness; and as the interest of the story depends rather on the development of character and motive than on the narrative, it may not be amiss to give here a brief sketch of a part of it. The hero, Ward Bennett, is at the outset commander of an expedition in search of the Pole. He and his lieutenant, Dick Ferriss, are the backbone of the party. Bennett, however, is the moving spirit of the whole thing; a man of gigantic frame and strength, and tremendous brute force of will. As he opposes this stubborn personality to the silent, immobile forces of the Arctic world, he somehow reminds one of a polar bear, shaggy, relentless, cruel, ready to crush all that lies in his way. Yet the man is not really cruel, except when the resistless current of his will is turned in some one direction. At heart he has the simplicity of the savage without the subtlety of that child of nature, and this is apt to be true of the civilized man in whom civilization is only a veneer.

Finally, when the expedition seems on the point of failure, when Bennett and his friend lie momentarily expecting death, they discover that both love the same woman, and Bennett is told that his love is returned. Ferriss is moved to this falsehood by a desire to solace the last moments of his friend. The party is rescued, however, and both men live to return to the city which is their home.

Lloyd Searight, the heroine, is a woman rich in her own right, who has founded a home for trained nurses, and lives and works there, on the same terms as other inmates, and subject to the orders of the head nurse. We meet her first as she battles single-handed for the life of a little girl. Just as she is assured that the child will live the news of the rescue of the Arctic expedition comes to her, and the reader is made acquainted with the fact that she really loves Bennett, although Ferriss did not, as he pretended, know of this love. Just here is a debatable point. Lloyd Searight is a woman of a totally different type from the ordinary heroine of fiction. She is a strong, beautiful, self-reliant woman, full of lofty ideals and high purposes, the sort of woman upon whom others of her sex are apt to lean; a woman who, in any circumstances and under the most trying conditions, can be trusted to keep her word; a woman who, with all her strength, is thoroughly endowed with a motherliness which prevents her from ever becoming masculine. There is a question whether just this type of woman would, naturally, be attracted toward a man of Bennett's type. In real life the strong woman is apt to take such a man for a friend and comrade, not for a lover. Her love is kept for the man who understands her, who is sensitive enough to know her thoughts almost before she knows them herself, and who may have weaknesses which appeal to her strength. Lloyd Searight has only two parallels in American literature, and both are creations of Elizabeth Stuart Phelps. These two are "Dr. Zay" and "Avis." Miss Phelps' work does not compare with Mr. Norris' in power and finish, but in the portraits of these two women she has been absolutely truthful. Avis is tricked into marriage through pity, Dr. Zay drawn into it through the chivalry of her lover. In neither case has Miss Phelps made the error of supposing that her heroine would be attracted by mere strength, by the possibility of being conquered and ruled. Mr. Norris has made his heroine a worshiper of force. On the general principle that men and women are apt to admire most what they do not possess themselves, the chances would be considerably against these two falling in love with each other.

However, the novelist has selected for his hero and heroine characters of such unusual types that they may be exceptions to the ordinary rule. The whole plot, moreover, depends on the battle of these two strong wills. This first happens when Bennett, with his elemental directness, attempts to come to an understanding with Lloyd. He tells her that he knows of her love for him and she denies ever having admitted it. He treats her denial as a piece of coquetry and fails to see how this accusation of falsehood insults her. The matter ends in temporary estrangement. The next conflict between them—the real emotional crisis of the book—comes when Bennett discovers that the woman he loves is in charge of a case of malignant typhoid fever, which has already overcome two nurses. He goes to the house, finds her alone, at breakfast, and demands that she give up the case. Her conscience and her professional honor both forbid this. She tells him that the patient is Ferriss, his best friend and one who has been to her almost a brother. He has but a moment to make the terrible choice between her life and Ferriss', and he makes the decision instantaneously, as his habit is. He refuses to listen to her arguments or her pleadings, or to allow her to leave the room. The result is that Ferriss dies. This chapter is one of the most remarkable, not only in the present work, but among Mr. Norris' writings thus far. The subject is one which presents great difficulties, and it must be said that he has handled the whole in a masterly way.

The reader is carried by an impetuous rush of the narrative from this chapter to the close of the book. The relation between the two personalities, the masculine and the feminine, both magnificently strong in their own way, is one which few modern authors could have pictured. Mr. Norris has done it. The character of Lloyd, while exceptional, is in some respects typical, and in its portrayal the author has shown a subtle and quick intuition and a depth of insight which is rare among novelists. Many men have drawn the primitive woman of strong personality; many others have pictured the wayward, charming, tender, lovable woman of civilized life, but the heroine who, with all the refinements and complexities of civilization, yet possesses the sincerity, strength and depth of feeling of primitive womanhood, is rare in fiction. The woman with a purpose has too often been labeled "strong-minded," and caricatured. Lloyd Searight is this woman, drawn without a hint of caricature, sympathetically, appreciatively, and, in the main, truly. This in itself would make Mr. Norris' book somewhat unusual. Add to this the still more remarkable character of the hero, the powerful descriptions in the chapters dealing with the Arctic regions, the absolute realism of the emotional scenes, and the slight, sketchy, but perfect, picture of Adler, the faithful henchman of Bennett, and it must be seen that if "A Man's Woman" is not a great novel it surely has some of the elements of one.

But the book cannot be described; it must be read to be appreciated. It is not even possible to quote from it; the descriptions lose half their force when separated from the tumultuous swiftness of the narrative. Mr. Norris has proved that he can introduce and handle unusual, original material; in other words, he has something new to say. He has proved over and over again his ability to draw character, to make the children of his brain live and move before us; and in this last novel he has shown an extraordinary ability to understand the character and motives of a very uncommon woman. There is no other American writer in the field who has done all this. It is but reasonable to expect that, in time, this California genius will do much more.

James L. Ford. "Pseudo-Realism." *Providence Journal*, February 25, 1900, p. 15.

In his delightful "Fables in Slang," Mr. George Ade characterizes a certain type of modern novel in the following words:

> The dull, gray Book, or the Simple Annals of John Gardensass, A Careful Study of American Life. In Chapter 1, he walks along the Lane, stepping first on one foot and then on the Other, enters a House by the Door, and sits in a four-legged wooden chair, looking out through a Window with Glass in it. Book denotes careful Observation. Nothing happens until Page 150. Then John decides to sell the Cow. In the final chapter he sits on the Fence and Whittles. True Story, but What's the Use?

In the last sentence of this inimitable bit of literary criticism Mr. Ade has given voice to a feeling that often enters my soul as I plod wearily through the pages of the novel of the modern realistic school, wondering why the author has written so many words and fearful lest I may inadvertently skip some of the "strong bits" that have compelled the admiration of the critical wiseacres. I am moved to speak of this now because within the past fortnight I have read two books of the John Gardensass variety, both of which denote careful observation and suggest the question, "What's the use?"

The pages of "Averages" are not numbered beyond the 400 mark, yet I who have climbed over each and every one feel as if there must have been 4000 of them. If it was as hard work to write this book as it is to read it, then Miss Eleanor Stuart deserves a golden crown for her industry; moreover, she is an adept in the art of carefully observing everything that is not worth telling about. Her story deals with a woman who has written a book called "The World's Woe," and who seems to be affected with a mania for the society of hopelessly commonplace and stupid persons. She gives a dinner party, lasting several chapters, at which nothing is said or done that is worth putting on paper, and in a subsequent chapter she moves into the country, and is there visited by members of her chosen circle, who vie with one another in tediousness. At last her husband dies, and, although I am not much of a theologian, I am certain that he is now in a land which furnishes him with livelier company than he ever found at his own fireside.

I am told that this story owes its title to the fact that it deals not with the extremes of society, but with its average constituent parts, and I know that its publishers have the effrontery to describe it in their advertisements as "brilliant." I am told, moreover, by certain apostles of realism, that to describe anything precisely as it is is the highest form of literary art. That is not what I call literary art, however. I call it cataloguing, and I would just as soon read a description of every tomato can and coal scuttle, every bit of kindling wood and scrap of newspaper found in a vacant lot as to trudge through the story of "The World's Woe" dinner party again.

I cheerfully give Miss Stuart credit for her industry and good intent, but such qualities are too rare to be put to such unworthy use. She can gain nothing from the printing of "Averages," except a reputation for "cleverness," and it is so easy to be clever in this town. Any woman can become clever by simply going about and asking people if they have read "Red Pottage."

"A Man's Woman," by Frank Norris, contains only 286 pages, and is superior to "Averages" in point of interest as well. It deals with phases of life which in the hands of a skilled literary artist might become interesting and well worth writing about. Unfortunately for himself, however, Mr. Norris has been commended by insincere or misguided persons, for what they call his "strong bits"—a term which has come to signify anything grossly unpleasant—and now, in the belief that we cannot have too much of a good thing, he has given us a novel made up entirely of "strong" writing that becomes wearisome after the first chapter.

His book opens with nearly fifty solid pages devoted to a description of the sufferings of an Arctic exploring expedition. On the first day one of the dogs dies and they eat his body, on the next the carpenter dies and is buried in the snow, on the next the chief engineer's hands are frozen off, and on the next they eat their boots. So the horrors are piled up on one another until, from very weariness and disgust, we turn to the middle of the book to see if there is to be any relief.

The few survivors of the expedition, having been rescued, the scene changes to the hospital in which the heroine is employed as a nurse. This heroine is the "man's woman" about whom the story has been constructed, and her name is Lloyd Searight. It is a fact worthy of comment, by the way, that the women with unsexed names who infest the pages of modern fiction are invariably uninteresting, and this one is as worthless, from the reader's point of view, as a dull, realistic writer can make her. Lloyd is a rich woman, whose desire to "be something" has made her a professional nurse. At the moment of her introduction to us she is on her way to assist the surgeon who is to operate on a little girl for hip disease, and those who know the resources of "strong" writing will readily believe me when I say that in the description of that operation not a single revolting detail is spared the reader.

At the conclusion of this operation Lloyd is courted by an Arctic survivor whose hands have been frozen off, and after that, her favorite horse, whom of course she manages to perfection, tries to bolt with her and is killed by the other Arctic explorer, who crushes his skull with a hammer. This cheerful incident is followed by an enlivening medical report on a typhoid fever case, in which the handless lover dies under circumstances that would be hideously distressing were the reader not already hardened to horrors of every description.

The subtle and resourceful Mr. Norris then favors us with another typhoid case, in which the other explorer is nursed back to life by Lloyd, who marries him and serves as his amanuensis until the close of the book, when we see him starting cheerfully on his second voyage in search of the pole.

In the words of Mr. Ade, "What's the use" of all this horror? That it is admired by persons of a certain school of what they think is thought cannot be denied; but on the other hand, these very persons have the effrontery to sneer at Dickens as a man who did not know his business. If Mr. Norris has been unfortunate enough to fall into this way of thinking, let him read about the killing of Nancy Sikes—the most brutal thing that Dickens ever wrote—

and see for himself how skillfully and with how much blended pathos and humor the great novelist led his readers up to that scene. There is no skipping pages there, no yawning, no turning over the pages to see "how long this thing is going to last anyway."

The sad, bitter truth about the whole matter is that neither Miss Stuart nor Mr. Norris has any sense of humor. Miss Stuart has no descriptive powers and no knowledge whatever either of the art of story telling or of the resources of the English language. She is merely clever. Mr. Norris, however, shows a certain degree of literary skill in his descriptions of the suffering of the ice-bound explorers. I should call him a literary mechanic capable of occasional excellent jobs. If he were an artist, however, he would not have written "A Man's Woman," but would have sought for his peculiar gifts congenial employment in some honest, well-paid labor, such as the preparation of catalogues of undertaker's supplies.

"A Man's Woman." *Public Opinion*, 28 (March 1, 1900), 281–82.

There are, no doubt, as many different definitions of a man's woman as there are men. Yet, while we recognize that Mr. Norris's attempt at generalization must be a vain one, we are none the less curious to hear his opinion. We note in the first place that he has not presented a composite of feminine graces and virtues, but a woman strikingly individual in every particular. Even her beauty is of an extraordinary type:

> She was tall and of a very vigorous build, full-throated, deep-chested, with large, strong hands and solid, round wrists. Her face was rather serious; one did not expect her to smile easy; the eyes dull blue, with no trace of sparkle and set deep under heavy, level eyebrows. Her mouth was the mouth of the obstinate, of the strong-willed, and her chin was not small. But her hair was a veritable glory, a dull-red flame, that bore back from her face in one great, solid roll, dull red, like copper or old bronze, thick, heavy, almost gorgeous in its sombre radiance.

It is not, however, upon the dull blue of her eyes or the dull red of her hair that Lloyd Searight's claim to the title of "man's woman" rests, but upon the absence of certain qualities usually classified as essentially feminine. Her lover speaks of her as "a great, strong, noble, man's woman, above little things, above the little, niggling, contemptible devices of the drawing-room," with no place in her life for "pretty graces, petty affectations, petty deceits, and shams, and insincerities." As the story progresses we find that her strongest claim rests upon an in-seeing sympathy which makes her husband understand so clearly the needs of a man's nature. The man in the case is quite as extraordinary in his way as the woman. Here is Mr. Norris's description of him:

> Bennett was an ugly man. His lower jaw was huge almost to deformity, like that of the bull-dog, the chin salient, the mouth close-gripped, with great lips, indomitable, brutal. The forehead was contracted and small, the forehead of men of single ideas,

and the eyes, too, were small and twinkling, one of them marred by a sharply defined cast.

Bennett is not a prize-fighter, as Mr. Norris's description might easily lead one to believe. He is the leader of a Polar expedition, iron-hearted, iron-strong. His every act indicates a force and a power of mind that stops at nothing to attain its end, that rushes straight to its object, breaking down resistance, smashing through obstacles with a boundless, crude, blind, Brobdingnag power. The stupendous force of merciless nature that keeps him from the goal of his ambition, the north pole, he regards as his enemy and the enemy of science, and his keenest joy comes from pitting his strength against "the titanic primal strength of a chaotic world." No doubt he was first drawn to Lloyd Searight because he saw in her strong-willed obstinacy something to overcome. Even after they had acknowledged their love for one another there was a tremendous clash of wills. For Lloyd, too, had an enemy to wrestle with, and her enemy was disease and death. She had devoted her fortune to building a hospital, and her life to the profession of a nurse, because she wanted with all her soul to count in the general economy of things; to choose a work and do it. To *do* things had become her creed. Yet with Bennett there could be no compromise, no half measures, and at a most critical moment she abandoned her work for him. Not to be outdone in generosity, he offered to give up his career for her, but she refused to let love stand between him and a God-given task. When he was asked to take charge of another expedition she was the first to bid him to go.

Mr. Norris is an acknowledged realist, yet the reader of "A Man's Woman" is scarcely conscious of the fact. There are, to be sure, a few touches of ultra-realism, and we fancy a critical analysis would reveal touches of idealism and symbolism as well. But one reads the story with scarcely a thought as to what school of fiction it belongs. He thinks only of the battle of life as fought by this strong man and this strong woman, the development of each character under the influence of the other, the faithful friendship of the two men who have faced death together. Three scenes leave an indelible impression—Bennett watching over his men, the living and the dead, the night before the rescue of the expedition, Lloyd's struggle for the life of a child, and the scene between Bennett and Lloyd outside the room where his friend Ferriss lay dying. This—the crucial point of the story—is handled in a masterly manner that redeems all its minor weaknesses.

"A Man's Woman." *The Outlook*, 64 (March 3, 1900), 486.

The author of "McTeague" again in his new novel finds it necessary to his ideas of realism to present the most repellent and brutal narratives of human suffering. The details of the agonies endured by his Arctic heroes are heart-rending enough, but those of the experience of his trained nurse in a serious operation upon a little girl can only be described by the words sickening and disgusting. Such a description out-Zolas Zola, and has no legitimate place in a work of fiction. It only proves that the author has carefully "got up" the special knowledge involved. It is in no way a requisite part of plot or purpose. Those who read further than this chapter will find that Mr. Norris handles an original fiction-motive with distinct power, and shows a decided advance over "McTeague" in the development of character.

"A Man's Woman."
The Independent, 52 (March 8, 1900), 611.

As a story of Arctic ice, boreal adventure, frozen extremities, dire suffering, heroic courage, intense love and flamboyant sentimentality, *A Man's Woman* is worthy of distinct notice. It is not literature, but the story telling is excellent; a strong interest is maintained until near the end, when there comes a weakening on account of a strained sentimental attitude assumed by the heroine, who, after marrying the hero, sends him back again into the ice-pack to undergo once more his horrible experiences. The story thus closes lamely; but there is a great deal of force in its earlier chapters. The author has a fine genius, which makes itself distinctly felt.

"Frank Norris's 'Man's Woman.'"
The Argonaut, 46 (March 12, 1900), 8.

Frank Norris has taken one of the much-discussed questions of the day, the attitude to be taken by husband and wife each toward the career the other has chosen, for the central theme of his latest novel, "A Man's Woman." The husband is an Arctic explorer, and the woman a trained nurse—neither of which vocations is compatible with uninterrupted domesticity—and Mr. Norris's solution of the question is the same that has been found most acceptable since Adam delved and Eve spun: the woman gives up her own career and yet sends the husband out on his frigid search for fame.

Lloyd Searight, the woman, has endowed a home for trained nurses, and enrolled herself on its staff. Ward Bennett, the man she loves, and Dick Ferriss, his dearest friend, return from a polar expedition, and, Ferriss contracting typhoid fever, Lloyd is sent to nurse him. The case is a most malignant one, and two nurses have succumbed to the infection. At a critical stage of the disease Bennett learns that Lloyd is the nurse, and, in spite of urgent calls from the servant momentarily at the sick bed, forcibly prevents her from attending the patient. Through this negligence Ferriss dies. Lloyd's love for Bennett is stunned—she thinks it dead—and Bennett himself sinks with the fever, and Lloyd nurses him. He tries to drive her from his bedside, as he had from his friend's, but she is the stronger, and nurses him back to life. They marry, and in time she helps him to another expedition to the pole.

The pictures of the explorers' sufferings and struggles in the frozen north, with which the book opens, are extraordinarily vivid, and equally lifelike are the scenes in which Lloyd is shown in her duties as a trained nurse. Mr. Norris has evidently collected his data with the painstaking care of another Zola. But the strain of this painstaking is apparent in every page, and there is not a passage in the book that it is a pleasure to read. As to the mental battles through which Lloyd struggles when Bennett breaks her career and when she forces herself to return to the nurses' house and state the facts to her companions—there are pages and pages of these semi-delirious ramblings that are wearisome. Mr. Norris has got it all in, undoubtedly. What he should have done is to leave in only the salient points.

One can not but take exception, too, to Mr. Norris's title, "A Man's Woman." Brute force is not the modern concept of true manliness, and Ward Bennett is, by his primitive directness of thought as well as by his simian features and physique, little better than a human gorilla, and it is an insult to the race to apply to a female whose love for a male, evoked solely by his force, survives what was in intent the murder of his friend, the high title of "a man's woman."

"A Man's Woman." *Baltimore Sun*, March 12, 1900, p. 10.

Mr. Norris tells the story of an Arctic expedition in which the explorers suffered torture almost beyond description. Ward Bennett, the commander of the expedition, returns to America and marries Lloyd Searight, the "Man's Woman." Despite the dangers, she sends him off to the North Pole again—her ambition that the American flag might be the first to be planted there outweighing her fears and love. "A Man's Woman" is a strong story and a subtle one in some portions.

" 'A Man's Woman,' by Frank Norris." *Chicago Inter Ocean*, March 12, 1900, p. 4.

This story opens with as graphic a description of the terror of a Northern winter among the ice floes as was ever written. It is amidst these perils where men are making their perilous journey toward the pole that the reader is introduced to the heroine, Lloyd Searight, "a man's woman." A ship had been wrecked, and the crew had been adrift upon the ice floes, working like slaves with the dogs at their sledges, forever pulling southward, and when at last the sun revealed himself long enough for them to get their latitude, they found they had been drifting northward all the time they had wearily been pulling southward. The men lay dead about them, the living dogs had long been fed from the bodies of their dead comrades, and now the men were reduced to dog meat when the introduction took place. Just then Adler, one of the men, tore open the flap and shouted: "Three steam whalers off the floe, sir; boat pulling off. What orders, sir?" Bennett drew himself up. "My compliments to the officer in command. Tell him there are six of us left. Tell him—tell him anything. Men!" he cried, his honest face growing radiant, "make ready to get out of this. We are going home—home to those who love us, men." The story here breaks, and the lengthy third chapter introduces us more fully to the heroine, as she receives telegrams from both Bennett and Ferriss of "Rescued," and the romance proper begins. It is just the kind of story that cannot be epitomized.

It is a strong story, which solves the unanswered problems in many a real life—how two opposite careers of man and wife can be solved.

"A Man's Woman."
Boston Evening Transcript,
March 21, 1900,
p. 12.

This is a strong book with two "tremendous" episodes, the account of an arctic expedition during the last days of despair, sickness and death, and the other, a minute description of a heroic surgical operation. The hero is a man of iron will and characteristic jaw, whose virility brings the remnant of his followers home from the land of polar cold and darkness and conquers a young woman—who leaves a rival to die because this despotic person will not permit her to go back to the bedside she had been attending as a nurse. Finally, after they have been married for some time, the arctic fever returns and when he is tempted to take charge of a new expedition to find the north pole his wife bids him godspeed. Considering the temper of the gentleman, the old story of the condition of domestic affairs in the Franklin household which made it easy for Sir John to go to any sort of cool place recurs to the memory. Mr. Howells thinks Mr. Norris "has arrived," a rather meaningless bit of ungrammatical slang. He may possess potencies of success, but so far he seems not to have acquired the qualities for a right start upon the literary career, a sense of harmony, proportion and atmosphere, with that element of restraint which is the foundation of style and the perception that beauty and truth are one. To encourage brutality, black and white crudities, sketchiness, in literature is a kind of crime. Instead of being sovereigns of the East, it might be well for us to become its pupils. It is a curious fact that the white man's ideals are lower than those of the yellow race today, and that we are rather drifting away from the refinement which the ancient civilizations have guarded. It would be helpful to some of our writers to study their art in Japan. Much modern work is simply barbarous.

"Books."
St. Paul Pioneer Press,
March 25, 1900,
p. 23.

"A Man's Woman," by Frank Norris, published by the Doubleday & McClure Co., is a powerful story, very well told, of the struggle between two strong wills, a man's and a woman's. Ward Bennett, scientist and Arctic explorer, and Lloyd Searight, professional nurse, are both possessed of unusual force of character, of tremendous power of will amounting in the man even to brutality. Neither has ever met real defeat, neither has ever been broken. They love each other and inevitably their strong wills clash. The man's brute force triumphs in the conflict, but at terrible cost to both, and it is this very triumph which in the end overthrows his strength. This seems almost like a paradox, but it is not really so. The woman, in spite of her strength, is conquered by outward circumstances, by the man's power, but the man, whom no obstacle can daunt, no other will break, is brought low, beaten, humbled, by the terrible consequences of his own act. "Beaten, beaten at last; defeated, daunted, driven from his highest hopes, abandoning his dearest ambitions. And how, and why? Not by the enemy he had so often faced and dared, not by any power external to himself; but by his very self's self, crushed by the engine he himself had set in motion, shattered by the recoil of the very force that for so long had dwelt within himself. Nothing in all the world could have broken him but that." But the woman, gathering herself together after the bitterness and shame of the terrible consequences of her defeat in the very moment when duty was the strongest, the woman, voluntarily renouncing her own work for the man's sake, became the help and the inspiration which lead him back to his old strength of purpose. This is the theme of the story. There is little plot, if we mean by that term complication of outward incident. The interest is mainly what is usually called in literature psychologic. Yet the idea which is worked out is a definite one. Unlike many of the modern realistic books in which the study of character is the all-important thing, something is actually accomplished here. The characters do not wander aimlessly through the book without any apparent reason for their being there. They all bear a real relation to the central theme that is worked out. The book is extremely, brutally realistic. The minute description of the Arctic explorer's experience is terrible, too terrible to be pleasant reading. There are also other places which are almost as unpleasant, the description of the operation, for instance. There is, indeed, less excuse for this last passage and for all the details of medical practice which are given in such abundance than for the horrors of the Arctic expedition. The latter serve, in some measure, to make us appreciate Bennett's character, but there are any number of sick-room details which might just as well be omitted without in any way injuring the characterization of Lloyd. Not that the book is ever offensive morally, it is not. The realism, unpleasant as it sometimes is, is brutal but not vicious. Moreover, the general theme and the situation into which it leads are essentially dramatic.

There is not much to find fault with in the construction of the story. It is in the whole well knit together, although there is undoubtedly at times an unnecessary amount of minute detail. There is not an incident, however, which does not bear in some way upon the main theme of the story. It is of course in the portrayal of the central characters, Lloyd, Bennett and Richard Ferriss, that the best work is done. In fact these characters are the story, and they are masterly creations, although by no means entirely pleasing. Especially is this true of Bennett, who is self-centered, brutal, almost insane at times, in his strength. On the other hand, Lloyd Searight is certainly a noble type. There is much careful analysis of these two figures, yet it is to be especially noted that their analysis never becomes morbid. There is no taint of the pathological in the book for all its realism. It is sane and healthy and the characters innately noble. On the whole it may be said that it is a remarkable study of character, unusually well written, full of dramatic power, but frequently disagreeably realistic.

"Hints for Spring Reading."
St. Louis Republic, March 25, 1900, [p. 11], "Magazine Section."

For a really unpleasant story, read "The Monster" by Stephen Crane. There are, however, touches here and there that are not unpleasant, and some of the situations are saved by a grim humor. Another unpleasant story is Frank Norris's "A Man's Woman." Mr. Norris can reel off horrors, but he has many virtues. His man's woman is not a man's woman at all; she is too strong-minded, and the man is not a woman's man.

"Notes of a Novel Reader."
The Critic, 36 (April 1900), 352–53.

It may be that there are people so misguided as to apply to "A Man's Woman" that much-abused adjective, "realistic." It is the last word in the world to describe what Mr. Norris has done. He has created an improbable man and an impossible woman, put them into an unimaginable situation, and then breathed the breath of life into them. They live and move, there is no doubt of that. They are vital, vivid, colossal if you like, but they are no more realistic than the Yellowstone Park or the Grand Canyon of the Colorado. That is, they are freaks of Nature, not her normal products. But they are worth while.

The grip which Mr. Norris gets upon your attention is a thing in itself, and deserving of study. This unreal book is perfectly convincing. The unsympathetic characters hold your interest tensely, though they never succeed for a second in winning a morsel of your affection. The writer's method is the exact reverse of, for instance, Barrie's. The latter demands that his readers love his characters at once. If you are obdurate and do not love them, you stand in imminent danger of being bored by them at times, but few indeed are the readers whose affections escape the snares set for them by Tommy and the rest. Neither Lloyd Searight nor Ward Bennett is lovable for an instant, but then they are not uninteresting for an instant either. Bennett is an Arctic explorer, "having more the look of a prize-fighter than of a scientist." "His lower jaw was huge almost to deformity, like that of the bulldog, the chin salient, the mouth close-gripped, with great lips, indomitable, brutal. The forehead was contracted and small, the forehead of men of single ideas, and the eyes too were small and twinkling, one of them marred by a sharply defined cast."

Ward Bennett is "masterful" beyond anything ever dreamed of in the philosophy of the late Edward Fairfax Rochester. The sub-title of the book might have been "And a Woman's Man," for this hero in his ugliness and his primeval force is a good deal nearer the type that most women will accept as worshipful than Lloyd Searight is to the average man's ideal of femininity. The title of the story is a challenge. What constitutes a man's woman? When a woman uses the term she means some one who is unwilling to win popularity among her sisters—which must always be bought by character; tenderness, quick intuitions, and absolute square-dealing in regard to the emotional property of another woman being perhaps the favored virtues—when she can obtain admiration from the other half of the race by cheaper means. Lloyd Searight is a great Brunhilde creature with a glory of copper-colored hair and dull blue eyes, large-handed, deep-chested, serious. She studies nursing and employs part of her fortune in building a Nurses' Agency where her theories can be carried out. She is not animated by philanthropy or a love of humanity, but by a desire to count in the general economy of things. She, too, is stubborn, masterful, and insolent in conscious power. She is as far from any ideal of a man's woman heretofore presented as the east is from the west. Perhaps, if man were to create woman from his inner consciousness, he might turn out something so big, simple, and serious as this, because he would not have the material at hand for a composition more alluring, subtle, dear. It would almost seem that no one but Providence has the touch which is desirable in fashioning the creature feminine.

After her lover has been returned to her from the horrors of starvation within the Arctic circle, and, later, from the clutch of fever, Lloyd sends him away again into the hell of the frozen North, because it is "his work," and she deems it needful to his soul's health. Providence would repudiate such a woman, and the reader's indignation is boundless. But when indignation has exhausted itself, interest still remains. Whether we like what he does with it or not, such lavish power as Mr. Norris shows is an exhilarating spectacle. His prodigious, brutal beings are tonic as the great West itself is tonic, and the air in which they live and breathe yields an intoxicating oxygen.

"Spring Flowers of Fiction." *The Book Buyer*, 20 (April 1900), 237–38.

A Man's Woman is a book that, notwithstanding its merits, is disappointing. It holds the attention from first to last, but the impression it leaves is one of discontent. This "man's woman" is not exactly what men seek in the higher womanhood whose flower brings them a greater happiness than any they have known before; and she is decidedly not the ideal "man's woman" of women's dreams. This is, at least, a consensus of opinion of feminine readers of the story. Mr. Norris, we believe, made the mistake of setting out to write a "strong" book; and when a writer naturally so virile as the author of *McTeague* deliberately sets about the strengthening of his strength, the result is almost inevitably brutality. This book is brutal; so was *McTeague*, but the latter was a child of the slums; the strength of the leaders of men, of whom Mr. Norris's Arctic explorer is one, is of a different kind, or, at least, we like to think so. The climax of the story is ingeniously invented, but it is not life, not even drama: it is lurid melodrama, worthy of Sardou at his worst. It is this element that both attracts and repels the reader, but the ultimate judgment is not a favorable one. However, Mr. Norris has only deferred our expectations of him, not killed them. *A Man's Woman* leaves our opinion of the possibilities of his talent unchanged.

"A Man's Woman." *New Orleans Times-Picayune*, April 8, 1900, p. 7, part 3.

There is a good deal of sheer, inconsiderate brutality about this story. It is not pleasant, and it neither stimulates the fancy nor lightens the heart. The man in question is an Arctic explorer, with "the look of a prize fighter, rather than of a scientist." He has a "lower jaw square almost to deformity, the chin salient, the mouth close-gripped, with great lips, indomitable." Lloyd Searight is an equally unusual type. She is a great, big, deep-chested, yellow-haired, serious person, with more money than sense, who builds a hospital and works as a trained nurse, not through motives of philanthropy, but simply that she may be a factor in the economy of the world. After her lover has returned to her from the horrors and starvation of the arctic, she sends him back again, because it is his work, and that kind of thing is needful for his soul's health. Both these people are hopelessly unreal, and the situations in which the author places them are improbable to the last degree. Yet Mr. Norris has command of so vivid and vital a style, and has a gift of such genuine characterization, that the reader's interest is riveted from the first page to the last. He won't like the book, but he will not be able to stop reading it.

Charles F. Lummis. "That Which Is Written: Beauty and the Brute." *Land of Sunshine*, 12 (May 1900), 385.

More varied and therefore more satisfactory than *Blix* or *McTeague*, Frank Norris's latest novel, *A Man's Woman*, has all the strength and all the grimness one has come to expect in the work of this young California writer. There is a good deal of originality in the plot; and the drawing of the three chief characters is vivid. "Bennett," the hero, is an enormous brute; an impossible iron mastery fit to clutch even the frozen North by the throat. If any of our arctic explorers were really of his mold, the pole would have been conquered already. "Ferriss," his lieutenant and victim, is more normal and doubtless more admirable. As for the heroine, "Lloyd," she is decidedly "a man's woman" done by a man; and yet inspiring in her way. The description of the horrors of the Freja expedition in search of the Pole is rather tremendous; and all in all the book is of very uncommon force.

"A Man's Woman." *Overland Monthly*, 35 (May 1900), 476.

There is much strength in Mr. Norris's latest book. There is also much brutality, and unnecessary brutality at that. Some forty pages at the beginning are occupied by a vividly realistic description of the sufferings of an Arctic expedition in dire straits. Nothing is omitted, even to the smell. The various smells contributing to the particular and distinct odor, as it were, are described as smells of drugs, moldy gunpowder, dirty rags, unwashed bodies, stale smoke, scorching sealskin, soaked and rotting canvas, and finally, the catalogue being exhausted, as "every smell but that of food." Truly the city of Cologne, of perfumed notoriety, cannot be compared with this.

We have harrowing descriptions of a surgical operation, a dog-fight, or, at all events, a sequel to a dog-fight, the smashing of a horse's head with a geological hammer, a typhoid case, and other little episodes of a nearly-equally-stimulating nature. Then, as if the horrors had failed for want of invention, the diary of the ill-fated expedition is set down, and such cheerful notes as "Metz died during the night,"—"Hansen dying,"—"Still blowing a gale from the northeast,"—"A hard night," meet the eye. There can be no complaint of lack of incident in a book which manages to pack this into the compass of two hundred and eighty-six short pages. The book is, nevertheless, unquestionably interesting. It is an intensely thrilling and exciting story. But the whole effort to create bigness, to make great, overwhelming effects, is so obvious that there is an air of exaggeration rather than of real power. One feels in the country of the Brobdingnagians. What reason can there have been for making the hero of the story a burlesque, a man whom one would laugh at in the street? Here he is—six feet two—the look of a prize-fighter rather than a scientist—ugly—lower jaw huge almost to deformity—chin salient—mouth close-gripped, with great lips— indomitable—brutal—forehead contracted and small—eyes small and twinkling, one of them marred by a sharply defined cast. Why that cast at all, Mr. Norris? But if we must have it, why not a slight one? The heroine herself must have been a striking object. She had copper-colored hair, dull blue eyes, and a dull glow forever on her cheek. And the way that hero and heroine work themselves into each other's affections borders upon the titanic. No *dolce far niente* for them, no dawdling at ease in paths of idle dalliance, but violent if grotesque conflict as to who is to prevail, and in one instance an unseemly struggle, with the life of the hero's best friend at stake. That the friend dies is inevitable. He could not decently have done anything else, in Mr. Norris's book. Finally, the woman gives the man back again to the horrors of the Arctic winter. Here the author really strikes a noble note. One cannot but sympathize with "A Man's Woman," even if she is so unnecessarily repulsive. She has good stuff in her after all, and makes the very best of the inevitable. In spite of Mr. Norris, however, his hero must of necessity have gone back to the North sooner or later, and if the lady with the dull blue eyes had objected, so much the worse for her.

[Charles F. Lummis]. "In Western Letters." *Land of Sunshine*, 13 (June 1900), 18.

Frank Norris, the hard-handed young man who writes novels as it were rolling off a log—grim and strong and well-carried novels, like *McTeague* and *A*

Man's Woman, which certainly do not smack of youth or ease—was born in Chicago in 1870. He was educated in the University of California (class of '94), but did not graduate; having neglected to be born with that vermiform appendix of the brain which harbors the higher mathematics. So he finished his year at Harvard (class of '95). His first ambition had been to be an animal painter; and in 1888–90 he studied art in Paris. Doubtless if he had gone on he would be an admirable painter of grizzly bears; but he came to see more in writing them. *McTeague* was begun in 1895; and in 1896 Mr. Norris returned to San Francisco to become associate editor of *The Wave*, on which he performed prodigies of "copy"—"an average of 30,000 words a week, including one short story," for two years. He found this shotgun productivity a most beneficial training—as it is, so far as concerns the habit of concentration. In the fall of '97 he left *The Wave* to finish *McTeague*, which powerful though ghastly novel he wrote in 100 days. In 1895 he was sent to South Africa by the San Francisco *Chronicle*; but got embroiled in the Uitlander row, and was deported by the Boers. In 1897 he was called to New York to take a place on the staff of the S. S. McClure Co., and was sent to Cuba to "do" the war for *McClure's Magazine*. When Doubleday & McClure split up, Mr. Norris went with the former, on whose staff he now is, working at his usual pressure. He was married February 12, 1900, to Miss Jeannette Black, of San Francisco; and is living in New York. Counting his age, his pressure and his quality, it is not at all unreasonable to look to Mr. Norris for achievement which will overshadow even the two man-books by which he has compelled so general attention and praise.

"A Man's Woman." *The Literary World*, 31 (July 1, 1900), 140.

A Man's Woman, by Frank Norris, best can be characterized in a slang phrase as "piling on the agony." The hero, a man of iron with the lower jaw of a bull-dog, the heroine, larger in soul, as well as physically, than the average of women; the retreat of an Arctic exploration party gradually succumbing to dreadful hardships and approaching starvation; a surgical case in detail; two cases of typhoid fever; such incidents warn readers what to expect.

"A Man's Woman." *Academy and Literature*, 59 (October 20, 1900), 362.

The probable has happened: we have here a novel that opens in the Arctic regions. Readers of *Shanghaied, McTeague,* and *Blix* will follow Mr. Norris anywhere. But in the third chapter we are in Calumet-square, and "the heat had been palpitating through all the City's streets since early morning." We have glanced at the end of the story; it is most quietly effective.

"Our Library Table."
The Athenaeum, October 27, 1900, p. 547.

"Two characters of extraordinary power" are represented in a volume entitled *A Man's Woman*, by Mr. Frank Norris (Grant Richards). The lady was "a grand splendid man's woman," "tall and of a very vigorous build—full-throated, deep-chested, with large, strong hands and solid, round wrists." She was a hospital nurse, of heroic proportions, and an American. He, too, was an American, a great explorer of the Arctic regions, endowed with indomitable will and a manner "like the slow, still moving of a piston." These two strong characters "clashed violently together," and between them they cost a good man—*her* patient and *his* coadjutor—his life. Of this they repent, and then marry. After which he once more pursues his Arctic avocations, being urged thereto by a desire to do better than the English expedition. The nerves of every one in the book seem to be exceedingly highstrung, and they suffer proportionately. The crises and ordeals are of constant occurrence, and would suffice for half a dozen volumes of fiction. The writer shows intimate acquaintance with the details of a surgeon's work and hospital nursing, and one operation on the upper part of a lady's leg is described with painful minuteness. The book is carefully written, but it is not pleasant reading.

"A Man's Woman."
Bookman (England), 19 (December 1900), 90–91.

Mr. Norris's work has always the saving grace of individuality. Faulty in design, and uneven in workmanship, the story is vigorous and the characters striking and unconventional. The action is spasmodic, and in one part of the book is overburdened with medical technicalities, no doubt correct, but certainly superfluous. Both the man and the woman—for the other characters are mere dummies—are finely conceived and finely drawn. Mr. Norris seems to be fond of studying abnormal types, realising them with singular clearness. The hero, with his fierce strength and intense passion, recalls the heroine of Mr. Norris's earlier book, "Shanghaied," a book superior to this in smoothness and mechanism. "A Man's Woman" hardly fulfils the promise of "Shanghaied," but to call it disappointing is to pay a high compliment to Mr. Norris. Incidentally we have a quarrel with him over the title of the book. We deny that she was "a man's woman" at all. She might have been "*the* man's woman," but that was different. As an ideal, the heroine seems to us as impossible as the needlessly maligned "fluffy doll."

Notes

The Epic of the Wheat

THE OCTOPUS

A STORY OF CALIFORNIA

BY

FRANK NORRIS

NEW YORK
DOUBLEDAY, PAGE & CO.
1901

The Octopus

"Literary Notes." *Washington Times*, November 11, 1900, p. 8, part 2.

"The Octopus" is the significant title selected by Frank Norris for the novel he has just completed and which will shortly be published by Doubleday, Page & Co. It is the longest and those who have been permitted to read it in manuscript pronounce it the strongest work that has thus far come from his pen. It forms the opening of a trilogy of novels which is to treat the subject of wheat under the three phases of production, transportation, and consumption, and paints the evils of railroad monopoly in no uncertain colors, the personality and methods of the late Collis P. Huntington being made the subject of a full length portrait. The training of Mr. Norris for the writer's trade has been a varied and adventurous one. He was born in Chicago thirty-odd years ago, and spent his boyhood there and in California. His first ambition was to become an animal painter, and with that in view he studied for two years at the "Atelier Julien" in Paris, but returned to America in time to enter and be graduated at the University of California in the class of '94. After that he studied for a year at Harvard, and then, as a correspondent for a San Francisco newspaper, journeyed to South Africa, where he had a hand in the Uitlander uprising. When that movement met with speedy failure he was compelled by the Boers to leave the Transvaal, but not before he had nearly died of fever in a hospital at Johannesburg. He returned to San Francisco to become one of the editors of a weekly paper called the "Wave," and early in 1898 came East, bringing with him the manuscript of 'McTeague." Since then he has been writing almost without interruption, but during the war with Spain went again to the front as correspondent for "McClure's Magazine" and did successful battle with a second attack of fever in a Santiago hospital. Mr. Norris is a rapid and methodical writer, counting 3,000 words of copy a fair day's task, but he comes to his work after careful preparation and with a full mind, and prunes and revises with infinite care. Though "McTeague" was written in one hundred days, its author had been two years collecting the material for it, and the same careful and honest workmanship has marked the making of all his books.

"Minor Fiction." *Washington Times*, March 10, 1901, p. 10, part 2.

"The Octopus," the new novel by Frank

Norris, published by Doubleday, Page & Co., is to be the beginning of a remarkable undertaking. Though a novel complete in itself, this will be the first of a trilogy of the epic of the wheat, or, three related novels, the first dealing with the production of wheat, the second with its distribution, and the third with the consumption of American wheat in Europe, altogether forming the story of a wheat crop from the time of its sowing in California, through the stock exchange gambling based on it in Chicago, to its use as the relief of a European famine. This new novel, dealing with the fight of the railroad "octopus" and the wheat growers, is said to raise the standard of this author's work, and may go further to make Mr. Norris, dealing with modern California wheat, what Bret Harte was to the early gold country.

I. F. Marcosson.
"Some Observations on Books and People."
Louisville Times,
March 16, 1901,
p. 10.

My young friend, Frank Norris, inaugurates an unusual literary work next week, when his most ambitious effort so far, "The Octopus," will make its appearance. It is the first of a trilogy of novels on the wheat problem. Indeed, it may be termed the epic of the wheat, beginning with the days of the growth in the golden West, through the stages of cultivation, sale and then to the turmoil of the stock market, through all the checkerboard of the speculative world, even to Europe. It is a daring thing to attempt, but those who have watched the work of this brilliant young Westerner have no fear of the outcome.

It has been my pleasure to hear some of this new book and it insures big things. Norris is perhaps the most promising of all the young men in American fiction. He believes in a new West, not only in the drama of life, but in the sphere of fiction. And that region is a land of promise in more ways than one. It is filled with the teeming life of a varied kind and back of it is the rich history of Spanish days, the rare color of a glorious climate and the wealth and luxuriance of picturesque landscape.

"Books and Their Makers."
New York Evening Sun,
March 30, 1901,
p. 5.

In "The Octopus: a Story of California" (Doubleday, Page & Co.), Mr. Frank Norris has produced a remarkable novel, which is a great advance in conception and workmanship on "McTeague," but, like it, "The Octopus" repels while it charms and fascinates the reader. The author tells us that his new novel is the first part of a Trilogy to be known as the Epic of the Wheat; the second part, in another novel, is to treat of the Chicago pit or grain market; and the third, of a famine in Europe which is relieved by a great wheat harvest in the New World. "The Octopus" is, of course, the Trust, which in the Story of California is the Pacific & Southwestern, a railroad running through the great wheat farms of the San Joaquin Valley in Tulare County. We are introduced to a typical California ranch community—the wheat farms out there still being known as ranches, for cattle used to be raised on the vast plains in the old days. There is Magnus Derrick, an ex-politician of the old school, proprietor of the Los Muertos ranch, who is known as the Governor; his son, Harran, the ranch manager, a handsome, manly young fellow, whose brother Lyman is an ambitious lawyer-politician in San Francisco; Annixter, the eccentric and aggressive youngster who owns the Quien Sabe ranch; Osterman, a harum-scarum neighbor who has a talent for political intrigue; Vanamee, the sheep herder and range rider, a mystic; Father Sarria, the Mission priest; Hilma Tree, the comely dairymaid on Quien Sabe ranch, who is the belle of the valley; Dyke, the black-listed railroad engineer; Caraher, the Anarchist saloon-keeper; Presley, the man of ideals and poet, a protégé of Magnus Derrick; and, last but by no means least, S. Behrman, the lawyer of Bonneville, representing the Pacific & Southwestern Railroad in its dealings with the ranchmen, who, in each case, own but half of their wheat farms, the alternate sections belonging to the company under its grant. For these alternate sections the ranchers understood that they would have to pay at the rate of $2.50 an acre when called upon by the company.

Mr. Norris is evidently familiar with the San Joaquin Valley and its people, and he makes his readers at home among them. We soon learn that war to the knife is going on between the ranchmen and the P. & S. W. over the question of freight charges, but the author does not permit such a practical and sordid condition to interfere with the human treatment of his characters, their habits, loves and hates, their amusements and quarrels, while he makes us feel that the storm is gathering that will burst in a great tragedy—if the Octopus is not battled.

The ranchmen, worried and exasperated by the exactions of the company, determine to form a league, raise a corruption fund, and elect two of the three railroad commissioners. They have had two years of bad crops, and unless rates are lowered a good crop will not save them from bankruptcy. All their dealings with the Octopus are through S. Behrman, the big-paunched attorney of Bonneville, whom insults never ruffle and who puts on the screws with an odious courtesy. He is the pawnbroker turned lawyer and banker, and naturally is an object of loathing. Magnus Derrick, the "Governor," holds out against the project of buying delegates for a long time, but at last yields to the argument that the only way to beat the company is to follow its example of playing dirty politics. The election comes on and the League elects two of the railroad commissioners, one of whom is Lyman Derrick, the lawyer son of the "Governor." When the Commission draws up its rates, the San Joaquin Valley is as badly off as ever. There is an average reduction of 10 per cent, but it has been obtained by scaling down charges 30 to 50 per cent in counties where no wheat is carried. The tariff along the P. & S. W. remains the same. The League has been betrayed by Lyman Derrick and he has been bought by the Octopus with the promise of the nomination for Governor. Upon the heels of this reverse for the League comes the news that the Octopus wants $27.50 per acre for the alternate sections on the ground that improvements have made the land valuable. The improvements were made by the ranchmen, and ruin stares them in the face. In the courts the contest goes against them. They buy rifles and drill with the determination to resist the seizure of their property by the Sheriff. When the day of trouble comes most of the Leaguers lose their nerve, and but eleven make a stand. In the fight that follows most of them are killed. The Octopus gets their wheat lands in the end, and S. Behrman installs himself in the best ranch. These are the dry facts, the argument of the story; but Mr. Norris never lets his reader's interest in the fortunes of his characters flag. He has a power of graphic description which holds the attention always, and he is a magician in the use of words. The close and sympathetic observer is revealed in almost every sentence. Here, for instance, is a picture of Hilma Tree, the young girl, whom the uncouth and violent Annixter marries in spite of himself: "She was charming, delicious, radiant of youth, of health, of wellbeing. In her eyes, wide open, brown, rimmed with their fine thin line of intense black lashes, the sun set a diamond flash; the same golden light glowed all around her thick, moist hair, lambent, beautiful, a sheen of almost metallic lustre, and reflected itself upon her wet lips, moving with the words of her singing. The whiteness of her skin under the caress of this hale, vigorous morning light was dazzling, pure of a fineness beyond words. Beneath the sweet modulation of her chin, the reflected light from the burnished copper vessel she was carrying set a vibration of pale gold. Overlaying the flush of rose in her cheeks, seen only when she stood against the sunlight, was a faint sheen of down, a lustrous floss, delicate as the pollen of a flower or the impalpable powder of a moth's wing. She was moving to and fro about her work, alert, joyous, robust, and from all the fine, full amplitude of her figure, from her thick white neck, sloping downward to her shoulders, from the deep, feminine swell of her breast, the vigorous maturity of her hips, there was disengaged a vibrant note of gayety, of exuberant animal life, sane, honest, strong."

Of tragic incidents in Mr. Norris's story there is no lack, not including the battle between the Leaguers and the Sheriff's posse, which is grewsome in its realism. There is the tragedy of the mystic sheep herder's love, which has no relation to the general theme, but has a powerful fascination for the reader, who yet has to confess to a feeling of the uncanny; there is the madness of Dyke, the blacklisted engineer and ruined hop grower, who holds up a train on the P. & S. W. and is hunted down with bloodhounds, and there is the duel in the barn at the merrymaking, between Annixter and Delaney, the rum-crazed cow puncher. In the closing paragraphs of his book, Mr. Norris justifies the Octopus on the principle of the greatest good to the greatest number. "Falseness dies," he says, "injustice and oppression in the end of everything fade and vanish away. Greed, cruelty, selfishness and inhumanity are short-lived; the individual suffers, but the race goes on. Annixter dies, but in a far distant corner of the world a thousand lives are saved" (that is, by the movement of the wheat crop). "The larger view always and through all shame, all wickedness, discovers the truth that will, in the end, prevail, and all things, surely, inevitably, resistlessly work together for good." This is not convincing, after the sombre picture of the lives of the San Joaquin ranchers, which Mr. Norris paints for us. They were ground down and harshly used, but the concluding paragraph of "The Octopus" is probably a confession that the subject had overwhelmed the author, and he could conceive no remedy.

"Huntington in a Novel That Pictures the Part the Southern Pacific Played in the Grim Tragedy of Mussel Slough."
San Francisco Examiner, April 6, 1901, p. 3.*

Magnus Derrick farms ten thousand acres of wheat in the San Joaquin valley. He is the central figure in the new romance by Frank Norris, "The Octopus," published by Doubleday & Page. It is the epic of the wheat, the story of the long struggle of the farmers with the Southern Pacific Company, its blood and tears, its soiled politics and remorseless conditions. The keynote of the book is struck in the following paragraph. Harran, son of Magnus speaks:

"Why Not Hold Us Up?"

"Ulsteen gave his decision yesterday," he continued, reading from his father's letter. "He holds, Ulsteen does, that 'grain rates as low as the new figure would amount to confiscation of property, and that, on such a basis, the railroad could not be operated at a legitimate profit. As he is powerless to legislate in the matter, he can only put the rates back at what they originally were before the Commissioners made the cut, and it is so ordered.' That's our friend S. Behrman again," added Harran, grinding his teeth. "He was up in the city the whole of the time the new schedule was being drawn, and he and Ulsteen and the Railroad Commission were as thick as thieves. He has been up there all this last week, too, doing the railroad's dirty work, and backing Ulsteen up. 'Legitimate profit, legitimate profit,'" he broke out. "Can we raise wheat at a legitimate profit with a tariff of $4 a ton for moving it 200 miles to tidewater, with wheat at 87 cents? Why not hold us up with a gun in our faces, and say, 'Hands up!' and be done with it?"

These farmers whom Mr. Norris has selected for his examples are men of large enterprises, of brains, breeding and education, conducting great farms with an army of men working scientific machinery under perfect discipline. Here is the sketch of one of them who comes as near being the hero of the tragedy as anybody:

Brains to His Boots.

Annixter, who worked the Quien Sabe ranch—some four thousand acres of rich clay and heavy loam—was a very young man, younger even than Presley, like him a college graduate. He looked never a year older than he was. He was smooth-shaven and lean built. But his youthful appearance was offset by a certain

---

*This item presents a classic example of how a book review can be made to serve the purposes of yellow journalism. A sensational drawing of Delaney's ride into Annixter's barn is featured. A sketch of C. P. Huntington, the model for Shelgrim, is also presented. The *Examiner* seized the opportunity afforded by *The Octopus* to lash out at the Southern Pacific interests. The "review" and illustrations fill an entire page.

male cast of countenance, the lower lip thrust out, the chin large and deeply cleft. His university course had hardened rather than polished him. He still remained one of the people, rough almost to insolence, direct in speech, intolerant in his opinions, relying upon absolutely no one but himself; yet, with all this, of an astonishing degree of intelligence, and possessed of an executive ability little short of positive genius. He was a ferocious worker, allowing himself no pleasures, and exacting the same degree of energy from all his subordinates. He was widely hated and as widely trusted. Every one spoke of his crusty temper and bullying disposition, invariably qualifying the statement with a commendation of his resources and capabilities. The devil of a driver, a hard man to get along with, obstinate, contrary, cantankerous; but brains! No doubt of that; brains to his boots.

This overpowering atmosphere of wheat in which the human being is absorbed has its natural result on one who although surrounded by it is yet not of it—that is to say, on Derrick's wife thus:

Ten Thousand Acres of Wheat.

But this new order of things—a ranch bounded only by the horizons, where, as far as one could see, to the north, to the east, to the south and to the west, was all one holding, a principality, ruled with iron and steam, bullied into a yield of 350,000 bushels, where even when the land was resting, unplowed, unharrowed, and unsown, the wheat came up—troubled her, and even at times filled her with an undefinable terror. To her mind there was something inordinate about it all; something almost unnatural. The direct brutality of 10,000 acres of wheat, nothing but wheat as far as the eye could see stunned her a little. The one-time writing teacher of a young ladies' seminary, with her pretty deerlike eyes and delicate fingers, shrank from it. She did not want to look at so much wheat. There was something vaguely indecent in the sight, this food of the people, this elemental force, this basic energy, weltering here under the sun in all the unconscious nakedness of a sprawling, primordial Titan.

Magnus Derrick Depicted.

This is Magnus Derrick.

But Magnus was in every sense the "prominent man." In whatever circle he moved he was the chief figure. Instinctively other men looked to him as the leader. He himself was proud of this distinction; he assumed the grand manner very easily and carried it well. As a public speaker he was one of the last of the followers of the old school of orators. He even carried the diction and manner of the rostrum into private life. It was said of him that his most colloquial conversation could be taken down in shorthand and read off as an admirable specimen of pure, well-chosen English. He loved to do things upon a grand scale, to preside, to dominate. In his good humor there was something Jovian. When angry, everybody around him trembled. But he had not the genius for detail, was not patient. The certain grandiose lavishness of his disposition occupied itself more with results than with means. He was always ready to take chances, to hazard everything on the hopes of colossal returns.

The Railroad's Handy Man.

Behrman is the man who does the dirty politics of the railroad in that region. He is a banker and money lender at the county seat and this is his picture:

> He was a large, fat man, with a great stomach; his cheek and the upper part of his thick neck ran together to form a great tremulous jowl, shaven and blue-grey in color, a roll of fat, sprinkled with sparse hair, moist with perspiration, protruded over the back of his collar. He wore a heavy black mustache. On his head was a round-topped hat of stiff brown straw, highly varnished. A light-brown linen vest, stamped with innumerable interlocking horseshoes, covered his protuberant stomach, upon which a heavy watch chain of hollow links rose and fell with his difficult breathing, clinking against the vest buttons of imitation mother-of-pearl.
> S. Behrman was the banker of Bonneville. But besides this he was many other things. He was a real estate agent. He bought grain; he dealt in mortgages. He was one of the local political bosses, but more important than all this, he was the representative of the Pacific and Southwestern Railroad in that section of Tulare county. The railroad did little business in that part of the country that S. Behrman did not supervise, from the consignment of a shipment of wheat to the management of a damage suit, or even to the repair and maintenance of the right of way. During the time when the ranchers of the county were fighting the grain-rate case, S. Behrman had been much in evidence in and about the San Francisco courtrooms and the lobby of the Legislature in Sacramento.

The story opens just at the beginning of the winter rains. The Derricks are in a hurry to begin plowing. A shipment of eastern-made plows arrives for them at the Bonneville depot. They want to get them at once but that is not the railroad's way of doing business as Behrman explains:

> "It looks a trifle like rain," observed S. Behrman, easing his neck and jowl in his limp collar. "I suppose you will want to begin plowing next week?"
> "Possibly," said Magnus.
> "I'll see that your plows are hurried through for you then, Mr. Derrick. We will route them by fast freight for you and it won't cost you anything extra."
> "What do you mean?" demanded Harran. "The plows are here. We have nothing more to do with the railroad. I am going to have my wagons down here this afternoon."
> "I am sorry," answered S. Behrman, "but the cars are going north, not, as you thought, coming

from the north. They have not been to San Francisco yet."

Magnus made a slight movement of the head as one who remembers a fact hitherto forgotten. But Harran was as yet unenlightened.

"To San Francisco!" he answered, "we want them here— what are you talking about?"

"Well, you know, of course, the regulations," answered S. Behrman. "Freight of this kind coming from the Eastern points into the State must go first to one of our common points and be reshipped from there."

Harran did remember now, but never before had the matter so struck him. He leaned back in his seat in dumb amazement for the instant. Even Magnus had turned a little pale. Then, abruptly, Harran broke out violent and raging.

"What next? My God, why don't you break into our houses at night? Why don't you steal the watch out of my pocket, steal the horses out of the harness, hold us up with a shotgun; yes, 'stand and deliver; your money or your life.' Here we bring our plows from the East over your lines, but you're not content with your long-haul rate between Eastern points and Bonneville and San Francisco and return. Think of it! Here's a load of stuff for Bonneville that can't stop at Bonneville, where it is consigned, but has got to go up to San Francisco first by way of Bonneville, at 40 cents per ton, and then be reshipped from San Francisco back to Bonneville again at 51 cents per ton, the short-haul rate. And we have to pay it all or go without. Here are the plows right here, in sight of the land they have got to be used on, the season just ready for them, and we can't touch them. Oh," he exclaimed in deep disgust, "isn't it a pretty mess! Isn't it a farce! the whole dirty business!"

Corporation's Bad Faith.

The farmers had taken up their ranches on the invitation of the railroad company which owned the alternate sections under the congressional grant. The corporation, before its title was perfected, invited settlement on the land in order to make freight for the road. These invitations took the form of circulars in which the price was placed at $2.50 an acre. The farmers regarded these circulars in the light of a contract on the faith of which they spent thousands and ten thousands of dollars improving these holdings. Yet about this time rumors began to get about that the corporation would not keep faith. To ascertain the truth Annixter interviewed Cyrus Ruggles, the railroad land agent at Bonneville:

"Well," observed Ruggles decidedly, tapping the end of his pencil on his desk and leaning forward to emphasize his words, "we're not selling now. That's said and signed, Mr. Annixter."

"Why not? Come, spit it out. What's the bunco game this time?"

"Because we're not ready. Here's your check."

"You won't take it?"

"No."

"I'll make it a cash payment, money down—the whole of it— payable to Cyrus Blakelee Ruggles, for the P. and S. W."

"No."
"Third and last time."
"No."
"Oh, go to the devil!"
"I don't like your tone, Mr. Annixter," returned Ruggles, flushing angrily.

"I don't give a curse whether you like it or not," retorted Annixter, rising and thrusting the check into his pocket, "but never you mind, Mr. Ruggles, you and S. Behrman and Genslinger and Shelgrim and the whole gang of thieves of you—you'll wake this State of California up some of these days by going just one little bit too far, and there'll be an election of Railroad Commissioners of, by, and for the people, that'll get a twist of you, my bunco-steering friend—you and your backers and cappers and swindlers and thimble-riggers, and smash you, lock, stock and barrel. That's my tip to you and be damned to you, Mr. Cyrus Blackleg Ruggles."

Uninvited Guest Came Also.

Annixter has built the biggest barn in all the San Joaquin, and there shall be cakes and ale, dancing and jollification. He gives a big ball in the new barn, to which the whole country was invited, with a single exception. The uninvited guest is a cowpuncher and bronco buster, who has a grudge against Annixter. The uninvited guest came also, and this is how:

He came with the suddenness of an explosion. There was a commotion by the doorway, a rolling burst of oaths, a furious stamping of hoofs, a wild scramble of the dancers to either side of the room, and there he was. He had ridden the buckskin at a gallop, straight through the doorway and out into the middle of the floor of the barn.

Once well inside, Delaney hauled up on the cruel spadebit, at the same time driving home the spurs, and the buckskin, without halting in her gait, rose into the air upon her hind feet and coming down again with a thunder of iron hoofs upon the hollow floor, lashed out with both heels simultaneously, her back arched, her head between her knees. It was the running buck, and had not Delaney been the hardest buster in the county, would have flung him headlong like a sack of sand. But he eased off the bit, gripping the mare's flanks with his knees, and the buckskin, having long since known her master, came to hand quivering, the bloody spume dripping from the bit upon the slippery floor.

Delaney had arrayed himself with painful elaboration, determined to look the part, bent upon creating the impression, resolved that his appearance at least should justify his reputation of being "bad." Nothing was lacking—neither the campaign hat with up-turned brim, nor the dotted blue handkerchief knotted behind the neck, nor the heavy gauntlets stitched with red, nor—this above all—bear-skin "chaparejos," the hair trousers of the mountain cowboy, the pistol holster low on the thigh. But for the moment this holster was empty, and in his right hand, the hammer at full cock, the chamber loaded, the puncher flourished his teaser, an army Colt's, the lamplight dully reflected in the dark blue steel.

Duel at the Ball.

Annixter has his pistol in his coat pocket. He fires at Delaney through the coat. They fight a duel amid the wild confusion. With the last shot in his pistol Annixter hits Delaney's wrist. The cow puncher falls from his horse, runs for the door and escapes almost before anybody knows what has happened.

Tidings That Foretell Ruin.

It was an eventful social function. Before the party separate letters arrive notifying the farmers that the railroad has fixed the price of their lands at $27 an acre. That means ruin, and this is how the news is received:

> It was not alone the ranchers immediately around Bonneville who would be plundered by this move on the part of the railroad. The "alternate section" system applied throughout all the San Joaquin. By striking at the Bonneville ranchers a terrible precedent was established. Of the crowd of guests in the harness room alone nearly every man was affected, every man menaced with ruin. All of a million acres was suddenly involved.
>
> Then suddenly the tempest burst. A dozen men were on their feet in an instant, their teeth set, their fists clenched, their faces purple with rage. Oaths, curses, maledictions, exploded like the firing of successive mines. Voices quivered with wrath, hands flung upward, the finger, hooked prehensile, trembled with anger. The sense of wrongs, the injustices, the oppression, extortion and pillage of twenty years suddenly culminated and found voice in a raucous howl of execration. For a second there was nothing articulate in that cry of savage exasperation, nothing even intelligent. It was the human animal hounded to its corner, exploited, harried to its last stand, at bay, ferocious, terrible, turning at last with bared teeth and upraised claws to meet the death grapple. It was the hideous squealing of the tormented brute, its back to the wall, defending its lair, its mate and its whelps, ready to bite, to rend, to trample, to batter out the life of The Enemy in a primeval, bestial welter of blood and fury.

* * *

> "Fight! How fight? What are you going to do?"
>
> "If there's a law in this land——"
>
> "If there is, it is in Shelgrim's pocket. Who owns the courts in California? Ain't it Shelgrim?"

Decide to Go into Politics.

The farmers decide to go into politics and fight the railroad with its own weapons. They will elect railroad commissioners in their own interest. They buy delegates enough in the State convention to nominate two of their own men, as they supposed. One of these is Lyman Derrick, a son of Magnus, who is a young lawyer in San Francisco, but secretly in the pay of the railroad company. Lyman Derrick is elected easily, the corporation making no opposition.

The farmers triumph, but Annixter is fearful. As he says, it was "too easy."

Trail of the Bloodsuckers.

Mr. Norris has a fad for symbolism, as may be sure from his description of an incident in Lyman Derrick's office shortly after the election:

> It was a commissioner's official railway map of the State of California completed to March 30th of that year. Upon it the different railways of the State were accurately plotted in various colors, blue, green, yellow. However, the blue, the yellow and the green were but brief traceries, very short, isolated, unimportant. At a little distance these could hardly be seen. The whole map was gridironed by a vast, complicated network of red lines marked P. and S. W. R. R. These centralized at San Francisco and thence ramified and spread north, east and south to every quarter of the State. From Coles, in the topmost corner of the map, to Yuma in the lowest, from Reno on one side to San Francisco on the other, ran the plexus of red, a veritable system of blood circulation, complicated, dividing, and reuniting, branching, splitting, extending, throwing out feelers, offshoots, tap roots, feeders—diminutive little bloodsuckers that shot out from the main jugular and went twisting up into some remote country, laying hold upon some forgotten village or town, involving it in one of a myriad branching coils, one of a hundred tentacles, drawing it, as it were, toward that center from which all this system sprang.

Shooting Peas at a Battleship.

Lyman Derrick and his colleagues in the railroad interest being a majority of the commission formulate a grain rate tariff, making an average 10 per cent cut all over the State, but the reductions only apply to mountain stations that ship no wheat. Rates from San Joaquin Valley points are not touched, but the commissioners have technically complied with their pledges. Genslinger, the editor of the country paper in the pay of the railroad, tells Magnus how little he knows of politics:

> "Oh, we know all about that," answered Genslinger, smiling. "You thought you were electing Lyman easily. You thought you had got the railroad to walk right into your trap. You didn't understand how you could pull off your deal so easily. Why, Governor, Lyman was pledged to the railroad two years ago. He was the one particular man the corporation wanted for Commissioner. And your people elected him— saved the railroad all the trouble of campaigning for him. And you can't make any counter charge of bribery there. No sir, the corporation don't use such amateurish methods as that. Confidentially and between us two, all that the railroad has done for Lyman, in order to attach him to their interests, is to promise to back him politically in the next campaign for Governor. It's too bad," he continued, dropping his voice, and changing his position. "It really is too bad to see good men trying to

bunt a stone wall over with their bare heads. You couldn't have won at any stage of the game. I wish I could have talked to you and your friends before you went into that Sacramento fight. I could have told you then how little chance you had. When will you people realize that you can't buck against the railroad? Why, Magnus, it's like me going out in a paper boat and shooting peas at a battleship."

Story of Mussel Slough.

The ejectment suits in the courts go against the farmer. These lands are put up for sale and are sold by the railroad to deserving buyers. It is the story of Mussel Slough. The farmers band together in a league to resist by force the installment of the railroad tools on their land. Yet they allow themselves to be taken by surprise. A bloody fight follows:

> With the words, he dropped to one knee, and, sighting his rifle carefully, fired into the group of men around the buggy.
>
> Instantly the revolvers and rifles seemed to go off of themselves. Both sides, deputies and leaguers, opened fire simultaneously. At first, it was nothing but a confused roar of explosions; then the roar lapsed to an irregular, quick succession of reports, shot leaping after shot; then a moment's silence, and, last of all, regular as clock ticks, three shots at exact intervals. Then stillness.
>
> Delaney, shot through the stomach, slid down from his horse, and, on his hands and knees, crawled from the road into the standing wheat. Christian fell backward from the saddle toward the buggy, and hung suspended in that position, his head and shoulders on the wheel, one stiff leg still across his saddle. Hooven, in attempting to rise from his kneeling position, received a rifle ball squarely in the throat, and rolled forward upon his face. Old Broderson, crying out, "Oh, they've shot me, boys," staggered sideways, his head bent, his hands rigid at his sides, and fell into the ditch. Osterman, blood running from his mouth and nose, turned about and walked back. Presley helped him across the irrigating ditch and Osterman laid himself down, his head on his folded arms. Harran Derrick dropped where he stood, turning over on his face, and lay motionless, groaning terribly, a pool of blood forming under his stomach. The old man Dabney, silent as ever, received his death, speechless. He fell to his knees, got up again, fell once more, and died without a word. Annixter, instantly killed, fell his length to the ground, and lay without movement, just as he had fallen, one arm across his face.

League Fell to Pieces.

The league fell to pieces. Conservative people shook their heads and said they were law-breakers. The corporation took pains to assist this impression. Mr. Norris writes:

> Instantly Bonneville had been isolated. Not a single local train was running, not one of the through trains made any halt at the station. The mails were not moved. Further than this, by

some arrangement difficult to understand, the telegraph operators at Bonneville and Guadalajara, acting under orders, refused to receive any telegrams except those emanating from railway officials. The story of the fight, the story creating the first impression, was to be told to San Francisco and the outside world by S. Behrman, Ruggles and the local P. and S. W. agents.

The railroad is triumphant all along the line. Magnus Derrick goes out of his mind; Behrman takes possession of the big ranch, harvests grain that Magnus planted, builds an elevator at Port Costa and as a small installment of poetic justice is smothered to death by the wheat pouring into the hold of his own ship.

The Philosophy of Huntington.

In the background of the glaring tragedy stands the mysterious, resourceful figure of the man who directs. Mr. Norris calls him Shelgrim:

"Believe this, young man," exclaimed Shelgrim, laying a thick, powerful forefinger on the table to emphasize his words, "try to believe this—to begin with—that railroads build themselves. Where there is a demand sooner or later there will be a supply. Mr. Derrick, does he grow his wheat? The wheat grows itself. What does he count for? Does he supply the force? What do I count for? Do I build the railroad? You are dealing with forces, young man, when you speak of the wheat and the railroads, not with men. There is the wheat, the supply. It must be carried to feed the people. There is the demand. The wheat is one force, the railroad another, and there is the law that governs them—supply and demand. Men have only little to do in the whole business. Complications may arise, conditions that bear hard on the individual—crush him maybe—but the wheat will be carried to feed the people as inevitably as it will grow. If you want to fasten the blame of the affair at Los Muertos on any one person, you will make a mistake. Blame conditions, not men."

I.F.M. [Isaac F. Marcosson].
"Frank Norris, Realist: Something About the Brilliant Young Author of 'The Octopus.'"
Louisville Times, April 6, 1901, p. 13.

The publication of "The Octopus," just brought out, once more attracts attention to Frank Norris, one of the most striking figures in American fiction. On this latest work he has staked much. It is his most ambitious effort, and from a glance it may be said that the hopes raised, first on a knowledge of the story and then on a genuine confidence in the ability of the author, will not be in vain. "The Octopus" is the first of a trilogy of American stories, the whole to form an epic of the wheat problem. It is a tremendous undertaking, but those who know Norris realize that he is made of the stuff that enters into the composition of those capable of doing big things. More will be said of this book later.

The belief was expressed in this paper with the publication of "Moran of the Lady Letty" that Frank Norris would be a forceful factor in the writing of books. It has been a pleasure to watch his success, how he has grown from a writer of a mere story of an adventure at sea to the dignity of being the most conspicuous of the American realists. The way to the height has been marked by several books, remarkable for their variety and notable for their cleverness.

If you met Norris for the first time you would believe that he was a serious, studious sort of young man. Something in the modesty of his demeanor and the reserve of his manner hides the real force that is behind it all. His eyes are keen and his hair is tinged with gray, and yet he has hardly turned thirty. Within the years of his life he has known many exciting experiences.

Norris was born in San Francisco, the place which he has made the background for most of his earlier work. On attaining manhood he entered journalism and became a member of the staff of the San Francisco Examiner. During the Jameson raid he was sent to South Africa for his paper, and together with some other correspondents was expelled from the country. He made a trip to the Klondike for his newspaper, and roughed it considerably. Later he was editor of "The Wave," of San Francisco.

Shortly after the publication of his first book he moved East, and he has made his home in New York ever since. He has every confidence in the literary future of his native West; in a new California fiction, not reeking with the atmosphere of mining camps or aglow with the golden sunsets, but with the new life and the new social conditions which have grown out of the mighty Western civilization. And it may be said that he has been the brilliant herald of this evolution. He is a discriminating student of humanity, a vivid colorist, a realist of the sentimental kind, who knows how to ingenuously present the grim actualities of life with a background of finer things. Each year has been a ripening of his art; each book has witnessed a step in his work, until to-day he is among the foremost of our younger writers.

Wallace Rice. "Norris's 'The Octopus.'" *Chicago American*, April 6, 1901, pp. 5–6, "Literary and Art Review."

Frank Norris has written a novel, as fascinating, as repellent, as multifarious, as misshapen as the marine monster from which it gains its name of "The Octopus" (Doubleday, Page & Co.). Sufficiently absorbing to hold the reader with something of the Wedding Guest's insistence, once it is taken up, it leaves him with precisely the opposite impression with which Coleridge's masterpiece is laid down. It is wonderfully clever, and only where the author permits himself vain repetitions does its interest flag; but its philosophy is hideous, and the book is as certainly at war with itself as its characters are with one another. To its composition every crime lends its bad interest—rape, murder, train robbing, bribery, corruption in politics, prostitution, inordinate greed, lust for gold and lust for blood. In his characters, for the most part, vice is rebuked and morality upheld. To those who depart from the accepted standard, romantic justice, as unusual in life as it becomes customary here, is meted out with fine particularity. The bad man is killed with a rifle shot, the train robber is sentenced for life, the briber goes down into the darkness of insanity, the corruption-monger is strangled in his own accumulating wealth. Everywhere Mr. Norris shows himself to be animated by high principle in his treatment of his characters. But in the underlying principles which he demonstrates at the end, the babyish plea of elemental force and destiny is entered for the arch-devil of them all, and the other lessons go for naught.

"The Octopus," like Mr. Norris' other well-known books, is a work of realism. Its foundation facts are derived from the history of the Southern Pacific Railroad, and almost all the story revolves around the machinations of the officials of that great monopoly. In this the author becomes a public benefactor—at least in intention. How difficult it will be for him to persuade Americans of the substantial truth of his indictment against such a corporation may be known to him, yet the fate which befell Messrs. Merwin and Webster's "The Short-Line War" two years ago will be interesting in this connection. The two authors came upon an attempt on the part of Jay Gould to grab one of the feeders of the Erie Railway, an independent company, as it appeared in the records of one of the courts in New York State. Finding the account more fascinating than anything they could plan for themselves, they made a careful investigation, and in writing the romance held themselves closely to the demonstrable facts.

The book was read by one of the leading officials of the Burlington Road at my instance, and he told me afterward that he himself had been through precisely such an experience in the West, identical with the narrative to such an extent that he knew every move of the warring factions in the corporation before he reached them. In the face of this, in spite of the double occurrence of just such depredations as the book disclosed, the New York Evening Post dismissed the story as incredible—the New York Evening Post at that time being controlled by the Villard interests. Mr. Norris makes a far more serious indictment against the Southern Pacific than this. He quotes actual documents to prove the wickedness of the position taken by its officials in ousting the men whom it induced to settle on its lands by what turned out to be the falsest of false pretenses; but he does not stop there. The Octopus has as many branches as its namesake. It controls the Railway Commission, it controls the Legislature, it controls the courts. In drawing his indictment against it in the earlier part of the book Mr. Norris does unconsciously the thing he represents the commissioners as doing corruptly; he raises his rate so high that it is certain to be rejected at the bar of public opinion. If his novel be one with a purpose, and that the exposure of infinitely corrupt corporation methods, it is self-defeated on the instant. He himself seems aware of this later in the book, for his most intimate character says: "Tell the people five years from now the story of the fight between the League of San Joaquin and the railroad and it will not be believed."

This is the chief fault to be found with the construction of the book—and a book with a self-defeated purpose can hardly be called a book at all, even though, as here, it abounds in vivid descriptions, insistent characterizations and abounding interest. There are other faults, more noticeable in a book serving so realistic a purpose than in any other. Priests of the Roman Church do not quote the Protestant translations of the Scriptures, for example, as Father Sarria does here. The episode of Vanamee and Angele Varian, poetic and engrossing though it be, has no possible relevance in this work, nor is it in any way bound up in the rest of it. The sandwiching of the account of the dinner in the house of a millionaire and of the starving of a mother in the street is felt to be a trick, a tour de force, rather than literature—the literature that Mr. Norris affects to despise in more than one place in his pages, as though his book could have illiterary vitality.

But, as was intimated before, the philosophy of the book is its weakest point. After all the sin and suffering and death of its earlier pages, the whole question of personal responsibility for crime is dismissed by the archfiend of them all in these words: "Try to believe this—to begin with—that railroads build themselves. Where there is demand, sooner or later there will be a supply. Mr. Derrick, does he grow his wheat? The wheat grows itself. What does he count for? Does he supply the force? What do I count for? Do I build the railroad? You are dealing with forces, young man, when you speak of wheat and the railroad, not with men. There is the wheat, the supply. It must be carried to feed the people. There is the demand. The wheat is one force, the railroad another, and there is the law that governs them—supply and demand. Men have only little to do in the whole business. Complications may arise, conditions that bear hard on the individual—crush him maybe—but the wheat will be carried to feed the people as inevitably as it will grow. Blame conditions, not men."

It need not be pointed out that this hideous doctrine, the doctrine that would justify a Nero and damn an Antonine, can be urged in favor of any crime that ever was hatched in warped and brutal brains. It is the doctrine of personal irresponsibility, of a conscienceless world, of a godless universe. It is the plea of organized greed and unrestrained lust in all ages. Most unfortunately it is the plea which Mr. Norris represents as wholly converting the most intelligent character in his book, the character with which he asserts the greatest degree of personal intimacy and for which he makes the greatest appeal for the reader's sympathy.

"Books & Authors." *Atlanta Constitution*, April 7, 1901, p. 8, "The Sunny South" supplement.

Frank Norris's new novel, which will bear the imprint of Doubleday, Page & Co., is a narrative of the war between the California wheat growers and the railroad trust and is called "The Octopus." The story is said to be full of local color, as may be judged from some of the characters, such as Angele Varian, an ill-fated girl who was loved by Vanamee, the sheep herder and range rider; Hilma Tree, the dairy girl on Annixter Ranch; Magnus Derrick, the governor, proprietor of Los Muertos Ranchos, and his son Harran and others, all of which have an exceedingly delightful melodramatic savor.

George Hamlin Fitch.
"Books for Spring."
San Francisco Chronicle,
April 7, 1901,
p. 28.

In "The Octopus" Frank Norris has written the first part of what he calls "the Trilogy of the Epic of the Wheat," and it is issued in a large volume of 652 pages by Doubleday, Page & Co. of New York. It is founded on the well-known Mussel Slough conflict between the settlers of the San Joaquin valley and the Southern Pacific Railroad Company, and it is noteworthy as the first attempt to put into fiction the struggle between a body of farmers and a great corporation. Mr. Norris has attempted to picture on this enormous canvas the production of wheat. In a second volume, entitled "The Pit: A Story of Chicago," he proposes to describe a great "deal" in wheat, and in a third volume, "The Wolf: A Story of Europe," he will deal with the relieving of a famine in the Old World by shiploads of American wheat. This large plan has a flavor of Balzac in it, but Mr. Norris is more nearly akin to Zola than to the father of French realism. He has Zola's fondness for iteration and reiteration of special traits of a character until the man or woman actually lives before one's eyes, and he also has Zola's habit of working up a hundred petty details that have no other value except to give realism to his story and to excite interest in the various characters. Some of this incidental elaboration could be cut out with profit, as the taste of the novel reader of the period does not incline to fiction of the dimensions that Dickens and Thackeray produced. But if one has the time he will find that all these digressions have their value and all go to produce their effect. In his minor characters and in his descriptions of scenes on the great wheat ranches of the San Joaquin, Norris resembles Hamlin Garland more than any other American writer. He has Garland's power of painting a vivid scene in a few words, and that keen dramatic sense that enables him to bring out his points in dialogue that has in it the sweat and dust of the field and the road. Norris makes no attempt to idealize this hard life in a country that has so few redeeming features in the long dry season, and his humor is rough, reminding one of the farce of the period rather than of genuine comedy. But his pathos is real, and only once, toward the end, when he contrasts the starving in the city streets of the old woman from Mussel Slough with the plenty at the millionaire's dinner table, does he indulge in the devices of the theater.

The story is crowded with characters and with incident. Magnus Derrick, the big ranch owner, his sons and the neighbors who finally unite to defy the railroad—all these men are sharply and clearly drawn. Equally vivid are the sketches of the country editor who receives his subsidy; Behrman, the representative of the railroad, who also does a large business in mortgages on wheat land; Dyke, the blacklisted railroad engineer; Vanamee, the sheepherder and mystic, and Father Sarria, the mission priest. Upon Annixter, the young ranch owner, the novelist has expended his skill and the wooing of Hilma Tree, the pretty young dairy maid, furnishes much of fun as well as the sentiment of the story. Vanamee, a college graduate whose mind has been unhinged by the tragedy that ruined the life of the simple country girl that he loved, is a fine character, and he and the priest and the poet Presley lend the spiritual element that is so conspicuously lacking in most of the other characters. Dyke, the blacklisted engineer, is also a fine character, simple-minded, warm-hearted, devoted to his child, but when ruined by the unexpected advance in railroad freight rates, he becomes a dangerous man, holds up a train and makes a desperate fight to resist capture. The unctuous S. Behrman, the railroad agent, is a finished sketch. The man is not so much immoral as unmoral; he has a greed that is insatiate, and his own instincts urge him on to follow to the letter the orders of his employers. He is the visible sign and symbol of the great corporation and as such is hated and feared, but he bears a charmed life and retribution only overcomes him at the end, when he is smothered in the wheat of which he has defrauded the ranchers of the valley. And over against all these characters, dominating the whole book, is Shelgrim, a striking portrait of the late head of the Southern Pacific Company, with his passionate devotion to work, his enormous executive force, his sympathy with his employees and his keen interest in art and literature.

It is impossible in the limits of this article to give even an outline of the plot. It must suffice to say that all the incidents lead up to that lamentable and deadly conflict between the settlers and the railroad agents which produced so powerful an effect at the time and which left a legacy of hatred and misunderstanding for years. The great plain of Tulare county, in the heart of the San Joaquin valley, is the scene of the story. Here we see the rich black soil turned over by the great gang-plows and the seed sown; and here before the harvest is ripe occurs the fight that made the Mussel Slough dark and bloody ground. All the phases of ranch life and all the distinctive features of the scenery of this huge inland valley are reproduced here with the fidelity of the camera. The burning sun, the steel blue, cloudless sky, the dusty road, the tawny fields stretching away to the horizon, the ugly water tanks—all these points in the landscape are bitten into the memory by the art of the novelist. Here is a specimen picture:

> All about him the country was flat. In all directions he could see for miles. The harvest was just over. Nothing but stubble remained on the ground. With the one exception of the live oak by Hooven's place there was nothing green in sight. The wheat stubble was of a dirty yellow; the ground, parched, cracked and dry, of a cheerless brown. By the roadside the dust lay thick and gray, and on either hand, stretching on toward the horizon, losing itself in a mere smudge in the distance, ran the illimitable parallels of the wire fence. And that was all; that and the burnt-out blue of the sky and steady shimmer of the heat.
>
> The silence was infinite. After the harvest, small though that harvest had been, the ranches seemed asleep.... There was no rain, there was no wind, there was no growth, no life; the very stubble had no force to rot. The sun alone moved.

All the latter part of the story moves as did the final chapters of "McTeague" after the murder—swiftly, surely and with a momentum that carries the reader along. The whole story of the fight is handled with great skill, and equally strong, but more melodramatic, is the picture of the end of the unspeakable Behrman—strangled and buried by the wheat in the hold of the ship Swanhilda. Perfect also as a picture and as showing the traits of each character is the strong scene of the dance in the barn and the fight between Annixter and the drunken cowboy. As a whole, the book is the strongest that Norris has yet written. It is full of the vitality of real life. It is written with a pen of iron, in the virile style that made Kipling famous. It lays hold upon the reader, and no one who takes it up will ever be able to efface it from the memory.

I. F. Marcosson.
"The Epic of the Wheat."
Louisville Times,
April 13, 1901,
p. 13.

This is a time of new and mighty forces in literature—of quick and strenuous changes in life. The historian in fiction, wearied of the superficialities of conventional society, reaches back to the elemental resources of nature for his inspiration to find therein a vast and thrilling background out of which there leap the terrific impulses that shape all human endeavor and regulate human relation.

Back to the soil then for primordial instincts; back to the toiler for the real values of life. Call it realism if you will; cower before its vividness; shun its minute details, but it is life nevertheless—bare, unvarnished, unsentimental—stripped of romantic glamour and vivid with actuality.

Frank Norris has been the most brilliant exponent of this realism in American fiction, and in his new book, "The Octopus," he reaches what is so far the fullness of his powers. His story is a terrific protest against the oppression of a community by a great railroad; it is a stinging indictment of a trust, that fastened its tentacles in the rich soil of a great country and wrote the story of its success in the life's blood of its martyrs.

All that Norris has done before is but an introduction to this book, which is a truly monumental work, one to rear itself among its contemporaries like a prophet of old rose above his fellows in the majesty and dignity of his inspiration. For "The Octopus" is historic and prophetic, sounding a splendid new note. It is a masterful and impressive performance, to command interest and to compel admiration. It is likewise the first of a trilogy of novels which is to embrace the epic of the wheat and in this first book Norris has laid a magnificent cornerstone for his undertaking.

* * *

Norris has been the herald of a great Western civilization; the artist of a passionate and tumultuous life. The root of his art is planted in his native California and the color and glow of that place is in all his work. It is in that land that he lays the scene of his new story; it is across the San Joaquin valley that "The Octopus" marks its scarlet trail.

The story of this remarkable novel is founded upon history, upon what is known as the Mussel Slough affair—when the wheat growers of the valley, stung to defiance by the extortions of the railroad, unable to endure their oppression any longer, rose in their indignation and came in conflict with the railroad which they believed was trying to defraud them of their land. There was a bloody encounter and the railroad retired, master of the situation.

Out of this then Norris has constructed the fabric of his work, drawn from a dramatic episode in the story of a band of tillers of the soil. There is nothing like "The Octopus" in our fiction. Something in its splendid earnestness brings it before you in all the fearful sincerity of a document in evidence.

Its story may be told in a paragraph or it may be spun out to a volume of great proportions. It is not so much in the actual narrative that this book is valuable; it is in the treatment of the theme, and the lessons that it teaches.

* * *

"The Octopus" is a novel without a hero; a romance without a heroine. In this book nearly all men are free and equal and it is difficult to find a low figure. It is a group of powerful, compelling men; men who do big things, who meet great odds, who make a tremendous struggle. The reek of blood is in it; the note of defiance is heard throughout. But the stronger triumphs and the weaker meets defeat.

It is an old oppression in the story of man that had reached down through all the ages, an old spectacle where the Titan has stood with the whip-lash of organized power. A truly pathetic sight it is, and Norris unfolds it with rare detail and terrible earnestness.

It is useless to comment on his people. Each character is etched with unerring hand and stands against the background of the narrative a vivid and lifelike figure. There is no play in this story; it is all tragically serious. Men do not smile when they are fighting the battle of their life; when they see the hand of the oppressor reach out for the fruit of hard endeavor.

Norris gives a remarkable impression of the force, the power, the crushing domination of the trust in the first part of his book, when a monster passenger engine driven at record speed through the valley of San Joaquin cuts through a flock of sheep that had gathered on the track. He sees there "the symbol of a vast power, huge, terrible, flinging the echo of its thunder over all the reaches of the valley, leaving blood and destruction in its path; the Leviathan with tentacles of steel, clutching into the soil, the soulless Force, the iron-hearted Power, the Monster, the Colossus, the Octopus."

* * *

There is a multitude of figures in this story, and the temptation is strong to linger over them. Straight through the gamut of life goes the novelist from the rancher sweeping the trackless plains to the iron-hearted President of the great power that rides to the death through the wheat-growers' valley. The way from inferior to superior is marked by a splendid company, and each man in his life plays many parts, the whole a tragedy of tremendous energy.

But there is behind this book something keener, truer or more vitalizing than the mere story; something that stirs the consciousness to a new and thrilling realization; the hopelessness of the struggle of man against a great power.

Never before perhaps has such a demonstration been made in a book. It is intensely dramatic, intensely real. It has been fortunate that it remained for Norris to sound this note; to utter the protest of oppressed man against his oppressor.

There is no veneer of sociological condition; no glamour of pathetic isolation.

Norris has reached down into the actual life of a real and throbbing condition and paints it as he found it. And it is the sort of realism that we want in our fiction; it is this sort of truth that we want in books.*

The Bookworm. "World of Letters: A Great Novel." *Town Talk*, 9 (April 20, 1901), 25–26.

"The Octopus" is the first of the three novels which are to compose what Frank Norris has chosen to call "the Trilogy of the Epic of the Wheat." As outlined by the author, "The Octopus, a story of California," deals with the production; "The Pit," a story of Chicago, takes up the distribution, and the third, "The Wolf," a story of Europe, will tell of the consumption of American wheat, and "will probably have for its pivotal episode the relieving of a famine in the Old World community." The story of "The Octopus" is founded on the Mussel Slough affair which took place some twenty-five years ago. It was the culmination of an infinite number of encroachments and aggressions on the part of the railroad company, which fi-

*The remainder of the review is illegible for the most part. What can be gleaned is that Marcosson finds in *The Octopus* a proof that realism need not always be "grimy" and "shocking." The episodes involving Vanamee include finely handled sentiment and convincingly depicted notions of ideal love. He concludes by opining that Norris has not disappointed his readers' expectations: Norris is clearly a "new and virile force" in fiction; *The Octopus* is a vivid, colorful, and "superbly conceived" work of art.

nally led to armed resistance on the part of the settlers in the lower San Joaquin valley, and the shooting of farmers by the railroad forces very much as Mr. Norris has set forth in his book. The conflict shook the State as perhaps no other occurrence since the breaking out of the civil war has done, and in many of the rural communities, for years afterward, the talk of establishing railroad communication would call forth violent opposition. Mr. Norris has a large subject, and he has wisely taken a large canvas on which to paint his picture. There are twenty-seven characters, each distinct and individual, and the story is told in six hundred and fifty-two pages of absorbing narrative. "The Octopus" is not a book to be lightly taken in hand in a spare half hour while waiting for the dinner bell. It is to be undertaken in no spirit of levity. There is tragedy in the air from the first page to the last. Bonneville, the railroad town, is typical of a score of minor communities dependent on the great corporation for their very existence, and Genslinger, editor of the *Mercury*, is even yet a familiar character. In fact, it is commonly regarded as an open secret that the railroad company is the real editor and owner of at least one paper in every settlement along its lines. S. Behrman—he is always spoken of as S. Behrman—is another well known and easily recognized. He is the corporation's handy man, the local banker and money lender, and the local agent for the company.

He was a large, fat man, with a great stomach; his cheek and the upper part of his thick neck ran together to form a great tremendous jowl, shaven and blue-grey in color; a roll of fat sprinkled with sparse hair, moist with perspiration, protruded over the back of his collar. He wore a heavy black moustache. On his head was a round-topped hat of stiff brown straw, highly varnished. A light-brown linen vest, stamped with innumerable interlocked horseshoes, covered his protuberant stomach, upon which a heavy watch chain of hollow links rose and fell with his difficult breathing, clinking against the vest buttons of imitation pearl.

Magnus Derrick, who holds Los Muertos rancho, and is looked to for leadership by the other farmers, is as much of a contrast in appearance as in character.

> The Governor was all of six feet tall, and though now well toward his sixtieth year, was as erect as an officer of cavalry. He was broad in proportion, imposing an immediate respect, impressing one with a sense of gravity, of dignity and a certain pride of race. He was smooth-shaven, thin-lipped, with a broad chin, and a prominent, hawk-like nose—the characteristic of the family—thin, with a high bridge, such as one sees in the later portraits of the Duke of Wellington. His hair was thick and iron-grey, with a tendency to curl in a forward direction just in front of his ears. He wore a top-hat of grey, with a wide brim, and a frock coat, and carried a cane with a yellowed ivory head.

Harran Derrick is the son of his father and the active manager of the ranch. Annixter, another of the farmers, is in his way as much of a brute as McTeague or Bennett of Mr. Norris' former stories, but in Annixter the brute is tamed, and the man comes uppermost at last, through his love for Hilma Tree.

> He was a ferocious worker, allowing himself no pleasures, and exacting the same degree of energy from all his subordinates. He was widely hated and as widely trusted. Everyone spoke of his crusty temper and bullying disposition, invariably qualifying the statement with a commendation of his resources and capabilities. The devil of a driver, a hard man to get along with, obstinate, contrary, cantankerous; but brains! No doubt of that; brains to his boots.

Caraher, saloon keeper, preaching anarchy and advocating the use of dynamite, has his indirect grievance against the railroad corporation, and Dyke, the discharged engineer who invests his savings and mortgages his homestead in order to establish a hop ranch, only to find himself beggared by a doubling of freight rates, are other characters who figure prominently. Presley, the poet, friend and protégé of the Derricks, and Vanamee, the mystic, have little to do with the story, yet the reader will be loth to spare them, or Father Sarria, the mission priest. It would be useless to attempt to give, in the space of a brief article, even a skeleton of the plot or a list of the stirring incidents of the story. It is a chronicle of contrasts. There is always the black shadow in the background, the skeleton at every feast, the tenacle of the octopus reaching out to grasp. The rejoicing in the first rain, after a dry season, is spoiled for the Derricks because the implements they need for their work, though already at the Bonneville depot, must be hauled to San Francisco and back in order that the company may collect the additional freight; Presley's day of dreaming closes with the slaughter of the herd of sheep which had wandered out on the track and were run down by the engine; Annixter's barn dance, ending with the news that the railroad company had fixed the price of its "sections" at more than ten times the price it had intimated when the settlers were induced to go on the land; Magnus and Harran Derrick with their elation at the suggestion of the Orient as a new market crushed by the adverse decision of the court; Annixter's return to Quien Sabe with his bride and the hold-up of the train by Dyke, crazed by his absolute ruin brought about by freight rates which were practical confiscation; the meeting of the League when so much was expected because the farmers thought they had two of the three railroad commissioners with them, only to find that Lyman Derrick, the son of Magnus, had betrayed them all and belonged, body and soul, to the enemy; Osterman's rabbit drive coming to a close in the tragedy of the irrigating ditch, and even the little picnic planned by the Annixters spoiled by the running down and capturing of the old friend and neighbor, Dyke, with S. Behrman conspicuous; the grand dinner at the railway magnate's mansion, and Mrs. Hooven, widow of one of the murdered ranchers, starving in the street. In the hands of a less skilful writer than Mr. Norris the result would be forced and unreal. But Norris has left the incidents to tell the story and there is nothing theatrical in his methods. When S. Behrman meets his fate, smothered in the hold of the ship loading with the wheat from Los Muertos, which the charitable ladies of San Francisco have bought to send to the relief of famine-stricken India, there seems to be a providence at work after all. There are some wonderfully truthful descriptions of the landscape of the San Joaquin valley under different conditions—the dry, stubble fields, and the white dust of the dry season, the viscid 'dobe after the rain, the first tender green when the wheat has come, and the glorious gold of the harvest. The plowing and planting, and the harvesting are all painted by a master hand. Chapter 1 of Book II is a satirical photograph of San Francisco society—"San Francisco! It is not a city—it is a Midway Plaisance." One would need to quote it entire to do it justice. Mr. Norris has made as much use of the sense of smell in this book as in its predecessors, but happily all its odors are not unpleasant. The flowers of the Seed ranch counteract in some degree the more unpleasant smells which are almost as insistent in print as in reality. Much of the description, as well as the constant repetition and reiteration of personal traits and characteristics could be spared by the hasty reader, but "The Octopus" is not a hasty reader's book. Those who think it adds interest to their reading to find living counterparts for characters in fiction can easily identify the people who sat to the author for their portraits. Indeed, for that matter, many of the incidents are chronicles of real happenings. "The Octopus" should settle the question of Frank Norris' right to a place in the front rank of writers. The book is furnished with an excellent map of the country around Bonneville, by which the story can be accurately followed.

"The Octopus: A Story of California."
The Outlook, 67 (April 20, 1901), 923–24.

A book certain to arouse favorable and unfavorable comment, to be liked and disliked, to be looked at from many varying points of taste and thought, but at all events not a book to be passed over as slight, trifling, or merely amusing. Following Zola in his great trilogy of Paris life, Mr. Norris has attempted a trilogy of novels on wheat production and consumption; "The Octopus" tells of the fierce struggle between the wheat-raiser and the railroad which must bear the wheat to the market; a second novel will have the Chicago wheat-pit as its central point; a third, probably the relief of famine in the Far East by the wheat from the Far West. What economic value is to be attached to this "prose epic" of the contest between the great California wheat-raiser who looks out upon his ten thousand acres of growing wheat and the railroad which puts on "all the freight the product can bear," and thereby (in the story at least) drives the producer to bribery, bloodshed, and ruin, depends entirely upon the typicalness of the case presumably put forward as of general application. Certainly the reader must feel inclined by the vivid, dramatic narrative to the belief that a railroad system having a monopoly because of no business competitor, a carrier upon which the public at large depends for service, should be forced to submit to public supervision, even in the matter of rates, to prevent positive oppression. Mr. Norris's treatment of his subject is broad and comprehensive in its general plan, but in its detail minutely realistic. Sometimes this minuteness becomes annoying, as when, with the Maeterlinck-like repetition, he insists on mentioning a certain woman's "three-cornered white forehead" whenever he refers to her, or invariably tells us, when his would-be poet mounts his bicycle, that the handle-grips were made of cork; indeed, as Wagner has a musical phrase for every person or idea, so Mr. Norris seems bound to repeat certain descriptive phrases whenever his personages reappear in the tale. There is much, too, besides the trilogy-design that suggests Zola here: the eloquent reiteration of the lifelikeness of the earth smiling to the plow, teeming with the seed, giving birth to the harvest, often reminds one of "La Terre" and "Fécondité;" so does the rapid cumulative piling up of descriptive phrases in important passages. We have commented on the quite needless coarseness and brutality of two of this author's other stories; that element is less prominent here, and where it does occur is less willful, more a part of the general purpose. The latter part of the story seems to us not entirely to sustain the force and really tremendous energy of the earlier half; such a scene as that where, in alternate paragraphs, the railroad capitalists revel in wine and talk art while their starving victim dies on the street is, from the literary point of view, distinctly "yellow." A carping critic might find plenty of points for attack upon individual things in the book; yet, judging it as a whole, it is extraordinary in its grasp and in its vivid depiction of things pleasant and unpleasant, of people who (much as one dislikes some of them) are flesh and blood, not wooden pegs upon which to hang a sentimental or historical romance, of the conflict of elemental passions and forces.

"Books: To Read or Not to Read: An Epic of Wheat." *Overland Monthly*, 37 (May 1901), 1050–51.

Tolstoi succinctly, if somewhat dogmatically, says: "The art of our time can be and is of two kinds—1, art transmitting feelings flowing from a religious perception of man's position in the world in relation to God and to his neighbor—religious art in the limited meaning of the term; and 2, art transmitting the simplest feelings of common life, but such, always as are accessible to all men in the whole world—the art of common life—the art of a people—universal art." It is to this latter standard that Mr. Frank Norris' latest book, "The Octopus," conforms. It involves a great idea. It carries the Titan-like shadow of human outlines such as moves in the works of the great Frenchmen, Zola or Hugo, or in Millet's peasant pictures, smacking of the life of the soil. It treats of those qualities of human nature which are not exclusive properties of one class, but are common alike to the nature of the club man and the laborer. Following after the Zolaesque trilogy idea, "The Octopus" is only the first of a projected series of novels forming together "The Epic of the Wheat." They are not to conflict with one another, the first involving a story of the production of wheat, the second, "The Pit," a story of Chicago, will relate to the distribution, and the third, "The Wolf: A Story of Europe," to the consumption of American wheat. The encircling plot in the book is "The Octopus"—the "Pacific and Southwestern Railroad"—the "Road" of which Shelgrim, its President, says, sitting in his city office: "Control the road! Can I stop it? I can go into bankruptcy if you like. But otherwise if I run my road as a business proposition, I can do nothing. I can *not* control it. It is a force born out of certain conditions, and I—no man—can stop it or control it. Can your rancher stop the wheat growing? He can burn his crop, or he can give it away, or sell it for a cent a bushel—just as I could go into bankruptcy—but, otherwise, his Wheat must grow. Can anyone stop the Wheat? Well, then, no more can I stop the Road." Ground under the merciless heel of this force, Mr. Norris' characters live life as we all know it—love simply and strongly, carry on the ceaseless, world-old struggle of the male for maintenance of the family, fight, weep, sin, die, hate. The medium of observation in the novel is the eye of one Presley, an Eastern college graduate, who had an insatiable ambition to write a poem of "the West, that world's frontier of Romance, where a new race, a new people—hardy, brave and passionate—were building an empire; where the tumultuous life ran like fire from dawn to dark, and from dark to dawn again, primitive, brutal, honest, and without fear." But his enjoyment of the vast beauty of the grain fields is continually broken into and roughly jarred by the thunder of the hideous locomotives hurtling their dominating way across the ranchmen's acres. "He searched for the True Romance, and in the end, found grain rates and unjust freight tariffs." Here is what the author also found, but to him they spelled the poetry of realism.

Two sub-plots hold our interest: the delicate love idyll of Vanamee and Angele Varian, touching upon phases of the most modern psychological thought, the shadowy world of the mind, and the wholesome romance, fresh, simple, strong, natural, between "Buck" Annixter and Hilma Tree. He is an aggressively masculine, youthful, obstinate, healthy animal, reclaimed through his love for her beauty, purity, and good sense. In Hilma, Mr. Norris shows again how well he can portray a beautiful woman. In this he is easily the peer of Kipling. In fact, we doubt if that great writer of short stories will ever write a novel which in the handling of complex forces in modern life, creation of character, or realism, will equal "The Octopus."

Shelgrim, the President of the Road, playing the part of spider in his den in the midst of the system he has created, though remarkable appears only in a very small portion of the story: which is for the most part placed in a region of ranches, of which the largest is called Los Muertos, down in the San Joaquin Valley, not more than a day away from San Francisco. The life on the ranches until consumed by the Octopus, is of an easy-going, out-door, good-natured sort. Annixter lies in a hammock on his porch eating prunes and reading David Copperfield; he marries the daughter of his dairy keeper; the big dance he gives in his great barn is a tremendous rollicking affair, interrupted by the entrance of a farm-hand on horseback, who fights a duel, there and then, with the proprietor, and which is enlivened by a punch so strong as to be popularly dubbed "the fertilizer." "But Presley," Mrs. Derrick murmured when he explained to her his "Song of the West," whose truth, savagery, nobility, heroism, and obscenity had revolted her, "that is not literature." "No," he had cried between his teeth, "no, thank God, it is not." But it is life, we add. There is life in the personality of Hilma Tree, from which "there was disengaged a vibrant note of gaiety, of exuberant animal life, sane, honest, strong." There is life in the unscrupulous, ambitious, fashion-ably garbed figure of Lyman Derrick, the young San Francisco lawyer. "His office was on the tenth floor of the Exchange Building . . . below him the city swarmed . . . around Lotta's fountain the baskets of the flower sellers . . . set a brisk note of color. . . . But to Lyman's notion the general impression of this center of the city's life was not one of strenuous business activity. It was a continuous interest in small things, a people ever willing to be amused at trifles, refusing to consider small matters—good natured, allowing themselves to be imposed upon, taking life easily—generous, companionable, enthusiastic; living, as it were, from day to day, in a place where the luxuries of life were had without effort; in a city that offered to consideration the restlessness of a New York, without its earnestness; the serenity of a Naples, without its languor; the romance of a Seville, without its picturesqueness." And here live the families of the unregenerate rich, dining in luxury, while unfortunates starve on the streets—of the book. The situation as depicted in Mr. Norris' virile, trenchant, galvanized phrase, is well worth serious attention. Whether or not one agrees with Presley's conclusion that "men were naught, death was naught, life was naught; Force only existed—Force that brought men into the world, Force that crowded them out of it to make way for the succeeding generation, Force that made the wheat grow, Force that garnered it from the soil to give place to the succeeding crop."

"A Short Guide to New Books: The Octopus." *The World's Work*, 2 (May 1901), 782.

We are glad to be able definitely to recommend "The Octopus" as being a book of special interest and merit. The author, Mr. Frank Norris, has taken for his motive a wheat crisis, which occurred in the San Joaquin Valley, California, some twenty years since, and around it was woven a story treating of "the People" and "the Trust" from a very unusual and convincing point of view. Combined with this thoroughly practical aspect is an extraordinary blending of realism, mysticism, idealism, pessimism, and optimism and directness—a cosmopolitan disregard for predominance of tone—and an equal, forceful style of construction. None of the sunlight or shadow of Californian life and atmosphere is lost. If a note of immaturity sounds at times, it is more pleasing by way of contrast than otherwise, and does not detract from a book which leaves one with careful and distinct impressions and thoughts of a strong book, strongly written.

Frederic Taber Cooper. "Frank Norris's 'The Octopus.'" *Bookman* (America), 13 (May 1901), 245–47.

There is a character at the outset of Mr. Norris's new volume, the poet Presley, who is haunted by the dream of writing an epic of the West. His ambition is to paint life frankly as he sees it; yet, incongruously enough, he wishes to see everything through a rose-tinted mist—a mist that will tone down all the harsh outlines and crude colours. He is searching for true romance, and, instead, finds himself continually brought up against railway tracks and grain rates and unjust freight tariffs. All this is quite interesting, not because Presley is an especially important or convincing character, but because it is so obviously only another way of stating Mr. Norris's favourite creed: that realism and romanticism are, after all, convertible terms; that the epic theme for which Presley was vainly groping lay all the time close at hand if he could but have seen it, not merely in the primeval life of mountain and desert, and the shimmering purple of a sunset, but in the limitless stretch of steel rails, in the thunder of passing trains, in the whole vast, intricate mechanism of an organised monopoly.

No one is likely to quarrel seriously with this position. There certainly is a sort of epic vastness and power in many phases of our complicated modern life when treated in a broad, sweeping Zolaesque fashion—in the railroad, the stock exchange, the department stores when they are set before us like so many vast symbols, titanic organisms, with an entity and a purpose of their own. It is only when we come down to details, the petty, sordid details of individual lives, that realism and romance part company. Yet no one knows better than Mr. Norris that it is these very details which give to every picture of life its true value and colour, and he himself has often given them to us with pitiless fidelity. There are few writers of to-day who could cope with him in giving the physiognomy of some mean little side-street in San Francisco, of painting with a few telling strokes a living picture of some odd little Chinese restaurant, of making us breathe the very atmosphere of McTeague's tawdry, disordered, creosote-laden dental parlour, or the foul, reeking interior of Bennett's tent on the ice fields of the far North. It is a trifle exasperating to find a man who can do work like this deliberately choosing every now and then, after the fashion of his poet Presley, to look at life through rose-coloured glasses, instead of adhering fearlessly to the crude colours and the harsh outlines. It was this tendency which betrayed him into the melodramatic ending of *McTeague*; in real life the big, dull-witted dentist would probably have perished miserably in a gutter or a garret, if he had succeeded in evading the hangman; but it suited Mr. Norris's purpose better to apotheosise him, to drive him out into the midst of the alkali desert, forming, as it were, the one human note in a sort of vast symphony of nature. In the present work there is nothing quite so glaring, yet we detect the same underlying spirit. It is felt not alone in the vein of mysticism which runs through the book, the whole episode of Vanamee, the lonely, half-distraught shepherd invoking the spirit of his lost bride across the wide expanse of prairie. It is felt still more in the lack of vivid character drawing in *The Octopus*, in a certain blurring of the outlines, that suggests a composite photograph, in the substitution of types for individuals. In more than one way Mr. Norris is farther away from real life in *The Octopus* than he was in *A Man's Woman*, just as in that novel he was farther away than in *McTeague*.

The truth is that *The Octopus* is a sort of vast allegory, an example of symbolism pushed to the extreme limit, rather than a picture of life. Mr. Norris has always had a fondness for big themes; they are better suited to the special qualities of his style, the sonority of his sentences, the insistent force of accumulated noun and adjective. This time he has conceived the ambitious idea of writing a trilogy of novels which, taken together, shall symbolise American life, not merely the life of some small corner of a single State, but American life as a whole, with all its hopes and aspirations and its tendencies, throughout the length and breadth of the continent. And for the central symbol he has taken wheat, as being quite literally and truly the staff of this life, the ultimate source of American power and prosperity. This first volume, *The Octopus*, dealing with the production of wheat, shows us a corner of California, the San Joaquin Valley, where a handful of ranchmen are engaged in irrigating and ploughing, planting, reaping and harvesting, performing all the slow, arduous toil of cultivation, and at the same time carrying on a continuous warfare against the persistent encroachment of the railroad, whose steel arms are reaching out, octopus-like, to grasp, encircle and crush one after another all those who venture to oppose it. It is quite likely that Mr. Norris has been careful of his facts, that he has some basis for his presentment of the railway's acts of aggression, the unjust increase of freight tariffs, the regrading of land values, the violent evictions—in short, that his novel is well documented. From the symbolic side, however, the literal truth is unimportant. The novel typifies on a small scale the struggle continuously going on between capital and labour, the growth of centralised power, the aggression of the corporation and the trust. But back of the individual, back of the corporation, is the spirit of the nation, typified in the wheat, unchanged, indomitable, rising, spreading, gathering force, rolling in a great golden wave from West to East, across the continent, across the ocean, and carrying with it health and strength and hope and sustenance to other nations—emblem of the progressive, indomitable spirit of the American people. Such, at least, seems to be Mr. Norris's underlying thought, and he has developed it in a way which compels admiration, even from those who find *The Octopus* as a story rather disappointing. Especially deserving of cordial praise is the manner in which the two underlying thoughts of his theme are kept before the reader, like the constantly recurring *leit-motivs* of a Wagnerian opera. First, there is the *motiv* of the railroad, insistent, aggressive, refusing to be forgotten, making its presence felt on every page of the book—in the shril' scream of a distant engine, in the heavy rumble of a passing freight train, in the substantial presence of S. Behrman, the local agent, whose name greets us at the outset of the story in large flaring letters of a painted sign on a water-tank, "S. Behrman has something to say to *you*," and whose corpulent, imperturbable, grasping, personality obtrudes itself continually, placid, unyielding, invincible. Now and then we have a clear-cut picture of the road itself, as in the graphic, ghastly episode of an engine, ploughing its way through a flock of sheep, which had somehow made their way through the barbed-wire fence and wandered upon the track.

The pathos of it was beyond expression. It was a slaughter, a massacre of innocents. The iron monster had charged full into the midst, merciless, inexorable. To the right and length [sic], all the width of the right of way, the little bodies had been flung; backs were snapped against the fenceposts; brains knocked out. Caught in the barbs of the wire, wedged in, the bodies hung suspended. Under foot it was terrible. The black blood, winking in the starlight, seeped down into the clay between the ties with a prolonged sucking murmur.... Abruptly Presley saw again in his imagination the galloping monster, the terror of steel and steam, with its single eye, cyclopean, red, shooting from horizon to horizon; but saw it now as the symbol of a vast power, huge, terrible, flinging the echo of its thunder over all the reaches of the valley, leaving blood and destruction in its path; the leviathan, with tentacles of steel clutching into the soil, the soulless Force, the iron-hearted Power, the Monster, the Colossus, the Octopus.

And, secondly, there is the *motiv* of the wheat underlying that of the railroad, yet ever present and unchanged throughout the long and fluctuating struggle.

Men—motes in the sunshine—perished, were shot down in the very noon of life, hearts were broken, little children started in life lamentably handicapped; young girls were brought to a life of shame; old women died in the heart of life for lack of food. In that little, isolated group of human insects, misery, death and anguish spun like a wheel of fire.

But the wheat remained. Untouched, unassailable, undefiled, that mighty world-force, that nourisher of nations, wrapped in Nirvanic calm, indifferent to the human swarm, gigantic, resistless, moved onward in its appointed grooves. Through the welter of blood at the irrigation ditch, through the sham charity and shallow philanthropy of famine relief committees, the great harvest of Los Muertos rolled, like a flood from the Sierras to the Himalayas, to feed thousands of starving scarecrows on the barren plains of India.

Such, in brief, are the purposes of Mr. Norris's book. It is full of enthusiasm and poetry and conscious strength. One can hardly read it without a responsive thrill of sympathy for the earnestness, the breadth of purpose, the verbal power of the man. But as a study of character, a picture of real life, of flesh and blood, it must be frankly owned that *The Octopus* is disappointing. A few of the characters are good, they promise at first to win our sympathies—characters like the slow, tenacious German, Hooven; the tall, commanding figure of Magnus Derrick, the "governor," to whom life was one huge gamble; the coarse-fibred, combative young farmer, Annixter, with his scorn of "feemales" and his morbid concern over the vagaries of a stomach which would persist in "getting out of whack." But, taken as a whole, the characters do not wear well; they come and go, love and suffer and die, and their joy and their misery fail to wake a responsive thrill. An exception, however, must be made in the case of S. Behrman. He, at least, is consistently developed and consistently hated. From first to last he has appeared invincible, out of reach of law, of powder and shot, of dynamite. And the final episode, where he is struck down at the very summit of his ambition, caught in a trap by his own wheat, and pictured writhing, struggling, choking to death miserably in the dark hold of the ship, beaten down and lashed by the pitiless hail of grain as it pours with a metallic roar from the iron chute, is a chapter tense with dramatic power—a scene for which a parallel must be sought in the closing pages of *Germinal* or the episode of the manhunt in *Paris*. Whatever shortcomings *The Octopus* may possess, this one chapter goes far toward atoning for them. It gives a glimpse of Mr. Norris at his best, and holds out a hopeful promise for the future volumes of the trilogy.

"The Trilogy of Wheat." *Bookman* (America), 13 (May 1901), 212–13.

We reproduce in these pages two views of the wheat region in the San Joaquin Valley, California, the scene of Frank Norris's new novel, *The Octopus*. The book itself, the first of the long-promised trilogy of American Wheat, is reviewed at some length elsewhere in this issue, but it offers such an excellent text for a discussion of symbolism in fiction that we feel inclined to write a few words of our own in addition.* Mr. Norris's indebtedness to Zola has often been made the subject of comment. Not merely has his literary creed been obviously based upon the author of the Rougon-Macquart, but even his style, the very swing of his sentences, the manner in which he marshals his adjectives, gaining a sort of cumulative emphasis from groups of ponderous synonyms, frankly show the influence of Zola. Yet nowhere has this influence been so marked as in *The Octopus*, and nowhere has it been so little to his advantage. And this is because it is the influence of Zola the symbolist, the author of *Paris* and of *Fécondité*, rather than the old-time Zola of *Nana* and of *L'Assommoir*.

Of course symbolism is not a new tenet in Zola's literary creed. In every volume of the Rougon-Macquart series there is some central idea, some one symbol which is dwelt upon and emphasized until it haunts the reader like an obsession; some vast personification: the Bourse in *L'Argent*, the Halles in *Le Ventre de Paris*, the railroad in *La Bête Humaine*; it is an effect which Mr. Norris himself reproduced with some success, with the symbol of gold constantly recurring, in the pages of *McTeague*. But in *Paris*, Zola went a step farther, and attempted to symbolise not merely one phase of Parisian life, but the whole motley, complex life of the capital. Each phase of life is represented in that book by a single character, and the plot is arranged with great ingenuity, so that the paths of all these characters, many of them so remote one from another, touch and cross and coincide at intervals, sufficiently at least for the purposes of a sustained story. Undoubtedly *Paris* was in many ways a remarkable *tour de force*; at least it probably carried this sort of symbolism, this attempt to epitomise the life of a nation within the limits of a single volume, as far as it is likely to be carried. And yet it left a great deal to be desired. Taking them character for character, the personages in *Paris* do not approach in human interest those of Zola's earlier volumes of *Pot-Bouille* or *Germinal*; and this is because they are generalised, because they stand for types and not merely for individuals. Tolstoi, in *Resurrection*, without attempting anything half so ambitious, has come far nearer to success, because in the vast army of characters whom he introduces, and who cover the whole field of Russian life, there are no general types; each and every one of them is a separate human being, sharply differentiated from the rest, and even those who come upon the scene for a moment only and then pass on not to reappear again, leave with us the desire to know something further of their lives. In *The Octopus* Mr. Norris has obviously taken *Paris* rather than *Resurrection* for his model; but he has not had the advantage of Zola's experience of twenty-two years' study of national life. We feel safe in suggesting that if *The Octopus* had been the final summing up of a series of twenty volumes chronicling the history of an American Rougon-Macquart family, it would have come considerably nearer than it does to being a candidate for the title of Great American Novel.

*See Cooper review, which precedes.

A. Schade Van Westrum. "A Novelist with a Future." *The Book Buyer*, 22 (May 1901), 326–28.

Mr. Frank Norris disappointed the expectations he had roused with his crude, powerful "McTeague," when he followed it up with "Blix" and "A Man's Woman"—two respectable, average performances, books of little color or weight. He has redeemed himself in *The Octopus*, the first of a "trilogy of the Epic of the Wheat," which will deal with (1) the production, (2) the distribution, and (3) the consumption of the American cereal. *The Octopus* deals also, and principally, with the war between the wheat-grower and the railroad; it is historic, for none can fail to recognize the tragic episode here recounted, with the great transcontinental railroad builder who but recently laid down the burden of his giant task as the central force. The second book, "The Pit," will probably have an equally strong basis in a recent Chicago "corner" in wheat; the third, "The Wolf," will have its scene laid in Europe, but of this Mr. Norris himself does not appear to be quite certain at the present moment. It will, however, certainly deal with a famine in an Old World community, and its relief by American wheat. The trilogy will tell the story of a crop from the time of its sowing in the West to that of its consumption across the ocean.

The trilogy has come to be much beloved of modern novelists. D'Annunzio practices his art in trilogies; Zola has developed its possibilities to the utmost. And just here it may be well to notice the unmistakable influence of the great Frenchman upon the young American:

> There it was, the Wheat, the Wheat! The little seed long planted, germinating in the deep, dark furrows of the soil, straining, swelling, suddenly in one night had burst upward to the light. The wheat had come up. It was there before him, around him, everywhere, illimitable, immeasurable. The winter brownness of the ground was overlaid with a little shimmer of green. The promise of the sowing was being fulfilled. The earth, the loyal mother, who never failed, who never disappointed, was keeping her faith again. Once more the strength of nations was renewed. Once more the force of the world was revivified. Once more the Titan, benignant, calm, stirred and woke, and the morning abruptly blazed into glory upon the spectacle of a man whose heart leaped exuberant with the love of a woman, and an exulting earth gleaming transcendent with the radiant magnificence of an inviolable pledge.

This is pure Zola, and there is much of it. In fact, Mr. Norris appears to be saturated with Zola's method. The trick of repetition of certain adjectives, phrases and descriptions, so wearisome in "Fécondité," is here, too, but kept within bounds; and the grouping of the masses on the enormous canvas is entirely after the masterly manner of the Frenchman. But where could have been found a better method to follow? Mr. Norris is not an imitator: there is much in this book that is entirely his own—its best passages, in fact—but the influence is visible, nor could it have been ignored, once it was felt. If Mr. Norris falls short of the cumulative grandeur of Zola, it is not because his talent is inferior, but because he is a far younger man, for the maturity of power only comes with years and practice. He has in him the root of the matter, and the will and talent to make it blossom and bear fruit. Inevitable comparison with the French master at so early an age is sufficient tribute to a young man's gift. In *The Octopus* Mr. Norris fixes his place in American literature as the most promising of its coming novelists.

He succeeds in filling his canvas; of that there can be no doubt. But he still lacks the insight gained from experience, the power to make deductions, to generalize, and to coordinate his observations. He stands before one of the greatest problems of the day—the trust; he records the upbuilding work it does, the havoc it creates, but the lesson escapes him. He is but one of many of us watching modern economic developments, expecting vaguely some climax; he is not a leader sent to guide us out of the slough, nor does he pretend to be. He has his young enthusiast, Presley, as Zola has his Abbé Froment; and with Presley he stands silent, bewildered, when the head of the Octopus—the railroad—speaks, as he was wont to speak in real life:

> "Believe this, young man," exclaimed Shelgrim, laying a thick, powerful forefinger on the table to emphasize his words, "try to believe this—to begin with—*that Railroads build themselves.* Where there is a demand, sooner or later there will be a supply. Mr. Derrick, does he grow his wheat? The Wheat grows itself. What does he count for? Does he supply the force? What do I count for? Do I build the Railroad? You are dealing with forces, young man, when you speak of Wheat and the Railroads, not with men. There is the Wheat, the supply. It must be carried to feed the People. There is the demand. The Wheat is one force, the Railroad another, and there is the law that governs them—supply and demand. Men have only little to do in the whole business. Complications may arise, conditions that bear hard on the individual—crush him, maybe—*but the Wheat will be carried to feed the people* as inevitably as it will grow. If you want to fasten the blame of the affair at Los Muertos on any person, you will make a mistake. Blame conditions, not men.
>
> "You are a very young man. Control the road! Can I stop it? I can go into bankruptcy if you like. I can do nothing. I can *not* control it. It is a force born out of certain conditions, and I—no man—can stop it or control it. Can your Mr. Derrick stop the Wheat growing? He can burn his crop, or he can give it away, or sell it for a cent a bushel—just as I could go into bankruptcy; but otherwise his Wheat must grow. Can anyone stop the Wheat? Well, then, no more can I stop the Road."

Having been wrought up to anarchy and bomb-throwing by the highhanded oppression of the wheat-growers in California, ending in bloodshed and ruin, Mr. Norris's young hero stands undecided before the colossus whose work endures to the greater prosperity of the country; immature enthusiasm, a warm heart dominating an untrained, inexperienced brain, has no argument to offer to moderate, philosophic old age. "One cannot make an omelet without breaking the eggs," said Napoleon, and he who must make the omelet because a nation needs it for its sustenance will never be understood by him who wishes to save the eggs. A clear view of the truth as he must see it is not yet for Presley: he is too young. And the facts of history prevent Mr. Norris from ending his tale with a climax of poetic justice. One of the railroad's eggs is broken, too, it is true, but it is a bad one. This episode, by the way, is Zolaesque symbolic melodrama.

But, after all, does Zola offer us a solution in his trilogy that begins in "Lourdes" and concludes in "Paris"? His Abbé Froment, who, unable to banish misery from his own little parish, yet wished to teach the Pope how to make the whole world happy, ends with a somewhat confused Fourierism, after having laid down the burden of the career he had chosen. And we must not forget that, whereas in his case we are able to judge the completed work, we know of Mr. Norris's nothing but its beginning. He may join the prophets and the theorists, but, so far as can be seen now, it is with conditions, not with theories, that he will concern himself. He presents the two sides of a mighty problem which alone the world can see: there is a third side, which may bear the solution, but we have merely made guesses at it from the days of Lassalle and Marx to those of Henry George and Tolstoy, and Bellamy, and Mr. Howells, and Zola.

Thus far about Mr. Norris's subject. His treatment of it is daring in its proportions. He has his limitations, but they are easily forgotten in the bold handling of the whole. There is true drama in it, and true poetry—groping after life in its largest meaning, a feeling for mother earth that, often symbolic, like Zola's, comes near to understanding.

Thrice welcome is this book. Compared with it, certain much advertised "successes" of recent years will dwindle to their true proportions. Far better is it to produce such independent work under the moulding influence of Zola than to copy Dumas or Thackeray in historical romance. Mr. Norris has deliberately shouldered the difficulties of a trilogy planned on an enormous scale. He is young, he is ambitious, and his undoubted talent may carry him through. He should have our good wishes in the completion of his task; he deserves success, and it may be that he will command it. But through it all we fear that our economic outlook will not be widened or deepened by him. He may write three notable novels; he will not find a new way. Eggs will still have to be broken if we are to have omelets, even after the completion of this Epic of the Wheat. It is given to but few of us to be novelists and economic thinkers both. Meanwhile we all must be beholden to him for the novel of the season.

"The Promise of a Great Story."
The Argonaut, 47 (May 13, 1901), 8.

When the Great American Novel is written it will be upon the lines that Frank Norris has attempted to follow in "The Octopus: A Story of California." All the elements of romance are in this book, and more, for it has a purpose beyond entertainment. The passions of its characters have full play, untrammeled by conventions, its field is gloriously ample, bright and warm in the sunlight, dark and cold in the shadow. Its theme almost justifies the title, "An Epic of the Wheat." Yet the work is lacking in some vital qualities. It is a painting of historical importance by one who has not yet acquired great skill in outline and perspective, one who has not yet learned the secrets of harmony in color. Full credit may be given for the genius that seized upon its central idea, for the judgment that selected from a wealth of accessories some best suited to the picture, for the sense of dramatic strength that formed the group of figures in its foreground, for the art that made its atmosphere almost real. And with this appreciation there is still room for the wish that it had been reserved for a riper knowledge, for a surer hand.

The story follows the fortunes of four or five families settled in the San Joaquin Valley, and with the interests of those whose future rests upon ownership of the fertile soil and bounteous harvests are mingled the aims, successes, and failures of many others. Labor in the fields by owner, overseer, and hands, rude sports and homely entertainments, the softening influence of beauty, tenderness, and requited love—these are the gentler passages in the chronicle. But there are more stirring motives and events. Unjust and cruel treatment of employees, the deceit and tyranny of those in temporary places of authority, the disgrace of political corruption, the greed and unrestrained power of a great corporation—all these work for sorrow, defeat, and death in the more stirring chapters. Much of the tale is true. Its tragic phases are not overdrawn.

Two more books are to follow this, continuing the epic of the golden grain. One will have to do with transportation and distribution, its scenes laid in Chicago among dealers and speculators.

The third will show the need and use of a cargo of wheat in a famine-stricken community abroad. Mr. Norris has undertaken a task that will try his powers to the utmost. "The Octopus" is stronger and better than "McTeague," the most forceful and least artificial of his earlier works. His admirers, and they are many, may confidently hope for even higher accomplishments in his next volume.

"The Octopus." *The Independent*, 53 (May 16, 1901), 1139–40.

Mr. Norris's "Epic of the Wheat" will consist of three novels, quite distinct in plot, and having no connection except that they all relate to wheat, its production, distribution and consumption. *The Octopus* is the first of the trilogy, and deals with the issues between the California wheat growers and the railroad trust.

If the author has any political doctrines, they are not clearly defined. He simply dramatizes a tragic situation. Apparently he has been shocked into an impression of Western life with its monstrous quickenings and vast travails; and he writes under the impetus of a strong and morbid excitement. The flaw in the book is that too much emphasis at the beginning has destroyed the possibility of proper emphasis at the close. The author has not enough personal self-restraint for his theme. He grows a trifle hysterical in the end: Sorrow is overdone. Justice fails him, and he unconsciously appeals to the mob for sympathy.

But *The Octopus* has qualities that lift it out of the rank of commonplace fiction. There is a breadth in the conception like the bigness that pervades the West. It takes in comedy and tragedy, nature and man, the tender heart and the inexorable law, the little home and the world, the grain of wheat and the big, warm earth that enfolds it, the railroad and the sheep crushed upon its track. The earth is as much a character in the story as any other. The author has earthy instincts and powers of interpretation that give life and meanings profound to the clods beneath his feet. He clears away everything but the earth and sky and his *dramatis personae*. The effect is tremendous, but it is not the power of true art. The final impression on the reader is that the individual human will has no sway or freedom, but is beaten down by inanimate force. Mr. Norris expresses the idea in his own vigorous language thus:

> Colossal indifference only, a vast trend toward appointed goals. Nature was, there, a gigantic enigma, a vast cyclopean power, huge, terrible, a leviathan with a heart of steel, knowing no compunction, no forgiveness, no tolerance; crushing out the human atoms standing in its way, with Nirvanic calm, the agony of destruction sending never a jar, never the faintest tremor, through all the prodigious mechanism of wheels and cogs.

No better comment on the last impression of the book could be written. It is our favorite contention that the aim of art is to enlarge the human will, not to contract it. In this enlargement lie both the joy and the morality of true literature.

As for the men in this world of "wheels and cogs," their hearts are with the wheat in the earth. They affect neither virtue nor modesty, and their humor is Brobdingnagian. They are coarse and vital, and, but for the author's obsession by the demon of blind force, might have stood forth as elemental human beings. As it is, the author's own lack of balance enters too deeply into their composition. Annixter is at the first a unique and powerful creation; but his sudden conversion to domestic modesty is grotesquely contrary to human nature; it is the handiwork of a man inexperienced in life. To offset the brutal materialism of his world Mr. Norris has introduced into his society two romantic characters—a poet and a seer. The poet is intended to sustain the same relations to the story as were held by the chorus in the old Greek tragedies. He interprets for the reader by struggling to understand conditions himself. The conception is a good one, but made somewhat ineffective by the crude contrasts in the situation and by a failure to comprehend the true poetic nature. The idea of his great poem which stirs the nation is evidently borrowed from the widely bruited doggerel verse called "The Man with the Hoe." The mysterious seer is well and powerfully drawn in the earlier chapters, but dwindles away somehow into regions of the most artificial and unconvincing supernaturalism.

No man, it is sometimes said, can write a great book now. The world has become too colossally great; there is too much brain power, judgment and taste to compete with; but, despite its manifold crudities, this book contains scenes of real beauty, and elements of power that only need to put off hysterical license to rival anything written in recent years. What the author needs most is not ideas, but the temper and patience of a calmer and more massive personality.

"The Book and the Public."
Town Talk, 9 (May 18, 1901), 24–25.

It is good to be able to chronicle that "The Octopus" called for a second printing within four days of its appearance. Whether it be that the reading public will always choose a good book when there is one to be had, or whether it merely helps to mark the passing of the swashbuckler hero, and the pseudo-historical novel, the announcement is equally gratifying. It was the late H. C. Bunner who said: "And yet, it seems to me, a good deal of public respect ought to be accorded to the public that has given to Shakespeare a recognition sole and single in the annals of literature. And if that public once in a while chooses to amuse itself by purchasing a few hundred thousand copies of 'Mr. Binks of Nevada,' I cannot see that any more serious importance attaches to such a freak of taste than we are accustomed to attribute to a fleeting popular fancy for a new beverage or to a novelty in the way of personal adornment. Unfortunately, the condescending literary man too often takes these vagaries for true indices to the capacity of the public to put a sound valuation upon literature; and it is from this misconception of the true state of the case that he is frequently tempted to offer to the public a book that is positively disrespectful." One form of the disrespectful book has flooded the markets of late, almost to the exclusion of all else—the book which is a palpable imitation of something that has achieved success, and which is evidently put forward for no other purpose than for "the money that is in it." It is a material age, and the author, like any other laborer, is worthy of his hire. Bare backs and empty stomachs have little concern with "art for art's sake," and pot boilers are as well known in literature as elsewhere in Bohemia, but the pot boiler of the real artist is still a work of art, though it may not be of the highest type, and is not to be considered in the same category as the mechanical efforts of the hewers of wood and drawers of water who have forsaken their proper callings, and who can do no more and no better than to copy the model which offers them the fewest mechanical difficulties. What the profession of letters needs is a guild or association of some sort which will prevent these machine-made and run-in-the-mould products from ever reaching the dignity of print. It is manifest, already, from the tone of Eastern reviews, that the railroad question, as it has affected California is not understood beyond our own State line, and it is only begging the question to find fault with Mr. Norris for raising the social status of the San Joaquin farmers. It makes no difference in the strength of the book that it is not exactly and minutely true to local history—whether it was actually beans instead of hops that was the infant industry strangled at its birth, or whether the settlers on the "Railroad sections" were Hoovens or Derricks, or in what particular terms they addressed the company's agents, the facts remain practically the same. Even if "The Octopus" had no shadow of a foundation in fact, it is none the less a great book—a good thing well done, and in spite of the dragging in of Tolstoi and Zola by way of comparison a book that stands alone and needs no bolstering.

"The Epic of the Wheat." *Boston Evening Transcript*, May 22, 1901, p. 18.

In "The Octopus," Mr. Frank Norris has not written, as his publishers proclaim, "A Story of California." Locality is a mere incident. He has written a story of the world, a story of the struggle between the powers of capital and the power of labor, a story of the elemental warfare of man with nature, of contending forces, Titanic, inhuman, an inevitable trend toward an appointed goal, a vast and terrible conflict of powers, symbolizing the whole of the struggle for existence.

It is true that this first of a trilogy of novels deals with the production of wheat in California; the second, is to deal with the Chicago wheat pit; and the third, at present but ill-defined in the consciousness of the author, is to have for its central idea the relieving of a famine in an Old World community, the trilogy forming the story of a crop of wheat from the time of its sowing to the time of its consumption. This novel deals with an actual incident in California known as the "Mussel Slough Affair," when the wheat growers of the San Joaquin Valley came into actual contact with the railroad ("the Octopus") which was trying to defraud them of their land. Yet after all, it is not the mere story of a crop of wheat which Mr. Norris is writing. He is dealing with the greatest developments of modern economic life; whether or not we will have, from this trilogy, some clew to the problem over which mankind has been guessing, with such leaders as Marx and George and Tolstoi and Bellamy and Howells and Zola, is yet to be determined.

Beginning with the young poet, Presley, who is seeking to write an epic of the West, Mr. Norris introduces his first motif, the Railroad. It comes into the situation as the poet has all but grasped his theme, and seems to him the discordant note in the whole grand opera. The sordidness of the lives about him repels him. Only when he comes to live in the Epic of the Wheat, does the poet see that the material has been ever at his hand; not in the story of the Spanish grandee holding the power of life and death; not in the tragedy of Vanamee's strange love; not in the beautiful Angele Varian; not in the story of the Long Trail, the baking desolation of the desert, the midnight vigils under the silent stars; not the fierce life of the forgotten towns, not in the old Mission, with its Fathers planting the sacramental elements of wheat and oil and wine, but in the strenuous life of the people about him, in the plexus of steel rails that spread over the State, complicating, dividing, reuniting, branching, throwing off feelers, involving remote towns in its myriad branching coils, its hundred tentacles drawing the lifeblood of the country into that vast stomach, dominated by an intelligence without a heart. Constantly recurrent, this motif is insistent, aggressive, dominating the pages, and holding the reader enchained by its omnipresent symbolism of human power.

Along with this there is the second motif, never changing and refusing to be forgotten, constantly intermingled with that of the railroad. It is that of the Wheat:

> Men—motes in the sunshine—
> perished, were shot down in the

very noon of life, hearts were broken, little children started in life lamentably handicapped; young girls were brought to a life of shame; old women died in the heart of life for lack of food. In that little, isolated group of human insects, misery, death, and anguish spun like a wheel of fire.

But the wheat remained. Untouched, unassailable, undefiled, that mighty world-force, that nourisher of nations, wrapped in Nirvanic calm, indifferent to the human swarm, gigantic, resistless, moved onward in its appointed grooves. Through the welter of blood at the irrigation ditch, through the sham charity and shallow philanthropy of famine relief committees, the great harvest of Los Muertos rolled, like a flood from the Sierras to the Himalayas, to feed thousands of starving scarecrows on the barren plains of India.

It is inevitable that this work should be compared with that of Zola, and the comparison itself is a tribute to the genius of the younger man. He lacks the power to deduce, to generalize, to bring into a coherent plan the observations of his experiences. But let us be patient. He stands, like the rest of us, watching the Problem of the Ages, groping for light in a world darkened by the smoke of fierce conflict. He is not an imitator of Zola, although he has the same method of repeating phrases, descriptions and adjectives. Even this is not tiresome, and he only emphasizes characteristics which make his people sharply defined and consistent. His striving is always for the light, and though he has not yet found it in this first book of the Epic, he may yet catch some gleams in other corners of the world. Now, indeed, he concerns himself merely with conditions, and once he runs up against the blank wall behind which the Power has intrenched itself, when the head of the Octopus speaks to the poet:

"Believe this, young man," exclaimed Shelgrim, laying a thick, powerful forefinger on the table to emphasize his words, "try to believe this—to begin with—that railroads build themselves. Where there is a demand, sooner or later there will be a supply. Mr. Derrick, does he grow his wheat? The wheat grows itself. What does he count for? Does he supply the force? What do I count for? Do I build the railroad? You are dealing with forces, young man, when you speak of wheat and the railroads, not with men. There is the wheat, the supply. It must be carried to feed the people. There is the demand. The wheat is one force, the railroad another, and there is the law that governs them—supply and demand. Men have only little to do in the whole business. Complications may arise, conditions that bear hard on the individual—crush him, maybe—but the wheat will be carried to feed the people as inevitably as it will grow. If you want to fasten the blame of the affair at Los Muertos on any person, you make a mistake. Blame conditions, not men."

From this presentation of the philosophy of life the poet recoils in terror. The new conception stupefies him. No one, then, is to blame for the men killed at the irrigation ditch. Forces, condition, laws of supply and demand are the enemies, after all. No, not enemies. There is no malevolence in nature. It is, then, a gigantic engine, a leviathan with a heart of steel, knowing no compunction, no forgiveness, no tolerance; crushing out the human atom standing in its way, "with Nirvanic calm," the agony of destruction sending never the faintest tremor through all that prodigious mechanism of wheels and cogs.

If the respect for truth has prevented Mr. Norris from ending his tale with a climax in which justice is done, if in his youth he has no answer to the colossus whose work will endure for the final upbuilding of his country; if this book offers nothing in the way of amending the situation—of altering those conditions, those forces, those laws of supply and demand which alone were responsible for the blood shed at the irrigating ditch, for the women driven to lives of shame or starvation, for the broken hearts left behind after the Octopus has sucked the life-blood from the land—we must remember that he is not as yet the seer or the theorist, but that he is presenting us, in this first work, the conditions only of the mighty problem. He does not pretend to be the leader sent to guide this people in their dealings with that mighty modern force, the trust.

"The Octopus" is the symbolism of the strenuous American life. Wheat, the staff of life, well forms the central symbol, and entirely apart from its bearing upon the story typifies the genius of production, the spirit of the nation, spreading and gathering power, going over seas and carrying health and sustenance to other peoples, emblematic of the spirit of the American people. The book is full of enthusiasm and consciousness of power, and no one can read it without being thrilled through and through with the earnestness of the man in grappling with the problem as Ajax defied the lightning. The love story is not important, whether it be that of beautiful Angele Varian and her hopeless lover, Vanamee, or of the coarse, aggressive young farmer Axminster [sic], with his brutal passion for Hilma Tree turning to a pure and sanctified devotion. The wheat itself typifies the Resurrection and the Life. Magnus Derrick, regarding life as a huge gamble, and doing evil that good may come; Lyman, the railroad commissioner, selling his birthright for a mess of pottage; Hooven, the stolid Dutch farmer; Vanamee, the recluse of the desert; all these are motes in the sunbeam. As characters in the vast drama they play their parts and play them well, but the characters are subordinated to the theme; primarily it is, as the railroad president says, with conditions and not with men, that the story deals.

There is one exception. S. Behrman, the agent of the railroad, is, while a symbol of the means by which the Octopus achieves its ends, a gross creature of flesh and blood. He is developed with rare consistency. Safe from bullets, from dynamite, and out of the reach of the law, he at last becomes the object of poetic justice in a chapter which is one of the great pieces of symbolic melodrama, like the struggle of Jean Valjean in the sewer, the man-hunt in Paris or the closing pages of "Germinal." Struck down in the hour of his triumph by the very grains of wheat that pour upon him in the hold of the ship, choking in the dust and beaten down to his death by the power which has made him what he is, S. Behrman is made the central figure of a chapter that stands out as a piece of literary workmanship of the very first order, grim, terrible and never to be forgotten.

Mr. Norris has done his best. He has

given us a novel which will live after other "books of the year" have been laid by and forgotten. And best of all, he holds the promise of better things yet in the remaining numbers of the trilogy, this "Epic of the Wheat," which Doubleday, Page & Co. have been fortunate in putting before the public.

J. B. Kerfoot. "The Latest Books." *Life*, 37 (May 30, 1901), 455.

In *The Octopus*, by Frank Norris, we have the most notable piece of fiction that has come from the hand of any American writer during the past year. It deals with the troubles between the wheat growers of California and the railroad, and is the first of three books intended by the author to constitute "the epic of the wheat." The story is one of compelling interest and carries the reader far beyond petty regrets for its overwhelming tragedy.

Jack London. "The Octopus." *Impressions Quarterly*, 2 (June 1901), 45–47.

There it was, the Wheat, the Wheat! The little seed long planted, germinating in the deep, dark furrows of the soil, straining, swelling, suddenly in one night had burst upward to the light. The wheat had come up. It was before him, around him everywhere, illimitable, immeasurable. The winter brownness of the ground was overlaid with a little shimmer of green. The promise of the sowing was being fulfilled. The earth, the loyal mother who never failed, who never disappointed, was keeping her faith again.

Very long ago, we of the West heard it rumored that Frank Norris had it in mind to write the *Epic of the Wheat*. Nor can it be denied that many of us doubted—not the ability of Frank Norris merely, but the ability of the human, of all humans. This great, incoherent, amorphous West! Who could grip the spirit and the essence of it, the luster and the wonder, and bind it all, definitely and sanely, within the covers of a printed book? Surely we of the West, who knew our West, may have been pardoned our lack of faith.

And now Frank Norris has done it; has, in a machine age, achieved what has been peculiarly the privilege of the man who lived in an heroic age; in short, has sung the *Epic of the Wheat*. "More power to his elbow," as Charles F. Lummis would say.

On first sight of the Valley of San Joaquin, one can not help but call it the "new and naked land." There is apparently little to be seen. A few isolated ranches in the midst of the vastness, no timber, a sparse population—that is all. And the men of the ranches, sweating in bitter toil, they must likewise be new and naked. So it would seem; but Norris has given breadth to both, and depth. Not only has he gone down into the soil, into the womb of the passionate earth, yearning for motherhood, the sustenance of nation; but he has gone down into the heart of its people, simple, elemental, prone to the ruder amenities of existence, growling and snarling with brute anger under cruel wrong. One needs must feel a sympathy for these men, workers and fighters, and for all of their weakness, a respect. And, after all, as Norris has well shown, their weakness is not inherent. It is the weakness of unorganization, the weakness of the force which they represent and of which they are a part, the agricultural force as opposed to the capitalistic force, the farmer against the financier, the tiller of the soil against the captain of industry.

No man, not large of heart, lacking in spontaneous sympathy, incapable of great enthusiasms, could have written *The Octopus*. Presley, the poet, dreamer and singer, is a composite fellow. So far as mere surface incident goes, he is audaciously Edwin Markham; but down in the heart of him he is Frank Norris. Presley, groping vaguely in the silence of the burning night for the sigh of the land; Presley, with his great Song of the West forever leaping up in his imagination and forever eluding him; Presley, wrestling passionately for the swing of his "thundering progression of hexameters"—who is this Presley but Norris grappling in keen travail with his problem of *The Octopus,* and doubting often, as we of the West have doubted?

Men obtain knowledge in two ways: by generalizing from experience; by gathering to themselves the generalizations of others. As regards Frank Norris, one can not avoid pausing for speculation. It is patent in this, his last and greatest effort, he has laid down uncompromisingly the materialistic conception of history, or, more politely, the economic interpretation of history. Now the question arises: Did Frank Norris acquire the economic interpretation of history from the printed records of the thoughts of other men, and thus equipped, approach his problem of *The Octopus?* or, rather, did he approach it, naive and innocent? and from direct contact with the great social forces was he not forced to so generalize for himself? It is a pretty question. Will he some day tell us?

Did Norris undergo the same evolution he has so strongly depicted in Presley? Presley's ultimate sociological concept came somewhat in this fashion: Shelgrim, the president and owner of the Pacific and Southwestern, laid "a thick, powerful forefinger on the table to emphasize his words. 'Try to believe this—to begin with—that railroads build themselves. Where there is a demand, sooner or later there will be a supply. Mr. Derrick, does he grow his wheat? The wheat grows itself. What does he count for? Does he supply the force? What do I count for? Do I build the railroad? You are dealing with forces, young man, when you speak of wheat and railroads, not with men. There is the wheat, the supply. It must be carried to feed the people. There is the demand. The wheat is one force, the railroad another, and there is the law that governs them—supply and demand. Men have only little to do in the whole business. Complications may arise, conditions that bear hard on the individual—crush him, maybe—but the wheat will be carried to feed the people as inevitably as it will grow.'"

One feels disposed to quarrel with Norris for his inordinate realism. What does the world care whether Hooven's meat safe be square or oblong; whether it be lined with wire screen or mosquito netting; whether it be hung to the branches of the oak tree or to the ridgepole of the barn; whether, in fact, Hooven has a meat safe or not? "Feels disposed" is used advisedly. In truth, we can not quarrel with him. It is confession and capitulation. The facts are against us. He *has* produced results, Titanic results. Never mind the realism, the unimportant detail, minute description, Hooven's meat safe and the rest. Let it be stated flatly that by no other method could Frank Norris or anybody else have handled the vast Valley of the San Joaquin and the no less vast-tentacled *Octopus*. Results? It was the only way to get results, the only way to paint the broad canvas he has painted, with the sunflare in his brush.

But he gives us something more than realism. Listen to this:

Once more the pendulum of the seasons swung in its mighty arc.

* * *

Then, faint and prolonged, across the levels of the ranch, he heard the engine whistling for Bonneville. Again and again, at rapid intervals in its flying course, it whistled for road crossings, for sharp curves, for trestles; ominous notes, hoarse, bellowing, ringing with the accents of menace and defiance; and abruptly Presley saw again, in his imagination, the galloping monster, the terror of steel and steam, with its single eye, cyclopean, terrible, flinging the echo of its thunder over all the reaches of the valley, leaving blood and destruction in its path; the leviathan, with tentacles of steel clutching into the soil, the soulless Force, the iron-hearted Power, the monster, the Colossus, the Octopus.

* * *

The direct brutality of ten thousand acres of wheat, nothing but wheat as far as the eye could see, stunned her a little. There was something vaguely indecent in the sight, this food of the people, this elemental force, this basic energy, weltering here under the sun in all the unconscious nakedness of a sprawling, primordial Titan.

* * *

Everywhere throughout the great San Joaquin, unseen and unheard, a thousand ploughs upstirred the land, tens of thousands of shears clutched deep into the warm, moist soil. It was the long, stroking caress, vigorous, male, powerful, for which the Earth seemed panting. The heroic embrace of a multitude of iron hands, gripping down into the brown, warm flesh of the land that quivered responsive and passionate under this rude advance, so robust as to be almost an assault, so violent as to be veritably brutal. There, under the sun and under the speckless sheen of the sky, the wooing of the Titan began, the vast primal passion, the two world-forces, the elemental Male and Female, locked in a colossal embrace, at grapples in the throes of an infinite desire, at once terrible and divine, knowing no law, untamed, savage, natural, sublime.

Many men, and women, too, pass through the pages of *The Octopus*, but one, greatest of all, we can not forbear mentioning in passing—Annixter. Annixter, rough almost to insolence, direct in speech, intolerant in his opinions, relying upon absolutely no one but himself; crusty of temper, bullying of disposition, a ferocious worker, and as widely trusted as he was widely hated; obstinate and contrary, cantankerous, and deliciously afraid of "feemale women"—this is Annixter. He is worth knowing. In such cunning fashion has Norris blown the breath of life into him, that his death comes with a shock which is seldom produced by deaths in fiction. Osterman, laying his head on his arms like a tired man going to rest, and Delaney, crawling instinctively out of the blood-welter to die in the growing wheat; but it is Annixter, instantly killed, falling without movement, for whom we first weep. A living man there died.

Well, the promise of *Moran* and *McTeague* has been realized. Can we ask more? Yet we have only the first of the trilogy. *The Epic of the Wheat* is no little thing. Content with *The Octopus*, we may look forward to *The Pit* and *The Wolf*. We shall not doubt this time.

"The Novel of the West." *Washington Times*, June 2, 1901, p. 8, part 2.

When the name of Frank Norris appeared among those of younger American novelists two or three years ago, some of those who read his first romances prophesied that he would be great some day, and when his latest book, "The Octopus," was announced as the first of a trilogy of novels dealing with the development of wheat interests in this country, it was awaited with considerable interest. The obvious thing was that the young novelist had attempted something great; the thing which was not so certain was whether, as the unconventional hero of his present work would say, he had "bit off more than he could chew."

The salient quality of the book is that nobody can help reading it through. It grasps the attention like tentacles and has some of the uncanny fascination of its namesake. It is not a pleasant book. It is not a cheerful book. Its language is not classical, nor are its characters conventional, and the author seems to be possessed by a sort of savage contempt for some of the people who are likely to form his public. There is a "public be d—d" way with him which is not ingratiating. Yet this is not a pose, and it can therefore be easily forgiven. He may have a contempt for society, but he does not thrust it down your throat. He is too much interested in business.

The octopus in question is the Pacific and Southwestern Railroad, and the book is a history of the fight between this organization and the ranchers whom, one by one, it ruined, some of them body and soul. It makes of one man a murderer, of another a martyr, of another a corrupt politician; it wrecks the life of one woman, drives another to a life of shame, and another to starvation in the street. There is something like Zola about Mr. Norris, as many of his critics have remarked; but it is Zola with all the Gallicism taken out of him, purified, strengthened, set in the clean, fresh air of the West, which seems as good for cuttle fish and other anachronistic monsters as it is for wholesome things. Left alone with no adequate foe, the railroads gobbled Lower California, and grew large on their rich fare as the kangaroo developed in the isolated land of Australia, out of all reason. It is life which is the master, life and the principles of growth, and the silent, ceaselessly growing wheat fattens the monster corporation as it might have enriched the blood of the people, and in time past did so strengthen them. The men of the West, when they fight, fight great foes; they are not hampered by the pettiness of a divided struggle. Possibly, to some such unhindered fight with gigantic enemies Norris owes his own great though crude strength. He impressed many readers of his earlier books as a man who was stronger than his work, and hence awkward; who was clumsy in handling material sometimes from its very richness. At any rate, this is the first of his books in which he can be said to have handled it easily and artistically, missed no point, drifted into no vagueness, allowed no worship of mere strength to blind him to beauty.

The book is great. There is no doubt of that. If it is not the best work its author can do, he will be the great American novelist when he comes into his own. There is a reserve about it that hints something more to come.

Norris is a realist, in the most brutal, uncompromising way; but he is also a poet. The poetic touch in "McTeague" was what saved the book; but he has managed his imagination in this book with a surer and more skillful hand. He has introduced an exquisite idyl of the hills, shifting into fearful tragedy, and then into refined, almost esoteric beauty, in the story of Vanamee and Angele Varian. He has, with a grim and stern determination, sacrificed everything to the essential strength and fineness of his plot; he has let no touch of pathos, of cruelty or of squalid coarseness escape which could add to the force of his denouement; hence the denouement is not only strong, but inevitable. It is one of those books for which it is not possible to imagine a change in any detail of the plot. The logic of events and of character make every step necessary. In this the author has shown that power of intuitive perception which alone entitles a man to be called a genius.

He has shown the same unerring instinct in the selection of his types. Magnus Derrick, the Southern man and natural leader of men, holding to the ideals of Calhoun's time, keeping the daring and gambler's instinct of 'Forty-nine; Lyman Derrick, the facile product of new conditions; Presley, the student and dreamer; Annixter, the brutal, uncouth, semi-savage man of the West, the spirit of fight incarnate; Hilma, the primitive peasant of the Old World with the refinement of the American girl giving her a charm indescribable; Hooven, the illiterate little German farmer; Dyke, engineer and railroad man to the ends of his fingers, such a man as might have taken the "Yellow Mail" of Spearman's latest story over the mountains; Vanamee, the mystic shepherd, brooding under the shadow of a crime not his own; even Mrs. Cedarquist, the fashionable woman of San Francisco, that city which is described in a phrase as "not a city, but a Midway Plaisance," by this free-handed, cynical Westerner—there is not one of these people, or of the minor characters, in whom a note rings false.

As for the descriptive passages and the dramatic scenes, the book is so crowded with them that it is of no use to quote. In spite of its unusual length there is not an ounce of padding in it. The author, by contrast with more superficial writers of romance, seems at first slow in getting into the swing of his narrative; but it is like an ocean greyhound getting out of the tangle of smaller craft around. All his first chapter is necessary.

Above all, the thing is new, absolutely new; theme, characters, material, style, all are without dog-ears. There is no previous novel which touches any of them. The subject has seemed too big to handle; the people are individuals as well as types, and an individual cannot be conceived and drawn twice. There is but one Newcome; there is but one Magnus Derrick.

An additional proof of the essentially poetic truth of Norris' conceptions is the fact that the fight with the Octopus puts every character, one after another, to the test. Whatever is mean, or cowardly, or base, or weak in any man or woman comes to light in the struggle with a gigantic and subtle enemy. The one person who remains untouched by its pollution is perhaps Hilma, saddened and martyred by it, but not corrupted. Annixter, through his love for her, also escapes demoralization, but either that or death was inevitable. Without Hilma he might have been debased; with her, he became a martyr. Yet this enemy, this force—silent, superhuman, polluting—is no respecter of persons, and in the end kills its willing and prosperous servant as remorselessly as its enemies. The final thought of the book is brought out with a marvelous delicacy of touch, and so naturally that it escapes the opprobrium of a moral.

It is the wheat, after all, which has wrought this evil, the silent, impersonal power of life, crushing the few to feed the many, wrecking the ranches of Lower California to feed the millions of India.

The man who can see at once details and causes, minute phenomena and mighty laws, is the man for whom this materialistic yet idealizing generation of Americans has been waiting. "McTeague" and "The Octopus" indicate this ability in Norris. It remains for him to do what these seem to promise.

"Writers and Books." *Boston Evening Transcript*, June 12, 1901, p. 19.

Many reviewers and readers of Frank Norris's first book of his Trilogy, "The Octopus," have speculated upon the economic theories which the novelist might hold. In a personal letter to a Boston man, Mr. Norris thus explains his position: "I do not think I shall attempt any solution of the problem involved in 'The Epic of the Wheat.' The novelist, of necessity, deals rather with conditions than with theories, and I think I shall leave to the political economist the solutions of the problems of the 'present discontent.'"

Charles F. Lummis. "That Which Is Written." *Land of Sunshine*, 15 (July 1901), 58.

Powerful and surprising as a couple of the former novels of Frank Norris have been found, this young California writer has raised his sights above *McTeague* and *A Man's Woman*, and shot as true in his latest, *The Octopus*. If he can carry the two remaining members of his projected Trilogy of Wheat on as high a plane, it will be an astonishing performance. If too visibly determined by Zola, and often too diligently brutal in style, it has rather tremendous strength and scope, and its local coloration of the "Octopus" is almost historical. This tragic picture, which to the stranger will seem a travesty, is really a find handling of the abominable conditions which made Californians hate not railroads, but the *kind* of railroad they knew—here thinly masked as the "Pacific and Southwestern." The historic Mussel Slough slaughter, the "all-the-traffic-will-bear" policy, the corruption of legislatures, the shameless confiscation and robbery of individuals—all these are painted to the life. The character-drawing is less inevitable than the description, perhaps. "Magnus Derrick," the wheat king, "S. Behrman," the characteristic railroad tool, and "Vanamee," the recluse, are the most striking figures. "Annixter" seems a willful exaggeration at first, though his transformation by love for "Hilma" is more convincing. The diaphanous device of "Presley" as a Markham and Man-with-the-Hoe seems hardly good workmanship. And it must be confessed that Mr. Norris is not yet so sure-handed with women and love-stories as with rough-hewn men. "Hilma" is the marble for a big statue; but her Pygmalion lacked the glow which should have informed the work of the Chisel. But all in all the book is a most uncommon one in grasp and force and depth of current; such an energy, in fact, as very few American authors can either summon or harness.

"The Octopus." *Boston Evening Transcript*, July 31, 1901, p. 12.

No one who studies society can well be oblivious to an increasing mood of fatalism. It finds expression negatively in general complacence with what is, and in the lack of deep and sustained hatred of evil by individuals and communities. Whatever is is right, broadly speaking, say poets, clergy and statesmen. Evil is but good in the making. It is a lesser good. Law governs all. The individual is impotent, indeed he is a negligible quantity compared with society as a whole. Nationalism is the dominant thought of the hour, and destiny is its keyword. Fortunately here and there voices are raised deprecating the extinction of the individual and pointing out the dangerous tendencies of the hour; and of this sort was Bishop Lawrence's recent baccalaureate sermon to the graduating class of the Institute of Technology.

To account for the latest form of fatalism one has only to bear in mind the aboriginal instinct in man to look upon himself as an automaton, a pawn in the game of life, and then to remember that a superficial acquaintance with science on the part of the masses has created the impression that there is an exact parallelism between the reign of law in the physical world and in the spiritual world.

Convinced that heredity and environment have foreordained him to be what he is, and finding in current poetry and philosophy, and in not a little theology of the day, that good is inextricably mixed with evil, it is not surprising that the modern man loses belief in his power to choose his own destiny and skill in divination between right and wrong.

This turbid state of mind and conscience is seen in discussions of economists in dealing with the trust problem, in the pulpit utterances of men discussing race problems, and in the writings of poets. Thus William Watson, in his latest poem "Achievement," ashamed and wrathful at British extermination of the Dutch republics, nevertheless comes round to say—

We have raised up heroes where we
 found but hinds,
We have ravaged well, our rapine is not
 vain.
Redder from our footprints the wild rose
Of freedom shall afresh hereafter
 spring,
And in our own despite are we the sires
Of liberty, as night begets the day.

It is this teaching, whether serious or in bitter jest, that some good from all evil comes which is dangerous, as we conceive it. Especially so if found in the literature of the masses, in the fiction of the day or in the public press or in the pulpit. Therefore it is with mingled regret and gratitude that one lays down Norris's story "The Octopus." Gratitude, because it gives indisputable proof of the author's power to deal with vital, present-day problems in a bold, gripping, realistic way, too minutely and sordidly realistic at times possibly, but in the main admirable. Seldom has the futility of fighting the devil with his own weapons been more vividly or terribly portrayed than in Magnus Derrick's downfall. No story of our American life yet written begins to compare with this story in its depiction of the remorselessness and cruelty of which a great corporation may be guilty if it chooses to be. As you read it your blood boils, and you yearn to have Behrman the Jewish tool of Shelgrim—the millionaire captain of industry—meet his doom long before he does, in a way awful and ironically just.

The cumulative moral effect of the narrative is such that you instinctively compare it with all the sermons you have heard during the past year, and then begin to understand why it was that one of the country's most gifted and popular preachers recently admitted in conversation that the novelist—along with the editor—is to be the great ethical teacher of the twentieth century, the clergymen hereafter to occupy a subordinate place. Such is the power of the story as a story. So splendidly moral is it as depiction of the evil of evil.

But, alas! the author is not content to tell the story. He must preach, moralize, attempt to deal with the mystery of evil. He is not content to let the conscience of his readers draw the inevitable moral. Instead of stopping with the scene which describes the death of Behrman by suffocation in the hold of a vessel which is bearing his wheat to India, Presley the poet—not unlike Edwin Markham in some aspects of his career—is permitted to reappear and moralize, and he comes round to the lame conclusion that despite all the satanic procedure by which the wheat farmers have been despoiled of their own, it is atoned for by the fact that the wheat grown on their ranches saved the lives of starving Indians or hungry Americans and Europeans. The implication of the last chapter of the book is that all the corporation did in spoiling the individuals was inevitable, the necessary method of conducting the transportation business.

It does not require very keen ethical discrimination to point out in reply that wheat is in itself unmoral; that whether stolen or honestly owned if delivered in India it will save life. It by no means follows as night the day that a corporation without a rival in the Southwest needed to cheat land settlers, bribe judges, juries and legislators, evict tenants, murder honest men, disrupt families, etc., in order to get cheap wheat for the benefit of the American consumer. Such conduct is not the inevitable fruit of competitive business, or even of monopoly administration. If it were, revolution would be upon us.

The keynote of this corporation's conduct is to be found in Behrman's reply to Dyke, the ungratefully treated ex-engineer, the deceived and ruined hop-grower, as, in his mingled despair and wrath, he presses Behrman to expound the principle on which the corporation imposes its freight rates. Behrman blurted out at last these pregnant words: "All the traffic will bear." In this he showed a spirit of mingled greed and envy as old as Cain, a deliberate willing to do wrong on the part of his superiors for which they were morally responsible; and not the workings of an inevitable, economic law, which made tyranny and villainy necessary.

If Mr. Norris in the other two forthcoming novels of his trilogy on wheat will be content to tell his story and let the average reader draw his or her own moral he will do well. Humanity has struggled too hard in its upward course toward ethical ideals to be easily converted now into belief that men like Shelgrim and Behrman are workers together with God for humanity's betterment, when they resort to such devices as are depicted in "The Octopus." The net result of a life like Shelgrim's may be beneficial, but even so, there is no use in trying to extenuate particular sins because of the total outcome. It is quite proper to believe with Presley that "all things, surely, inevitably, resistlessly work together for good." But the danger of popular exposition of that comfortable optimism is that your man in the street soon begins to reason that Cain was not so much worse than Abel, Pharaoh than Moses, Nero than Marcus Aurelius, Saul than Paul, Ananias than Stephen, Napoleon than Washington, Parnell than Gladstone, Guiteau than Garfield; and the result is individual and national deterioration in morals.

A.H.
"Talk About Books."
The Chautauquan, 33 (August 1901), 539.

The conflict between wheat producers and the railroad is the subject of Frank Norris's novel "The Octopus." The ranchmen are caught in the grip of the road that controls their land, their means of transportation, the popular vote, the courts, and the press. The struggle is not with men, but with a power that crushes all opposition, impersonally and inevitably. The only hope is that, though individuals are overwhelmed, the force of the wheat is strong enough to prevail in the end. As an attempt to depict in its large meaning the life of the west and the problems of our mercantile civilization, the book is worthy of commendation. It touches what is vital and characteristic. The characters are well drawn—strong, practical, whole-souled men and women, not at all the primitive nature-born, brutal beings the author makes them typify in his paragraphs of picturesque comment. We cannot accept their final destruction by the railroad. To lose property unjustly is hard, but it need not make men criminals nor cringing turncoats. The book is called an epic, but its view is too partial to justify the title. Whatever the hostility of producer and transporter, there is a closer, more vital interrelation and dependence.

"Book Reviews."
Canadian Magazine, 17 (August 1901), 392–93.

Naturally enough, the aspects of industrialism creep into modern fiction, and the fight of the shippers against railway rates is one of the real problems of the day. In "The Octopus" we have this phase of economic disquietude worked out. In a certain district of California the landed proprietors decide to grow wheat on a large scale, but being at the mercy of one railway whose rates are so high as to preclude all profits to the growers they decide to fight the monopoly. The first engagement is political in character: they elect a state railway commission pledged to lower rates. To secure this commission bribery has been used against the wishes of the more prudent, who, however, finally succumb to the temptation. But, as is so often true, the end does not justify the means. The commission plays them false. Then the railway, which owns large tracts of these growers' lands, exacts a price which ruins the nominal owners. When violence is resorted to the details of the bribery come out and public opinion turns against the harassed farmers. They lose their homes, their reputation and finally their lives in the contest against the giant power of a big corporation. It is a sad story of wrong met in a wrong way. It is well called an epic of the wheat, and one's sympathies go out to the minor victims, chiefly women, who fall in the general catastrophe. To relieve the gloom of the tragedy there are some bright pictures of Californian life and western humour. The author is at times rather discursive, but of his powers of description there is no doubt.

"A Wheat Trilogy: Frank Norris Starts It with a Story of the Grain Growing, Called 'The Octopus.' "
Munsey's Magazine, 25 (August 1901), 76.

With "The Octopus," Frank Norris has put himself a long stride ahead of the author of "McTeague." In lieu of the life story of a San Francisco dentist, we have for the theme a Homeric struggle between a band of men and a corporation, the farmers and the railroad, with the man *Presley* to play the part of Greek chorus, pointing out the significance of it all, and giving the author a mouthpiece for his reflections and his righteous anger.

The railroad is the villain of the piece, a villain of the coal black, unmitigated type that gets hissed by the gallery; but unlike most villains, it is triumphant at the close. Those who have followed the bitter struggle between the farmers of California and the Southern Pacific Railroad Company are rereading history in "The Octopus"—though history of a somewhat partisan type, for the State owes the railroad vast benefits as well as vast grudges. The incidents of which the book is built are strong and vital, though there is occasional affectation in the style; and at points the narrator rises to a bigness and simplicity that makes it human drama of a high type.

Two novels are to follow "The Octopus"—"The Pit, a Story of Chicago," and "The Wolf, a Story of Europe," completing a trilogy which will be known as "The Epic of the Wheat." It is difficult to see what Mr. Norris or Zola, or their readers gain from the linking of novels into trilogies, though possibly their publishers think that it increases their sales.

"American Literature." *Saturday Review* (England), 92 (August 31, 1901), 280.*

Two ventures in fiction of widely differing method and spirit are Mrs. Wharton's "Crucial Instances" and Mr. Frank Norris's "The Octopus." Mrs. Wharton has been so close a student of Mr. Henry James that her work, although strongly individual in temperament, has borne evident marks of a dominating influence; in this latest book there are signs of emancipation, which are the more

*Reprinted in "Writers and Books," *Boston Evening Transcript*, September 21, 1901, p. 19.

welcome because Mrs. Wharton has gifts of perception and characterization of a high order. "The Octopus" is a novel of crude and almost barbaric force; showing in many parts the deep impress of Zola, both in method and manner, but disclosing also great vigor of imagination, dramatic feeling and a deep sense of reality.

William Morton Payne. "Recent Fiction." *The Dial*, 31 (September 1, 1901), 136.

Mr. Frank Norris has evidently determined to become the American Zola. The brutal realism of his first books indicated a marked intention of following in the footsteps of his French prototype, and all that was needed to make the parallel complete was the invention of some large scheme of social portrayal which should link together a series of semi-independent novels. Such a scheme he has now elaborated, and the general subject of the projected series is indicated by "The Epic of the Wheat," its collective title. Three books are planned, dealing respectively with the production, the distribution, and the consumption of our chief agricultural product. The first book of the series "The Octopus," is a story of the struggle between the wheat-growers of California and the railroad company upon which they are dependent for access to their market. "The Pit," taking us to Chicago, will follow; and "The Wolf," shifting the scene to Western Europe, will complete the trilogy. This is a large conception, and Mr. Norris has dealt with its first phase in a manner that cannot fail to win respect and even admiration, in spite of the defects of a method that is essentially inartistic. With him, as with M. Zola, realism means the piling up of great masses of trivial fact, reporting in place of true characterization, and the enforcement of his argument by the bludgeon rather than by the rapier. Allowing for all that may be urged against the methods of railway companies in general, and in particular against the methods of the corporation that has held California within its constricting tentacles, we think that Mr. Norris has shown himself too evidently a partisan of the agriculturist, and has failed to deal impartially with the forces that contend for mastery in his pages. If only he had given the devil his due, we might be willing to admit the diabolic character of the corporation which he assails; as it is, we are rather inclined to sympathize with the octopus, which stands, after all, for practices that come within the form of law, whereas the practices of the wheat-growers stand for the most part without the law, and illustrate nearly every form of violence and anarchy. If the writer means to preach anything, it is that a certain degree of outrage justifies individuals in taking the law into their own hands, and that is the most dangerous sophistry that now confronts our civilization. We have little doubt, for example, that if Mr. Norris were writing of an earlier generation in California, he would be on the side of the Vigilance Committees rather than on the side of law and order. But his book is made an impressive one by virtue of its mere bulk and overwhelming particularity, as well as by certain dramatic episodes that are presented with remarkable vividness and intensity of feeling. And the vein of mysticism that crops out here and there is not only distinctly Zolaesque, but also provides a welcome relief from the oppressive atmosphere of the narrative.

"The Octopus."
Academy and Literature, 61
(September 7, 1901), 193.

This is the first story in Mr. Norris's promised trilogy of the "Epic of the Wheat." What has an octopus to do with wheat? Everything, when, as in this case, the Octopus is a tract of country in California which goes by that name. Mr. Norris gives a very business-like air to this novel by including a map of the Octopus district, and a list of the characters. These number twenty-seven. We have Magnus Derrick (the "Governor"), proprietor of the Los Muertos Rancho, his wife, his two sons, his neighbours and friends, and many humbler folk. Dipping into the book we find the loading of a grain ship put to a tragic use. The novel, it should be explained, is complete in itself. The scene throughout is California.

"Literary Review for 1901."
The Current Encyclopedia, 1
(September 15, 1901), 367.

Nothing done by any writer of English in several years shows more crude power than "The Octopus" of Mr. Frank Norris. It is the first of a number of recent works of fiction, and the only one not written by a professed journalist, which has for its object the exposure of one or another social iniquity. The "Octopus" here is the Southern Pacific Railway, and the deeds described relate to the seizure of lands in the San Bernadino Valley by that powerful and unscrupulous corporation. Mr. Norris's work is always powerful, painstaking and realistic. His style savors overmuch of the methods of M. Zola, but his theme is similar and he himself still in early youth. This book is the first of a promised sequence of three, the others to deal with a grain corner in Chicago and with a famine in Europe, respectively.

[William Dean Howells.] "Editor's Easy Chair." *Harper's Monthly Magazine*, 103 (October 1901), 824–25.

... the poet may not be bidden, and wherever one is a poet that is a reason for his being there, in fancy as in fact. Mr. Frank Norris is a poet among the California wheat-fields, where he has woven a prodigious epic of how they lie bound by the irons of a hated railroad. His novel "The Octopus" is an epic of Zolaesque largeness; but Mr. Norris is a poet of native note, and he owes to the great romantic realist nothing but the conception of treating a modern theme epically. That was what he did, as to the place, in his "McTeague," and that is what he has done, as to the action, in "The Octopus." All that happens, happens around the oppression, ruthless, mechanical, increasing, of the land by the road, and the characters are the means direct and indirect of the infliction and affliction. They are not the less personalities because of their typical function; they are each most intimately and personally real, physically real, but also psychically real. Their material presence is enforced by the recognition of some distinctive and characteristic trait, which is repeated again and again in the very same terms till it is wrought into the reader's consciousness inseparably from the idea of this and that personality. It is a method that does its work, but we think it would be well for Mr. Norris to ask himself if it is not a trick. Apart from this he has the power of compelling our assistance at the actions and emotions of his characters; and they are very vital emotions, very vital actions. He gets back to something primitive, something primeval in his people; they love and hate with a sort of cave-dweller longing and loathing, yet with a modern environment of conscience that tells on them at last in fine despairs and remorses. The book has moments of drama which in the retrospect expand immensely, so that the afternoon of the rabbit hunt and the evictions and the fight of the embattled farmers with the legal agents of the road seem a vast, wretched epoch of one's own. The stir of dumb cosmic forces is felt through all, but these are, if anything, a little too invited, though their presence is of great imaginational consequence. Certain episodes, loosely or not at all related to the main purpose, we would prefer to have another time rather than lose altogether. For the most part the story is compactly and strongly built; it stands firmly, and it marches to the end with an awful, automatic, inexorable trend, like a piece of relentless mechanism endowed with organic activity. But the end is the fall of the great leader of the farmers, who perishes morally and spiritually because he has consented to employ the bad means of the road for the good aims of the land; it is not the death of the road's local manager, choked, drowned, buried in the avalanche of wheat which has [been] robbed from the farmers. That is a bit of the melodrama towards which Mr. Norris dangerously tends in his hours of triumphs. Other defects his book has, but with them all it is a great book, simple, sombre, large, and of a final authority as the record of a tragical passage of American, of human events, which, if we did not stand in their every-day presence, we should shudder at as the presage of unexampled tyrannies.

"The Octopus." Review of Reviews (England), 24 (October 1901), 423–24.

This is a horrid story, horrid but clever. From the first page to the last it is one story of unadulterated horror, and although the villain is killed off in original fashion in the last chapter but one, the expiation is inadequate. "The Octopus" is, nevertheless, not without its uses. It may enable English readers to understand something of the mainspring of the populist and Bryanist movement in the United States, and as a social study it is worth examination; but any one who wishes to read a novel for the sake of enjoyment had better give "The Octopus" a wide berth. It is a horrible tragedy, a tragedy in which the economic forces reign supreme. If you can imagine Aeschylus sensationalised, and the Greek drama re-dressed as a modern novel, you can imagine something of the sombre note which is audible on every page of this most depressing book. "The Octopus" is the first of a trilogy of novels which, when complete, will form what the author calls "The Epic of the Wheat." "The Octopus," a story of California, where the wheat is grown, is to be followed by "The Pit," a story of Chicago, where the wheat is sold, and the series will conclude with "The Wolf," a story of Europe, where the wheat is consumed. When complete, the three novels will form the story of a crop of wheat from the time of its sowing as seed in California to the time of its consumption as bread in a village of Western Europe. As "The Wolf" will have as its central episode a famine in an old-world community, readers who determine to go conscientiously through Mr. Norris's trilogy will sup full of horrors, horrors unrelieved—if we may judge by the first volume—by a single gleam of light.

"The Octopus" is the name which Mr. Norris gives to the Railroad Trust, personified for the purpose of the story in the Pacific and South-Western Railroad of California, which serves the great wheat-growing district of San Joaquin.

The purpose of the story is to drive home into the mind of the reader the conviction that the farmers are absolutely helpless in the grasp of the railroad octopus. Again and again the moral is enforced that, in the words of one of the characters, it is no use to buck against the railroad. The railroad comes off victorious every time. I will not attempt to tell the story on which Mr. Norris has hung the various familiar incidents in the war which rages without ceasing between railroads and their customers in the Far West. Suffice it to say that we have all the familiar methods illustrated and described by which a railway, having got a district into its power, squeezes the life-blood out of the unfortunate farmers, and by resorting to every artifice of fraud, corruption, or force, stamps out opposition and reigns absolute despot over the country-side. Quite early in the book there is a description of an express engine dashing through a flock of sheep. The page is worth quoting, not only as illustrating Mr. Norris's style, but because it sounds the keynote of the whole book.

The railroad itself is personified by the monster locomotive, which rushes like a fiend from the nether pit across the idyllic beauty of the country-side. The hero and almost the only surviving person in this tragic drama was revelling in the benediction of the stars and the beauty of the dream-sleep of the earth, when suddenly there was an interruption. He had only time to jump back upon the embankment when:—

> A locomotive, single, unattached, shot by him with a roar, filling the air with the reek of hot oil, vomiting smoke as sparks; its enormous eye, cyclopean, red, throwing a glare far in advance, shooting by in a sudden crash of confused thunder; filling the night with the terrific clamour of its iron hoofs.

While the earth was still vibrating with the roar of the engine and the echoes of its frantic gallop upon her fair valley, the quivering glare of its fires lost itself in the night, and even the distant humming of its wheels was no longer heard—

> But the moment the noise of the engine lapsed, Presley—about to start forward again—was conscious of a confusion of lamentable sounds that rose into the night from out the engine's wake. Prolonged cries of agony, sobbing wails of infinite pain, heart-rendering, pitiful.

The noises came from a little distance. He ran down the track, crossing the culvert, over the irrigating ditch, and at the head of the long reach of track, between the culvert and the Long Trestle, paused abruptly, held immovable at the sight of the ground and rails all about him.

In some way the herd of sheep—Vanamee's herd—had found a breach in the wire fence by the right of way, and had wandered out upon the tracks. A band had been crossing just at the moment of the engine's passage. The pathos of it was beyond expression. It was a slaughter, a massacre of innocents. The iron monster had charged full into the midst, merciless, inexorable. To the right and left, all the width of the right of way, the little bodies had been flung; backs were snapped against the fence posts; brains knocked out. Caught in the barbs of the wire, wedged in, the bodies hung suspended. Under foot it was terrible. The black blood, winking in the starlight, seeped down into the clinkers between the ties with a prolonged sucking murmur.

Presley turned away, horror-struck, sick at heart, overwhelmed with a quick burst of irresistible compassion for this brute agony he could not relieve. The sweetness was gone from the evening; the sense of peace, of security, and placid contentment was stricken from the landscape. The hideous ruin in the engine's path drove all thought of his poem from his mind.

What happened to these unfortunate sheep happens to all the characters in this story. The railroad smashed over them all, and we are never allowed to escape from the image of that galloping monster, the terror of steel and steam, with its single eye of cyclopean red shooting from horizon to horizon; and we are taught to see in it the symbol of a vast power, huge and terrible, which leaves blood and destruction in its path,—the leviathan with tentacles of steel clutching into the soul, the soulless force, the iron-hearted power, the monster of the Colossus, the Octopus.

Mr. Norris has not studied for nothing in the school of Zola, and his style often smacks of the straining rhetoric of Victor Hugo. However painful the story may be, the mere pain which it produces is a testimony to its extraordinary power. It is a hideous nightmare which he compels us to realise. Even the Wheat itself, which he personifies almost as much as the Railroad, seems to come under a kind of curse, while as for the railroad, it looms before us as an absolute devil, a mechanical fiend, more terrible than any of the loathly worms which figure in mediaeval romances, who spread their long length across the country-side, and battened upon the unfortunate peasants in the midst of whom they had made their lair. It is never pleasant to be made to realise hell, but Mr. Norris, in this book, has burnt a little bit of it into the memory and imagination of men.

William L. Alden. "London Letter." *New York Times*, October 5, 1901, p. 722, "Saturday Review of Books and Art."

London, Sept. 15.—Mr. Frank Norris's book, "The Octopus," has made a true literary sensation here. I have not yet seen a single review that did not praise it warmly. Fault is found with it in certain respects, but the real greatness of the book is gladly acknowledged.

It has been suggested that Mr. Norris would never have written "The Octopus" if Zola had not previously written his wonderful novels. Probably this is true. The conception of the world as governed by the forces of nature and industry which lies at the basis of "The Octopus" is essential to the conception which runs through Zola's work. The wide scope of Mr. Norris's "epic of wheat" is Zolaesque, and Mr. Norris has undoubtedly copied some of the mannerisms of Zola, and caught something of his style. We may frankly admit all this, for it is nothing to Mr. Norris's discredit. It is the rarest of all events that a newly created book is written. One book begets another. One author dates his ancestry back to some other author. Nine-tenths of all the books that have been written during the last century would not have been written had not other and earlier books appeared.

* * *

It is one thing to imitate an author, and quite another to derive inspiration from him. Mr. Norris has not imitated

Zola except in certain trivial matters. He follows the methods of Zola, just as nearly all historical novelists follow the methods of Scott. He is moved to write the "epic of the wheat" by the spirit of Zola breathed upon him through the books of the great Frenchman, but "The Octopus" is none the less great because it is begotten by "La Terre" and "Germinal." It would not have been written had Mr. Norris never read Zola, but it would have been a great pity if he had read instead the writing of some smaller man, and gained a milder and less desirable inspiration.

* * *

The resemblance between Mr. Norris and Zola interests me, partly because I have a very great admiration for Zola, and partly because the matter of conscious or unconscious plagiarism has for many years been an especial study of mine. It is so easy to accuse an author of borrowing from another, and the accusation is so fatal, that it ought never to be lightly made. Mr. Norris is certain to be accused openly of having imitated Zola, and it is well that the distinction between imitation and legitimate descent should be emphasized. Mr. Norris is of the family of Zola. That is all that need be said about the relationship between the two. If any one, in order to defend Mr. Norris, pleads that he has in no way followed Zola, the defense would be a mistake that in the end would injure rather than benefit Mr. Norris.

"The Octopus."
The Athenaeum, October 5, 1901, pp. 447–48.

"McTeague" and "Blix" are novels which have given Mr. Norris some standing in England; but, creditable as these were, they by no means prepared one for so important a piece of work as "The Octopus," which is launched as the first volume in a grandiloquently named "Trilogy of the Epic of the Wheat": "The Octopus, a Story of California"; "The Pit, a Story of Chicago"; and "The Wolf, a Story of Europe." European critics may be pardoned a smile over the nomenclature: "The Epic of the Wheat," "A Story of Europe"! A smile is justifiable, but let it for catholicity's sake be good-humoured, courteous, and a genuine smile, rather than a masked sneer. "The Octopus" is not a fully formed work; it has not lain quite long enough in the mental womb of its inception. Thus the critic, if he cared to dwell upon such things, could point out instances of over-fluency, the tautology which springs from uncooled enthusiasm, lack of restraint, and a verbosity which has robbed certain passages of the dignity belonging of right to the situations they describe. The girl Angele Varian, for instance, is hardly once mentioned in these pages (and mention of her is not infrequent) without the phrase, "Her wide forehead made three-cornered by her plaits of gold hair." Regarding a statement upon p. 126, one would like to ask Mr. Norris whether over in America it is really possible that a horse can be shod in five minutes. "The leviathan with tentacles of steel clutching into the soil, the soulless Force, the iron-hearted Power, the Monster, the Colossus, the Octopus." The author may safely leave such laboured piling of effect to weaker men, whose work, lacking the body of his, demands more of stucco and paint. We note a tendency towards the flamboyant which Mr. Norris will have time to get well in hand and under control before setting about the completion of his trilogy. In this and similar matters his work will derive great benefit from a strong and consistent use of the curb. The fifth chapter of "The Octopus" is a long and strong chapter of fifty pages. It was a most unfortunate blunder to weaken and encumber it by closing upon two rushing pages of *résumé* of all that had gone before. All these blemishes are on the generous, opulent side, and have their root in the fact that the author is too close to the idea which possessed him. The critic points them out, but only with such kindly meant deprecation as that with which his comrades charge a gallant soldier with recklessness, and in the confident hope that the remaining two volumes in the wheat trilogy may be relieved of the handicap they involve.

"The Octopus" is a powerfully visualized picture of the evil wrought by great monopolies or "trusts." In this case the monopoly is a railway, its prey the wheat-growers and other producers in California. A list of the twenty-seven principal characters and a map of the district dealt with in the story form a serviceable frontispiece. The reviewer can recall no line of sentimentality in the book. Its handling of plain, elemental male characters, such as Magnus Derrick and Annixter (the best realized figure this), is consistent, strong, and altogether creditable. If it be true that it is not wisely described as an epic, it is equally true that it is a powerful and tragic piece of fiction.

"The Octopus: A Story of California."
The Spectator, 80 (October 5, 1901), 486.

For those who must have sensation *The Octopus* will do better, and *The Octopus* is really an exceedingly interesting book. Not, as the title suggests, a tale of adventure by sea, but a study of the conflict between the old civilisation of the ranch and the new enterprise of the railway contractor in the heart of California. Mr. Norris writes stirringly, and his pages are full of moving incident and vivid description. He has passion and pathos, and if his touch is sometimes a little too hot and heavy, it must be recognised that, on the other hand, he is never dull. A short preface explains that this volume is the first of three books, each complete in itself, which are to give us together the "Trilogy of the Epic of the Wheat."

Talcott Williams. "Fiction Read and Written in 1901." *Review of Reviews* (America), 24 (November 1901), 589–91.

If sheer power carried to great popularity, Mr. Frank Norris would be leading all the rest in "The Octopus." Mr. Norris is still young. He gripped attention with "McTeague." "The Octopus" is born of his Western work as a journalist. The late C. P. Huntington is in it, and Mr. Edwin Markham's familiar poem suggests an incident. The Southern Pacific and the wheat-grower wrestle in it for the mastery. The book has that crowded sense of elemental forces Zola gives. It spares nothing; it asks much. Coincidence is carried to catastrophe. But the mere story does not attract, and for all its force has aspects of the pamphlet, and the public, which avoids argument with its novels, after months has not found this book out. It is, after all, but one of a group on the topics bred by social issues. Miss Mary E. Wilkins has put the grind of New England factory life into "The Portion of Labor," with slow, minute, photographic detail. A subdiscussion of the social question has been interwoven by Mrs. Helen Campbell in her international novel "Ballantyne." Municipal aspects of the struggle with street railroads appear in "The Autocrats," by Mr. Charles K. Lush. Mr. F. A. Adams has written, quite seriously, a wild extravaganza in "Kidnapped Millionaires." "The Warners," by Gertrude Potter Daniels, attempts the Chicago aspect of trusts.

These are sufficiently immediate, but this is the growing note of our fiction. The mere novel of social incident has almost ceased.

"Literature." *Illustrated London News*, 119 (November 2, 1901), 660.

Mr. Frank Norris has given us in "The Octopus" what he calls "the epic of the wheat." His book has many merits and some defects, among which excessive length is not the least. But when we remember that Mr. Norris is the creator of "Blix," and that he is absolute master of the love idyll, we are inclined to think it a pity that he should fritter away his time in producing Zola-esque realism of an inferior quality. About wheat and wheat-growing Mr. Norris obviously knows a great deal, and he handles the inner poetic aspect of his theme with real power. About the Railway Trust—against the tyranny of which his book is one long protest—we are content to believe that he is well informed, and in his righteous campaign we wish him well; but of love, one might say, Mr. Norris knows practically everything, and the story of Annixter and Hilma Tree redeems and distinguishes "The Octopus." When we first meet with Annixter he is a hard-headed, self-seeking, but capable young man, who looks upon the fair sex as "fool, feemale women"—not, perhaps, very promising material out of which to create a hero. And yet, as the story develops, we mark step by step the process of transformation; see the love which consumes him—gross at first almost to brutality—burn ever more clearly, until at last all that is base disappears. So great is Mr. Norris's power in this direction, so delicate and just is his perception, that we cannot at this moment recall the name of any other writer who has these qualities in a like degree. Why, then, should Mr. Norris waste himself upon side issues?

"Literature: Books of the Year."
The Independent, 53 (November 21, 1901), 2778.

But perhaps the most magnificent literary shortcoming of the year is Mr. Frank Norris's Epic of the Wheat, *The Octopus*. There are characters in the book which call to mind the ancient Greek tragedies. But the author does not understand the restraint of that noble art. He is bent upon death and destruction; and if, as he declares, this volume is the first of a trilogy on Wheat, little will be left in the world to hope for by the time the last one appears.

Frederic Taber Cooper. "Literature, American and English."
The International Year Book: 1901 (New York: Dodd, Mead & Co., 1902), pp. 449, 452–53.

While a survey of the fiction of 1901 shows that the general tendencies are substantially the same as in the years immediately preceding, the resulting impression as a whole is distinctly encouraging, and the exceptional quality of just a few unique volumes stamps the past season as a notable one. In this country the remarkable vogue of the colonial novel, which began two seasons ago with *Richard Carvel* and *Janice Meredith*, has continued unabated, notwithstanding frequent prophecies to the contrary; while the substantial reward which awaits a successful story of this type has proved an irresistible temptation to more than one well-known novelist, who, like Miss Wilkins and Miss Jewett, had hitherto been identified with novels of a very different quality. A work of far more significance and interest is being accomplished by a group of earnest writers, mostly of the younger generation, in the novel of contemporary life. This group includes men of such different methods and ideals as Will Payne, Robert Herrick, and Frank Norris, all striving in their several ways to depict certain vital phases of typically American life and character. ... The most serious attempts in fiction of the past year, understanding fiction in the sense of an interpretation and criticism of contemporary life, have been made by [virtual] newcomers in literature. Unlike that earlier group of writers, Miss Wilkins and Miss Jewett, George W. Cable, Charles Egbert Craddock and Octave Thanet, each of whom stood definitely and unmistakably for a narrow section of American life, laying on their local color with the minuteness of a miniature painter, these newcomers in fiction strive frankly for scenes and characters which will typify American life as a whole. Consequently, they are compelled to work in bolder, broader lines, in a more impressionistic style, and it is not surprising that the results are at times somewhat crude. It is interesting to find that a majority of this group go to the west, from Chicago all the way to the Pacific slope, for types and scenes which they consider representatively American. The biggest and boldest effort of the year, even if in some ways it was a mistake, was Frank Norris's *Octopus*. Two years earlier, the publication of *McTeague* had stamped Mr. Norris as a realistic writer of considerable promise, an avowed disciple of Zola, whose use of some central, symbolic idea in each novel, he imitated frankly and effectively. *The Octopus* is a far more ambitious and comprehensive effort. It forms the first part of a trilogy, *The Epic of the Wheat,* in which the author planned to symbolize American life as a whole, its resources, its aspirations, its destiny. This first volume deals with the wheat in the grain, its luxurious growth in the wide, fertile stretches of the San Joaquin Valley; the prolonged struggle of the farmers against the aggression of the local railroad, which typifies the eternal struggle between capital and labor, and by loans and foreclosures and unjust freight-rates, little by little gets the farmers into its power, until its very rails seem to their excited imagination like vast tentacles stretching out octopus-like to seize and swallow up the land. But while the individual succumbs, the wheat remains, emblem of American prosperity, rising and augmenting and gathering strength to roll eastward like a vast golden wave, across the continent and across the ocean, to bring health and wealth and strength to other nations. This in brief seems to be the basic idea in Mr. Norris's new symbolic novel, and thus stated it contains a certain degree of impressiveness. The difficulty lies in the execution; since it is very difficult to develop effectively these big central ideas without at the same time sacrificing the human interest of the individual characters; and it is just here that some critics have found Mr. Norris's book disappointing. Two volumes which bear a striking resemblance in their inception, central characters and development of plot up to a certain point are Will Payne's *Story of Eva,* and Theodore Dreiser's *Sister Carrie.* . . .

" 'The Octopus: A Story of California.' " *Saturday Review* (England), 93 (March 8, 1902), 304.

Mr. Norris' main theme is of a Frankenstein description. The railroad built over a limitless wheat-growing area, octopus-like, crushes men to death. Whilst he awakens the most active of our sympathies on behalf of the broken hearts and blighted homes of the victims of the railroad and its agents, he leaves an impression of the inevitability of the series of tragedies which he describes. Mr. Norris' style lacks reserve; his words, especially the adjectives, rage with cyclonic fury. How much of this is redolent of the Californian soil and how much it mars or heightens the effect of the narrative the individual reader will determine for himself in accordance with his knowledge of the life around which the book is written.

Henry W. Boynton. "Literature and Fiction." *Atlantic Monthly*, 89 (May 1902), 708–9.

Mr. Norris's latest story is a more pretentious sort of work. It boasts a good deal of preliminary apparatus—a note explaining that this is the first of a trilogy, duly billed as The Epic of the Wheat, a list of personae, and a map of the region in which the action takes place. Photographs of a California wheat-field and a patent reaper and a tintype or two of the leading persons would have left still less for the imagination to do. But the author is a confessed realist, and his style, as well as his method, bears the Gallic hall-mark: "His smooth-shaven jowl stood out big and tremulous on either side of his face; the roll of fat on the nape of his neck, sprinkled with sparse, stiff hairs, bulged out with greater prominence. His great stomach, covered with a light brown linen vest, stamped with innumerable interlocked horseshoes, protruded far in advance, enormous, aggressive." This Mr. S. Behrman is eventually, in accordance with that poetic justice which even the realist cannot always resist, smothered to death in the hold of a wheat steamer. By that time the reader has learned so much about S. Behrman's person that (and this time the poetic justice reacts, perhaps, against the story-teller) he is more pleased to be personally rid of an obnoxious animal than to have that story-world rid of the villain whose machinations have caused most of its troubles.

Hilma Tree we first know as a physically attractive animal, subtly colored after the manner of D'Annunzio's creatures: "Under her chin and under her ears the flesh was as white and smooth as floss satin, shading delicately to a faint delicate brown on her nape at the roots of her hair. Her throat rounded to meet her chin and cheek, with a soft swell of the skin, tinted pale amber in the shadows, but blending by barely perceptible gradations to the sweet warm flush of her cheek. The color on her temples was just touched with a certain blueness where the flesh was thin over the fine veining underneath. Her eyes were light brown . . . the lids—just a fraction of a shade darker than the hue of her face—were edged with lashes that were almost black." So much for the lust of the eye; presently we find the mystic Vanamee, many years after the death of his betrothed, recalling her in terms of another sense. He dwells habitually upon that "faint mingling of many odors, the smell of the roses that lingered in her hair, of the lilies that exhaled from her neck, of the heliotrope that disengaged itself from her hands and arms, and of the hyacinths of which her little feet were redolent." This is the sort of romantic vulgarity of which only the realist of the French school is capable. The world has pretty much stopped demanding that the Great American Novel shall be cast in an altogether new mould, but may still require it to be free from the method and manner of distinctly alien literatures. There are certain racial prescriptions of taste and style which cannot be safely ignored. Whatever is true of his manner, Mr. Norris's persons are certainly indigenous, and give the book its power. Presley and Vanamee one might have met elsewhere, but the Derricks, Annixter, and, above all, Hilma Tree,—what is the value to creative fiction of world-movements and commercial problems compared with such breathing human nature as this?

B. O. Flower. "The Trust in Fiction: A Remarkable Social Novel." *The Arena*, 27 (May 1902), 547-54.

In "The Octopus," Mr. Norris has produced a novel of American life exhibiting the strength, power, vividness, fidelity to truth, photographic accuracy in description, and marvelous insight in depicting human nature, together with that broad and philosophic grasp of the larger problems of life, that noble passion for justice, that characterize the greatest work of Emile Zola, without that sexualism or repulsive naturalism which the French writer so frequently forces upon his readers, and which is so revolting to the refined and healthy imagination.

"The Octopus" is a work so distinctly great that it justly entitles the author to rank among the very first American novelists. All the characters are real, living men and women, in whose veins runs the red blood of Nature. With one exception, each individual thinks, speaks, acts, and lives in harmony with the nature attributed to him. A noble consistency pervades the volume. Even individual inconsistencies are such as we all find in our own lives. The exception referred to is found in the pitiful sophistry accredited to the great railway magnate, Shelgrim, in which he seeks to shift from his head and the heads of the responsible directors, to the insensate railroad, the blame for the frightful and widespread ruin—the wanton slaughter of brave, loving, and industrious fathers, brothers, and husbands, the destruction of once happy homes, the driving of men to crime and of women and girls to starvation and ruin—that was the direct result of calculating and premeditated deception and gross injustice, rendered possible only by bribery and wholesale corruption. When Shelgrim refers to the despoiling of the farmers of their homes, and to the death and ruin that had marked the recent tragedy, as due to the insensate railroad or to blind forces, and not to corrupt individuals, when he compares the railroad with the growing wheat, which unconsciously supplies the world with life-giving bread but is without responsibility for its beneficence, he not only insults the intelligence of the poet, but belittles himself in a way quite inconceivable by the utterance of such palpable sophistry. Nor is it imaginable that Presley, even though sick, distraught, and on the verge of nervous collapse, would for a moment have been impressed by such shallow twaddle and false similes. No; Shelgrim was no man to father such pitiful and absurdly fallacious reasoning before a free and intelligent man, though he doubtless did inspire precisely such utterances from the editors of his hireling press and the advocates paid by the railroad to retail such inane talk to voters too sodden and brutalized by long hours and hard toil to be able to see clearly or reason logically.

With this single exception the *dramatis personae* of the volume think, speak, act, and live in exactly the way you and I, given similar characters, temperaments, and environment, would have thought and acted.

But "The Octopus" is far more than a

strong, compelling, and virile story of American life: it is one of the most powerful and faithful social studies to be found in contemporaneous literature. It is a work that will not only stimulate thought: it will quicken the conscience and awaken the moral sensibilities of the reader, exerting much the same influence over the mind as that exerted by Patrick Henry in the House of Burgesses of Virginia, and by those noble utterances of James Otis, Samuel Adams, and John Hancock just prior to our great Revolutionary struggle.

"The Octopus" is founded on a piece of actual history, stern, tragic, and ominous—the "Mussel Slough Affair"—in which the farmers of the San Joaquin Valley were dispossessed by the railroad company, and in their attempt to protect their roof-trees several persons were cruelly murdered. Though, perhaps, in some respects the author cannot be said to have painted the action of the railroad company as darkly as the cold facts of history would warrant, he has on the whole shadowed forth the central facts in a striking manner; while his marvelous descriptive power enables him to bring the case before the reader in so vivid a way that the scenes will long linger—gloomy and disquieting pictures—in memory's halls.

The dark deeds connected with Mussel Slough are typical of many tragic passages that have marked the rise, onward march, and domination of corporate greed—as, indeed, the story is thoroughly typical of the mighty struggle between the people and the trusts.

The tragedy of Spring Valley, Illinois, so vividly related by Mr. Henry Demarest Lloyd in his "A Strike of Millionaires against Miners," and the dark and criminal history of the Standard Oil Company, as described by Mr. Lloyd in his "Wealth *vs.* Commonwealth," are other typical illustrations that will suggest themselves to thoughtful readers as expressing the same savage, brutal, unjust, lawless, and demoralizing spirit that has marked the aggressive march of corporations, monopolies, and trusts.

It remained for Mr. Norris, however, to present in a bold, striking, and powerful romance a concrete illustration, true in spirit, method and detail, of the conflict that has been waged between the trusts and the people.

II

The novel opens in the great San Joaquin Valley, one of the world's mighty wheat-fields, where ranches are like principalities, where not a single blade is seen turning the soil, but battalions of plows moving forward with military precision, simultaneously turning hundreds of furrows. Here it is that the standing wheat is cut, threshed, and sacked by a single great machine. Here it is that farming is carried forward on as colossal a scale as is to be found on the face of the globe.

And into this valley, lured by seductive railroad pamphlets, many men of wealth have come to call from the brown earth her golden harvest, even as some of them had previously called forth gold and silver from the fastnesses of the Sierras.

The circulars of the railroad company had been framed, as later events proved, cruelly to deceive the settlers. They read:

> The Company invites settlers to go upon its land before patents are issued or the road is completed, and intends in such cases to sell to them in preference to any other

applicants and at a price based upon the value of the land without improvements. In ascertaining the value of the lands, any improvements that a settler or any other person may have made on the lands will not be taken into consideration; neither will the price be increased in consequence thereof.... Settlers are thus insured that in addition to being accorded the first privilege of purchase, at the graded price, they will also be protected in their improvements.... The lands are not uniform in price, but are offered at various figures from $2.50 upward per acre. Usually land covered with tall timber is held at $5.00 per acre, and that with pine at $10.00. Most is for sale at $2.50 and $5.00.

The fact that the land mentioned as being above $2.50 an acre was the timbered land, which was usually held to be worth $5 an acre, while that covered by valuable pine trees was $10 an acre, appeared fair and reasonable. Such land was valuable from the very start, while the wide sterile plains of the valley were worthless until improved, cultivated, and in many cases irrigated; and the pledge that improvements should not be considered when the price of land was given seemed to deceive the honest farmers. The railroad had not yet received the title to the land. When it did the settlers should have the opportunity to buy on the favorable terms.

With this promise Magnus Derrick, the most commanding figure among the ranchers, popularly known as "the Governor" throughout the valley, and his favorite son, Harran, had taken up a vast tract containing tens of thousands of acres and known as the Los Muertos Rancho. Annixter, a college graduate who had come into a fortune, had secured the Quien Sabe Rancho, while Osterman, another young man of means, had secured another immensely fertile property. Old man Broderson and other farmers had come into the valley, bringing their all, staking everything on these new homes. Buildings rapidly rose, as extensive as the means of the ranchers would enable them to erect. Drains and irrigating ditches were made that cost fortunes to dig; and the desert was transformed as by magic into fields of gold that later fed the world.

From the first the railroad had proved to be an "organized appetite." It had carried out the policy of charging in freight tariff "all the traffic would bear." A State Commission had been elected, which it had been believed would be loyal to the people; but here, as everywhere else, were the evidences of the corrupting touch of the railroad corporation. The Commission had made a rate so absurdly low that no road could carry the freight except at a loss. The road refused to abide by the schedule, claiming that it amounted to confiscation. The courts upheld the railroad and ruled that, as they had no power to make rates, the only thing to be done was to put the rates back to the old exorbitant figure.

In the opening chapters we find the leading ranchmen assembled at the home of Magnus Derrick in consultation. Many things had recently occurred to exasperate the farmers. That very day Magnus and Harran Derrick had discovered their car-load of new plows, ordered months before, side-tracked at Bonneville. They had just arrived in time for work, as the autumn rains had set in; but while making the arrangements to have them taken to Los Muertos, S. Behrman, the representative of the railroad, appeared, reminding the farmer that it was a rule of the railroad that all freight had to go to the terminal point and then be shipped back to its destination. This rule was to give the railroad the advantage of the exorbitant short-haul rates; and therefore, though the plows were badly needed, though they were sidetracked at their destination, they could not be touched until they were taken to San Francisco and re-shipped back to Bonneville. And this incident was only one of a number of occurrences in which the greed and unjust aggressions of the railroad were exasperating the farmers. The action of the Commission and the judgment in regard to rates of the wheat tariff satisfied the ranchers that the company's corrupting influence was being exerted in every department of the State government; and some one suggested that they fight the devil with fire—that, as they had exhausted every honorable and legitimate means of warfare, they should now meet the railroad on its own field and secure a commission of their own through bribery.

Magnus Derrick repels with indignation this proposition, but the others urge that no other hope remains to the farmers but to secure the nomination of two commissioners who can be relied upon as being loyal to their interests. A certain Mr. Darrell, in the southern part of the State, they believe to be such a man, and for the other they settle upon Magnus Derrick's elder son, Lyman, now a rising lawyer in San Francisco. Young Derrick, unfortunately for the Farmers' League, has political ambitions. He aspires to be Governor, and two years before received assurances of favor from the great railroad company, provided he would be loyal to them. This, of course, was not known to the League. Finally the election came off, and the ranchers' board was triumphantly elected.

In the meantime rumors are circulated that the road is at last ready to grade the land. The farmers have been impatient to get the title to their land, and at first hail the news with satisfaction. They have taken the land, which would have been a drug at $2.50 an acre, but, by draining, irrigating, planting with trees, and improving by the erection of fine buildings, they have raised its value to fully $15 an acre. Soon the rumors of the regrading of the land are coupled with the intimation that the railroad company, in violation of its pledge, proposes to charge the settlers a price quite equal to the worth of the land with all its improvements.

The dramatic first act of the story closes with a ball at the new barn of Annixter, where all the country is well-nigh present. It is a highly sensational and thrilling time, culminating with telegrams being handed to the ranchers by which they are informed that the company demands from $20 to $27 an acre for their holdings—a price that will mean worse than ruin to them.

From this time on the movement is swift and the action frequently highly dramatic. The raising of Annixter from the plane of self-absorption and low ideals to that of exalted manhood, under the reforming influence of a noble woman's love; the ruin of Dyke through the road's advancing the rate on hops, and the tragic aftermath; the work of the new railroad commission; the visit of Lyman and the tremendously dramatic scene in the home of Magnus Derrick, in which the betrayer of the people is denounced and disowned by Magnus—all are vividly described. Then comes the great rabbit chase and picnic gotten up by Osterman, followed immediately by the supreme tragedy, when the officers, at the instigation of the railroad, begin evicting the farmers from their homes, while the latter resist to the bloody end.

Then the scene is shifted to San Francisco, and we catch a glimpse of Shelgrim and are present at a banquet given by one of the millionaire directors of the railroad, where the costliest of imported wines and viands of the rarest are served; while without poor old Mrs. Hooven, widowed by the railroad, and her little daughter, starving and sick, are begging for a crust of bread.

After a last glance over the San Joaquin Valley we find ourselves on the steamer that is loading with wheat for famine-stricken India; and here we come face to face with one of the strongest situations in modern fiction. The highly dramatic death of S. Behrman, weird, uncanny, and terrible, is as great a piece of work as Victor Hugo's vivid description of Gilliatt's struggle with the octopus, in his "Toilers of the Sea." S. Behrman, the smooth-tongued, remorseless, relentless man, who is at once the type of the soulless and cruel railroad corporation and its efficient tool, rising to opulence through the wheat that he has plundered from honest industry, is at last swallowed up, crushed, suffocated, destroyed by that same wheat.

III

"The Octopus" is a work of genius. Not only is it a powerful romance of compelling interest—thrilling, dramatic, and so graphic that its various shifting scenes stand out clear-cut and unforgettable, but as a social study it possesses a historical value equaled by few works of fiction. It is, broadly speaking, typically historical not only of the great railroad corporation, whose story is so well known on the Pacific Coast, but of the railroad corporations of the United States, and of the trusts in general.

It is part of the settled policy of the complacent tools and servants of corporate power to seek to discredit all such pictures, even though they know full well that for more than a quarter of a century the baleful influence of corporate greed has been felt throughout the length and breadth of the land, not only in the levying of unjust tributes on the poor but in the debauching and corruption of government in all its ramifications. "The Octopus" shows in a vivid manner how this supreme tragedy—this lowering of the political ideals from the fundamental demands of justice, honesty, and freedom to subserviency to capitalistic aggression—has been accomplished in the United States. It is very easy for apologists and beneficiaries of corporate corruption to seek to discredit such pictures as "fiction." The facts on which this novel is based, however, were a terrible reality; and the methods by which the great railroad power became well-nigh omnipotent on the Pacific Coast have been indicated by the publication of letters of C. P. Huntington to General Colton. These communications, it will be remembered, were made public in the famous suit brought in Santa Rosa, California, to decide whether the widow of General Colton had been fairly dealt with by the railroad company, in whose confidential service the General had long been engaged. In these letters we have a startling revelation of how the railroad magnates tampered with officials, how they made and unmade committees, how they worked in Congress through the press, how neither Governors, Congressmen, statesmen, members of the Cabinet and judges, the Associated Press, nor the editors of the country escaped the argus eyes of the railroad officials.

The bribery by the wholesale issuance of railroad passes and the enormous sums of money needed to "fix things" or "convince" legislators—these and other things are more or less baldly set forth in these memorable letters, in which Thomas Scott and C. P. Huntington figure as warring chiefs.

And when we turn from the Pacific slope the same facts meet the eye everywhere. The amazing admissions of Jay Gould before the investigating committee of the New York Legislature in 1873 startled the nation for a brief period, and the report of this committee was a sickening revelation of gigantic corruption. The exorbitant prices paid by our own all too complacent Post Office Department for the rental of cars and the hauling of mails have been for years a national scandal. It was this shameful plundering of the people for the railroads, permitted by the Post Office Department, that called for the following impressive words in the halls of the United States Senate from one of the Eastern Senators:

> "The fact is, Mr. President, that the great power of these corporations who control everything, who are powerful enough to make and unmake public men, is so omnipotent that no executive officer has been found in the last twelve years, except in the single case of Postmaster-General Vilas, who has attempted to reduce the compensation for mail transportation; and within six months after he had left the Department every economy that he introduced had been wiped away, and the companies received not only what they had received before but their compensation was increased. Never, during my long service in this body, except in this one instance, have I known of a Postmaster-General making a *bona fide* effort to control this railroad extortion, which every one knows to exist."

The recent exhibition of the subserviency of the machinery of justice in New York City to the New York Central Railroad is another striking illustration of the facts that Mr. Norris so eloquently emphasizes in his novel.

But it must not be imagined that "The Octopus" is primarily a social study. It is above all a great literary creation. The author is at all times the artist. Only on rare occasions, like the following for example, do the characters moralize. Here, however, we have the great California manufacturer, Cedarquist, thus referring to the supreme peril of the Republic:

> "If I were to name the one crying evil of American life, . . . it would be the indifference of the better people to public affairs. It is so in all our great centers. There are other great trusts, God knows, in the United States, besides our own dear P. and S. W. Railroad. Every State has its own grievance. If it is not a railroad trust, it is a sugar trust, or an oil trust, or an industrial trust, that exploits the People, *because the People allow it*. The indifference of the People is the opportunity of the despot. It is as true as that the whole is greater than a part, and the maxim is so old that it is trite—it is laughable. It is neglected and disused for the sake

of some new ingenious and complicated theory, some wonderful scheme of reorganization, but the fact remains, nevertheless, simple, fundamental, everlasting. The People have but to say 'No,' and not the strongest tyranny, political, religious, or financial, that was ever organized could survive one week."

Mr. Norris unfolds a mighty drama, which concerns our own time. He paints colossal pictures so vividly that there is small need for didactic moralizing about them. One feels from the first that he is in the presence of a great artist, a man of real genius; and though there is more of shadow than of sunshine in the highly dramatic romance there are many passages of great beauty. The descriptions of Nature and her marvelous works, the portraying of Vanamee, and the wonderful transformation of Annixter are typical examples of the beauty and poetry that abound in this volume.

"The Octopus" is a novel that every reader of *The Arena* should possess. If it is impossible for you to procure more than one work of fiction this season, my advice—my unhesitating advice—is to buy "The Octopus," read it aloud to your family, and then lend it to your neighbors. In so doing you will be helping to awaken the people from the death-dealing slumber that has been brought about by the multitudinous influences of corporate greed, controlling the machinery of government and the opinion-forming agencies of the Republic.

A. L. Muzzey. "Book Notices." *The Public*, 5 (May 3, 1902), 64.

"The Epic of the Wheat" is to include "The Octopus," the subject of our present notice, and later "The Pit, A Story of Chicago," and "The Wolf, A Story of Europe." If this "Trilogy," when completed, sustains the power of the first volume, it will place our American author in the front rank with writers of the great novels which have touched the deepest problems of human life. "The Octopus," dealing with the war between the wheat grower and the railroad trust in California, is one of the strongest works of fiction recently published, although it appears not to have attracted as wide attention from reviewers as its literary style deserves—the fearless arraignment of the great railroad powers possibly laying some restraint on writers for the conservative press. The author of "The Epic of the Wheat" is a poet in the conception of his plan and in his vivid coloring of the scenes presented with photographic clearness to the eye of the reader. His delineations of character are equally vivid and strong, and the dramatic action of the story brings out the individual qualities of each with a distinctness of detail that makes us witnesses of living personalities enacting real scenes. That the wrongs and injustices described are literal facts in all their details would doubtless be denied by the powers inflicting them; but there is no question about the author's own point of view, and his convictions are expressed with a burning earnestness that communicates to the sympathetic reader the fire of a moral purpose to lend a hand in the conflict with evil. The temptation and after suffering of the noble Magnus Derrick, the wrongs of Dyke and Annixter and Hilma touch us as if they were personal friends, and we feel our hearts throb with the grief and indignation that moved Presley to his passionate speech to the league after the tragedy. We even shudder before the Nemesis of poetic judgment in the fate of S. Behrman, who, gloating over the wheat as it rolled in a cataract from the elevator into the great hold of the transporting ship, accidentally loses his poise and plunges through the hatch and down the iron chute to the vast cavern where in slow agony he is at length overwhelmed by the rich flood for whose treasure he had bartered his soul. He had borne a charmed life against the wrath of the wronged, only to find at last the exact measure of justice. But as Vanamee says, with the wisdom learned in silence:

> "The good never dies. The evil dies. Cruelty, oppression, selfishness, greed, these die; but nobility, but love, but sacrifice, but generosity, but truth, thank God for it, small as they are, difficult as they are, difficult as it is to discover them—these live forever—these are eternal.... What is it that remains when all is over? Look at it all from the vast heights of humanity—'the greatest good to the greatest number.' What remains? Men perish, men are corrupted, hearts are rent asunder, but what remains untouched, unassailable, undefiled? Try to find that, not only in this but in every crisis of the world's life, and you will find, if your view be large enough, that it is not evil, but good that in the end remains."

" 'The Octopus' by Frank Norris." *Sunday Call*, November 9, 1902, p. 1, magazine section.*

The recent sad and sudden death of Mr. Frank Norris marks the loss to the English speaking world of one of the greatest writers of the day. As an author he was just in his prime. His last novel, "The Octopus," published last year, has been recognized both here and abroad as the closest approximation to the great American novel of anything that has ever appeared from the pen of any writer.

As a Californian Mr. Norris made a name that brings the greatest credit to his State; and as the author of "The Octopus," Mr. Norris wrote the strongest book on California ever published.

This novel, under the author's primal idea—so disastrously interrupted by his death—was intended to be the first in a series of three books devoted to that greatest of all world forces, wheat. This story concerns itself with the growing of the wheat. It was Mr. Norris' idea to have the second book a novel with Chicago as a center and the motif of the book was the handling of wheat by the brokers in the pit; while the third book of the trilogy should tell of the final distribution of wheat in Europe.

Fortunately "The Octopus" is com-

*This is an introduction to a serialization of *The Octopus*.

plete in itself, and as a matter of fact would naturally be the most interesting of the trilogy for us of California; for Mr. Norris chose as the scene for this book the most immense wheat fields known the world over—our own plains of the San Joaquin Valley. The story concerns itself with the life of the farmers of the great plains and their struggles not only with soil and against the mishaps of weather, but also against the ravenous sharks of the business world who hover around to tear away the profits from the tiller of the land.

As a novel this is the nearest approach to the great American novel so long sought for by critics and public. As a story, it will keep you sitting up nights until you have finished it. The character studies in this book are peculiarly Californian, and particularly accurate and convincing.

Immediately upon the death of Mr. Norris, realizing the great interest that would naturally be awakened in his last novel, "The Octopus,"—a masterpiece of fiction—The Sunday Call forthwith made arrangements at great expense with Mr. Norris' publishers for the exclusive rights of "The Octopus" for the Pacific Coast.

Therefore the publication of "The Leopard's Spots" has been temporarily postponed and now "The Octopus" will be published in as large installments as is compatible with the importance of the other many and varied features of The Sunday Call Magazine Section.

"The Octopus" will be followed by "The Gospel of Judas Iscariot," by Aaron Dwight Baldwin, which has created a tremendous furor in both Europe and America. It throws a new light on the strange life, the character and motives of this, the most bitterly execrated man in either the biblical or profane history of all ages.

It shows the splendors, the vices and follies, the wars and the feasts, and the sports and pleasures of Rome as they have never been shown before, and tells of the coming of Christ and his long and glorious struggle to establish his kingdom of heaven on earth, and the remarkable part Judas played in his crucifixion.

Then will come "The Leopard's Spots," by Thomas Dixon Jr.; "When Knighthood Was in Flower," by Charles Major; "The Gentleman From Indiana," by Booth Tarkington; "Tainted Gold," by Mrs. C. N. Williamson, whose "Mystery Box," published a few weeks ago in The Sunday Call, was one of the best stories in this remarkable series; "The Turnpike House," by Fergus Hume, etc., etc.

Just ponder over that list of books, as well as the names of the writers, and remember you get all those stories free with The Sunday Call. Other announcements will be made later.

The Epic of the Wheat

THE PIT

A STORY OF CHICAGO

BY

FRANK NORRIS

NEW YORK
DOUBLEDAY, PAGE & CO.
1903

The Pit

Frederic Taber Cooper. "Frank Norris." *Bookman* (America), 16 (December 1902), 334–35.

It is a sad coincidence that Zola's death should have been followed so soon by that of his most earnest disciple in this country, Mr. Frank Norris. When he left New York recently, after revising the last proofs of his forthcoming novel, *The Pit*, Mr. Norris intended to start with his wife on a journey around the world, sailing from California in one of the many tramp steamers that carry wheat to the Mediterranean. Incidentally, he expected to collect material for the third volume of his trilogy, *The Wolf*. Mrs. Norris's health, however, necessitated a change of plans, and he settled down for the winter on a ranch, where, as he recently wrote to an Eastern friend, he "could shoot bears from his front door." Here he was suddenly stricken down with appendicitis, dying in a San Francisco hospital on October 25.

There is no danger of making an overstatement in saying that [the death of] Mr. Norris is a serious loss to American letters. Although barely thirty-two years old, he had achieved enough to show that his talent was not of the meteor order, no mere flash in the pan, burning out with his first book. On the contrary, he has left at least two volumes which are likely to endure, and which gave promise for the future unsurpassed in brilliance by any American writer of his years. In looking back over Mr. Norris's career, one cannot help being struck with the almost feverish impatience that he showed to reach his highest goal to do his biggest, most ambitious work without delay. It seems now almost as though some premonition reached him of the exceeding brevity of time allotted him. Yet with this impatience was coupled an admirable restraint, an indefatigable industry. Having once determined that Realism was the true creed, he adhered to it in the face of strong temptations. It is not generally known that the nucleus of *McTeague* was written as part of the university work during Mr. Norris's term of post-graduate study at Harvard, and that it was conscientiously elaborated and polished for four years before the public were allowed to see it. *Moran of the Lady Letty*, the author's one bit of almost pure romanticism, was dashed off in an interval of relaxation, and became his first published book. Its popular success suggested that an easy avenue to fortune lay open along that line, for Norris had a lively gift for inventing stories of the blood-and-thunder order, and often amused his friends by reeling off sword-and-buckler plots by the yard. In his published work, however, he conscientiously adhered to his creed, and only occasionally made concession to his inborn love of romanticism—a weakness that he frankly admitted. When a friend once expostulated with him for the gross improbability of the closing chapter of *McTeague*, where the murderer, fleeing from justice into the burning heat of an alkali desert, carries with him a canary, that continues to sing after thirty-six hours without food or water, Mr. Norris frankly admitted the absurdity, but said that he could not resist the temptation, for the scene made such a dramatic contrast. "Besides," he added whimsically, "I compromised by saying that the canary was half-dead, anyhow."

As already stated, Mr. Norris was an avowed disciple of Zola, and there can be no doubt that the influence of *Rome* and *Paris* and *Fécondité* did him serious harm. Even the fully ripened power that produced *Le Quatre Evangiles* could not make the principal characters anything more than lay figures, animated pawns with which to work out certain specified sociological problems on a vast human chess-board. The same defect, in magnified proportions, was responsible for the failure of Norris's *Octopus*. Certainly the fault did not lie with the underlying scheme of this Trilogy of the Wheat, unless the inherent bigness of the scheme was in itself a mistake. A characteristic of Norris was his love of big ideas, his insistence upon some great central symbol that would bind a novel together into one firmly knit whole. In *McTeague* the symbol is gold; the whole book is filled with a flood of yellow light—the floating golden discs that the sunlight through the trees casts upon the ground; the huge golden tooth that swings before McTeague's dental parlor; the golden dreams of the crazed Mexican girl; the hoarded gold that finally causes Trina's death. But probably not one reader out of a hundred grasps the idea that lurked somewhere in Mr. Norris's brain, that *McTeague* was a California novel, and gold the most fitting symbol he could devise for that State.

Later on he grew more ambitious. A single State no longer satisfied him. What he wanted was a symbol which should sum up at once American life and American prosperity. His friends are still fond of telling of the day when he came to his office trembling with excitement, incapacitated for work, his brain concentrated on a single thought, his Trilogy of the Wheat. "I have got a big idea, the biggest I ever had," was the burden of all he had to say for many a day after.

It would be an unkindness to dwell upon the brilliant promise of this Trilogy, and the undisguised disappointment felt by those who had the most confidence in Norris when *The Octopus* appeared, if it were not for the fact that what he failed to do then he has done, and done brilliantly, in his second volume, *The Pit*. In it Mr. Norris has remained true to his scheme; wheat, the central symbol, chief source of the nation's growth and wealth, is visible on every page, but subordinated and in the background. The interest of the story is concentrated not upon symbols, but on the central characters—flesh-and-blood characters such as Mr. Norris never before succeeded in drawing. In all his earlier books there is something unpleasantly primordial, Titanic, monstrous about his heroes and heroines. In *The Pit* he gives evidence that somehow and somewhere he had lately been gaining a truer insight into the hearts of his fellow-men, and especially his fellow-women. And this insight he has used in his new book without in any way detracting from the central plot—a gigantic attempt to corner the world's supply of wheat, to force it up, up, up, and hold the price through April and May and June, until finally the new crop comes pouring in and the daring speculator is overwhelmed under the rising tide, "a human insect, impotently striving to hold back with his puny hands the output of the whole world's granaries." There can be little question that, as a drama of mad speculation, *The Pit* is the nearest approach to Zola's *Argent* that has yet been made in English.

Frederic Taber Cooper. "Literature, American and English." *The International Year Book: 1902* (New York: Dodd, Mead & Co., 1903), pp. 408, 410.

The leading American novels of 1902 do not lend themselves readily to classification. If any one type can be said to predominate it is that of the novel of modern western life—a forceful, virile type, of which *The Pit*, by the late Frank Norris, is the most conspicuous example. And yet two of the strongest books of the year, the two which attracted most attention from critics in England, were historical novels, both written by women—*The Conqueror,* by Mrs. Atherton, and *The Valley of Decision,* by Mrs. Wharton. . . .

Much of the best talent in this country is being devoted to novels of the West— either the strenuous pioneer life of the plains, the mines and forests, or the equally interesting social life of western cities, where the veneer of culture is still comparatively thin. Two notable examples of their respective types are *The Virginian*, by Owen Wister, and *The Pit*, by the late Frank Norris. In spite of the number of books embodying the cowboy in all possible forms, from the roughest caricature to the most photographic fidelity, there was hitherto no one story which could be pointed out as the novel, par excellence, of the cowboy. This at last Mr. Wister has produced. . . .

Whatever else may be said for or against the late Frank Norris, it must be conceded that he came nearer than any other writer of his generation to reproducing in English the epic bigness of theme and the epic sweep of style that characterized the novels of Emile Zola. Norris was never satisfied with halfway measures; he was not happy until he found a symbol that would sum up in a single word all American life—Wheat; and he was so engrossed in this central symbol that he made the mistake of subordinating everything else to it. Zola could paint vast cycloramas, but in them the actors in the central tragedy always stood out in sharp relief. In *The Octopus* of Norris the principal actors seem to sink into the background, to lose themselves and become submerged under the waving fields of yellow grain. *The Pit*, Mr. Norris's last book, finished just before he died, is in this respect a notable forward stride. Wheat is still the symbol, but it is subordinated to the interest of human actors in the book. It is a story of the attempt of one man to corner the wheat market of the world. He buys and buys and the price soars steadily up; he holds on through April and May, and his fortune seems made. He holds on a day too long, and all of a sudden the new wheat comes pouring in, an overpowering flood, rising higher and higher, gradually submerging the man who is depicted standing there, like a feeble insect, striving with outstretched hands to hold back the granaries of the world. No other story of Chicago can fairly be placed in the same category. . . .

"Frank Norris and Edwin Lefevre."
Bookman (America), 16 (January 1903), 441–42.

A graphic little story regarding the late Frank Norris has reached us, which goes to prove that the most convincing touches in fiction are not necessarily copied from life and that even an avowed realist may sometimes be misled. During his last year in New York, Mr. Norris formed a rather close friendship with Edwin Lefevre, the author of *Wall Street Stories*, and it was at one time agreed between them that Mr. Lefevre should revise the proofs of Mr. Norris's story, *The Pit*, in all the chapters relating to the wheat market, receiving due credit in the preface for his share of the work. As it turned out, they never succeeded in coming together for that purpose, and the plan was abandoned. But frequently, at Mr. Norris's request, Mr. Lefevre explained the intricacies of stock markets, speculations, corners and the like; and one night he found himself launched upon an eloquent description of a panic. He described the pandemonium reigning on the floor of the Exchange, the groups of frenzied, yelling brokers, the haggard faces of men to whom the next change of a point or two meant ruin. And then he followed one man in particular through the events of the day, and pictured him groping his way blindly out from the gallery, a broken, ruined man. So far, Mr. Lefevre had told only what he had seen, all too often, with his own eyes. But at this point, carried away by his own story, he yielded to the temptation to fake a dramatic conclusion, and he told how the man was still striding restlessly, aimlessly along the corridor, when the elevator shot past and some one shouted "Down!" and the ruined man, his mind still bent upon the falling market, continued his nervous striding, gesticulating fiercely and repeating audibly, "Down! down! down!" "There you are!" interrupted Mr. Norris, springing up excitedly; "there you are! That is one of those things that no novelist could invent!" And yet, adds Mr. Lefevre in telling the story, "it was the one bit of fake in my whole description."

Isaac F. Marcosson. "Frank Norris' Last Book: Lamented Young Novelist at His Best in 'The Pit'—The Wheat Motive Again."
Louisville Times, January 3, 1903, p. 7, section 2.

The death of Frank Norris was a serious loss to American literature. He was just coming to his own; there was a rich ripening of his brilliant art, and those who possibility for the great American novelist [sic]. It is with a sadness higher than that usually aroused by a posthumous book that comment is passed on his last work, "The Pit," which is about to be brought out. In the consideration of this volume there is all that touching pathos that the cutting off of a young career inspires and the ineffable regret over what might have been accomplished. Yet "The Pit" needs neither sympathy nor sentiment to make it stand as a distinct achievement and a worthy memorial to the rare talents and soaring [sic].

Readers have been permitted a glimpse of "The Pit" in its serial form, but now the whole massive work appears, a fitting link in that trilogy of the epic of the wheat upon which Norris set his heart and concentrated all his energy. All his efforts find artistic fruition in this work. While it lacks the heroic proportions and magnificent sweep of "The Octopus," yet it encompasses the whole scope of the plan undertaken by Norris—to flash on his canvas the lights and shadows of the struggle for supremacy on the wheat exchange.

* * *

In November, 1901, when the reading world was debating whether "The Octopus" was a splendid waste of energy or an enduring work, Norris was already busy with "The Pit." The whole drama of the wheat problem was unfolded in his mind and he was eager and hungry for the second section of his work. At that time he wrote me his first outline of the story; wrote the condensation out at length in his little cramped hand. That extract is now before me and after the perusal of the book it is evident that he did not vary one detail in the original conception of the story. In that outline, in commenting on the wheat motive, which was the dominant one, he wrote the following prophetic words: "The wheat motive is continued the same as in "The Octopus"—a great and resistless force moving from west to east, from producer to consumer; benevolent and beneficent as long as it is unhampered, but destroying all things and all individuals who attempt to check or divert it."

In "The Octopus" it was the tragedy of the production; in "The Pit" is the tragedy of the market. In that first story of the wheat country it was the man Behrman who was finally engulfed in the ocean of the grain; in this second and last story it is Jadwin, the speculator, who is buried under the crash of his corner on May wheat. The lessons are the same; the treatment remains forceful and dramatic.

There is less action in "The Pit" than in "The Octopus." The reader misses a certain melodramatic touch; a phase of the vivid imagery which marked "The Octopus," but in its stead there is the more refined, more sustained art, at once appealing and impressive. The story deals with the attempt of Jadwin to corner the market. He does so, but narrowly misses losing his wife. Finally in the darkness of disaster and with the wreck of his fortune about him he sees gleaming through the murk the love light long kindled in the eyes and heart of his wife. The crash comes at a time when the wife, stung by neglect, is about to waver. It is developed in masterly fashion and is an incident long to be remembered.

"The Pit" touches human nature at its most sensitive point; an old life's tragedy is unfolded in rare and enthralling fashion. The sorrow of the worship of Mammon, the ethics of commerce, the whole drama of love all pass before the reader.

* * *

"The Pit" is Norris' most human and most emotional work. There is none of the reek of "McTeague." None of the blood conflict of "The Octopus." Here and there is a touch of that blithe spirit which pervaded "Blix." It is a genuine novel. It is little short of a masterful story. In this book Norris dissects a woman's heart for the first time in a book. In Laura Dearborn, who marries Jadwin, and who becomes the martyr of a man's compelling ambition to make money, he reveals a woman of lovely charm and all too human sometimes.

Norris throws strong lights on the Chicago Board of Trade. He got his material first hand, and in many ways it is the best story dealing with commercial life that we have had. He writes of "the pile of the Board of Trade building; black, monolithic, crouching on its foundation like a monster Sphinx, with blind eyes, silent, grave, crouching there without a sound, without sign of life, under the night and in the drifting veil of the rain."

What need is there to write of "The Pit" as a book? It is rather a document in evidence of the life's work of one of the rarest and most fascinating figures in that small group of American writers whose ideals were high; whose art was true; whose work is certain to endure. Back of this book is great tragedy; the spectacle of his young life suddenly cut off. Norris will be held in affectionate remembrance by all whose privilege it was to know him and by that steadily increasing circle of readers to whom "The Pit" will now come as a fitting farewell he can only be held in sincere admiration. One might paraphrase the beautiful German line and say "He lived and he labored" and his work was not in vain.*

---

*Reproduced with this review was a section of a letter by Norris in which he discusses the structure and focus of *The Pit*.

"New Books and New Announcements." *New York Herald*, January 3, 1903, p. 14.

The most important work of fiction in immediate sight is "The Pit," by the late and lamented Frank Norris, a novel of life and wheat speculation in Chicago, which Messrs. Doubleday, Page & Co. will publish on January 15.

Though complete in itself, this continues "The Epic of the Wheat," begun by "The Octopus" which was to have been rounded off by a third volume that will now, alas! never see the light.

Edwin L. Shuman. "In Realm of Books: Frank Norris' Chicago Novel, 'The Pit,' His Last and Strongest Work." *Chicago Record-Herald*, January 3, 1903, p. 10.

About the middle of January the last novel of the late Frank Norris will be issued in book form, under the title "The Pit: A Story of Chicago." I have had the privilege of reading an advance copy, and have been impressed with the power of the story. It is more convincing than "The Octopus," more pleasing than "McTeague," more dramatic than any of Mr. Norris' other works. It shows that he was gaining a firmer grasp of his art, and was in the way of becoming one of our greatest novelists. The undeniable excellence of "The Pit" emphasizes the regret one feels over his untimely death.

Mr. Norris shaped his methods largely after those of Zola, and, like him, had planned a trilogy of novels with a purpose. They were to embody "The Epic of the Wheat." The first, "The Octopus," dealt with the war between the wheat grower and the railroad trust. The second, "The Pit," depicts a gigantic wheat corner on the Chicago Board of Trade. The third, to have been called "The Wolf," was to deal with the sufferings of European peasants through a famine caused by such a corner. Unhappily, the trilogy must remain incomplete, but "The Pit" is a good novel, and able to stand alone.

Like Zola, Mr. Norris had adopted the "catalogue method" of writing. Instead of depicting a scene in a few clear-cut and suggestive lines, he massed detail on detail. This method has its strong and weak points. It inevitably makes heavy reading in spots, but it lends itself to strong dramatic effects. Both of these qualities are seen in "The Pit." The descriptions are sometimes wearisome, especially in the first half of the book, but the powerful dramatic movement at length sweeps away all detraction and leaves one thrilling with the scenes enacted before one's eyes. "The Pit" is by all odds the greatest novel yet written about the commercial life of Chicago.

* * *

The opening scene is a grand opera night at the Auditorium, where we meet all the chief characters. Curtis Jadwin, the daring wheat speculator, falls in love with Laura Dearborn. Laura has two other lovers, who make things interesting, and the girl's character shows forth in its weakness and strength in her relations with these suitors. But Jadwin's masterful nature sweeps all obstacles aside, and we see Mr. and Mrs. Jadwin happily ensconced in a palace overlooking Lincoln Park before the story is many chapters old.

Then come the dramatic developments. Jadwin, a most lovable fellow, and simply devoted to Laura, gets deeper and deeper into speculation on the board. As his battles become fiercer and his involuntary neglect of his wife increases an insidious danger besets Laura in the form of an earlier lover. We see two tragedies bearing down upon Jadwin, one in the pit and the other in his home. Yes, and there is a third, for the terrible strain drives sleep and appetite from him and threatens to unsettle his mind. The skill with which these themes are developed and brought to a smashing climax in a Board of Trade panic constitutes the greatness of Mr. Norris' novel.

* * *

The author has used the local color of Chicago freely and for the most part accurately, though Clark street is spelled throughout with a redundant "e." A good example of his descriptive methods is found in passages such as this:

> All the life of the neighborhood seemed to center at this point— the entrance of the Board of Trade. Two currents that trended swiftly through LaSalle and Jackson streets, and that fed or were fed by other tributaries that poured in through Fifth avenue and through Clark and Dearborn streets, met at this point, one setting in, the other out. The nearer the currents the greater the speed. Men, mere flotsam in the

flood—as they turned into LaSalle street from Monroe or even from as far as Madison—seemed to accelerate their speed as they approached. At the Illinois Trust the walk became a stride; at the Rookery the stride was almost a trot. But at the corner of Jackson street, the Board of Trade now merely the width of the street away, the trot became a run, and young men and boys, under pretense of escaping the trucks and wagons of the cobbles, dashed across at a veritable gallop, flung themselves panting into the entrance of the board, were engulfed in the turmoil of the spot, and disappeared with a sudden fillip into the gloom of the interior.

Thus it went day after day. Endlessly, ceaselessly, the Pit enormous, thundering, sucked in and spewed out, sending the swirl of its mighty central eddy far out through the city's channels.

There is more imagination than realism in such passages, but is not this the secret of the genuine romancer?

The insidious lure of the speculative habit is embodied in the fate of one of the characters, Mr. Cressler, who has "reformed" and inveighs against the evils of speculation only to fall from grace in the end and go down to ruin and suicide when caught on the wrong side of his friend Jadwin's corner. The cruel barbarity of the battle in the pit is brought out in many places, and in the following bit of Cressler's talk we get a glimpse of the theme which the author intended to embody in his third novel:

> It's like this: If we send the price of wheat down too far, the farmer suffers, the fellow who raises it; if we send it up too far, the poor man in Europe suffers, the fellow who eats it. And food to the peasant on the continent is bread—not meat or potatoes, as it is with us. The only way to do so that neither the American farmer nor the European peasant suffers is to keep wheat at an average, legitimate value. The moment you inflate or depress that, somebody suffers right away. And that is just what these gamblers are doing all the time, booming it up or booming it down. Think of it, the food of hundreds and hundreds of thousands of people just at the mercy of a few men down there on the Board of Trade. They make the price. They say just how much the peasant shall pay for his loaf of bread. If he can't pay the price he simply starves.

* * *

"The fascination of this pit gambling is something no one who hasn't experienced it can have the faintest conception of," says Cressler. "I believe it's worse than liquor, worse than morphine. Once you get into it, it grips you and draws you and draws you, and the nearer you get to the end the easier it seems to win, till all of a sudden, ah! there's the whirlpool. 'J.,' keep away from it, my boy."

But Jadwin could not keep away, nor could Cressler himself. By degrees we see the great corner in May wheat working to its climax, squeezing, ruining, killing those who fall under its crushing power. Jadwin runs the price up to $1.50 a bushel and reigns supreme. Then he loses his head and undertakes to carry the deal over to July wheat. But the earth itself is against the great speculator now. With superb nerve he mortgages all his property, and fights like a Titan against the new crop that comes pouring in upon him from every wheat state in the West.

The author pictures Jadwin deluged and borne down by a symbolic flood of wheat. Pandemonium reigns on the board, and the final scenes are exciting and impressive. The events are overwrought, no doubt, and the vast forces that the author makes you see sweeping through the building are not visible to the ordinary mortal, but the triumph of the novelist is that he has succeeded in humanizing these tense scenes. You never lose interest in Jadwin or his wife or any of the others whose fate hangs upon the outcome.

I imagine "The Pit" will interest men more than women, though the love story is a vital and engrossing part of the book. Wheat dominates everything, and unless one be interested in the workings of the Board of Trade one is likely to resent its interruption of the romance. But this is a fine, strong piece of fiction, just the same—one of the best of its kind.

"Books of the Week." *New York Herald,* January 10, 1903, p. 12.*

The book of the week, or, rather, of next week, for it is here reviewed from an advance copy, is Frank Norris' "The Pit." Indeed, it promises to be the book of the year, mayhap of the decade. Enthusiastic critics may even declare that

*Reprinted in part in "The Pit," *The Literary News,* 24 (February 1903), 34.

it comes close to being the great American novel to which we have all been looking forward for—how many years?

In the death of Frank Norris, which occurred in San Francisco on October 26 of last year, American literature lost its greatest potentiality in fiction. The word "potentiality," though it has been defamed by all ignoble use, is really the best for our present purpose. Doubtless it would be more accurate to confine its use to the future sense as indicating possibilities, but the world has determined to use it also in the sense of present performance.

And Mr. Norris was not only a shining promise for the future. He had given us excellent performance, so excellent that no young man of anything near his age had outstripped. His "McTeague" came near being a masterpiece. Many good critics insist that at all events it was his masterpiece. But the voice of authority generally concedes that distinction to "The Octopus," the first of a contemplated trilogy which was to deal with the epic of the wheat. In England (and it is a commonplace that English opinion is a sort of posterity to ourselves) it was hailed almost as the one great novel that America had produced in a decade. Now comes a posthumous novel, "The Pit," the second in the series, which Messrs. Doubleday, Page & Co. will publish on January 15. The third, which was to have been called "The Wolf," perished in embryo when the busy brain of the author was stilled in death.

Mr. Norris, as we learn from his publishers, was a reader for their house when the idea for this trilogy came into his mind.

One day, they tell us, Norris came to a member of the firm almost trembling with enthusiasm.

"I've got a great idea," he said, and he

told his plan of "The Epic of the Wheat," perhaps the largest constructive task any American novelist has ever given himself.

The first novel was to deal with the war between the wheat grower and the Railroad Trust, the second would be the fictitious narrative of a "deal" in the Chicago wheat pit, while the third would probably have for its pivotal episode the relieving of a famine in an Old World community. In other words, the three novels, each complete and distinct in itself, were to be connected together in their relation to, first, the production; second, the distribution; and third, the consumption of American wheat. When complete, they would form the story of a crop of wheat from the time of its sowing as seed in California to the time of its consumption as bread in a village of Western Europe.

The publishers encouraged Mr. Norris in his project. The reception accorded to "The Octopus," as already indicated, fully justified them in this encouragement.

Both "The Octopus" and "The Pit" show distinct traces of Zolaesque influence. This does not mean that Norris followed Zola into the cloacal mysteries. He made no studies in morbid moral pathology. He did not gloat over the seamy side of human nature. But he looked at men and their motives, as exhibited in the clear light of day, with the calm and serene gaze of the social philosopher. He possessed the X-ray of genius. He could detect the secret springs of human action. He could make them visible to the multitude. In "The Octopus," however, he had been more the disciple. In "The Pit" he is more the prophet of a new dispensation. In the first he had become, in an inoffensive sense, the American Zola. In "The Pit"
he becomes more distinctively the founder of a new school, which may preclude a French Norris.

He has recovered his balance, in other words. He is no longer swayed to the right or the left by his great predecessor. He stands on his own feet. He allows his imagination free play. He fuses his conceptions into harmonious accord in his own alembic. He touches the mystery of life with a poetry and a dramatic intensity which are wholly his own.

In "The Octopus," as in most of Zola's novels, there are a crowd of characters, each sharply individualized, but confusing and distracting at a first perusal. In "The Pit" the characters who count may be numbered on your fingers, and dominating them all are the hero and the heroine, Curtis Jadwin, capitalist and speculator, who brings about the corner that constitutes the crisis, and Laura Dearborn, the woman whom he loves and marries, and who is whirled, an innocent victim, into the maelstrom of his own creation. To the comedy and the tragedy, the romance and the melodrama of these two central figures all the others are artistically subordinated.

They are a vividly imagined couple. Laura, because through her feminine complexity she was the more difficult of the two to manage, is perhaps the greater triumph. Her coquettish heartlessness before she discovered that she had a heart, her self-surrender when she found herself immutably in love with the man whom she had married without the consciousness of love, are alike admirably presented. Yet she is no faultless monster. When baffled in the endeavor to win from her husband the external evidence of the passion he really feels, but which is subordinated and for the moment almost overwhelmed by his greater passion for speculation, she turns in despair to the lover who has not only the inner feeling, but the outer semblance, and she is only saved from moral wreck by the financial wreck that overtakes her husband. Her victory is based upon her husband's defeat.

The whole story moves swiftly and inevitably to the final catastrophe through a series of intensely dramatic scenes. Laura's sensations at the opera and in her desolated home are as acutely described as the sensations of her husband in the whirl and toss of the wheat exchange. Take as an example the really great scene in which Jadwin's triumphs are swallowed up in defeat. The corner is smashed. All his calculations have come to naught. The wheat has broken from his control. "For months he had, in the might of his single arm, held it back, but now it rose like the upbuilding of a colossal billow. It towered, towered, hung poised an instant, and then, with a thunder as of the grind and crash of chaotic worlds, broke upon him, burst through the pit and raced past him, on and on to the eastward and to the hungry nations. And then, under the stress and violence of the hour, something snapped in his brain."

Crazed with the imminence of his peril, he strives against the torrent of the wheat.

"There in the middle of the pit, surrounded and assaulted by herd after herd of wolves yelping for his destruction, he stood, braced, rigid upon his feet, his head up, his hand, the great bony hand that once had held the whole pit in its grip, flung high in the air, in a gesture of defiance, while his voice, like the clangor of bugles sounding to the charge of the forlorn hope, rang out again and again, over the din of his enemies:—

" 'Give a dollar for July—give a dollar for July!'

"And then, all at once, the pit, the entire floor of the Board of Trade, was struck dumb. All at once the tension was relaxed, the furious struggling and stamping was stilled. Landry, bewildered, still holding his chief by the hand, looked about him. On the floor, near at hand, stood the president of the Board of Trade himself, and with him the vice president and a group of the directors. Evidently it had been these who had called the traders to order. But it was not toward them now that the hundreds of men in the pit and on the floor were looking.

"In the little balcony on the south wall opposite the visitor's gallery a figure had appeared, a tall, grave man in a long black coat—the secretary of the Board of Trade. Landry with the others saw him, saw him advance to the edge of the railing and fix his glance upon the wheat pit. In his hand he carried a slip of paper.

"And then in the midst of that profound silence the secretary announced:—

" 'All trades with Gretry, Converse & Co. must be closed at once.'

"The words had not ceased to echo in the high vaultings of the roof before they were greeted with a wild, shrill yell of exultation and triumph that burst from the crowding masses in the wheat pit.

"Beaten, beaten at last, the great bull! Smashed! The great corner smashed! Jadwin busted! They themselves saved, saved, saved! Cheer followed upon cheer, yell after yell. Hats went into the air. In a frenzy of delight men danced and leaped and capered upon the edge of the pit, clasping their arms about each other, shaking each others' hands, cheering and hurrahing until their strained voices became hoarse and faint.

"With one accord they leaped upon him. The little group of traders was swept aside. Landry alone, Landry who had never left his side since his rush from out Gretry's office, Landry Court, loyal to the last, his one remaining soldier, white, shaking, the sobs strangling in his throat, clung to him desperately. Another billow of wheat was preparing. They two—the beaten general and his young armor bearer—heard it coming. Hissing, raging, bellowing it swept down upon them. Landry uttered a cry. Flesh and blood could not stand this strain. He cowered at his chief's side, his shoulders bent, one arm above his head, as if to ward off an actual physical force.

"But Jadwin, iron to the end, stood erect. All unknowing what he did, he had taken Landry's hand in his, and the boy felt the grip on his fingers like the contracting of a vise of steel. The other hand, as though holding up a standard, was still in the air, and his great detoned voice went out across the tumult, proclaiming to the end his battle cry:—

" 'Give a dollar for July—give a dollar for July!'

"But, little by little, Landry became aware that the tumult of the Pit was intermitting. There was sudden lapsing in the shouting, and in these lapses he could hear from somewhere out upon the floor voices that were crying:— 'Order—order, order, gentlemen!'

"But again and again the clamor broke out. It would die down for an instant in response to these appeals, only to burst out afresh as certain groups of traders started the pandemonium again by the wild outcrying of their offers. At last, however, the older men in the Pit, regaining some measure of self-control, took up the word, going to and fro in the press repeating 'Order! Order!' "

"The Epic of the Wheat—The Pit." *Indianapolis News*, January 10, 1903, p. 8.

It is with mingled feelings of regret and admiration that many readers will approach the last novel of Frank Norris. The second in his never-to-be-completed trilogy which, justly, but perhaps a trifle grandiloquently, he named "The Epic of the Wheat." The trilogy started with "The Octopus: A Story of California"; the second number is the present volume: "The Pit: A Story of Chicago"; and the third and last book was to have been "The Wolf: A Story of Europe." The idea was a noble one in its conception. Wheat was the main topic, the inspiration of these novels; wheat, not only as it affects and has affected American life and character and institutions, but as it, with its vast power and resistless movement, affects Europe. The first volume dealt with the production of wheat in the great grain fields of the West; "The Pit" deals with the distribution of the grain, and the last novel—never to be written now—was to have dealt with the consumption of American wheat. Completed, the trilogy would have formed the story of a crop of wheat from the time of its planting as seed in California to the time of its consumption as bread in a village of western Europe.

In his first story, "The Octopus," Mr. Norris wrote fiction, but he dealt broadly with facts. His story was based

The Pit

on facts taken from historical records, but they were facts dealt with imaginatively; facts tinged with romance and made known through fictitious characters. The present volume is all fiction; the fictitious narrative of a "deal" in the Chicago wheat pit; a fictitious deal by fictitious characters, but in its main thread and incidents eminently typical and precisely what might have been.

Close to the title page of the novel is printed a list of the principal characters in the novel; just as at the theater the names are printed on a play-bill. They are few: Curtis Jadwin, capitalist and speculator; Sheldon Corthell, an artist; Landry Court, broker's clerk; Samuel Gretry, a broker; Charles Cressler, a dealer in grain; Mrs. Cressler, his wife; Laura Dearborn, a protégé of Mrs. Cressler; Page Dearborn, her sister and Mrs. Emily Wessels, aunt of Laura and Page.

These are the dramatis personae, but prominent among them stands out the figure of Curtis Jadwin, typical American, self-made, self-reliant, doggedly honest, fearless; who, not from any desire for wealth, but simply for the reason that he has ambition to be leader in the great speculative game, acts as a human dam for the great tide of wheat coming from the West, halts it at Chicago and holds it there by the sheer force of his power and genius until the want of it is felt not only in the remotest hamlet in the United States, but in India, in Europe—all over the world.

Laura and Page Dearborn are two New England girls, left orphans, with a competency, and they take a house in Chicago and live there with their aunt, Mrs. Wessels. Page does not figure much in the story except as a foil to her sister. Laura is a typical American girl, attractive, well educated, a trifle ambitious. She attracts men. At the beginning of the story she is all but engaged to Sheldon Corthell, the artist; she suffers the admiration of Landry Court, the broker's clerk, and she meets for the first time with Curtis Jadwin. Jadwin is unlike any man she has ever met. Uneducated, unpolished, yet he has a dignity that attracts her, a force that compels her admiration, and after a strange wooing he wins her for his wife and when he has married her wins her love.

There is a mansion prepared for Laura, facing Lincoln Park; there is travel abroad and Laura is very happy—until the wheat enters into her life. Samuel Gretry and Jadwin have been boys together, and one day Gretry tells Jadwin that he has advance information from France of an impending war. The news will not be made public for twenty-four hours. Jadwin buys wheat, and in twenty-four hours makes $50,000. This affects him little, but by and by he is drawn into speculating, on the bear side of the market, and having keen judgment and remarkable shrewdness, every deal he makes wins. Then, one day, he turns bull and begins to buy; he establishes private correspondents in Europe wheat, right and left, running the price up and up until one day sitting alone with Gretry in the office they figure out that there are less than a hundred million bushels of wheat in the entire country. Gretry says he has a lot of short wheat on his books:

> Jadwin was silent a moment, tugging at his mustache. Then suddenly he leaned forward, his finger almost in Gretry's face.
> "Why, look here," he cried. "Don't you see! Don't you see—"
> "See what?" demanded the broker, puzzled at the other's vehemence.
> Jadwin loosened his collar with his forefinger.

"Great Scott! I'll choke in a minute. See what? Why, I own ten million bushels of this wheat already, and Europe will take eighty million out of the country. Why, there ain't going to be any wheat left in Chicago by May! If I get in now and buy a long line of cash wheat, where are all these fellows who've sold short going to get it to deliver it? Say, where are they going to get it? Come on, now, tell me where are they going to get it?"

Gretry laid down his pencil and stared at Jadwin, looked long at the papers on his desk, consulted his penciled memoranda, then thrust his hands deep into his pockets, with a long breath. Bewildered, and as if stupefied, he gazed again into Jadwin's face.

"My God!" he murmured at last.

"Well, where are they going to get it?" Jadwin cried once more, his face suddenly scarlet.

"J," faltered the broker, "J, I—I'm damned if I know."

And then, all in a moment, the two men were on their feet. The event which all those past eleven months had been preparing was suddenly consummated, suddenly stood revealed, as though a veil had been ripped asunder, as though an explosion had crashed through the air upon them, deafening, blinding.

Jadwin sprang forward, gripping the broker by the shoulder.

"Sam," he shouted, "do you know—great God!—do you know what this means? Sam, we can corner the market."

And so they do, or rather Jadwin does, for Gretry is only the broker, the faithful lieutenant. Wheat goes up, up, up—a dollar-thirty—a dollar-forty—a dollar-fifty—a dollar-sixty. "By heavens," cries Jadwin, "I'll make her touch the two-dollar mark."

There is a bear clique formed against Jadwin, who has become the biggest man in the pit, but Jadwin anticipates the clique, and when the bears make an assault on his line he sells, too, sells two bushels for every one they sell, and at the right moment buys in again at a low price the wheat he has sold at a high one, until the bears are routed, foot and horse, and he is left master of the field.

But, in the meantime, Laura Jadwin is left alone in her great house, with her army of servants. Corthell, who has gone to Europe on Laura's marriage, returns and becomes her cavalier and Jadwin, far from jealous, is glad that Laura has companionship. Hurt, aggrieved, not understanding the absorbing passion of her husband, Laura listens to the lovemaking of the artist and an elopement is among the possibilities. One feels sorry for Laura, who has so much to tempt her, and is so deserving of sympathy, but it is Jadwin and his gigantic plans that are more absorbing.

Jadwin's corner is an immense success—his wealth has increased until he himself does not know what he is worth, but with it all there has come a certain numbness of brain, a stupor which has robbed him of his farsightedness, and he is completely master of the market when he takes an insane idea to "swing this deal right over into July." It is in vain his friends and advisors protest; they tell him that the new crop coming in will swamp him. He tells them they are crazy and he goes on in his determined way. But what was prophesied comes to pass. It is in vain for him to try to stop. His wife pleads with him to quit. "Corner wheat!" he cries. "It is the wheat that has cornered me. It's like holding a wolf by the ears, bad to hold on, but worse to let go." There comes the fatal day on which it is imperative that Jadwin shall hold up the price of wheat. He mortgages all his real estate and throws that into the balance; he works his enormous credit to its last fraction. The tide pours in from all the wheat-raising States; the market gets beyond his control; the dam breaks; the golden grain comes pouring in and Jadwin goes down in the wreck.

In "The Octopus" it will be remembered there was one of the characters who was watching the wheat pour in a golden stream from the enormous elevators into the hold of a ship. He slipped and fell and the grain in a relentless stream poured in on him; held him by the legs; rose higher and higher, to his neck, to his mouth, choking his frantic cries; burying him beneath it and blotting him out forever. So, in the present story:

> Jadwin was in the thick of the confusion by now. And the avalanche, the undiked Ocean of the Wheat, leaping to the lash of the hurricane, struck him fairly in the face.
>
> He heard it now; he heard nothing else. The Wheat had broken from his control. For months he had, by the might of his single arm, held it back; but now it rose like the upbuilding of a colossal billow. It towered, towered, hung poised for an instant, and then, with a thunder as of the grind and crash of chaotic worlds, broke upon him, burst through the Pit and raced past him, on and on to the eastward and to the hungry nations.

* * *

> Beaten; beaten at last, the Great Bull! Smashed! The great corner smashed! Jadwin busted! They themselves saved, saved, saved! Cheer followed upon cheer, yell after yell. Hats went into the air. In a frenzy of delight men danced and leaped and capered upon the edge of the Pit, clasping their arms about each other, shaking each other's hands, cheering and hurrahing, till their strained voices became hoarse and faint.

And the stricken man goes home to his palatial mansion—his no longer, and sitting with his wife he has neglected for so long for the wheat which has engulfed him at last, they are reunited.

It is a great story, but it is more than a story; it is a philosophic study of certain phases of American life. It is big; it has the bigness of the American continent, the bigness of the American spirit in it, and for this reason, if for no other, comes as near being the real American novel as any that has gone before. It is little short of marvelous, the insight into human nature possessed by this young writer, who has died too soon; on every page his remarkable keenness and sureness of observation are apparent; his characters live and move with all the frailty and mistaken impulse that rule humanity. The tale breathes the very atmosphere of Chicago, the great clearing-house for the West; the bustling, untidy city, whose spirit of unrest, of "hustle," of progressiveness, is the true American spirit, felt and respected now to the uttermost parts of the earth. How all this has been captured and set down in a single novel it is hard to say, but it has been done, and the result is here in a book that will be widely read; that will stand out as a worthy thing in the great flood of American fiction. Reading this book, and swayed by its power, the world will, more than ever, regret the untimely taking off of its author—with his work yet undone.

George Hamlin Fitch. "Good Reading."
San Francisco Chronicle, January 11, 1903, p. 18.

After careful reading of "The Pit"—the last work by the late Frank Norris—one feels more keenly the loss to American letters by his death, just when he was coming into the full sense of his mastery of the story-teller's art. This second volume of what the author called the Epic of the Wheat is issued by Doubleday, Page & Co. of New York in French gray boards, with title in paper label, not a pleasant binding for library shelf or table. It is illustrated with a portrait of Norris, with pipe in mouth, reading by a student's lamp. It is a good profile view, but in some way no one ever associates Norris with domestic ease. Rather would one have had a front view with the strongly marked eyebrows and the brooding eyes that seemed to have many unwritten stories in their depths.

This young California novelist several years ago conceived the idea of making a series of three romances out of the history of wheat. The first, which he called "The Octopus," was devoted to the struggle between the grain-growers in the San Joaquin valley and the railroad company, which finally culminated in the Mussel Slough tragedy. The second was "The Pit," a story of a gigantic deal in wheat in Chicago which affected the markets of the world and brought the pinch of hunger to peoples on the other side of the globe. The third was "The Wolf," a picture of famine in India, which was to be relieved by the generosity of the New World. The subject was certainly epic in character, and the two volumes that were completed by the young author show that had life and strength been given him he would have done even finer work in the third volume than in the other two.

In his first book Norris reproduced with absolute fidelity the peculiar people, the strange climatic conditions and the remarkable scenery of that great interior valley of California, where many of the old-time wheat farms were larger than the average European prince's domain. No one before him had ever been able to make real the tremendous battle between organized capital and the individual wheat farmer, except perhaps Bailey Millard in his fine short story, "A Notch in a Principality." But this romance of Norris', powerful as it was, was not well wrought out. Characters were introduced which had no bearing on the plot and there was tedious iteration and reiteration of certain traits of mind or body—an offensive mannerism borrowed from Zola. There was also a too evident fondness for the grim and ghastly realism that shocks rather than impresses the reader. But all through the book one was struck with the tremendous force of the writer's descriptions, as well as with his masterly grasp of the essential parts of his story. Annixter, the young California wheatgrower, a rough ashlar whom no refinement could ever make polished, will stand as a type of the best qualities of the young manhood of the State, and the book is crowded with descriptions that are photographic in their fidelity to nature and life.

In his second story, "The Pit," Norris has developed a character as strong and as masterful as his San Joaquin wheat rancher. This is Curtis Jadwin, graduate of the hard life of a Western farm, and when we first see him, a man of mature years, owner of a large amount of income-paying real estate in Chicago, and an occasional dabbler in grain speculation in that mighty maelstrom of legalized gambling, the Chicago wheat pit. Jadwin has had a common-school education, and from his association with big financiers he has gained that training which marks him as a man of affairs. He is large, massive, slow of movement, but direct, plain spoken, self-centered. His huge figure and wide-spreading plans dominate the book and color and shape the lives of all with whom he comes in contact. He is not a natural gambler, but his associations and his few early successes lure him on until the speculative fever enters into his blood. Then when the mania gets a firm grip on him he moves on to the logical end, more and more possessed by the demoniac force of the fiercest passion the world knows, until the climax comes in a great smash-up of a wheat deal that aimed at nothing less than cornering the bread supply of the entire world.

To make a story like this interesting, a story which deals in so much technical detail of board of trade methods and the shrewd devices of wheat speculators, required great art. That Norris has succeeded will be the verdict of anyone who reads his book with care. It is admirably developed, and the most truthful features are the almost despairing efforts of the old broker to withstand the temptation to plunge into pit speculation and make a great fortune in a few weeks. The analysis of the American speculator has never been so well done. Old Cressler is even more striking in his fidelity to real life than Jadwin himself. Here is a broker, doing a large commission business and with ample fortune, who has refrained from speculation for twenty years because at the outset of his career a deal narrowly missed carrying away all his gains. Yet in his old age, when the great bear operator in the Chicago pit invites him to take a share in a deal that cannot fail, he first declares that he is afraid to venture in where he once narrowly escaped ruin, and ultimately risks his whole fortune in the venture. The bear raid, which was really directed against Jadwin, though Cressler did not know it, fails, and Cressler, who is Jadwin's closest friend, puts a bullet through his brain.

Jadwin's case is complicated by his marriage. When the book opens Jadwin is one of a theater party that hears a great opera singer. In the party is a young girl, Laura Dearborn, with whom the middle-aged bachelor is greatly impressed. She is bright, frank, eagerly intelligent, and at the same time very womanly. With the same force and tenacity that he pursues a business deal Jadwin carries on his courtship until the girl is fairly overcome by his persistence. Yet she cannot fail to see his generosity, his goodness and his great love for her. These more than atone for his faults and though she is much attracted by an artist named Corthell she finally marries Jadwin. With her wedding day comes the great love that she hoped to feel before that ceremony. Jadwin proves to be an ideal husband until the grip of speculation is fastened upon him. Then, as always happens in real life, the passion for gambling subdues all other passions. The man forgets his home obligations and in her bitter revolt at this neglect the wife welcomes the attentions of her old artist lover. He is still in love with her, but only the sentimental side of the woman is attracted to him. It is bad art to make her plan to forsake her husband just on the eve of his downfall. No woman of Laura's force of mind and character could do so suicidal a thing as that and one is glad when the call for her services to aid the stricken man diverts her from so foolish an act.

All the details of Jadwin's gradual absorption in the game of cornering the wheat supply of the world are worked out with rare skill. One follows it as one follows a real game that is full of exciting episodes, and the climax in the great wheat pit, when the bull leader who has made hundreds submit to his dictation is at last overthrown, is splendidly dramatic. The one who stands by Jadwin to the end, Landry Court, a young broker, is an excellent character; so, too, is Page Dearborn, Laura's younger sister. In fact, there are half a dozen characters so true to life that one recognizes them as belonging to a well defined American type. It is impossible to take any incident of this story from its contents without hurting it, but one may quote this description of the center of speculation in Chicago as it first appeared to Laura, and again as she saw it when leaving the city with her husband to begin life anew further West:

> And all at once, intuitively, Laura turned in her place, and raising the flap that covered the little window at the back of the carriage, looked behind. On either side of the vista in converging lines stretched the tall office buildings, lights burning in a few of the windows, even yet. Over the end of the street the lead-colored sky was broken by a pale, faint haze of light, and silhouetted against this rose a somber mass, unbroken by any glimmer, rearing a black and formidable facade against the blur of the sky behind it.
>
> And this was the last impression of the part of her life that that day brought to a close; the tall, gray office buildings, the murk of rain, the haze of light in the heavens, and raised against it, the pile of the Board of Trade building, black, monolithic, crouching on its foundations like a monstrous Sphinx with blind eyes, silent, grave—crouching there without a sound, without sign of life, under the night and the drifting veil of rain.

"Frank Norris's Last Novel."
The Argonaut, 48 (January 12, 1903), 23.

"The Pit" is a masterly work. No one can lay it down without profound regret that the hand that wrote it, the quick intelligence that conceived it, are no more. It is a remarkable book, and, had Norris lived, that he would have written a greater book, we believe. But Frank Norris is dead, and the trilogy, so largely planned, so well begun, so strongly continued, will forever remain a lamentable fragment—as appealing in its incompleteness as the winged victory.

The most excellent thing in "The Pit" is the character-drawing. From Jadwin (a triumph in naming, by the way) the strong man whom the Pit o'erwhelms, down to Aunt Wess, the old-fashioned body with a mania for counting things, and whose recurrent phrase, "Well, I don't want to say anything," is exquisitely characteristic—yes, down to the very cat which soberly makes her toilet by the abandoned wheat pit, while the afternoon sun floods through the west windows—each character is real. There are scores of little touches, those vivid bits which flash like lime-lights on a personality. There are dozens of incidents and isolated scenes, each of which, lifted from its context, would lose but little. Such is the boudoir conversation between Laura Dearborn, the "heroine," and Mrs. Cressler—a conversation narrated with rare understanding of feminine subtleties, of those conventional round-about routes of thought that obtain between women, even when each knows precisely what the other is thinking. Another fine piece of description is the rehearsal for amateur theatricals; another is the scene in which Page, Laura's younger sister, who has the "journal habit," is told by Laura of her approaching marriage, and writes in her diary: "Oh, love is so beautiful—so beautiful, that it makes me sad. When I think of love in all its beauty, I am sad, sad like Romola in George Eliot's well-known novel of the same name." Isn't that the raw girl in her 'teens to the life?

The word "detached" comes naturally in speaking of the pages and paragraphs narrating incidents which are as clear-cut as cameos. And here lies, perhaps, the fault of the book. The shadow of the final tragic chapters in which is described the fall of Curtis Jadwin, who tries to corner wheat, though it lies over the beginning of the book, does not persist during the intermediate portion. The incidental *divertissement* is not subservient to the tragic theme. All events do not seem to face toward, and lead up to, the climax. The incidents are detached. Another thing which detracts somewhat is the fact that the reader is not kept "in suspense." It is plain early that Jadwin will speculate, that he will fail, that he will carry his friends down with him. The book could end no other way. And so the tragedy loses a little of its force. But taken altogether, the book is very strong, will undoubtedly be very popular, and will have no small effect in bringing into further discredit the evil of gambling on the price of wheat.

"A Significant Novel." *The Outlook*, 73 (January 17, 1903), 152–53.

Those who keep in touch with the life, not of a section, but of the country as a whole, and are sensitive to the stirrings of the spirit over the length and breadth of the continent, have felt for several years past that we are approaching another and more comprehensive expression of American life in books. One of the results of the journalistic treatment of literature, now so prevalent, is the attempt to take account of stock every week and to measure accurately the rise and fall of the tide of creative power from year to year. In the nature of things this is impossible; but the fact that it is impossible does not deter a great many people from pronouncing final judgments on literary conditions and prospects. When the tide recedes, these critics are sure that the artistic impulse in America has spent itself, or that the country has ceased to produce the material of which art is made. They are confident that commercialism, or the practical spirit, or the decay of the love of the beautiful, or absorption in material activities, has drained the springs of inspiration, and that nothing can be hoped from America in the future except a civilization which is content to work with its hands and leave other civilizations to work with the soul.

Nothing could be more short-sighted or lacking in the historical spirit than these predictions. Again and again in literary history the rise and fall of the tide of creative power have left their marks; again and again, when the vital force which blossoms in every art has receded and left the earth bare and bleak, it has come back with a rush and sweep unknown before, while the elegists were chanting its funeral dirges. No one can feel deeply the tremendous forces which are at work in the life of this country to-day without being confident that, sooner or later, those forces will find their expression in literature. Such a tide of energy as that which has been steadily mounting since the Civil War cannot find utterance for itself in material activities. Sooner or later, it reaches the higher levels of the soul, and intensity of action is translated by men of genius into intensity of aspiration.

At the very time when the press finds it difficult to keep the record of the material growth of the country, so rapid and so vast is it, there has come and gone a man with the original insight, the profound sympathy, the touch with his hand, which are the prime elements of power in a great man of letters. It is easy to overestimate the significance of a writer, like Frank Norris, who dies at the very beginning of his career; and it is too soon to pass final judgment upon the work which he has left; but it must be quite clear, even to those who differ widely from the young novelist in his methods and his point of view, that the author of "The Octopus" and "The Pit" brought to the study of American life that power of looking beneath the surface, of touching the great realities, of seeing the dramatic and ethical aspects of contemporary movements, which constitute original force in literature. While other men were saying that there can be no poetry or romance in a country so engrossed in business affairs, so absorbed in gigantic practical enterprises, Frank Norris fastened upon one of the most engrossing, colossal, and in a sense tyrannical of these activities, saw how every great outgoing of energy relates itself to many laws of life, and how impossible it is for men to work lavishly and with sublime forgetfulness with their hands without engaging their souls; and, equipped with this insight, guided by this sympathy, Norris was artist enough to seize the dramatic aspects of the raising of wheat, its transportation, and its final distribution. It was an immense theme, demanding the energy of a Zola and the genius of a Tolstoi.

It is not surprising that a man who died at thirty-two should not have shown a complete mastery of his material, and should have failed perfectly to co-ordinate all the parts of his great design. What is significant is the fact that he saw under the surface of American life the deep and inexhaustible human interest; and that he had the genius to recognize the epical quality, not of life in Russia or in France, but on the wheat-fields of the Far West and in the exchange in Chicago.

That he had the faults of a young writer is clear enough. "McTeague" was the book of a very young man, who could not discriminate clearly between what was essential and what was nonessential, and, in his attempt to tell the truth as he saw it, was willing to drag in incidents which were not only disagreeable but absurdly out of place in any formal study of character. The book was significant, not as a finished piece of art, nor as a faultless piece of workmanship, but as disclosing a determination to see things as they are, and to deal with them, not only from first-hand knowledge, but with first-hand directness and power. When "The Octopus" appeared, it registered an immense advance on all its predecessors. It was far from being a finished piece of work. The influence of Zola was evident on almost every chapter; it lacked concentration; there were departures from good taste in it, and there was lack of restraint; but, on the other hand, there were the tread and swing of a powerful man, exploring, with open mind and heart, a great new field.

The second story in the trilogy which Norris planned shows a still greater advance on the work which preceded it. There are signs of immaturity in "The Pit." The lighter phases of life with which it deals are not always touched with a light hand; Norris had still much to learn in the delicate art of social portraiture. But in the handling of his main theme "The Pit" shows the touch of a master. There is a current in the story which is almost irresistible, and which mounts at times to the height of a flood. Such power is not common anywhere in the literature of the world, and it has very rarely appeared in this country. No such searching study of the absorbing, tyrannical, destructive fascination of speculation has ever before appeared. In its vivid description of relentless energy, made up of a thousand details, each one of which contributes to the impressiveness of the general effect, one is no longer reminded of Zola, from whose influence Norris had evidently broken away, but of Balzac. There is no imitation of the method of the older writer on the part of the younger writer; but there is the same thoroughgoing, searching study of all the phenomena contributing to a tremendous impressiveness in the total result.

"The Pit," which bears the imprint of Messrs. Doubleday, Page & Co., will be widely read for its human interest; it ought to be widely read for its searching exposure of one of the perils which menace American growth and manhood in the country. It would be premature to hail "The Pit" as the great American novel. It has evident faults; but its insight, its power of imagination, and its tremendous energy ought to silence those who have been ready to declare that the material of great art does not exist on this continent; and it will confirm the hopes of those who believe that there is to be another literary development in America in the near future not less characteristic of the hope of the New World than was the fine, aspiring, noble-minded literature of a past generation.

"Books and Men Who Make Them." *Chicago Inter Ocean*, January 19, 1903, p. 7.

"The Pit," by the late Frank Norris, is at hand from the press of Doubleday, Page & Co., New York.

As all who keep informed on current fiction know, "The Pit" is the second volume of a series of three planned by Mr. Norris, the trilogy to be called: "The

Epic of the Wheat." In this connection it is of interest to quote part of a statement of the plan made by Mr. Norris under date of June 4, 1901, in New York:

The Trilogy of the Epic of the Wheat includes the following novels:
"The Octopus: A Story of California."
"The Pit: A Story of Chicago."
"The Wolf: A Story of Europe."
These novels, while forming a series, will be in no way connected with each other save only in their relation to (1) the production, (2) the distribution, (3) the consumption of American Wheat. When complete, they will form the story of a crop of wheat from the time of its sowing as seed in California to the time of its consumption as bread in a village of Western Europe.
The first novel, "The Octopus," deals with the war between the wheat grower and the Railroad Trust; the second, "The Pit," is the fictitious narrative of a "deal" in the Chicago wheat pit; while the third, "The Wolf," will probably have for its pivotal episode the relieving of a famine in an Old World community.

Mr. Norris died Oct. [25], 1902, in San Francisco. Before beginning his trilogy he had written some very readable fiction, "Moran of the Lady Letty" was his first. It was a little fantastic, but strong, and it attracted attention to the author immediately. "McTeague," "Blix," and "A Man's Woman" are his other novels. Many think that "McTeague" was the best of these, but it is no more than fair to say that the author showed growth with every effort. Certainly "A Man's Woman" was a story worthy of his pen, and when "The Octopus" appeared it was hailed as the best of his work. In England it was said to be the American novel of the decade.

However that may be, "The Octopus" was sufficiently good to assure a warm welcome for "The Pit," the second of the trilogy. "The Wolf," it is stated, was not even begun.

Characters of "The Pit."

The principal characters in "The Pit" are few. First there is Curtis Jadwin, a typical self-made Chicago man. At the beginning of the story he is a capitalist whose large and legitimate business interests keep him busy. He is an honest man, with a kind heart and fine impulses, despite his lack of what the world calls polish. Laura Dearborn is a beautiful and talented young woman, transplanted from Massachusetts to Chicago. She is about 22 when the story opens, and she has not yet "found herself," as Kipling would say. She has three lovers—Sheldon Corthell, Landry Court, and Curtis Jadwin. Corthell is an artist, and a very lovable type of his kind. He appeals to all that is artistic in Laura Dearborn, and to the woman in her. Landry Court is one of the staff of a big commission house on the board of trade. He is just a nice, jolly young fellow, a good business man, but in other walks of life as irresponsible as a schoolboy. Laura likes him and is nice to him on the older sister plan. Jadwin, last in the field, is attracted at first sight, makes up his mind that he wants her for his wife, and sets out to get her with the same persistence that marks him in business. Charles Cressler is a commission man on the board of trade. Early in his career he made a large fortune, tried to corner wheat, and was

The Pit

lucky to get off without losing all. Warned by this experience, he sticks to commission and lets speculation alone. Jadwin and Cressler are firm friends, while Laura is a sort of protégé of Mrs. Cressler. Page Dearborn is a younger sister of Laura, and Mrs. Emily Wessels is the aunt and chaperon of the Dearborn girls, who are orphans with a comfortable estate of their own. Samuel Gretry is a board of trade broker, who is much in evidence in the later scenes.

The Heroine.

The story opens at the Auditorium on a grand opera night. The Dearborn girls, with their aunt, are discovered waiting in the inner vestibule for the Cresslers, who have invited them to sit in their box. The Cresslers are late, and this gives the author a chance to describe the scene and the three women. Here is his description of the heroine:

> She was a tall young girl of about 22 or 23, holding herself erect and with fine dignity. Even beneath the opera cloak it was easy to infer that her neck and shoulders were beautiful. Her almost extreme slenderness was, however, her characteristic; the curves of her figure, the contour of her shoulders; the swell of hip and breast, were all low; from head to foot one could discover no pronounced salience. Yet there was no trace, no suggestion, of angularity. She was slender as a willow shoot is slender—and equally graceful, equally erect.
> Next to this charming tenuity, perhaps, her paleness was her most noticeable trait. But it was not a paleness of lack of color. Laura Dearborn's pallor was in itself a color. It was a tint rather than a shade, like ivory; a warm white, blending into an exquisite, delicate brownness toward the throat. Set in this paleness of brow and cheek, her deep brown eyes glowed lambent and intense. They were not large, but in some indefinable way they were important. It was very natural to speak of her eyes, and in speaking to her her friends always found that they must look squarely into their pupils. And all this beauty of pallid face and brown eyes was crowned by and sharply contrasted with the intense blackness of her hair, abundant, thick, extremely heavy, continually coruscating with somber, murky reflections, tragic, in a sense vaguely portentous—the coiffure of a heroine of romance doomed to dark crises.

The crowd thins out, the overture begins and still the Cresslers do not come. Finally Page sees a man also evidently waiting and recognizes in him Mr. Jadwin, who is to be one of the party.

> They saw a gentleman of an indeterminate age—judged by his face he might as well have been 40 or 35. A heavy moustache, touched with grey, covered his lips. The eyes were twinkling and good tempered. Between his teeth he held an unlighted cigar.

Laura wants Page to speak to him about the situation, but Page sees that Mr. Jadwin does not remember her and declines. Finally Laura does and addresses him. For an instant as she approaches an expression of suspicion, almost distrust, comes into his face.

Whereupon Laura puts on her "grand manner" and proceeds to get even as women know how to do. At that moment in come the Cresslers with Mr. Corthell and Mr. Court, crying "The bridge was turned." So everything is all right at last and they go up to their box.

A Note of Impending Tragedy.

But while Laura was waiting in the vestibule she heard the first note of the tragedy that impends all through the book:

> Directly behind them two men, their faces close together, elaborated an interminable conversation, of which, from time to time, they could overhear a phrase or two.
>
> "—and I guess he'll do well if he settles for thirty cents on the dollar. I tell you, dear boy, it was a smash!"
>
> "—never should have tried to swing a corner. The short interest was too small and the visible supply was too great."
>
> Page nudged her sister and whispered: "That's the Helmick failure they're talking about, those men. Landry Court told me all about it. Mr. Helmick had a corner in corn, and he failed today, or will fail soon, or something."

It was a wonderful night for Laura, as is the first night of grand opera for any romantic, imaginative, high-strung young woman. She sat spellbound, her hands clasped tight, her every faculty of attention at its highest pitch. Never was this first night to be forgotten, this world of perfume, of flowers, of exquisite costumes, of beautiful women, of fine, brave men. She looked back with immense pity to the narrow little life of her native town she had just left forever. How easy it was to be good and noble when music such as this had become a part of one's life. All things not positively unworthy became heroic, all things and all men. Landry Court was a young chevalier, pure as Galahad. Corthell was a beautiful artist-priest of the early Renaissance. Even Jadwin was a merchant prince, a great financial captain. And she herself—ah, she did not know; she dreamed of another Laura, a better, gentler, more beautiful Laura, whom everybody loved gently and tenderly, and who loved everybody, and who should die in some garden far away—die because of a great love—of a broken heart—and all the world would be sorry and weep over her when they found her dead and beautiful amid the flowers in some far off place where it was always early morning and there was soft music. And she was so sorry for herself and so hurt with the sheer strength of her longing to be good and true and noble and womanly that the tears ran down her cheeks and dropped on her tight-shut, white-gloved fingers.

But even as the soprano sang of love and declared that the stars and the night-bird together sang "He loves thee," and the music died away fainter and fainter, till voice and orchestra blended together in a single, barely audible murmur, vibrating with emotion, and sentiment, and romance, she heard in a hoarse masculine whisper the words:

"The shortage is a million bushels at the very least. Two hundred car loads were to arrive from Milwaukee last night—"

Then the lights went up and the act was over, and when Laura came to see was out in the foyer and Corthell was making love to her, and evidently about to ask her to be his wife. He had got as far as telling his love, and she had said that she was glad that he loved her, when Page and Landry joined them, and it was time for the next act.

A Drama of Real Life.

In the next intermission Laura stayed in the box, and Jadwin had a chance to make himself agreeable. She guessed by his manner that paying attention to young girls was for him a thing altogether unusual. As she sat and listened to him she could not help being a little attracted. He was a heavy-built man and would have made two of Corthell. His hands were large and broad—the hands of a man of affairs who knew how to grip, and, above all, how to hold on. Those broad, strong hands and keen, calm eyes would enfold and envelop a purpose with tremendous strength, and they would persist and persist and persist, unswerving, unwavering, and untiring, till the Purpose was driven home. And the two long, lean, fibrous arms of his! What a reach they could attain, and how wide and huge, and even formidable, would be their embrace of affairs!

And then, abruptly, between two phases of that music drama of passion and romance, there came to Laura a swift and vivid impression of that other drama that at that very moment was working itself out close at hand, equally picturesque, equally romantic, equally passionate; but more than that, real, actual, modern—a thing in the very heart of the life in which she moved. And here he sat, this Jadwin, quiet, in evening dress, listening good-naturedly to this beautiful music for which he did not care, to this rant and fustian, watching quietly all this posing and attitudinizing. She was astonished. This was the man she promised herself she would humble for that first mistrustful stare at her. Corthell made her feel her sex. With Jadwin she felt his manhood more than her womanhood; he made her feel that she had a head as well as a heart.

Driving home to the North Side, they turned up to La Salle street from Jackson boulevard. They found the office buildings lighted from basement to roof. Through the windows could be seen clerks and book-keepers at work in their shirt sleeves, though it was long after midnight. The sidewalks were full, and messenger boys ran to and fro. It was the Helmick failure in full blast.

Laura looked, suddenly stupefied. Here it was, then, that other drama, that other tragedy, working on there furiously, fiercely through the night, while she and all those others had sat there in that atmosphere of flowers and perfume, listening to music. Suddenly it loomed portentous in the eye of her mind, terrible, tremendous. Ah, this drama of the "Provision Pits;" where the rush of millions of bushels of grain and the clatter of millions of dollars, and the wild shouting of thousands of men filled all the air with the noise of battle. Yes, here was drama in deadly earnest—drama, and tragedy, and death, and the jar of mortal fighting.

* * *

Laura turned and looked back. On either side of the vista in converging lines stretched the blazing office buildings. But over the end of the street the lead-colored sky was rifted a little. A long, faint bar of light stretched across the prospect, and silhouetted against this rose a somber mass, unbroken by any lights, rearing a black and formidable facade against the blur of light behind it.

And this was her last impression of the evening. The lighted office buildings, the murk of rain, the haze of light in the heavens, and against it the pile of the Board of Trade Building, black, grave, monolithic, crouching on its foundations like a monstrous sphinx with blind eyes, silent, grave—crouching there without a sound, without sign of life under the night and the drifting veil of rain.

Chicago, the Great.

The preliminaries of the story run along smoothly. "The Pit," as the subtitle sets forth, is "A Story of Chicago," and the author therefore works in graphic bits of description by way of letting Laura learn to know her new home. Mr. Norris took one thing at least close to his heart: That Chicago was the heart of the nation, as shown by the following:

> Or, again, it was South Water Street—a jam of delivery wagons and market carts backed to the curbs, leaving only a tortuous path between the endless files of horses, suggestive of an actual barrack of cavalry. Provisions, market produce, "garden truck," and fruits in an infinite welter of crates and baskets, boxes and sacks, crowded the sidewalks. The gutter was choked with an overflow of refuse cabbage leaves, soft oranges, decaying beet tops. The air was thick with the heavy smell of vegetation. Food was trodden under foot, food crammed the stores and warehouses to bursting. Food mingled with the mud of the highway. The very dray horses were gorged with an unending nourishment of snatched mouthfuls picked from backboard, from barrel top, and from the edge of the sidewalk. The entire locality reeked with the fatness of a hundred thousand furrows. A land of plenty, the inordinate abundance of the earth itself emptied itself upon the asphalt and cobbles of the quarter. It was the Mouth of the City, and drawn from all directions, over a territory of immense area, this glut of crude subsistence was sucked in, as if into a rapacious gullet, to feed the sinews and to nourish the fibers of an immeasurable colossus.

> Suddenly the meaning and significance of it all dawned upon Laura. The Great City, brooking no rival, imposed its dominion upon a reach of country larger than many a kingdom of the Old World. For thousands of miles beyond its confines was its influence felt. Out, far out, far away in the snow and shadow of northern Wisconsin forests, axes and saws bit the bark of century-old trees, stimulated by this city's energy. Just as far to the southward pick and drill leaped to the assault of veins of anthracite, moved by her central power. Her force turned the wheels of harvester and seeder a thousand miles distant in Iowa and Kansas. Her force spun the screws and propellers of innumerable squadrons of lake steamers crowding the Sault Ste.

Marie. For her and because of her all the Central States, all the Great Northwest, roared with trafffic and industry; sawmills screamed, factories, their smoke blackening the sky, clashed and flamed; wheels turned, pistons leaped in their cylinders; cog gripped cog; belting clasped the drums of mammoth wheels, and converters of forges belched into the clouded air their tempest breath of molten steel.

It was Empire, the resistless subjugation of all this central world of the lakes and the prairies, Here, midmost in the land, beat the Heart of the Nation, whence inevitably must come its immeasurable power, its infinite, infinite, inexhaustible vitality. Here, of all her cities, throbbed the true life—the true power and spirit of America; gigantic, crude with the crudity of youth, disdaining rivalry; sane and healthy and vigorous; brutal in its ambition, arrogant in the new-found knowledge of its giant strength, prodigal of its wealth, infinite in its desires. In its capacity boundless, in its courage indomitable, subduing the wilderness in a single generation, defying calamity, and through the flame and debris of a commonwealth in ashes rising suddenly renewed, formidable, and Titanic.

"The Pit."

Here is one of his descriptions of the Pit—the board of trade:

> Often Jadwin had noted the scene, and, unimaginative though he was, had long since conceived the notion of some great, some resistless, force within the Board of Trade Building that held the tide of the streets within its grip, alternately drawing it in and throwing it forth. Within there, a great whirlpool, a pit of roaring waters spun and thundered, sucking in the life tides of the city, sucking them in as into the mouth of some tremendous cloaca, the maw of some colossal sewer; then vomiting them forth again, spewing them up and out, only to catch them in the return eddy and suck them in afresh.
>
> Thus it went, day after day. Endlessly, ceaselessly, the Pit, enormous, thundering, sucked in and spewed out, sending the whirl of its mighty central eddy far out through the city's channels. Terrible at the center, it was, at the circumference, gentle, insidious, and persuasive, the send of the flowing so mild that to embark upon it seemed devoid of all risk. But the circumference was not bounded by the city. All through the Northwest, all through the central world of the Wheat, the set and whirl of that innermost Pit made itself felt; and it spread and spread and spread till grain in the elevators of Western Iowa moved and stirred and answered to its centripetal force, and men upon the streets of New York felt the mysterious tugging of its undertow engage their feet, embrace their bodies, overwhelm them, and carry them bewildered and unresisting back and downwards to the Pit itself.
>
> Nor was the Pit's centrifugal power any less. Because of some sudden eddy spinning outward

from the middle of its turmoil, a dozen bourses of continental Europe clamored with panic, a dozen Old World banks, firm as the established hill, trembled and vibrated. Because of an unexpected caprice in the swirling of the inner current, some far-distant channel suddenly dried, and the pinch of famine made itself felt among the vinedressers of Northern Italy, the coal miners of Western Prussia. Or another channel filled, and the starved moujik of the steppes, and the hunger-shrunken coolie of the Ganges' watershed, fed suddenly fat and made thank offerings before ikon and idol.

There in the center of the Nation, midmost of that continent that lay between the oceans of the New World and the Old, in the heart's heart of the affairs of men, roared and rumbled the Pit. It was as if the Wheat, Nourisher of the Nations, as it rolled gigantic and majestic in a vast flood from West to East, here, like a Niagara, finding its flow impeded, burst suddenly into the appalling fury of the Maelstrom, into the chaotic spasm of a world-force, a primeval energy, blood-brother of the earthquake and the glacier, raging and wrathful that its power should be braved by some pinch of human spawn that dared raise barriers across its courses.

By Way of Preliminary.

A preliminary development of the story is that Gretry induces Jadwin to go into a grain deal, showing him that there is no chance to lose. Jadwin at first refuses, though he sees that the deal is a good one. He says:

"I know, Sam, and the trouble is not that I don't want to speculate, but that I do—too much. That's why I said I'd keep out of it. It isn't so much the money as the fun of playing the game. With half a show I would get in a little more and a little more, till by and by I'd try to throw a big thing and the big thing would throw me."

But Jadwin went in, just the same, and pulled out $50,000.

In the meantime all three of Laura's lovers were making love to her. The girl was not a flirt, but she liked to be loved. But one fateful night Corthell again proposed, and Jadwin asked her to be his wife, and Landry Court dared to kiss her on the cheek as he said good-night in the hall. This brought the girl up with a round turn. She went over the situation, was ashamed to find that she had more or less encouraged all three men, decided that she did not want to marry at all, and sat down and wrote all three lovers. She told Landry Court that she never wanted to see him again, apologized to Corthell and dismissed him, and told Jadwin that his suit was hopeless, intimating that she hoped they would still be friends.

The behavior of the three men was characteristic. Landry wrote her an abject and tear-stained apology. The artist sent her a box of Jacqueminot roses, with a single line of farewell. When she got back from a long walk she found Jadwin waiting for her; he had been sitting in the house for two hours.

This being the case, it will not surprise the reader to learn that in the end she did marry Jadwin. He made a surprisingly satisfactory husband for even such a romantic and impulsive young woman as Laura. Then the story jumps three years, during which the Jadwins have been to Europe and the husband has surrounded her with everything that heart could wish and love suggest.

Beginning of a Corner.

During this time, also, Jadwin had more than once speculated in wheat. He no longer needed Gretry's urging to spur him. He was "blooded to the game." He had developed into a strategist— bold, of inconceivable effrontery, delighting in the shock of battle, never more jovial, more daring, than when under stress of the most merciless attack. It was a bear season and had been for three years. It was a saying on the board that all that was necessary to make money was to sell wheat.

Then, all of a sudden, Jadwin turned bull and began to buy. Gretry called him a fool, but Jadwin had worked out the problem for himself and would go his own way. He did, and he cleaned up $500,000 in one day. That very day Corthell returns from Europe and is invited to dine with the Jadwins. Jadwin does not return till late and there is a graphic description of the scene when he comes in and announces his success. It is pregnant with a sense of coming disaster. The lonely wife, hurt by her husband's rapidly increasing absorption in speculation; the sympathetic artist, loving her as devotedly as ever, and appealing to the very side of her that her husband is neglecting; the capitalist, flushed with his triumph and blind to the possibility of disaster either in his business or in his home— The three make a vivid scene.

Then, one day, Gretry and Jadwin were in the broker's office figuring on the situation. They figured out that there are less than 100,000,000 bushels of wheat in the entire country. Gretry says he has a lot of short wheat on his books:

Jadwin was silent a moment, tugging at his mustache. Then suddenly he leaned forward, his finger almost in Gretry's face.

"Why, look here!" he cried. "Don't you see? Don't you see—"

"See what?" demanded the broker, puzzled at the other's vehemence.

Jadwin loosened his collar with his forefinger.

"Great Scott! I'll choke in a minute. See what? Why, I own 10,000,000 bushels of this wheat already, and Europe will take eighty million out of the country. Why, there ain't going to be any wheat left in Chicago by May! If I get in now and buy a long line of cash wheat, where are all these fellows who've sold short going to get it to deliver it? Say, where are they going to get? Come on, now, tell me, where are they going to get it?"

Gretry laid down his pencil and stared at Jadwin, looked long at the papers on his desk, consulted his penciled memoranda, then thrust his hands deep into his pockets, with a long breath. Bewildered, and as if stupefied, he gazed again into Jadwin's face.

"My God!" he murmured at last.

"Well, where are they going to get it?" Jadwin cried once more, his face suddenly scarlet.

"J," faltered the broker, "J, I—I'm damned if I know."

And then, all in a moment, the two men were on their feet. The event which all those past eleven months had been preparing was suddenly consummated, suddenly stood revealed as though a veil had been ripped asunder, as though an explosion had crashed through the air upon them, deafening, blinding.

Jadwin sprang forward, gripping the broker by the shoulder.

"Sam!" he shouted, "do you know—great God!—do you know what this means? Sam, we can corner the wheat market!"

Jadwin, King of Wheat.

Well, Jadwin was right; the market could be cornered. And he proceeded to do it. But he had to do it under cover, for when he had made his $500,000 coup he had promised his wife that he would let speculation alone. And he had made a brave fight to keep his word, but the fascination of the pit had been too strong for him. So presently the papers had much to say of the Unknown Bull who dominated the market in May wheat. Soon it was figured out that this unknown Napoleon of Wheat had actually cornered the May market. Then it became known that this Czar was Jadwin. Fame beyond estimation was his. The press talked of little else and exploited him in a thousand ways. Deputations of farmers came all the way from the Far West to make him presentations and tell him how mortgages were being paid off, new farming implements were being bought, new livestock purchased, and new areas seeded. All these deputations blessed the name of Jadwin.

And why not? He had forced wheat up to $1.50 and a wave of prosperity was sweeping through the great wheat belt. One letter said:

—and, sir, you must know that not a night passes that my little girl, now going on 7, sir, and the brightest of her class in the county seat grammar school, does not pray to have God bless Mr. Jadwin, who helped papa save the farm.

As for Jadwin himself, his wealth increased with such stupefying rapidity that at no time was he able to even approximate the gains that accrued to him because of his corner. It was more than $20,000,000 and less than $50,000,000. That was all he knew. Nor were the everlasting hills more secure than he from the attack of any human enemy. Out of the ranks of the conquered there issued not so much as a whisper of hostility. Within his own sphere no Czar, no satrap, no Caesar ever wielded power more resistless.

"Sam," said Curtis Jadwin at length to the broker, "Sam, nothing in the world can stop me now. They think I've been doing something big, don't they, with this corner. Why, I've only just begun. This is just a feeler. Now I'm going to let 'em know just how big a gun C. J. really is. I'm going to swing this deal right over into July. I'm going to buy in my July shorts."

The Beginning of the End.

That was the beginning of the end of Curtis Jadwin, King of Wheat. To corner wheat is possible, but to no man is it given to corner wheat twice. The very prosperity that he had created in the wheat belt was his undoing. Nature again took a hand in the July deal, and this time she was his enemy.

In "The Octopus" one of the characters was watching the wheat pour in a golden stream from the enormous elevators into the hold of a ship. He slipped and fell, and the grain poured in on him; held him by the legs; rose high and higher to his neck, to his mouth, choking his frantic cries; burying him beneath it, and blotting him out forever. So with Jadwin:

> Jadwin was in the thick of the confusion by now. And the avalanche, the undiked ocean of the wheat, leaping to the lash of the hurricane, struck him fairly in the face.
>
> He heard it now; he heard nothing else. The wheat had broken from his control. For months he had, by the might of his single arm, held it back; but now it rose like the upbuilding of a colossal billow. It towered, towered, hung poised for an instant, and then, with a thunder as of the grind and crash of chaotic worlds, broke upon him, burst through the pit and raced past him, on and on, to the eastward and to the hungry nations.

But to know the full measure of the undoing of Curtis Jadwin you must read "The Pit" for yourself. For, you see, there were infinite possibilities of disaster in the situation; it was not financial disaster only that threatened. And just by way of a hint as to the possibilities it may be ventured that Cressler, lured back at last into the game of the Pit, was found with a bullet hole in his temple.

Extended remarks about the faults of this posthumous novel of Frank Norris do not seem fitting. For one thing, it evidently lacks the final revision that the author, had he lived, would have given its pages. His Chicago geography, for instance, is woefully faulty. And one may notice some careless writing in the extracts given.

But by way of praise there is much to be said. "The Epic of the Wheat" was nobly planned. If the execution fall short of the plan it must be remembered that "The Epic of the Wheat" is an heroic subject. Yet "The Pit" is not small. On the contrary, it is big with the bigness of our American spirit, now felt and respected to the uttermost ends of the earth. It is more than a story: it is a study of life in certain phases distinctly and emphatically American—which is to say of the West and of Chicago. Indeed, one would say that "The Pit" comes nearer to setting forth the atmosphere of Chicago—the great, hustling, untidy clearing-house of the West—than anything that any other man has written.

When Frank Norris died he was called a "potential" genius. "The Pit" shows that he was a genius, undisciplined, but on the way to do great work of an enduring kind. Many writers outlive their fame. Frank Norris died too soon. His death is a distinct loss to American literature.

G.H.S.
"Books of the Day: *The Pit:* Frank Norris's Last Novel."
Boston Evening Transcript,
January 21, 1903,
p. 16.

By the death of Frank Norris, at the age of thirty-two, American literature lost its greatest known potentiality. This is not to say that there are not greater writers left, of the older generation, or greater yet to be known. But the first great work of the trilogy of the "Epic of the Wheat" which Mr. Norris wrote and which Doubleday, Page & Co. have published—"The Octopus"—gave us to see that here was an author who would bring great things into our American literature, and who must be regarded as by far the most promising of our American writers. The word "promising" is used advisedly, for if "The Octopus" was not the long expected "great American novel" in actual fact, it was near enough to it to lead us to hope that the man in his maturity might produce the expected thing. No one else had written so near American life in the same way, and the one thing that inevitably struck the reader of this first work of the trilogy was that here was an author of genuine force, a man who was working out a great idea because he could not help doing so, a potentiality in American letters.

But alas! the hand of the writer was stayed by death, and "The Pit," the second volume of the Epic, is the last. As a trilogy the work cannot be judged. No one knows what he might have done with the third volume and so "The Pit" must stand by itself. There are certain inherent difficulties in dealing with the trilogy, which has ever been a favorite literary form among great writers. The success of the trilogy depends so much upon the continuity of the central idea, that the thing must be carried to a logical conclusion for the reader to feel the entire force of the argument. Mr. Norris had happily finished "The Pit," but he had not even outlined the third volume, "The Wolf," which was to complete his trilogy dealing with the production, the marketing and the distribution of a crop of wheat. So if "The Pit" seems to lack something of the interest of "The Octopus," it might be attributed to the fact that the latter took us by surprise. The scene was less familiar, and the struggle of the farmers with the railroad was less generally known than the conflict of the wheat pit, which has not been neglected by other writers of fiction. We must consider the two volumes together as only a part of a grand whole, and the finished volumes give the strongest of evidence that the trilogy would have been an accomplishment in American letters to stand when other books have been forgotten, and the authors' names, now prominent before the public, are but dimly remembered.

The criticism has been made that there is no particular merit in the idea of following a crop of wheat from its production through the markets of the world to the consumer. It is claimed that the raison d'être of a work of art ought not to rest upon an abstract idea. Why not? The novelist, according to Mr. Norris's own idea, is dealing with life, with the eternal verities, and only a work founded upon the immutable can of itself hope to survive. I have before me a letter of the late novelist, in which he says:

"I do not conceive it within the province of the novelist to furnish solutions for existing problems, or to point the way to a solution. The novelist, by nature, cannot be a political economist. It is the province of the novelist to describe life as it is, to tell the thing as he sees it, leaving it to the political economists to find a remedy for the problems of life."

The reader of the "Epic of the Wheat" must bear in mind this attitude of the writer. Furthermore, he must know that Mr. Norris was a symbolist. To his mind, wheat represented the nourisher of the world, and the production of the wheat crop, in "The Octopus," dealt with a world-old question, the struggle of Capital and Labor. "The Pit," dealing with the marketing of the wheat, symbolized Competition, the strenuous expression of our virile American life. "The Wolf," which was to deal with the distribution of the wheat crop to a famine-stricken district in Western Europe, was to be built around the idea of the Struggle for Existence. These are eternal verities—the things which press in forever upon the mind of the thoughtful man and insistently demand consideration. The plan of treating these in a series was not a fanciful one. The idea of production, of distribution and consumption might be applied to cordwood in the Maine forests, and thereby furnish as good novels, if one has the skill to apply that idea so that the reader shall see that behind it stands the enduring truth, and the Life itself is described, and not the outward symbol of it alone.

Mr. Norris spoke of his undertaking as "a very heavy task," when he started upon the writing of "The Pit." He appreciated the loss of the fresh ground which he had in "The Octopus," but it is the more to his enduring fame that he has shown no falling off in power. His skill of execution is as great as in the first book of the trilogy, and his portraiture is equally strong, although no one character stands out as distinctly as does the fat railroad agent in "The Octopus." This perchance demonstrates his fidelity to truth. His Chicago speculator is a masterpiece, but he is not the only figure in a larger world than that of the San Joaquin Valley and due attention has been given to other characters who play their prominent parts in the life of the great gray city. It is not that his character of the speculator is less distinct, but that other characters are more so, and there are fewer of them than in "The Octopus."

"The Pit" is a simple enough story in outline. Laura Dearborn, a young girl from Worcester county, in Massachusetts, goes to live in Chicago, and on her first night at the grand opera meets Curtis Jadwin, a successful real estate dealer. Even in the opera box she hears some talk about the wheat market, and thus the first motif for the novel is introduced. Norris deals, like Zola, in the splendid antithesis of life; on the one hand the amenities of life, the artistic side of humanity, the splendor of wealth, and on the other the fierce, grim battle for existence which obtrudes itself into the Italian opera. Laura comes to understand this antithesis as she sees how the city imposes its dominion upon half a world:

"It was a life in which women had no part, and in which, should they enter it, they would no longer recognize son or husband, or father or brother. The gentle mannered fellow, clean minded, clean handed, of the breakfast or supper table, was one man. The other—who and what was he? Down there in the murk and grime of the business district raged the battle of the street, and therein he was a being transformed, casehardened, supremely selfish, asking no quarter; no, nor giving any. Fouled with the clutchings and grapplings of the attack, besmirched with the elbowing of low associates and obscure allies, he set his foot toward conquest, and mingled with the marchings of an army that surged forever forward and back, now in merciless assault, beating the fallen enemy under foot, now in repulse, equally merciless, trampling down the auxiliaries of the day before in a panic dash for safety; always cruel, always selfish, always pitiless."

Laura, beautiful and accomplished,

has three lovers, one an artist, who appeals to her romantic side, another a young fellow who has yet his fortune to make, but who is "chummy" and boyish, and the third, Curtis Jadwin, who ultimately wins her by his masterful manner. Only until after they are married does she feel sure of her love for her husband, and her life is ideal until her husband enters the field of speculation. He soon neglects his brilliant young wife, and the artist comes again upon the scene. Starving for love, Laura is about to leave her home with the artist, when her husband comes home to her, a ruined man. The hour of his failure is her triumph.

But the main line of the story follows the operations of Jadwin in the Chicago wheat market. From a successful bear operator he becomes a bull, and through this the story moves swiftly and surely to the inevitable catastrophe. Jadwin becomes a mysterious force, cornering the wheat supply of the world. But led by his pride, believing himself invincible, he attempts to carry the corner too long, and essays a repetition of his success—a success bought at the cost of the execrations of wheat consumers in the Old World and the suicide of one of his dearest friends.

"But he knew the danger—knew just how terrible was to be the grapple. Once that same day a certain detail of business took him near to the entrance to the floor. Though he did not so much as look inside the doors, he could not but hear the thunder of the Pit. Out of that hideous turmoil he imagined there issued a strange unwonted note, as it were, the first rasp and grind of a new avalanche just beginning to stir, a diapason more profound that any he had yet known, a hollow, distant bourdon as of the slipping and sliding of some almighty and chaotic power.

"It was the Wheat! the Wheat! It was on the move again. From the farms of Illinois and Iowa, from the ranches of Kansas and Nebraska, from all the reaches of the Middle West, the wheat, like a tidal wave, was rising, rising. Almighty, blood-brother to the earthquake, coeval with the volcano and the whirlwind, that gigantic worldforce, that colossal billow, Nourisher of the Nations, was swelling and advancing.

"There in the Pit its first premonitory eddies already swirled and spun. If even the first ripples of the tide smote terribly upon the heart, what was it to be when the ocean itself burst through, on its eternal way from West to East? For an instant came clear vision. What were these shouting, gesticulating men of the Board of Trade, these brokers, traders, speculators? It was not these he fought; it was that fatal New Harvest; it was the Wheat; it was—as Gretry had said—the very earth itself. What were those scattered hundreds of farmers of the Middle West, who, because he had put the price so high, had planted grain as never before? What had they to do with it? Why, the wheat had grown itself; demand and supply, these were the great laws the wheat obeyed. Almost blasphemous in his effrontery, he had tampered with the laws, and had roused a Titan. He had laid his puny human grasp upon Creation, and the very earth herself, the great mother, feeling the touch of the cobweb the human insect had spun, had stirred at last in her sleep, and sent her omnipotence moving through the grooves of the world to find and crush the disturber of her appointed courses."

The description of the final act in this grand tragedy is a tremendous piece of work. It is of a part with those scenes which remain in literature as indelible pictures of fiction, like the retribution which overtakes S. Behrman in "The Octopus," the closing scene in "Germinal," or the struggle of Jean Valjean in the sewer. There is a touch of symbolism, too, in the final words of the book, a repetition of the words which close the first chapter, where Laura, as she raises the carriage curtains to look out, in driving home from the opera, sees the scene of her husband's ultimate downfall.

"And this was the last impression of the part of her life that that day brought to a close; the tall, gray office buildings, the murk of rain, the haze of light in the heavens, and raised against it, the pile of the Board of Trade Building, black, monolithic, crouching on its foundations like a monstrous sphinx with blind eyes, silent, grave—crouching there without a sound, without sign of life, under the night and the drifting veil of rain."

"Books of the Week: An Epic of the Wheat." *Public Opinion*, 34 (January 22, 1903), 121.

In this story of the wheat pit Mr. Norris has written his last and best book. His power of comprehending and depicting large movements without ignoring or obscuring the necessary details shows to good advantage, and the mingling of the humorous and the tragic in human affairs, the general incongruity of life, appears in accurate proportion and vivid colors. He has boldly attacked a familiar and difficult—perhaps difficult because familiar—arena in which to array his characters, the wheat pit of the Chicago board of trade. In the character of the speculator, Curtis Jadwin, who attempts to corner the world's supply of wheat and fails only because the wheat was grown faster than he could buy it, he has had an easy task. Strong but simple-minded, country-bred but the equal of any man on the floor of the board of trade in subtlety and the strategy of the market, his distinguishing traits are so few and so easily seen that Mr. Norris has not found it a serious matter to present a life-like picture of him. With Laura, his wife, the case is very different. Ambitious, high-bred, complex, craving attention, but with a strain of the Puritan in her, she might well have baffled even the cleverness of Mr. Norris. That he has painted her clearly and impressively without any appearance of straining for effect or overemphasis is the highest tribute that could be paid to the quality of his genius. In her he has drawn a high type of the American woman whose virtues are positive without being strident, and whose faults are virtues carried to extremes.

It is in his character work that Mr. Norris shows the greatest advance over his earlier manner. It has required fewer strokes of the pencil, less color, less dependence on details of feature and character to present a satisfactory picture. Formerly he seemed to be possessed with the fear that his readers might not see the characters exactly as he saw it, a fear that is not entirely absent in some of the descriptive passages of this book. This added lightness of touch is used to advantage in the delineation of the minor personages of the cast. This is especially true of Landry Court, the young broker's clerk, who, Sheldon Corthell says, always impresses him as "though he had just had his hair cut." This young gentleman, when Page Dearborn, still in her teens, confides to him that she has frequent fits of brooding melancholy, recklessly responds: "Well, so have I. At night, sometimes—when I wake up. Then I'm all down in the mouth, and I say, 'What's the use, by Jingo?' " The artist, Sheldon Corthell, with whom Laura at times always imagines herself to be in love, is also well portrayed.

The narrative leads easily and naturally from the opening chapter, where the discussion of the latest failure on the board is mingled with the strains of Italian grand opera, through the marriage of Jadwin and Laura and her awakening to the fact that she is really in love with her husband, the gradual enticement of Jadwin into speculation in wheat and the consequent estrangement of the couple, and reaches its climax in the great corner in wheat, which sent the price soaring and brought upon Jadwin's head the unqualified praise of the farmers and the equally unqualified execration of everyone else and collapsed finally in a smash that buried Jadwin and his fortune and caused the suicide of his closest friend. In describing the break of the corner Mr. Norris is perhaps too insistent that his readers shall understand the situation. The scene is graphic, almost sensational. Jadwin has gone down into the wheat pit in a last vain effort to stay the toppling price that is falling before the inrush of the new wheat from the western farms. "Jadwin was in the thick of the confusion by now. The wheat had broken from his control. For months he had, by the might of his single arm, held it back; but now it rose like the upbuilding of a colossal billow. It towered, towered, hung poised for an instant, and then, with a thunder as of the grind and crash of chaotic worlds, broke upon him, burst through the pit and raced past him, on and on to the eastwards and to the hungry nations."

The end is tragic in a way, but it is impersonal tragedy. Bankruptcy and poverty are visited upon the daring speculator and his followers, although their courage is apparently unbroken. With indomitable cheerfulness they go back to their gambling as soon as they have recovered their breath, or turn their attention to less risky occupations. In nothing is the conception more typically American and modern than in the last glimpse that we catch of Jadwin, the ruined speculator, rising with his spirit unbroken from the wreck of his fortune.

"The Heart of the Nation, Norris Calls Chicago." *Brooklyn Daily-Eagle*, January 22, 1903, p. 12.

We present to-day two reviews of the late Frank Norris' new novel, "The Pit." The first is a criticism of his style; the second is a surrender to the irresistible attraction of his story-telling.

"The Pit" (Doubleday, Page & Co., $1.50) is a story of Chicago by the late Frank Norris, whose novel, "The Octopus," won for him a cosmopolitan reputation as the most ambitious and the most painstaking of American novelists. His recent death was, of course, the occasion for much talk about the "promise" nipped in the bud, but Norris quite fulfilled his promise. He would not have done better, and he probably would have done worse, if he had had time to write as much as Zola,

The Pit

and as his manner happened to be the manner of Zola, his reputation would not improbably have dwindled away more quickly than his invention. The world has long since tired of Zola, although the fascination of a pioneer name always outlasts critical judgment, and we shall probably see as big a rush for the forthcoming "Truth" as there was for "Nana." But Norris began where Zola ended; he inherited the tired feeling which the name of Zola had begun to produce. Perhaps it was fortunate for the abiding reputation of Norris that destiny foreclosed on his ambition when it did. "The Octopus" and "The Pit," to say nothing of "McTeague" and "Moran" are classical contributions to American fiction which will remain colossal by the very reason of their loneliness.

Norris, His Rhetorical Redundancy.

The impression felt after the first hundred pages of "The Pit" is one of disappointment. There is the harsh amateurism of the realist who does not know when not to say a thing; who intrudes superfluous description where it mars the content and interrupts the narrative; and who, worst fault of all, is redundant, pleonastic, in the determination to be impressive. Norris, like Zola, was deficient in delicacy and finesse; unable to produce effects by suggestion, he hammered them out by force. As examples, here are two taken at random:

"Within there, the Board of Trade Building, a great whirlpool, a pit of roaring waters spun and thundered, sucking on the life tides of the city, sucking them in as into the mouth of some tremendous cloaca, the maw of some colossal sewer; then vomiting them forth again, spewing them up and out, only to catch them in the return eddy and suck them in afresh."

In this passage each figure of the metaphor is repeated twice by means of identical synonyms. Cloaca is Latin for sewer, maw and mouth, vomit and spew are the same things.

"It was the debris of the battle field, the abandoned impedimenta and broken weapons of contending armies, the detritus of conflict, torn, broken and rent, that at the end of each day's combat, incumbered the field." (Crumpled telegram on the floor of the Exchange.)

This again is mere reiteration and verbosity. It is importing the manner of the pulpit into the quietude of the closet.

Similarly injudicious is the manner in which the abstract reflections are forced onto the narrative of facts:

"As Jadwin crossed Jackson street, on his way to his broker's office on the lower floor of the Board of Trade building, he noted the ebb and flow that issued from its doors, and remembered the huge river of wheat that rolled through this place from the farms of Iowa and ranches of Dakota to the mills and bakeshops of Europe."

As Jadwin was a dealer in real estate, and not a novelist, it is improbable that he made these reflections. Straining probability for the sake of airing an idea falls short of the finest workmanship.

Norris, His Mastery of Detail.

But the little prejudices inspired by the first contact with Norris' manner vanish before the irresistible hypnotism of his genius. There is nothing affected or exaggerated in his astonishing closeness of observation and the masterly exactitude of his descriptions. Leaving aside the splendid picture of a morning at the Wheat Pit (Chapter 3), a picture which will be quoted, we dare swear, in anthologies of the next century, here is an admirable little specimen of the Norris Zolaism—the habit of making everything real even at the risk of superfluity:

"Jadwin came in his double seated buggy, his negro coachman beside him and the two coach dogs, Rex and Rox, trotting under the rear axle. His horses were not showy, nor were they made conspicuous by elaborate boots, bandages, and all the solemn paraphernalia of the stable, yet men upon the sidewalk, amateurs, breeders, men who understood good stock, never failed to watch the team go by, heads up, the check rein swinging loose, ears all alert, eyes all alight, the breath deep, strong and slow, and the stride, machine like, even as the swing of a metronome, thrown out from the shoulder to the knee, snapped on from knee to fetlock, from fetlock to pastern, finishing squarely, beautifully, with the thrust of the hoof, planted an instant, then, as it were, flinging the roadway behind it, snatched up again, and again cast forward."

Detail like this, well enough in a horse biography or a trotting text book, is, of course, entirely out of place and intrusive in the description of a tea party; but when there is so much of it, applied to all sorts of matter, it is dignified into specialism and makes of a novel a sort of cyclopedia or moving picture of contemporary life.

Norris, His Belief in Chicago.

"The Pit" is an ordinary society novel with a love story, but without a plot, filled up with the incidents of the social and commercial life of Chicago and portraits of a number of persons representative of American fashion and finance. Not the least important of the phases of life depicted is that dealing with the speculation in wheat on the Chicago Stock Exchange and Mr. Norris makes this topic the occasion for some impressive, if trite, reflections.

In one passage he predicts that Chicago will become the metropolis of the United States, as the hub of the biggest wheel in commerce, the wheel which moves the food.

"It was Empire. The resistless subjugation of all this central world of lakes and prairies. Here, midmost in the land, beat the Heart of the Nation, where inevitably must come its unmeasurable power, its infinite, infinite, inexhaustible vitality. Here, of all her cities, throbbed the true life—the true power and spirit of America; gigantic, crude with the crudity of youth; disdaining rivalry; sane and healthy and vigorous; brutal in its ambition, arrogant in the new found knowledge of its giant strength, prodigal of its wealth, infinite in its desires."

* * *

"The Pit" is enthralling—enthralling. It marks the top notch in the real American novel—the novel of business. It describes how a man named Jadwin succeeded in cornering May wheat and went smash in trying to carry the corner over into July Wheat. The cornering of wheat—or gigantic speculations toward that end—is an old story, and a story that has been admirably told by hundreds of newspaper reporters. But the late Frank Norris—laurels on his lamented grave!—has made more than a newspaper story of it. He has made of it an epic. He has shown how insidiously the craze of speculation seizes a great mind—how ambition o'erleaps itself as Napoleonically in finance as in war. Jadwin began as a "bear"; he was triumphant when he cleared half a million in one day. But he couldn't stop. This is how the "corner" began:

"Jadwin was silent a moment, tugging at his mustache. Then suddenly he leaned forward, his finger almost in the broker's face.

" 'Why, look here,' he cried. 'Don't you see? Don't you see—'

" 'See what?' demanded Gretry.

"Jadwin loosened his collar with a forefinger.

" 'Great Scott! I'll choke in a minute! See what? Why, I own ten million bushels of this wheat already, and Europe will take eighty million out of the country. Why, there ain't going to be any wheat left in Chicago by May! If I get in now and buy a long line of cash wheat, where are all these fellows who have sold short going to get it to deliver it to me? Say, where are they going to get it? Come on now, tell me, where are they going to get it?'

" 'My God!' murmured Gretry at last."

Accordingly, in May, Jadwin, the "unknown Bull," held all the wheat, in America. He had bought it at about 90. It quickly mounted to a dollar; but at a dollar, a dollar and a half, a dollar and one the panic stricken bears found there was no wheat to be had. Then they "tumbled"; Jadwin had positively cornered the market. He could make his own price—and he made it capriciously at anything over $1.50, meaning winnings of over $20,000,000 in a month.

But then infatuation, accompanied by the dread prompter of mental breakdown, struck him. Instead of realizing—and that was difficult, for the price would break should he unload—he determined to corner the next crop also and send the price to two dollars. It was here that nature stepped in, and here that Norris works off the immense if fantastical "problem" which formed the inspiration of the trilogy.

Jadwin was no longer fighting men—he was fighting the law of growth, the law of supply and demand. The growth of wheat is as indispensable and as inevitable as the continuance of population. When prices are inflated new areas come under cultivation; the flood of grain pours into the market in volumes too immense and too rapid for any single financier to control. The supply of "visible" in July exceeded all Jadwin's calculations; the bears were sure of covering their "shorts," and they sold, sold, sold, until Jadwin and his broker suddenly found themselves distressed for the actual cash necessary for margins and storage, although they possessed $40,000,000 worth of wheat.

Then—the market "broke." In the midst of a veritable pandemonium Jadwin, the Great Bull in person, went on the floor of the board, deserted by his brokers.

"Give a dollar for July—give a dollar for July!" he cried.

But every one knew that he had no longer a dollar to give. "Yah-h-h. Yah-h-h, he's done for, busted; busted!" was the howl that greeted him.

One rises from the perusal of this enthralling story so much under the grip of its wonderful virility and realness that one's disposition is all for unbridled praise. But of course there are other things in literature beside the stock speculations of uneducated business men. There are multitudes of "cultured" readers who will merely resent this glorification of what, to their glasshouse lives, is "commonplace"—the view of those for whom commerce has no romance. The ordinary novel reader will very possibly say of it that its love story would not have been half bad if it were not so frequently interrupted by cryptic allusions intelligible only to stockbrokers.

"The Book Worm." *Saturday Night* (Toronto), 16 (January 24, 1903), 4.

Frank Norris, the young Western novelist whose untimely death was so much regretted by readers from the Atlantic to the Pacific, completed the second of the three books which he called "The Epic of the Wheat," before his sudden taking off. The story ran as a serial in a United States publication, and has been recently published in book form, and Morang presents it to Toronto readers in a neat get-up, with three full ears of golden wheat as a significant crest. The second of the trilogy is called "The Pit," and is the story of manipulation of the harvest (so beautifully told of in the first book, "The Octopus") by the speculators in Chicago. Apart from the faithful story of the wheat, the graphic history of the "corner," the gruesome results of speculation on the minds and morals of men, there is a woman, who is drawn with a fascinating and frank touch. A Chicago product of speculation is Laura, the wife of the great Bull, the Wheat King, Curtis Jadwin, and Norris, after laying bare her selfishness, her false culture, her almost dissolutisms, leaves her with her steps set in the right way, but a fearsome doubt in the mind of the reader about her staying powers. Chicago life is so lightly sketched that only one who knows it can fully see the fidelity of the portrait. Little side touches recall and verify remembrance, and make one realize how close and keen were the observation and deduction of Frank Norris. The impetus of the wheat and its deadly power to crash him who manipulates it against its divine way to nourish and sustain life, recalls the terrible fate of the greedy oppressor in "The Octopus." That worthy was sucked into the hold of a great ship and smothered in the grain he had acquired by injustice and cruelty. Curtis Jadwin, the Wheat King, held the traders of the wheat pit in his grasp, squeezed them dry and cast them aside. Hear him when he reaches after Scannel, the broker who played unfair years ago and made wreck of wretched Hargus, his partner: "I'm laying particularly for Dave Scannel. I'll wring him bone dry. If I once get a twist of that rat I won't leave him hair nor hide to cover the wart he calls his heart." And he made his words good, the episode of Scannel's retribution being the strongest in the story. One follows the inflation of the wheat, breathless and amazed, and when the collapse comes occurs the touch recorded as in "The Octopus." "He had laid his human, puny grasp upon Creation, and the very earth herself, the great mother, feeling the touch of the cobweb that the human insect had spun, had stirred at last in her sleep, and sent her omnipotence, moving through the grooves of the world, to find and crush the disturber of her appointed courses. It was the Wheat, the Wheat." As one reads Norris's strong, convincing, graphic sentences one feels a fresh and keen sense of deprivation in recalling that "The Epic of the Wheat" will never be finished by his master-hand.

Emily S. Bouton and Elizabeth Ayres. "Literature: The Second Book of the 'Epic of the Wheat.'"
Toledo Daily Blade, January 24, 1903, p. 18.

Since The Octopus by Frank Norris aroused and thrilled the literary world two years ago, its many readers have almost breathlessly awaited the promised appearance of the second of the trilogy of which that was the first. Mr. Norris has conceived the idea of following the wheat from its growth and harvesting in the great fields of the west, to the heart of the centralized market in Chicago, thence over the seas to the hungry people of other lands.

The first story was published and made a strong impression. The second finished shortly before the death of the author, has just come from the press. It is entitled The Pit, and it is fitly named. With a wonderful realism he has pictured the gambling in wheat which forms so large an element in the business life of the Windy City, and not only the business life, but through its effects the social and home life of the people. It is a powerful story, one that grips and possesses the reader to its very end. The action is more centered than in The Octopus; the atmosphere more stifling, for, instead of great fields with the broad expanse of blue sky above, and the rush of the wind across the bending grain, the scenes are confined to the Pit and the Chicago homes of the actors therein.

The characters are few in number and well sustained. They are first grouped together in a party at the Auditorium Theatre, where the Italian Opera Company is giving one of its popular performances. First are the two sisters, Laura and Page Dearborn, the former the real heroine of the story. She is very beautiful: erect, slender, graceful, with doe brown eyes, whose glow is "lambent and intense"; a paleness that is always noticeable, and yet does not seem a lack of coloring; and abundant hair of the most pronounced murky blackness. Page, the sister, is a young girl of seventeen, with beauty quite as noticeable in its promise as that of Miss Dearborn. The two are orphans, new comers in Chicago, and under the care of their father's friends, the Cresslers, whose present guests they are.

Landry Court, another of the party, is a keen young fellow connected with the brokerage staff of the great firm of Gretry, Converse & Co., the latter being a vital factor in the story. "He made friends almost at first sight, and was one of those fortunate few who were favored equally of men and women." Another young man is Corthell, thus described:

> He was a lightly built man of about twenty-eight or thirty; dark, wearing a small, pointed beard, and a moustache that he brushed away from his lips like a Frenchman. By profession he was an artist, devoting himself more especially to the designing of stained windows. In this his talent was indisputable.

> He [Jadwin] was a heavy-built man, would have made two of Corthell, and his hands were large and broad, the hands of a man of affairs, who knew how to grip, and, above all, how to hang

on. Those broad, strong hands and keen, calm eyes would enfold and envelop a Purpose with tremendous strength, and they would persist, unswerving, unwavering, untiring, till the Purpose was driven home. And the two long, lean, fibrous arms of him: what a reach they could attain, and how wide and huge and even formidable would be their embrace of affairs.

With these people Mr. Norris plunges his readers into the midst of events that vibrate with intensity. His grasp upon the situations is something tremendous in scope. He feels little things, as well as the great, and thus makes his pictures vital with meaning. Here is his description of a scene in South Water street. It was a jam of delivery wagons and market carts, with a "infinite welter" of crates and baskets, boxes and sacks upon the sidewalk:

> The gutter was choked with an overflow of refuse cabbage leaves, soft oranges, decaying beet tops. The air was thick with the heavy smell of vegetation. Food was trodden under foot, food crammed the stores and warehouses to bursting. Food mingled with the mud of the highway. The very dray horses were gorged with an unending nourishment of snatched mouthfuls picked from the backboard, from barrel top, and from the edge of the sidewalk. The entire locality reeked with the fatness of a hundred thousand furrows. A land of plenty, the inordinant abundance of the earth itself, emptied itself upon the asphalt and cobbles of the quarter. It was the Mouth of the City, and drawn from all directions, over a territory of immense area, this glut of crude subsistence was sucked in, as if into a rapacious gullet, to feed the sinews and to nourish the fibres of an immeasurable colossus.

Laura looked forth each day upon the scene around her in the "Great Grey City" and suddenly its significance dawned upon her.

"There is something terrible about it," she murmured to herself, "something insensate. In a way it doesn't seem human. It's like a great tidal wave. It's all very well for the individual so long as he can keep afloat, but once fallen, how horribly quick it would crush him, annihilate him, how horribly quick and with such horrible indifference. I suppose it's civilization in the making, the thing that isn't meant to be seen, as though it were too elemental, too primordial; like the first verses of Genesis."

The pictures Mr. Norris draws of The Pit are startling in their realism. He shows how men change in character from the kind, thoughtful home lover of the evening to the case hardened, supremely selfish fellow of the day, down in the murk and grime of the business district, who asks and gives no quarter. He depicts the way in which the gambling desire clutches his hero, and grinds every other instinct and wish, until he sees nothing but the oceans of wheat which come pouring into Chicago, the power of which he determines to direct.

The character of Jadwin and the subtle way in which the fever of speculation arises within him, until it dominates his life, his love for Laura and everything most dear to him, are wonderfully pictured. There can be nothing more powerful than the chapters describing his struggle for supremacy in The Pit, nothing that can hold the nerves at a greater tension, than the detail of the days in which the one thought surging through his brain came to be wheat, wheat, wheat, repeated with unvarying rhythmic regularity.

It is not impossible to find in this wonderful story expressions that are far from being good English, but they have no more effect upon its strength than bubbles upon the top of the waters of a swiftly flowing river.

The third book must now remain to the end unwritten. The two left behind are sufficient to show the genius of the man who so early left the theater of human action. Could he have lived to write The Wolf, in which the central thought was to have been the relieving of a famine in a village in the Old World, it would, doubtless, have been as thrilling and moving as are The Octopus and The Pit.

It is said that Mr. Norris made little money from his books, but from his publisher's report his widow will reap the benefit of his splendid work.

"Frank Norris's Latest Novel."
New York Evening Sun, January 24, 1903, p. 5.

"Alone, on the edge of the abandoned Wheat Pit, in a spot where the sunlight fell warmest—an atom of life, lost in the immensity of the empty floor—the gray cat made her toilet, diligently licking the fur on the inside of her thigh, one leg, as if dislocated, thrust into the air above her head." Thus by a touch of contrast akin to genius is the effect heightened of one of Frank Norris's descriptions in his last novel "The Pit" (Doubleday, Page & Co.), of a day of battle and turmoil on the floor of the Chicago Board of Trade. It is the second novel in the Trilogy of the Epic of the Wheat, now, alas! never to be finished. The first in the series, "The Octopus," which dealt with the war between the wheat growers and the Southern Pacific Railroad in California, was hailed as the most virile and thoroughly American novel that had been written in many a long day, and veteran critics like Mr. Howells greeted the rising star with the generous prediction that it was destined to eclipse all others in our literary firmament. What Mr. Norris's work would have been at his maturity, if he had been spared to realize his plans, which were ambitious, can only be conjectured. That it was steadily growing in power, feeling and scope of treatment is shown by the evolution from "McTeague" to "The Pit." In the first the expression of his art was crude, coarse, and sometimes brutal, and he repelled when designing to impress the reader with his realism. Mr. Norris was surer of himself in "The Octopus," where he wrote about the California he was most familiar with; and in his last novel he held himself well under control, even in the throes of description when he rises to great heights of imaginative writing.

"The Pit," as Mr. Norris explained in explaining the plan of the Trilogy, is the fictitious narrative of a "deal" in the Chicago wheat pit. It was his design to illustrate the folly of attempting to corner wheat and to suggest the immorality of it; incidentally to show that the passion for speculation may become so absorbing as to alienate the love of a devoted woman. In "The Pit" the wife of Curtis Jadwin, the Napoleon of the Board of Trade, who buys and sells millions of bushels of wheat, is not unfaithful to him but she is perilously near the brink of infidelity at times. The drama revolves around these two characters—Jadwin, the self-reliant, robust, strenuous and daring man of business, whose conscience is deadened by his passion for gambling on a gigantic scale; and his wife, Laura, an imaginative, impulsive and capricious young woman, whose instincts are good but who does not know herself, and is unstable and steadfast, constant and fickle, fixed and mutable by turns, but feminine in all her moods and fancies.

Jadwin, who had made his fortune in real estate, was the soul of caution until Gretry, of Gretry, Converse & Co., the commission house, argued him into a deal on the strength of a private tip from Paris to raise the import duty on wheat. No one hated speculation more than Jadwin's friend Cressler, who said one day:

"If we send the price of wheat down too far, the farmer suffers, the fellow who raises it; if we send it up too far, the poor man in Europe suffers, the fellow who eats it. And food to the peasant on the Continent is bread—not meat or potatoes, as it is with us." And in an outburst of resentment, for he has lost a fortune in speculation and abandoned it, Cressler said: "I believe it's worse than liquor, worse than morphine. Once you get into it, it grips you and draws and draws you, and the nearer you get to the end the easier it seems to win, till all of a sudden, ah! there's the whirlpool. 'J,' keep away from it, my boy."

Jadwin turned to Miss Laura Dearborn, whom he had determined to make his wife, and said with a laugh:

"Charlie means all right, but now and then some one brushes against him and opens that switch."

When Gretry got his tip about the French duty on wheat he sent for Jadwin. Passing through the customers' room on his way to the private office Jadwin saw a broken, seedy old man doubled up in a chair and eating a sandwich with a trembling hand.

"I say," said Jadwin, when he sat down opposite the broker, "I saw an old fellow outside in your customers' room just now that put me in mind of Hargus. You remember that deal of his, the one he tried to swing before he died. Oh,—how long ago was that? Bless my soul, that must have been fifteen, yes, twenty years ago."

"I guess that was Hargus you saw out there," answered the broker. "He's not dead. Old fellow in a stove-pipe and greasy frock coat? Yes, that's Hargus."

Jadwin was dumfounded.

"And he's not dead? And that was Hargus; that wretched, broken—whew! I don't want to think of it, Sam."

But the unpleasant fact did not deter Jadwin from going into the wheat deal, after protesting that it was a risky business. He made $50,000 sure money, and afterward he could not keep out of the market, ultimately planning to corner wheat and running the price up to $1.40 before the crash came which ruined him. Cressler, the man who hated speculation, had been induced by Crooke, the great bear, to go in on the other side, and losing a second fortune, killed himself.

Laura Dearborn, although she had more than a liking for Corthell, the artist, had to capitulate to the persistent Jadwin, who wouldn't talk of anything else but his suit, and won a dubious yes after he had been told no a hundred times. Telling Mrs. Cressler of her engagement, Laura said:

"And when I finally said I would marry him, why, Mrs. Cressler, he choked all up, and the tears ran down his face, and all he could say was, 'May God bless! May God bless you!' over and over again."

But when Laura became Mrs. Jadwin she learned to love her big-hearted unconventional husband, who worshipped the ground she trod on and whose every thought was of her until he was caught in the snare of the cornered wheat pit again and lost his senses in the mad whirl of profits—for until the end came this Napoleon never lost a battle. Then he neglected his wife and forgot his magnificent home, and almost broke her heart. There was the inevitable intruder, the man who had loved her passionately before marriage—the artist Corthell. Only the ruin of her husband by the collapse of the great corner saved Laura from herself, and then she went out with him from their luxurious home which had been sold under the hammer to begin life again.

Sombre is the tragedy of Jadwin's downfall, but magnificent his courage in defeat. And in the day of triumphs his generosity is royal. To decrepit old Hargus he restores his fortune, wringing from Scannel, the man who had ruined him, a check for the amount—Jadwin had caught the scoundrel short of wheat and put the screws on him. But when Jadwin was threatened with overthrow he could not get a dollar out of Hargus.

"I—I don't lend my money," said the old miser, hurrying from his tainted presence.

We know nothing more powerful in contemporary fiction than Mr. Norris's description of the titanic battles in the wheat pit which ended in the Waterloo of Curtis Jadwin, the "Great Bull." For example: "Jadwin himself, the great man, the 'Great Bull' in the Pit! What was about to happen? Had they been too premature in their hope of his defeat? Had he been preparing some secret, unexpected maneuver? For a second they hesitated, then, moved by a common impulse, feeling the push of the wonderful new harvest behind them, they gathered themselves together for the final assault and again offered the wheat for sale; offered it by thousands upon thousands of bushels; poured, as it were, reapings of entire principalities out upon the floor of the Board of Trade.

"Jadwin was in the thick of the confusion by now. And the avalanche, the undiked Ocean of the Wheat, leaping to the lash of the hurricane, struck him fairly in the face.

"He heard it now; he heard nothing else. The wheat had broken from his control. For months he had, by the might of his single arm, held it back; but now it rose like the upbuilding of a colossal billow. It towered, towered, hung poised for an instant, and then, with a thunder as of the grind and crash of chaotic worlds, broke upon him, burst through the pit and raced past him, on and on to the Eastward and to the hungry nations.

"And then under the stress and violence of the hour something snapped in his brain. The murk behind his eyes had been suddenly pierced by a white flash. The strange qualms and tiny nervous paroxysms of the last few months all at once culminated in some indefinite, indefinable crisis, and the wheels and cogs of all activities save one lapsed away and ceased. Only one function of the complicated machine persisted; but it moved with a rapidity of vibration that seemed to be tearing the tissues of being to shreds, while its rhythm beat out the old and terrible cadence: 'Wheat-wheat-wheat, wheat-wheat-wheat,'

"Blind and insensate, Jadwin strove against the torrent of the Wheat. There in the middle of the Pit, surrounded and assaulted by herd after herd of wolves yelping for his destruction, he stood braced, rigid upon his feet, his head up, his hand, the great bony hand that once had held the whole Pit in its grip, flung high in the air, in a gesture of defiance, while his voice like the clangor of bugles sounding to the charge of the forlorn hope, rang out again and again, over the din of his enemies:

" 'Give a dollar for July—give a dollar for July!' "

"Frank Norris's Story of 'The Pit.' "
New York Sun,
January 24, 1903,
p. 7.

The late Frank Norris's novel, "The Pit: A Story of Chicago" (Doubleday, Page & Co.), is overflowing realism relieved by some rather high and fanciful descriptive flights. In its general style it is like "The Octopus" that went before it in the trilogy of stories planned under the ambitious title of "The Epic of the Wheat." In the words of the author's prospectus, it is "the fictitious narrative of a 'deal' in the Chicago wheat pit." We find it hardly as ample and as picturesque as the Californian story, "The Octopus," which dealt with the growing of the wheat and the war between the wheat growers and the railroads, but it is still an exceptionally vigorous and good story. For the jaded novel reader there was much reward in "The Octopus," and there is a definite continuation of that reward here.

The new story has for its opening scene the Auditorium Theatre in Chicago on a grand opera night. The heroine, Laura Dearborn, is in attendance, and so is the hero, Curtis Jadwin. They are interesting characters both, and the interest of them is brought out in very skilful and artistic manner. The grand opera itself is treated with the humor which many believe that it deserves. "The tenor held the stage—a stout, short young man in red plush doublet and gray silk tights. His chin advanced, his arm extended, one hand pressed to his breast, he apostrophized the pavilion, that now and then swayed a little in the draught from the wings." Corthell, the painter, the "beautiful artist-priest of the early Renaissance," the hero next to Jadwin, nodded his head in approval, and he knew. Landry Court, the "young chevalier, pure as Galahad," also liked it, though he was moved to say critically, "He's not in voice to-night. Too bad. You should have heard him Friday in 'Aida.' " As for Laura, she shut her eyes when the tenor sang his passion to the soprano. "Never had she felt so soothed, so cradled and lulled and languid. Ah, to love like that! To love and be loved. There was no such love as that to-day." But amid the generous applause which rewarded the soprano and the tenor, and even as the soprano came out again and again on the balcony of the pavilion and bowed, could be heard fragments of unflattering conversation, such as "one hundred and six carloads"—"paralyzed the bulls"—"fifty thousand dollars." Still another impression that we may remark is that afforded by Laura's aunt, Mrs. Wessels, who kept wondering and saying, "I don't see why the young man, the one with the pointed beard, didn't marry that lady and be done with it. Just as soon as they'd seem to have it all settled, he'd begin to take on again, and strike his breast and go away. I declare, I think it was all kind of foolish."

On her way home from the opera Laura remarked in the murk of rain and against the haze of light thrown by Chicago upon the heavens "the pile of the Board of Trade Building, black, grave, monolithic, crouching on its foundations, like a monstrous sphinx with blind eyes, silent, grave—crouching there without a sound, without sign of life under the night and the drifting veil of rain." That the author was satisfied with this description of the Board of Trade Building is shown in the circumstance that the closing paragraph of the story is an exact repetition of it.

On page 62 we find a description of the city of Chicago in the same large, rhetorical vein. It was while she was in South Water street that Laura suddenly conceived the meaning of Chicago. "The Great Grey City, brooking no rival, imposed its dominion upon a reach of country larger than many a kingdom of the Old World. For thousands of miles beyond its confines was its influence felt. Out, far out, far away in the snow and shadow of northern Wisconsin forests, axes and saws bit the bark of century-old trees, stimulated by this city's energy. Just as far to the southward pick and drill leaped to the assault of veins of anthracite, moved by her central power. Her force turned the wheels of harvester and seeder a thousand miles distant in Iowa and Kansas. Her force spun the screws and propellers of innumerable squadrons of lake steamers crowding the Sault Sainte Marie. For her and because of her all the Central States, all the Great Northwest, roared with traffic and industry; sawmills screamed; factories, their smoke blackening the sky, clashed and flamed; wheels turned; pistons leaped in their cylinders; cog gripped cog; beltings clasped the drums of mammoth wheels, and converters of forges belched into the clouded air their tempest breath of molten steel.

"It was empire, the resistless subjugation of all this central world of the lakes and the prairies. Here, midmost in the land, beat the heart of the nation, whence inevitably must come its immeasurable power, its infinite, inexhaustible vitality. Here, of all her cities, throbbed the true life—the true power and spirit of America; gigantic, crude with the crudity of youth, disdaining rivalry; sane and healthy and vigorous; brutal in its ambition, arrogant in the new-found knowledge of its giant strength, prodigal of its wealth, infinite in its desires. In its capacity boundless, in its courage indomitable; subduing the wilderness in a single generation, defying calamity, and through the flame and the débris of a commonwealth in ashes, rising suddenly renewed, formidable and titanic."

Jadwin was a representative figure in this heart of empire. He operated in the Board of Trade Building. Though unimaginative, he had often, within that building, thought of it as "a great whirlpool, a pit of roaring waters," that "spun and thundered, sucking in the life tides of the city, sucking them in as into the mouth of some tremendous cloaca, the maw of some colossal sewer; then vomiting them forth again, spewing them up and out, only to catch them in the return eddy and suck them in afresh."

This was the Pit of the title, the centre of speculation in wheat. As it seemed to

Jadwin, so it was. "Thus it went, day after day. Endlessly, ceaselessly, the Pit, enormous, thundering, sucked in and spewed out, sending the swirl of its mighty central eddy far out through the city's channels. Terrible at the centre, it was at the circumference gentle, insidious and persuasvie, the send of the flowing so mild that to embark upon it, yielding to the influence, was a pleasure that seemed all devoid of risk. But the circumference was not bounded by the city. All through the Northwest, all through the central world of the wheat, the set and whirl of that innermost Pit made itself felt; and it spread and spread and spread till grain in the elevators of western Iowa moved and stirred and answered to its centripetal force, and men upon the streets of New York felt the mysterious tugging of its undertow engage their feet, embrace their bodies, overwhelm them, and carry them bewildered and unresisting back and downward to the Pit itself.... Wheat, Nourisher of the Nations, as it rolled gigantic and majestic in a vast flood from West to East, here, like a Niagara, finding its flow impeded, burst suddenly into the appalling fury of the maelstrom, into the chaotic spasm of a world force, a primeval energy, blood-brother of the earthquake and the glacier, raging and wrathful that its power should be braved by some pinch of human spawn that dared raise barriers across its courses."

The wheat overwhelmed Jadwin. He went under. As the story has it, "the avalanche, the undiked Ocean of the Wheat, leaping to the lash of the hurricane, struck him fairly in the face." We have tried to give some little idea both of the realism and the rhetoric here. The story is a love story as well as a story of business. Corthell, the artist, makes the contrast, of course, to Jadwin, the wheat speculator. Laura was one to inspire love either in a romantic and artistic or in a practical "business" person. The story carries out in reasonable measure the promise which was in "The Octopus." The reader will not be disappointed in it. There is more power in it, after all, than there is in a dozen stories with which we could find no particular fault.

"Books That Are Being Read at This Time." *St. Paul Globe*, January 26, 1903, p. 8.

Had Frank Norris lived he might have achieved who knows how much? As it is, he has left behind him at least one book which, though it may go through the popular stage, will nevertheless be read generations from now. It is a pity that the "Epic of Wheat" was destined never to be finished, for those who have read "The Octopus" and "The Pit," the first two of the proposed trilogy, are keenly disappointed not to see the finish. For inasmuch as "The Octopus" was a far greater production than any of his previous books, so does "The Pit" excel "The Octopus." The first of the trilogy deals with the war between the wheat grower and the railroad trust; the second, "The Pit," is a fictitious narrative of a "deal" in the Chicago wheat pit, and the third, "The Wolf," which will never appear, was to have had for its pivotal episode the relieving of a wheat famine in an old world community.

"The Pit" has been running in the Saturday Evening Post, where "The Octopus" was also published, and from the beginning of its first chapters has aroused a widespread interest. It is a story which appeals to almost every class of people. The business man who seldom "wastes time" over novels may read it and find there a deep interest in the throbbing life of the pit so vividly described. And still it is a tale of "human interest"—not in the yellow journal meaning of the term—but full of human interest because its characters are real, every-day people who act as real people do, not as they should, sometimes, but there is not a character in the book who is not always human.

The characters in the story are not too numerous, as is so often the case with stories of the day; in reality there are but nine people whom the reader is called upon to interest himself in, and it is difficult to choose which of these is the most interesting. Probably Curtis Jadwin, a typical self-made man, is the most prominent character. He is not one of the perfect self-made men one sometimes reads of, but never meets, for he too is human. He is first of all good, and secondly, full of business. He chose the girl he wanted to marry and married her because he loved her. He started in with wheat gambling just for a pastime, became engrossed, forgot his wife, was deaf to her pleading for a little of his time, and finally learned his lesson by a loss of everything he had. It was one of those times when wheat was forced higher and higher, threatening every moment to fall; but Curtis Jadwin, confident but half crazed, risked his every penny on its going still higher, and lost it all. His confidence and perseverance were characteristic of the man though they ruined him, as they caused the death through suicide of his best friend, Charles Cressler, who also failed in a big deal.

Laura Dearborn, whom Jadwin married, is the kind of a character that reminds the reader of some acquaintance. The casual reader might have called her weak, but she was not, not more than any other woman is weak. For is not every one weak in a sense? She was a sentimental girl, fond of admiration, one of the women to whom love is as essential as bread and butter. Besides Jadwin she had two other suitors, as totally different from each other as they were from Jadwin. One, an artist, Sheldon Corthell, takes the place of the villain in the story, only he was not a villain; though, during the time of her husband's neglect of her he begs her to go away with him. Landry Court was a bright young business man, boyish, who loved her in a chivalrous manner. All proposed to her on the same evening and, not meaning to be a flirt, she encouraged all of them, withholding any fixed answer from all. At the close of this day she bethought herself of her peculiar conduct, was ashamed of herself, and wrote to each of them a note refusing his offer of marriage. Court and the artist ceased their courting, but Jadwin went ahead and married her, even succeeding in making her love him. And they lived very happily until he became so deeply engrossed in wheat.

There are several other rather interesting people brought into the story. But none can appreciate the descriptions of the pit, full of life as they are, unless he has stood in the balcony overhanging the screeching mob in the pit and seen for himself how true a picture the book has given of this part of Chicago life. It seems almost too real, too horrible, too noisy to be true to the reader who has never seen for himself.

"The Pit."
Baltimore Sun,
January 29, 1903,
p. 8.

Have you read "Moran of the Lady Letty"? This was the first novel of Frank Norris, and it is a novel of worth.

Have you read "Blix" and "A Man's Woman"? Two more novels worth your reading are these works of the dead man.

Have you read "McTeague," the most brutal novel ever written by an American, and the most typical in its morbidness and its naked force of the novels left us by the man who stood first among American writers in his representation of the sordidness of life. "McTeague" is a gruesome book—a book that causes one to shudder; yet it is a book of power.

Have you read "The Octopus"? It is the strongest novel of life in the wheat country of the Southwest and the most bitter arraignment of the methods of railroads possessing monopolies that has ever been published. "The Octopus" is a novel that is written in a fashion that takes hold of the reader and compels, not woos, his interest.

Have you read "The Pit," the last and not the least of the books that form the legacy of the dead author to American literature?

Six books, in all, are these novels of Frank Norris, and six of as powerful books as were ever written. Here are their names again: "Moran of the Lady Letty," "McTeague," "Blix," "A Man's Woman," "The Octopus," and lastly, "The Pit." But if the author had lived there would have been, at least, a seventh, and that would have been "The Wolf," which, with "The Octopus" and "The Pit," would have formed "The Epic of the Wheat," a trilogy which, even though incomplete, has won for Frank Norris the place which his admirers always believed within his reach. Although "The Wolf" was not written, the dead man has done enough to win for himself the regard of critics, even of those tardy critics that are only now ungrudging in their praise. Time was—and that not so long since—when the present reviewer was one of the few who hailed Norris as the master of realistic novelists, and then we were a byword in the mouths of not a few of our brethren who, now that the man is dead, find words almost insufficient to voice their praises of his genius. Perhaps the praise is better late than never, but Norris' books are the same today as they were when they were first written. Yet many of those who praise now found little to praise then. For example: "McTeague" was well-nigh a flat failure from the publisher's standpoint, and from the Atlantic to the Pacific critics cut it to pieces. "The Octopus," that seems at the present time to be ranked, well-nigh unanimously, as among the very best of American novels, was never appreciated by the general public, and won extremely faint praise from the majority of critics, and the publishers found that it was far from profitable to themselves or to the author. But all at once the public awoke to the realization that Norris is an author to whom their attention has not been sufficiently called, and critics awake to the realization that they have missed an opportunity; therefore public and critics vie with each other in good words for one whom they reviled or neglected when he was living, and they jostle each other in their efforts to praise or to buy his books.

"The Pit" is in a manner the continuation of "The Octopus," and yet it is [in] no way connected with that work. It is a continuation in that "The Octopus" has for its subject wheat—the grain being in the hands of the producer and the transporter. In "The Pit" the subject is wheat, and it is in the hands of the speculators. The story of "The Octopus" is of the plains of the Southwest and the characters are those who are concerned with raising wheat on a gigantic scale and conveying it to the markets. In "The Pit" the story centers around the wheat pit in Chicago, and the scene of the story is essentially one of Chicago. Yet the characters of the story have that broad humanity that makes them belong as much to the town of the reader as the town of "The Pit." The men and women whom Frank Norris has drawn have their activity in Chicago because the author has chosen so to place them, but he might as well have placed them in New York or New Orleans, in San Francisco or in San Antonio, in Portland, Maine, or in Portland, Oregon. This much for the broad humanity of the characters, but local color is another thing, and the story is full of local color and that of Chicago. The men may be of any place, the women may be of any place, but "The Pit" can be of but one place, and that, Chicago. The story is one of love, of fond and tender love, of a man for a woman and a woman for a man. It is a story that shows the love in the heart of the man gradually stifled by the love for business, and it shows a woman's heart growing faint beneath the neglect of one she loves; but in the end—the end in "The Pit" is the best that Norris ever accomplished—love triumphs and casts aside the clogs of monetary ambition and hearts are united in a love that disregards advantage. The course of the story is full of dramatic situations. It is replete with those realistic descriptions that give to the works of Norris their peculiar strength. We do not care how or where the dead novelist got the technique of the book. This man and that man have claimed the credit of the suggestions concerning financial affairs that Norris worked into shape, but we are satisfied with their effect. Effectiveness is the crowning merit with all of the work of Norris. His novels have in them the force that compels. "Brutal," say critics, and we own to the charge. Brutal was Norris, as was Zola, but the work of the American possessed a ring of truth that never, to us, seemed present in the work of the Frenchman, and again to us—and we have read Zola in the original as well as in translation—the work of Norris is immeasurably superior in effectiveness. Page after page of the work of Zola is a dreary word-waste, but in the pages of Norris every word counts. The work of Norris uniformly possesses a virility that the work of Zola too often lacked, and when Norris threw aside the mysticism that now and again clouded 'The Octopus" he was unapproachable as a realist. "The Pit," with its excitement, its love, its tragedy, its human interest, is a book that will stand among the foremost of the virile books of American literature.

"Books: The Pit."
Detroit Times,
January 31, 1903,
p. 3.

Perhaps few novels written in this day and generation have the greatness of scope which characterizes the work of the late Frank Norris, than whom few men in literature were more sincerely or deeply lamented. Mr. Norris had a strong, realistic style, which was reaching its zenith, when death came. At first, he had been hailed as the Zola of America, a promise which he fulfilled in truth to life, to an extent, though his work never or seldom, purposely portrayed the disgusting.

"Moran of the Lady Letty" had been a bright, virile story and "Blix" and "The Man's Woman" readable tales. In "McTeague" he displayed the strong touches of rugged realism, but the tale was so unattractive, its characters almost repulsive, that its value was rather in what it prophesied, than what it consisted.

But in "The Octopus" and "The Pit" Mr. Norris had come fully into his own. On these two novels, his reputation will stand, and we feel justified in saying that it is a reputation that will not die the early, but not untimely death, of the fame of the majority of our writers.

The cause of this is stated in our first paragraph. Mr. Norris's novels have scope. They are not limited to one or two phases of life, but boldly delineate, many of the currents and the counter currents of this great modern thing that we call Civilization.

In this, Mr. Norris has followed the manner of the older novelists, Thackeray, Dickens, Eliot and the others. One cannot call his style leisurely, rather it is exhaustive, but it lacks all trace of the sketchy hurriedness common to many writers. And in this, Mr. Norris deserves not only admiration, but a goodly share of praise, and the pity of it is that we are not able to give honor to whom honor is so justly due. After he had made more or less of a name for himself, Mr. Norris did not take a mean advantage and foist off a lot of hack work, but with restraint, he set himself faithfully to his task, and the fruit of it is "The Octopus" and "The Pit."

It was Mr. Norris' intention to write a trilogy called "the epic of the wheat." The first, "The Octopus," told of the growing of the wheat in California, and the great fight between the growers and the railroad. The second, "The Pit," deals with the selling of the wheat in Chicago. The third, "The Wolf," was never written. It was planned to have in it an account of the using of the wheat in a famine-stricken community in Europe. The stories are, however, each complete in itself.

"The Pit" is both a good, interesting story, and a bold, graphic picture of the whirling commercial life of the Chicago wheat pit, rolled into one, and blended so skillfully as to form one compact whole, which, while it is a novel, is also a glowing picture of life.

The characters are strong, in that they are reasonably differentiated. They are depicted with ten times the care that is common in the writing of the day. Laura, the heroine, is a girl of varying motives, and varying desires, as girls in real life are apt to be. Her men friends are all portrayed with skill, and are true both in type and the individuality.

The striking thing in the book, it occurs to us, is the tremendous moral and economical lesson involved. Whether placed there by design or no, the question comes constantly home to the reader: What has the Chicago wheat pit gambler done to merit wealth? He toils, indeed, but he certainly does not spin. He neither produces nor aids in the distribution. Contrariwise, he makes a disgraceful sustenance by making the farmers sell wheat at ruinously low prices if he be a "bear," or making the starving peasants of far-off lands pay exorbitant prices, if he be a "bull."

Jadwin, the grain speculator, is a nice fellow, no doubt about that. But what has he done that his wife should have all the good things, while these, His children, want for bread? He has not added one iota to the world's happiness. There may be some consolation for us, when a man earns wealth in legitimate business—though in that line, monstrous wealth is impossible—but when a man gambles and wins, and when society sets the mark of respectability on that gambling and calls it "business," then, indeed, do we, "the heathen," rage.

All this Mr. Norris shows to us and we can cordially commend "The Pit" to you, if you want to be awakened to some facts of modern interest. In many ways it is doubtful if the year will see a novel to equal it. Beyond question, it is literature.

"The Pit: A Dispassionate Examination of Frank Norris's Posthumous Novel."
New York Times, January 31, 1903, p. 66, "Saturday Review of Books and Art."*

Just how much American literature lost by the death of Frank Norris is a difficult question, to which there will be many answers, none conclusive. That the work he had already done contained much of promise and something of achievement will probably be admitted by all. Opinions will differ widely as to the extent of the achievement, and achievement is, after all, the only safe

*See p. 283 for Mary L. Patteson's response to this review.

basis of judgment, while recognition of a young author as "promising" is criticism not the less severe because in kindly form.

Clearly as Mr. Norris had proved himself to be a story teller with stories to tell, he had not revealed either the inerrant taste of genius or the patient industry of enlightened talent. He was in a hurry to do great things, and, conscious of strength, did not take the pains to acquire the technical skill upon which perfection of detail depends. His books, in consequence, were remarkable rather than admirable, or, at least, more remarkable than admirable, and one sometimes gets from them the impression of reading a first draft manuscript instead of the printed page. They evidence what it is customary to call fatal facility, and seem to be written at high speed and left uncorrected.

If this seeming is deceptive, and Mr. Norris did in reality give his books the careful revision without which the conscientious artist is never content, then there is a chance that his work would have been "promising" to the end of a long life, as it was to the end of one pathetically short. For there was not much difference between "McTeague" and "The Octopus," so far as literary finish went, and now comes "The Pit," with all of the small faults as well as all of the large virtues of its predecessors. Nature made Mr. Norris a marvelously accurate observer of the life around him, and to this gift added the creative imagination, but she did not endow him with an instinctive knowledge that the right word is worth a long search, and he had not discovered it for himself. He appreciated only too well the colossal effects produced by Zola, and imitated that master's devices only too successfully, for in imitating the devices he often missed the effects. Perhaps he had read both too much and too little; if he had read less his style would have been original, because he would not have thought anything about style, and if he had read more he would have been able consciously to make a style of his own—which comes to the same thing.

But Mr. Norris was what he was, and there is small profit in regretting, and less in resenting, that he was not something else. He followed a happy inspiration when he planned "the epic of the wheat," and, as "The Octopus," which dealt with the growing and the growers of what means more to humanity than any other product of the soil, was no common book, so "The Pit," which shows the fierce excitements of speculation in the staff of life, is something more than merely a piece of picturesque and vigorous writing. That it is an absolutely accurate picture of the Chicago Board of Trade and the men who contend therein is likely to be questioned by those with much personal knowledge of both, but that matters little to the rest of us, for grain brokers and their clients, or patrons, or customers, or whatever it is that grain brokers have, are at least as interesting as Mr. Norris saw them as they are in reality, and the novelist, even the realistic novelist, has the best of rights to leave history and statistics to the historians and the statisticians, and to consult only his own conscience—and needs—in regard to the amount of exaggerating and emphasizing he should do. He would not have claimed that Curtis Jadwin, his hero, is the ordinary speculator in wheat, or that every, or even any, attempt to "corner" that useful staple has passed through precisely the phases he records; but certain as it is that there are not many Jadwins, there is no obvious reason why there should not be one of them, and, given the one, the recorded "corner" would follow naturally enough.

Business has its adventures as well as its adventurers, nowadays, and the growing tendency of novelists to substitute the comedy and tragedy of business for those of war, hunting, and other similarly antiquated forms of activity is proof of great wisdom on their part, especially as "heart interest" combines as logically and inevitably with business as with the other occupations.

It does so in "The Pit," which includes among its numerous personages several entirely comprehensible women—every one of whom, for a wonder, could safely submit her "past" to the inspection and commentary of publics even more censorious than that of Chicago is supposed to be. The reader hardly sees, perhaps, why so many men fell in love with Laura Dearborn, or why the well-matured Jadwin thought himself so lucky to win her away from his less wealthy rivals; but real life is full of mysteries of that sort, and surely the realistic novelist is under no obligation to ignore the fact that unexpected results are often reached by the solution of personal equations. Laura made quite as good a wife as the somewhat priggish grain gambler deserved. Among the minor characters—Board of Trade men of various ranks and ages, the inevitable pair of youthful lovers, a maiden aunt bewildered by millions, and the like—are several that were carefully conceived and projected, and not the less sympathetic because they are the immemorial "types" of fiction and the stage, newly costumed, each serving the familiar purpose. Indeed, if one looks below the surface of "The Pit" one soon realizes that not much more than its properties is new.

"The Octopus" seemed to be for the most part the product of actual experience, and the wheat was an essential feature of the story, but the second book of the "epic" reveals the use of second-hand information as to the methods and language of the grain speculators. The author's material was well studied up, not unconsciously acquired and thoroughly possessed. Had the third volume of the proposed series been written, the deterioration from the first would probably have been still more marked, for Mr. Norris was able to acquire a closer knowledge of Chicago than he would have obtained in regard to a European village stricken with famine, which was to have been the scene of a book called "The Wolf," and dealing with the consumption of the wheat raised in California and made the object of a ruthless gamble beside Lake Michigan.

While on his own ground and voicing the wrongs of his own people, Mr. Norris won easier pardon for his verbal infelicities than when he wandered into new fields and imagined emotions instead of feeling them. The war between the wheat growers and the Pacific railways was something worth getting excited over; as much can hardly be said of a laborious demonstration that speculation in the necessities of life, when conducted on a large scale, is an immoral practice, and very wearing on the nerves of the speculator. The demonstration at best is not entirely convincing, and so far as it does convince it was unnecessary. Mr. Norris would have gone much further in the time allotted him if he had taken himself a little less, and his chosen profession a little more, seriously. He was a preacher turned novelist—a preacher, that is, of elementary sociology and economics, and his magnificent powers of observation and description were allowed to run wild in order that he might hasten to tell the world some true things that were not new and some new things that were not true.

Florence Jackson. "More of the Strenuous Life." *Overland Monthly*, 41 (February 1903), 156–57.

It is of the life we know best, or think we do, that we like best to hear. More readily can we put ourselves in touch with it, feel a near relation to and part of it, if it is so familiar that we can say to ourselves, though we would not to anyone else: "Yes, yes, that is the way life seems to us." Thus it is that the latest work from the pen of the ever-to-be-mourned-for Frank Norris, strikes a chord of instant response in the readers who are his countrymen and who live the strenuous life he saw and painted. And this story of eager rushing, modern thought and deed, thrills us because we are a part of it, though to few it is given to see, before it is pointed out as he saw it, that the poetry and romance to be found in the strong motives and deeds of what is called a matter-of-fact age, are as stimulating to high effort and noble aspiration as were feats of arms and chivalry in an older time. Through the musing of Laura Dearborn on the night of the opera and of the reported failure of a great financier, we are made to see in "The Pit" how vividly the author felt these influences of clashing emotions and motives. He shows their magnetic power to impress, and through the wonderful strength of words that seem to be hurled like javelins to spear his thoughts and hold them up to view, he compels the reader's enthusiasm for the bewildering forces of restless and agitating life, a life so truly American, and this story so truly descriptive of it that, as a chronicle of actual conditions which distinguish this country from all others and are not to be found in just this state elsewhere, Mr. Norris' work may be ranked as perhaps more distinctively original than any other that has been given to the country within the last decade. The style, the verbiage, is truly American; that is, it contains that sound of the matter-of-fact, common places, which is a note in every-day life all over the United States, and inextricably mixed with the picturesque and romantic that all would find though few seek. Now and then a word, a phrase, in the midst of the most virile construction and nearly perfect expression, shows a lack of attention to every detail of art, to every rule of counterpoint, that causes a break in the harmony of a passage. To such a worker, time only would bring the skill, unconsciously used, that would complete the full major melody. For Norris gives no minor strains to make the ear watchful for their meaning, or to lure the heart with a "divine sadness." He has heard the deep-toned swell of the voice of humanity with its chant and dirge and glory of civilization, and triumph of despair, or of success, and he has set it down as he heard it—a chronicle, which an epic must ever be, of events and of persons, stirring, vibrating with the life of which it sings. Pity, indeed, that such a writer could not have lived to give the real literature of his language such lyrical expression as would bring his work to the highest standard of art! The completed trilogy of "The Epic of the Wheat" would have shown, what he seemed to feel so intensely, that the desires and the necessities of men draw them together from all quarters of the globe, and make them alike debtors and creditors of one another.

Albert Bigelow Paine. "Frank Norris's 'The Pit.'"
Bookman (America), 16 (February 1903), 565–67.*

Frank Norris died leaving his trilogy unfinished. It was to consist of three novels—*The Octopus, The Pit*, and *The Wolf*. *The Octopus*, a story of wheat raising and railroad greed in California, was published in 1901. It belonged to no school of American letters, but immediately made a place for itself. It had its faults—the faults of youth and prodigal abundance—the faults that belong to the land of sun and harvest of which he wrote. And yet to-day it seems that these very faults are a part of its charm, and on the whole, one would not have the book altered or revised in a single line.

And now there comes the second of the trilogy, *The Pit*—a story of wheat markets and speculative greed in Chicago. *The Pit* is a book of fewer pages than *The Octopus*, also of fewer characters, of less lavish conception. It is the skilled work of the mature artist who pursues his idea in a straight line, gaining impetus and power with every page, rising at last to fine and triumphant achievement that brings the reader to his feet, takes him out of himself, leaves him at last in the realization that a big

*Reprinted in condensed form, with the same title, in the *Bookman* (England), 23 (March 1903), 246–47.

book—a bit of real literature—is in his hands.

The progress of Curtis Jadwin—the picture of that supreme moment in the Pit where he stands alone with the bears tearing at his throat—these things are not easily surpassed. From the vast periphery of the world the golden tide of grain is whirled into the fierce maelstrom of La Salle Street, where at the central point stands Curtis Jadwin, the towering figure about which every other character in the book is made to revolve. Masterful, good natured, daring, lucky, with little of culture and no very delicate sense of honesty in the matter of a deal, he is the typical Chicago wheat trader whose Pit education is acquired by leaps and bounds until with clear far-seeing brain and limitless confidence in his own judgment and good fortune, he is able to "swing a corner" in the world's greatest cereal, and hold the food supply of nations in his grasp. Every other character in the book is accessory to Jadwin. Sam Gretry, the broker; Landry Court, the clear-eyed, clean-hearted young trader; the Cresslers; old Hargus, the derelict—a bit of drift flung up by the maelstrom—these are some of the figures, drawn to the life, that revolve and eddy and swing about the great speculator—himself caught and flung by the Pit's mighty whirlpool, until the roar of the Exchange, the grind and clatter of the street, the very beating of his heart and throbbing of his brain echo but the one refrain. "Wheat, wheat, wheat—wheat, wheat, wheat!"

In *The Pit* as in *The Octopus* love has its part in the story, but with a difference. In *The Octopus* the love element, beautiful though it was, was incidental. In *The Pit* the love, if less beautiful, is of deeper importance, seldom lost sight of, never forgotten, by the reader.

The character of Laura Jadwin—an intellectual creature of moods, chasing her own elusive personality in the pursuit of self analysis, actress to her finger tips, sincere in her very insincerity—is one that men will love, women will discuss, and all remember. With Corthell, the artist—an artist in whom we do not quite believe—she forms a picture apart from the others, wherein that side of her character but slightly understood by Jadwin is given its opportunity for a development that seems likely to lead beyond even the swirling outreach of the Pit, which, in common with Corthell, she detests. In her great house, alone, without companions or sympathy, with all the world at her beck, and yet with no single thing that she can hold to her heart and call her own, the reader's broadest sympathy goes out to Laura Jadwin, and he is ready (mind, we say *he*) to forgive her anything.

We wish we had been called upon to forgive her; that Norris had found it within his conception to let her go out with Corthell into the night, and brought Curtis Jadwin, broken in body, mind and purse, to his vast desolate home.

"Old girl—Honey!"

How that feeble cry in the gloom would have told, with only the echo of the empty dark to answer.

We wish, too, that Laura Jadwin might once have looked down from the visitor's gallery upon the fury of the Pit—that she could have been Curtis Jadwin in the moment of his Waterloo. It is true, she had little interest in this phase of the life about her, but her art instinct, her woman's curiosity, her love, such as it was, for the man himself, might have prompted her to witness "the greatest fight in the history of La Salle Street," where Curtis Jadwin faced the ravening bears alone. We all along expected that she would do this, and we feel that Norris expected it, too. Perhaps when this time came she would not go. She was a creature of moods, and the author is not always master of his own characters.

And this may account for the ending Norris may have planned, her flight with Corthell, yet found it impossible to make her go. As to the object of her affection perhaps Norris himself knew little. That she loved Curtis Jadwin, we have no further evidence than that she told him so, under certain favourable conditions.

The fact that later she made the same statement to another man, with an equal fervour and against all social canons, lessens the value of this testimony. We love Laura Jadwin, and we feel that Norris loved her, too. But he must have found in her a perverse and difficult heroine.

The Octopus, The Pit, The Wolf—the big conception of one capable of making of it a big reality. The first two have come to us out of the author's youth and strength. The third, *The Wolf*, will never be written.

Yet to those who have read *The Octopus*, and shall read *The Pit*, it will not seem that the author has left his work undone. In *The Octopus* he gave us the scope and magnitude of his full conception. In *The Pit* he more than once projects his thought into the scene and atmosphere of the book that was to follow. Indeed, the final story is suggested throughout, while in one place we are given a brief but graphic picture of the Wolf itself—the famine abroad, resulting from wheat shortage and Pit speculation—"the loaf small as the fist and costly"—the bitterness of the cry for bread. Through the bellow and roar of the Pit we hear the bark and snarl of the Wolf—the gaunt cry of hunger—we picture for ourselves the deadly misfortune of crop failure—the blighting curse of greed. Perhaps it is better that these things should be suggested than amplified. Their detail, as depicted by Frank Norris, would have been masterly, sombre, terrible. Perhaps unconsciously he felt that this book would never be written, and so, without knowing it, made the writing unnecessary. His great work seems completed as it stands;—the Epic of the Wheat is finished.

The Octopus and *The Pit*—two fine novels of a great new century. Already *The Octopus* has become for the time at least, a part of our literary history. *The Pit*, just given to the public, is certain of a welcome and a hearing. In many ways it is better than *The Octopus*,—better technically—more direct—shorter—going surer to the mark. Better, but not bigger. It will please many more people, and many people more. Its characters live and breathe, struggle and die. Only, they breathe the narrow, smoke-laden, vitiated atmosphere of La Salle Street, instead of the measureless golden anodyne of California, and then, where shall we find another Annixter, another Hilma Tree, another S. Behrman?

"The Pit."
Book News Monthly, 21 (February 1903), 437–38.

The deep regret that was and still is being felt throughout this country for the loss of Mr. Frank Norris is in no degree diminished upon a perusal of Mr. Norris's posthumous novel, "The Pit." This work is the second volume in the great trilogy so admirably planned and begun by the brilliant young author, a series of novels that was to form an "Epic of the Wheat." The first volume was "The Octopus" and no one who read it could deny that here was a mighty wielder of the pen, a gifted novelist such as America had not heard the voice of for many years. Mr. Norris was only a young writer, but already he had developed a maturity that placed him far beyond more aged heads and gave him a precedent over many of those of older name and fame. In short, Genius, which had for so long veiled her face in the land of America, as far as the novel was concerned, had once again beamed forth in gladsome greeting and touched her magic wand to one of whom Nature might again stand up and truly say, "This was a man." For it is not only Frank Norris, the brilliant novelist, who commands our deepest respect and highest admiration, but it is the man whose wonderful personality compels our regard, whose force of character sweeps us into new realms and mightier, a man scrupulously true to his ideals, a man who, laboring unweariedly in his chosen field of high art, swerved not, whom nor fame nor money could lure to paths of lower plane, to fields of greater profit, to the sacrifice of adherence to the cause unto which he had consecrated his powers.

It was no mean task to which Frank Norris applied himself when he sat down to pen an epic of the wheat. It involved problems and intricacies in American economic life that required not only vast breadth of imagination and novelistic grasp, but that called as well for an earnest study of conditions as they exist and an irreproachable accuracy in knowledge of difficult affairs. Not only must American life in its social aspects be satisfactorily portrayed, but the mighty questions of certain financial phases must be perfectly set forth and brought to a fitting issue.

In "The Octopus" Mr. Norris showed the wheat in its growing stages. The farmer who sowed the seed, his anxieties in regard to the weather and the crops, the influence of railroad corporations, the blighting force of the mailed hand upon the country-folk were vividly depicted and the first act in the mighty drama of grain growing, grain buying and grain selling, of importation and exportation, of agricultural industry, speculation and consumption was enacted.

"The Pit" is the second act in the thrilling story. It is the picture of the speculator, of the Board of Trade and never in fiction have we been brought so forcibly face to face with the madness of the Stock Exchange as in this novel. Chicago is the scene of the action, the chief characters are men of business enterprise and wealth, the hero is a multi-millionaire who corners the wheat only to find himself later cornered by the wheat, after a signal triumph and a magnificent fight. The Chicago Board of Trade, with the wheat pit in particular, is placed before us, and the contrast between the drama of romance as enacted upon the stage and the immense and more important drama that day by day involves men and money with the terrible reality of its implacable grasp, is irresistibly forced upon us. In the heroine most of all is the contrast set forth; it is in her peculiar double character, her fluctuations from ideality to reality, that we see the startling comparison in all its significance. Laura Dearborn is a creation, she is something new in the woman of fiction, but she is the truest of the true to life. Mr. Norris could make characters; he could make them live before us, he could give us a subtle intimacy with their innermost personalities and give it without lengthy psychological analysis or tedious play with soul problems and tendencies. The effect for which Mr. Henry James is ever striving and barely succeeds in bringing to pass after a number of hours passed in wearisome reading is obtained by Mr. Norris in a page, and an interesting page at that, while the intense grip of situation, the thrilling power of exciting scene make the work of the latter not only satisfying but absorbing from beginning to end. And all this, too, without the sacrifice of artistic skill, without a lapse from good, refined, even elegant style. Mr. Norris's mode of expression is distinctively his own, but it measures up to a high standard in novelistic art. It has clarity, it has force, it has purity, it has dignity, is has easy flow that makes easy reading. It all causes one to wonder why a man of such unique endowments should have been cut off in his very prime, swept away, as it were, in the very moment of his triumph, in that moment when his full powers lay right at his command, and when he was so industriously striving to put them to best and safest use.

A. Schade Van Westrum. "Second Canto of the Epic of the Wheat." *The Lamp*, 26 (February 1903), 54–56.

When "Moran of the Lady Letty" appeared it was singled out by the discerning critics as a decidedly clever "minor novel." The public agreed to some extent with the reviewers, then the story passed the way of much current fiction, and its author discovered that, while he had made a beginning, he had his spurs still to win. He wrote "McTeague," and with it took the deciding step. Frank Norris began to be talked about more seriously as a coming man. "Blix" came and went, an experiment in another field and in another manner. Norris did not return to it. His "Man's Woman" closed the first period of his career, ended all too soon by death. In this story of an arctic explorer he carried to its extreme limit his conception of the man who achieves, of the strenuous life stripped of all the safeguards that civilization has put around it, of the master who must be brutal for his own sake and that of his followers.

The transition from the first to the second and last period of Norris's activity is striking. His view broadened, his insight deepened, his grasp strengthened. Social unrest we have always had with us—religious, political, or economic. In our day the discontent takes the economic form. Norris saw the wheatfields of California and the struggle between the agriculturist and the railroad magnate. Then his glance travelled midway across the continent to the Chicago wheat pit, another stage of the progress from the producer to the consumer; and, last of all, he saw the staple of man's food nourishing the masses of Europe. The trilogy may well have suggested itself without the aid of Zola's series of three, which deals, strangely enough, with the oldest social unrest, the religious as well as with the industial one. Norris began to plan the Epic of the Wheat, which was to be told in three prose narratives—"The Octopus," dealing with the war between the wheat-grower and the railroad trust; "The Pit," a narrative of a corner in wheat in the Chicago wheat pit; and, last of all, "The Wolf," a story of the relief of a European famine by the American grain, which now will never be written.

Norris found his own material; for his method of treatment of it he went direct to Zola, whose influence had been traceable in his earlier work. "The Octopus" is saturated with the Zolaesque manner, its symbolism, its repetitions of attributes and phrases. And, truth to tell, no better model could have been found for the handling of so vast a subject than the Titanic French naturalist. "The Octopus" grew into an epic, forcing attention.

"The Pit" is now added to it, the last work of Frank Norris. The trace of Zola is still perceptible in it here and there, but it is the trace of the school, rather than of the Master; in meaning and atmosphere this story, like "The Octopus," is strikingly American. The descriptions of the neighborhood of the Chicago Board of Trade, in the early part of the book, may be insisted upon a little too much, but later on one learns to value the technical meaning of this appeal to the memory. When Norris comes to the excitement and rush of the "corner," his picture is all life and action in scenes now perfectly familiar. Here is the strenuous life in its most modern form told dispasionately, with all the impartiality, the minuteness of observation of the realist, yet with a force that carries the reader along.

The story is remarkably well balanced. Its women are as interesting, as well seen, as its men. Laura Dearborn, who becomes the speculator's wife, and her younger sister Page are types of the present-day American young woman, while yet remaining individuals. The American woman's rival, as Paul Bourget came to see when he visited us, is business on an enormous scale, before whose allurement the attractions of women pale into insignificance. Laura Dearborn, self-centred, thrown upon her own resources by her husband's pursuit of the golden glamour, finds herself; her sister is dealt with in a lighter vein, not unworthy of Mr. Howells in its humor and gentle sympathy; the culture, which is still an exotic among the mass of our busy men, who look upon its votaries not without suspicion, is cleverly represented by an artist in stained glass. The magnificently true proportions of the story will lead many of its readers at first into a misconception of its vast scale. But its true values will gradually disclose themselves, for it is one of the finest, strongest pictures yet penned of our present-day life, with its strong, if hidden, distinction between the male and the female element. And the very excellence of the story makes more poignant the regret over our loss of the most promising of our younger men-of-letters. Norris made his indelible mark upon our literature before he died. He might have served it so much longer in the maturity of his great and studiously cultivated talent.

Owen Wister.
" 'The Pit—A Story of Chicago': The Last and Best Novel of the Late Frank Norris."
The World's Work, 5 (February 1903), 3133–34.

Two hearts, that should beat as one, estranged by prosperity, and by adversity united in the happy and solemn end:

this, stated in its simplest terms, is the theme of "The Pit"—a theme as old as the hills, and all the better for being so. Ingenuity, surprises, novel twists of plot, these also belong to legitimate art; but it is never upon them that the soundest art relies; great artists always concern themselves with the usual, not with the unexpected; with the familiar rather than with the exceptional; and are recognized by their simplicity, not by their complexity. Mr. Norris has chosen a situation that belongs to all time, and has given it a treatment which belongs entirely to himself. This is what we ask of the strong writer, and it is only the strong writer who can do it.

A man of action, shrewd, self-made, and successful in affairs, to whom speculation has so far been no more than a distrusted and occasional pastime, meets and marries the first woman who has seriously interested him. He outstrips his competitors with ease; he conquers her with no very great difficulty. She is not sure how much she loves him, and her own words, "Do you suppose you can say 'no' to that man?" summarize the quality of his wooing, which is but little presented on the scene. That both are large enough natures for a fine and understanding union is shown by one simple and beautiful page after they have come out from church after being married.

But a friend has recently drawn him into certain transactions in wheat so profitable that his latent relish for such excitement is awakened. This starts the crack in their happiness.

If I leave all for thee, wilt thou exchange
And *be* all to me? Shall I never miss
Home-talk and blessing?

Her heart, like every natural woman's, had asked this of her husband, and the answer is—his deepening preoccupation in his wheat gambling ventures, his increasing absences from her. He was rich already when he married her, rich beyond need of greater wealth; but the lust of the chase is on him, and hence he gives her more and more the luxurious things she does not want and less and less the only thing she craves—the home-talk and blessing. Sometimes her appeals for his companionship (she makes but few, being proud) bring him to her for awhile, filled with desire to make amends; but his brief resolves evaporate like mist in the hot glare of speculation. Repeated triumphs lead him on, flatter his vanity, stimulate his sense of power and his thirst for more power. Each new campaign is on a scale more huge; to see his enemies outgeneraled, to graze ruin and make half a million instead, all this gives him sensations so poignant and delicious that he grows to require it like some hypodermic injection. Deprived of it, his powers sink flaccid and unelastic. Especially after one victory, when he comes home declaring it shall be his last—that he is done with this debauch of nerves—is the abstinence shown to be a strain greater than his endurance can any longer sustain. He fidgets in idleness; tries books, driving, the theatre, his country place, all quite in vain. These things cannot hide him from his ennui, do not bite sharp enough to stimulate him. He goes back to the wheat pit, and this is the beginning of the end.

Presently the markets of the world are throbbing with his vast operations. The fortune that still attends him makes the annihilation of those who stand in his way; he himself becomes the storm centre, while through his brain sweep the vertiginous currents of trade and strategy which he has set going and could not stop if he would.

To such demands mortal strength is unequal. His judgment grows bloodshot, his human feelings grow bloodshot, his sleep deserts him, and his appetite; and whenever he is not in action, night or day, the words "wheat, wheat, wheat" sing perpetually in his head; so that he goes flying forward through the weeks with the dread of illness coming behind him and the beckoning illusion of his omnipotence in front. These pages are so powerful that they drag the reader in their sweep even as the wheat drags the hero, even as Dickens and Zola and Tolstoi drag one with an interest and a suspense that are like a joyful riot of pain.

And the man's lonely wife meanwhile? She sits deserted in her uptown magnificence, sharing in her husband's life no longer, knowing nothing of his thoughts, his doings, his hopes or his fears, not even seeing his face any more, but keeping company with empty, expensive furniture. He has ceased to come home at all, but makes his visits to her by telephone, sleeping in a hotel room as close to the Board of Trade as he can get. So for her also a pit opens—a pit of desperation, that she struggles back from. The end is happy.

Stripped of accessories, such is the story; nor do accessories seem to count for much in looking back upon this book. It belongs to a group of financial novels certain of which are familiar to most of us—"Mammon and Company," for instance, and "The Market Place" and Mr. Hope's new story. Very different from each other, all in their way take up the same thread of modern speculation and thus furnish a proper measure by which to gage "The Pit."

I think Frank Norris has outstripped them all. I do not think any one of them compares with him in emotional interest or in grasp of the subject. His study of the quite special technicalities presented seems far more thorough than any of theirs, even Harold Frederic's, whose book has strength. Mr. Frederic's pirate financier is a success; Mr. Benson's is a failure, though he tried hard; Mr. Hope does not try at all, but plays more on the surface; and it is the speculating woman who is the object of his brilliant attention.

When it comes to the accessories, to drawing-room small talk, to a certain light sureness of touch in presenting men and women of the world, we have nobody, except Edith Wharton, who can do it right. Hope and Benson do it very right. Harold Frederic is clumsy at it, and Frank Norris is behind Harold Frederic. From this inadequacy in accessories may be excepted one comedy scene where a young girl and grown man discuss love, literature and themselves. It is very pleasant.

Concerning the art of "The Pit" certain other reserves are to be made; but if they are all made they will leave still untouched the great main story, strong, passionate, vivid—livid, I had almost written—with interest. The author's firm hand and long reach stretch into tragic depths of the human soul far beyond the compass of the other financial novels I have named.

You have noticed, have you not, how many novels we read, how few we remember? They are little pleasure-bridges by which we cross a mental gap and go on, and that's all. This is one sort of novel, and a good sort, too. Have you noticed how, even though we may think of these stories during the hour that we read them, we never think of their authors for a minute? Their existence does not occur to us.

But there is another, a rarer kind of novel, the kind written by what we call a master. The sure symptom of such a novel is not so much that you remember *it*, but that you think of its *author*. You feel the force, the personality, the attitude toward life, that lie behind the printed words; the story is but a medium through which you have met *somebody*. Frank Norris is somebody. In his first novel, the sea story, this was evident at once. In "McTeague" his strength had grown; in "The Pit" he has risen on stepping-stones to higher things. Such a raw device as (for example) the recurrent descriptive phrase is no longer employed; and his last word to us shows him on the road to have become a master.

There is a marble group called "Death Arresting the Hand of the Young Sculptor." When I think of this group I think of Frank Norris and lament the great loss to our national literature that his death has brought.

Bailey Millard. "Outline of 'The Pit,' Frank Norris' Last and Best Novel." *San Francisco Examiner*, February 1, 1903, p. 10.

"The Pit," the sixth, last and best of the novels on which Frank Norris expended his brief literary life, has come from the publishing house of Doubleday, Page & Co., and is as welcome to the reviewer as all strong, tense, colorful romances must ever be. That it will be equally welcome to the public I am firmly convinced. In all great centers of civilization, where the hum and drone of traffic are pervasive and familiar, the book will go with a bound, because of the truth of its pictures of trade, which will make a strong appeal to this materialistic age, full of its strenuous and arrogant commercialism. Nor need there be any fear for the universality of its appeal, for the vivid love story it contains will captivate the imagination of all story lovers, from the happy "hobo" to the miserable millionaire.

There were many people who bent over the interminable pages of "The Octopus" with lassid interest, and for whom its tiresome prolixity and irritating discursiveness could have no sort of interest; "McTeague" shocked the Puritanical element among the novel readers, and "Moran" was too exciting for those who had fed upon the Howells gruel. None of the objections to his other work can be urged against this novel of Norris'; none except the elemental ones respecting the author's philosophy of life, or rather his lack of it, and the fact that he never was an artist of a contemplative and meditative nature, or one who made a close study of values, but rather one who dashed down his impressions of form and color and hurried on to the next sketch. These were temperamental attributes of a romance writer who could do his three thousand words a day every day in the week, and, while one need not look for technical perfection in work thus turned out, it more than makes up to the reader in its spontaneity of expression and tenuity of thought; and when one reflects that to the great mass of plain people who constitute the novel-reading public Mr. Norris' vocabulary will appear as something very scholarly and even recondite, there need be no misgivings as to a little looseness, not to say, recklessness, of rhetoric.

Curtis Jadwin, the great central figure of "The Pit," is at first a solid business man of Chicago and an eminently respectable one. His character seems to be drawn somewhat on the lines of that of John D. Rockefeller, for he is a Sunday school superintendent and a man of much probity as to the details of his conduct, but unscrupulous as to the essence of his operations. We should follow his money-grubbing history with as little interest as that of the "rise" of any other nuzzling creature of the sordid alleyways of trade but for the fact that he is elevated into deserving prominence as the suitor for the hand of a cultured young woman named Laura Dearborn. It is his devotion to Laura that makes the man, for he is seen to acquire taste in art matters through her and to become imbued with a real desire for self-improvement. As to Laura, one may judge of her physical make-up from the following description:

> She was a tall young girl of about twenty-two or three, holding herself erect and fine with dignity. Even beneath the opera cloak it was easy to infer that her neck and shoulders were beautiful. Her almost extreme slenderness was, however, her characteristic; the curves of her figure, the contour of her shoulders, the swell of hip and breast were all low, from head to foot one could discover no pronounced salience. Yet there was no trace, no suggestion of angularity. She was as slender as a willow root is slender—and equally graceful, equally erect.

The story opens at the opera, where all Chicago has gone to hear a great singer. The crush of society people and their toilets are material which Norris employs very neatly, for, though no great lover of social forms, he had made a thorough study of the ways of "the higher classes" and the polite world generally. Here his touch is sure. He seems to delight in long descriptions of the clothes people wear and the way they wear them, and is not behind Henry James in his appreciation of the little touches of toilet which mark the distinction between people who know how to dress and those who do not. Dwellers in our genial climate will follow with interest the description of the interior of an Eastern theatre on a cold night and of the picture there presented:

> Everywhere the eye was arrested by the luxury of stuffs, the brilliance and delicacy of fabrics, laces as white and soft as froth, crisp, shining silks, suave satins, heavy gleaming velvets, and brocades and plushes, nearly all of them white—violently so—dazzling and splendid under the blaze of the electrics. The gentlemen in long, black overcoats, and satin mufflers, and opera hats; their hands under the elbows of their women-folk, urged or guided them forward, distressed, preoccupied, abjuring their parties to keep together, in their white-gloved fingers they held their tickets ready. For all the icy blasts that occasionally burst through the storm doors, the vestibule was uncomfortably warm, and into this steam-heated atmosphere a multitude of heavy odors exhaled—the scent of crushed flowers, of perfume, of sachet, and even—occasionally—the strong smell of damp seal skins.

Curtis Jadwin is one of the three men who are making love to Laura Dearborn. The others are Landry Court, who is connected with a brokerage firm, and Sheldon Corthell, an artist. Of all these Laura thinks while she sits in the theatre. Under the spell of the music Landry Court is a young chevalier, pure as Galahad; Corthell is a beautiful artist-priest of the early Renaissance, and Jadwin is a merchant prince, a great captain of trade. She is not sure which of her lovers she likes best, but she inclines toward Corthell, the artist, as she is a girl somewhat given to grand manners and always sensitive to high art impressions.

We see her in the streets of dirty, windy Chicago. She is not satisfied with the town, being more interested in the less raw and crude cities of New England. The black smoke that closes every vista of the business streets oppresses her and the soot that stains linen and gloves each time she stirs abroad is a never-ending discomfort.

"But the life was tremendous. All around, on every side, in every direction, the vast machinery of the Commonwealth clashed and thundered from dawn to dark and from dark to dawn. Even now as the car carried her farther into the business quarter, she could hear it, see it, and feel in her every fiber the trepidation of its motion. The blackened waters of the river, seen an instant between stanchions as the car trundled across the State street bridge, disappeared under fleets of tugs, of lake steamers, of lumber barges from Sheboygan and Mackinac, of grain boats from Duluth, of coal scows that filled the air with impalpable dust, of cumbersome schooners laden with produce, of grimy rowboats dodging the prows and paddles of the larger craft, while on all sides, blocking the horizon, red in color and designated by Brobdingnag letters, towered the hump-shouldered grain elevators."

Laura is seen to be a very high-strung, sensitive and really serious girl, and is probably Norris' best feminine creation. When one of her lovers tries to kiss her she bursts into an angry passion, and in her reflections upon the episode, accuses herself of flirting with the three of them. They have all made her offers of marriage, and she now sits down and writes letters refusing each one of them. Corthell takes his rejection very seriously and runs away to Europe. Court, who is forbidden in her house, is also dejected by his dismissal, but opposition only strengthens the determination of the business-like Jadwin to win the haughty young woman for his wife. He sets to work with this end in view and so assiduously does he apply himself that he makes her his wife, although one feels all the while that the artist, had he been at hand and pressed his suit, would have been the likelier man.

While the love story is progressing Jadwin is getting much interested in wheat operations and is becoming a great figure in the market, a sort of "Old Hutch," as it would seem. When he marries Laura he is well on the road to great wealth and is able to give her everything she wants except happiness. She is willing to care for him a great deal, but he neglects her shamefully. With him now it is all "wheat, wheat, wheat." He is going forward madly in his speculations and is very anxious to control the market.

When the old artist lover returns on the scene the neglected wife receives him cordially. They are discussing art and music in the lowered lights of the drawing-room and she is aware of the attraction which he still has for her—an attraction increased by the sympathy of their interests and the spiritual kinship which she feels for him, when the husband breaks in, turns on all the electric lights and gives vent to a loud jarring note, the announcement that he has made half a million in the market. Here is the picture:

> "Are you here, Laura? By George, my girl, we pulled it off, and I've cleaned up five—hundred—thousand—dollars!"
>
> Laura and the artist faced quickly about, blinking at the sudden glare, and Laura put her hand over her eyes.
>
> "Oh, I didn't mean to blind you," said her husband, as he came forward. "But I thought it wouldn't be appropriate to tell you the good news in the dark."
>
> Corthell rose, and for the first time Jadwin caught sight of him.
>
> "This is Mr. Corthell, Curtis," Laura said. "You remember him, of course?"

Jadwin is wedded so closely to the wheat market that his neglect of Laura becomes worse and worse, and the artist lover, whose character degenerates visibly toward the end of the story, does not hesitate to take advantage of the situation. Laura is a marble monument of unhappiness. Her husband piles gifts upon her; she has everything that a woman might wish, except her husband's kindly care and attention.

> Her desires were gratified with an abruptness that killed the zest in them. She felt none of the joy of possession; the little personal relation between her and her belongings vanished away. Her gowns, beautiful beyond all she had ever imagined, were of no more interest to her than a drawerful of outworn gloves. She bought horses till she could no longer tell them apart; her carriages crowded three supplementary stables in the neighborhood. Her flowers, miracles of laborious cultivation, filled the whole house with their fragrance. Wherever she went deference moved before her like a guard; her beauty, her enormous wealth, her wonderful horses, her exquisite gowns made of her a cynosure, a veritable queen.
>
> And hardly a day passed that Laura Jadwin, in the solitude of her own boudoir, did not fling her arms wide in a gesture of lassitude and infinite weariness, crying out:
>
> "Oh, the ennui and stupidity of all this wretched life."

Jadwin, full of business affairs, does not come home on her birthday and she greatly feels this slight, because she has looked forward to the day as one on which he could not fail to devote himself to her. But the artist is there. He makes mad love to her and she reluctantly gives her consent to fly with him on the morrow. But this desperate ending of her weary home life never comes, for her husband, who has been trying his best to control the breadstuff market, is hard hit and losing ground rapidly. There is a tremendous flurry in wheat, owing to the panicky condition of the foreign markets, and the bears are pressing the great speculator very hard. Then comes that sort of description of the wheat pit which the reader has been looking for instinctively all along. Norris must have studied the scene during some disturbance of the market to have been able to make his story such a vivid picture. It reminds us of Markham's "Wall Street Pit" and the lines—

I see a hell of faces surge and whirl,
Like maelstrom in the ocean....
Is this a whirl of madmen ravening
And blowing bubbles in their
    merriment?
Is Babel come again with shrieking
    crew
To eat the dust and drink the roaring
    wind?
And all for what? A handful of bright
    sand
To buy a shroud with and a length of
    earth?

Jadwin here shows himself as an heroic figure, and one cannot help feeling a certain sort of pity for the poor, hunted spectacle of him. But he dies hard, as witness:

> Jadwin was in the thick of the confusion by now. And the avalanche, the undiked ocean of the Wheat, leaping to the lash of the hurricane, struck him fairly in the face.
>
> He heard it now, he heard nothing else. The wheat had broken from his control. For once he had by the might of his single arm held it back; but now it rose like the upbuilding of a colossal billow. It towered, towered, hung poised for an instant, and then, with the thunder as of the crash and grind of chaotic worlds, broke upon him, burst into the pit and raced past him, on and on to the eastward and to the hungry nations.
>
> And then under the stress and violence of the hour something snapped in his brain—the murk behind his eyes had been suddenly pierced by a white flash, the strange calms and the tiny nervous paroxysms of the past few months, all at once culminated in some indefinable crisis and the wheels and cogs of all activities save one lapsed away and ceased. Only one function of the complicated machine persisted, but it moved with a rapidity of vibration that seemed to be tearing the tissues of being to shreds, while its rhythm beat out the old and terrible cadence:
>
> "Wheat — wheat — wheat, wheat — wheat — wheat!"
>
> Blind and insensate, Jadwin strove against the current of the wheat. There in the middle of the pit, surrounded and assaulted by herd after herd of wolves, yelping for his destruction, he stood braced and rigid upon his feet, his head up, his hand, the great bony hand that once held the whole pit in its grip, flung high in the air in a gesture of defiance, while his voice, like the clangour of bugles sounding to the charge of a forlorn hope, rang out again and again over the din of his enemies:
>
> "Give a dollar for July—give a dollar for July!"

But he cannot hold back the mighty, irresistible tide that rushes in upon him. His day as the ruler of the market is done. Yet he is slow to give up. He makes a last grand rally and then yields to his enemies.

> Beaten; beaten at last, the great bull smashed! The great corner smashed! Jadwin busted! They themselves saved, saved, saved!

Cheer followed cheer, yell after yell. Hats went up, into the air. In a frenzy of delight men danced and leaped and capered upon the edge of the pit, clasping their arms about each other, shaking each others' hands, cheering and hurrahing till their strained voices became hoarse and faint.

Some few of the older men protested. There were cries of:

"Shame! Shame!"

"Order—let him alone!"

"Let him be; he's down now. Shame! Shame!"

But the jubilee was irrepressible; they had felt the weight of the bull's hoof, the rip of his horn. Now they had beaten him, had pulled him down.

"Yah-h-h! Whoop, yi, yi, yi! Busted, busted, busted! Hip, hip, hip, and a tiger!"

"Come away, sir! For God's sake, Mr. Jadwin, come away," Landry was pleading with Jadwin.

After which, of course, the loving, high-minded Laura, losing sight of her artist, is all wifely sympathy and affection. She still has her own private funds and with these they journey to the great West to rebuild their broken fortune. There the tale ends.

A strong, well-knit, well-told, vivid, real and vital story of human life and love, full of stimulating passages and strong, stirring pictures—a story wrought out of an intense nature, gifted with eyes that saw into the heart of things. Those of us here on the western rim, who had boasted of Norris and looked to him proudly to uphold our art standard, shall not fail of our applause, although it falls upon the dull, cold ear of death. For we know that the spirit of him whom we applaud is smiling upon us from its height and sharing with us the satisfaction we feel as a literary community in his work as an artist in letters.

"The Pit—A Story of Chicago."
Philadelphia Inquirer, February 1, 1903, p. 14, "Second Section."

The late Frank Norris planned a trilogy which should encompass the whole story of wheat. "The Octopus," dealing with the raising of wheat and its transportation to market, was published two years ago and made a distinct success. The octopus was the railroad and the story dealt with the troubles of the farmers by reason of high rates, discriminating rates, and of monopoly in owning the elevators, making practically only one purchaser for the grain. It was a long story and, though of undoubted power, was faulty in that it took a long time to get at the human interest.

"The Pit" deals with the selling of wheat in the Chicago mart and has no other connection with "The Octopus" than that the commodity is the same. "The Wolf" was to have been the third story and was to deal with a famine in Russia. This will never be written.

"The Pit" is undoubtedly the best work by Norris, and is one of the strongest of recent American novels. The writer had his art more securely developed and his construction is distinctly better than in anything that has been done by him. It is a great story, though it is much to be feared that the casual reader will not find it out. As a mere tale of a man who loved, made a fortune and went broke in speculation it is not new and not particularly entertaining. It has been told a thousand times with better detail and much more superficial charm. The power of the book lies in its characters and in the psychological development of Jadwin, the chief actor in the drama. It may be also said to lie in the psychology of wheat itself, for never before has an inanimate commodity become so real a character, and that a dominating one, in fiction. Gold is always in stories and it has ruined many, but gold seems like a simple thing in its powers for evil compared with wheat, the harmless necessary staff of life.

The argument of the story is briefly that once a speculator in wheat, always a speculator in wheat. It is "wheat—wheat—wheat—wheat—wheat—wheat" that, like a demon, takes possession of the man who speculates in it. It forms his thoughts night and day. It drives from him all sense of caution, all sense of right and wrong, all feeling of moral obligation, takes him from his wife, leads him to desert his home—and for what? To make money? No, simply because there is no escape. If the author is to be believed, alcohol, with all its terrors, is harmless beside the love for wheat speculation. It is an insidious monster that enters the soul unawares and finally dominates and usually destroys it.

The story of Jadwin is that of a strong, resourceful man of business, who loved a woman of rare qualities and compelled her to love him by his many engaging and fundamental qualities of mind and soul. Accustomed to occasionally taking a flyer in wheat on a rather large scale, he got into the pit gradually, under the leadings of his broker friends. Once fairly enmeshed in the tendrils of speculation he loses his best qualities for the moment and is with difficulty recalled by his wife for a time. Then he plunges in worse than ever and makes the old-timers stare by his boldness. Finally he accomplishes the greatest corner of the age and makes millions, whereupon his friends urge him to desist. It is too late. He goes in to make more and loses all, but it is after all a gain, since he comes to himself and finds himself and finds his wife, and in comparative poverty, they start out once more, little regretting the splendor that brought them no happiness and nearly wrecked both their lives, morally and physically.

One can see from this that it is a book of fundamental things. It sounds the emotions and the motives of action deeply, and it rings true in every case. There may be those who care little for the details of speculation and may not be able to follow it, but there will be none who cannot see the one increasing purpose of the book, which is to show that even so good a thing as wheat may be the mainspring of great evil and that so powerful a thing as love may be strangled by a passion for a commodity.

This is quite the book of the new year and if the remaining eleven months have anything so powerful for good it will be a notable year indeed.

"Wit and Wisdom from Some of the Popular Books of the Season." *Spokane Spokesman-Review*, February 1, 1903, p. 17.

"I tell you the fascination of this pit gambling is something no one who hasn't experienced it can have any conception of. I believe it is worse than liquor, worse than morphine. Once you get into it, it grips you and draws you and draws you, and the nearer you get to the end the easier it seems to win, till all of a sudden, ah! there's the whirlpool!"—Frank Norris in "The Pit."

"New Books." *Washington Post*, February 2, 1903, p. 7.

A life of peculiar and extraordinary promise ended with the death of Frank Norris on October 25 in San Francisco, at the age of thirty-two. In the group of fine young intellects revealed in recent years his place is well to the front. Unlike his brilliant young contemporaries, most of whom are at their best in the telling of pleasing and agreeable tales, Frank Norris' strongest work is rarely of the "charming story" variety. "McTeague," the first real expression of the power that was in him, is a gloomy and depressing study of unbalanced natures, but human in every fiber. Greater by far, however, is "The Octopus," the first volume of a trilogy designed by Norris to be the epic of the wheat from the field, through the market, to the mouths of the hungry, and a book of earnest and powerful purpose. "The Octopus" fittingly prepared the way for the second volume of the trilogy, "The Pit," the manuscript of which was completed just before the death of the author.

"The Pit" is a story of the Chicago grain pit. Unlike Norris's earlier novels, the important characters in this book are few in number, and dominating them are the hero and heroine, Curtis Jadwin, capitalist and speculator, who brings about the corner that constitutes the crisis, and Laura Dearborn, the woman whom he loves and marries. To these central figures all the rest are artistically subordinated.

Jadwin is not a villain. He is simply spurred on by ambition and the love of the great commercial combat, the story of which is presented with wonderful realism. Even a reader who knows nothing of stock market mysteries cannot fail to grasp the situation, and an interest that is almost personal is aroused as to the outcome. The wife is neglected, home and friends apparently forgotten, while the madness of speculation possesses the man.

The coquettish heartlessness of Laura before she discovers her real self, her complete surrender when she realizes that she is in love with the man she has married without the consciousness of love, are alike admirably described. Yet Laura is not faultless. When baffled in her earnest endeavor to win from her husband evidence of the love he really feels for her, but which is overwhelmed for the time by his greater passion for speculation, she turns in despair to the lover who has not only the inner feeling, but exhibits freely the outer semblance as well, and she is barely saved from moral wreck by the financial wreck that overtakes her husband.

The writer of a review of this book in "The Bookman" (Albert Bigelow Paine), wishes "that Norris had found it within his conception to let her go out with Corthell into the night, and brought Curtis Jadwin, broken in body, mind, and purse, to his vast, desolate home.

" 'Old girl—Honey.'

"How that feeble cry in the gloom would have told, with only the echo of the empty dark to answer."

Will many readers sympathize with Mr. Paine in this abnormal taste for dramatic effect? One hopes not. After the torture of the nervous strain both Jadwin and Laura had endured it would seem that even the mildly sympathetic reader will find Mr. Norris' ending of the story more to his liking, and, with an unmistakable sense of relief, will watch them go together out into the world to start life anew. Surely the most unreasonable longing for dramatic effect must find abundant satisfaction in the picture of Curtis Jadwin when he stands alone in the pit, with the bears tearing at his throat, his triumphs swallowed up in defeat. "The wheat has broken from his control. For months he had, in the might of his single arm, held it back, but now it rose like the upbuilding of a colossal billow. It towered, towered, hung poised an instant, and then, with a thunder as of the grind and crash of chaotic worlds, broke upon him, burst through the pit, and raced past him, on and on to the eastward and to the hungry nations. And then, under the stress and violence of the hour, something snapped in his brain. . . .

"There in the middle of the pit, surrounded and assaulted by herd after herd of wolves yelping for his destruction, he stood braced, rigid upon his feet, his head upon his hand, the great, bony hand that once had held the whole pit in its grip, flung high in the air in a gesture of defiance, while his voice, like the clangor of bugles sounding to the charge of the forlorn hope, rang out again and again, over the din of his enemies:

" 'Give a dollar for July—give a dollar for July!'

"With one accord they leaped upon him. The little group of his traders was swept aside. Landry alone, Landry, who had never left his side since his rush from out Gretry's office. Landry Court, loyal to the last, his one remaining soldier, white, shaking, the sobs strangling in his throat, clung to him desperately. Another billow of wheat was preparing. They two—the beaten general and his young armor-bearer—heard it coming; hissing, raging, bellowing, it swept down upon them. Landry uttered a cry. Flesh and blood could not stand this strain. He cowered at his chief's side, his shoulders bent, one arm above his head, as if to ward off an actual physical force.

"But Jadwin, iron to the end, stood erect. All unknowing what he did, he had taken Landry's hand in his, and the boy felt the grip on his fingers like the contracting of a vise of steel. The other hand, as though holding up a standard, was still in the air, and his great detoned voice went out across the tumult, proclaiming to the end his battle-cry:

" 'Give a dollar for July—give a dollar for July.'

"But, little by little, Landry became aware that the tumult of the pit was intermitting. There was sudden lapsing in the shouting, and in these lapses he could hear from somewhere out upon the floor voices that were crying: 'Order—order, order, gentlemen.'

"But again and again the clamor broke out. It would die down for an instant, in response to these appeals, only to burst out afresh as certain groups of traders started the pandemonium again by the wild outcrying of their offers. At last, however, the older men in the pit, regaining some measure of self-control, took up the word, going to and fro in the press, repeating, 'Order, order.'

"And then, all at once, the pit, the entire floor of the board of trade was struck dumb. All at once the tension was relaxed, the furious struggling and stamping was stilled. Landry, bewildered, still holding his chief by the hand, looked about him. On the floor, near at hand, stood the president of the board of trade himself, and with him the vice president and a group of the directors. Evidently it had been these who had called the traders to order. But it was not toward them now that the hundreds of men in the pit and on the floor were looking.

"In the little balcony on the south wall, opposite the visitors' gallery, a figure had appeared, a tall, grave man in a long black coat—the secretary of the board of trade. Landry, with the others, saw him, saw him advance to the edge of the railing, and fix his glance upon the wheat pit. In his hand he carried a slip of paper.

"And then in the midst of that profound silence the secretary announced:

" 'All trades with Gretry, Converse & Co. must be closed at once.'

"The words had not ceased to echo in the high vaultings of the roof before they were greated with a wild, shrill yell of exultation and triumph, that burst from the crowding masses in the wheat pit.

"Beaten; beaten at last, the great bull! Smashed! The great corner smashed! Jadwin busted! They themselves saved, saved, saved! Cheer followed upon cheer, yell after yell. Hats went into the air. In a frenzy of delight men danced and leaped and capered upon the edge of the pit, clasping their arms about each other, shaking each others' hands, cheering and hurrahing till their strained voices became coarse and faint."

"The Wolf," the final volume of the trilogy, as planned by Mr. Norris, will never be written. Yet it is a question whether the work can be regarded as unfinished. Mr. Paine in his review truthfully says: "In 'The Octopus' he gave us the scope and magnitude of his full conception. In 'The Pit' he more than once projects his thought into the scene and atmosphere of the book that was to follow. Indeed, the final story is suggested throughout, while in one place we are given a brief but graphic picture of the wolf itself—the famine abroad, resulting from wheat shortage and pit speculation—'the loaf small as the fist and costly'—the bitterness of the cry for bread. Through the bellow and roar of the pit we hear the bark and snarl of the wolf—the gaunt cry of hunger—we picture for ourselves the deadly misfortune of crop failure—the blighting curse of greed. Perhaps it is better that these things should be suggested than amplified. Their detail, as depicted by Frank Norris, would have been masterly, somber, terrible. Perhaps unconsciously he felt that this book would never be written, and so, without knowing it, made the writing unnecessary. His great work seems complete as it stands—the epic of the wheat is finished."

"Books of the Day." *Chicago Daily News*, February 5, 1903, p. 11.

Frank Norris' death, deeply regretted as it was at the moment, becomes a cause for public mourning when his last book is read. Born in Chicago and passing his boyhood and early youth here, he has repaid whatever debt to the city arises by reason of this in the most generous manner by this posthumously published story, "The Pit," the second volume of "The Epic of the Wheat," of which "The Octopus" was the first volume and the third will forever remain unwritten. "The Octopus" dealt with the wheat-growers in southern California and their relations to the Southern Pacific railways. It was a most ambitious book, though seriously hampered by its author's admiration of the methods of Emile Zola, realism in the Zolaistic sense of the word, filled with mannerisms strikingly like those of the Frenchman's, and using the actuality of a desperate fight between the railway and the farmers to tell a tale of the greatest interest.

"The Pit," too, has its basis in fact, the corner in wheat which Joseph Leiter failed in several years ago standing forth as the salient truth underlying the fiction. But it shows a literary maturity chiefly in its refusal longer to accept the methods of Zola as its own, which the other lacked. It is compact as well and the romantic and poetic episodes which interrupted the flow of the earlier narrative are lacking here. It abounds in minor and unimportant inaccuracies, due to the author's having been out of the city so long, and in many instances it is plain that a partial rewriting of passages would have improved the style of the book. That these were not corrected is a pity and the responsibility must rest with the publishers for them. Appearing originally as a serial the reader will be assured that Norris, had he lived, would have made all the changes needful, for a more conscientious and painstaking literary artist has never lived.

But, at worst, the errors are slight and do not seriously mar the enjoyment certain to come from the book. It holds a romance of interest in addition to the thrilling story of the strategy which underlies the control of the wheat supply of the world. This romance begins with the attraction a man of great means suddenly feels toward a young girl who has just come to live with kinsfolk in Chicago after passing her earlier life in a New England village. Curtis Jadwin meets Laura Dearborn at a box party in the Auditorium and leaves little doubt from the beginning that he intends to make her his own. Two other men are in love with her before the book has gone through many pages, a rich artist, Sheldon Corthell, and a young fellow in one of the commission offices on the board of trade, Landry Court. It is indicative of Norris' art that the light conversation of the party in the box where these characters meet is interrupted on all sides by the discussion of a deal in wheat which has just proved unsuccessful, sounding the note which is to pervade the book.

The same qualities which had made Jadwin successful, the artist a dilettante and the broker's clerk at the beginning of his career throw Laura Dearborn into Jadwin's arms, not so much apparently because she loved as that he was too little unaccustomed to failure to tolerate refusal. With marriage, however, love came, and Laura is her husband's devoted friend, with hardly a waver of sentiment, even when he neglects her grossly after the passion for speculation has seized him and the attempt to run the corner begins.

The moral lesson of the book is powerfully yet incidentally drawn. One of the characters, a friend of all the principals in the story, has been bitten once in a grain deal and he tries hard to keep Jadwin from immersing himself in speculation, only to fall its prey at the close. Nor does Jadwin enter upon his course with any intention of becoming a speculator. His property has been acquired largely through the purchase of city land—itself a speculative enterprise, to be sure, but less so for those who had the foresight to see the possibilities of Chicago's growth than for those in cities less remarkable. The end of the book is conventional but happy. Tragical as its possibilities were, Norris chose not to avail himself of them. The book reads more pleasantly because of this and there can be little doubt that it comes closer to the truth, as it has been seen. But there will be a controversy regarding its suitability here—the old one of true truth and fictional truth.

What Chicagoans will like best about the book, in all likelihood, is the embodiment in it of the real spirit of the place. No one could come here a stranger and arrive at the heart of things as Norris has, dig out the grain of gold from all the sordidness, the gem of beauty from the reek and ruck, and hold it glowing before the world as it is held here. Some of the Chicago novelists whose lives have been spent here have failed in this, but it is because they have not possessed, in addition to such knowledge as Norris', the power of comparison which his long residence elsewhere gave.

J. B. Kerfoot. "The Latest Books." *Life*, 41 (February 5, 1903), 108.

It was hardly to be expected that the second novel in Frank Norris's trilogy of The Wheat should equal *The Octopus*, yet in spite of this realization *The Pit* is a disappointment. In the California story, the impotence of the human atoms before the impersonal power of the Octopus, at first dimly discerned, became little by little omnievident and unescapable, till tragedy was justified by its own grandeur. In *The Pit*, the current of the action is clogged and interrupted by petty detail, till the roar of the maelstrom of the Pit is drowned by the nearer bickerings of a mere love story.

"The Pit." *The Independent*, 55 (February 5, 1903), 331–32.

From the broad, fertile fields of California where the wheat is raised, and from the battle with the great railway that strangled the land in its arms like a huge octopus, we are carried in this second novel of Mr. Norris's trilogy to the Pit, in the Chicago Board of Trade Building, where the wheat is sold and where men rage like demons in the buying and selling of it. From the first chapter, where the heroine, newly arrived in Chicago, beholds through the murk of rain and many glimmering lights that sinister Building, "black, grave, monolithic, crouching on its foundations, like a monstrous sphinx with blind eyes, silent, grave,—crouching there without a sound, without a sign of life under the night and the drifting veil of rain,"—to the last paragraph, where, as she leaves the city, the same somber mass blocks her vision through the same "drifting veil of rain," always it dominates the story, a symbol of stern, inhuman, tremendous force. It is blind and voiceless, but it is more instinct with artistic life than the men who plot and rave beneath its roof, than the women whose happiness and misery, without any will of their own, are held within its grasp.

This, indeed, is the deliberate purpose of the author's art; he is a late imitator of the naturalistic school dominated by Zola, whose aim was to represent human beings as lost in the current of some great, overpowering, brutal force. And it is characteristic of things American that we should welcome an imitation of such a literary movement after its career is run in France and other ideals have come to the front. In part Mr. Norris is notably successful in his attempt. The origin and growth of Jadwin's corner in wheat seize the reader's attention and will not let it go; the climax of the story, when the crash comes and Jadwin, broken in health and mind, comes out into the Pit to stay the fatal storm, is a powerful piece of writing. We shall not soon forget the picture of his impotence as he stands repeating with mechanical monotony the fatal words: "Wheat—wheat—wheat!" But it is characteristic of the story, as of all such stories, that we read it impatiently, hurrying through the intermediate scenes in our eagerness to reach the conclusion which we have foreseen from the beginning. Our interest, moreover, from first to last is less involved in the individual characters than in the contest of great impersonal forces. Just as the characters of *The Pit* are associated with the selling of wheat do they become real. Jadwin is the most vital of all; even Crookes, tho he appears but once or twice in the story, is alive and distinct. As we move further from the center, however, the persons, the heroine and her sister and the others, become more and more shadowy until we reach that feeble caricature, the artist Corthell. There is displayed in places a tremendous energy of description, but the final impression of the book is not far from a glorification of the basest passions in the American character.

"The Editor's Table."
Kennebec Journal (Augusta, Maine), February 7, 1903, p. 6.

This is a continuation of the "Epic of the Wheat," begun by Mr. Norris in "The Octopus" although it is entirely complete in itself. The brilliant young author whose wonderfully clear and vivid pictures of the social and business life of the great western metropolis had arrested the attention of the whole country, corrected the last proof of "The Pit," only a month before his untimely death. Strong as were the literary and dramatic qualities of "The Octopus," we feel that this latest and last work of Mr. Norris is justly entitled to rank as his best.

It is a wonderful story, of the strenuous, restless, nerve wearing life, that finds a field of activity in the wheat and corn pits of the Chicago Board of Trade Building. Out of it breathes the living spirit of the great city by the lakes, and the maelstrom on La Salle street. It is real. Its characters are genuine flesh and blood people—not the shadows of romance, or the idealistic figures of a purely imaginative world. There is not one affected line—not one false note between the covers of this book. It impresses us not merely by its wonderful grasp and effective grouping of detail; not merely by its clear and subtle analysis of character and motive, but rather by its atmosphere of truth, its frank and unreserved genuineness. It is the work of one who had personally lived among his characters, and who had the power to portray them with the rare skill that belongs only to the master of his art.

The graphic story of Curtis Jadwin's "corner" on wheat, gives the most complete and dramatic picture of such a spectacle, with all that it involves, that has ever appeared in print. In its special field it is, and we are inclined to think it will always be, a classic.

"The Pit" is certainly entitled to rank as a truly great novel, which will give the readers of the future, a closer and accurate conception of conditions as they exist today in the metropolis of the great West, with its wonderful resources, its insatiate commercial greed, and its restless speculative spirit, that knows no pause, and remorselessly crushes its victims, as beneath the wheels of a juggernaut.

"With Some Authors You Have Known." *Atlanta Constitution*, February 8, 1903, p. 8, "The Sunny South" supplement.

When Frank Norris died he was called a "potential" genius. "The Pit" shows that he was a genius, undisciplined, but on the way to do great work of an enduring kind. Many writers outlive their fame. Frank Norris died too soon. His death is a distinct loss to American literature.

W. L. Courtney. "Books of the Day." *London Daily Telegraph*, February 11, 1903, p. 6.

A short time ago the literary world heard with no little regret that Mr. Frank Norris was dead. Not only the readers of "The Octopus," but also those who knew something of the imperfect but brilliant sketch, "Shanghaied," and the more mature novel entitled "McTeague," had become aware that in Mr. Norris we had a novelist of rare promise, destined not only for an American, but for a much wider public. "The Octopus" was, it will be remembered, the first part of a Trilogy dealing with wheat. The production of the wheat in the golden plains of California was to be succeeded by its distribution in the Board of Trade offices in Chicago, and its consumption in some old-world community. It is a matter for congratulation that, though we shall never, in all probability, see the third section, to which the author gave the name of "The Wolf"—the relief, that is to say, of the wolf of hunger by the supply of the staff of life—the second instalment of the Trilogy, which is called "The Pit," was left complete, and is today published by Mr. Grant Richards. It is not quite so good as "The Octopus," but perhaps that was inevitable from the nature of its subject. The charm of the earlier narrative lay in its beautiful delineation of country, its wide and picturesque grasp of all the natural elements of the great cornfields, and also in the precise and distinct portrayal of some of the characters involved in the plot—Annixter, for instance, who began by being a coarse piece of matter, and was purified and heightened by love; or the old farmer, Magnus Derrick, gradually tempted to join the movement of revolt against the all-encroaching tyranny of the railroad. In "The Pit" Mr. Frank Norris has not quite the same chances, or possibly he deliberately neglects them. When the wheat arrives in Chicago, it becomes a matter for speculation with the bears and the bulls of the Chicago market. Naturally, we have no such appropriate background as we found in "The Octopus," suggested by the yellow glory of the cornfields. The mise-en-scène is only Chicago itself—grandiose, big, overpowering in the magnificence of palatial mansions and broad thoroughfares, but also in essence vulgar and commonplace. The material pursuit of wealth is of course rampant in Chicago. The men who succeed are the men who can afford to live in the palaces. The "Pit" itself, where all the chaffering of the market goes on, is a hideous arena of sordid aims and interests. Listen to the description which Mr. Norris himself gives:

> Often Jadwin had noted the scene, and, unimaginative though he was, had long since conceived the notion of some great, some resistless force within the Board of Trade building that held the tide of the streets within its grip, alternately drawing it in, and throwing it forth. Within there a great whirlpool, a pit of roaring waters, spun and thundered, sucking in the life tides of the city, sucking them in as into the mouth of some tremendous cloaca, the maw of some colossal sewer; then vomiting them forth again, spewing them up and out, only to catch them in the return eddy, and suck them in afresh.... All through the North-West, all through the central world of the wheat the set and whirl of that innermost pit made itself felt; and it spread and spread and spread till grain in the elevators of Western Iowa moved and stirred and answered to its centripetal force, and men upon the streets of New York felt the mysterious tugging of its undertow engage their feet, embrace their bodies, overwhelm them, and carry them bewildered and unresisting back and downwards to the Pit itself. Nor was the Pit's centrifugal power any less. Because of some sudden eddy spinning outward from the middle of its turmoil, a dozen bourses of Continental Europe clamoured with panic, a dozen old-world banks, firm as the established hills, trembled and vibrated. Because of an unexpected caprice in the swirling of the inner current, some far-distant channel suddenly dried, and the pinch of famine made itself felt among the vine dressers of Northern Italy, the coal miners of Western Prussia. Or another channel filled, and the starved moujik of the steppes, and the hunger-shrunken coolie of the Ganges' watershed fed suddenly fat and made thank-offerings before ikon and idol.

The nature of the scene which he has to describe has, it will be observed, its effect upon the author, limiting the powers of his imagination, setting bounds to his artistic capacity, and making his style crude and harsh and "impressionist" as perhaps the subject demands.

Yet there is no question that the work

of Mr. Frank Norris is nothing if not epical in character. As compared, for instance, with a man like Stephen Crane, whose genius, such as it was, was that of the episode, Mr. Norris possesses some of the large and elemental faculties which go to the composition of early and primeval romance. Mr. W. D. Howells has recently written about him in an American magazine, in which naturally enough he alludes to the obvious fact that Mr. Norris is a disciple of Zola. Certainly, it was from Zola that our author derived that power of grasping a whole series of events, of getting to the essential meaning of a city or community, or given civilization—something, too, of that mastery of detail which in the book before us makes the gilded squalor of Chicago streets live before our eyes. But while Zola is melodramatic, positive, realistic, Mr. Norris, with more imagination, has the epical instinct, sometimes letting his fancy roam far and wide in riotous freedom—always the disciple of the Muses, even though the Muse of his inspiration wears the smart tailor-made dresses of an American heroine. "The Octopus," for instance, was not only a history of actual personalities—the farmer, the railway magnate, the daredevil of the plains—but an idealised narrative in which the characters become typical, and the suffused atmosphere of the piece was such as has never been seen on sea or on land. Mr. Norris, in short, allows himself to dream with faculties which Zola was never able to cultivate, not even in "Le Rêve." The American writer is a realist with a difference, a man who lets his imagination play round the puppets when he draws, and therefore places them on a platform and pedestal far above the vulgar trivialities of every day.

The story of "The Pit" is conceived on simple and broad lines. Each of the characters is clearly designed, and the obvious nature of the plot and its dénouement is by no means unimpressive. The principal figure is a man called Curtis Jadwin, capitalist and speculator, a symbolic figure of the tragic drama, with all its implicit possibilities of death and devastation and ruin. He is, as we find him at first, a hard, straightforward, practical business man, a very Napoleon of trade, a kind of figure, which has become familiar to us in these modern days—an American of enterprise, full of gigantic ideas and practically unlimited audacity. It is his misfortune that such a man should ever fall in love, and we are aware from the outset that his wooing of Laura Dearborn is carried on at the peril of his own reputation and career. For the heroine, Laura Dearborn, is not a woman with whom everyone would be happy. Indeed, it is a weakness of the novel that her somewhat vacillating temperament should leave us in some doubt alike as to her virtues and her defects. She certainly was never born to be happy, because she had never tried to understand her own predilections and sympathies. Primarily her instincts were artistic; secondarily she believed herself intended to be a great lady. Of course, her beauty made her the object of general admiration, nor is it a matter of surprise that of her three admirers—Landry Court (a broker's clerk), Sheldon Corthell (an artist), and Curtis Jadwin (the speculator), it was the last who won her as his wife. From this point the evolution of the story is easy to foresee. Laura Dearborn marries the millionaire, loves him for his resolution, his pluck, his Imperial instincts in organisation and command, and also gains all the satisfaction of knowing that in his house she is the leading lady of Chicago. But the still small voice within her of artistic susceptibility is not quenched even by the pomp and pageantry of her social triumphs. If Curtis Jadwin is as clever domestically as he is financially, he will retain her affection; but if he puts his business first, and gives his wife only the second place, the horizon is sure to be black with clouds. And now we begin to see how the terrible nightmare of the Pit—that is to say, the gambling in wheat at the Chicago Board of Trade—broods over the fortunes alike of hero and heroine. What is the struggle that is going on in the magnificent palace to which Curtis Jadwin brings his bride? It is the desperate conflict between the speculative instinct and domestic peace. When a man, hardened in the ways of the world, accustomed to find his interest in the intricacies of commerce, deliberately adds to his responsibilities by taking to himself a wife, he ought to settle once for all the competing claims of the big world of trade and the little world of domestic felicity. Curtis Jadwin sincerely loved Laura Dearborn, but he loved gambling more; and so it comes to pass that the artist, Sheldon Corthell, once more comes on the scene, and the woman, who would have done anything for her husband if only he had shown the most fragmentary concern in her affairs, feels all the horrible temptations involved in a life of isolation and neglect.

There can only be two solutions of a problem like this. Either the husband loves his fortune or his wife. He may succeed in business, he may become the largest capitalist that the world has ever known, but the price he has to pay is the loss of Laura Dearborn. This, which is the natural catastrophe of a situation such as Mr. Frank Norris has devised, is not the one which he chooses to accept. He prefers the other horn of the dilemma. He brings his hero to condign grief, and then, when he is a ruined man, he will give him back the estranged affections of his wife. Curtis Jadwin, who had climbed, step after step, the dizzy ladder of speculation, finally conceives the insane idea that he can make a corner in wheat—that he can possess himself of all available stocks and dictate the price of the commodity to the world. The thing is impossible, as all his friends and much experience of Chicago gambling tell him. Then the hour of fate strikes, and Curtis Jadwin, capitalist and speculator, with the whole edifice of his fortune tumbling about his ears, comes back, broken and half-demented, to the arms of Laura Dearborn. The drama which Mr. Norris unrolls before our eyes is impressive just in virtue of its simplicity. But Chicago dominates, as was, perhaps, inevitable, the whole course of the narrative. The scenes of the Pit are graphic and realistic, but the more intimate and absorbing tragedy of human souls is subordinated to the appalling mechanism of blind commercial forces. For this reason, as has been already suggested, "The Pit" is inferior as a work of art to "The Octopus," but no one can deny its strength and absorbing interest. More than before we appreciate the misfortune which prevented this Trilogy from being developed into its final phase. Possibly the relief of some Old-World community, the victorious struggle against famine by a plentiful supply of wheat, which was to have been the subject of "The Wolf," might have restored to us that beautiful background of Nature for which the ugly splendour of Chicago affords but a poor substitute.

"New Books." *Edinburgh and Glasgow Scotsman*, February 12, 1903, p. 2.

It was a great misfortune for American literature that Mr. Frank Norris died before completing his "Epic of the Wheat." "The Octopus," wherein he began the "epic" with a story centering round the growing of the wheat and the war of the growers with the railroads, was a brilliant book which did much to increase the author's reputation on this side and to establish it more securely on the other; and now its promise has been more than fulfilled in the second of the series, which is the story of a great wheat "corner" and of the lives of men who "hustled" in the wheat "pit" of Chicago, buying and selling grain which they never saw or handled, winning and losing fortunes over "futures." The stress of American business life was never better reflected than in these pages, which are vivid as the cinematograph, so well has Mr. Norris caught the spirit of it all and so excellently has he adapted the rhythm of his graphic English to the rush of the racing commerce. The main interest of the story turns on the love of a beautiful and intellectual woman for a capitalist who has succumbed to the mania of wheat speculation and is attempting to create a "corner." Her love is stunted by the devotion of her husband to the markets. Neither does he return her love, nor can he give her the intellectual sympathy for which she craves—and then there happens what so often happens. An old lover reappears, an artist who has come "straight from Tuscany—and gardens and marble pergolas." Tuscany and Chicago! Heavens! One pardons her transgression. So the artist plays the organ to her and instructs her in art, and the meshes of the net are ever tightening around her, while her husband, blind to everything outside the wheat markets, is becoming more and more engulfed in the great tide of the grain, which finally is to overwhelm him as it has overwhelmed others who have tried to fight the laws of Nature. Thus in effective contrast are the realm of art and the world of commerce, the dreams of painters and the stern realities of the men who buy and sell. The end comes with the shattering of the "corner," and it should satisfy all who recognise the real man in Curtis Jadwin beneath the speculator and who are not so aesthetic as to wish to see their romantic longings realised at the cost of violation of a certain commandment. To Jadwin the "crash" brings financial ruin, but to his wife, and also to himself, enlightenment. The strength and picturesqueness of this drama of the "pit" are such that all must keenly regret the death of its young author before he was able to complete what would, without doubt, have been a brilliant trilogy."

"American Literature." *Saturday Review* (England), 95 (February 14, 1903), 206.

... The transition from Mr. Marion Crawford to Mr. Frank Norris brings out the wide diversity of point of view and manner which is a notable feature of the American novel-writing of the day. Mr. Norris' death a few months ago brought to a premature end a career of unusual promise. His earlier work was disagreeably hard in its realism and the dead level of literary values which it presented; but it was honest and sincere, and there was a touch of original power in it which seemed to promise much. Mr. Norris saw a great prose epic in the range, the complexity, the tremendous economic and social significance of the vast wheat-growing industry and he planned to write the epic in three novels. The first volume, *The Octopus*, we reviewed in our issue of 8 March last year; the second, *The Pit*, which has recently appeared, is a graphic and powerful study of wheat speculation in Chicago; the concluding story was to deal with the distribution of wheat and to describe a famine in some remote community in Europe. The plan was an ambitious one and Mr. Norris was too young a writer to carry it out with the masterful hand which it demanded; he was still too much under the influence of M. Zola to give his work complete individuality. His construction was sometimes at fault, his taste was uncertain, and his grasp of his rich materials was sometimes relaxed; but he had real force of imagination, he saw the dramatic possibilities of the life about him, and he gave abundant evidence of the possession of unusual strength and vigour.

"The Pit."
The Athenaeum, February 14, 1903, pp. 204–5.

Students of modern fiction probably remember the publication in the autumn of 1901 of a story called "The Octopus." It was the opening volume of a trilogy which its author dignified by the name of "The Epic of the Wheat." The present is the second volume of that projected trilogy, but between its publication and that of its predecessor the talented author was called to his last account. One is glad to have this second book, and grieved to think that the same hand can give us no more. "The Octopus" dealt well and powerfully, from the dramatic standpoint, with the production of wheat in the great league-long fields of the West, and with the war that is waged between railway monopolies and the producers, the men who make and the men who carry. The subject was a great one—a grand and elementary theme, well deserving epic treatment. We will not say that Mr. Norris's story was an epic, but it was, at any rate, a fine and inspired piece of fiction which dealt adequately with a great theme. The present volume is a drama descriptive of the handling of the wheat by the speculators who rule the markets from the Pit, the wheat division of the Board of Trade building in Chicago. These speculators, many of whom have never seen a field of wheat, are the men who to a great extent decide what the peasantry of many countries in the Old World shall pay for their loaves. By their devious ways, their deep-laid financial plots, their elaborate and complicated system of gambling, they decide whether the farmers of the Far West shall prosper for a season, and buy new buggies and "parlour-organs," or whether they shall suffer a spell of grinding anxiety and mortgage their land to supply their children with food. Nervous, sleepless, town-bred men in Chicago offices, their eyes fixed day and night upon the tape, or the dial which tells of the momently varying price of wheat—men whose horizons are bounded absolutely by the rise or fall of their banking accounts—decree that the hungry millions of the East shall feed full for a year, or be pinched by year-long hunger. And every day these little dollar-snatching demigods, whose powers are so great to make or mar their fellow-men in far outlying places, horde together and scream and yell, perspire and scramble, whine and bluster, truckle and jeer one with another, through long heated hours of high pressure, in the sordid theatre which is called the Wheat Pit in Chicago. They are made and they are broken, making and breaking, fattening and starving, thousands of better men as they rise and fall. The great river of wheat they fatten on streams steadily on, planted by man and ripened by nature for man's sustenance, unheeding and unchanged by the frantic mob about its banks, of men who seek to dam or hurry its volume to serve their own insignificant ambitions. The wheat supply is, as it were, a force of nature. Beside its clean might the wiles and plots of scheming men appear infinitely puny, infinitely sordid, a humiliating exhibition. In "The Octopus" Mr. Norris showed the grandeur of the wheat's growth and production, and in the light of that picture, the picture of man's first handling of it—the railway companies and transit agents—was grey, dingy, and saddening. The present book carries us further in the wheat's history, further from nature, and into the crowded heart of men's affairs. The picture becomes infinitely more dingy and saddening. Nature is far enough from the Chicago Pit. In his next book the author, had he lived, was to have carried us to the end of the wheat's journey, past the buyers of Europe to the mouths of the million-headed poor, whom the gentlemen of the Pit pinch or fatten at pleasure. That picture would probably have shown us hunger, and hunger is a terrible and an ugly power; but we think it would have been far less sordid, less mercenary, less mean, than this study of heartless speculation in the Pit. And that would be because, whilst the struggle for food is natural, primary, and wholesome, the fight for dollars, for unearned millions, among the gamblers of the Pit, is artificial, exotic, and unwholesome. The one is a bracing and productive pursuit, the other a nerve-shattering, death-dealing trade.

"The Pit" is a city story, and lacks the gloriously sunny open air of "The Octopus." It is not an epic, but it is a very powerful melodrama, and something of an object lesson for the many people of British origin whose eyes are turned towards the United States in admiring scrutiny of the commercial methods and gains of that country. If proof were needed, this book is in itself sufficing evidence of the fact that Frank Norris had more in him than literary promise. His literary methods were those of Zola, and the large conceptions which filled his mind and inspired his pen took no account of literary niceties. He had no time for the polishing of phrases; the question of style did not greatly trouble him. But he had a fine feeling for the bigness of things, for the grandeur of nature, and for the absorbing interest of life, bare life, with its millions of intersecting and conflicting currents. His death is a loss which we sincerely regret.

"The Pit."
The Spectator, 90 (February 14, 1903), 262–63.

The late Mr. Frank Norris, whose recent premature death removed one of the most impressive of the younger American novelists, conceived a plan which he unhappily did not live to complete. It was to write what he called a "Trilogy of the Epic of the Wheat." In the first novel, *The Octopus*, a story of California, he dealt with the war between the wheat-grower and the Railway Trust; *The Pit*, the novel before us, is a "fictitious narrative of a 'deal' in the Chicago wheat-pit"; while he intended the central motive of the third and concluding novel of the series, *The Wolf*, to be "the relieving of a famine in an Old World community." It remains to be added that the three novels, while forming a series, were "in no way connected with each other, save only in their relation to the production, the distribution, and the consumption of American wheat." The reader, therefore, who comes fresh to the second book labours under no serious drawback even if he has not read its predecessor; for not only is the scene shifted, but an entirely new set of characters is introduced. The organic unity of the whole scheme is thus combined with an independent treatment of its successive phases, and sufficient importance is attached to the subsidiary episodes, and to the character studies of personages not essential to the main current of the plot, to attract a reader who looks for a story without a moral behind it.

It is difficult, however, for any one who brings any intelligence to bear on the perusal of such a work as *The Pit* to escape the oppressive significance of Mr. Norris's picture of the conflict between the human and the inhuman elements in the America of to-day. The *dramatis personae* are dominated by the great forces at the back of them: by the teeming earth, the monstrous machinery of production and distribution, and (in the drama before us) by the colossal organisation of the great game of speculation. The absorption of the American business man in his occupation has often puzzled English observers. Mr. Norris enables us to understand it and realise the romance and fascination of a life in which there is no room for culture or leisure, and where men toil that their women-folk may have a good time. Seen through his eyes, Chicago loses the aspect of a chaotic wilderness of bricks and mortar, and is invested with a huge menacing and non-human personality in which the individual is dwarfed to nothingness. Take, for example, the passage giving impressions of the heroine shortly after her arrival in the Great Grey City:—

> But the life was tremendous. All around, on every side, in every direction the vast machinery

of Commonwealth clashed and thundered from dawn to dark and from dark till dawn. Even now, as the car carried her farther into the business quarter, she could hear it, see it, and feel in her every fibre the trepidation of its motion. The blackened waters of the river, seen an instant between stanchions as the car trundled across the State Street bridge, disappeared under fleets of tugs, of lake steamers, of lumber barges from Sheboygan and Mackinac, of grain boats from Duluth, of coal scows that filled the air with impalpable dust, of cumbersome schooners laden with produce, of grimy rowboats dodging the prows and paddles of the larger craft, while on all sides, blocking the horizon, red in colour and designated by Brobdingnag letters, towed the hump-shouldered grain elevators. Just before crossing the bridge on the north side of the river she had caught a glimpse of a great railway terminus. Down below there, rectilinear, scientifically paralleled and squared, the Yard disclosed itself. A system of grey rails beyond words complicated opened out and spread immeasurably. Switches, semaphores, and signal towers stood here and there. A dozen trains, freight and passenger, puffed and steamed, waiting the word to depart. Detached engines hurried in and out of sheds and roundhouses, seeking their trains, or bunted the ponderous freight cars into switches; trundling up and down, clanking, shrieking, their bells filling the air with the clangour of tocsins. Men in visored caps shouted hoarsely, waving their arms or red flags; drays, their big dappled horses feeding in their nose bags, stood backed up to the open doors of freight cars and received their loads. A train departed roaring. Before midnight it would be leagues away boring through the Great Northwest, carrying Trade—the life blood of nations—into communities of which Laura had never heard. Another train, reeking with fatigue, the air brakes screaming, arrived and halted, debouching a flood of passengers, business men, bringing Trade—a galvanising elixir—from the very ends and corners of the continent. Or, again, it was South Water Street—a jam of delivery wagons and market carts backed to the curbs, leaving only a tortuous path between the endless files of horses, suggestive of an actual barrack of cavalry. Provisions, market produce, "garden truck" and fruits, in an infinite welter of crates and baskets, boxes and sacks, crowded the sidewalks. The gutter was choked with an overflow of refuse cabbage leaves, soft oranges, decaying beet tops. The air was thick with the heavy smell of vegetation. Food was trodden under foot, food crammed the stores and warehouses to bursting. Food mingled with the mud of the highway. The very dray horses were gorged with an unending nourishment of snatched mouthfuls picked from backboard, from barrel top, and from the edge of the sidewalk. The entire locality reeked with the fatness of a hundred thousand furrows. A land of plenty, the inordinate abundance of the earth itself emptied itself upon the asphalt and cobbles of the quarter. It was the Mouth of the City, and drawn from all directions, over a territory of immense area, this glut of crude subsistence was sucked in, as if into a rapacious gullet, to feed the sinews and to nourish the fibres of an immeasurable colossus. Suddenly the meaning and significance of it all dawned upon Laura. The Great Grey City, brooking no rival, imposed its dominion upon a reach of country larger than many a kingdom of the Old World. For thousands of miles beyond its confines was its influence felt. Out, far out, far away in the snow and shadow of Northern Wisconsin forests, axes and saws bit the bark of century-old trees, stimulated by this city's energy. Just as far to the southward pick and drill leaped to the assault of veins of anthracite, moved by her central power. Her force turned the wheels of harvester and seeder a thousand miles distant in Iowa and Kansas. Her force spun the screws and propellers of innumerable squadrons of lake steamers crowding the Sault Sainte Marie. For her and because of her all the Central States, all the Great Northwest roared with traffic and industry; sawmills screamed; factories, their smoke blackening the sky, clashed and flamed; wheels turned, pistons leaped in their cylinders; cog gripped cog; belting clasped the drums of mammoth wheels; and converters of forges belched into the clouded air their tempest breath of molten steel. It was Empire, the resistless subjugation of all this central world of the lakes and the prairies. Here, midmost in the land, beat the Heart of the Nation, whence inevitably must come its immeasurable power, its infinite, infinite, inexhaustible vitality. Here, of all her cities, throbbed the true life—the true power and spirit of America; gigantic, crude with the crudity of youth, disdaining rivalry, arrogant in the new-found knowledge of its giant strength, prodigal of its wealth, infinite in its desires. In its capacity boundless, in its courage indomitable; subduing the wilderness in a single generation, defying calamity, and through the flame and the debris of a commonwealth in ashes, rising suddenly renewed, formidable, and Titanic. Laura, her eyes dizzied, her ears stunned, watched tirelessly. "There is something terrible about it," she murmured, half to herself, "something insensate. In a way, it doesn't seem human. It's like a great tidal wave. It's all very well for the individual just so long as he can keep afloat, but once fallen, how horribly quick it would crush him, annihilate him, how horribly quick, and with such horrible indifference! I suppose it's civilization in the making, the thing that isn't meant to be seen, as though it were too elemental, too—primordial; like the first verses of Genesis."

Laura Dearborn, who is a New Englander of a complex temperament, with artistic and histrionic aspirations, finds herself very soon confronted with the necessity of choosing between her three suitors,—Corthell, an artist;

Landry Court, a strange blend of the schoolboy and the keen man of business; and Curtis Jadwin, a self-reliant millionaire who has risen from obscure beginnings to a commanding position in Chicago. In the contest between the claims of culture, of boyish charm, and of strength of will the last-named naturally carries the day. Laura refuses all three, only to find that Jadwin will take no denial; and at last, yielding to his persistent importunity, she marries him first and falls in love with him afterwards. Now Jadwin's wealth is grounded on the solid basis of real estate, but he is at times a speculator on a large scale, and soon after his marriage the condition of the wheat market tempts him to gratify his gambling instinct more fully than ever before. The deeper he gets into the toils the more he neglects his wife, who wields all the spells of her womanhood in vain to recapture him, and at last, hungering for sympathy and humiliated by her ill-success, is on the point of eloping with the artist, when her husband's financial failure gives him back to her. There has never been any other woman for him: the Wheat Pit was the *belle dame sans merci*, and with the collapse of his schemes he comes to his right mind again. This is in very brief outline the plot of a really striking novel, written with a nervous energy attuned to its theme, but curiously devoid of charm or distinction of style. It derives value, however, apart from the grandiose conception of a soul-devouring and domesticity-destroying mammon-worship, from its being an essentially American product—in regard to structure, we admit, Zola's influence is obviously paramount—and from the light that it throws on the feverish concentration of the American temperament.

"The Romance of Commerce." *Academy and Literature*, 64 (February 14, 1903), 153–54.

Mr. Frank Norris had planned out a big scheme, and died after accomplishing but two-thirds of it. His idea was to write the epic of wheat, to trace its growing in the American West, its manipulation in Chicago, and its distribution in Europe. For he saw that commerce has its romance no less than warfare, and that the financial fighter is the modern equivalent to the knight in armour. Moreover, if man does not live by bread alone, bread is necessary, and its passage from the soil to the eater crosses innumerable interests. "The Octopus" was the first of the series, and dealt with the struggle between the farmer and the Railway Trust. This, "The Pit," is the second. On its way from grower to consumer the wheat has to pass through the Chicago Wheat Pit, where speculators gamble on the future price. Small material for romance, you may think, in the turn of the hand on the dial at the Chicago Board of Trade. But Laura, sitting in the Opera House, and listening to occasional scraps of talk over the Helmick failure, caught the romance underlying the market reports—

and abruptly, midway between two phases of that music drama, of passion and romance, there came to Laura the swift and vivid impression of that other drama that simultaneously—even at that very moment—was working itself out close at hand, equally picturesque, equally romantic, equally passionate; but more than that, real, actual, modern, a thing in the very heart of the life in which she moved. And here he sat, this Jadwin, quiet, in evening dress, listening good-naturedly to this beautiful music, for which he did not care, to this rant and fustian, watching quietly all this posing and attitudinising. How small and petty it must all seem to him!

And how American is the attitude of the girl, of Jadwin, of the writer! For it takes an American to see the romance that underlies the business operation. Laura had three lovers, an artist, a broker's clerk, and Jadwin—a capitalist. She chose Jadwin. And it was Jadwin who was caught in the swirl of the gamble on futures; Jadwin, who beat time with a hymn book to the singing of his Sunday school. For the story is of an attempted corner in wheat. In the Wheat Pit—and Mr. Norris draws a really wonderful picture of a morning on that central floor of the cereal world—they do not see the wheat, they would not know what to do with it if they had to store the wheat they buy. But they bet what wheat will cost a week or a month hence. And Jadwin saw his way to buying up all the visible supply. It was not the want of money, for he had enough; it was the gambler's passion; and Jadwin for a short spell had the world's loaves in his hands. Now there is a situation for a novelist. Jadwin, for a moment, is a Napoleon, an Alexander, a Providence with the instincts of a devil. But Cressler, the dealer, was right when he maintained that wheat cannot be cornered by any means:—

First, for the reason that there is a great harvest of wheat somewhere in the world for every month in the year; and second, because the smart man who runs the corner has every other smart man in the world against him. And, besides, it's wrong; the world's food should not be at the mercy of the Chicago wheat pit.

It's wrong, and it's impossible. Mr. Norris brings these two points home in the manipulation of his story. The impossibility and the wrongness both rest on the limitations of the individual. No man can keep an eye on every grain of corn that comes into the market. And the man who tries to corner the world's supply of wheat is in danger of sacrificing what is more valuable to himself. What shall a man profit if he gain the whole world's wheat supply and lose his own Laura?

We have read this story with great interest, for it is one of the few that hit the balance of a man's life, which wavers ever between the world of action and the world of sentiment. We have read it, too, with a keen sense of regret that Mr. Norris did not live to complete his scheme. He was one of the very few novelists who have seen the romance underlying the market reports.

"The Pit."
Times Literary Supplement (London), February 20, 1903, p. 56.

The publication of a posthumous work by Frank Norris is likely, we think, to raise once more the question as to the responsibility of literary executors. In certain cases it hardly matters if they search a dead author's waste-paper basket for work that the author himself wished to destroy. We should not be less indebted to Charles Dickens than we are at present if the rake of the literary ragman gathered up more of his poorest journalism and gave it to the world as further "Sketches by Boz." But what will not harm a giant may be fatal to a smaller being; and the publication of *The Pit* (Grant Richards, 6s.) by the author of "The Octopus" is obviously a mistake from every literary point of view. For the merest tiro in criticism cannot read the first paragraph of the book without perceiving that a rough draft has been put upon the public for a finished work. It would have been kinder to suppress the book altogether, or to give the world only those portions of the story on which the writer had worked with a certain care. And in saying so much, a much greater blot than mere lack of revision is indicated. The epic of the Chicago wheat-pit has no artistic relationship to the remainder of the book, for the women of the story are without life, and parasitic to the theme, which is that of a wheat-corner engineered by the chief male character. Mr. Norris himself seems to have been conscious that there were big books to be written in which the love of women could rightly play no part. Deep in his mind he must have seen that his conception of the Chicago wheat maelstrom, which is certainly not without its grandiose elements, was such a story. But he yielded against his own convictions, and by introducing extraneous women, who are no more than puppets, he destroyed his own effect. That such a woman as Laura Dearborn ever existed is the merest dream of a man who has no conception of more than one woman in the world. That one woman he drew in "Blix." Much of the rest is frankly Zola, though less obviously so than in his previous and better book, "The Octopus." But in that he drew California, with which he had more than a tourist's acquaintance. The heart of Chicago he never touched, and he makes it a mere giant of pasteboard. He worshipped power with the passion of a woman, but never succeeded in drawing it. Yet even in "The Pit" there are indications that he might in the end have attained to strength rather than violence.

"Literature."
Illustrated London News, 122 (February 21, 1903), 282.

"The Pit," the story of a gigantic "deal" and an equally gigantic failure in the Board of Trade Building in Chicago, will not enhance the reputation won for the late Frank Norris by "Shanghaied," "McTeague," and "The Octopus," the first of the projected Trilogy of the Epic of the Wheat, of which the present volume is the second. When writing of the actual operations in the wheat-pit, Mr. Norris not only shows very considerable power of description, but undoubtedly holds the attention; in the remainder of his story, however, the crudity of his staccato method—effective, perhaps essential, in the fiction of statistics of which "Calument K." is so excellent an example—because at once apparent, and occasionally strikes a jarring note. Mr. Norris would have done well, indeed, had he confined his narrative to the commercial side of Mr. Jadwin's character; had he, in a word, made his novel entirely a story of the Pit, for the wheat-gamble dominates his book as it dominates the personages in it. Beside it, the question of Jadwin's love for, and subsequent neglect of, his wife, and the love affairs of Sheldon Corthell, Landry Court, and Page Dearborn are episodes that, all-important as they are to those concerned, are of comparatively little moment in the estimation of the reader. The Pit, and the Pit alone, is the subject that fascinates; it is the triumph of eighths and quarters over sentiment. Mr. Norris had a great ambition, but an ambition, unhappily, only partially revised.

Thomas R. Bacon. "The Last Book of Frank Norris." *Impressions Quarterly*, 4 (March 1903), 12–14.

It is impossible for any one, especially for a Californian, and more especially for one who had known Frank Norris, and had carefully and somewhat anxiously watched his career in the field of letters, to speak of his last book in a thoroughly scientific spirit of criticism. There was so much in him, not only of promise but of accomplishment, that we are appalled by his inability to go on. Yet this terrible fact is only an illustration of the doctrine which he always preached, in his early romantic story as in his most realistic novel, that the world is stronger than the individual, that though at times "men are masters of their fate," the great courses of the universe go on, resistless, inevitable. He knew two things: first, that the individual has self-sovereignty; second, that the universe is run by law, a law which is absolutely certain, and which takes up into itself, and uses for its own ends the aberrations of the human will. Whether he ever tried to solve the paradox involved in this antinomy, there is no evidence in his books. He seems to have accepted the facts in the case, and not to have troubled his soul about the problem of the ages,

Of providence, foreknowledge, will and fate,
Fixed fate, free will, foreknowledge absolute.

His own end illustrates. As Jadwin in the exercise of his will persisted in holding his corner until the irresistible rush of the wheat swept him away, fate and free-will working together, so Norris exercised his free-will in not heeding the physician's advice, and the forces of nature took him off. The form of nature's operation might have been an earthquake or a tornado or the cataract of the wheat; it happened to be appendicitis.

Norris started out in life with the avowed purpose of being a writer of fiction. He believed that he had it in him, and he turned all his energies to proving that he had. He went to college because he thought that he could get something there that would help him. He traveled, he studied, he read, he observed, with just this one aim in view. He did with his might the thing which his hand found to do. He was getting very near to the highest success, when the end came.

He was very conscientious in his work. He tried to investigate all the details of any matter of which he spoke. In this respect he was almost as careful as Balzac; yet his earlier work was full of blunders in just this regard. If he wanted to write of a ship, he studied a ship, and seems to have got a good understanding of the construction and working of a ship. If he wanted to write of a steam harvester, he carefully examined the machine in all its parts and operations. If he wanted to tell of the Chicago wheat pit, he looked at it with steady, discerning gaze until the thing became clear to him. But he could not thus examine all things, and to the very last he made queer mistakes about things which he had not yet observed. These mistakes grow fewer and fewer as he goes on. The only one I have noticed in his last book is his singular description of the early life of Laura Dearborn in Massachusetts. There are only a few lines; but more mistakes and misconceptions could hardly be crowded into so few lines. He knew nothing about New England; possibly he never could have known anything about it, though he had dwelt there many years. And the New England to which he tried to refer could never have known him.

He took Zola for his master. The positive character of that singular genius found an echo in his own way of looking at things. Like most enthusiastic disciples, he began by copying the faults as well as the strength of the master, but this last book shows that he had enough power of self-culture to outgrow the incidental faults while preserving the essential merits of Zolaism. While retaining the method, he has avoided the dirt which deforms Zola's most masterly work, and has thus demonstrated that the dirt is not an essential part of the method.

The Pit seems to me to show in many respects an advance in power and artistic sense upon *The Octopus*. It is more real, in the sense that it deals more with what is than with what might be. It is less extravagant, and, in the popular sense, less romantic. There are no such wild adventures, as indeed there hardly could be on such a different stage. The people are more real. It will probably be the judgment of most critics that the heroine is uninteresting, but that does not make her the less real. Most real persons are uninteresting. That may be a good reason for not putting them into novels, but it does not make them the less real. Some of the other persons are just as real and at the same time interesting. Jadwin is a very thoughtful and accurate picture of a good and able man, carried away by the passion for gambling on a large scale. The study of his mental, moral and physical deterioration under the influence of this passion is very well done. It is pitiful enough and real enough. But it is in the lesser persons that Norris has given us the last evidence of his skill in the portrayal of character. Page Dearborn is one of the sweetest, most natural and most vivid of girls to be found in fiction. Some of the young men in the book are live and real, and their defects are the defects of their qualities. I do not think that much can be said about Laura's persistent lover. He is simply a fool and a fake. I have a notion that Norris knew this and meant it.

But in these novels the portrayal of character and personal experiences are only incidents. The story may be tragic or comic, the individuals concerned may be good or bad, they may be happy or sorrowful,—whatever happens to them, our ears are always hearing the thunderous undertone of the moving wheat. The original conception of the trilogy indicates genius of a very high order. That Norris was able to express that conception in words, even partially and imperfectly, makes us think of what might have been,—could he have lived. But he could not.

His purpose was to follow the true romance of the wheat from its sowing in American soil, through the complications of transportation and manipulation, until the peasants and artisans of Europe consumed it, or failed to consume it and died. The first book told of the growing of the wheat in the San Joaquin Valley in California, and the tyranny exercised over the growers by the Southern Pacific Company, a tyranny which in these few years has largely passed away by the operation of natural law. But Norris was too intelligent a man to suppose that this tyranny was due to any peculiar malevolence on the part of the managers of that peculiar monopoly. He saw clearly that the conditions were not due to any wickedness or misanthropy on the part of individuals, but to the working of economic law, which is just as inevitable as the working of any other natural law. The interview between the half-crazy Presley and the president of the railway (whom he chose to call Shelgrim, but whom he might just as well have called by his own name) shows that in his indignation against the suffering which was caused by the monopoly, he never lost sight of the fact that the great men who were running the great business were really trying to do the best they could. That they had many unworthy agents, who used the power of their monopolistic position for their own selfish ends, is beyond question. The "S. Behrmans" are very familiar figures in California. We all know them. But he saw that economic law, like all other natural law, brings round its revenges. Many of the monopolists are good men and have consciences, though it is a little hard for ordinary people to understand how their consciences work.

The second book deals with the wheat as it passes through *The Pit*, where it is subject to the manipulations of the brokers. With sound judgment Norris chose an actual incident, which excited the interest of the world a few years ago. The personality is different; the antecedents and outcome are different, but the fact is actual. And a very appalling fact it is. That a private citizen of Chicago can by a word so raise the price of wheat in Italy that the people break out in riots over the cost of a loaf of bread is one of the most impressive facts in modern life. This is just what happened in reality as in the novel. A very romantic fact it is and Norris has used it with discretion as the foundation of his novel. But what does it all mean? The moral is that if a man "monkeys" too much with such a force as the wheat he is sure to get the worst of it. But this is only a touch on the surface of the problem.

That the operation of a natural law can be modified by an individual will, that the selfish whim of a man in Chicago can starve people in Europe is in itself a consideration so awful that it sets us at once face to face with the question of human life and human duty, and the use of mankind. What are we here for? Has man a mission upon this queer planet where he finds himself? If Norris had nothing else to do in this world, he did this one thing. He brings us to the solemn definition of the elements of simple morality.

Apparently man has a place and purpose here. The outcome of the study of history is that man is here to temper the operation of natural law, or mere force, by considerations of justice and mercy. That he can do so is so strange that it can fairly be called miraculous,—the standing miracle. That man can use the destructive lightning for beneficent ends, that he can use the explosive power of steam to make people live and prosper and be happy teaches us that man is of some use. He turns merciless powers to a merciful end, and thereby justifies his being.

The greatest invention of the nineteenth century was not the steamship nor the locomotive nor the telegraph nor the telephone, nor any one of the thousand uses to which steam and electricity have been applied. Neither was it the modern war-ship nor smokeless powder nor Bessemer steel, nor the sewing machine. It was the purely legal invention of the corporation of limited liability. This invention has made possible the wide utilization of the others. It is, on the whole, the most beneficent of inventions. It has brought life and living to millions who otherwise would have starved or would never have been at all. But through the inexperience of man the beneficence of the invention has been partly offset by incidental evils, so that many men have come to feel that corporations are, in themselves, evil. The tremendous power which our present corporation law allows a few individuals to accumulate in their hands is felt, and rightly felt, to be a menace to the public welfare. It makes the will of such individuals more potent in modifying the results of the action of natural law. Love of wealth, of power, of fame, of adventure, sways such men away from their best instincts. Instead of using their immense influence to mitigate the action of natural law by consideration of justice and mercy they seem to add emphasis to its cruelty. More than ever, it seems to some, "To him that hath is given, and from him that hath not is taken away even that which he hath."

I have taken this illustration because it is the basis of *The Octopus*. In *The Pit* we have other conditions of modern life that exemplify the same thing: the apparent influence of a single human will upon the fixed course of events, its control over the order of things. Of course, in a prolonged wrestle between a man and the universe, the universe will get the upper hand, but it seems sometimes as if it had to make a mighty effort, and the nature of things seems disturbed.

Norris had too much the instinct of the artist to attempt to solve or even discuss philosophical problems through the medium of fiction, but he states the factors of such problems with great distinctness as he tells his stories. The facts of modern life stare us in the face from his pages and set us thinking. That we shall have no more of this kind of "realism" from his hand is matter for keen regret.

The improvement in the last book over the other extends to the style. There were certain tricks and mannerisms in *The Octopus* which were annoying. I have a feeling (I may be quite wrong) that Norris had been reading the translation of Sienkiewicz's novels and had been infected by Mr. Curtin's attempts to reproduce Polish idiom in English. However this may be, such objectionable things are conspicuous by their absence from *The Pit*. On the contrary, the style is uncommonly clear and simple. Things are said in such a way that it is impossible not to understand the meaning, and the language has the beauty of sincerity.

The reading of *The Pit* adds the sharpest pang to the disappointment of his taking off. He did not bury his talent in the ground or hide it in a napkin. He employed it, and increased it tenfold. He faithfully did with it the best he knew how, and his best was very good.

Hamlin Garland. "The Work of Frank Norris."
The Critic, 42 (March 1903), 216–18.

The three books on which the fame of Frank Norris already rests are these—"McTeague," "The Octopus," and "The Pit." "McTeague," as its name implies, is an exhaustive study of two or three persons—one of which is a profound characterization. "The Octopus" is a presentation of sociologic conditions in California, and "The Pit" is a social and sociologic study of Chicago.

I began my acquaintance with Norris over the pages of "McTeague." The amazing particularity and unfailing interest of this grim story led me to a belief that its author could do anything—even write a "Trilogy of Wheat." Once a very wise and gentle man listened to a plan which involved several volumes—and at the end said quietly—very quietly: "Admirable—only be sure you don't lost interest in your plan." I thought of this when Norris outlined his scheme for the trilogy. It is to be forever incomplete, not because the author lost interest in its final volume, but because he is dead, and his master, Zola, is dead, and "The Wolf" remains only a title in Norris's last preface.

In the place of this third volume we may set "McTeague"—or rather it should come first, and "The Octopus" and "The Pit" be moved up the line—for there is no need of apology in dealing with "McTeague." In it is some of the best work Norris ever did, and as a whole it stands as a sort of preparation work—a superb thesis on the individual, leading to a consideration of the sociologic—the epic.

It is the study of a poor, badly equipped young man who painfully gains a certain place in society and struggling blindly and brutishly, fails to maintain it,—a lonely, harmless creature, dull, gross, and good-tempered, to whom law is a menace and poverty a never-absent, hellward-sloping gulf just at his feet. He has few helpers and no brethren, but has many enemies. He is at once tragic and comic. His history is of a kind with Daudet's "Jack" and Flaubert's "Madame Bovary." It is inexorable in its unrelenting lifelikeness. It is one of the most masterly studies in our literature, but the reader is forced at the end to ask "Of what avail this study of sad lives?" for it does not even lead to a notion of social betterment. It is gray, gray and cold, in tone. It ends in a desert, with two of its chief characters locked in death-grapple.

Norris's interest was not that of the ethical teacher, the reformer who turns on the light. He rejoiced in McTeague and Trina as terms in a literary theorem. Their sufferings lead to no conclusions. They are in the book because they appealed to his dramatic sense, his love for character. This book is without direct prototype. You may say it reminds you of Flaubert in treatment, or of Zola in theme, but in reality it is without fellow. Its originality is unquestionable. There are flaws in it, but they do not seriously detract from its essential greatness. It is vital and compelling on every page.

In "The Octopus" the intention is frankly sociologic. A map prefaces the story, a cast of characters is thrown upon a screen. The author is in the country and concerned with wide horizons rippling with vast wheatfields; he is dealing not with a few persons huddled into a flat, but with proud landowners in combination against a giant corporation. McTeague was a blind fighter, but the farmers in "The Octopus" are immense land lords, oppressors in their own right, banding together for purely mercenary reasons; had they all been really fighting for life, as was the poor engineer turned tiller of the soil, the book would have been heart-wringing. In every chapter *wheat* is taken for the motive, the ever-recurring refrain. The impersonal is uppermost; individuals are subordinated, inexorably crushed, or senselessly exalted as in life by blind forces.

At times the attempt to apply the methods of Zola is too apparent. We weary of adjectives which seem to have been taken directly from "La Terre." The motive is too insistent, the impersonal ceases at times to interest. The use of the refrain is Wagnerian, but it loses in effect at times. Perhaps it is not a trick, but it certainly is an artifice and legitimate enough. Reference to Trina and McTeague was often made in words to the same effect—in "The Octopus" the dead bride of Vanamee, Hilma Tree, Annixter, Behrman are announced by almost exactly the same phrases— wonderfully good phrases too— precisely as Wotan and Siegfried are announced by the same trumpet flares, varied to the flow of the orchestral score. This gives unity to the structure of the novel and produces a most vivid and powerful impression on the mind of the reader, but it also adds formality and fixedness— restricting free development. In the case of Magnus Derrick the artifice proved not merely ineffectual but practically impossible, for his was a dynamic characterization. He grew. Even Annixter (one of the most individual of all Norris's characters) breaks away from his old self. The phrase departs so widely from the original that it ceases to be recognized.

I do not know that I object to this repetition, but I do consider the constant use of adjectives in the style of Hugo and Zola a disfigurement. Their use was a survival of his boyish idolatry of the two men who labored to make the French language something more than the mincing periphrasis of court intriguers. "McTeague" may be said to partake of the method of Balzac. "The Octopus" certainly was founded upon "Germinal" and "La Terre." But there his indebtedness ceased—for McTeague, and Annixter and Trina and Derrick—for the throngs of marvellously realized characters in each of these books we are indebted to the keen eyes, the abounding insight, and the swift imagination of a born novelist. Norris studied life, or rather he absorbed it, without effort and without conscious design. "McTeague" is a mine of inexhaustible riches of observation. A second or third reading gives increasing wonder as to how the boy acquired so much knowledge and so much discernment.

It is not necessary to apologize at any point for Norris. It is not necessary in criticising some mistakes of judgment in "The Octopus" to say "He will become a great novelist." He was a great novelist. "The Octopus" is a bitter and sweeping arraignment of impersonal conditions—a sort of inexorable clash of forces, and while it rose higher on some sides than "McTeague," it fell below it on others—but it showed Norris's power in another way. It demonstrated his ability to transfer his scene as well as his characters. He was not bound to the slums of San Francisco. As he knew Polk Street, so he seems to present the San Joaquin Valley and its life, and this knowledge stood him in full hand. His first novel was worthy of his great plan. It is fairly tremendous.

He now permitted himself a greater display of power. He laid the scene of the second number of his Epic of the Wheat in Chicago. But here again he knew his ground. His boyhood had been spent in the great city of the Wheat Pit. He knew certain phases of it as the keen-eyed youth saw it, and he studied it later with definite purpose, with the eyes of the novelist, in preparation for his last book "The Pit." I saw a great deal of Norris during the time when this story was forming in his brain, and I confess I was more uneasy than he. He smoked his pipe and made merry and discussed everything else under the sun—and appeared quite at ease. He said he knew that it was, in a way, the most important test of his powers, and yet he seemed not to be taking pains. He appeared almost too confident of his powers.

But "The Pit" is a worthy successor to "The Octopus." It is sunnier and more hopeful than "McTeague," and less cumbrous and set of form and phrase than "The Octopus." It is, in fact, a superb study of Chicago on certain well-defined sides. *The wheat* is there, of course, by design, and is to my mind too much insisted upon, but the impersonal does not submerge and dissolve the characterization. It is there as a sound, a wind in the trees, a reminder, but the characters move to and fro, acting and reacting on each other, quite freely, quite naturally. The great speculator, Jadwin, is a most admirably drawn type of Western business man—worthy to be put beside "Silas Lapham." Laura Dearborn, if she has not the subtlety of emotional experience of Mr. Howells's Marcia Gaylord, is quite as vital. She does not convince at all points, but as a whole she is Norris's most important study of a woman.

"The Pit" does not pretend to be a society story of Chicago,—and it is unduly bleak on that side,—but as a presentation of the strong forces finding expression in its business centres it is thus far unrivalled. Henry Fuller's "Cliff Dwellers" is its worthiest companion-piece. The projected final volume, "The Wolf," would have been a more difficult problem than either of those preceding it, for it not merely prospectively dealt with foreign material, but it involved a succession of incidents rather than a dramatic clashing of interests. Norris would have written it had he lived, but its working-out offered peculiar dangers, it seems to me.

Thus far the reader will get only the grim side of Norris, but in "Blix," fortunately, is the author as his intimate friends knew him, boyish, fun-loving. He was the best company in the world. His eyes glowed with humor. His face shone with roguery and good cheer. His antic manner was never coarse, and his jocular phrases were framed in unexpected ways. He was always and constantly interesting, and to be in his company was to find the world better worth while.

Youth makes a savage realist, for youth has boundless hope and exultation in itself. When a man begins to doubt his ability to reform, to change by challenge, he softens, he allows himself to pity. Norris in "The Pit" is more genial, that is to say, more mature, than in "McTeague" and "The Octopus." He was thirty-two and successful. He was entering on a less inexorable period. He was not written out, as perhaps Stephen Crane was; on the contrary, his mind was glowing with imagery. His ideals were fine, his life without strain, and his small shelf of books will stand high in the library of American fiction.

"The Pit."
Current Literature, 34 (March 1903), 371.

The last book by the late Frank Norris and the second of his uncompleted trilogy, The Epic of the Wheat, is a vigorous, strong story, told with directness and power and conveying a lesson steeped in truth. The characters are drawn finely and firmly and with rare insight. The work but accentuates how great has been the loss of Mr. Norris to American literature.

"The Pit."
The Literary World, 34 (March 1903), 54.

From the dainty *Moran of the Lady Letty*, through the brutal *McTeague*, the breezy *Blix*, and the over-realistic *A Man's Woman*, up to the ten-league canvas of the *Epic of the Wheat*, of which *The Octopus* was the first panel and *The Pit* the second, with yet a third panel to be filled—this was the work of Frank Norris when Death summoned him. Any review of *The Pit* cannot but be tinged with a *de mortuis* color, and yet that is unfair to both the author and his public.

The Pit, as all know, is a continuation of the *Epic of the Wheat*. The *Octopus* showed the wheat in its stages of growth and transportation, and the effect of those stages on the lives of many. *The Pit* brings the wheat into the world of trade, and shows its commercial potentialities acting on the lives of many others—a totally different set of people, and yet the same wheat. The *locale* of the people of *The Pit* is narrower than that of its predecessor—the place Chicago and the Board of Trade—the folk, with a few exceptions, either wheat manipulators or their kindred. The book is a-tingle with the spirit of speculation—the keynote struck in the very first chapter goes vibrating through the story, at first with a low yet persistent hum, very like the fragments of trade chatter that reached the ears of Laura Dearborn through the music of the opera, then deadened by the love motives that follow, then breaking through the *viols d'amour*, at first feebly, then more boldly, then loud, then louder, then crashing out in full force, and sweeping away every other sound.

And what of the people who dance to the tune of the Wheat? They are many and diverse, yet individual. First comes Curtis Jadwin, the solid level-headed man of affairs, led into the pit half against his will, fascinated by and finally, seeking to be its master crushed and enslaved in it. His speech in the early part of the book against the futility of the idea of a wheat corner, compared with his frenzied utterances near the close: "Nothing in the world can stop me now ... I've got it all figured out, your 'new crop' ... we'll fight against the earth itself"—these two scenes alone show the development of the force of the pit. Other types of this are Cressler, the reformed plunger, who takes one more flutter in Wheat to his ruin and death; old Hargus, the decayed speculator, one of the most telling characters in the book, whom Wheat has long ago crushed and crazed; Gretry, the conservative broker, who warns Jadwin in vain; and young Landry Court, the boyish clerk, who fights for his firm in the wheat pit—all these are vivid pictures. Then outside the whirl of the "strenuous life" of trade calmly stands the debonair dilettante figure of Corthell, the artist, ultra-refined, sensitive and sensuous, whose love for Laura Jadwin is the submotif of the book. Add a few sketches of wheat traders, bulls, bears, lambs, and one has a bird's-eye view of the men of the story, in the drawing of which it is hard to find a fault.

The women are less happily drawn. Laura Dearborn, afterwards Mrs. Jadwin, is a complex figure whose complexity tangled up her creator. She is unplaceable and uncertain, and very inconsistent. By all that her character makes her out, she should have eloped with Corthell at the finish, instead of sharing a life of rehabilitation with the ruined Jadwin. But the dear Public, whose prophet is the *Saturday Evening Post*, would not have it so; and the result is that to the thinking reader Laura stands at the end with "Quitter" writ large and bold over her. Page, the serious-eyed sister, is merely "Blix" looking at life through a new pair of spectacles, and "Aunt Wess" is the usual type of the novelistic and dramatic "first old woman."

As a book *The Pit* is interesting; as a companion piece to *The Octopus* it is a bit disappointing. There is not enough of bigness, there is nothing in it that equals the scene of the Gerards' dinner and the death of the German woman, or the scene of S. Behrman's end, crushed by the wheat he had accumulated, or the closing paragraph of *The Octopus*. Yet despite this, it is a tale one will pick up and read to the end, with but one sense of lagging interest—in the middle of the first half of the story. After that there will be "nothing else doing," the swirl and rush of the pit will hold him in its grasp, as it did all who came within its ravenous reach.

"A Striking Novel."
Review of Reviews (England), 27 (March 1903), 304.

"The Pit" is a story of tremendous power and energy. It is the second of a trilogy of novels planned by Mr. Frank Norris, which, when completed, was to constitute an Epic of the Wheat, describing the production, the distribution and the consumption of the great nourisher of nations. "The Octopus" was a realistic, powerful, and even awful picture of the deadly warfare waged in the Far West of America between the grower of the wheat and the Railway Trust. "The Pit" possesses all the qualities of the first novel, but in it Mr. Norris handles his materials with greater skill. He has not gained complete mastery of the lighter sides of his theme, the opening chapters are somewhat crude, but when he approaches his central subject his grasp is undeniable. In "The Pit" the great flood of wheat has swept westward on its way to the crowded and hungry cities of Europe. It rushes and roars and swirls through the provision pits in the Chicago Board of Trade. It is here, where the rush of millions of bushels of grain and the clatter of millions of dollars and the tramping and wild shouting of thousands of men fill the air with the noise of battle, that the drama is played out. Curtis Jadwin, a wealthy Chicago business man, succumbs to the fatal fascination of speculating in wheat. He is thrilled with the sense of mastery and of power. He buys a million, five million, forty million bushels of wheat, then he corners the whole available supply; he dictates the price of wheat to the world; the farmers of the West grow rich; the poor of Europe starve at the lifting of his finger. Never for a moment does Mr. Norris lose sight of the human element that underlies the great commercial transaction. He describes powerfully, vividly the moral deterioration of the man, the terrible strain on nerve and brain, the gradual absorption of every thought, every feeling in the gigantic struggle to keep up the price of wheat, to outwit rivals, and to crush enemies. At last the inevitable crash comes, when the wheat breaks from his control, and, rising like a colossal billow, overwhelms him and races past him, on and on, to the eastward and to the hungry nations. It is a fearful and a thrilling climax, and in telling it Mr. Norris is at his best. His description of Laura, Jadwin's wife, is a fine piece of character drawing, showing keen insight and observation. In its way it is as remarkable as the picture of the great speculator himself. In the early death of Mr. Norris—he was only thirty-two—we have lost a writer of remarkable power and insight, and who seemed destined to exercise a powerful influence on American literature.

"Notable Books of the Day: The Epic of the Wheat."
Literary Digest, 26 (March 7, 1903), 353.

It is difficult to regard this work except through a sort of hallowing mist that the author's untimely death has cast about it. Yet the work is in no need of any extraneous influence to make a lasting impression. The conception is a strong one and the workmanship is stamped with sincerity on every page. Mr. Norris shows the influence of Zola and Howells, and his methods are those of the realists; but he has not felt compelled to limit himself to petty events and drearisome, commonplace characters. He was not afraid of strong dramatic situations, and in "The Pit," as well as in "The Octopus," there are scenes that remind one of Victor Hugo in his great passages.

As in "The Octopus," the Wheat itself is the *deus ex machina*. It was the Wheat that conquered the railway, "the octopus," and finally wreaked vengeance upon S. Behrman; and it is the Wheat that breaks down Jadwin in the flush of his vast success in the Chicago wheat-pit. What human power had failed to do, this mighty tide flowing from the farms of the West accomplished, and one sees in this tide a force like that of gravitation itself, and as ineluctable as fate. As one feels in the old Greek tragedies the implacable power of the gods back of human passions and making mock of human efforts, so one feels in this work the vast resources of nature as typified in the Wheat, back of the machinations of man and ready when the fulness of time has come to brush aside all such petty things as railroad corporations and millionaire speculators. It is a true epic.

The first half of the story moves slowly, and to most novel-readers will prove disappointing. Laura Dearborn and her three lovers are the principal characters here, and their relations to one another are interesting, but not absorbingly so. The best parts of this section of the story are in the nature of incidents, such as Laura's first night at the opera and the rehearsal for private theatricals at the Cresslers, and the conversation between Laura's sister Page, just budding into womanhood, and her first lover, Landry Court. But the real power of the author is developed after the marriage of Laura and Jadwin, when "The Pit" begins to drag him into its maelstrom of speculation, when he begins to neglect her, and she, piqued and outraged, almost throws herself into irretrievable ruin with an old lover, halting, however, on the very brink. Jadwin's stupendous operations on the 'change, the fights between the bulls and bears, are a sort of modernized "Iliad," and like the ancient tale, thrill with personal encounters, until Jadwin, overturning all opposition, is himself overwhelmed by a power more than human. Crushed, but not destroyed, he returns to sanity, to health, and to domestic joy, and the end is a happy, tho pathetic, one. It is one of the strongest works of fiction produced in America in recent years.

Mary L. Patteson.
"From Readers: 'The Pit.'"
New York Times,
March 7, 1903,
p. 158, "Saturday Review of Books and Art."*

The criticism of Frank Norris and his posthumous novel, "The Pit," which appeared in a recent number of *The Saturday Review of Books*, though dispassionate, I hardly consider clear-sighted or correct. I am glad that the reviewer left himself the loophole of escape from his rather sweeping statements in admitting that opinions will differ rather widely as to the extent of Mr. Norris's achievements. Considering the criticism that Mr. Norris was in a "hurry to do great things, and did not take the time he should to acquire technical skill," in the light of the recent sad event, we should be glad he was in a "hurry"; that before his untimely end he was able to give "The Octopus" and "The Pit" to American literature.

Undoubtedly "The Pit" is not equal to "The Octopus," but if Mr. Norris had written nothing but the later book, he still deserves to be ranked as a "reformer" among modern writers, as he has demonstrated the possibility of making a successful novel out of the great questions which are confronting us at the present time.

Those who have suffered from railroad monopolies, trusts, and other institutions which have menaced civic liberty, found in Mr. Norris a champion who voiced their wrongs by that far-reaching and most effective argument, the popular novel. As his reviewer admits his success as a story teller, I challenge his right to consider that the proper vocation of the author of "The Octopus" and "The Pit" was primarily that of a Socialist or a preacher. Arguing on such an hypothesis, the same could be said of Dickens, Harriet B. Stowe, and all authors who have used the popular novel as the means of agitating public reforms. I do not assert for Mr. Norris that he was a genius of the first rank: but his books, his Wheat Series, have attracted widespread interest among business men as well as politicians. He did not write of the "Blossoms of Chivalry" or of a "Stirring Passion" in a charming, dainty style, the finish and rhetoric of which we admire, but soon forget. The passion with which he was consumed was a real one, and when we lay down his books we remember them.

Mr. Norris did "take himself seriously." He did not cater to the gallery with the horseplay humor now in vogue. He had something to say, and he was not afraid to say it. Like Walt Whitman, his faults were typically American. He was not fastidious in his language. He was writing to the men of the country, to the lawmakers, and his object was to touch the heart, not to please the ear. Had he acquired a more finished style, he might have lost that forcefulness of expression which made his books throb with power and so roused his readers that they felt through all his shortcomings he was a man who had a "message."

*A response to the *Times* review on pp. 235–37.

"The Story of 'The Pit.'" *London Daily Express*, March 7, 1903, p. 4.

Frank Norris—wild, reckless, brilliant, Frank Norris—is dead. In his thirty-two years he had crowded enough of stirring incident to fill the lifetime of ordinary mortals.

In America they knew and admired him first as a San Francisco journalist, then as a war correspondent, lastly with an added fame as the author of "The Octopus."

He did not live to hear them praise "The Pit," the story of Chicago, which in its force and eloquence marked him as one of the best descriptive writers of our time.

The tale he tells is not in itself remarkable. But it is the surroundings in which he plunges his characters that are of great interest to Englishmen.

They are men and women of Chicago with whom he deals. We see how the American women stand apart, well dressed, cultivated, artistic, knowing nothing of the furious struggles of their husbands and fathers in the hunt for money. We see how even in their amusements business is never absent from the mind of the keen American men.

Jekyll and Hyde.

From the time when they leave school, in their pleasure, in their love-making, in their living, and almost in their dying, the struggle for gold is part of their existence.

Ah, these men of the city, what could women ever know of them, of their lives, of that other existence through which—freed from the influence of wife or mother, or daughter, or sister—they passed every day from nine o'clock till evening? It was a life in which women had no part, and in which, should they enter it, they would no longer recognise son or husband, or father or brother. The gentle-mannered fellow, clean-minded, clean-handed, of the breakfast or supper-table was one man. The other, who and what was he?

Down there, in the murk and grime of the business district, raged the Battle of the Street, and therein he was a being transformed, case-hardened, supremely selfish, asking no quarter; no, nor giving any. Fouled with the clutching and grappling of the attack, besmirched with the elbowing of low associates and obscure allies, he set his feet towards conquest, and mingled with the marchings of an army that surged for ever forward and back; now in merciless assault, beating the fallen enemy under foot; now in repulse, equally merciless, trampling down the auxiliaries of the day before in a panic dash for safety; always cruel, always selfish, always pitiless.

The "Pit" from which the novel draws its name is the wheat market on the Chicago Produce Exchange. The "pits" are the arenas in the centre of the Exchange wherein the brokers stand during 'Change hours, and it is into this whirlpool of speculation that the characters are drawn.

There is nothing on earth quite like the Pit of Chicago. It is where the wheat that gives a living to the western farmer is sold; it is where the wheat that feeds millions of people in the Old World is sold. To corner the supply means vast prosperity to the western producers, and frightful suffering in the east, where the food of the nations rises by leaps and bounds.

The Unregarded Public.

The caprice of the speculator may bring the pinch of famine among the vinedressers of Northern Italy, the coal miners of Western Russia, or the very poor in our own East End. But these are things of which the plungers in the wheat market do not think.

In the struggle for existence among the bulls and bears the public have no place. They are indefinite millions, timid, innocent people, as much out of place in the Pit as puppies in the cage of panthers. In the mutual struggle it is no matter if they crush them to death by the mere rolling of their bodies. Charity, mercy, consideration for others—they have no place in the Pit of Chicago.

Here is the picture of the place in full action upon the morning when great speculations were forward:—

> The official reporter climbed to his perch in the little cage on the edge of the Pit, shutting the door after him. By now the chanting of the messenger boys was an uninterrupted chorus.
>
> From all sides of the building and in every direction they crossed and recrossed each other, always running, their hands full of yellow envelopes. From the telephone alcoves came the prolonged, musical rasp of the callbells.
>
> In the Western Union telegraph booths the keys of the multitude of instruments raged incessantly. Bare-headed young men hurried up to one another, conferred an instant, comparing despatches, then separated, darting away at top speed. Men called to each other half-way across the building. Over by the bulletin boards, clerks and agents made careful memoranda of primary receipts, and noted down the amount of wheat on passage, the exports, and the imports.

The Overture.

> And all these sounds—the clatter of the telegraph, the intoning of the messenger boys, the shouts and cries of the clerks and traders, the shuffle and trampling of hundreds of feet, the whirring of telephone signals—rose into the troubled air, and mingled overhead to form a vast note, prolonged, sustained, that reverberated from vault to vault of the airy roof, and issued from every doorway, every opened window, in one long roll of uninterrupted thunder.
>
> In the Wheat Pit the bids, no longer obedient of restraint, began one by one to burst out, like the first isolated shots of a skirmish line. Grossman flung out an arm, crying:—
>
> "Sell twenty-five May at ninety-five and an eighth," while Kelly and Semple had almost simultaneously shouted, "Give seven-eighths for May!"
>
> The official reporter had been leaning far over to catch the first quotations, one eye upon the clock at the end of the room.

The hour and the minute hands were at right angles.

Then suddenly, cutting squarely athwart the vague crescendo of the floor, came the single incisive stroke of a great gong. Instantly a tumult was unchained.

Arms were flung forward in strenuous gestures, and from above the crowding heads in the Wheat Pit a multitude of hands, eager, the fingers extended, leaped into the air. All articulate expression was lost in the single explosion of sound, as the traders surged downwards to the centre of the Pit, grabbing each other, struggling towards each other, tramping, stamping, charging through with might and main.

Promptly the hand on the great dial above the clock stirred and trembled, and, as though driven by the tempest breath of the Pit, moved upward through the degrees of its circle. It paused, wavered, stopped at length, and on the instant the hundreds of telegraph keys scattered throughout the building began clicking off the news to the whole country, from the Atlantic to the Pacific, and Mackinac to Mexico, that the Chicago market had made a slight advance, and that May wheat, which had closed the day before at 93⅜, had opened that morning at 94½.

The story tells of how the hero Jadwin cornered the market; how as the price of wheat rose a wave of prosperity ran over Western America, where the farmers were buying carriages and the women parlour organs and furniture. Yet at the same time that Jadwin was swimming forward on the tide of his success loaves in Italy shrank as small as a fist, and women and children were dying of starvation.

In this Mr. Norris was only repeating history with small exaggeration. The picture that he draws of this great speculator is of immense power. Wheat, wheat, wheat—it ran chanting through his head, driving out sleep and love and human affections.

But in the end the corner broke in a scene which we might consider impossible if we had not already received more descriptions which show that it is not exaggerated:—

> The Pit was mad and drunk and frenzied; not a man of all those who fought and scrambled and shouted who knew what he or his neighbour did. They only knew that a support long thought to be secure was giving way, not gradually, not evenly, but by horrible collapses and equally horrible upward leaps. Now it held, now it broke, now it re-formed again, rose again, then again in hideous cataclysms fell from beneath their feet to lower depths than before. The official reporter leaned back in his place, helpless.
>
> On the wall overhead the indicator on the dial was rocking back and forth like the mast of a ship caught in a monsoon. The price of July wheat no man could so much as approximate. The fluctuations were no longer by fractions of a cent, but by ten cents, fifteen cents, twenty-five cents at a time. On one side of

the Pit wheat sold at ninety cents, on the other at a dollar and a quarter.

And all the while, above the din upon the floor, above the tremblings and shoutings of the Pit, there seemed to thrill and swell that appalling roar of the wheat itself coming in, coming on like a tidal wave, bursting through, dashing barriers aside, rolling like a measureless, almighty river, from the farms of Iowa and ranches of California, on to the east—to the bakeshops and hungry mouths of Europe.

Such is the story of the Pit, one of the most remarkable products of our modern civilisation.

"Books and Their Makers."
Boston Herald, March 8, 1903, p. 17.

"The Pit," which is the book of the moment in this country, with nothing for a really good second, is ranked in England, where it has just appeared, considerably below "The Octopus." Writing in the London Daily Telegraph, Mr. W. L. Courtney says that the nature of the scene Mr. Norris has to depict—Chicago, to wit—limits the powers of the author's imagination, sets bounds to his artistic capacity, and makes his style crude and harsh and impressionistic. The charm of the earlier book, he thinks, lay "in its beautiful delineation of country, its wide and picturesque grasp of all the natural elements in the great cornfields, and also in the precise and distinct portrayal of some of the characters involved in the plot."

Yet he considers that the work of Mr. Norris is nothing if not epical. Stephen Crane's genius, "such as it was," was that of the episode; Norris had "some of the large and elemental faculties which go to the composition of early and primeval romance." Mr. Courtney goes on to compare Norris with his master, Zola—to the advantage of the former. Norris has more imagination, as well as the epical instinct; he "allows himself to dream with faculties which Zola was never able to cultivate, not even in 'Le Rêve.' The American writer is a realist with a difference, a man who lets his imagination play round the puppets which he has drawn, and, therefore, places them on a platform and pedestal far above the vulgar trivialities of every day."

[William Dean Howells.] "The Last Work of Frank Norris."
Harper's Weekly, 47 (March 14, 1903), 433.

Time will no doubt undo the effect of death in taking the gifted young novelist from his task, so far as to relieve his last book from the appearance of challenging the primacy of his earlier and more masterly achievements. It is the present misfortune of his fame that the second drama of the three which he imagined for his greatly designed trilogy of The Wheat should follow haltingly upon the first with a pace which the third shall never come to help it mend. But it will be all the more the care, as it should be the generous will, of those who read *The Pit* to remember that we have had *The Octopus*, and that we were to have had *The Wolf*, in which the story of the food and famine of the world was, and was to have been, fully told. The first of these three was adequate, and the second is not adequate, but it is more adequate than it seems in the incomplete perspective. One may fancy in it the faltering of the hand unconsciously prophetic of fate, the impatience of him who fights with numbered days; for as Lowell said of Keats, "as we turn the leaves, they seem to warm and thrill our fingers with the flush of his warm senses, and the flutter of his electrical nerves, and we do not wonder he felt that what he did was to be done swiftly."

The book has the pathos of this apparent haste, and yet looked at with due reflection it has not the effect of a hastily imagined thing. The material is less picturesque and less dramatic than that of the book dealing with the growth and garnering of the wheat in the fields which were robbed as well as reaped. There is no such episode as the struggle of the farmer, gun in hand, with the railroad, but the descent into the Pit of the great Bull who has been destroying himself in his reckless play with the suffering of millions of men and women and children, is no mean incident, and the novelist has wrought it into fiction both strong and fine. The pity of the thing is that so much of the book relates to the unimportant society side of the business, to the half-cultured, half-ignorant, wholly egotistical woman who stands for the heroine, when its sole heroine should have been The Wheat. The author has not sufficiently mastered her personality, though he has almost done it, to let us feel that he feels her essential vulgarity; he has not shown us a rich nature depraved by the reckless game of the man fighting and tricking the hapless unhungered for the bread in their mouths, but a cheap nature ready to betray him for the flatteries and caresses of another cheap nature. The tragedy is not in the domestic story of Laura and Curtis Jadwin, but in that of the poor old Cresslers, who are dragged down with their wreck, and are sacrificed against their wills and principles to the insensate ambition of Jadwin. Before the story is finished, one has quite ceased to care for either of the Jadwins, whether she was ruined through her greedy vanity or he through his ruthless lust of power. Let her go with the meretricious esthete who makes love to her; let him fall under the feet of his enemies in the Pit; we cannot care, and we are not interested to know that they really go to a new scene to rehabilitate their unessential lives.

Perhaps if the author had taken time to think out his material a little more thoroughly he would have found a hint in it of immense importance to our imperfect civilization, a truth known dimly and dumbly to those who suffer the worst harm from the facts. It is not alone the luxury of our Jadwins which is vulgar; it is the Jadwins themselves who are vulgar, by whatever other names they call themselves in Chicago or New York, or by whatever difference of social circumstance they distinguish themselves from one another. It is for such brute state as theirs that the earth groans with harvests and her children with hunger, and we have not quite an assurance from the novelist that he senses their vulgarity. He leaves us to fear that somehow the woman's beauty, and the man's courage have blinded him. Yet there are passages and touches throughout the book that testify to his insight and his ability to paint the make as well as the manner of his people. There is excellent characterization in his work, and occasionally a robust and powerful dramatization. For him it is too late to inquire whether the savage mock-splendor of the Chicago which he portrays has not held for him the glamour that it may have worn for him in his earlier years, and whether he has not approached it with less detachment than he kept in dealing with the facts of his California story, which he saw with maturer eyes; but for the critic of his work, and for the student, the suggestion may have value.

The book wants balance, as we have hinted, and it is overweighted with fact of the less rather than the greater importance; it should have toppled, if at all, to the side of the wheat gambler—not the wheat gambler's wife. Where the work is with the scenes in the grain exchange, the Pit, it is always masterly, from that first glimpse of the Pit in the beginning, to that battle-piece at the last where Jadwin breaks with tradition and convention, and he, the great Bull, enters the arena in person, and fights the Bears to his death. In these moments, and such as these the book magnificently succeeds, but there are other moments when it is as true and still finer, such as those when it reveals the prim, pure, high nature of a girl like Page Dearborn; the gentle, motherly goodness of Mrs. Cressler; the flat, kind, commonplace of Mrs. Wessels. For the rest, one could have wished the material had been scanned by the severer eye of the author's later experience. It is on the society side that it is weak; it is not so weak on the social side; and on the human side it is worthy to stand with the author's greater work: not on the same level, indeed, and yet not fatally below it, as nine-tenths of our other fiction must. On what may be called the physical side, it is wonderful. You can see, hear, feel those people.

B. O. Flower. "The Pit." *The Arena*, 29 (April 1903), 440–42.

I

One takes up this volume with a feeling of deep sadness and lays it down with profound regret, born of the remembrance that the gifted author, in the flush of early manhood and possessing the genius that promised to place him in the very front rank of twentieth-century novelists, has been so recently stricken down by death. He was a strong, fine, manly thinker, a splendid type of the best young manhood of to-day—a conscientious writer with high ideals and gifted in an eminent degree with a realist's brain and a poet's imagination. He possessed the strength and rare power vividly to picture life as it really is that were exhibited by Emile Zola, and yet was free from the revolting naturalism that marred most of the great Frenchman's master works. He was far more than a mere realist. He possessed the imagination of the true poet. Hence, his created characters became colossal and typical, while the subtle charm born of idealism relieved his writings from the dead level of mediocrity that marks the work of those who essay to be realists but who are devoid of imagination and poetic feeling. We hailed Mr. Norris as emphatically the coming American novelist, and in his taking off experience a personal loss.

II

The reader will naturally compare "The Pit" with its companion volume, "The Octopus," and most critics have pronounced in favor of the last-written work. We confess, however, that we do not share these opinions; for, while "The Pit" is unquestionably more finished and at times evinces greater maturity in thought and expression, it lacks, it seems to us, much of the compelling force and tremendous dramatic power that marked "The Octopus." We have a feeling, in reading the two books, that the author must have spent far more time in the preparation of his first great work than on his last volume.

In "The Pit," Jadwin is a distinctly great creation, a typical Napoleon among speculators, of colossal proportions; yet to our mind he is not nearly so impressive a character study as Magnus Derrick, the overshadowing personality in "The Octopus." Then in "The Octopus" we have a number of powerfully drawn characters that impress their individuality in an unforgettable manner upon the mind. Annixter, Vanamee, S. Behrman, Cedarquist, Dyke, Osterman, Broderson, Hilma Tree—these are strong, typical characters, presenting not only distinct individualities but different view-points of life; and when compared with the little group of people who enter into "The Pit," and who are for the most part very conventional, it is difficult to see how any one can find in Mr. Norris's last book a work comparable to the great drama of the wheat as found in the San Joaquin Valley story.

Nevertheless "The Pit" is a great novel, instinct with present-day American life. The story deals chiefly with the Chicago wheat pit, the great gambling center or Wall Street of the Middle West. The overshadowing central figure, Curtis Jadwin, is in the opening chapters a remarkably successful real estate dealer, who is deeply interested in a large Sunday-school composed of little waifs in one of the poorer districts of Chicago. Moody, he explains, got him interested in the work. Jadwin is a natural organizer, a strong, daring man of exceptional business power and judgment. His friend Cressler warns him against ever dabbling in stocks. It means ruin in the long run, he explains. Cressler has spoken by the cards, having been one of the tens of thousands of victims of this same pit.

Jadwin early becomes deeply attached to Laura Dearborn, a striking though at first not a very lovable young woman. This lady already has two suitors—an artist named Sheldon Corthell, and a young broker, Landry Court. They all propose and are refused. The young broker takes his defeat philosophically and marries the heroine's sister. The artist folds his tent and flees to Europe. Jadwin immediately begins siege for the capture of the resisting heart. In the long run he wins the prize, and for a time all is joyous.

Jadwin, however, in spite of his determination, has been drawn into the maelstrom of speculation. The Pit has thrown its fatal spell over his imagination. Here for a time success follows success, until he is regarded as the most formidable speculator of the great city. Beginning as a "bear," he eventually becomes the "Great Bull" of the Pit; and at last with him, as with the multitude of other men who are seduced by the fascinating charm of this great Western gambling center, the Pit claims him as its own.

There are men of cold, calculating, and phlegmatic temperament who can gamble or drink or use opium for years, and yet appear to be little influenced. But not so with another class—men of keen imagination, of idealistic and poetic temperament, of high-strung and nervous organism. When one of this class comes under the spell of a potent stimulant, whether it appeals primarily to the physical appetites or to the mental faculties and imaginative world, the results are much the same. The man becomes the victim of the spell, the slave of the illusion. It is all one whether it be hasheesh, absinthe, whisky, lust for power, the dominion of sensual appetites, or the mania for gambling and speculation. In time the baleful spell fills the mental world as darkness fills the windowless cell; and thenceforth, for a time at least, the man, be he ever so great a genius, is the slave of the illusion. Seldom has a novelist given so strong an illustration of this tremendous fact as has Mr. Norris in his portrayal of the career of Curtis Jadwin.

After the fascination of the wheat pit has thrown its spell over his brain, the man becomes transformed. We hear no more of the Sunday-school; his wife is neglected; all those things which he before most enjoyed become for him stale, flat, and unprofitable. The mania for gambling drives out well-nigh all else. He becomes as much the slave of the Pit for a time as man ever becomes of drink, of opium, or of the hallucinations of well-defined insanity. And seldom indeed has the essential evil of stock gambling been more vividly portrayed than in this work. Barring Zola's great novel entitled "Money," which is also concerned with stock gambling, we know of nothing in contemporaneous fiction more impressive than this work.

During the days when the mania for speculation is holding the "Great Bull" in its deadly grasp, his whole nervous nature is so overwrought that it verges more and more toward complete collapse; while his beautiful but neglected wife is drifting toward the most perilous quicksands upon which a wife can wreck her life. The artist has returned; he has become a constant visitor at the Jadwin house; he notes the neglect and unhappiness of Mrs. Jadwin; he makes love to her, and all but persuades her to fly with him. At the critical moment, however, just as she is on the verge of deserting her husband's home, Curtis Jadwin is overtaken by complete ruin. The wheat destroys his fortune as in "The Octopus" it destroyed the life of S. Behrman; and with the sweeping away of his enormous wealth comes nervous and mental collapse. He is brought to his home more dead that alive. Laura, instead of flying with the artist Corthell, faithfully nurses her husband back to health. It is a long, weary task, but by no means devoid of sweetness, as through the convalescence the two are drawn again together. Jadwin is ruined, but the little fortune that Laura possessed before her marriage has remained intact, and the two determine to move West and begin again. The volume closes with the train bearing them from the great Mistress of the Lakes.

All the principal characters are drawn with the fidelity that makes the reader feel that they are real, living human beings. The book is one of the most convincing documents in modern romance.

F.C.B.
"Talk About Books."
The Chautauquan, 37 (April 1903), 100.

It seems to the writer that a considerable amount of captious criticism has been given to "The Pit," by the late Frank Norris. Comparison with "The Octopus," the first book of a proposed trilogy styled "the epic of the wheat," is inevitable, but it would appear to be short-sighted judgment which declares one to be more powerful than the other. If the same manner had characterized each book, criticism of effectiveness would be better grounded. Nowhere have we found such a picture of the domination of the American speculative instinct and practice in nature's production as Norris paints in "The Pit." Nor can we admit that Chicago atmosphere has been misrepresented or bunglingly presented. The sacrifice of a wife—a contradictory creature, real at least so far as masculine ideals of the day conceive the position of the American woman—heightens the tragedy of business. Stronger fiction than this, in our opinion, has not been produced by writers of this generation in America.

William Morton Payne.
"The New Books."
The Dial, 34 (April 1, 1903), 242–43.

The ambitious purpose of the late Frank Norris to write "the epic of the wheat" in a series of three novels must now remain unfulfilled. The plan of this trilogy, it will be remembered, was to embrace the production of the world's chief food staple, its marketing in the great central city of America, and its consumption in some far-off region of Europe. The first of these pictures we had, in "The Octopus," and reviewed at the time of its appearance; the second we now have, in "The Pit"; the third we shall never have, although we know that it was to be called "The Wolf," and may well believe that it offered to the novelist a finer opportunity than either of the other two. "The Pit" is called "a story of Chicago," but one must not hastily infer that the suggestion of the title is scriptural, for by it nothing more sinister or infernal is meant than the wheat-market, with its speculative fever and frenzied conflict. As far as the story has private interest, both central situation and moral are familiar enough. Charles Dudley Warner's novels, and those of many other writers, have preached effectively upon the same text. But the author has arrived at something more than private interest, for he has sought to dramatize the clash of commercial arms and the shock of speculative battle, giving to the impersonal forces brought into play the principal share of our attention. We cannot say that the attempt has been altogether successful. In this respect "The Pit" seems less successful than "The Octopus" was, and it was only a very qualified praise that we were able to bestow upon that earlier work. Both books are strained, turgid, and unconvincing. The posthumous book, moreover, shows signs of hurried writing, and has evidently lacked the revision that the author would have given it had he lived.

Mr. Henry Kitchell Webster is another novelist who seeks his themes in the strenuous business life of today. His "Roger Drake, Captain of Industry" is a capital story of its kind; the material is well under control, and the plot is skilfully managed. It does not attempt to do so big a thing as is attempted in "The Pit," and it seems to us, in consequence of this restraint, the better novel of the two. But we are deeply suspicious of all these attempts to base works of fiction upon the money-making motive. Balzac did it successfully, because he was a genius of the first rank, but our recent American efforts in this direction seem to be little more than a sort of journalism, and none of them possess the elements of permanent interest.

"More Novels." *The Nation,* 76 (April 2, 1903), 276.

If Mr. Wister is the Novelist Laureate of the Cowboy, the late Mr. Norris should have held the same title as to Wheat, whose epic he has sung with magnificent force and stir. "The Pit" offers a wondrously vivid representation of the swirl and pull of the "undiked Ocean of the Wheat" as it surges round the Chicago Board of Trade. Reading, one seems to be at the mercy of an appalling whirlpool, and to see one's maddened fellow-beings wheeling, whirling, sinking, then hurled from the maelstrom to fall back and begin again the horrid circuit. Hideously real is the deal in the wheat pit, with all its side issues, its demoralizations and tragedies. The vociferous note of Chicago's works and ways is ever at the reader's ear. The rushing interest of the story holds his attention like a vise, while he seems to be fixed in the heart of a factory with all harsh sounds clanging and all machinery roaring, not only in respect of the pages given to the business life of the Great Gray City, but in the scenes of so-called domestic quiet. The portraits are good, in a style of ultra-detail. The development of the two-souled heroine makes a strong study and companion-piece to that of her husband, the great speculator. A Titan he, fighting Titans, beaten only, as his arch-enemy says, by Wheat itself. For the novel reader who looks for poetic justice, the sword of judgment falls too lightly on him, the "Great Unknown Bull," who wrecked so many lives in wantonness. One would like to see him at least repentant. For poetry, we must look farther—to the flow of the great stream of the wheat from the seed to the hungry markets of Europe—a sight made finely visible by the writer's imaginative yet direct way of seeing and saying. And there is a powerful moral in the spectacle of commercial gambling and its victims. But how unlovely a world is even the better part of a world where Bigness is the deity! In vain do music, art, books, nature, put in their pleas. The fingerprints of the great gods Size and Noise are on every page.

Harriet Waters Preston. "Lady Rose's Daughter: The Novels of Mr. Norris." *Atlantic Monthly*, 91 (May 1903), 691–92.

It seems odd indeed to turn from the staid elegance and essential artificiality of the novel of patrician manners (which hath its perennial charms, no less, for the savage republican breast, and which Mrs. Ward [in *Lady Rose's Daughter*] manages about as well, after all, as any other living writer) to the two most impressive and memorable works of fiction recently published in America; I mean The Octopus and The Pit by the late lamented Frank Norris. The very names of these books are boldly sensational, chosen deliberately, as it would seem, to attract the democracy of the reading world. Their action takes place far down,—at the very roots of organized society. They deal with the most primitive, humble, and universal of human needs,—the production of that daily bread which is the staff of man's life in the body. How the grain on which our common sustenance depends is planted in hope and harvested in fear, only to be exploited far away, at great commercial centres, by speculators who supply or deny it, for their own selfish gain, to the multitudes who toil at the base of the social pyramid,—such was the broad theme which Mr. Norris proposed to himself in his Epic of the Wheat.

For a good while after the first appearance of The Octopus, not much was said aloud about the book. It was a thing painful to read and disquieting to remember; moreover, it was confessedly but the fragment of a more comprehensive scheme. I am not sure that The Octopus can in any proper sense of the term be called a romance. It is a vision, a revelation, an eruption of the subliminal verities, a peep into the red crater over which we lightly walk. It is also, in some sense, a manifesto and a prophecy. It has no central plot, although it quivers from end to end with the throes of human tragedy, like the soil of a volcanic region, in an unquiet time. I may record my own impression—based on some personal acquaintance with the scene of the drama—that the tremendous indictment which it brings against one among the monster monopolies at whose aggrandizement we all tremble, is absolutely just; and that there is no case of cruelest oppression, no phase of the mournful and manifold ruin so passionately portrayed that has not its grim parallel in contemporary experience. But the San Joaquin valley is, after all, only a small corner of earth,—a secluded spot fenced in by mountain walls,—and it seemed that allowance ought to be made for the fact that Mr. Norris had dreamed an epic, and had in him, beyond a doubt, the makings of no mean poet. For all his unflinching grasp of ugly fact, his candor of spirit, and the controlled quietude of his prevailing tone, one felt that the first number of his trilogy had been conceived upon heroic lines, and invested with a more or less colored atmosphere. Moreover, the final catastrophe of the tale, so daringly imagined, so novel in its horror, and yet so fit,—the doom of the coarse villain, who was, after all, but the instrument of a securely defended syndicate of iniquity,—appeared to exemplify a justice more poetic than probable.

But when, after the silence of a year or two, Mr. Norris took up his pen again in The Pit, and resumed his gallant crusade, one saw, at a glance, how the youthful paladin had altered and matured. He had dropped the dithyrambic note, and in this which was destined to remain the last word of his grave parable he speaks as a seer no longer, but as a man of the Western world,—alert, collected, fearless, and with powers fully ripe.

The Pit is the Chicago wheat-pit; and the sometime dreamer of the far Californian valley with its fathomless fecundity and the daze of its perpetual sunshine holds his own without effort amid the din of our biggest marketplace, and evinces a nervous grasp of its most complex affairs. And it is not the victim of the monopolist for whom he is pleading now so much as for the monopolist himself whom he warns of his own soul's peril.

The Pit is a better constructed and more efficiently handled narrative than its predecessor, but it is also more like other books. The love story that runs through it seems a deplorably common one, until we come, at the very end, to the unexpectedly sane and hopeful resolution of the trite intrigue. The actors in the piece are all rather vulgar,—at best but half taught and superficially civilized. Nevertheless—and it is to my mind one of Mr. Norris's chief points of distinction as a writer—there is nothing vulgar in his manner of portraying them. He does not gloat or smack his lips—as how few of our native novelists can wholly refrain from doing!—over the inordinate splendors of their new found luxury. He reports the faulty grammar of their loose though graphic speech quite simply,—with no airs of patronizing apology, or affected appeal to remote academic tribunals. These are his own kindred whom he sees attacked by a strange madness, and in peril of a deeper [pit] than the wheat-pit through their overmastering greed for anyhow-gotten riches. What matters it how they dress or talk if only they be rescued and rehabilitated? The solemnity of the issues involved and his own concentrated moral conviction make all questions of mere taste appear trivial in the author's eyes; and he moves through the lakeside palaces of Chicago with a detachment as complete and a *ton* as admirable as were ever Mrs. Ward's in any ducal mansion of them all!

For to those piercing young eyes of the great writer we have lost it was given for one moment, before their light went out, to see this teeming and formless American life of ours "steadily" and to "see it whole." It lay bare to his brief clairvoyance with all its vast resources and capacities in flux, its immense potentiality for both good and evil; above all with those heavy obligations to the race and the future, attaching to the focal place from which it can move no more, in the intricately woven web of the world's unified fate. The vision faded and the *Illuminé* passed on, even before he could render intelligible to his countrymen the whole of what he saw. But his broken message remains full of import, and it is idle to indulge in unavailing regret over the part that was never spoken.

A fitting motto for the unfinished trilogy might be found in those ringing lines, familiar to us all of the elder generation,—the manliest perhaps ever penned by the cloistered sage from whom the author of Lady Rose's Daughter derived by natural inheritance her first, and her best inspiration:—

Charge once more then, and be dumb!
Let thy comrades when they come,
When the forts of folly fall
Find thy body by the wall.

Hugh Herdman. "The Pit." *Pacific Monthly*, 9 (June 1903), 393.

A perusal of Frank Norris' "Octopus" thoroughly convinced one of the unusual ability of the young author. There was something in his work far above what one usually expects in these days. Clearness of vision was it? Or virility of thought? Or courage in expressing his convictions? Perhaps all of these, and more. Discerning critics saw in him many of the qualities which characterize Zola and Balzac, and predicted for him unmeasured success.

Accordingly, when "The Octopus" stood forth as pre-eminently the most virile novel that had appeared for years, predictions of even greater success seemed to be justified. There were few who doubted that, strong and rugged and true as is "The Octopus," it is but the first and consequently the least powerful, of his contemplated trilogy on Wheat. The others could not fall below the first— the author would see to that. With confident anticipations of pleasure, then, we all looked forward to the publication of the second of the trilogy, "The Pit."

But just then came the sudden death of the gifted Californian, and hope drooped low. It was known that he had finished "The Pit"—that was some consolation—but now we all realized that it was the completed trilogy, and not "The Pit" alone, that we were anticipating. But with these two, which are but parts of a greater unfinished whole, we must be content. Our life's work is, after all, but a part of what we intended to do.

"The Octopus" tells the story of the growing of the wheat; "The Pit" that of the sale of it. The pit is the Chicago wheat pit, and the story which is woven about that as the center is full to overflowing with the energy which is concentrated in that maelstrom. Mankind seems possessed with the phrenzy of speculation, and the reader is caught and borne irresistibly into the eddy. This demon of speculation lays its clutches on the hero and all but disrupts his home, and is prevented from making a tragedy of his and his wife's life only by the sovereign power of love. With all the strength and vigor and clearness of Zola, Frank Norris has laid bare the heart of the speculator and the evil that he does. He has shown ignoble passions in the making and in the working, but alongside of these he has displayed the love that wells up in the heart of a man and the heart of a woman. He has written a strong story, a story true to the elements of life, but a clean story.

"Books of the Year." *The Independent*, 55 (November 19, 1903), 2741.

The Pit was the second volume of Frank Norris' trilogy, which he called "The Epic of the Wheat." In some ways it was a stronger book than "The Octopus," and showed the increase of the author's power, as well as his weakness as a literary artist. He was the one man of note in America seriously affected by Zola's influence without suffering the taint of his bestial genius. And it is a coincidence that they both should have passed away during the same year. Zola's last novel, *Truth*, was based upon the Dreyfus affair. And in this story he appears to have reached the final decadence of his creative faculty. Beginning with the hypothesis that man is the product of heredity and environment, he multiplied the individual, and became the interpreter of the animalized life of the resultant leprous mass. He had a genius for obscenity. But he suffered the natural revulsion of age and experience from this degradation of his imagination, and in this last story turns dully to the contemplation of abstract ideas. With the passing of Zola the literary art of our times is delivered from the further influence of a gifted but degenerate mind.

A DEAL IN WHEAT

AND OTHER STORIES OF THE NEW AND OLD WEST

BY
FRANK NORRIS

Illustrated by
Remington, Leyendecker, Hitchcock and Hooper

NEW YORK
DOUBLEDAY, PAGE & COMPANY
1903

A Deal in Wheat

"Stories of the East and West."
The Argonaut, 53 (September 26, 1903), 325.

Ten of Frank Norris's short stories have been reprinted in one volume under the title of the opening one, "A Deal in Wheat." This, as may be guessed, is an episode evolved from the results of Mr. Norris's researches after material for "The Pit."

It is followed by four characteristically Western sketches, in which the characters converse with great gusto in the easy, unstudied, and roughly graphic vernacular of the cow-puncher.

"A Memorandum of Sudden Death" is Mr. Norris in a mood of dramatic imaginativeness. This story recalls in diary form the thoughts and emotions of a noted writer, one of a group of white men beset on the desert by a superior number of Indians, and doomed to certain and cruel death.

There are four stories of sea-life, in which Mr. Norris shows his familiarity with the character and dialect of the rough sailorman. A ghostly vision figures in one of these sea-stories, something which is rarely treated in our brisk, matter-of-fact epoch. Mr. Norris has handled it very effectively and with some notably good descriptive writing, but with the lurking and ineradicable skepticism that belongs to the times.

A couple of love-stories with Mexican heroines round out a collection which is as a chart, recording the eager ardor and boundless curiosity with which this promising young writer had turned his bright, investigating gaze upon the more novel phases of our Western life.

"Tales of Norris: A Volume of Posthumous Stories by the Author of 'The Pit.'"
New York Times, 52 (September 26, 1903), p. 652, "Saturday Review of Books and Art."

"A Deal in Wheat" is the first and the shortest of these stories by the late Frank Norris. The title, of course, suggests Chicago and "The Pit," but the fact is that the stories which have already appeared in magazine form, are with one exception concerned with the gun-firing, cow-punching West of the plains, or the semi-piratic seafaring West of the Pacific Coast, not with the new West of the grain exchange and the gambler in breadstuffs.

They are forceful, dramatic, high-colored tales, done for the most part in the mongrel, garish, yet wonderfully enlivening dialect which fiction has assigned to the cow-punching hero and the three-card monte man. Of the latter not the least is Peg-Leg Smith, who here storms and sins and gets his grim punishment. This Peg-Leg could not endure to hear another man swear, but that he straightway erupted streams of rabid rage and his sidearms spat bullets as a hot frying-pan grease. But, says the story teller, using his lingo:

> This yere prejudice agin profanity is the only thing about this yere Peg-Leg that ain't pizen bad, and that prejudice, you got to know, was just along o' his bein' loco on that one subjeck. Just the same as some gesabos has feelin's agin cats or snakes, or agin seein' a speckled nigger.

An effective thing is the "Memorandum of Sudden Death," a manuscript supposed to be written in the pauses of the tragedy by a man of literature, one of a body of troopers and scouts, dogged, surrounded, and picked off by hostile Indians upon the plains. Written so, and found beside the bodies and given to the world just as the doomed man wrote it, it is a thing that readers will remember, a thing surely hard to do, yet, one must think, singularly well done.

For the seafaring tales, they have a charm of their own. They deal gently with the shady doings of the Three Black Crows—undertakers of illicit "propositions" from Alaska to the Horn involving imminent risk of the neck and finances by the Pacific and Oriental Flotation Company of San Francisco, Cyrus Ryder, President. The three smuggle arms to Central American revolutionists with adroit petticoated assistance; they steal otter skins of fabulous price from Russians, (first filling the Russians with a wonderful champagne made by the Pacific and Oriental Flotation Company out of Rhine wine, effervescent salts, raisins, rock candy, and alcohol,) and sail on the trackless seas of the South Pacific to a nameless island with a 200-year-old skeleton in its closet and a treasure alongside. This is the story of the "Ship that Saw a Ghost"—the story of a two-century-old derelict. A stout steam freighter she was, this ghostseer, the Glarus by name, and thenceforth she lay at the San Francisco docks, "never to smell blue water again or to taste the trades—no pilot to take her out, no Captain to navigate her, no stoker to feed her fires, no sailor to walk her decks." For the seafaring man has his fancies—"and the Glarus is suspect. She has seen a ghost." It is a good yarn, and there is in it some work after the inspiration of the Ancient Mariner which is as fine of the kind as one often reads. Certainly the reader will carry away in his mind a ghost of his own in the haunting memory of an etching of a lone, lonely sea and the ancient, tattered, crumbling ghost ship rippling the water beneath her rotten bows—moving across the track of it with never a wind astern. The spinal chills and thrills, that mysterious vibration of the nerves which comes upon the touch of the Thing Unseen—incomprehensible, contradictory of logic—these the reader will have as he reads, if he is not a man entirely machine-made. For there is still a skill—and Mr. Norris had it—to remind the most skeptical that there is more in the earth and heaven than steam and electricity can move or modern steering wheels govern.

"The Ghost of the Crosstrees," on the contrary, is an explained ghost—a night-robed sleep walker—sleep-walking being a childish survival in the one of the Three Black Crows—and "The Riding of Filipe" is a Mexican tale of a woman scorned and a good horse that did not fail at need. Which is the prize plot of melodrama.

Altogether, they are stories worth while—these of the dead romance of the buccaneer West by this dead romancer of that wonderful episode in civilization.

"A Deal in Wheat." *Book News Monthly*, 22 (October 1903), 123.

This volume is a collection of short stories by the late Frank Norris, who everyone will doubtless remember, died within the last year just as he had achieved fame in the literary world by the production of his "Epic of the Wheat" in three volumes, entitled "The Octopus," "The Pit," and "The Wolf," the last of which has not yet been published.

Mr. Norris was a man who did not believe in writing on a subject until he had made himself familiar with every detail, and it was while he was making a study of the Chicago wheat pit that he gathered the data for the story which furnishes the title to the present collection.

The remainder of the tales in the book are miscellaneous in subject, some being romantic, such as only the author could pen, and others being various pictures of life in its many different phases drawn with the virility, the command of language and the wide knowledge of human nature and conditions, the manifestations of which only make the premature death of the author more lamentable.

"Books of the Week." *The Outlook*, 75 (October 10, 1903), 373.

The least artistic of this posthumous collection of Mr. Norris's stories is the one giving title to the volume. As a vigorous protest against existing conditions it might by some thinkers perhaps be given first place—hardly as a finished production in a book of this sort. The reason for its selection for the position is obvious, however, in view of the success of "The Pit." A far better story in the present volume is "The Passing of Cock-Eye Blacklock." There are a half-dozen or more besides, all of the familiar Western flavor. One or two are very good indeed.

"A Deal in Wheat." *Times Literary Supplement* (London), October 23, 1903, p. 304.

Mr. Frank Norris, whose views on the novelist's responsibilities are discussed in another column [see pages 311–12], was young when he died, and so much might be deduced from internal evidence in any one of his books. But it is doubtful whether any work of his would carry conviction so strongly upon this point as *A Deal in Wheat* (Grant Richards, 6s.), a posthumous collection of stories dealing with the West and with the sea. It is, perhaps, a hard thing to say, but it is certainly a true one, that, even at his best, he never quite escaped from the very obvious influence of other writers, and in this particular volume it is made quite plain that he almost always wrote at second hand, and was under obligations to men as well known as Stevenson and as little known as Mr. Lewis, who wrote "Wolfville" and "Wolfville Days," and who has made one class of Western types peculiarly his own. The sketch, or anecdote, which furnishes the title for the book is no more than a study for his wheat books, and it might with advantage have been put in the waste-paper basket. The best story in the volume is, perhaps, the humorous "Passing of Cock-eye Blacklock," which is unadulterated "Wolfville." In the sea stories, which possess no particular merit, there are comments drawn straight from Stevenson's "Wreckers." The whole volume is, indeed, compact of rather boyish plagiarisms, and can do nothing to increase the writer's reputation, which must ultimately rest on "The Octopus" and "McTeague," both of them excellent books in their way.

Frederic Taber Cooper. "The Sustained Effort and Some Recent Novels."
Bookman (America), 18 (November 1903), 311–12.

If Mr. Conrad is an example of an author who always knows his own distance, and gauges his stride accordingly, the late Frank Norris is a good example of an author who lacked that knowledge. Mr. Norris took himself and his work with great seriousness; his ideal in fiction was a lofty one, and he was steadily, persistently, indomitably, working towards it—indeed, in the opinion of many of those who best know his work, he had already crossed the threshold of achievement. Yet, whatever place is ultimately assigned him in the history of American letters, this at least is sure—that he was first and last an artist who depended upon bold lines and sweeping brush strokes, and that he could not be true to himself if hampered by a narrow canvas. To look to Frank Norris for short stories is as incongruous as to set a Rodin to carving cherry pits, or a Verestchagin to tinting lantern slides. Yet it does not follow that the recently published collection entitled *A Deal in Wheat* were not worth preservation. On the contrary, they are full of the keenest interest to all students of contemporary letters. No one but Norris could have written them; every page breathes forth the uncrushable vitality of the man. But to call them short stories is to misname them. They impress one as fragments, rather splendid fragments too, trials of the author's strength, before he launched forth upon a really serious work. Take, for instance, the opening story, which gives the title to the volume. It was palpably written for practice, a sort of five-finger exercise in preparation for Mr. Norris's last volume, *The Pit*—and from this point of view it is brimful of interest. But taken as a story, it is at once too long and too short. Mr. Norris attempted in it to cover altogether too much ground; he might with advantage have stopped some pages sooner than he did—and yet, at the end there remains a sense of incompleteness. In the whole collection, there is just one story that stands out, unique and forceful—"A Memorandum of Sudden Death"—and in this the effect is achieved at the expense of probability. It is a good illustration of the length to which his occasional accesses of riotous romanticism would carry the author of *Moran of the Lady Letty*. This "memorandum" is a fragment of a journal supposed to be written by a wounded soldier, one of a small band of troopers who have been surrounded and followed, day after day, by a band of hostile Indians, through desolate miles of sand and sage, until the final attack is made. Granting that a United States trooper, with one or two bullets in him, and his comrades lying dead and dying around him, could go on recording passing events with the accuracy, the minuteness, the astonishing atmosphere, of this story, one must admit that this is Mr. Norris's nearest approach to the artistic unity of an ideal short story.

A good example of how much may be done with a modest one or two talents is afforded by Elia W. Peattie's unpretentious little volume, *The Edge of Things*. The author is in no sense a long-distance writer; she is best at ease in the simple, short story—and she knows it. And so, in undertaking a more sustained effort, she has frankly adopted the short story form, developing her plot through a series of more or less connected pictures, each complete in itself, yet each forming an essential part of the whole. Her style is simple, too; she is not prodigal of words and phrases; and yet it is a question whether even Norris has pictured with more compelling power the desolation of the Southwestern desert lands, and the morbid influence they have upon men who try to live too long in these regions which are literally the "edge of things." The central theme is not without interest, it concerns a young fellow from the East, who goes out there full of brave plans for building up a golden fortune from his sheep ranch. And then, after a time, luck goes against him, and his sheep die, and his funds run low, and the horror of the desert seizes him, and he thinks he is going mad, like many another poor fellow whose fate he hears of. But from this he is saved by a simple air-castle that he weaves during his hours of loneliness. In the old adobe house, to which he has temporarily fallen heir, he finds a woman's glove; and later, scratched on the wall, a verse in a woman's writing. And from these trifles he reconstructs a personality, and fills the place with the companionship of an imaginary form and face. And for the sake of rounding out the story, the girl whom he has constructed in his day-dreams turns out to be a real person after all. But the value of the book is not in the story, but in the atmosphere, the wonderful sense that you have of loneliness and isolation and endless monotony.

"A Deal in Wheat." *Current Literature*, 34 (November 1903), 626.

This volume contains a number of Frank Norris's short stories which appeared in different periodicals and magazines. They are all strong, virile stories, and, with the exception of the

"A Deal in Wheat." *Literary News*, 24 (November 1903), 322–23.

These stories, fragmentary and dissimilar as they are, are another proof of the loss that the American world of letters, if not of literature, suffered in the early death of Frank Norris. As the sub-title states, they are all stories of the West, both old and new, the West of the cowboy, the miner, and the rancher. The same power of vivid portraiture that characterized his more important work is in evidence here and also his strong Americanism, in spite of his assumed resemblance to the later French realists. The first story in the volume, which gives the title to the collection, is one of the least impressive, but it has the quality of dramatic sympathy and insight that marked the two volumes in his unfinished trilogy of the wheat. For the others, it need only be said that they are excellent examples of true realism, which may be described as a species of literary photography combined with the artist's faculty of discernment and interpretation. The occasional straining for effect and insistence on a particular point of view on the reader's part that marred some of his longer stories is almost entirely absent here. first, have to do with frontier and western life. An interesting volume not unworthy to be compared to Bret Harte's or Kipling's at their best.

S.D.S., Jr. "A Deal in Wheat and Other Stories." *The Reader*, 2 (November 1903), 635–36.

One story in this volume stands out clearly and distinctly as reaching the high level of Frank Norris's very best work. Not in the comprehensive sense of the novel, with broad far-reaching sympathies and characterizations, but with special attention to the presentation of one tragic episode, and of one man whose life's ending was the acme of honorable tragedies. It is well to disregard the title story—titular, in fact—to speak of the achievement, the masterpiece that is called "A Memorandum of Sudden Death." "A simple setting forth of a young man's emotions in the very face of violent death," which came, of course, to the suppositious writer. It is enough to say that every single sensation, every thrill of pain or pleasure that one individual member of a forlorn hope, one soldier on an Indian trail, hopelessly encompassed by his savage enemies, found within him nerve and actual physical force sufficient to record, in throbbing intervals of agony, the details of the throes of death, are given. Up to the very end there is no false note, no mawkish sentimentality; there is nothing but the honest record of the ebbing of an honorable life.

The story that gives the book its name may possibly have suggested the theme—or have been a part of the suggestion—of Mr. Norris's projected trilogy—the "Epic of the Wheat." It has to do with the subject to which his later life's energies were devoted. In itself it has more of promise than performance, and it is difficult to consider it otherwise than in the shadow of its successors. It is a good story of its kind, but Norris has made so many other bigger things happen in his bigger books that this particular ruination of an individual through trade manipulations seems comparatively trivial. There are other stories in different veins—eking out the volume: some of them display qualities of humor that might well have been carried forward. Some of them show a knowledge of the sea, its charm and its compelling mystery that one would hardly have expected from this author—in his latter phase an apostle of the fact, if ever there was one. Conclusively, there is this to be said about these stories as a whole: they reflect the experiences, the life, the observations of a man who had gone over the world. A man whose impulse and desire was always to see the light, and yet who could not be blind to the shadow that is the light's inevitable companion. A writer who has made his mark upon the literature of our time, and who will be remembered as one of the most honest and conscientious, as well as most capable chroniclers of his time.

"A Deal in Wheat."
Academy and Literature, 65 (November 7, 1903), 500, 502.

In this volume Mr. Norris maintains the wealth of colour and colossal vitality which one has learned to associate with his realistic stories of western life. His style, disproportionate and cramping if confined to the four walls of humdrum, is well suited to the vastness of the Sierras and to the loneliness of the high seas. "A Deal in Wheat" is the first of ten stories of leather-lunged men of the Western States. This first story, which gives the title to the book, is full of bustle and rings true, but is somewhat difficult to understand unless one is familiar with the language of the Stock Exchange. As a character-sketch "Bunt" is quite a creation: he is described as a "horse wrangler, miner, faro dealer and bone gatherer"; and in Bunt's mouth many of the shorter stories are put. He has a wealth of expression: "one 'greaser' is the kin wot'ud steal the coppers off his dead grandmother's eyes." A fine bit of work which alone makes the book worth reading is a "Memorandum of Sudden Death," the last record of a sporting journalist who enlists in the U.S. Cavalry in order to gain experience. He is killed in the process. With three other troopers he finds himself cut off by a band of hostile Indians, and between the intervals of firing his last cartridges, wounded to death, the horses shot, his companions killed, he calmly writes this memorandum of sudden death. Well, it is the best story in the collection, and it is immaterial who found the loose sheets of the MS., or whether the notes were written in pencil or ink. A "Bargain with Peg Leg" also makes good reading, but it ends with a regrettable and very old story. Mr. Norris drew men for men; for the feminine world and its influences on the tides and affairs of men he had little mention in this book. His women are poor things: one starves, another loves her husband's employer, and a third is a man, in disguise!

"A Deal in Wheat, and Other Stories."
The Athenaeum,
November 7, 1903,
p. 613.

The author of "The Octopus" and "The Pit" would not, we think, have given to the stories which fill this volume the honour of publication in book form. Yet, since he is no longer with us, we are inclined to consider the publication justifiable. The stories are a good way below the level of his best work, but they are characteristic, full of muscular force and energy. They are not original work, in the sense that the never completed trilogy on wheat was. The motif in one of them is really *vieux jeu*, we mean the story which ends with: " 'The joke of it was,' finished Bunt, 'that they hadn't any blanket.' " In one or two others, which deal with the seafaring adventure, we find an entire lack of originality, matter and manner being both so strongly derivative as to read almost as parody. The opening story, from which the book takes its title, is in the author's characteristic vein, and presents strongly his hatred of that soulless form of commerce in which dwellers in cities, who never see wheat, gamble in the world's food supplies, ruining producers and buyers alike in their mad thirst for speculative gains.

"Frank Norris' Short Stories."
San Francisco Chronicle,
November 15, 1903,
p. 8.

"A Deal in Wheat and Other Stories" is the title of a volume of Frank Norris' short stories, the main one evidently a study for "The Pit." This tale is interesting and it contains some dramatic scenes but it proves very conclusively that Norris was not at his best in the short story. He needed the opportunity to reiterate his main points in various ways until at last he had made an ineffaceable impression upon the reader's mind. These eleven stories are all good as brief studies of life and character but they will be forgotten when "The Octopus" and "The Pit" are well remembered.

"The Book Buyer's Guide."
The Critic, 44
(April 1904),
382.

These are not to be ignored because they are short stories while their author was famed as a writer of long ones. They are quite good enough to command attention, independently. Doubtless the title story will be anticipated with most interest by Mr. Norris's admirers, because of its having been a kind of preliminary sketch written during the preparation of "The Pit." Yet it is by no means the best in this collection of striking and unhackneyed tales, which are rather the more interesting for not being in the ordinary short-story manner. There is a background of the West in all the stories, strongly and competently sketched in. The characters, too, are set forth with an admirable ease that suggests that their author knew a great deal more about them than he told.

Mr. Norris liked the unusual and the dramatic. He also liked horrors, which he handled ably, if not always discreetly; and he liked to place them in near and perilous juxtaposition to comedy. "A Bargain with Peg-Leg" is eminently characteristic of its writer. The story that is likely to be remembered the longest, however, is that striking "Memorandum of Sudden Death," in which Mr. Norris surpasses his ordinary level of performance in achieving an effect of extreme horror without affronting description of material unloveliness and unsightliness. It may or may not be likely that a young United States trooper with an interest in writing fiction should have kept a journal, in concise, vivid fragments, up to the very moment of his death at the hands of Indians who had been following him and his companions across the desert for four days. At all events, such a question would never occur while reading the story, which is the important point.

It is to be regretted that the delightful stories of adventure which deal with those modern San Francisco pirates, the "Three Black Crows," and their cruises in behalf of the "South Pacific Exploration Company," were not published separately. In geniality and humor they are greatly ahead of much of Mr. Norris's more ambitious work.

The author of "The Pit" is not at his best in writing a love story, but the two included in this collection are to be commended. The faults of Mr. Norris's novels, faults of structure and of taste, do not appear in this admirable volume, which is a most prepossessing medium through which to view a writer who has had no lack of praise.

THE RESPONSIBILITIES OF THE NOVELIST

AND OTHER LITERARY ESSAYS

BY

FRANK NORRIS

NEW YORK
DOUBLEDAY, PAGE & COMPANY
1903

The Responsibilities of the Novelist

"Frank Norris on the Responsibilities of the Novelist."
Literary Digest, 25 (December 20, 1902), 831–32.

A pathetic interest attaches to two posthumous articles by Frank Norris, which appear in the current issues of *The Critic* and *The World's Work*. They represent some of the last work that he ever did; but they are so buoyant and virile, they seem so prophetic of work he was yet to do, that it is difficult indeed to imagine that the hand that wrote them is already still.

The novel, declares Mr. Norris, in his article in *The Critic*, is "the great expression of modern life." It may be superseded in the future by a higher form of art, but to-day it is "essential—because it expresses modern life better than architecture, better than painting, better than poetry, better than music.... It is that thing which, in the hand of man, makes him civilized and no longer savage, because it gives him a power of durable, permanent expression." We quote further:

"How necessary it becomes, then, for those who, by the simple art of writing, can invade the heart's heart of thousands, whose novels are received with such measureless earnestness—how necessary it becomes for those who wield such power to use it rightfully. Is it not expedient to act fairly? Is it not in heaven's name essential that the people learn, not a lie, but truth?

"If the novel were not one of the most important factors of modern life, if it were not the completest expression of our civilization, if its influence were not greater than all the pulpits, than all the newspapers between the oceans, it would not be so important that its message should be true.

"But the novelist to-day is the one who reaches the greatest audience. Right or wrong, the people turn to him the moment he speaks, and what he says they believe."

In view of the great responsibilities involved, continues Mr. Norris, how is it possible for novelists to look so frivolously upon their craft? Why do we not brand as "disreputable" the novelist who is "in literature for his own pocket every time"? Mr. Norris continues:

"The people have a right to the truth as they have a right to life, liberty, and the pursuit of happiness. It is *not* right that they be exploited and deceived with false views of life, false characters, false sentiment, false morality, false history, false philosophy, false emotions, false heroism, false notions of self-sacrifice, false views of religion, of duty, of conduct, and of manners.

"The man who can address an audience of one hundred and fifty thousand people who—unenlightened—*believe what he says* has a heavy duty to perform, and tremendous responsibilities to shoulder; and he should address himself to his task not with the flippancy of the catch-penny juggler at the county fair, but with earnestness, with soberness, with a sense of his limitations, and with all the abiding sincerity that by the favor and mercy of the gods may be his."

In his article in *The World's Work*, Mr. Norris considers the "neglected epic" in American life—the story of the conquest of the West. Here again are involved the "responsibilities" of writers who have failed to record the heroism of their own people. We quote:

"The young Greeks sat on marble terraces overlooking the Ægean Sea and listened to the thunderous roll of Homer's hexameters. In the feudal castles the minstrel sang to the young boys, of Roland. The farm folk of Iceland to this very day treasure up and read to their little ones handwritten copies of the Grettla Saga chronicling the deeds and death of Grettir the Strong. But the youth of the United States learn of their epic by paying a dollar to see the 'Wild West Show.'

"The plain truth of the matter is that we have neglected our epic—the black shame of it be on us—and no contemporaneous poet or chronicler thought it worth his while to sing the song or tell the tale of the West, because literature in the day when the West was being won was a cult indulged in by certain well-bred gentlemen in New England who looked eastward to the Old World, to the legends of England and Norway and Germany and Italy for their inspiration, and left the great, strong, honest, fearless, resolute deeds of their own countrymen to be defamed and defaced by the nameless hacks of the 'yellow-back' libraries. . . .

"The great figure of our neglected epic, the Hector of our ignored Iliad, is not, as the dime novels would have us believe, a lawbreaker, but a lawmaker; a fighter, it is true, as is always the case with epic figures, but a fighter for peace, a calm, grave, strong man who hated the lawbreaker as the hound hates the wolf. . . .

"He died in defense of an ideal, an epic hero, a legendary figure, formidable, sad. He died facing down injustice, dishonesty, and crime; died 'in his boots'; and the same world that has glorified Achilles and forgotten Travis finds none so poor to do him reverence. No literature has sprung up around him—this great character native to America. He is of all the world-types the one distinctive to us—peculiar, particular, and unique. He is dead, and even his work is misinterpreted and misunderstood. His very memory will soon be gone, and the American epic, which on the shelves of posterity should have stood shoulder to shoulder with the 'Hemskringla' and the 'Tales of the Nibelungen' and the 'Song of Roland,' will never be written."

"Books and Their Makers."
Boston Herald, February 15, 1903, p. 38.

From [Doubleday, Page & Co.] we are to have a volume of essays containing the "Literary Essays" of the late Frank Norris. These papers are supposedly the clever and pungent articles which Mr. Norris contributed to the Critic. The "Complete Memorial Edition" of Mr. Norris' works is to appear in eight volumes, limited to 150 sets.

"The Pit," by the way, sprang into popularity from the day it was issued. Within a week the fourth edition was ready, and preparations had been made to print a fifth edition of 20,000 copies as quickly as several establishments could manufacture them. The book well deserves its success.

"A Mine of Thought." *Public Opinion*, 35 (October 22, 1903), 536.

These essays are the expressions of a novelist of high ideals who united with that fact the advantage of being numbered with the unostentatious "arrived." "For the million, life is a contracted affair," explains Mr. Norris, "they trust to the novelist for expansion. It is essential that he should not lie. . . . He moulds public opinion." The essay "A Neglected Epic" shows the inspiration under which he was writing when he was taken away. "What has the conquest of the west produced in the way of literature," he bemoans. "The dime novel, the wild west show! Now the time has gone by." But those who have been caught in the fascination of the epic of the wheat feel that he was in a way of creating literature. The volume is a mine of thought which, we fear, none but he could work properly.

"The Novelist as Preacher." *Times Literary Supplement* (London), October 23, 1903, p. 304.

The late Mr. Frank Norris was known as the author of vast romances on the wheat trade of America, agriculture, freights, railways, farmers, rifles, and villains. What romance and instruction as to life and manners and economics could be extracted from his materials he conscientiously gave. His novels were by no means deficient in intelligence and vigour, but were written in a noisy tub-thumping style, many sentences concluding with three adjectives piled upon each other, as "he was grim, ferocious, truculent." With several excellent qualities Mr. Norris could not be suspected of critical genius or of refined learning. His essays on "The Responsibilities of Novelists" display Mr. Norris taking his office very seriously. He must have been interviewed a great deal, and taught to think of the art of fiction with great solemnity. His style includes such gems as "phenomenally large circulations." Like Mrs. Proudie he rejoices in "surely, surely," and, for all we know, had been "destined to the pulpit," which he would have adorned. He speaks of a manuscript "lost under peculiarly distressing circumstances"; the worn verbal coinage of the American newspaper supplies his rhetoric. He thinks that "the esthetic cult" is equivalent to "persons of aesthetic culture," and that it takes a verb in the plural—"The esthetic cult have no conception." He actually avers that "the best class of novels proves something." The mathematician could not see what "Paradise Lost" proved; nor can we. The idea that anything can be proved by a work of fiction is the standing delusion of the modern didactic novelist; as if one were to write a romance to prove that Bacon was, or was not, Shakespeare, or to demonstrate the unity of the Iliad, or a theory of the origin of totemism. Such novels, religious, social, political, or metaphysical, are simply long-winded tracts, and prove no more than does "Meat in the Pan, or the Young Butcher Boy Rescued." "The Novel" is placed on a level with the pulpit and the Press— and is as useful as the pulpit as an instrument of scientific demonstration. Mr. Norris, however, was perfectly solemn about "the Novel" and its influence on "the People." The people does not read "the Novel," men of any class rarely read it, and, when they do, it is for entertainment, which they seldom get. "The People" is actually said to prefer Flaubert to Goncourt! The people never heard of either of them, and, in America, does not know French. Mr. Norris's French is all wrong in the accents. He is justly severe on the odious, trashy, historical novels, which, in America, have been advertised into large popularity among "Little People." "Do these Little People know that Scott's archaeology was about one thousand years 'out' in 'Ivanhoe'?" They do not; nor do we. The slips in "Ivanhoe" are obvious—Zernebock has no business there—but Scott knew more archaeology than all later novelists put together, though he did not always choose to be constant to what he knew. Bad as the popular medieval and other historical novels recently published in America are, they are morally harmless, much better reading than the malevolently mendacious newspapers, if Mr. Norris describes them correctly. Mr. Norris finds that Mr. Howells alone is left as the American novelist. Hawthorne, an infinitely higher name, has not enough of "a vigorous original Americanism." So much the worse for Americanism, if her greatest and most original writer of romance is not sufficiently American. The American girl "is not an active animal," she is always in the house, and "as like as not reading," and what she reads is "the feeblest, thinnest, most colourless, lucubrations," or novels. We are impatient of the colossal conceit of pampered novelists, weary of their talk about themselves, their trade, their cosmic influence. Except in a very few cases, they have no influence; they only fill with their preachments the minds of some women who know not their right hands from their left, in matters intellectual. Only they, not "the People," "believe" the novelist. The rest of mankind does not believe a word he says, and merely asks him to entertain them, a duty to which he prefers preaching and talking about himself. "The United States do not want and do not need scholars," says Mr. Norris grandly. The United States have them, whether they want them or not; have far more sound scholars than novelists whose pages an educated man takes the trouble to cut open. But the scholars help to maintain a standard of reading high above the tub-thumping novel; they do their work, they hold their tongues. To them Mr. Norris's honest, ignorant, noisy essays in criticism are a deplorable but unimportant example of degeneracy.

"The Responsibilities of the Novelist."
The Spectator, 91 (October 31, 1903), 710.

Mr. Norris takes the American point of view, and what he says has, accordingly, to be occasionally modified by the English reader. Nevertheless, this same reader, if he has written, or proposes to write, a novel—and how great a multitude are these two classes combined—will find it useful.

"The Rambler."
The Lamp, 27 (November 1903), 342–44.

The late Frank Norris's literary essays, marshalled handsomely between covers, under the title "The Responsibilities of the Novelist," impress one, on the first browsing, with a sense of vague regret. Here is something that should not have been; yet one knows not at first exactly what nor why. But, as you read, the feeling grows that this book would never have appeared had the author lived to decide the question for himself. The essays are good—amazingly good, some of them; their sanity never fails; their simplicity and force lack nothing; they are fresh, leisurely, progressive, healthy. But they are young and uneven. Norris was a man who grew fast. There are five years between some of these essays, written, according to the bibliography in the back of the volume, only a few months apart. The book's entire contents was dashed off within two years, and in that time Norris grew ten. We venture the prediction that none of the essays in the present volume would have passed muster of this growing author for admission to his ranks of books. Already, had he lived till now, would the best and latest of them have seemed trivial and partial in his eyes.

And yet, considered apart from the personality and rapid development of their writer, these essays are profitable. If they solve no problems, if they open no new fields, if they add nothing to the sum or the statement of truth, they at least restate familiar facts and conditions with singular clearness and force, delightful freshness, unerring selection, and complete sanity. And not the least of the pleasure they give is the melancholy contemplation of a mind that, had it survived, would inevitably have been in front of the literary movement the beginnings of which are already, in the opinion of many, at hand.

We quote, as an example of Frank Norris's character and quality as a man of letters, the final paragraphs of his essay on the responsibilities of the novelist:

"The Pulpit, the Press, and the Novel—these indisputably are the great moulders of public morals to-day. But the Pulpit speaks but once a week; the Press is read with lightning haste, and the morning news is waste-paper by noon. But the Novel goes into the home to stay. It is read word for word; is talked about, discussed; its influence penetrates every chink and corner of the family.

"Yet novelists are not found wanting who write for money. I do not think this is an unfounded accusation. I do not think it asking too much of credulity. This would not matter if they wrote the

Truth. But these gentlemen who are 'in literature for their own pocket every time' have discovered that for the moment the People have confounded the Wrong with the Right, and prefer that which is a lie to that which is true. 'Very well, then,' say these gentlemen. 'If they want a lie, they shall have it'; and they give the People a lie in return for royalties.

"The surprising thing about this is that you and I and all the rest of us do not consider this as disreputable—do not yet realize that the novelist has responsibilities. We condemn an editor who sells his editorial columns, and we revile the pulpit attainted of venality. But the venal novelist—he whose influence is greater than either the Press or the Pulpit—*him* we greet with a wink and the tongue in the cheek.

"This should not be so. Somewhere the protest should be raised, and those of us who see the practice of this fraud should bring home to ourselves the realization that the selling of one hundred and fifty thousand books is a serious business. The People have a right to the Truth as they have a right to life, liberty, and the pursuit of happiness. It is *not* right that they be exploited and deceived with false views of life, false characters, false sentiment, false morality, false history, false philosophy, false emotions, false heroism, false notions of self-sacrifice, false views of religion, of duty, of conduct, and of manners.

"The man who can address an audience of one hundred and fifty thousand people who—unenlightened—*believe what he says*, has a heavy duty to perform, and tremendous responsibilities to shoulder; and he should address himself to his task, not with the flippancy of a catch-penny juggler at the county fair, but with earnestness, with soberness, with a sense of his limitations, and with all the abiding sincerity that by the favor and mercy of the gods may be his."

The bibliography in the back of the book shows that in a period short of twelve years from his beginnings, Mr. Norris published fifty articles and essays, sixty-nine short stories, four poems, and six novels.

"Frank Norris' Essays." *San Francisco Chronicle*, November 1, 1903, p. 8.

There is much strong, vigorous writing in "The Responsibilities of the Novelist and Other Literary Essays," by Frank Norris. Most of the chapters appeared in the Critic and other New York periodicals during the last year of the young California novelist's life. These papers cover a wide range, but they all preach the creed that Norris illustrated in his own work. They all declare for originality, for description of the spirit of the life that the author really knows, for sincerity and absolute truth to nature. They are good to read, and one who has been interested in the brilliant young author of "The Octopus" and "The Pit" will find here something of the same spirit that flashes out in those stories.

Francis Thompson. "The Responsibilities of the Novelist, and Other Literary Essays." *Academy and Literature*, 65 (November 7, 1903), 491.

Here is a volume of essays on his own art by an American novelist who died "just as he really promised something great," and had in two novels (of which "The Octopus" was the first) partially achieved it. An author on his art may be right or wrong, but is always supremely interesting. For he writes of the one thing which he has most deeply and lovingly studied; and even if he go astray about its general principles, he reveals incidentally how he himself envisaged his art. This and a vital earnestness are the main interests of Mr. Norris's essays. We have encountered little in the book which has not been said, at one time or another, and well said, by English critics. But it is uttered with fiery zeal, with a gallant directness and downrightness in place of the cultivated and tempered critical suavity, and with the burning conviction of a man enunciating a new gospel. Such it may be in America; and even here it acquires a certain force of novelty by the forthright homespokenness of the author.

At the same time there is little of critical balance and comprehensiveness. He starts, for instance, by inveighing against those who would have the novelist on no account "write down to his audience"—would have him independent of his readers. On the contrary, says Mr. Norris, more than all others he should defer to his audience, should "feel his public" and watch his every word—"in a word, possess a sense of his responsibilities." Yet in the very next essay he vehemently asserts: "The eye never once should wander to the gallery, but be always with single purpose turned inward upon the work, testing and re-testing it that it rings true." He scorns those who "find out what the public want, and give it to the public cheap." He applauds the novelist who "never truckled," who is "independent of fashion and the gallery-gods." Yet he has previously said that "the People pronounce the final judgment," the People "are the real seekers after truth." He answers himself, and supplies the antidote to his own rash statements. For clearly he confused a just reverence for one's auditory and the responsibilities imposed by one's auditory with the popularity-mongering departure from the irreversible principles of art. It is against the latter alone that any true critic protests. And he shows that he is just as disdainful of outside opinion where the laws of art are concerned as the most fastidious critic could exact. As to the assertion about the People, it has been answered in these columns time and again.

Such is what we mean by his lack of critical balance. But he cries truths impressively, if not newly. His protest against the venal novelist—that "the People have a right to the truth as they have a right to life, liberty, and happiness," and that the lying novel is a more potent agent of falsehood than pulpit or press—this is a thing even more needed in America than here. The same may be said of his protest against the empty romance. The essence of romance is not clothes and externals, but the seizing of the spirit of an age. "Ivanhoe" is a huge anachronism in the matter of costume. And why not realism even in the historical novel, he asks? It is a fruitful hint, and there is a fortune for the novelist who can achieve it. But, indeed, did not Thackeray and George Eliot endeavour it? Romance, he exclaims, is everywhere, is under our feet, if novelists could see it. This determination to drag to the surface the romance inherent in the most sordid-seeming matters of modern life was the inspiration of the novel which made him famous. Bearing on his own work, also, is the essay concerning novels with a purpose. They are, he thinks, the greatest kind of novel; but the moment the novelist becomes wrapped up in his purpose, the novel fails. It must be his motive; but his main pre-occupation must be with his story and characters. Surely the truth is that any artist who sincerely develops a piece of life must involuntarily assume an attitude towards life; and in the exposition of that attitude will develop a philosophy of life the more effectual for being unconscious. That is the best "purpose." But we have said enough to show that here is a book worth reading in right of its artistic energy and earnestness.

"The Responsibilities of the Novelist."
The Nation (England), 77 (November 19, 1903), 411–12.

This collection of short papers written by the late Frank Norris expresses great zeal for his profession, and an ingenuous conviction that, if practised in conformity with his theories, it is an indispensable agent in the progress of humanity towards perfection. Personal ador for his work is the interesting quality of the book, compelling the attention and sympathy even of readers who permit themselves to smile at the author's self-sufficiency, and who may be bored by his clamorous manner of making the simplest statement.

After Mr. Norris's death the opinion was generally expressed that we had lost a good novelist who would surely have become a great one. Speculation on what might have been is never very profitable, but in this instance was perhaps justified by the imaginative force and eager spirit evident in Mr. Norris's published fiction. Assurance of his splendid possibilities can hardly survive the republication of these casual papers, which had better have been allowed to perish, for they show defects—defects of knowledge, of judgment, of taste—that militate against achievement of greatness in any direction. Such defects, it is true, might have been modified by time, but they seem to be rooted in an unconscious ignorance, showing itself in disparagement of things Mr. Norris did not know, of advantages and accomplishments that he did not possess, in a total absence of personal background and of attachment to a past that should stand for an older self, from which one's feelings and theories may derive strength and value.

It seems ungracious to dwell on the imperfections of a writer who in his short span of life went far, and it would be superfluous to do so, were it not that his work expresses in an extreme fashion some regrettable idiosyncrasies of young American writers, especially of those who come out of the West. Few of them have Mr. Norris's native force, but they have similar faiths, and can shout them as vociferously as he, even in self-contradiction. For them the Declaration of Independence marks the dawn of time; their country, besides being "God's own country," is his only one; at their birth, Truth (which they never define but always spell with a capital letter) came up from the bottom of her well to salute them; according to them "The People, The Plain People," are (as they delight to say, "in the last analysis") the appointed infallible judges of all things, and, the judgment of literature being their special function, they have decided offhand, yet finally, that "mere literature" must go. The prose style of this happily confident band is an experimental (perhaps accidental) blend of many ostentatious styles (Carlyle, Dickens, Macaulay), and their vocabulary is largely their own.

Every one of Mr. Norris's articles illustrates some of these idiosyncrasies. About the Truth and the Plain People and the duty of the novelist to provide the one for the other, his concern is shrill:

> In the larger view, in the last analysis, the People pronounce the final judgment. The People, despised of the artist, hooted, caricatured, and vilified, are, after all, and in the main, the real seekers after Truth. . . . Is it not, in Heaven's name, essential that the people hear not a lie, but the Truth? If the novel were not one of the most important factors of life; if it were not the completest expression of our civilization; if its influence were not greater than all the pulpits, than all the newspapers between the oceans, it would not be so important that its message should be true. . . . Yet novelists are not found wanting who write for money. I do not think this is an unfounded accusation. I do not think it asking too much of credulity. This would not matter if they wrote the Truth.

The strain comes o'er the ear like the voice of the great Chadband, demanding to know: "What is the T-r-ewth? Is not a lie. No!"

Mr. Norris is very hard on his brethren who wilfully trick the Plain People, offering a lie in glittering armor; but, on the whole, he concludes that it is better for Americans to read them than not to read at all, because "books have never done harm." The only Americans who may not read are the modern novelists. They are peremptorily forbidden such recreation, lest they should not be able to address the Plain People simply and intelligibly. "Books have no place in his equipment, have no right to be there—will only cumber and confuse him." The writer himself has indeed suffered no little confusion from the reading of books, either too much or too little. In a paper called "A Neglected Epic," he laments the failure of contemporary Americans to celebrate in epic form "the conquering of the West, the subduing of the wilderness beyond the Mississippi," and mentions the achievements in that way of other and earlier races. Why, he wonders angrily, has no great bard sung the Alamo, where Texans fought and died for several things enumerated, much more honorable than "loot and the possession of an adulteress"; and why, again, is "Achilles, murderer, egotist, ruffian, and liar," a hero, while the apparently immaculate name of Bowie "is perpetuated only in the designation of a knife"? Clearly, Mr. Norris did not read enough to be disturbed by a Homer question, or by any suggestion that national epics have not been written at the moment when the action celebrated was going on. He seems to think that Homer sat before the beleaguered city while the great fight waged, calmly inditing an immortal tale; that Tasso accompanied the crusaders to Jerusalem; and that *trouveres* were singing the songs of Roland when he blew his horn for succor at Roncesvalles. Though epics seemed to him desirable productions, he may have thought that to know anything about their history savored of scholarship, a thing he despised and distrusted. "The United States," he writes, "in this year of grace nineteen hundred and two, does not want and does not need scholars, but Men—Men made in the mould of the Leonard Woods and the Theodore Roosevelts." And, pursuing the subject hotly, he quotes "so high an authority as Dr. Patton of Princeton, who has recently said that nowadays men do not go to college to become scholars, and that it was time and money wasted to try and make them such." This was an indiscreet speech for any professor of any university to make, and if Dr. Patton should read the works of Mr. Norris and many of his contemporaries, he might come to fear that the responsibilities of a professor may be almost as solemn as the responsibilities of a novelist.

"The Responsibilities of the Novelist." *The Athenaeum*, November 28, 1903, p. 718.

The Responsibilities of the Novelist, by Frank Norris, contains close upon thirty short essays upon literary topics. The title of the book is that of the first, and is well chosen, for the reason that it strikes a note which runs all through the volume; "The True Reward of the Novelist," "The Need of a Literary Conscience," and similar titles, show the general trend of the writer's thought and attitude. It is a very readable and characteristic book, full of the strenuous and frank enthusiasm which marked all that the author did in life—of the faults which usually go with such temperaments as his was, and which are never on the niggard side and never paltry. Thus, in considering the responsibilities of the novelist, the author argues:—

> But the novelist to-day is the one who reaches the greatest audience. Right or wrong, the People turn to him the moment he speaks, and what he says they believe.

Yet later, in the heat of demonstrating that the retail bookseller of

America is a literary dictator, he says:—

> Author, critic, analyst, and essayist may hug to themselves a delusive phantom of hope that they are the moulders of public opinion, they and they alone, &c.

As a strenuous man must, he wrote generally as a partisan, and it may well be that he exaggerated somewhat the influence wielded nowadays by the popular novelist. But his contentions remain good and wholesome.

Hamilton W. Mabie. "Studies in Literature." *The Outlook*, 75 (December 1903), 829–30.

Mr. Bagehot somewhere says that as a result of the teaching of Greek and Latin in the English public schools the boys did not always learn those languages, but they became convinced that there are such languages. Books which deal with literary subjects are not always literature, but they involve recognition of the fact that there is such a thing as good writing, and they evidence the existence of a widespread interest in it. When that interest shall take a foremost place in the minds of those who govern by virtue of superior intelligence is simply a question of time; sooner or later the expression of the soul of a people becomes a matter of necessity. In this country many have become impatient because the adequate voices are so late in speaking, and some have begun to despair; but there is no occasion either for impatience or despair. Art was never born in a day, and there are good and sufficient reasons why Americans should be later than other peoples in producing the most sensitive and perfect flower of civilization. We have said some true and deep things already, and we have said them in a language which has not lacked beauty or nobility; we must give the great processes of growth time to run their course before we demand the ultimate insight and power. Meanwhile we are dissatisfied with our achievements, and that is a good sign; and we are groping about eagerly, if somewhat blindly, for the larger products and the deeper forces of art, and that is a better sign.

If Mr. Frank Norris had lived, the collection of his short papers issued in book form by Messrs. Doubleday, Page & Co., under the title "The Responsibilities of the Novelist," would probably have remained unpublished; now that he has gone, at the beginning of a very promising career, they are interesting as disclosing his ideals of art and his discontent with existing conditions. The papers are short, and have the newspaper rather than the book quality; they are fragmentary, discursive, and brusque in style. They must be read in connection with "The Octopus" and "The Pit" in order to be understood. Mr. Norris made the mistake, at the beginning of his career, of confounding crudity with strength, and delicacy and refinement with weakness. He had the consciousness of the possession of individual force, and he felt deeply the vital connection between life and art. He looked for force, virility, bold speech, original power; and these things are rare in current literature; its excellences are of another kind.

Norris began with an omnivorous appetite for life and a very untrained instinct for art. His early stories were powerful, but in a very elementary way; they dealt with coarse forms of life in a blunt, crude fashion. But as he went on toward clearer vision and deeper knowledge he began to distinguish between the really characteristic and the essentially vulgar, and to learn the secrets of that art which is the very quintessence of power without a suggestion of raw energy. He had long passed out of the blacksmith stage of hammering his themes by main force, and had given substantial evidence not only of remarkable growth but of unusual power, and when his career was arrested he seemed to stand on the threshold of a notable artistic achievement.

These papers must be read in the light of this brief history of a powerful mind working itself clear of a tendency towards raw individualism in selection and construction. They are often crude in form and rough in style; they were written for the moment in the speech of that moment; they are full of rash judgments, of misconceptions of the relations of the books of the time to the conditions of the time; they are not, in themselves, of permanent value. But when all these things have been said, it must be added that this volume is highly significant of that reaction against imitation, conventionality, and commercialism in book-making in which all young writers of real power share, and which is prophetic of the better things which are to come.

Mr. Crothers's volume of essays, "The Gentle Reader," which bears the imprint of Messrs. Houghton, Mifflin & Co., is in another vein, and would perhaps draw the fire of some of Mr. Norris's young contemporaries, who would charge it with a too easy surrender to old-time standards, a too facile adoption of old-time methods. The title suggests slippered ease, indoor content, and class distinctions; it recalls the time when reading was a privilege, not a necessity, and writers spoke chiefly to a small circle of readers.

Now, it must be confessed that these essays do not deal with elemental passions, burning questions, the turbulent contentions of contemporary business life; it must be confessed that they have the air of having been written in a library, and that they assume a considerable familiarity with books and history on the part of the reader. But shall there be no quiet places in the world, no ease of mood, no play of the mind, no charm of humor or grace of manner in modern writing? In order to be strong must we cease to be good company to our friends and agreeable persons to our generation? Mr. Crothers is, by reason of his quiet humor, his easy, restful touch, his fine idealism, a writer peculiarly adapted to speak to a restless time and to remind it that there were good things before our age, and that if wisdom is not to perish with us we must take time to ripen as well as to stir and storm through our allotted years.

"Norris—The Responsibilities of the Novelist." *The Critic*, 43 (December 1903), 576.

Mr. Norris was very serious, very "up-to-date," and not in the least ambiguous in these essays on the art and the trade of novel-writing and a variety of allied topics. He made, however, no effort to cultivate the essay as a literary form and the preeminent value of these papers lies in their being the sincere expression of a clever and successful novelist's opinions. Many of the essays originally appeared in *The Critic* and will not need recalling to its readers. The book contains a complete bibliography of Mr. Norris's works.

"The Responsibilities of the Novelist." *Out West*, 19 (December 1903), 688.

A number of Frank Norris's later essays, mostly upon various phases of literary work, are published under the title, *The Responsibilities of the Novelist*. They are always vigorous, often polemic, and, without exception, show marks of haste and lack of preparation. Mr. Norris held high ideals of the power and duty of the writer of fiction, and worked steadily towards them. The value of his work as essayist lies mainly in his formal statement of his self-imposed standard as novelist. The proof-reader has made some exceptionally bad blunders.

THE THIRD CIRCLE

BY
FRANK NORRIS
AUTHOR OF "THE PIT," "THE OCTOPUS," ETC.

INTRODUCTION BY
WILL IRWIN

LONDON: JOHN LANE, THE BODLEY HEAD
NEW YORK: JOHN LANE COMPANY
MCMIX

The Third Circle

"Stories by Frank Norris."
New York Times Review of Books,
May 29, 1909,
p. 339.

"Sixteen Stories by Frank Norris: 'The Third Circle.'"
San Francisco Call,
June 13, 1909,
p. 7.

The collection of sketches and short stories by Frank Norris entitled "The Third Circle" (John Lane Company, $1.50) has a melancholy as well as an artistic interest, for it makes evident once more the loss American literature sustained in the early death of the author. The tales are sixteen in number and include publications in various magazines, from the San Francisco Argonaut in 1891 to Everybody's in 1902. Nearly all of them have their scenes laid in San Francisco of the last decade of the nineteenth century and give brief glimpses of life, sudden snatches of light and color, as the author saw them in his walks about the city. None is of much importance in itself, but all are of interest in the view they give of a novelist in the making. And all of them show more or less of those qualities of close observation and vivid rendering which made distinctive his later novels. Will Irwin contributes a brief preface.

As illustrative of the road by which a novelist often reaches his goal the collection of 16 short stories by Frank Norris issued under the title of "The Third Circle" should awaken an interest at once absorbing and profitable. That brilliant, incomprehensible and powerful sketch which gives the book its name tells, as many readers will remember, of the visit of an eastern girl, Harriet Ten Eyck, and her lover, young Hillegas, to the restaurant of the Seventy Moons in the Chinese quarter of San Francisco.

Hillegas descends to the lower story of the restaurant in search of the Chinese boy from whom they had ordered tea, and on his return finds Harriet Ten Eyck vanished as utterly as if the earth had engulfed her. The tale, though possessing inevitable crudities, is a foreshadowing of the extraordinary force and penetration which enabled the writer to see straight to the heart of things and to depict them in the nervous, forcible English which invariably finds its mark. Into his trenchant phrases Norris has managed to infuse much of the inscrutable mystery and melancholy of the east while filling his pages with purely western atmosphere. The terror, rush and finality of the tale are indescribable.

The 15 other stories which comprise Norris' earlier work in this direction range from the tragic note of "Little Dramas of the Curbstone," portrayals of everyday happenings seen through a poet's eyes, through the infinite and subtle pathos of "Toppan," a clever, intellectual fellow married to the woman "who never could understand," but whom he loved nevertheless and for whom he sacrificed his career, to the inimitable American humor of "This Animal of a Buldy Jones." Splendidly skeletonized, these few tales have the merit of a set of fine etchings, where the process of elimination has been carried out to the last possible degree. No one can read these 16 stories without being moved to emotion of some sort. Their tragedy grips you with a sense of illumination; their comedy arouses light-hearted laughter; their pathos stirs something deeper than tears. The tearing apart of the citadel of human nature, as evidenced in his later works, had its beginning here, and in his portrayal of the men and women he chose as subjects the primal instincts, the unconscious basic motives, the age old tendencies of mankind, are laid bare as with a scalpel. The imaginative and descriptive forces at work in "Little Dramas of the Curbstone" rise at times to Zolaesque heights, and if Norris had lived to write the novel of San Francisco which is to place the city before the world in its curiously interwoven social aspects the literary world might have been richer by a book that would have lived.

The volume has an introduction by Will Irwin, friend and comrade of Norris in the old hack days, when Irwin, Norris and Cosgrave, with half a dozen others, worked and strove for success side by side. It is rather a singular fact that of this circle three of its members should have gone east to achieve success, Norris' fame coming immediately on the publication of his first novel, Cosgrave winning honors as the editor of Everybody's Magazine and Irwin achieving marked distinction first as the managing editor of McClure's and afterward in connection with Collier's Weekly and the Saturday Evening Post. Of the trio it was Norris who won his spurs first. His beginnings as a writer were made in San Francisco on the Wave, and it is of these youthful, lucky, easy going days together that Irwin speaks thus in his introductory words. . . .*

"The Third Circle." *The Nation,* 88 (June 17, 1909), 607.

However skeptical some of us may have been as to the absolute excellence of the late Frank Norris's young achievement, few can have doubted that he was on the way to excellence. There was a confident ardor about him that seemed almost a guarantee of success. "I am going to make you people sit up," he said to a friend at the very beginning of his career. The friend thought the remark in rather bad taste, but in due time found himself "sitting up." Norris was thinking in trilogies when death cut him off.

*Here follows the essay by Will Irwin. See "Introduction," *The Third Circle* (New York: John Lane, 1909), pp. 7–11.

His precocity was still manifesting itself, he was pushing a little ahead of his powers. "The Pit" and "The Octopus" must stand, after all, as astonishing exercises rather than as portions of an unfinished masterpiece, but there is no mistaking the power in them, or the promise.

The stories here collected are, says Mr. Irwin in his spirited introduction, "the longest and most important of his prentice products.... They are an incomparable study in the way a genius takes to find himself." This is putting it strong: the claim is scarcely borne out by the contents of the volume. They seem rather to show how a reporter with a realistic bent may become a writer of brilliant magazine stories. We do not gather that these exhibits are here reprinted in chronological order. As they stand they display not so much growth as versatility. They are extremely clever, and, with three or four exceptions, patently "magazinable." The list of copyrights printed at the beginning of the book shows in what different markets Norris succeeded in placing his work. But it is the three or four exceptions which to our mind are most individual and striking. Three of them were, we gather from Mr. Irwin, written before the rest, and stand first in the book. The horror of the incident narrated in "The Third Circle" is intensified by the grim and pithy manner of its telling. The writer has no notion of commenting or enlarging upon his facts: it is enough to present them. "The House with the Blinds" and "Little Dramas of the Curbstone" are not properly stories at all, but sketches of certain chance-seen episodes of city life, each of them with its mystery over the solution of which the artist is perfectly non-committal.

These vivid bits of romantic realism appeared in the San Francisco *Wave*, when Norris was sub-editor thereof—before the East had heard him and summoned him in its peremptory way to stand and deliver the fruits of his fresh talent.

He succeeded in transplanting that talent without destroying it; but we cannot help thinking that much of the matter in the present volume is reliquian of a temporary surrender, or semi-surrender. It would be interesting to know when the story called "Dying Fires" was written. Here we read of a Californian sub-editor, with a genius for comprehending the life about him, who writes a novel which has life and nature in it. An Eastern publisher accepts it, and the young Californian is presently called to the editorial staff of the publisher's magazine. He comes to New York, and falls in with a set of third-rate "authors," who, with their pretensions and affectations, so confuse, mislead, and altogether bedevil the young fellow that he turns from life to phrases. His second novel is as feeble as it is sophisticated. After a time he realizes his mistake, goes back to the Sierras, and "with such sapped and broken strength as New Bohemia had left him, strove to wrest some wreckage from the dying fire." But the last spark is quenched, and "there remains only a little heap of bitter ashes." Happily, there was no such end of the matter for Norris: his torch burned brighter, and he bore it with steadier hand, to the last.

"Frank Norris' 'Third Circle.'"
The California Weekly, 1 (June 25, 1909), 485.

San Francisco life before the earthquake of 1906, with its terrible conditions in the Chinese quarter, and the countless incidents that made thinking men and women thrill with excitement and horror, form the subject of the late Frank Norris' "Third Circle," to be published shortly by John Lane company. The book contains an introduction by Will Irwin, Mr. Norris' intimate friend and associate on the San Francisco Wave. In this introduction Mr. Irwin tells how he and Mr. Gelett Burgess stole into the Wave office by night, after the paper had died a natural death, and took away one of the old files containing the work of Mr. Norris. Mr. Irwin shows how eminently fitted, both by natural talent and newspaper training, Mr. Norris was to write of the life depicted in "Third Circle."

Randolph Edgar.
"'Studio Sketches of a Novelist."
The Bellman, 7 (July 17, 1909), 862–63.

"Don't write a Colonial novel. Don't write a Down East novel. Don't write a Prisoner of Zenda novel. Don't write a novel. Try to keep your friends from writing novels." *From "The Volunteer Manuscript," by Frank Norris.*

The author of these lines of advice, had he lived to reach the full development of his powers, undoubtedly would have attained a position among the greatest of American novelists. For this reason, his "Third Circle," a posthumous collection of short stories and sketches, is of peculiar value, since in its sixteen tales one can trace the unfolding of his mental qualities and gradually see them increasing in force and clarity. In nearly every one can be seen those powers of close observation and vivid rendering that made distinctive his later works.

Frank Norris, it will be recalled, died seven years ago, a comparatively young man, preparing what in all probability would have been his masterpiece. Despite his untimely end before he had remotely approached the maturity of his powers, he had realized in fiction, as no one had yet done, the Western type. Bret Harte had drawn the pioneer, but that generation had passed away to be succeeded by the capitalist, the railroad builder, the speculator, the journalist and even the poet and painter. And each of these types in the peculiar guise of our new Western civilization, Norris had embodied in his brilliant and realistic stories.

Altogether the list of his works, including novels, poems and short stories and essays, numbers over a hundred, only one quarter of which has, until the recent publishing of "The Third Circle," found its way into book form. "The Third Circle" is composed almost entirely of Norris's earliest work written for such papers as the San Francisco Wave and the Argonaut. They are, with few exceptions, taken from life in San Francisco, though one of the most notable of the collection, "Son of a Sheik," written by Norris while yet a student in the University of California, has for its hero a son of the desert who, having received an education in Europe, has become cultivated and civilized. In a moment of stress he stands forth stripped of his education, his untamed fighting spirit aroused and the battle-cry of his race leaping unbidden to his lips.

In the brief preface, which is a pleasing tribute to Frank Norris's genius, Will Irwin writes: "It used to be my duty as sub-editor of the old San Francisco Wave to 'put the paper to bed.' We were printing a Seattle edition in those days of the gold rush and the last form had to be locked up on Tuesday night, that we might reach the news stands by Friday. Working short-handed, as all small weeklies do, we were everlastingly late with copy or illustrations or advertisements; and that Tuesday usually stretched itself out into Wednesday. Most often, indeed, the foreman and I pounded in the last quoin at four or five o'clock Wednesday morning and went home with the milk wagons—to rise at noon and start next week's paper going. For Yelton, most patient and cheerful of foremen, those Tuesday night sessions meant steady work. I, for my part, had only to confer with him now and then on a 'caption' or run over a late proof. In the heavy intervals of waiting I killed time and gained instruction by reading the back files of the Wave, and especially that part of the files which preserved the early, prentice work of Frank Norris. It was a surprising study of the novelist in the making. 'The studio sketches of a great novelist,' Gelett Burgess had called these ventures and fragments. Burgess and I, when the Wave finally died of too much merit, stole into the building and took away one set of old files. A harmless theft of sentiment we told ourselves... When we had them safe at home we spent a night running over them marveling again at these rough creations of blood and nerve which Norris had made out of that city which was the first love of his wakened intelligence, and in which, so woefully soon afterward, he died."

Mr. Irwin compares this work of Frank Norris to a complete collection of Rembrandt's early sketches, the full technique and co-ordination is not yet developed but all the basic force and vision is there. "The Third Circle" affords the reader an incomparable study of the way a genius takes to find himself.

[Jeanette Gilder.] "The Lounger." *Putnam's Magazine*, 6 (August 1909), 629–33.

When I received the advance-sheets of a book called "The Third Circle," by Frank Norris, I picked it up but laid it down again, saying to myself: "What does this mean? There can't be more than one Frank Norris, and he has been dead, alas! for years." Then I picked it up again, and saw that this Frank Norris whose name was on the title-page was the author of "The Pit," "The Octopus," etc., and then I knew that it was *the* Frank Norris. There was an introduction by Will Irwin, and a frontispiece portrait which there was no gainsaying. There were the far-seeing eyes, the sensitive mouth, the artistic hands of the Frank Norris that I had known so well, not so very many years ago. This book is made up mainly of San Francisco stories. Will Irwin in his introduction tells us that it used to be his duty, as editor of the old San Francisco *Wave*, to "put the paper to bed." They were, he tells us, printing a Seattle edition in those days of the Alaskan gold rush, and the last form had to be locked up on Tuesday night, that the paper might reach the newsstands by Friday. Being shorthanded, as all such offices are, everything was late, and, instead of getting to press on Tuesday night, it was usually Wednesday morning before the last quoin was pounded into place.

While Irwin was waiting for the forms to be made up, he killed time by reading over the back files of the *Wave*, especially that part which preserved the early prentice work of Frank Norris. "He was a hero to us all in those days," writes Mr. Irwin, "as he will ever remain a heroic memory—that unique product of our Western soil, killed, for some hidden purpose of the gods, before the time of full blossom." A year before this time, Norris had gone East to look after the publication of his novel "Moran of the Lady Letty." That wise man of the East, S. S. McClure, always had his eye on the West. He read the *Wave*, as he read almost everything that was published, and he read "Moran of the Lady Letty." He immediately sat down and wrote to the author and told him to come to New York and he would publish his book, and that he wanted him to write for *McClure's Magazine*; that, in short, he wanted to be his literary godfather, which in re-

ality he became. But before he wrote "Moran of the Lady Letty," Norris had written a number of short stories for the *Wave*, some longer than others, but most of them comparatively short, and it is these stories that Mr. Irwin has collected and brought together in this book.

According to Mr. Irwin, Mr. J. O'Hara Cosgrave, "owner and editor and burden-bearer of the *Wave*, was in his editing more an artist than a man of business. He loved 'good stuff'; he could not bear to delete a distinctive piece of work just because the populace would not understand. Norris then had a free hand. Whatever his thought of the day, whatever he had seen with the eye of his flesh or the eye of his imagination, he might write and print."

Gelett Burgess, another San Franciscan, calls these stories "the studio sketches of a great novelist"; and it was he, with Will Irwin, who rescued them from a fiery grave. To quote again from Mr. Irwin:

> Burgess and I, when the *Wave* finally died of too much merit, stole into the building by night and took away one set of old files. A harmless theft of sentiment, we told ourselves; for by moral right they belonged to us, the sole survivors in San Francisco of those who had helped make the *Wave*. And, indeed, by this theft we saved them from the great fire of 1906. When we had them safe at home we spent a night running over them, marvelling again at those rough creations of blood and nerve which Norris had made out of that city which was the first love of his awakened in-

telligence, and in which, so woefully, soon afterward he died.

The nucleus of some of his novels will be found in these stories, for the saving and publication of which we owe Mr. Irwin a debt of gratitude. Norris wrote too little for us not to want every scrap from his pen; he never wrote carelessly, and he never wrote a line without a thought in it. After he came to New York, even after the publication of several of his novels, he was not making a great deal of money, nothing like what he ought to have made with his reputation, and he was obliged to do other writing than that of fiction. We engaged him to do a monthly turn for the *Critic*, as *Putnam's Magazine* was then called. It was a sort of go-as-you-please, having the general title of "Salt and Sincerity." The title was a good one, for everything that Norris wrote was sincere, and the salt brought out its flavor. The dramatisation of "The Pit," and its successful production as a play, helped Norris financially, I imagine, more than any of his novels. While he was immensely admired by the few, he did not get the vogue that would ultimately have come to him could he have lived longer and gone on writing.

In some ways I like these short stories of Norris's better than his longer ones. Perhaps, after all, like that other famous San Franciscan, Bret Harte, he was a short-story writer. Bret Harte, if you remember, wrote but one novel, and it would have been just as well if he had not written that. These stories of Norris's are clearer-cut than his novels, less detailed, but what is there is mighty good. The little bits of description, either of places or men, could hardly be improved upon. I am surprised that the *Wave* did not have a circulation equal to that of the *Saturday Evening Post*, for I don't see how any one could have read one of these stories without wanting to read them all. Turn to "The House with the Blinds," and see if it does not whet your appetite for more:

It is a thing said and signed and implicitly believed in by the discerning few, that San Francisco is a place wherein Things can happen. There are some cities like this—cities that have come to be picturesque—that offer opportunities in the matter of background and local color, and are full of stories and dramas and novels, written and unwritten. There seems to be no adequate explanation for this state of things, but you can't go about the streets anywhere within a mile radius of Lotta's fountain without realizing the peculiarity, just as you would realize the hopelessness of making anything out of Chicago. Fancy a novel about Chicago, or Buffalo, let us say, or Nashville, Tennessee. There are just three big cities in the United States that are "story cities"—New York, of course, New Orleans, and, best of the lot, San Francisco.

Here, if you put yourself in the way of it, you shall see life uncloaked and bare of convention—the raw, naked thing, that perplexes and fascinates—life that involves death of the sudden and swift variety, the jar and shock of unleashed passions, the friction of men foregathered from every ocean; and you may touch upon the edge of mysteries for which there is no explanation—little eddies on the surface of unsounded depths, sudden outflashing of the inexplicable—troublesome, disquieting and a little fearful.

Or, the opening of the "Third Circle":

There are more things in San Francisco's Chinatown than are dreamed of in heaven and earth. In reality there are three parts of Chinatown—the part the guides show you, the part the guides don't show you, and the part that no one ever hears of. It is with the latter part that this story has to do. There are many good stories that might be written about this third circle of Chinatown, but believe me, they never will be written—at any rate not until the "town" has been, as it were, drained off from the city, as one might drain a noisome swamp, and we shall be able to see the strange, dreadful life that wallows down there in the lowest ooze of the place—wallows and grovels there in the mud and in the dark. If you don't think this is true, ask some of the Chinese detectives (the regular squad are not to be relied on). Ask them to tell you the story of the Lee On Ting affair; or ask them what was done to old Wong Sam, who thought he could break up the trade in slave girls; or why Mr. Clarence Lowney (he was a clergyman from Minnesota who believed in direct methods) is now a "dangerous" inmate of the State Asylum. Ask them to tell you why Matsokura, the Japanese dentist, went back to his home lacking a face. Ask them to tell you why the murderers of Little Pete will never be found, and ask them to tell you about the little slave girl, Sing Yee. Or—no; on the second thought, don't ask for that story.

These stories belong to the history of San Francisco—of that city as it was before the great fire, and as it will never be again. San Francisco will rise, phœnix-like, from her ashes and spread her wings over her hills; but she will never again have the romance about her streets and buildings that she had in the days when Norris wrote these stories. It is the San Francisco of the past—the mysterious, romantic, gruesome San Francisco, if you will—where "things happened" that could happen in no other city in this country. I am sorry that no one has written of New York as Norris has written of San Francisco. We must have the plots for just as many strange stories here, but we have not had the storytellers. I don't mean to say that no stories have been written around the out-of-the-way places of this city, for any number of them have been. Mr. Janvier and O. Henry have written some delightful ones; the late H. C. Bunner wrote some, and the later Theodore Winthrop wove romances around Washington Square and the old University building; still, the great New York novel—I don't mean of society, such as "The House of Mirth," but of the whole city, as we find London in "Bleak House"—has yet to be written. San Francisco should be proud of Frank Norris, and should do something to honor him—put up a tablet, or a statue, or name a street or a park after him.

"The Third Circle."
The Academy, 77 (August 14, 1909), 419.

Those who have read that inimitable little romance "Blix," and the other more famous books of Frank Norris, will be prepared to find good and notable work in this posthumous collection of short sketches. The early newspaper efforts of an author naturally do not contain the best portion of his talent, but there is sufficient originality and cleverness in many of these pieces to foreshadow the success which was to attend the publication of "The Pit" and "The Octopus"—novels which flung, as upon a screen in flaming letters, some of the sins and sorrows of American money-hunting. No wonder that among those capable of judging fine literature the premature death of this brilliant young writer from across the water brought a feeling of deep sadness and regret.

Mr. Will Irwin, who was with Norris in his early days on the staff of the San Francisco *Wave*, contributes an introduction that is full of interest. The editor of the *Wave* was one in a thousand. "He loved 'good stuff'; he could not bear to delete a distinctive piece of work just because the populace would not understand." He was more an artist than a man of business. Therefore the literary work of his young subordinate appealed to him strongly, and obtained a hearing which more "business-like" editors might have denied to it. The tales themselves, rescued from the files of the *Wave*, vary greatly, as might be expected. Two or three stand out from the rest as worthy of special notice:

"The Third Circle," the title-story, has a masterly description of San Francisco's Chinatown as it used to be; and "Toppan" is a wonderful little psychological study of the way of a clever man with a mediocre maid. Not one is without interest, although the virtue of brevity is often exemplified remorselessly. Most of them betray the young man's leaning toward the tragic side of life, but their main fascination will only be felt by those who are familiar with the author's more mature work; to such persons as may here find their first introduction to Norris's writings the stories will make little more than the ordinary appeal.

"The Third Circle."
The Athenaeum, August 21, 1909, p. 206.

There are some sixteen stories or sketches brought together in this book, and if it were not that they are posthumous papers, we should have questioned the wisdom of preserving some of them. They represent the early work of a clever writer, whose life, unfortunately, was not long enough to admit of the maturing of his talents. Combined with the somewhat feverish energy which came to him in Western America, Frank Norris had a fine feeling for romance, and a serious appreciation of the writer's obligations which would probably have carried him far. The sketches here presented are rather journalistic than literary; but they contain imaginative touches, and interesting evidence of a writer's progress towards realization of his powers. They were written between 1891 and 1902, for publication in various American journals.

" 'The Third Circle.' " *Saturday Review* (England), 108 (August 28, 1909), 264.

This is a collection of short stories by the late Frank Norris, rescued from newspaper files by an admiring friend. The stories do not show Mr. Norris at his best, but they were well worth collecting. The author had the seeing eye and the gift of conveying vividly what he saw. It is strange to note with what persistency his mind turned to tragedy. Was it some foreboding of the tragic brevity of his career?

Sidney G. P. Coryn. "Books and Authors." *The Argonaut*, 65 (September 11, 1909), 168.

The first of sixteen short stories gives its name to the volume, stories that are now so well known as to need no further word of commendation. It is interesting to note that the *Argonaut* holds the first position in point of time among the copyright acknowledgments that preface the volume. The first of these dates is 1891 and it relates to a story published that year in the *Argonaut*. Other *Argonaut* dates are 1894 and 1895, and soon after came the call of the East, as it has come to so many other California writers.

"The Third Circle." *The Spectator*, 103 (September 18, 1909), 425.

This is a series of remarkable sketches and short stories by the late Mr. Frank Norris. As suggested in the introduction, they are especially interesting as showing the growth of his talent, but they are well worth reading for their intrinsic merit. The first one, "The Third Circle," gives an absolutely horrifying account of the disappearance of an English girl in Chinatown, San Francisco, and the story called "The Caged Lion" will also thrill its readers. The account of the sudden extinction of the electric light, and the consequent failure of the trainer's influence over his lions, is most dramatically given. The last story, "The Guest of Honour," is perhaps too fanciful, though its presence at the end of the book cannot fail to be touching. The anthropomorphism which sees death personified as an individual is not altogether attractive, but the account of the annual dinner, with its gradually diminishing number of guests, is very striking. The book, altogether, is well worth reading, even though the sketches are unequal.

"Norris, Frank. The Third Circle."
ALA Booklist, 6 (October 1909), 56.

Sixteen short stories and sketches gathered from several western periodicals. Not equal to the author's more mature work, but entertaining, and interesting as showing his early versatility and realistic bent.

"Reviews."
The Sewanee Review, 17 (October 1909), 501.

When Frank Norris died, in 1902, it was felt elsewhere as on the Pacific Coast, that a story writer of unusual strength and power had been lost to American literature. As the author of *The Pit* and *The Octopus*, he will long be remembered. In the present volume bearing the title of the initial sketch, the effort is made to collect and preserve "the longest and most important of his prentice products" written within the decade previous to the gifted author's early death. There are sixteen sketches in all and each is entitled to the place given it upon its own peculiar merits rather than, as was the evident intention of the editor, of exhibiting therein the growth and development of the author's imagination and technique.

"The Third Circle."
Bookman (England), 37 (October 1909), 54.

Nine times out of ten it is a mistake, or something worse, to go dredging into the back numbers of old magazines and newspapers and bringing to light the prentice work of an author who has become sufficiently famous to make such an enterprise commercially worth while; in the tenth case it is entirely justifiable. This is one of those tenth books; it would have been a thousand pities if the stories and sketches salved in "The Third Circle" had been left to their dusty oblivion in the files of the San Francisco *Wave*. Such things as "A Reversion to Type," and "The Third Circle" itself, a grim and subtle study, are almost as good as the best that Norris did in those later days when he was writing "McTeague" and "The Octopus." In "Shorty Stack, Pugilist," in the "Little Dramas of the Curbstone," in the slightest sketch the book contains there are touches of character, of imaginative realism and knowledge of the underside of human life which are instinct with a promise that Norris had only half realized when his short life ended. There is enough of brilliant work in these pages to make a reputation, and even to add somewhat to a reputation that is already made.

VANDOVER AND THE BRUTE

BY
FRANK NORRIS

DOUBLEDAY, PAGE & COMPANY
GARDEN CITY   NEW YORK
1914

Vandover and the Brute

"Keeping Up with the Literary Game." *New York Sun,* April 4, 1914, p. 8, section 2.

It comes as a pleasant surprise to hear that there is going to be another Frank Norris novel. So many years have elapsed since the death of Mr. Norris that hopes of a posthumous novel had about faded away. According to the explanation of the long delay in issuing the book, at the time it was completed, in 1896, the author considered the time was not ripe for such realism and put the manuscript away in storage in San Francisco.

Came the earthquake and fire of 1906. Mrs. Norris was away in Germany. The storage company, when the fire was drawing near, dumped a great number of crates, boxes, bales, &c., on a vacant lot in the Presidio, beyond the rage of the fire. The box containing the manuscript was not marked, and lay for years unclaimed. All the other Frank Norris manuscripts and papers (which were in the possession of his brother, Charles Norris) were burnt in the fire. And it was not until August, 1913, that Charles Norris came into possession of the manuscript of "Vandover and the Brute," which is now about to be published.

This book is said to have been "finished" satisfactorily to the artistic conception of the author. In view of which he is faring better in posthumous publication than that other student of realism, the late David Graham Phillips, who doubtless would have preferred that much of his miscellaneous manuscript had somehow perished.

"Wide Range of Themes Covered by New Fiction." *New York Sun,* April 4, 1914, p. 5, section 2.

Vandover and the Brute, by Frank Norris. A posthumous novel by the author of *The Pit*. Intensely realistic, the study of the gradual vanquishment of a man by the brute within him by reason of the weird, uncanny form which it takes in his imagination. The novel shows all the best qualities which marked this author as one of the country's most promising at the time of his death.

"Reviews of Current Novels: A Long Lost Novel by Frank Norris." *New York Evening Post,* April 11, 1914, p. 4, part 3.

The great attraction of Frank Norris is that, direct in method, he is finely imaginative in content; but here we have realism in immature roughness. Its intrinsic value is small beside its importance in filling the chief gap in our knowledge of Norris's development. The first completed novel, it was twin in conception with "McTeague," having been begun in 1894, Norris's senior year at the University of California, and finished in 1895 at Harvard. With neither "Vandover" nor "McTeague" was Norris satisfied. He laid the first away indefinitely, and in 1898 completed and published "Moran of the Lady Letty" before he had quite reworked the second. Ideas and ambitions were then crowding fast, and within a twelvemonth after "McTeague" two more novels—"Blix" and "A Man's Woman"—were published; the conception of a tripartite Epic of the Wheat seized him, and in 1901 came "The Octopus"; and in 1902 his death occurred a few months before the issue of "The Pit." How this first novel, which still awaited remodelling, was stored in a chest in San Francisco, miraculously saved from earthquake and fire, and identified, is told by Charles G. Norris. He also apologizes for its want of finish in the statement that "just as much as 'McTeague' was changed and improved before it was published, so 'Vandover and the Brute' would have been altered and rewritten were the author here to bring to its revision his riper judgment," to which he adds his opinion that it has some passages as fine as anything Norris afterward wrote.

A general outline of the book leaves its faults uppermost. There are characters stressed at the beginning who unaccountably drop; there are incidents that shed no light on the central theme of the book; there are currents that lead us to look for crises never fulfilled, gross improbabilities, patches of empurpled realistic description, the crude horrors of a literary youth fed on Zola and the Goncourts, and an ending loosely melodramatic. But through the novel still breathes strong sincerity, and every chapter shows clear and fast-budding gifts of characterization, construction, and narration. Vandover is a rich, motherless San Francisco youth who studies at Harvard and there explores life, cultivates a dilettantish talent for art, is left his own master by his father's death, sinks ambition and integrity in slothful luxury, goes from stage to stage of riotous living until money and health are gone, and is discovered at the end a dazed, brutish daylaborer, subject to attacks of lycanthropy, cleaning a row of tenements belonging to a one-time friend who has cheated his property from him. The book begins with the full stage of characters, drawn in ultra-detail, which distinguished "The Pit." There is a girl, Turner Ravis, who is introduced with a care presaging an important part, and disappears in 100 pages; there are young men, friends of Vandover, who similarly drop away; his father is a mere sketch; by the middle of the volume the author's powerful moral theme has run away with his pen, and Vandover is centre of a kaleidoscopic yet fateful action in which the outside world figures hazily.

Yet there is no monotony, and a deepening interest attaches to his course. He begins with self-indulgence, the sensuous pleasures of the stomach and armchair; his great impulse towards evil comes with a surreptitious course in the lower world, and betrayal of one of his girl friends, whose suicide drives him to southern California to recuperate; a wreck is brought in for no reason but the description of brutality and hysteria; he takes a studio on his return, is shunned by his friends, and plunges downward.

But the unflinching moral conviction of the book lifts it to a place not far below "McTeague" as a powerful private study, and as a demonstration of Norris's ability, even at twenty-five, to strain out the essential subjective significance in the bare outlines of commonplace life and make it searchingly intense. Like "McTeague," private study that it is, it has rudiments of the epic spirit in the social studies of the wheat trilogy. Undoubtedly, this quality also is derived from Zola, whose greater novels never lacked an epic touch. The novel's very faults claim relationship with Norris's later merits. The irrelevancies, as some of the scenes in the low-class "Imperial" café, and the gross melodrama, as the attacks of lycanthropy, were to be pruned away. His realism, asserting its sincerity, was to learn to add artistic restraint to unblenching grasp of ugly fact, and control itself into quietude of tone. The merits of this first book show the inborn genius of the most promising figure in the literary quarter-century, surpassing Stephen Crane in sturdiness and absence of nervosity; and its defects, compared with his later achievement, give us a new basis for tracing the growth of the skill and vision that were to fade at thirty-two.

"Novel by Frank Norris." *New York Times Review of Books*, April 12, 1914, pp. 181–82.

Something over a decade ago William Dean Howells quoted apropos of Frank Norris's work,

The unfinished window in Aladdin's palace
Unfinished must remain,

and added words of keen regret that it must be so—that a man who had not only shown signs of possessing actual genius, but who in earnestness and singleness of purpose stood out giant-wise among American writers, should have left us, his message only half delivered. And now, after praise and blame are for the most part alike silent, the long arm of coincidence reaches back across the years and rescues for us a few words more.

"Vandover and the Brute" was written nearly twenty years ago, almost simultaneously, we are told, with "McTeague." Plots and ideas for other novels supervened, and "Vandover," unrevised, was temporarily shelved. At the time of the San Francisco earthquake and fire the manuscript was in a storage warehouse that was burned to the ground. Its contents, though, strange to say, thrown out, hit or miss into a vacant lot, escaped injury, and in the course of time the crate containing the manuscript found a resting place in another storehouse, where it remained for years, unlabeled, unidentified, awaiting a claimant. Only recently has the mystery been solved, and the manuscript, from which even the author's name had been cut, possibly by some autograph seeker, has been recognized as unquestionably the long-missing work of the long-dead author.

It is only fair to say, in extenuation of the not infrequent roughnesses and crudenesses in the book, that it appears to be practically the author's first draft. In the ordinary course of events it would have been subjected to much chiseling and polishing before it was presented to the public, which of course, it has not received. The idea of the novel is so big, however, it stands so firmly upon the fundamental things in human nature, that we may well confine ourselves to a consideration of Mr. Norris's intent in the matter and let the details of its execution go.

It is the story of a sensitive, artistically inclined boy, with—to begin with—a very small Brute indeed hidden in the recesses of his soul. But there was no one, unfortunately, to warn him it was a Brute—instead, everybody ignored the fact that it was there at all—and it grew bigger. And as it grew bigger the boy, Vandover, grew weaker, until finally he became completely Brute, and to all intents and purposes there was no more Vandover. Briefly and balkily, that is all there is to it—but that is all there is to the tragedy of a large part of the human race.

There have been many tales told of the multiple personalities which sleep in us, of which probably the most gripping is Stevenson's famous romance. But all such stories have one fundamental weakness, looked at as moral documents; they are stories of fatality, not of cause and effect. The manifestations of multiple personality bear no relation to the man's voluntary inward life, which is all of him that really matters. "Vandover," on the other hand, is a story of growth, of evolution. In spite of our modern theorists on freedom—who aren't so very modern after all; one Nero was a consistent expositor of the cult—genuine growth, in the sense of desirable growth, is conditioned by inhibition, by restraint. Where these are lacking, something else grows; something invariably ugly, melancholy, and finally destructive—the brute in man. It is not merely a coincidence that every primitive race has its legend of the alternative from a living human being, the wer-animal.

It may be objected that the hero's final lapse into one of the most horrible of all forms of madness is inartistic; that it reduces the parable to too concrete a form, and overemphasizes the already obvious moral. Perhaps; yet one cannot help feeling that in a story of this sort there is something deeper than literary values to consider, and that the author's instinct was right. The figure of Vandover in his seizures, naked, four-footed, running up and down his room, his head low and swinging, is unspeakably frightful, yet it knits up his past and his future in the mind of the reader as nothing else could do. It makes the twilight of history articulate and links its cry of instinctive terror to the warning of the science of to-day.

One wonders what the reception of this book would have been had Frank

Norris devoted himself to its completion and publication twenty years ago. One thing is certain, it would have created a tremendous sensation. At that time the social evil had not become a fashionable topic of dinner-table conversation, and the episode of Flossie and young Haight, minor as it is, would have been a veritable bombshell. This episode, by the way, is a blemish, not because it dealt with the subject of "Damaged Goods" before "Damaged Goods" was thought of, but because it is unnecessary and out of balance. The main theme of the book, the usurpation of the throne of a man's soul by the wolf of desire, is strong enough to stand alone, so strong, indeed, that the intrusion of a distracting motive is as irritating as the buzzing of a fly at a funeral.

It shows how far we have traveled from the standards of twenty years ago that "Vandover and the Brute" will find few readers to-day to question its morality, or even its propriety. Frank Norris, to whom art meant truth, and truth art, would be glad to know (as perhaps he does) that his first book, the book he must have loved, and to which he perhaps dreamed of returning when he should have perfected a method worthy of it, appears at last in a time that judges it, not by conventional and artificial standards, but on the simple basis of the truth there is in it, and the quality of its technique. The latter, as we have explained before, it is not only kinder but fairer to leave undiscussed, though there are parts, notably the description of the shipwreck, that are superbly written; the truth in it will speak for itself.

"Current Fiction: *Vandover and the Brute*." *The Nation*, 98 (April 16, 1914), 432–33.

The great attraction of Frank Norris is that, direct in method, he is finely imaginative in content; but here we have realism in immature roughness. Its intrinsic value is small beside its importance in filling the chief gap in our knowledge of Norris's development. His first completed novel, it was twin in conception with "McTeague," having been begun in 1894, Norris's senior year at the University of California, and finished in 1895 at Harvard. With neither "Vandover" nor "McTeague" was Norris satisfied. He laid the first away indefinitely, and in 1898 completed and published "Moran of the Lady Letty" before he had quite reworked the second. Ideas and ambitions were then crowding fast, and within a twelvemonth after "McTeague" two more novels—"Blix" and "A Man's Woman"—were published; the conception of a tripartite Epic of the Wheat seized him, and in 1901 came "The Octopus"; and in 1902 his death occurred a few months before the issue of "The Pit." Mr. Charles G. Norris tells how this first novel, which still awaited remodelling, was stored in a chest in San Francisco and was miraculously saved from earthquake and fire.

Vandover is a rich, motherless San Francisco youth who studies at Harvard and there explores life, cultivates a dilettantish talent for art, is left his own master by his father's death, sinks ambition and integrity in slothful luxury, goes from stage to stage of riotous living until money and health are lost, and is discovered at the end a dazed, brutish day-laborer, subject to attacks of lycanthropy, cleaning a row of tenements belonging to a one-time friend who has cheated him of his property. The book begins with the full stage of characters, drawn in ultra-detail, which distinguished "The Pit." There is a girl, Turner Ravis, who is introduced with a care presaging an important part, and disappears in 100 pages; there are young men, friends of Vandover, who similarly drop away; his father is a mere sketch; by the middle of the volume the author's powerful moral theme has run away with his pen, and Vandover is centre of a kaleidoscopic yet fateful action in which the outside world figures hazily.

Yet there is no monotony, and a deepening interest attaches to his course. He begins with self-indulgence, the sensuous pleasures of the stomach and armchair; his great impulse towards evil comes with a surreptitious course in the lower world, and betrayal of one of his girl friends, whose suicide drives him to southern California to recuperate; a wreck is brought in for no reason but the description of brutality and hysteria; he takes a studio on his return, is shunned by his friends, and plunges downward. But the unflinching moral conviction of the book lifts it to a place not far below "McTeague" as a powerful private study.

E.F.E. [Edwin Francis Edgett]. "Norris's Posthumous Novel." *Boston Evening Transcript*, April 22, 1914, p. 8, part 2.

Almost twenty years after its writing, and more than ten years after the death of its author, "Vandover and the Brute" discloses the consummate skill of one who was both a story teller and a chronicler of life. When Frank Norris died in the autumn of 1902 at the age of thirty-two he had been widely hailed as a novelist of genius and power and the claim was wholly justified by his work. He had written "Moran of the Lady Letty," "McTeague," "The Octopus," and a few other stories long and short, and "The Pit" followed a few months after his death. He was a firmly avowed disciple of Zola, a vigorous believer in the truth-telling impulse of fiction, and a rare representative of the ambitious young man who sees an artistic goal ahead of him and who is bound to conquer it. "I do not see the necessity of transporting us to a hopelessly squalid scene," wrote one protestant, "unrelieved by a single grace or loveliness, for the mere sake of drawing a vivid picture that is not, when completed, fit for the ladies and children of the family to look at." Whereupon to this and to all like opposition, Mr. Norris made reply that he was "telling the truth as he saw it, independent of fashion and the gallery gods," and that he would be able to say: "I never truckled. I never took off the hat to fashion and held it out for the pennies. By God, I told them the truth. They liked it or they didn't like it. What had that to do with me? I told them the truth; I knew it for the truth then and I know it for the truth now. And that is his reward—the best that a man may know; the only one really worth the striving for."

And now in "Vandover and the Brute" Mr. Norris again writes eloquently with the pen of the born novelist and with the spirit of the rigorous realist. Its writing was almost coincident with "McTeague," although that story was begun first and finished later. It was written in part while he was studying at Harvard in 1895 and when he was only about twenty-five years old. It extends to three hundred and fifty pages and it is filled with character and incident. Whether from the prentice-hand of a young man of twenty-five or from the practiced pen of a middle-aged man of fifty, it is a notable story and a notable study. It takes a boy from childhood to manhood, and from year to year it reveals the successive stages of his moral and physical degradations. It might have been more coherent and more compact if its writer had lived to revise it, but he could never have made it more forceful or more truthful. Other writers have accomplished the same purpose—notably Mr. Maxwell in "In Cotton Wool" and Mr. Dreiser in "Sister Carrie"—and have accomplished it well, but none of them has excelled Mr. Norris in knowledge of life or in ability to disclose it by means of the printed page.

It is foolish to speculate what "Vandover and the Brute" might have become had Mr. Norris lived. It is by no means perfect as it is, but it is complete, and we venture to say that he could not have bettered it. His youth discloses itself in his lavish wealth of incident, in the abundance of sensations, in the unrestraint with which he describes successive crucial moments in Vandover's life, but if we search the writings of older and more experienced writers we shall find them no less unreticent. It is an inspiration to read "Vandover and the Brute" because it overflows with the spirit of a young writer who in making an early experiment in fiction finds himself already a master of his art. To have written such a story at such an age is in itself proof of the genius that impels an ambitious man in the right direction. Mr. Norris needed not the teachings of the schools, although he was ready and willing to profit by them, to make himself a writer of fiction. The ability was born in him. "McTeague" shows it in every line, and so does "Vandover and the Brute."

A period of about twenty-five years is passed in the action of "Vandover and the Brute," and through its entirety we follow the life of a boy and man who was possessed of so weak a will that he invariably allowed himself to drift helplessly along the tide of circumstance. If for a moment he was impelled to breast it, he invariably succumbed as soon as the effort became apparent. He was supported by his father well into manhood, his income after his father's death was sufficient for his needs, and from year to year he lived the life of an idler. He had ambitions to become an artist, but he never carried them beyond a meagre beginning. He got through Harvard, he returned to his father's home in San Francisco, and there he dwelt, frequenting disreputable resorts and indulging in all kinds of profligacy until he reached the gutter, a physical, an intellectual, a moral derelict.

In its sense of the flight of time, the story is perfect. The reader feels the impulsive downward progress of Vandover, but he feels at the same time that Vandover is what he is and what he becomes from the very beginning. Whether the story moves leisurely along from day to day, or whether it flies onward over long spaces of time, it is still following every moment of Vandover's career. This, for instance, is a typical passage: "All at once Vandover rushed into a career of dissipation, consumed with the desire of vice, the perverse, blind, and reckless desire of the male. Drunkenness, sensuality, gambling, debauchery, he knew them all. He rubbed elbows with streetwalkers, with bookmakers, with saloonkeepers, with the exploiters of lost women. The bartenders of the city called him by his first name, the policemen, the night detail, were familiar with his face, the drivers of the nighthawks recognized his figure by the street lamps, paling in the light of many an early dawn. At one time and another he was associated with all the different types of people in the low 'sporting set,' acquaintances of an evening, whose names grew faint to his recollection amidst the jingle of glasses and the popping of corks, whose faces faded from his memory in the haze of tobacco smoke and the fumes of whisky; young men of the city, rich without apparent means of livelihood, women and girls "recently from the East" with rooms over the fast restaurants; owner of trotting horses, actresses without engagement, billiard-markers, pool-sellers, and the sons of the proprietors of halfway houses and 'resorts.' " This is by way of summing up, but even more effective are the vivid scenes that the novelist describes in all their detail. A shipwreck, an evening at the opera, an attempted suicide, a gambling game, all these and many other events are visualized with extraordinary clearness by the novelist.

With all his realistic ardor, Mr. Norris never loses sight of the effect of his shifting scenes upon the reader, and he describes each and every one of them with a particularity that is never commonplace. We see Vandover in the midst of all his surroundings, in his father's home, in retreats, in hotels, in restaurants, and in fact in all his haunts. "The house was set in a large well-kept yard." This of the house on California street where Vandover lived with his father during many years. "The lawn was pretty; an enormous eucalyptus tree grew in one corner. Nearer to the house were magnolia and banana trees growing side by side with pines and firs. Humming birds built in these, and one could hear their curious little warbling mingling with the hoarse chirp of the English sparrows which nested under the eaves. The backyard was separated from the lawn by a high fence of green lattice-work. The hens and chickens were kept here and two roosters, one of which crowed every time a cable car passed the house. On the door cut through the lattice fence was a sign, 'Look Out for the Dog.' Close to the unused barn stood an immense windmill with enormous arms; when the wind blew in the afternoon the sails whirled about at a surprising speed, pumping up water from the artesian well sunk beneath. There was a small conservatory where the orchids were kept.

Altogether, it was a charming place. However, adjoining it was a huge vacant lot with cows in it. It was full of dry weeds and heaps of ashes, while around it was an enormous fence painted with signs of cigars, patent bitters and soap."

Vandover is the principal character in the story, and none of the other characters in it have any existence apart from their relation to him. The novel is a novel of Vandover's world. The friends of his Harvard days, the associates of his life in San Francisco, his companions in their prosperous years and those he consorts with in his final and horrible adversity are distinct entities, with personalities as well as names, but it is only as their lives touch Vandover's that we see them. Mr. Norris has accomplished what many other and more expert novelists have sought vainly. He has concentrated his attention and the reader's interest upon one man and one man alone, and he has compelled us to follow him to the bitter end.

Apologies for "Vandover and the Brute" because it is a posthumous novel, a first novel, a youthful novel, an unrevised novel, are unnecessary. It is a novel of which any writer might be proud, and it emphasizes strongly the great loss suffered by American letters in Mr. Norris's untimely death.

"Wealth of New York and Poverty of San Francisco Basis of New Books." New York Herald, April 25, 1914, p. 17.

A certain interest is attached to "Vandover and the Brute" (Doubleday-Page) as the posthumous novel of the late Frank Norris. For this reason, if for no other, it will have a strong appeal for the wide circle of readers of "The Pit" and "The Octopus." who regarded their author as one of the strong writers of American fiction.

A foreword to the new novel explains that it was written nearly twenty years ago, at about the time that "McTeague" was taking shape under the same pen. This I can really believe, as the work is less mature than Mr. Norris' later books, "The Pit" and "The Octopus."

According to the foreword, the influence of Zola is apparent throughout the story, but it would be more accurate to say that the author at this young and impressionable period of his life—he had just been graduated from the University of California and was taking post-graduate work at Harvard—was under the spell of that school of native realism in which detail and so-called "atmosphere" played an important part. The magazine writers were largely responsible for this school of writing, and the younger novelists were studying the art of describing everything of no importance with the greatest possible care. To enumerate the contents of a garbage box without missing a single banana peel was a triumph of literary endeavor in those days, and in this magic art the author of "Vandover and the Brute" excelled. Later in his career he learned the importance of greater things.

The story that comes to us now so many years after it was written is merely the life history of a man of good parentage and upbringing who goes to Harvard from San Francisco, returns to the last named city and, through idleness and dissipation, gradually deteriorates until he reaches the last point of poverty and degradation. His life is one long struggle between his better nature and the brutal appetites that are in almost every human being. Sometimes Vandover gains the upper hand and sometimes he succumbs to his lowest instincts. Drink, gambling and women are the evil forces with which he contends.

He returns from college to find himself in an excellent social circle and with the best things of life fairly within his grasp. His father is a lawyer and capitalist who has invested his money in real estate and is enabled to maintain for himself and his son a luxurious home. But Vandover does not care for business. Art, which has a special charm for the lazy temperament, has a strong appeal for him and he establishes himself in a studio where he works in desultory fashion, devoting a great deal of his time to novel reading, society and other pleasures. He has many "nights out" with his young friends, and the author gives us detailed accounts of the saloons that they visit and the drinks that they absorb, and that, too, without missing a single cocktail. A tragic episode in the young man's life ends his association with reputable society and hurries him on the downward way. He drinks more and more and takes to gambling, eating up first his income and then his principal and growing shabbier and shabbier until he becomes a mere vagabond on the water front. It is all very true and all very sad and the story has its own impressive moral. But is such a man worth writing about? It seems to me that he was hardly worth the saving, and I confess that I had no tears to shed when I saw the last of him.

"Books and Their Writers." *Louisville Courier-Journal*, April 27, 1914, p. 6.

After passing through vicissitudes enough to discourage any ordinary manuscript, the story of "Vandover And The Brute" has finally been brought to light. Its history reads like a romance; written by Frank Norris in 1895, it was misplaced, in some manner, supposed to have been burned during the San Francisco earthquake, and at last recovered in circumstances that would not be believed if they had been made a subject of fiction. As George G. Norris [sic] points out, in the preface, the author would, doubtless, have made many changes if his death had not untimely removed him from his literary labors. The question cannot but arise, in the reader's mind, whether it is ever fair to publish posthumous and unrevised works—to reveal what a writer has discreetly consigned to obscurity. In this case, however, the injustice done Mr. Norris is not so great as that perpetrated upon some other literary lights, as "Vandover" teems with those characteristics we have learned to recognize in his other works. It is a gloomy and somber story. Circumstance seems an implacable demon of destruction, subjugating the will, and involving even the one decent young man of the narrative in hopeless misery. A ferocious fate seems hovering over humanity. Even in this, perhaps his earliest novel,

Norris shows a Zolaesque passion for minutia, which leads the reader through mazes of horror. Coming, as it does, at the time when there seems to be a public passion for revelation of revolting details of some phases of life, "Vandover" is in accord with the general tendency of this class of literature. The principal character is a young man who, artistically gifted, has no moral stamina, no fixed principles, no potent ambitions; who offers to life only that negative surface upon which circumstance writes with unsparing hand. Undoubtedly the lesson Mr. Norris would enforce is a salutary one, and it is so dismally poignant that it cannot fail to impress—if only the right class of readers will be benefited by it.

The gradual development of "The Brute," which gains strength and substance from every concession, and finally devours the man, is told with that force and particularity of which Mr. Norris was master, and the picture needs no hortatory comment.

P.M.P.
"A Morbid Genius."
Syracuse Post-Standard, May 2, 1914, p. 4.

The late Frank Norris was an uncommon fellow, and the manuscript of his story, "Vandover and the Brute," went through uncommon experiences. It was known when Norris died that he had left a manuscript behind him, but the San Francisco earthquake had intervened, and it was supposed that the manuscript had been destroyed in that tremendous catastrophe. Through an odd string of circumstances it has come to light, and Doubleday, Page & Co. now publish it. It was the first book of this talented Californian. He had begun writing it in the year when he finished his college course. He knew that it would not do for a first novel. In the preface his literary executor quotes him as putting into the mouth of the sincere novelist the words "I told them the truth. They liked it or they didn't like it. What had that to do with me? I told them the truth. I knew it for the truth then and I know it for the truth now."

Vandover is a man of great talent, great capacity for good, but he is overpowered by a propensity to the one particular form of evil which eats the heart out of the best character, the best brain, the best intentions. The long struggle to overcome this form of temptation ends in complete defeat. Vandover at the end is washing dirty floors, with just enough intelligence to manage that simple task, his magnificent heritage gone forever. The brute has conquered. Vandover has become the brute. This is tragedy. It is written with a mournful and almost frenzied intensity. It is the truth—for that percentage of mankind who unfortunately happen to be overpowered by the brute that is in them. Perhaps it conveys a lesson; though it was not designed for any such purpose. Mr. Norris's work has been compared with that of Zola. The comparison seems fair enough, but it must be examined by one who has less dislike than the present writer for the realism of melancholy.

John Macy.
"Frank Norris,
Vandover and the Brute:
Some Notes on His
Later Work."
Boston Herald,
May 9, 1914,
p. 4.

Frank Norris was the most important American novelist of his generation. He accomplished much and he promised more. In the twelve years since his death only one man has given us books which equal his in sincerity and depth of purpose—Mr. Theodore Dreiser. When Doubleday, Page & Co. announced that an unpublished manuscript of Norris's had been recovered and that it was his first completed novel, one waited for it with mingled hope and misgiving. He had not found time or impulse to revise it and it was the work of a young man just out of college. One would read "Vandover and the Brute" because Norris wrote it, and because the first steps of a man who finally arrived are interesting to trace. Never was moderate expectation more agreeably disappointed. The case-hardened professional reader, who, like the surgeons, cannot permit his nerves to be affected by his daily task, lay awake all night impelled to the end of the book.

If Norris had failed in "Vandover" he might have contemplated the failure with satisfaction; for the theme he chose is so great that to have conceived it in youth is honor enough, and not to have worked it out completely is no disgrace. The book has faults; counsel would advise it to plead guilty on several counts. The nice girl of the story is drawn with uncertain strokes. There are signs of effort in the exposition of Vandover's character. No author under 35 or 40 could know enough to make all the steps of Vandover's descent self-evident. But the defects of the book are those of a large intention not quite realized. It is not the defects that would have insured the rejection of the book by any American publisher to whom Norris might have submitted it. It is the merits of the book that would probably have rendered it "unavailable" in the nineties. There is no way of proving it, but one can be fairly sure that if Norris had sent this book to publishers twenty years ago, he would have wasted his postage stamps.

For he dares to be a disciple of Zola. He sends a man to the dogs with more regard to character and circumstance than to the allurements of a happy ending. He makes an innocent man victim of a dread disease—fifteen years before any of us heard of Brieux. His conception of "love interest" excludes the merry wedding bells; indeed, in his earnest pursuit of an idea, he forgot his nice young girl and let her disappear from the story, as if it were not his business to know what became of her. If the seriousness of his work, his lofty idea of the duty and pleasure of a novelist, his tragic sense of life were inharmonious with the prevalent spirit in American literature at the close of the nineteenth century, he revealed in "McTeague" and allowed to lie buried in "Vandover" some qualities which even American readers must respect. In the first place he has the gift of sustaining and increasing the power of a story, the art of crescendo. I remember no work of his which falls off after a good beginning. "Vandover" gets better and better as it proceeds. If Norris knew this to be true, he might have felt sure of his calling, for when a tyro lacks real power, he almost invariably puts what stuff he has in the first part of his book and weakens toward the end.

Another power which Norris disclosed in this early novel is objectivity in the management of character. The young writer, who knows little except himself, is likely to make his people think as he thinks, so that they are but variously labelled packages of his opinions. From the first Norris's imagination was strong enough to endow his personages with individual temperaments, motives, habits of thought and modes of speech; they lead their own lives; they seem to be out of control. And that is the most difficult, the most wonderful illusion that a creator of fiction can produce.

A third virtue which he was to exhibit to a greater degree in the later books marks "Vandover" as the work of a born novelist, the sensory reality of the scene. Whether he learned the trick from Zola or whether his experience as an art student taught him how to visualize things, he knew how to present persons as if they had air on all sides of them, streets as if they could be walked upon, even an entire city, San Francisco, as an organism with a life and visage peculiarly its own. He is never guilty of the young writer's vice of seeming to "do a description." He uses his eyes and is perhaps youthfully conscious that he sees life in an individual way and is not a victim of other people's trite observations. A minor example of his resolution to see things as they are, to penetrate sham and hypocrisy and convention, is his description of the entrance of a factory. "In front on either side of the main entrance were white stone medallions upon which were chiselled the head of a workman wearing the square paper cap that the workman never wears, and a bent-up forearm, the biceps enormous, the fist gripping the short hammer that the workman never uses."

The author of "Vandover and the Brute" is a stern young moralist who portrays the struggle in the individual between good and evil. In "The Octopus" and "The Pit" Norris became a student of the social structure, of the contests between forces, economic and natural, in which the individual is ruined or succeeds, finds his hour of happiness and meets his hour of death. To say that these books are an epic of Daily Bread is not to misuse a large word. The story of wheat is the history of an empire, of vast migrations, conquests, and disasters, controlled, as all national movements and private destinies have been controlled, by the mute motive of hunger. Wheat is a fact and a symbol. It drowns the individual Berhman, who for the moment is the personal representative of the great impersonal system, the esurient Octopus; it inundates the grain market and makes havoc of Jadwin's fortunes. Viewed singly these deaths and failures are but accidents of the game; perhaps Behrman's death is too obviously accidental. But seen more deeply they are typical, inevitable, poetically just.

The last page of "The Octopus," conceived upon a plane of eloquence from which a fall would be easy, has a Whitmanian breadth of vision. "The WHEAT remained. Untouched, unassailable, undefined, that mighty world force, that nourisher of nations, wrapped in Nirvanic calm, indifferent to the human swarm, gigantic, resistless, moved onward in its appointed grooves. Through the welter of blood at the irrigation ditch, through the sham charity and shallow philanthropy of famine relief committees, the great harvest of Los Muertos rolled like a flood from the Sierras to the Himalayas to feed thousands of starving scarecrows on the barren plains of India."

From Bret Harte to Jack London many writers of unquestionable talent have sent us stories of the great West, its ranches, deserts and mines. If a general fault may be charged, subject to many exceptions, it is that they seem to have their eyes upon a New York or Boston publisher rather than upon their subject; they have packed their goods for the eastern market and have adulterated life with spurious romance. Three men above all others have looked at some aspects of the West with honest and perspicacious vision; two were humorists, Mark Twain and O. Henry, and the other was Norris, who had little humor except of the kind that does not make one laugh. There is no legitimate ground for quarrel with any piece of good writing, whatever the author's mood or general view of life. It will always be a pleasure to read Bret Harte; he was an artist in his kind, but of a tradition that has passed in every country except America. It is still a pleasure to read Mr. Jack London, and one has faith that he has not wholly capitulated to the many-headed god of popularity. But if fiction is to be taken seriously and held accountable as a record of life as well as an entertainment, we shall, in our old age, look back for a glimpse of the true West to the wise jokers, Mark Twain and O. Henry, who, each in his generation, laughed foolish romance out of countenance; and we shall look back also to the sombre realism of Norris. He was the one trained American novelist (trained of course in France) who happened to live in California and to write of the life he knew. His ranchers, bad men, Mexicans, train robbers seem to be drawn from life.

The frontispiece of an English edition of "The Octopus" is a picture of a duel between a man on horseback and a man on foot. If one saw that picture in a magazine one would carefully avoid reading the story. But the episode in Norris's text which the picture illustrates is different. It is different in one supremely important respect; it is not merely an exciting scene narrated for its own sake, it is deeply rooted in the social soil from which it springs and it invites the eye to look past it to a broad human landscape.

George Hamlin Fitch. "Realism That Repels: An Unrevised Early Story by Frank Norris Published." *San Francisco Chronicle*, May 17, 1914, p. 31.

It is a dangerous thing to unearth an early piece of work by a well-known writer and give it to the world, for the world has fixed the place of every writer who is dead, and does not take kindly to any new thing which may upset its estimate. Luckily, there is seldom any danger of such a reappraisement from the scraps which are brought to light by relatives or admirers of men of genius. Usually a man publishes during his lifetime all that he regards as worth printing. If anything is found among his effects, it may be set down as something which he did not value, or something that he looked upon merely as apprentice work.

Now, the brother of Frank Norris is responsible for the publication of an early story by the author of "McTeague" and "The Octopus." It is entitled, "Vandover and the Brute," and is brought out by Doubleday, Page & Co. of New York. In an introduction by Charles G. Norris we are given the curious facts in regard to this work, which the author evidently did not regard as fit to print without careful revision. The manuscript was among certain goods that were supposed to have been burned in the great fire in San Francisco. Afterward, it was found that several crates had been transferred before the fire, but the cutting out of the name of Norris from the title page led to the discarding of the manuscript until recently a junior member of the publishing firm took up the manuscript, and, after reading a few pages, recognized the author's style.

The story was written while Norris was taking a post-graduate course in English at Harvard. He had already written most of "McTeague," but had not revised "Vandover and the Brute." It seems to have been an effort on the part of young Norris to show how a young man of artistic inclinations and much real goodness of character was gradually dragged down by the brutal side of his nature. It is an elaborate study of the moral effect of yielding to the temptations offered by unworthy associates. Yet this study has very small value because the author was too young to properly appreciate cause and effect. He was wholly under the influence of Zola, but this was a subject which demanded the full power of his master. The result is that much of the realism with which the book is packed is offensive, because it produces only disgust in the reader.

Vandover is a young man who did not deserve the severe punishment dealt out to him by his literary creator. If Norris had been older and had had more knowledge of life he would have been the first to see that a man of Vandover's type does not fall so deeply into vice as he had made him plunge. Nor would he have made this young fellow responsible for the suicide of a pleasure-loving young woman, when faced with the sure prospect of shame. In fact, much of the book seems to have been the result of the observation of a man of Puritan strain, who had had very little experience of real life. It is to this lack of experience that we owe the tedious descriptions of the drinking, gambling and other vices of the immature Harvard students, who evidently regarded themselves as "perfect devils," from the Byronic point of view.

In the same way, many disagreeable episodes are introduced, apparently only for the sake of their ghastly Zolaesque realism. Such is the incident of the wreck of the coast steamer, with the brutal beating to death of the poor Jew, who tried to get aboard of the small boat in which Vandover is one of the survivors. There is fine descriptive work in this incident, but it has absolutely no bearing on the story. Another most repulsive incident, which has no moral value, is that of the physical contamination of young Haight, one of the finest characters in the book.

With a party of young Harvard men, he has dropped into a questionable resort, frequented by women of uncertain reputation. He has had no relations with women; he has kept himself apart. Yet he attracts one of the frail habitués, who kisses him on the mouth. Earlier in the evening he had cut his lip with a broken wine glass, and the result of this young harlot's kiss was loathsome blood infection that practically ruined his life and prevented him from marrying the girl whom he loved and for whose sake he had lived a cleanly life. Such things as this may occur, but, thank heaven, they are not common, and any one with any knowledge of life revolts against having them dragged into fiction, just as he objects to such a book as "My Little Sister," written to appeal to the hysterical people who believe in the wildest flights of the imagination of those who make moral or literary capital out of the crusade against the so-called "white slavery."

The publishers declare that this unrevised early work of Frank Norris is valuable in a moral way to every one who is "fighting the eternal fight between good and evil in his own soul." This does not seem to me to be true. The story has no value from a moral point of view, because of its manifest exaggerations and because of the illogical results of the hero's misdeeds. He is punished out of all proportion to his deserts, and the youngest reader will feel this as well as the most mature.

It is evident that Frank Norris realized this fatal defect of the book and felt that it could not be remedied. No amount of revision would have removed this vital fault. "McTeague" has much in it that is coarse and repulsive, but the plot is logical and convincing. In this story of Vandover the horrors are piled up in such a way that they fail to impress one as real. The only result of reading the book is to produce a profound depression and disgust with this semblance of life, which has no more connection with life as it is lived by ordinary people than the foul dens of the Barbary Coast or the unspeakable resorts of Commercial street have with the homes of decent San Franciscans.

This passion for realism in literature which Zola did so much to stimulate has produced many works that fortunately have had only a brief life. Frank Norris in his youth was strongly influenced by the author of "L'Assommoir" but he soon recovered, or he would have never given the world such great works as "The Octopus" and "The Pit." This early book, which is now brought out without his consent, will add nothing to his fame. In fact, it is a pity that it should have been published.

Herbert Bashford. "The Latest in Literature." *San Francisco Bulletin*, May 23, 1914, p. 14

"Vandover and the Brute," by Frank Norris, the most brilliant novelist California has yet given to the world and who during an altogether too brief lifetime added luster to American letters, has had a somewhat romantic history, according to Charles G. Norris' introduction to the novel.

This story was completed in 1895,

the earlier chapters having been written while the author was a student at Harvard. That the novel failed to find favor with the publishers is not surprising, as American fiction at that time did not possess those natural and strongly realistic features which have since lifted it from the fairy tale class and given it the strength and virility of life. The manuscript of the story was packed away in a crate. This was placed in storage. Owing to the fact that the warehouse was burned in the fire of 1906, it was assumed that the manuscript had been destroyed, but later it was discovered that certain boxes and crates had been removed from the warehouse just before the flames reached it. Eventually the manuscript was found and the story which should have been published years ago is now offered to the public.

"Vandover and the Brute," like the author's more finished novel, "McTeague," shows clearly the influence of Zola. In conception the story is big—one of those powerful themes of human interest which appealed so strongly to the author of "The Octopus," and which he invariably handled with such downright earnestness and sincerity as to stamp him a really great writer. While this novel, written in the days of his youth, has certain technical blemishes, it contains many passages which show a mental grasp, a knowledge of psychology and a keen insight into human nature that would be regarded as extraordinary even in a writer of mature mind.

The gradual dominance of the brute nature in Vandover is powerfully depicted—his slow, inevitable yielding to the baser passions and desires, the pangs of conscience at having been the cause of a young girl's suicide, his grief at the death of his heart-broken father and his certain degeneracy, resulting in mental and physical decay. Vandover is a study. His grosser nature is constantly warring against his better self and it proves the victor. He has moments of regret, of high resolve, but the brute within regains its hold and finally drags him down.

The soul-struggle of Vandover is powerfully portrayed and, while the craftsmanship is by no means equal to that of the author's later works, the novel shows clearly the marks of genius—a remarkable creation considering the youth of the novelist, and one which is to be commended to all lovers of virile, gripping fiction.

"Vandover and the Brute." *The Outlook*, 107 (May 30, 1914), 264-65.

This story was commenced by Frank Norris when he was doing postgraduate work in the English Department of Harvard University, and completed after his return to San Francisco. It was packed in a crate and stored in a large storehouse in that city. The earthquake came and was followed by the fire, and it was assumed that the manuscript had been destroyed. It came to light later in one of a number of boxes that had been moved just before the fire.

It is in every way a remarkable piece of work for so young a man. It is written in a style of such unadulterated realism that it is quite unnecessary for the "Foreword" to point out the influence of Zola. The story is Zola-esque in the extreme; the marvel is, however, that so young a man should know so much about the kind of life that is described. It is distinctly a story of ability and promise; it is also a story of the most unpleasant nature written in a most unpleasant style. It is in no sense an immoral tale; on the contrary, like "L'Assommoir," it is intensely moral: but it is brutally frank. It is not necessary to follow a young man through a prolonged bath of mud or to know all the details of the stages of vice by which he went to the bottom. The closing chapters of the story are remarkable as pictures of the physical disintegration which follows moral disintegration. They have a terrible precision as well as a terrible significance; but they hardly belong in a work of fiction. Reading this book is very much like being in a charnel-house and seeing a human body disintegrate. It is a repulsive, shocking spectacle. Frank Norris learned that, and, without losing his force, saw the artistic mistake he had made. When he wrote "The Octopus" and "The Pit," he had gone a long way in the direction of getting a larger perspective on life than when he wrote "Vandover and the Brute."

Frederic Taber Cooper.
" 'Vandover and the Brute.' "
Bookman (America), 39 (June 1914), 444–45.

Those whose privilege it was to know Frank Norris in the few brief transition years between the Nineteenth Century and the Twentieth, and to watch his rare and virile powers slowly find themselves and compel recognition of his brilliant and short-lived promise, find themselves facing a painful duty when asked to review his long lost posthumous novel, *Vandover and the Brute*. One thing seems certain: had Norris lived, this early work might have served him profitably as a source-book of youthful impressions, college-day spontaneity which, when once lost, is gone irretrievably:—but he would never have made the colossal blunder of publishing it in its present form. Until he became known, he, of course, could not have found a publisher for a work so audacious; and by the time that he had made a name and secured his public, his awakened understanding of his art would have forbidden the publishing of a piece of sheer apprentice work,—powerful in streaks, Zolaesque in the sheer surface mannerisms and a startling frankness of theme which he never again sought to attain, and yet revealing, in countless subtle ways, his lack of full understanding of his self-elected model. The briefest and simplest way of defining *Vandover and the Brute* is to say that Norris was gropingly trying to do what Mr. W. B. Maxwell has done of clear purpose and with masterly execution in his much debated volume, *In Cotton Wool*. Both these books tell the life of a man who always chooses the line of least resistance, the man who, starting out with high ideals and brilliant opportunities, finds it easier, month by month and year by year, to yield to the brute side of human nature that is perpetually striving to drag us down. The fatal weakness of *Vandover and the Brute* is its lack of explanation: there is nothing to account for the hero's weakness of will. There is no hint of any defective heredity, no evidence that there was anything especially vicious in Vandover's environment. His college course was fairly normal; he had his lapses, but they were comparatively rare. The only abnormal thing about him at this time was an unhealthy supersensitiveness of conscience, a tendency to magnify out of all proportion his occasional departures from the strait and narrow path. Furthermore, luck played a large part in Vandover's slow disintegration. If he had not lost his mother when a mere boy; if a certain girl had not committed suicide; if he had not been shipwrecked at a crucial moment; if his father had not succumbed to heart-failure; if he had not had a scoundrel for a friend; if,—we might go on indefinitely with the swelling list of "ifs." In real life, the issues are often complicated by apparently wanton intrusions of fate; but the novelist who knows his art tries to keep the issues clear; he says, accidents may happen, but let us work out the problem without their help. Norris had not yet learned this when he was breaking himself in by writing *Vandover and the Brute*, and that is why, for the sake of his reputation, it ought to have been issued for private circulation only and placed in the hands of the few who would have regarded it as a human document and nothing more.

"Current Thought in the New Books." *Review of Reviews* (America), 49 (June 1914), 761.

"Vandover and the Brute" pictures the gradual descent of a man to utter degradation through constant yielding to sensuous appetite. Vandover was an ordinarily good sort of a boy,—rather talented, in fact,—but as he grew older he loved to be lazy,—to eat, sleep, and be self-indulgent. He thought he had to be amused continually and disliked being bored and worried. "He liked to have a good time." Naturally he drifted downward along the lines of least resistance. Slowly the brute developed, slowly he was dragged by dissipation into the clutches of that frightful obsession known to physicians as *lycanthropia mathesis*. He became a wolf-man at periodic intervals, the victim of the beast which lived in his flesh.

This unusual book was written by the late Frank Norris previous to 1895. The manuscript went through the San Francisco earthquake and fire; the signature was cut from the title sheet by an autograph hunter and the authorship of the manuscript remained unknown until the junior member of a storage firm that had charge of certain boxes of the author's effects read the manuscript and recognized the style as that of Norris. The working out of the theme is crude, in a way, but very powerful. Its realism is not always palatable, but the reader never doubts for an instant that it is truth.

"Frank Norris's Werewolf."
Current Opinion, 56 (June 1914), 455-56.

Vandover was anything but a Fortunate Youth. For one thing, he was created by the late Frank Norris, and that pioneer of American ultra-realists did not give happy lives to the children of his brain. Like a perverted sun dial, he marked only the shady hours. "Vandover and the Brute" was written nearly twenty years ago, almost simultaneously with "McTeague." The manuscript—the author's first draft—was lost at the time of the San Francisco earthquake and has recently come to light and been published by Doubleday, Page and Company. The story is a variation of "Dr. Jekyll and Mr. Hyde," in which also Mr. Hyde triumphs. Vandover is a rich San Francisco youth who studies at Harvard, becomes something of a dilettante and very much of a libertine, wastes his money and health in riotous living and finally becomes a day-laborer subject to attacks of lycanthropy—that is, of that mania in which the sufferer believes himself to be a wolf, kills people, and drinks their blood. The "Brute" of the title is Vandover's worse self, the self which finally kills his better nature and drives him mad. As has already been said, the book is a first draft, and Norris would have changed and improved it had it been published during his lifetime. "There are characters stressed at the beginning," says the New York *Evening Post*, "who unaccountably drop; there are incidents that shed no light on the central theme of the book; there are currents that lead us to look for crises never fulfilled, gross improbabilities, patches of empurpled realistic description, the crude horrors of a literary youth fed on Zola and the Goncourts, and an ending loosely melodramatic." But the book has its value to all who are interested in the history of English realism and in the career of its brilliant and ill-starred author. In the review already quoted we read:

"The unflinching moral conviction of the book lifts it to a place not far below 'McTeague' as a powerful private study, and as a demonstration of Norris's ability, even at twenty-five, to strain out the essential subjective significance in the bare outlines of commonplace life and make it searchingly intense. Like 'McTeague,' private study that it is, it has rudiments of the epic spirit of the social studies of the wheat trilogy. Undoubtedly this quality also is derived from Zola, whose greater novels never lacked an epic touch. The novel's very faults claim relationship with Norris's later merits. The irrelevancies, as some of the scenes in the low-class 'Imperial' café, and the gross melodrama, as the attacks of lycanthropy, were to be pruned away. His realism, asserting its sincerity, was to learn to add artistic restraint to unblending grasp of ugly fact, and control itself into quietude of tone. The merits of this first book show the inborn genius of the most promising figure in the literary quarter-century, surpassing Stephen Crane in sturdiness and absence of nervosity; and its defects, compared with his later achievement, give us a new basis for tracing the growth of the skill and vision that were to fade at thirty-two."

"Derelict by Destiny."
Pall Mall Gazette (London), June 16, 1914, p. 9.

The author of "The Pit" died at thirty-two with a world of promise only partially fulfilled. A frank disciple of Zola, he came nearer than any man has done as yet to wringing romance out of the world of commerce. Harvard and Professor Gates taught him to write a better English than any American of his generation, and his service in the Jameson Raid showed his sympathies were with us at a time when Anglophilism was a rare plant in Western minds. And Norris was western of the West. He belonged more to California than to the Eastern States, and San Francisco is the hub of interest in his novels. When Presley in "The Octopus" projects a masterpiece—he is the one visionary in a row of books all stamped with the rankest realism—it is an Epic of the West, and West in the American sense of the term. Again, "McTeague," which is a drama of Californian gold and glitter, even to the hero's yellow hair. Even "The Pit," set down as it is in the marts of Chicago, strongly and frequently reminds one of the wheatfields of the Pacific slopes. Viewed as a conscious artist, who studied his medium and upheld his mission as devoutly as any ritual and religion, Norris turned out only one failure, and that was "A Man's Woman," and we cannot recall at the moment on which side of the Rockies that story rests.

These and other novels, a budget of marvellous short stories, and a couple of books of essays made a sum of triumph for a man who met his death so young. When he went, he left behind a novel which no firm would take, and the manuscript seemed to have perished in the earthquake fire of San Francisco, until by chance it turned up the other day. By this time, anything of Frank Norris's is welcome, and "Vandover and the Brute" has been hailed by his compatriots and admirers as the masterpiece it most assuredly is not. For a book written at twenty-five, it shows a most amazing precocity, and in any young writer might put extra girth upon his chest. But in that it was written at the same time as "McTeague," and the author was Norris, we can only say that it does not justify our expectations. Its name implies a struggle which is non-existent, for Vandover and the Brute are one. There is no conflict, and therefore no drama, in this steady supersession of good by evil. It is a paraphrase of Stevenson's terrible parable with the terror, the magic of vision, and the surprise left out. It reads like one of those exercises into which an artist puts all his taskwork. Vandover is a kind of whipping-boy with never a chance of grace or a compunctious visiting. There are pages when you perceive the author's half-admission that the thing comes desperately near to tedium, even in the writing.

Vandover is the son of an indulgent and prosperous widower, and takes to pleasure as a duck to water. Visions of success as an artist distract him now and then from the company and pursuits of his kind, and we feel a kind of genuine regret when he has to forgo the course of study in the Paris studios which, as we know, Frank Norris himself always regarded as one of the formative influences of his life. As it turns out, Vandover's experiences are of the emotional, and not of the aesthetic, order, and emotion with him means emotion at its worst. The compass that determines him revolves in a San Francisco restaurant, and, having engaged himself to one girl, and used another as a recreation, he seduces a third in a spirit of bravado, and is only pulled up when he learns soon afterwards that she has committed suicide. His father, all forbearance, counsels him to begin afresh; and a sea trip with a realistic shipwreck provides the necessary break. He returns to find "the governor" dead in his chair. The estate is no sooner set in order and transferred to him with the prospect of a competency than a suit is entered against him by the dead girl's father. The counsel engaged against him uses his old intimacy with Vandover in order to secure a settlement against him, and recurrent bouts of vice concur with rejection by his fiancée to reduce "Van" to a wreck of his former self. Gambling sweeps away the remainder of his fortune, and we leave him a derelict man-of-all-work, working for his lawyer friend at starvation rates, and drudging as the vilest of menials on the site where he had once been lord of the soil.

The fault with the novel is the old one of *a priori* misery. Predestination is as false in fiction as in theology, and Vandover fails to interest us because he never looks up and never once succeeds. Even when he tries self-destruction he fails:—

The night before he had been brave enough. How was it now that he could not call up the same courage, the same determination? When he thought over the wreck, the wretched failure of his life, the dreadful prospect of the future years, his anguish and his terror were as keen as ever. But now there was a shrinking of his every nerve from the thought of suicide—the instinctive animal fear of death, stronger than himself. His suffering had to go on, had to run its course. Even death would not help him. Let it go on; it was only the better part of him that was suffering. In a little while this better part would be dead, leaving only the brute. It would die a natural death without any intervention from him. Was there any need of suicide? Suicide! Great God! his whole life had been one long suicide.

A man of Vandover's force of character would at least have weighed the balance now and then between good and evil, and if he had deliberately chosen ruin, at least he would have rallied his forces with some show of wit and raillery. But of the buoyancy of vice there is none in Vandover. He settles down doggedly under the yoke, and never makes vice palatable or himself convincing. We cannot lay the story down once we have started, but this is not because of the inherent interest of the hero. We are merely fascinated by curiosity as to how Norris will handle the dreadful subject next. As it stands, this book is a disappointment, and if any one wonders what Norris would have done with his story had he lived, we are in no doubt whatever. He would have rewritten it, or burned it.

"New Books and Reprints."
Times Literary Supplement (London), June 18, 1914, p. 299.

This was written by the author of "The Pit" and "The Octopus," twenty years ago, when he was under the influence of a Zolaesque pessimism; and it depicts with force the losing struggle of a young man against his British instincts.

"Novels of the Season."
Literary Digest, 48 (June 20, 1914), 1494-95.

It would not have been fair to the memory of Frank Norris, who before his untimely death gave promise of becoming one of our foremost novelists and who produced "The Pit," "The Octopus," and others, to publish this book without a word of explanation. The work shows marks of college days, and was evidently written under that influence, but being an implacable arraignment of human frailty and too long for popularity, it was laid aside in San Francisco for other work. At the time of the earthquake, the boxes were supposedly burned, but were really carried to a point of safety. It was only within the last year that they were discovered and the MSS. identified. Without revision, and with all its unpruned crudities, it is still above the average work of the literary aspirant. Many would gladly have a claim to its authorship. One feels the gripping force of the story from the very beginning and, tho there is only a sketchy love element, and several characters are elaborately introduced and then apparently forgotten, there is no lack of interest. It is not a pleasant story, but a big and compelling one, full of forceful and dramatic situations.

" 'Vandover and the Brute.' "
Saturday Review (England), 117 (June 20, 1914), 805.

The issue of this novel, written by Frank Norris at the age of twenty-five, has an interest mainly personal. It shows us a novelist in the making. Frank Norris was only thirty-two when he died, but during the seven years that followed the writing of this book he matured in a remarkable way. "Vandover and the Brute" is a precocious effort which we imagine the author deliberately withheld from publication. It is a far cry from its crudity of style and conception to the finished smoothness of such novels as "The Octopus" and "The Pit," whereby Frank Norris established himself pre-eminently as the novelist of commerce, opening up a rich field of romantic discovery to many writers who have followed in his train. Those who have read the later works of Norris will find a certain pleasure and satisfaction in tracing in this youthful effort a foreshadowing of his powers.

Disappointing as the story is, it yet has some good straightforward vivid writing. It shows a sense of character, considerable facility in the handling of dialogue, and an almost slavish following of the methods of Zola. Frank Norris was always a realist, but here in his early days his work is glaring and ghastly, unrelieved by a sense of art or restraint. And in "Vandover and the Brute" he plunged with all the enthusiasm of youth into a subject too big for him, beyond his power to handle effectively.

The story turns on the eternal conflict of good and evil. The conception might have been taken from Stevenson's Jekyll and Hyde, for Vandover and the Brute are one, and the interest of the tale is purely psychological. We watch the crumbling away of a character rich in promise and opportunity, the gradual supersession of the man by the brute. Vandover, with everything in his favour to make for happiness, becomes the helpless slave of his own vices. At last, when he has thrown away his chance of love and lost his fortune by gambling, we are invited to look upon him as a menial in the place where he had once been master, on his hands and knees amid the sinks and tubs scrubbing the stains of grease upon the floor of the kitchen.

It is true the story awakens curiosity—but it is the kind of curiosity to know to what shifts the author will put his character next. Vandover himself never strikes us as real. We feel him a puppet obeying the strings pulled by a zealous master intent upon exhibiting his tricks. And the thing disappears flatly and ineffectively. It has neither glamour nor the magic of vision, and it should only be read by those who know the later work of Frank Norris.

"Vandover and the Brute."
Times Literary Supplement (London), June 25, 1914, p. 311.

To English readers "The Pit" and "The Octopus" are probably the two most familiar of the late Mr. Frank Norris's novels. His first book *Vandover and the Brute* (Heinemann, 6s.), which was written twenty years ago, is now printed for the first time after some curious adventures in MS. (it narrowly escaped destruction in the San Francisco earthquake), details of which Mr. Charles G. Norris gives us in his "foreword." Frank Norris had only lately graduated at the University of California when the conception of "Vandover and the Brute" obsessed him—a theme which might well have given pause to a young and untried writer—the terribly lonely, secret tragedy of a young man's losing fight against the baser part of his nature to the gradual atrophy of all his best instincts. Mr. Norris was at that time strongly under the influence of Zola; but throughout a story crowded with detailed realism a saving instinct preserves him from offending as Zola too often offended. "Sincerity" was and remained a watchword with him. Years later he held up to admiration the writer who could fairly say,

> I told them the truth. They liked it or they didn't like it.

What had that to do with me? I told them the truth. I knew it for the truth then, and I know it for the truth now.

Still there are many ways of telling the truth, and in the 1890's the judgment of the American publishers went against this "human document." For all that, the book, true to its author's creed, has undeniable good qualities. If it is, as Mr. Charles Norris puts it, "too strong to be always palatable," if its "sordid story marches mercilessly to its inevitable and sinister conclusion," it still shows a clear courage unaffected by the terror of its theme, a strong sense of pity and a certain tragic bleakness.

"Vandover and the Brute."
The Athenaeum,
June 27, 1914,
p. 886.

The publication of this posthumous work is a matter for great regret. It was written nearly twenty years ago, and the Foreword supplied by the author's brother contains much evidence, we think, that, had the writer had the chance of revising it for publication, excesses of repetition and detail as unsavoury as unnecessary would have been avoided.

As a story of degeneration it might have had its uses as a deterrent in certain quarters, were it not for passages which, we fear, will merely pander to any incipient depravity of mind. It is a strange jumble of callow work mixed with strongly portrayed incidents—that of a shipwreck being especially good. We would venture to suggest to those concerned in the present issue of the book that this edition should be reserved for fellow-craftsmen, who may at least learn from it things to be avoided, and that a fresh version, edited and revised for the general public, should be published.

"A Posthumous Novel."
The Nation (England), 15
(July 4, 1914),
536, 538.

About 1897, "the MS. of 'Vandover and the Brute' began its eastern visits," but "it was not in accord with the spirit of the day in literature," writes Mr. Charles G. Norris of this remarkable posthumous novel by Frank Norris, whose premature death, five years later, robbed America of one of its finest creative talents. The MS., rejected by the New York publishers, was put away in a box and warehoused; but, through some mistake, it was thought to have perished in the great fire of San Francisco. Not till 1913 was the rediscovered MS. identified as Norris's work.

"I never truckled; I never took off the hat to Fashion and held it out for pennies. By God! I told them the truth. They liked it, or they didn't like it. What had that to do with it?" is a passage quoted from one of Norris's essays by his brother, who adds that while Norris was writing "Vandover and the Brute," he knew that he should fail to find an American publisher to issue it. Why? Why this foredained boycotting of a fine, though by no means faultless, piece of fiction? The answer is that the subject itself, the life of dissipation which saps the will and rots the fibre of the hero, Vandover, is *tabu* to the good American, and that no matter how sincere the spiritual lesson or how brilliant the technical handling, the theme remains "unpleasant" to the average citizen.

It is curious, at the first glance, that only in the province of creative literature should these prohibitions and *tabus* be enforced. The American newspapers, which are perused calmly or eagerly by the most prudish readers, are replete with sensational reports of not only every species of love-crime but with accounts of the dissolute or depraved sexual acts of men and women in every class of society. Yet these very same readers will turn away, shocked, from a novel or a play which presents artistically, with depth and insight, a strictly truthful picture of sex relations. Why should this fine work of art excite the indignation of the very citizen who devours, with appetite, journalistic garbage? Partly, it is no doubt that the latter is in the stage of culture which tries to hide, or idealize or refine the claims of the senses. This is the theme of the novel before us, "the brute" in Vandover being "the terrible animal man," in Tolstoy's phrase, which, through self-indulgence and luxurious habits in youth, has gradually waxed formidable, sapping both the moral sense and the finer spiritual instincts. The theme is one familiar to ethical teachers from St. Augustine onwards, and particularly congenial, one would think, to a society still so markedly dominated as America by the legacy of Puritanic ethics. One can imagine how Hawthorne would have shrouded it with the chiaroscuro of his brooding fancy; how Poe would have spun from it a tale of haunting terror; how Mrs. Wharton would dissect its moral pathological issues as reflected in the glass of the self-distrustful Puritanic conscience.

But Norris was inspired by the example of the French naturalists, particularly by Zola, though no trace of the latter's taint of uncleanliness is discernible in him, and it is curious to note how San Francisco life falls into clear perspective, seen in the method reflected from the brilliant and clear-cut Latin atmosphere. In some ways, this picture of American manners is far more comprehensible than the home-grown article; one can criticize the emotions and ideas of the characters and the social habits that rule the community. One stands clear of that one-sided idealism, that cute, strident, and strenuous optimism, that sugary sentimentalism which are so overpowering in modern American literature. There is a real criticism of life, a real standard of moral value in "Vandover and the Brute," and the motives of the characters are not assessed by the measuring tape of conformity. But although the San Francisco atmosphere, the feel of the city, the look of the streets and houses and cafés, are rendered in brilliant descriptions, and Vandover and his little circle of friends are each cleverly characterized, there is a thinness, a lack of intimate warmth in the picture. As Mr. Charles G. Norris says, "the conception of the book is big—too big to be handled with the dexterity that the powerful theme of 'McTeague,' afterwards received from the more mature mind of its creator." When we remember that the novel is the work of a young man of twenty-five, we are more struck with the thoroughness with which he has mastered all the details of the steady degeneration of the victim's brain, through his moral indolence and loss of self-respect, than with the occasional artistic lapses of the narrative. Yet it is undeniable that the ethical stress discernible in the picture impairs its complete effectiveness. Vandover's ruin is brought about, first, by his seduction of the hysterical girl, Ida Wade, who commits suicide, and throws all the blame on him; and, secondly, by the failure of his artistic power to respond to his bidding when he sets himself to work in earnest. Youth lives with near and narrow horizons, and Norris has saddled his miserable hero with too many calamities, and drawn over-logically the moral lesson of the profligate's career. Nevertheless, the psychological analysis of a weak man's collapse in face of adversity, of the cumulative, down-dragging effect of evil habits on a neurotic subject, is essentially true; and no doubt Norris has constructed his picture from intimate observation of the effects of the profligate life led by certain of his college friends. The chief artistic flaw is that Vandover all along apprehends too clearly his own state and the successive stages of his moral atrophy; and his fear of the insatiable "brute" within him that is pulling him down to destruction is theatrically exaggerated. What is admirable in the treatment is the dry light incidentally shed on the American obsession of material success at any cost, symbolized by the figure of the acute, self-confident young business man, Charlie Geary. As Vandover falls lower and lower, his old college friend Geary climbs higher and higher, and each upward step is attained at the expense of someone weaker, less ruthlessly egoistic, than himself. At a critical moment, Geary basely betrays Vandover's confidence, and persuades him to sell to him, far below its value, a block of buildings, which Geary then develops into a valuable property. And the novel ends with an incisive piece of irony—the astute business man condescendingly giving his old chum—now starving and hopeless—a day's job, and directing him to scavenge well the sinks and drains and dust-pits of the cottage property out of which he has swindled him. "Vandover and the Brute" is a curious example, in short, of how a native American genius is prone to look to Europe to acquire artistic standards, and how it often has to appeal for recognition to a society whose shibboleths are not those of its own countrymen.

"A Study in Temperament."
Illustrated London News, 55 (July 4, 1914), 28.

An unimpeachable "moral" may condone the grossness of Zola, or the horror of Ibsen's "Ghosts," genius justifying the choice of subjects. Much the same argument might be advanced in regard to "Vandover and the Brute," by Frank Norris (Heinemann). Written nineteen years ago, after strange vicissitudes: peril by earthquake and peril by fire, the manuscript was discovered, the author identified. It is a terrible picture that the author of "The Pit" paints in this story, nothing less than the tragedy of a man wrecked, body and soul, by the brute element in his nature. There is a grim fascination in watching the descent of Vandover from his student days and ways at Harvard to his ultimate ruin. But, as in Zola and in Ibsen, this study of a lost soul has a power which impels respect for a method unpardonable in a mere horror-monger. The sting of the tragedy lies in the fact that Vandover is not wholly bad. He has some fine instincts, rather than qualities, but all are swept away by impulses of animal passion. He returns from Harvard to San Francisco, a "charming fellow," but before long the "brute" in him leads to debauchery; and to his major vice he adds drunkenness and gambling, sinking lower and lower. We see him in later stages obsessed by the illusion that he is a wolf, and we leave him a squalid, hopeless wreck. That the book is sincere, justifies scenes which are little less than an emotional orgy; though there are passages of beauty and pathos.

"Vandover and the Brute."
The Academy, 87 (July 4, 1914), 17.

The manuscript of this novel, supposed to have been destroyed in the great fire of San Francisco, was found in a crate of various contents with the name of the author cut away by some unknown autograph-hunter, and the book is now published with a brief foreword by Mr. Charles Norris, his brother. It is a crude, but powerful, story, not to be compared with "The Pit" or other works from the same hand, but with passages here and there which a critic might note as foreshadowing a splendid future. "The Brute" is Vandover himself, his lower nature, which in the end gains the mastery; but there was no need whatever to drag in the horrors of lycanthropy to deepen poor Van's downfall. Indeed, the very chapters which the young author evidently wished to make impressive fail entirely; they are simply unreal. It is admitted that the influence of Zola is strong in this first of Frank Norris's novels, but no one, as far as we know, has noticed that much of the book read extremely like a translation. Vandover, starting as a Harvard man, has every chance of success in life, but is especially susceptible to drink, gambling, and the influences of the saloon-life which he freely followed. His power as an artist is gradually sapped by nervous disease; and here the book goes to pieces. It is well worth reading for its admirable opening chapters and its description of the family and social life of the city of San Francisco. There is no escaping the suggestion of a fine ability half-developed, and the reader will once more regret that the author was fated so soon to leave an art of which he would have been a master.

"Man at His Worst: A Strong but Sincere Study."
Sketch (London), 87 (July 22, 1914).

Those of us who read this posthumous novel of Mr. Frank Norris will be able to share the emotions of the Early Victorian child set down before "The Fairchild Family." That small, pantalooned student of vice, accompanying Augusta Noble to her grave, having previously seen her burned alive through vanity, must have felt very much as a grown-up is likely to do who accepts Mr. Norris's view of the self-indulgent artist crawling on all fours and barking in maniacal imitation of a beast. After all, it is so human to desire to see the tilt of a new hat in the glass, and it is so human to desire comfort and ease; yet there is a little girl in sheets of living flame for having tip-tilted on a fender to look, while here is a man ruined and mad because, being a healthy animal, he—fed the brute. Of course, the Early Victorian child with observation must have discovered that it is not ever thus. The mirrors that receive attention, and nothing dramatic happens! Equally, the grown-up who has followed Vandover through his cycle of orgy will realise that, though Vandover's crimes may be common to many men, not many men share his punishment. The antique child and the grown-up might even go a step further and dwell on the quite horrible fates that have attended the most innocent and virtuous—pestilence, murder, not-at-all sudden death, even madness. Doubtless, the lady who wrote "The Fairchild Family" had an eye on Augustas and so forth, intending the moral as a preventive; however many charming children of the 'fifties may have been saved the vice of vanity by its means, it is extremely unlikely that that hardier growth, a Vandover with a potential brute, will read this story and refrain. It would be hard to put a finger on any one point of his career and say, "Here was the fatal indulgence"; more foolish than vicious, his nature developed evil as a consumptive develops phthisis. Remains, then, the artistic value of this gloomy canvas. It certainly possesses one: the proof lies in the reading, the steady turning of page after page, the undiminished interest, the concern which the final tragic phase awakes when the catalogue of sordid descents might so easily have dried up pity, in the sharp images which Mr. Norris's style impresses on the mind—above all, in its transparent, unaffected sincerity. "Vandover and the Brute" will not escape being dubbed a "strong" book, but it is really a sincere book. It may climb into the pulpit occasionally, but it is alive with the life of the street and the home and the restaurant. Nothing could be better than the short paragraph recording the death of Vandover's mother in a railway station, and the odd moment in which the odour of hot oil from an engine-room brought it back to him years afterwards. Not the least interesting thing about the story is the history of its manuscript; romance reeks in the chance by which it escaped the San Francisco fire, and the theft of its signature so nearly losing its identity: more romance than Mr. Norris, fiercely sincere, allows to creep into his entire book.

"The Degradation of a Soul."
The Independent, 79 (August 3, 1914), 173.

Sometimes the story of a manuscript is as interesting as its contents. A novel that had been lost for years, written by Frank Norris in 1895, that had passed thru the earthquake and fire at San Francisco, and been packed away in a crate with a wrong label, has recently been rescued and published. *Vandover and the Brute* lacks the author's revision, and is crude and unfinished in spots, yet it bears the impress of Frank Norris's genius. It shows the struggle for mastery in the soul of a man between the good and evil forces of his nature. Its painful realism recalls Zola, its plot reminds one of Stevenson in *Dr. Jekyll and Mr. Hyde* or Oscar Wilde in *The Picture of Dorian Grey*, but there is no touch of the supernatural in the steady downward pull of the Brute, and if the story repels we hear the voice of Frank Norris speaking out of the past: "I told them the truth. They liked it or they didn't like it. What had that to do with me? I told them the truth; I knew it for the truth then, and I know it for the truth now." A grim and bitter truth! But no one can dispute its power.

"Recent Reflections of a Novel-Reader."
Atlantic Monthly, 114 (October 1914), 525–26.

... The foregoing are distinctly serious-minded books, and there are yet more of them. Reformers all are the authors of *The Flying Inn, The Goldfish, The Congresswoman, Idle Wives, Vandover and the Brute*, and even *What Will People Say?* Each assails the thing that to him is anathema with such wit and adroitness as his brains allow....

There is no humor in *Vandover*. Written when Frank Norris was a college boy, it is little more than a medico-moral treatise of the school of Brieux. In its present shape it is too mediocre to be efficient or interesting, save as showing the writer's bent from the beginning....

Charles Knapp and J. L. Gerig.
"Literature."
The New International Year Book: 1914 (New York: Dodd, Mead & Co., 1915), p. 417.

... *Vandover and the Brute*, a posthumous novel from a strangely recovered manuscript by Frank Norris, depicts the degeneration of a soul....

Posthumous Items of Importance: A Checklist

H. M. Wright, "In Memoriam—Frank Norris: 1870–1902," *The University of California Chronicle*, 5 (October 1902), 240–45.

"Frank Norris, Novelist, Is Dead," *Oakland Enquirer,* October 25, 1902, p. 1.

"Death Ends the Career of Frank Norris," *San Francisco Chronicle*, October 26, 1902, p. 24.

"Death Stills the Pen of Frank Norris," *San Francisco Examiner*, October 26, 1902, p. 18.

"Frank Norris Passes Away," *Atlanta Constitution*, October 26, 1902, p. 9.

"Frank Norris, the Young Californian," *Springfield Republican*, October 26, 1902, p. 4.

Bailey Millard, "Writer Was Planning to Stay in California This Winter and Complete 'The Wolf' When Stricken by Appendicitis," *San Francisco Examiner*, October 26, 1902, p. 18.

I. F. Marcosson, "Some Recollections of Frank Norris," *Louisville Times*, October 27, 1902, p. 4.

"Norris," *St. Paul Dispatch*, October 27, 1902, p. 6.

Frank Morton Todd, "Frank Norris—Student, Author, and Man," *The University of California Magazine*, 8 (November 1902), 349–56; expanded from "The Farewell Tribute of a Friend to the Late Frank Norris," *Oakland Enquirer*, October 27, 1902, p. 5.

"The Week in a Busy World," *Atlanta Constitution*, November 2, 1902, p. 8, "The Sunny South" supplement.

"Norris Died Intestate: Royalties in His Books His Principal Estate," *San Francisco Chronicle*, November 2, 1902, p. 14.

"An Unfinished Literary Career," *Literary Digest*, 25 (November 8, 1902), 593.

William Dallam Armes, "Concerning the Work of the Late Frank Norris," *Sunset*, 10 (December 1902), 165–67.

"The Death of Mr. Frank Norris," *The World's Work*, 5 (December 1902), 2830.

Arthur Goodrich, "Frank Norris," *Current Literature*, 33 (December 1902), 764; for variant forms of the same, see "Frank Norris: The Estimate and Tribute of An Associate," *Boston Evening Transcript*, October 29, 1902, p. 14; and "An Unfinished Literary Career," *Literary Digest*, 25 (November 8, 1902), 593.

William Dean Howells, "Frank Norris," *North American Review*, 175 (December 1902), 769–78.

William Allen Wood, "A Golden Bowl Broken," *Phi Gamma Delta Quarterly*, 25 (December 1902), 157–63.

Thomas Wentworth Higginson and

Henry Walcott Boynton. *A Reader's History of American Literature*. Boston: Houghton-Mifflin and Company, 1903; pp. 254–56.

Charles S. Aiken, "Books and Writers," *Sunset,* 10 (January 1903), 245.

Gelett Burgess, "One More Tribute to Frank Norris," *Sunset*, 10 (January 1903), 246.

"Frank Norris," *Literary News*, 24 (January 1903), 9–10.

Arthur Goodrich, "Norris, the Man," *Current Literature*, 34 (January 1903), 105.

William Dean Howells, "Editor's Easy Chair," *Harper's Monthly*, 106 (January 1903), 328.

Bailey Millard, "A Significant Literary Life," *Out West*, 18 (January 1903), 49–55.

Henry Morse Stephens, "The Work of Frank Norris: An Appreciation," *The University of California Chronicle*, 5 (January 1903), 324–31.

"With Some Authors We Have Known," *Atlanta Constitution*, January 4, 1903, p. 8, "The Sunny South" supplement.

"Story of Frank Norris," *Spokane Spokesman-Review*, January 11, 1903, p. 17.

"The Late Frank Norris," *Atlanta Constitution*, January 25, 1903, p. 8, "The Sunny South" supplement.

"Literary Notes," *Spokane Spokesman-Review*, January 25, 1903, p. 17.

"Biographical Sketch of Frank Norris," *Book News*, 21 (February 1903), 443.

Florence Jackson, "Editorial Digest," *Overland Monthly*, 41 (February 1903), 152–53.

"Frank Norris; An Appreciation," *New York Herald,* March 1, 1903, p. 2, "Literary Section."

W. S. Rainsford, "Frank Norris," *The World's Work*, 5 (April 1903), 3276.

Nelli V. de Sanchez, "Books and Writers: Frank Norris's Memorial Seat," *Sunset*, 12 (April 1904), 560–61.

Milne V. Levick, "Frank Norris," *Overland Monthly*, 45 (June 1905), 504–508.

Denison Hailey Clift, "The Artist in Frank Norris," *Pacific Monthly*, 17 (March 1907), 313–22.

Frederic Taber Cooper. "Frank Norris," *Some American Story Tellers* (New York: Henry Holt, 1911), pp. 295–330.

Harry M. East, "A Lesson from Frank Norris," *Overland Monthly*, 60 (December 1912), 533–34.

Ernest Peixotto, "Romanticist Under the Skin." *The Saturday Review of Literature,* 9 (May 15, 1933), 613–15.

Index

A.H., 159–60
Abbot, Edward, 45–46
Abbot, Madeline Vaughn, 45–46
Academy, The, 21, 54, 75, 77–79, 331, 362
Academy and Literature, 107, 162, 269–70, 305–6, 315–16
Aiken, Charles S., 366
ALA Booklist, 333
Alden, William L., 166–67
Arena, The, 173–79, 289–92
Argonaut, The, 14–17, 64–65, 99–100, 144–45, 200–201, 299, 332
Armes, William Dallam, 365
Athenaeum, The, 26, 53–54, 108, 167–68, 264–66, 306, 318–19, 331–32, 359
Atlanta Constitution, 126, 259, 365, 366
Atlantic Monthly, 172–73, 294–96, 364
Ayres, Elizabeth, 223–25

Bacon, Thomas R., 272–76
Baltimore Sun, 59, 100, 232–33
Bangs, John Kendrick, 71–73
Banks, Nancy Huston, 49–50
Barry, John D., 35–37
Bashford, Herbert, 350–51
Beach, E. D., 44
Bellman, 326–27
Bonner, Geraldine, 14–17
Book Buyer, 44, 67–68, 104, 141–44
Book News Monthly, 240–42, 301, 366
Bookman (America), 49–50, 81–86, 137–41, 183–86, 238–40, 302–3, 352–53
Bookman (England), 23, 55, 108, 238n, 333
Bookworm, The, 131–33
Boston Evening Transcript, 38–39, 73–75, 101, 148–51, 156–59, 161n, 213–17, 340–42, 365
Boston Herald, 287, 310–11, 346–48
Boston Home Journal, 6
Bouton, Emily S., 223–25
Boynton, Henry W., 172–73, 366
Brooklyn Daily Eagle, 218–21
Buffalo Morning Express, 14, 32
Burgess, Gelett, 366

California Weekly, The, 326
Canadian Magazine, 160
Cather, Willa, 41–44, 68–69
Chamberlin, Joseph Edgar, 73–74
Chautauquan, The, 75, 159–60, 292
Chicago American, 124–26
Chicago Daily News, 255–57
Chicago Daily Tribune, 21
Chicago Inter Ocean, 4, 100–101, 203–13
Chicago Record-Herald, 188–91
Cincinnati Commercial Gazette, 4
Clift, Denison Hailey, 366
Columbus Dispatch, 4
Cooper, Frederic Taber, 54–55, 81–86, 137–40, 170–71, 183–86, 302–3, 352–53, 366
Coryn, Sidney, G. P., 332
Courtney, W. L., 259–62
Critic, The, 2, 48, 103–4, 276–79, 306–7, 321
Current Encyclopedia, The, 162–63
Current Literature, 279, 303–4, 365, 366
Current Opinion, 354–55

D., 74
Davenport, Eleanor M., 7–8
Detroit Free Press, 60

367

Detroit Times, 233–35
Dial, The, 161–62, 292–93
Dundee Advertiser, The, 21–22

E.F.E. (*see* Edgett, Edwin Francis)
East, Harry M., 366
Edgar, Randolph, 326–27
Edgett, Edwin Francis, 340–42
Edinburgh and Glasgow Scotsman, 23–24, 263

F.C.B., 292
Fitch, George Hamlin, 11–12, 60–61, 127–29, 198–200, 348–50
Flower, B. O., 173–79, 289–92
Ford, James L., 95–97

G.H.S., 213–17
Garland, Hamlin, 276–79
Gerig, J. L., 364
Gilder, Jeanette, 48, 327–30
Glasgow North British Daily Mail, 25
Goodrich, Arthur, 365, 366

Harper's Monthly Magazine, 163–64, 366
Harper's Weekly, 287–89
Herdman, Hugh, 296
Higginson, Thomas Wentworth, 365
Howells, William Dean, 18–20, 39–41, 163–64, 287–89, 365, 366

I.F.M. (*see* Marcosson, Isaac F.)
Illustrated London News, 76, 169–70, 271–72, 361–62
Impressions Quarterly, 151–54, 272–76
Independent, The, 13, 46, 65, 99, 145–46, 170, 257–58, 297, 363–64
Indianapolis News, 194–98
International Year Book, The, 54–55, 170–71, 185–86

J.D., 25–26
Jackson, Florence, 237–38, 366

Kennebec Journal, 258–59
Kerfoot, J. B., 151, 257

Knapp, Charles, 364

Lamp, The, 242–43, 313–14
Land of Sunshine, 51–52, 67, 105–7, 156–57
Levick, Milne V., 336
Life, 151, 257
Lippincott's Magazine, 2
Literary Digest, 282, 309–10, 357, 365
Literary Era, The, 51
Literary News, 191n, 304, 366
Literary World, The, 18, 35–37, 45–46, 107, 279–80
Literature, 18–20, 39–41, 71–73
London, Jack, 151–54
London Daily Express, 284–87
London Daily Telegraph, 24–25, 259–62
London Star, 25–26
Louisville Courier-Journal, 344–45
Louisville Times, 17–18, 33–35, 57, 70–71, 112, 123–24, 129–31, 186–88, 365
Lummis, Charles F., 51–52, 67, 105–7, 156–57

M., 74–75
Mabie, Hamilton W., 319–20
Macy, John, 346–48
Marcosson, Isaac F., 17–18, 33–35, 57, 70–71, 112, 123–24, 129–31, 186–88, 365
Michels, Ella S. C., 6–7
Millard, Bailey, 246–51, 365, 366
Munsey's Magazine, 20, 160–61
Muzzey, A. L., 179–80

Nation, The (America), 5–6, 293–94, 324–25, 339–40
Nation, The (England), 316–18, 359–61
New Age, The, 22–23
New International Year Book, The, 364
New Orleans Daily Picayune, 69–70
New Orleans Times-Picayune, 105
New York Commercial Advertiser, 57–58
New York Evening Post, 336–37
New York Evening Sun, 112–14, 225–28

New York Herald, 3–4, 188, 191–94, 343–44, 366
New York Sun, 228–30, 335
New York Times, 30–32, 86–88, 166–67, 235–37, 283, 299–301, 323, 337–39
New York Tribune, 29–30
North American Review, 365

Oakland Enquirer, 365
Oracle, K. B., 4–5
Out West, 321
Outlook, The, 12, 37–38, 61–62, 98–99, 134, 201–3, 301, 319–20, 351–52
Overland Monthly, 5, 6, 65–67, 105–6, 135–36, 237–38, 366

P.M.P., 345
Pacific Monthly, 74–75, 296, 366
Paine, Albert Bigelow, 238–40
Pall Mall Gazette, 355–56
Payne, William Morton, 161–62, 292–93
Peixotto, Ernest, 366
Phi Gamma Delta Quarterly, 365
Philadelphia Inquirer, 251–52
Pittsburgh Leader, 41–44, 68–69
Preston, Harriet Waters, 294–96
Providence Journal, 88–90, 95–97
Public, The, 179–80
Public Opinion, 12–13, 35, 65, 97–98, 217–18, 311
Publishers' Weekly, The, 1–3, 5, 11, 38, 49, 58
Putnam's Magazine, 327–30

Rainsford, W. S., 366
Reader, The, 304–5
Reader's History of American Literature, A, 366
Review of Reviews (America), 51, 168–69, 353
Review of Reviews (England), 164–66, 281
Rice, Wallace, 124–26

S.D.S., Jr., 304–5
St. Louis Republic, 103

St. Paul Dispatch, 365
St. Paul Globe, 230–31
St. Paul Pioneer Press, 58–59, 88*n*, 101–2
San Francisco Bulletin, 350–51
San Francisco Call, 180–81, 323–24
San Francisco Chronicle, 3, 11–12, 60, 91–92, 127, 198–200, 306, 314, 348–50, 365
San Francisco Examiner, 115–23, 246–51, 365
Sanborn, Annie W., 58
Sanchez, Nelli V. de, 366
Saturday Night, 222
Saturday Review (England), 26, 54, 161, 171, 263–64, 332, 357–58
Saturday Review of Literature, The, 366
Sewanee Review, The, 333
Shuman, Edwin L., 188–91
Sketch, 362–63
Some American Story Tellers, 366
Spectator, The, 21, 52–53, 76–77, 168, 266–69, 313, 332
Spokane Spokesman-Review, 252–53, 366
Springfield Republican, 365
Stephens, Henry Morse, 366
Story of the Files, The, 6–7
Sunset, 365, 366
Syracuse Post-Standard, 345

Thompson, Francis, 315–16
Times Literary Supplement, 271, 301–2, 311–12, 357–59
Todd, Frank Morton, 365
Toledo Daily Blade, 223–25
Town Talk, 131–33, 147

University of California Chronicle, The, 365
University of California Magazine, The, 7–8, 365

Van Westrum, A. Schade, 67–68, 141–44, 242–43

Washington Post, 253–55

Washington Times, 13–14, 46–48, 53, 62–63, 92–94, 111–12, 154–56
Wave, The, 4–5
Williams, Talcott, 168–69
Wister, Owen, 243–46
Wood, William Allen, 365
World's Work, The, 137, 243–46, 365, 366
Wright, H. M., 365

DATE DUE